APPLIED ANTHROPOLOGY
IN AMERICA

Applied Anthropology in America

SECOND EDITION

**Elizabeth M. Eddy
and William L. Partridge,
Editors**

Columbia University Press · New York · 1987

Library of Congress Cataloging-in-Publication Data

Applied anthropology in America.

Bibliography: p.
1. Applied anthropology—United States.
2. United States—Social policy.   I. Eddy, Elizabeth M.
II. Partridge, William L.
GN397.7.U6A66   1987   306   86-17535
ISBN 0-231-06372-5
ISBN 0-231-06373-3 (pbk.)

Columbia University Press
New York   Guildford, Surrey
Copyright © 1987 Columbia University Press
All rights reserved

Printed in the United States of America

Book design by J. S. Roberts

TO SOLON T. KIMBALL   (1909–1982)

Who taught that the study
of human behavior should
be of service to people

CONTENTS

PREFACE

A second edition of a well received book of contributed essays about applied anthropology offers an opportunity to reflect on developments which have occurred since the first edition was published in 1978. Perhaps the most noticeable event is the break with the past that has resulted inevitably from the dying out of the generation that participated actively in the applied anthropology programs of the London School of Economics and the International Institute of African Languages and Cultures during the 1930s, the United States government-sponsored programs and the early industrial studies which incorporated applied anthropologists during the depression and World War II years, and the founding of the Society for Applied Anthropology at Harvard in 1941. Since 1978, the deaths of such luminaries in the field as Gregory Bateson, Allison Davis, Adolphous Peter Elkin, Meyer Fortes, Geoffrey E. Gorer, Mlee Jomo Kenyatta, Solon T. Kimball, Gordon MacGregor, D'Arcy McNickle, Lucy Mair, Margaret Mead, Marvin Opler, Audrey I. Richards, Vera Rubin, Edward H. Spicer, W. E. H. Stanner, and Monica Wilson signal clearly that an era has ended. It reminds us too that contemporary applied anthropologists are members of a professional community with a distinguished tradition.

The generational succession has been accompanied by increased specialization within the field of applied anthropology, greater emphasis on the need for specific professional training and qualifications for careers in applied settings, and wider acceptance and recognition of anthropologists who pursue careers outside of museums and academic departments. In addition, considerable attention is being given to the theory and ethics of practice, the development of long-term data bases, cross-cultural analysis of change programs, the accumulation of data based on applied work, and the ways in which anthropologists can contribute more effectively to public policy. These emphases have been incipient in modern applied anthropology ever since its early beginnings. But, during the past decade, the seminal contributions of our forbears along these lines have come to unprecedented fruition.

Nine of the essays in this second edition are new, and three of the reprinted essays have been revised. The changes reflect not only the availability of newer and sometimes more sophisticated materials, but also the desire to represent the major areas of contemporary applied anthropology more adequately. The new essays on development anthropology, medical anthropology, evaluation research, policy studies, and theory reflect both the sustained interest in these fields over a long period of time and the extensive work in them during recent years. The revisions in the editors' introductory essay on the history of applied anthropology, William Foote Whyte's essay on organizational behavior reserach, and John H. Peterson Jr.'s essay on his work among the Choctaw incorporate new knowledge and developments that have appeared during the recent past. The remaining essays have been reprinted in their original form, except for minor editorial changes. These essays represent important attempts to conceptualize the theory and practice of applied anthropology which continue to be germane to current issues and concerns.

As in the first edition, this volume is limited to a consideration of applied anthropology as it is derived from social and cultural anthropology. Archaeologists, linguists, and physical anthropologists are making important contributions in applied fields, but their work is beyond our purview here. Moreover, this volume does not survey the entire field of applied anthropology within the sociocultural domain nor even within any of its specialized areas. Our intent here is purposively different from that of the general survey type of textbooks that are currently available on the topic of applied anthropology and in several of its specialty areas such as medical anthropology and educational anthropology.

The essays presented here address primarily several basic questions which confront *all* applied anthropologists regardless of their particular areas of practice. What contributions does applied work make to the construction and modifications of theory about sociocultural behavior? What are the uses of anthropology in professional practice outside of the classroom and traditional disciplinary research? How does anthropology apply to public policies related to human welfare? What are the ethics of practice?

The volume gathers together some of the more important recent attempts to respond to these and related questions. They document the significant differences between work in the academy and work in other types of settings. More importantly, they provide factual and substantial support for the fact that professional anthropologists today are making important contributions to theory, research, practice, and public policy. As students and graduates of anthropology departments become more involved in applied anthropology, it is important that they seek an understanding of what it entails so that they may know how best to prepare for and contribute to it. From the contributors to this volume, students and others may learn much that is important to the rethinking of both anthropology and the problems of our world if areas of mutual concern are to be redefined in ways that permit better solutions to problems than those now extant.

Both the earlier edition and the present edition of *Applied Anthropology in America* are dedicated to Solon T. Kimball, one of the foremost leaders in applied anthropology and in anthropological studies of American educational institutions and communities. The royalties from both editions have been used to establish the Solon T. Kimball Award for Public and Applied Anthropology within the American Anthropological Association. The first award was made at the 1984 annual meetings of the Association in Denver, Colorado.

Several people have contributed toward this edition. In particular, we wish to express our appreciation to Dr. Billie R. DeWalt for his helpful comments on the prospectus for the edition, to Maureen MacGrogan of Columbia University Press, and to Kathi Kitner and Phyllis Durell who struggled respectively with the bibliography and final typing of manuscripts.

INTRODUCTION

1

THE DEVELOPMENT OF APPLIED ANTHROPOLOGY IN AMERICA

William L. Partridge and Elizabeth M. Eddy

During the last sixty years, anthropology has changed from an esoteric taxonomy of primitive customs into a systematic, comparative, and holistic science of humankind. Its methods of study are derived from natural science, yet its subject matter is humanity. As both science and humanism, it keeps pace with changes in the conditions of human life which now engulf peoples all over the world. The most significant changes which

Elizabeth M. Eddy (Ph.D., Columbia) is professor emerita of anthropology at the University of Florida. She is a specialist in educational anthropology and has conducted fieldwork in hospital and school systems in the United States. She has served as associate project director of research at the New York School of Social Work, as project director of research at Hunter College in the City University of New York, and as director of the Urban Studies Bureau and chairperson of the department of anthropology at the University of Florida. She has been a consultant to the National Assessment of Educational Progress Project and to ABT Associates. She is a past president of the Council on Anthropology and Education and the Southern Anthropological Society. She is currently a councillor of the Society for Urban Anthropology.

William L. Partridge (Ph.D., Florida) is currently a consultant to the World Bank on the development of communities relocated by hydroelectric and irrigation projects. He has served as a consultant to the Inter-American Development Bank, the Pan American Health Organization, the Organization of American States, and the United States Agency for International Development, and has worked for the Institute for Development Anthropology. He has carried out extended field research in Colombia and Mexico and shorter assignments in Bolivia, Costa Rica, Guatemala, and India. Together with Antoinette B. Brown, he is conducting a long-term community study of the human ecology and health consequences of resettlement and development among the Lowland Mazatec of the Papaloapan River Basin in Mexico. He is former associate professor and chairperson at Georgia State University and has taught anthropology also at the University of Southern California. His major research interests are in community studies, community relocation, economic development linkages, and human ecology.

have affected anthropology are a rise in the power of new nations with hungry people, modern armaments, and few resources; the emergence of a world capitalistic economic system in which the flow of capital subsidizes efforts to achieve the social and political stability necessary to attract private sector investment; the unprecedented growth and scale of contemporary development programs; the massing of humanity in new urban and metropolitan settlement forms; a technology with the potential to feed the world or destroy industrial civilization; human consciousness of the limits of natural resources; a revolution in public health which brings the paradox of increased life expectancy and overpopulation; and systems of communication which bring news events from all over the world into the home even as they occur.

Problems of food production, ethnic relations, urban and regional planning, human migration and relocation, environmental protection, health care services, illiteracy, population control, aging, and many others which stem from these changes have stimulated the response which we call applied anthropology. Together with the growth of university programs in anthropology to create knowledge and train people to use it, increased specialization and interdisciplinary collaboration, increased awareness of professional responsibility to subjects of study, and a focus upon contemporary peoples and practical problems, applied anthropology is a recent development.

The term *applied anthropology* dates back to at least 1906, when it was used in the announcement of the establishment of a diploma program in anthropology at Oxford (Read 1906:56), and the term *practical anthropology* was used as early as the 1860s by James Hunt, the founder of the Anthropological Society of London (Rainger 1980; Reining 1962). But applied anthropology as we know it today is rooted in modern anthropology as it emerged in both the United States and Great Britain during the 1920s and 1930s.

This essay describes this development and devotes attention to the following questions: What is applied anthropology? How do applied anthropologists differ from other anthropologists?

What is Applied Anthropology?

There is no genuine theoretical or methodological distinction between "pure" and "applied" science. In popular thought, scientists engaged in pure research have little concern with potential uses of the results of their labor, and applied scientists are not concerned with making theoretical contributions. Yet, as any physician or biologist will testify, this neat distinction does not exist in actual scientific work. Physicians use theory daily in order to diagnose and treat clinical cases, and the results they obtain alter both theory and clinical practice. If this were not the case, they would still be using unicorn horn, leeches, and extract of human skull. Similarly, biologists utilize theory to develop pesticides permitting the control of fruit flies, and must modify theory when fruit flies multiply in the laboratory.

In science, the basic dialogue between theory and application is at the heart of any progress. Applications are in part determined by the adequacy of theory, and theory is accepted or rejected over the long run in relation to its utility in successive applications (Kuhn 1962). What is true of science generally is also true of the science of anthropology. The distinction between "applied" and "pure" anthropology is largely a fiction of popular culture. Both draw upon the same body of theory and methods that are commonly recognized as anthropological (Foster 1969; Clifton 1970; Naylor 1973; Bastide 1973; Goldschmidt 1979).

However, there is an important differentiation to be made between an "abstract" academic anthropology that is solely dedicated to theoretical and research interests identified by those within the academy and an "applied" anthropology that addresses the more immediate problems of the public outside of the academy. In Britain, the distinction was most clearly articulated by Malinowski (1929) and Radcliffe-Brown (1930); in the United States, it was noted by Arensberg (1947) in one of the early editorial statements in *Applied Anthropology* (later *Human Organization*), the journal of the Society for Applied Anthropology.

Historically, four features have distinguished applied from abstract anthropology. The first is that applied anthropologists study living cultures and contemporary peoples. The data they seek cannot be excavated in historical ruins, discovered in archives, or prodded from the memories of the aged. Insights gained from history or selective memories of the past may provide important perspectives for applied research, but they tell us little of how people today form social groups, accomplish tasks, survive in an environment, or solve problems.

In addition to research among living peoples—a type of research which engages many anthropologists who are not "applied"—applied anthropologists conduct research oriented toward the problems of those they work with and/or study. Their research stems from the needs of the people themselves, and these may range from such problems as mental illness, drug abuse, or food shortage, to such unconscious needs as dietary deficiency. In contrast, the problems posed for scientific investigation in abstract anthropology may or may not bear any relationship to the needs of living people. For example, the rage with which academic professionals attack one another over the diffusion of pottery in the first millennium B.C., the religion of the Cheyenne in the late nineteenth century, or the origins of Caribbean mortuary customs, all may bear little relation to the immediate problems of contemporary Hopi craftsmen, Cheyenne Baptists, or the laborers from St. Kitts who migrate to Galveston, Texas.

Third, applied anthropologists seek applications of their findings, data, and analyses beyond anthropology. Abstract anthropologists, on the other hand, find significance for their work in the debates which stimulated their forebears and continue to stimulate their peers. The ideas of past scholars define and give meaning to abstractions, define the procedures by which data are selected and collected, and restrict the focus of research within the bounds of historical tradition. Applied anthropologists utilize the same process of scientific abstraction or theory building, but these abstractions derive significance from their contemporary implications for the solution of problems among the public. As a consequence, applied anthropologists usually cross disciplinary boundaries, investigate problems which are novel to anthropological traditions, and select data for analysis on the basis of their relevance for current issues rather than ancient precepts.

Finally, there are notable differences in the career patterns of applied anthropologists as contrasted with those of abstract anthropologists. The latter are nearly always found in anthropology teaching and research positions with academic institutions or museums. Many applied anthropologists occupy similar positions, but those who remain within academic settings frequently hold appointments in departments other than anthropology or joint appointments in anthropology and another department. Moreover, they are likely to devote considerable professional time and effort to contract research and consulting work with nonacademic agencies and organizations. Today, the historic variance in traditional careers is more pronounced as significantly increased numbers of applied anthropologists become full-time employees of government agencies, corporations, and other institutions outside of the academy. Those who are so employed often call themselves *practicing* anthropologists in order to differentiate clearly their professional roles from those, whether applied or not, who primarily follow an academic career line.

The essays to follow in this volume will extend and clarify the above characteristics of applied anthropologists as they appear in the present. Before turning to them, however, it is necessary to examine the past and to trace the development of the distinction between abstract and applied anthropology and the phases through which it has passed. In doing so, we will illustrate further the contrast posed here and illuminate the varied responses of anthropologists to contemporary problems and issues.

We begin with a consideration of early American anthropology and the emergence of modern anthropology in America before examining the history of applied anthropology and the contemporary position of this subfield in our own and other societies. Even if it were possible to do so, it would not serve our purpose to describe all the details that are germane to the development of American anthropology, nor all the instances of work by applied anthropologists in America or elsewhere. Rather, our purpose here is to illustrate the major differences between abstract and applied anthropologists, to indicate the range of activities of applied anthropologists, and to present the current dilemmas of relating the science of anthropology to the problems of our times.

Early American Anthropology

When Lewis Henry Morgan, a lawyer from Rochester, N.Y., made his first trip to the Kansas and Nebraska Territory to study Indian kinship in 1859, the first white child born in the Territory was not quite thirty-one years old. John C. Fremont had explored the region only seventeen years earlier; the railroad would not arrive for another six years; Topeka was a mere cluster of houses. As it did in Europe, anthropology in America began to develop as a profession only after decades of colonial expansion. On both continents, anthropology represented a new science of man and a consolidation of research interests in prehistory, paleontology, comparative anatomy, and geology directed toward the integration of the study of man before the dawn of written history (Voget 1975).

The doctrine of progress, with the concomitant belief in the moral superiority of Western culture, was virtually unquestioned when anthropology was born in America. Throughout centuries of progress, the modern, "superior," "moral," social life of nineteenth-century industrialism was believed to have developed from "primitive," "immoral," "childlike" societies. Whether rooted in the Judeo-Christian belief of a divine plan of the creator or the newer belief in the power of human reason to direct human advancement that emerged from eighteenth-century European developmentalism, the doctrine of progress guided scientific inquiry and held the attention of a nation expanding westward. European social theorists were progenitors of many of the issues posed during that time. They included Comte, Spencer, Millar, Kames, Bachofen, Fustel de Coulanges, Sumner, Nietzsche, and others (Leaf 1979; Voget 1975; Harris 1968). None of these theorists had studied alien peoples firsthand for any extended period of time. Speculations about societies outside of the literate civilizations of Europe and Asia were generally without empirical foundation.

More fortunate than their European counterparts, American anthropologists found at their doorstep a living laboratory in which to study the postulated early stages of human evolution. American Indians, surviving on the outskirts of civilization's towns and cities and camped in the path of industrial expansion, provided important clues to the discovery of the invariant and determinant laws of both the divine plan for progress from "inferior" to "superior" morality and the mental stages of developmentalism through which "inferior" social institutions such as hordes, communal property, and "primitive" promiscuity evolved into democracy, private property, and monogamous marriage. The tools, foods, tribal laws, and words of American Indians were all signposts along the unilineal road of human progress, which only had to be generalized into stages by means of which all societies could be ranked. This was the purpose that drew Lewis Henry Morgan into the Kansas and Nebraska territories (White 1951, 1959a).

Morgan was the most outstanding but not the first early American anthropologist. The American Ethnological Society had been founded in 1842 in New York City. Composed of members of local historical and literary societies, it drew together professionals interested in geography, archaeology, philology, history, travelogue, and sometimes literary criticism. While a few members, such as E. G. Squier and H. R. Schoolcraft, carried out field research, most had no experience of this nature. Some, such as the Reverend Francis Hawkes, used the meetings to further racial determinism theories. The lack of coherent, explicit scientific criteria for defining the field of interest led to the demise of the society in 1870 (Bieder and Tax 1976).

The work of geologist and explorer Major John W. Powell, leader of the first United States Geological Survey of the western states and the first director of the Bureau of American Ethnology (founded in 1879 at the Smithsonian Institution), is probably the clearest example of the generalized, global, evolutionary nature of anthropology in nineteenth-century America. American Indian word lists, rainfall records, geological features, arrowheads, and anything else which could be recorded on paper or carried back to Washington were collected and stored by the Bureau. Although untrained in anthropology as we know it today, Powell and his staff were the first professional protoanthropologists in America to initiate ethnological studies of Indian cultures for use by the U.S. government's Bureau of Indian Affairs. As physical scientists, they hoped to contribute useful knowledge regarding what they foresaw would be the conflicts between native Americans and incoming Europeans. However, their preoccupation with reconstructing the earlier ways of life of Indians and with evolution resulted in little use of their work by governmental administrators (Kennard and Macgregor 1953). Moreover, their lack of explicit social scientific criteria for evaluating their collected evidence contributed to the decline of the Bureau as the focal point of American anthropology (Hinsley 1976, 1981).

Among the early American anthropologists, only Morgan achieved the objective of a synthetic, global schema of human evolution. His original interest in law led to study of the law, politics, and social organization of the nearby Seneca Indians (1851) and the discovery that kinship systems in North America and elsewhere displayed basic uniformities which crossed linguistic and cultural barriers (1871). Through his own fieldwork and a widespread network of correspondents, who were missionaries and others who lived among American Indians, Morgan gathered data to demonstrate that jural aspects of relations in "primitive" society were based on kinship, whereas those of modern society were established on property relations (1877). He described the transition from one organizational form to the other in terms of three stages of human progress: savagery, barbarism, and civilization.

Morgan's theory became one of the leading nineteenth-century concepts of unilineal evolution. He was the first American ethnologist to undertake field research in terms of specific theoretical problems. Yet he was not so much a pioneering leader in the development of American anthropology as he was its finest expression. For several decades, Jesuit priests, frontier missionaries, educated travelers, and learned professional men from eastern cities had written numerous treatises about native Americans, human nature, and progress. To counter Morgan's deterministic theory of evolution through a series of "ethnical periods," there were other equally deterministic theories which reached conclusions about native Americans on the basis of assumptions about the racial inferiority of "primitives," divine intervention, and the like. A member of the group to which Morgan read his scientific papers "could see nothing in it [the Iroquois kinship nomenclature] but the total depravity and perversity of the Indian mind—that it could ever have thought of such utterly absurd ways of characterizing relationships" (White 1959a). The period abounds with "armchair anthropologists" who had nothing to contribute to scientific debate other than inaccurate and secondhand impressions bolstered by deterministic theories grounded in the doctrine of unilineal progress from the ways of American Indians to those of the white man.

The deductive logic and determinism of late-nineteenth-century anthropologists did not come under scientific scrutiny until Franz Boas came to the United States from Germany in 1889. More than any other person, Boas deserves recognition as "the central figure in the emergence of American cultural anthropology" (Voget 1975:319, cf. Stocking 1974). His influence was no less seminal in physical anthropology and linguistics (Stocking 1974; Brace and Montagu 1965; Lowie

1937b). As Voget (1975:320) notes, estimates of Boas' influence sometimes overlook the fact that he was part of a new intellectual movement in the social sciences, stemming from German inductive empiricism. Having earned a doctorate in physics, with extensive training in geography and ethnology as taught in Germany, Boas represented the radical empiricists who placed faith entirely in the inductive method and tolerated only those generalizations which were supported by assemblages of data. It was not social theorists such as Durkheim or Simmel who inspired Boas, but natural scientists and geographers such as Alexander von Humbolt, Adolf Bastian, Theobald Fisher, Karl Ritter, and Rudolph Virchow (Stocking 1974; Kluckhohn and Prufer 1959; Smith 1959).

Through a lifelong dedication to empirical data collection and taxonomic classification, Boas challenged deterministic theories. His own extensive and intensive fieldwork and that of his students loosened the grip of theories of racial determinism, mental determinism, geographical determinism, and unilineal evolution upon American anthropology (Stocking 1968; Harris 1968:250–289). For nearly half a century, from 1896 until his death in 1942, Boas taught at Columbia University in New York City and during this time he transformed anthropology from a part-time occupation of untrained theorists to a scientific profession. Through his leadership, the American Ethnological Society was reactivated at the turn of the century, and the American Anthropological Association was founded in 1902 (Lesser 1976). He trained some of the most influential American anthropologists of this century: Alfred Kroeber, Robert Lowie, Melville Herskovits, Edward Sapir, Paul Radin, Irving Hallowell, Clark Wissler, Leslie Spier, Alexander Goldenweiser, E. Adamson Hoebel, Ruth Benedict, Margaret Mead, Ruth Bunzel, Ashley Montagu, Jules Henry, and Frank Speck (Harris 1968:251).

Franz Boas' major contribution was to map out the scientific field of anthropology as we know it today (Mead 1959). Dismissing generalization based on deductive assumptions as premature, he trained students as collectors of the ethnographic details of linguistics, physical anthropology, and ethnology, from which he hoped that generalizations would emerge. Faced with the expansion of industrialism, the steady decrease in the numbers of American Indians, and the threat that much of pre-European life would be lost, Boas launched a huge concerted salvage operation to record the "vanishing" cultures of North America. This was "to be done with almost no money, very few trained people, and no time to spare" (Mead 1959:30). As Murray Wax (1956) has pointed out, the price paid for such exhaustive data collection was that Boas was prevented from developing any major, integrated, theoretical synthesis based on the mountains of data collected. In the 1880s, the aim of his work was the search for cultural "laws," but by the late 1930s he had abandoned this goal (Kluckhohn and Prufer 1959:24). Rather, his "function became that of critic," the watchdog of a young science empirically too lean to support the weight of theory building (Wax 1956:63). The voluminous data are still mined today by anthropologists such as Claude Lévi-Strauss, who are specialists in the synthesis Boas anticipated.

In American anthropology, a distinction between abstract and applied anthropology did not exist in Boas' time. Application of scientific knowledge as a distinct pursuit and objective within the field only emerged later. But it was Boas himself who demonstrated that anthropological evidence could contribute to the solution of practical problems. Even before Boas began his attack upon determinism and deduction, American anthropologists were periodically seeking and finding practical applications of their knowledge.

In both the United States and Britain, the belief that anthropology has relevance for issues of public policy and welfare dates back to the emergence of the field as a scientific discipline at the turn of this century (cf. Frantz 1985). In British anthropology, however, a differentiation between abstract and applied anthropology was made as early as the 1920s. There, after anthropology had broken with nineteenth-century unilineal theories of evolution and the extreme diffusionist theories of Grafton Elliot Smith, W. J. Perry, and Fritz Graebner, the terms *practical* or *applied* anthropology were used by Malinowski (1929) and Radcliffe-Brown (1930) respectively to denote the emergence of social anthropology as a new branch of the discipline. As strong advocates of the study of human behavior and institutions in the contemporary world and extensive fieldwork in other cultures, both Malinowski and Radcliffe-Brown argued that the scientific data produced by this type of study would be capable of application by those concerned with the practical problems of planning administrative and development policies for native populations in the British colonies. To be a social anthropologist in England at this time was to be an applied anthropologist, and this situation did not change until after World War II.

Episodic Attention to Practical Problems

The relevancy of anthropologists' intellectual concern to practical issues of their time is normally quite tenuous. Nevertheless, events can give previously esoteric knowledge wider dissemination, and anthropologists who are disposed to do so can have significant impact upon popular and official thought about practical matters at particular moments in history.

In the early days of anthropology, for example, Henry R. Schoolcraft, a founder of the American Ethnological Society, married an Indian woman and spent years living among native Americans. Formerly the superintendent of Indian Affairs in Michigan, Schoolcraft was commissioned by the State of New York to carry out a census of Indians, after having spent nine years in New York intellectual circles (Bieder and Tax 1976:19). He was later appointed by the United States Congress to prepare a comprehensive statistical history of American Indians. *Information Respecting the History, Condition and Prospects of the Indian Tribes of the United States,* published between 1852 and 1857 in six volumes, was presented to President James Buchanan. It was the author's hope that public presentation of the facts "neither overrated by exaggeration nor underrated by prejudice" would lead to a less cruel policy toward native Americans (Schoolcraft 1857:vii).

Similarly, James Mooney, a Bureau of American Ethnology fieldworker, testified before Congress in 1890 on behalf of American Indians involved in the Ghost Dance, which was widely interpreted as preparation for war, and defended this indigenous response to forced acculturation (Wallace 1965:vi). Lewis H. Morgan, while primarily motivated by purely scholarly interest, published in popular magazines a defense of Indians against the "hue and cry" for their extermination following the Civil War and the westward surge of immigrant Americans (White 1959a:12, 18).

None of these scholars considered themselves applied anthropologists, nor is it likely that their colleagues thought of them as such. Practical application was not the objective of their scholarly interests but rather a result of the accumulation of anthropological knowledge which, due to circumstances of the day, became politically, ethically, or intellectually relevant to practical issues. Episodic applications to practical issues were largely the expression of personal commitments of individual scientists who functioned as knowledgeable experts in a field of public policy normally removed from the course of their daily work. These anthropologists were clearly a minority among their colleagues.

Franz Boas is another striking example of an anthropologist whose personal humanitarian beliefs and scientific knowledge found expression in his day. His humanism has been described as one of the primary factors that stimulated his thinking (Kroeber 1959:vii). Throughout his career, Boas was ardently committed to the promotion of human equality. He himself was a German immigrant who lived in New York during the early decades of this century at a time when racial prejudice against most immigrants, black Americans, and American Indians was virulently alive. Moreover, his lifetime spanned two world wars which evoked strong attacks on German-Americans.

Although Boas generally rejected deterministic theories as an explanation of sociocultural differences, those based on race provided a special focus for his scholarly endeavors. As early as 1898, in a report of the United States Commissioner of Education, he related the results of a study of the growth curves of Toronto children and an attempt to develop a standardized methodology for assessing the impact of culture in biological maturation. Physical measurements of nearly 18,000 immigrants representing five nationalities and eight occupational groups were reported in a second government report published in 1910. By documenting changes in the bodily shapes of the children of immigrants, Boas' study called attention to environmental influences on physical characteristics.

His book, *The Mind of Primitive Man* (1911) has been called the "Magna Carta of race equality" (Kardiner and Preble 1961:155). In *Anthropology and Modern Life* (1928), Boas attacked various forms of the belief that heredity determined behavior by devoting chapters to such topics as the myth of racial superiority, eugenics, and the inheritance of criminal traits. Toward the end of his life, he worked tirelessly and militantly on a range of anti-Nazi activities (Mead 1959:38–39). A month before he died, he spoke to the American Ethnological Society and urged it to "continue its active participation in anthropological work and contribute by the researches of its members and by its more popular activities to the difficult social problems of our times" (quoted in Mead 1959:35).

The implications of Boas' research to practical problems were and continue to be multiple. Yet, like Schoolcraft, Mooney, and Morgan, Boas was not an applied anthropologist. Useful applications of his knowledge were episodic, and the practical implications of his scientific work were implicit and largely the product of controversial issues which brought his research to public attention and personal convictions which encouraged him to address contemporary social problems. Nonetheless, the major portion of Boas' energy was devoted to abstract anthropology, and his fame is based on his methodological and substantive contributions to the profession and discipline of anthropology as an abstract rather than an applied science.

The Emergence of Modern Anthropology

Anthropology in the United States matured only when it was brought "out of the museums and into the mainstream of the social sciences" (Linton and Wagley 1971). This transition occurred between the mid-1920s and the mid-1950s. It was facilitated by the work of Ruth Benedict, Margaret Mead, Robert Redfield, W. Lloyd Warner, Melville Herskovits, Ralph Linton, and many others, as well as the very substantial contribution that such British social anthropologists as A. R. Radcliffe-Brown and Bronislaw Malinowski made to American intellectual thought and development.

By 1925, the exhaustive task of documenting the historical diffusion of culture traits among "vanishing" American Indians had reached a stage of development which permitted attention to be devoted to other problems. During the following decades, the taxonomic studies of early Boasian students were complemented by intensive systematic studies of single societies and cultures whose objective was that of explaining the functional relationships among various elements of social life. Boas himself pointed the way toward analyses of cultures as integrated functioning wholes, when he sent Ruth Bunzel to study the role of the individual artist at Zuni Pueblo in New Mexico in 1924, and Margaret Mead to study adolescents in Polynesia in 1925 (Mead, personal communication).

During the early 1920s, Margaret Mead was studying psychology at Barnard, where she took a course in anthropology from Boas in which Ruth Benedict was assisting. In 1923, she began her studies in anthropology under Boas at Columbia after completing a master's essay in psychology which had relevance for anthropological problems. After completing her dissertation, she won his support to begin fieldwork in 1925 (Mead 1972a:111–128). Boas encouraged her to study adolescence among American Indians, while Mead argued for a study of culture change in Polynesia. They compromised on a study of adolescent girls in Samoa (Mead 1972a:127–129).

When she left for Samoa, Mead was already convinced that anthropologists must study contemporary problems using contemporary tools while there still were "primitive" peoples among whom anthropologists could work. But she did not go to Samoa "to record the memories of old people." Rather, she went "to find out more about human beings like ourselves in everything except their culture" (Mead 1972a:292–293). She returned from Samoa in 1926 and wrote *Coming of Age in Samoa* (1928), which quickly became a best seller. By relating anthropology to psychology and including two chapters comparing the adolescent Samoan girl with her counterpart in the United States, Mead clearly emerged as a major leader in both modern American anthropology and in the relationship of anthropology to contemporary American problems.

There were still other influences upon anthropology in America during the 1920s. The most significant came from Great Britain and the school of anthropologists known today as functionalists. Bronislaw Malinowski and A. R. Radcliffe-Brown were among the first British anthropologists to carry out extended face-to-face research among "primitive" people in the language of the people themselves. Malinowski's *Argonauts of the Western Pacific* and Radcliffe-Brown's *Andaman Islanders* both appeared in 1922. Each explicitly rejected the search for origins, the taxonomic studies of trait distributions, and historical reconstructions. Instead, they focused upon the behavior of living people and the systematic interconnections among social structure, economics, religion, and politics through which primitive societies survived as a unified whole. The focus upon functional interdependencies between the various spheres of human experience in a culture made possible a systematic analysis of the traits which European and American scholars had heretofore merely collected. The question was no longer, "What is the origin and/or distribution of the mortuary rite?" but rather, "What function does the mortuary rite perform in this society which encourages its origins, persistence, and modification?" Moreover, extended fieldwork conducted in the language of the people provided anthropologists with more reliable data, a more comprehensive perspective on social customs, and an understanding of the meaning of human behavior in its natural context. The contributions of Malinowski and Radcliffe-Brown were unique in comparison to anything else going on in America at the time.

Fortuitously, 1922 also was the year when the young Beardsley Ruml was appointed director of the Laura Spelman Rockefeller Memorial (LSRM), a trust fund that had been established in memory of his wife by John D. Rockefeller, Sr., in 1918. Rockefeller had specified that the funds were to be used to advance social welfare. For Ruml, the way to accomplish this goal was through scientific social research. Under his leadership, the LSRM concentrated on the social sciences and public administration until 1929 when the Memorial was merged with the Rockefeller Foundation.

To develop the type of social research needed as a basis for more adequate policy decisions, Ruml moved boldly into the support of selected universities, research institutes, and fellowships for the training and promotion of collaborative relationships between the several social science disciplines, and the strong encouragement of closer contacts between social scientists and concrete social problems. He defined the social sciences as economics, sociology, political science, and the "related subjects" of psychology (in which he himself had been trained), anthropology, and history (Fosdick 1952; Fisher 1977).

In anthropology, the primary beneficiaries of LSRM funds were those who were engaged actively in collaborative relationships with other social scientists and using methodologies which brought them into direct contact with current social problems. Most notably, both Malinowski and Radcliffe-Brown quickly came to Ruml's attention as scientists who represented the type of anthropological research needed if the discipline was to become germane to contemporary societies.[1]

As early as 1924, LSRM officials accepted a proposal to participate in the planning of a center for anthropological research in Oceania. Consequently, when a new Chair of Anthropology was instituted at the University of Sydney in 1926, local funds were supplemented with generous LSRM monies awarded to the Australian National Research Council for anthropological fellowships, research, and visiting professors. The selection of Radcliffe-Brown for this position was an apt one and not solely because of his previous research among Australian aborigines. Although he was unknown to Rockefeller officials at the time he was appointed, his intellectual interests and previous professional activities in applied research and teaching at the University of Cape Town made him a congenial choice.

In London, 1924 was the year that Malinowski received an appointment to a Readership in Anthropology at the University of London (tenable at the London School of Economics). Subsequently, he was appointed to the first Chair in Anthropology at the University in 1927 (Firth 1957). Malinowski had received his training in anthropology at the London School of Economics (LSE) shortly before World War I.

Founded by Beatrice and Sydney Webb in 1894, LSE developed rapidly under the leadership of Sir William Beveridge, who was appointed Director in 1919. When Malinowski was appointed as Reader, it was the major academic center for social science research and teaching in Britain (Fisher 1977; Harris 1977). Given this background, it was predictable that Ruml would select LSE for major financial assistance. In fact, he viewed the School as a model for what he hoped to achieve in other academic settings.

Although Malinowski benefited from LSRM funds simply by being on the faculty at the right time, he himself was an entrepreneur of no mean ability. His linguistic abilities in several languages, the extent of his travels throughout the world, and his knowledge of both Amer-

1. The role of the Rockefeller Foundation in the development of social and cultural anthropology during the 1920s and early 1930s has been documented recently by Stocking (1984, 1985). The data presented here are based on Stocking's essays and on archival research on the history of British applied anthropology in which one of the authors (Eddy) is currently engaged.

ican and European scholarship combined to give him an exceptional range of knowledge (Firth 1957). Moreover, his own research in Oceania and his continuing personal ties to Australia through marriage enabled him to have intimate first-hand knowledge of anthropological and other developments there. All of these and other reasons contributed to the fact that by the late 1920s, Malinowski had become the major anthropological advisor to the Rockefeller staff.

In the late 1920s, Malinowski became a major figure in the newly established International Institute of African Languages and Cultures. The Institute represented a remarkable coalition of Roman Catholic and Protestant missionary societies, scientific and other organizations from more than eleven countries. It was primarily a scientific organization devoted to the study of the languages and cultures of African natives; the publication of studies on African languages, folklore and art; the collection and dissemination of information on linguistic and ethnological research and educational work in Africa; and the production of an educational literature in the vernacular.

The objectives included also the encouragement of "international co-operation in all questions connected with the mental development and technical advancement of the people of Africa" and the promotion of a "closer association of scientific knowledge and research with practical affairs." The constitution of the Institute provided that it "shall be entirely non-political and shall not concern itself with matters of policy or administration" (Smith 1934:4). It was within this context that Malinowski worked successfully together with J. H. Oldham, the internationally renowned missionary educator and first administrative director of the Institute, to gain considerable Rockefeller support for research monies and fellowships for the anthropological training of students from all over the world (including Africa) in a *practical* anthropology directed toward the problems of development in a rapidly changing colonial Africa.

Sponsored by the LSRM, Malinowski and Radcliffe-Brown made their first trips to America in 1926. Malinowski's trip was an extensive one and lasted for a six-month period. He taught for six weeks during the summer session at Berkeley and visited every major section of the United States. He also made a journey to Mexico, where he met Manuel Gamio. In addition to Berkeley, he touched base with several major universities and scientific institutions, including the University of Chicago, Columbia, Yale, Harvard, Howard, the Robert Brookings School, the Smithsonian, Duke, the University of North Carolina, and Tuskegee. He visited Hopi and Navajo reservations in Arizona and the Pueblo Indians in Santa Fe. In New York, he teamed up with Radcliffe-Brown and took part in several seminars with Boas' students. From New York, he made an excursion to Philadelphia to meet Elton Mayo, a close friend whom he had first met when he went to Australia en route to the Trobriand Islands. He concluded the trip by participating in the Social Science conference at Hanover, sponsored by the Social Science Research Council.

Radcliffe-Brown's trip was less of a marathon. He came to the United States from London on his way to assume his new post in Australia. As Malinowski had done, he met with Rockefeller Foundation officials and then made his way to Cleveland, the University of Chicago, Reno, Nevada (where he met Lowie), and San Francisco, where he visited with the president of Stanford University.

Both Malinowski and Radcliffe-Brown made subsequent trips to lecture and visit in the United States, and both eventually accepted academic appointments there. Malinowski received an appointment at Yale in 1939 and remained there until his untimely death in 1942; Radcliffe-Brown was appointed to the faculty at the University of Chicago in 1931 and stayed there until 1936 when he accepted a position at Oxford.

It was during their initial trips to the United States that W. Lloyd Warner first came in contact with Malinowski and Radcliffe-Brown. He was then a student of Lowie at Berkeley and Malinowski's lectures there during the summer of 1926 contributed significantly to his intellectual development (Lowie 1937a:xix). However, Warner was to be even more influenced by Radcliffe-Brown, who was searching for bright students to undertake research in Australia, recruited Warner, and arranged for him to receive one of the fellowships provided by the LSRM to the Australian National Research Council. As a result, Warner began three years of fieldwork among the Murngin. Though Lowie continued as Warner's American sponsor, Radcliffe-Brown directed his work on the kinship, economics, and religion of the Murngin. Warner emerged from the experience dedicated to the study of modern peoples and the methods of functional analysis. As he wrote a few years later:

When I went to Australia, I told my friends, Professor Robert H. Lowie and Professor Alfred Radcliffe-Brown, that my fundamental purpose in studying primitive man was to know modern man better; that some day I proposed to investigate (just how I did not then know) the social life of modern man with the hope of ultimately placing the researches in a larger framework of comparison which would include the other societies of the world. (Warner and Lunt 1941:3)

Warner returned from Australia to accept a position as instructor in Harvard's Department of Anthropology in 1929. There he met Elton Mayo, who in 1926 had been appointed associate professor and head of the Industrial Research Department in the Harvard Business School. Mayo had met Beardsley Ruml in 1922, soon after coming to the United States from Australia. The two quickly became close friends, and Ruml was largely responsible for establishing Mayo in academic life in the United States. Mayo's work at Harvard was fully funded by the LSRM (Kelly 1985b; Trahair 1984).

Together with L. J. Henderson, the physiologist, Mayo was one of the founders of the Committee on Industrial Physiology. His interests were in what he considered to be the deleterious effects of modern industrial society (Chapple 1953a:819; Richardson 1979 and essay 4 in this volume). Mayo was convinced that much of what was then called "fatigue" among factory workers was not physiological at all, but rather the result of social and psychological factors (Chapple 1953a:820). In 1930 Mayo brought Warner into the Committee, with an appointment in the School of Business and the Department of Anthropology, and together they generated the famous Bank Wiring Observation Room study.

A segment of a work department in the Hawthorne Plant of the Western Electric Company of Chicago was set aside for intensive observation and recording of social interaction among workers. Warner utilized for this study the techniques with which he had recorded Murngin funeral rites, marriage ceremonies, gathering expeditions, and hunting (Warner 1941). The systematic analysis of human interaction patterns pioneered by Malinowski and Radcliffe-Brown were applied to the least primitive aspect of modern society, to the very heart of industrial society (Chapple 1953a:820; Arensberg and Kimball 1965:218; Trahair 1984:245–246). The results demonstrated that fatigue could be reduced through manipulation of interactional variables, and became classic contributions to the field of human relations in industrial organization and business administration (Roethlisberger and Dickson 1939).

Within anthropology, these findings sparked an interest in the scientific investigation of human interaction (Chapple and Arensberg 1940). Exact techniques of micro-observation, classification, and recording of the periodicity, frequency, intensity, and duration of interaction sequences were developed as an outgrowth of functionalism and the recognition of functional interdependencies among elements of behavior. These techniques permitted observation of how minute changes in one element produce adjustments throughout the system.

Following his work at the Hawthorne Plant, Warner turned his attention to the utilization of anthropological methods for the study of modern American communities. The first study of this type in America had been undertaken by Robert and Helen Lynd in *Middletown* (1929), and Robert Redfield had already published *Tepoztlán* (1930), a study of folklife in a Mexican village. Funded by LSRM monies awarded to Mayo, Warner's study was and remains the most comprehensive of its kind to be undertaken in American society. His purpose was to explore the interconnections between family, work, and other systems of organization within the setting of community. An understanding of these functional interconnections was necessary in order to interpret the findings of the Hawthorne Study (Warner and Lunt 1941).

In a small New England town, Warner deployed Conrad Arensberg, Eliot Chapple, Allison Davis, Burleigh Gardner, Solon Kimball, and other Harvard anthropology students to undertake the study. The work began in 1931 and culminated in 1936 when Warner moved to the University of Chicago. Building upon the earlier work of the Lynds (1929) in Middletown, Warner and his students innovated technical tools such as the *Index of Evaluated Participation*. Rejecting a priori formulations based on income, housing, and level of education for determining social class, they analyzed social behavior, how groups were formed, who interacted with whom, and what the people of Yankee City felt were the significant divisions and groupings among them. The findings indicated that beyond the family, two significant social forms could be described which distinguished American community and culture: the corporation and the voluntary association (Warner and Lunt 1941; Warner and Low 1947). Individuals, families, and ethnic categories and groupings were articulated one to another through such institutions, and the importance of these organizational forms distinguished American culture as clearly as the Kula distinguished Melanesian culture.

Upon the completion of the Yankee City study, Warner's students, other colleagues, and Warner himself engaged in similar studies elsewhere. Arensberg and Kimball (1938) employed Warner's methods in their study of County Clare, Ireland, where, for the first time, they mapped out the social anthropological concept of community. Through analysis of the ongoing behavior of peasants, shopkeepers, tinkers, laborers, and others, they delineated a constellation of enduring social relationships in Irish rural culture and found these to be localized and perpetuated through community level social processes. Within the United States, Warner's influence was evident in a number of studies. These include John Dollard's study of *Caste and Class in a Southern Town* (1937); Davis, Gardner, and Gardner's study of family and racial divisions in *Deep South* (1941) and the differential access of human and nonhuman resources which characterized that community; Davis' (1948) comparative study of child-rearing which revealed the social and cultural bias in IQ testing; and Whyte's (1943) analysis of *Street Corner Society*.

During the years that Warner was undertaking his research in Australia, the Hawthorne Plant, and Yankee City, Ralph Linton was at the University of Wisconsin. While there, he established contacts with colleagues in sociology, social psychology, and psychology as well as with fellow anthropologists at Chicago. At Chicago he met Radcliffe-Brown, who introduced him to the functional approach and greatly influenced his intellectual development (Linton and Wagley 1971:37–38). Though he differed from both Radcliffe-Brown and Malinowski in many of his basic concepts, Linton developed a conceptual framework for viewing the social and cultural system as a response to the biological, psychological, and social needs of man and a lifelong interest in the problems of culture contact, diffusion, and acculturation. His textbook, *The Study of Man* (1936), was unlike any other available at the time (Linton and Wagley 1971:50) and it brought him into the forefront of anthropology. In 1937, Linton became visiting professor of anthropology at Columbia and then Boas' successor as chairman of the department. His new status gave expression to the increasingly important role that anthropology would assume not only at Columbia but elsewhere in the modern world.

The events set in motion by the work of Mead, Malinowski, Radcliffe-Brown, Warner, Linton, and many others during the 1920s and 1930s mark this period as a distinct one in the development of modern anthropology. The overemphasis on historical reconstruction yielded to studies of people within the context of the cultures in which they lived. There was increased concern with contemporary problems and closer relationships with colleagues in the social sciences—especially sociology, social psychology and psychology. The rise of social anthropology was accompanied by a functional approach to the understanding of cultural systems and attention to social structure and social organization.

For our purpose here, however, the significance of this era is that the florescence of research and theory which related anthropology to contemporary peoples laid much of the theoretical and methodological groundwork for the development of applied anthropology. Yet the work itself was concentrated primarily upon theoretical problems. The objective was to develop the knowledge necessary to understand society and culture, and most anthropologists still viewed the study of "primitive peoples" as a key to comprehending modern societies. Nevertheless, the pioneering work of Warner and those he influenced had extended anthropology to include ourselves, and Chapple and Coon's textbook, *Principles of Anthropology* (1942), encompassed all peoples, not only "primitives." Both "functional" and "historical" in outlook, it regarded anthropology as a science of human relations and interaction within social groups based on the natural science method of observing human beings within their environments and the use of the time scale to examine change. It foreshadowed a new anthropology in which contemporary peoples belonged.

Precursors of Applied Anthropology

We noted earlier that events external to anthropology can arouse interest in the application of anthropology to practical problems and also can result in significant episodic attention to social policy issues on the part of anthropologists whose primary commitment remains with abstract work within academe. In similar fashion, external events also can bring about a demand for anthropologists to become employees of governmental agencies, foundations, or other organizations and to become engaged in the task of applying their skills to the amelioration or solution of social problems. During the 1930s, for example, the number of Ph.D.s awarded in anthropology increased. But fresh Ph.D.s. faced a paucity of academic openings. Only a few schools offered instruction in anthropology, and even graduate departments were quite small. Thus many of the new graduates turned to other sources of employment (Ebihara 1985; Kelly 1985b).

Both in America and in other countries, governmental interest in the use of anthropologists and their data grew in strength. The crisis of colonialism created conditions which opened up opportunities for anthropologists as aides to administrators of native peoples. Jobs were suddenly available for anthropologists who were interested in social problems of living peoples and the formulation and implementation of policy. As Forde (1953:843–848) noted, government administrators in Africa were uninterested in information about tribal society until taxation and other compulsory schemes produced rebellion. In America, the situation was similar. The failure of colonial policy had been dramatically documented by a joint committee of Congress in 1867, which reported that native Americans were dying out, reservations were constantly being invaded by whites, and disease and starvation were a way of life (Officer 1971:27). No actions in defense of native Americans followed the report. In 1928, four years after American Indians were granted citizenship, the Meriam Report, commissioned by the Congress, documented the same conditions which were reported in 1867 (Officer 1971:41–42).

Following the election of Franklin Roosevelt as President in 1932, John Collier was appointed commissioner of the Bureau of Indian Affairs. Collier had been active in the defense of Pueblo land from white squatters in the 1920s. In his new position, he pushed through the Indian Reorganization Act or the Wheeler-Howard Act of 1934. This legislation has been the basis for Indian policy up to the present (Officer 1971:43–44). It provided that Indian lands would not be allotted any further, that land lost would be restored, that tribal governments would be formed, that loans would be made available to reservations, that the Bureau of Indian Affairs would hire Indians, but that the Department of Interior would retain control over reservation timber, soil, minerals, and tribal budgets (Officer 1971:43; Jorgensen 1971). The first intensive application of modern cultural anthropological concepts and methods to the problems of governmental administration was introduced by Collier when he employed anthropologists to aid in the implementation of these policies. During the same period, other anthropologists were hired in the Human Dependency Unit of the Technical Cooperation Group of the Soil Conservation Service. This unit was also linked to the Bureau of Indian Affairs and was assigned to the study of Indian lands with special attention to economic development, resources, social organization, education, and administrative policies (Kennard and MacGregor 1953:832–833; McNickle 1979; Kimball 1979; Kelly 1985a, 1985b).

It was logical to seek anthropologists to study American Indians and to make policy recommendations, since many of them had specialized knowledge about native Americans. However, most anthropologists at the time were ill-prepared to be of much service to either Indians or the government. Their interests were primarily with abstract problems and the past. As Malinowski (1929: note 4) remarked: "Even in the study of the fully detribalized and yankified Indian, our United States colleagues persistently ignore the Indian as he is and study the Indian-as-he-must-have-been some century or two back." Despite the fact that not all Indians were "detribalized," Malinowski accurately described the focus of the majority of American anthropologists. Tax (1937), Lowie (1922, 1935), Steward (1933, 1938), Swanton (1922), Densmore (1929), Murdock (1936), Benedict (1935), White (1932a, b), and other acknowledged experts on American Indians did not study the relationship between contemporary native Americans and the larger society into which they were systematically integrated. Rather, the focus of their analyses was the nonchanging aspects of indigenous cultures and the past. As one example, we will describe the interests of Robert H. Lowie, one of Boas' early students. His work on the Crow (Lowie 1912, 1922, 1935) provides a glimpse of the difference between abstract anthropology, to which Lowie's intellectual gifts were devoted, and the kinds of questions an applied anthropologist might have asked.

Although Lowie studied among living people, he did not study the contemporary cultural experiences of living people. The Crow were a seminomadic hunting people living in close symbiosis with sedentary maize agriculturalists previous to European contact. It was this period of Crow history which interested Lowie. He attempted to trace the diffusion of culture elements present among the Crow, to find out what the Crow had adopted from whom and what came out of their Hidatsa origins (e.g., the hot dance). He questioned old people about their childhood, and their memories became the vehicle for answers to abstract questions he had inherited from anthropological lore. He did not question them about their contemporary culture, although the reservation Crow carried a new culture quite different from that of their parents and grandparents—one which was partially comprised of elements contributed by traders, agents, missionaries, white settlers, the United States Congress, and the War Department. Had Lowie been an applied anthropologist, he would have given attention to this culture of the living people by examining similar theoretical issues (i.e., the diffusion of culture elements) within the contemporary context. His work would have examined the ideas, traits, and institutions in the day-to-day experiences of the generation that was then reaching maturity in a pluralistic society as members of a subordinate and confined subculture.

Moreover, Lowie's work was not oriented to immediate problems of consequence to the Crow or other parties to the reservation relationship. Among the tribes of the northern plains, the Crow were remarkable for their acceptance of allotment policies whereby plots of land were assigned to the heads of families for farming. Most tribes of seminomadic hunters rejected farming and, like the Sioux, ignored governmental orders to build European-style houses and plant European crops. In contrast, Department of Interior Reports during the 1880s reveal that the Crow cut hundreds of logs for building European-style houses on plots which they had already marked out and planted with European crops (Keller 1881; Armstrong 1882, 1883, 1884, 1885). Indeed, the Crow were so enthusiastic that their agents complained that there were insufficient technical personnel to show them how to build these new houses and that the Crow suspected the government of bad faith (Armstrong 1884:154). At the time of agent Armstrong's 1885 report, logs for 125 European-style houses had been cut and the Crow were awaiting further instructions (Armstrong 1885:345). Elsewhere in the United States, the allotment of Indian land and the attempts to instill European farming were spectacular failures and had disastrous consequences (Wallace 1969; Mead 1966). However, the important and different response of the Crow and its consequences did not interest Lowie at the time he worked among them. An applied anthropologist could hardly have ignored a problem of such central significance to the Crow, other Indians, the government, and other parties to the reservation relationship.

Finally, the uses of knowledge sought by Lowie were solely

within the circles of professional anthropology. The diffusion of moccasin designs, age societies, and the hot dance from one group to another in prereservation days could not have been of interest to the Crow or others concerned with reservation life. That such audiences should find his work of interest was not one of Lowie's considerations. Much more compelling was the interest of Clark Wissler, Alfred Kroeber, and other anthropologists who were concerned with reconstructing native life as if Europeans had never crossed the Atlantic Ocean.

In his choice of people, problems, and application for his studies, Lowie represented the mainstream of abstract anthropology. Nothing of immediate, practical value came out of his work for those he studied. This is not to say that Lowie's work and abstract anthropology are without value, for students of abstract problems have found, and will continue to find, a wealth of insights into the nature of religions, art, kinship, economics, and political processes in Lowie's work. From his contributions, there emerged important understandings of the nature of man, society, and culture, as the insights of Maine, Morgan, Smith, Frazer, Tylor and other early anthropologists were put to the test of scholarship. Eventually, if conditions permit, other uses may develop for the insights gained by Lowie. But this was not the case in early twentieth-century America.

The few anthropologists who did focus upon contemporary peoples stand out as notable exceptions. Margaret Mead (1966) conducted the first reservation-wide, household-by-household study of an Indian reservation in 1930, and painted a vivid picture of alienation and demoralization instilled by the reservation relationship, although it was personally a devastating experience for her (Mead 1972a:189–190; Howard 1984:133–135). Robert Redfield, Ralph Linton, and Melville Herskovits (1936) attempted to summarize the anthropological knowledge of acculturation and the culture change which results from continuous face-to-face contact among alien peoples. Even in the best anthropological studies of previous years, the focus was essentially upon native cultures or ethnographic areas. Relatively little was known of the structure of relationships which provided the conditions of contact between traditional Indians, progressive Indians, white ranchers, mining companies, farmers, land companies, the Department of Interior, the Public Health Service, missionaries, volunteer service workers, and other parties to the reservation relationship. Rather than descriptions and analyses of existing social relationships through which goods, services, and personnel moved on a reservation, anthropologists had concentrated upon only selected elements in a complex system.

When the government first hired anthropologists, therefore, there was little precedent for study of contemporary problems. Those who were hired were a minority willing to carry out innovative work. For example, Scudder Mekeel (1936) worked for the Bureau of Indian Affairs on problems of indigenous economic and political organization among the Sioux; and several others, including Gordon Macgregor (1946), worked in the Education Division of the Bureau on problems of socialization, child rearing, and enculturation among the Sioux. Morris Opler (1952) discovered that traditional leaders among the Creek of Oklahoma vigorously resisted implementation of the provision of the Indian Reorganization Act requiring political centralization. His recommendation that the revolving loan funds be decentralized and administered by traditional community leaders was initially rejected. When the centralization program failed, however, Opler's recommendation was finally adopted. John Provinse (1942) and Solon Kimball (Kimball and Provinse 1942; Kimball 1946, 1979), carried out land use and socioeconomic studies of resource interdependency among Navajo. They discovered a unit of socioeconomic organization the Navajo, the "outfit," which was a natural social unit by which the livestock enterprise was organized, and recommended that political and economic programs among the Navajo be organized along these lines. John Collier felt that the Provinse-Kimball discovery of natural social units which could form the basis of genuine cooperation among Navajo and government workers was extremely valuable. Of all anthropological research for the BIA, this discovery most fulfilled Collier's dream of preserving cultural integrity while building economically and politically viable Indian societies (Kelly 1980).

But the Provinse-Kimball advice went unheeded. The BIA lawyers and other government employees, having already created havoc several years earlier in the sheep reduction program, were committed to an existing policy and administrative structure. Not even Collier's enthusiasm for the recommendations could sway lower level employees. As Kimball (1946:16) reported:

It proved impossible to gain assent to proposals which would make the Navajos full participants in building and carrying through the program. If this was the situation under liberal policy and wise leadership, one can appreciate how much more difficult the problem will be elsewhere.

Kennard and Macgregor (1953:834) described the general response to anthropological perspectives as follows some years later:

From the anthropologists' insistence that functioning Indian life be recognized as a real force to be reckoned with, there arose a curious opposition on the part of the administrators to anthropologists themselves. The administrators, failing to understand the significance of expressions of traditional ways of behavior by Indian groups, assumed that anthropologists, in insisting on recognizing these, were arguing for the preservation of aboriginal Indian life. . . . This stems from one of the major tenets of the American people which underlies the idea of the American "melting pot," namely, that distinct behavioral differences cannot be tolerated.

Congressional budget cuts insured that anthropologists' services would be terminated. Opposition to anthropological work continued, and a few years later when Laura Thompson (1951), in collaboration with Collier and W. Lloyd Warner, undertook a massive interdisciplinary study of educational programs on twelve Indian reservations, interpreted the findings, and formulated policy recommendations, the response of the BIA was to ignore these findings and recommendations completely.

If anthropologists failed to be heard in administrative circles, the reasons lie partly with administrative prejudices and preference for familiar policy recommendations of BIA lawyers and career staff personnel. But they also lie within the narrow tradition of abstract anthropology. As Mekeel and Steward noted in 1936, the primary lesson of the BIA applied anthropology experiment was that even anthropologists with field experience had little or no knowledge of contemporary Indian social organization or problems. If they did, it was only because such knowledge had been acquired "inadvertently" (quoted in Kelly 1985b:129). From this experience, it became clear that narrowly conceived, piecemeal studies of only one element in a complex human relationship were inadequate. Anthropologists had too often concentrated on the past, and were vulnerable to the misperception of "arguing for the preservation of aboriginal Indian life." Anthropological holism, the approach which encompasses the total structural relationships among elements of an ongoing system of human interaction, revealed that the studies of natives in isolation from colonial administrative superstructures and the surrounding white society were not fruitful. Kimball (1946:8) summarized the lesson to be drawn from this period as follows:

Students of the science of human relations know that understanding, not of battles fought and won, but of reasons why colonial peoples are today in ferment, must come first from knowledge of the history and culture of the native groups, something of administrative organization and philosophy of the colonial powers, but basically there is need to examine the system of relations from which agreement or conflict arise as two peoples impinge upon each other.

The governmental work of anthropologists during the 1930s was instrumental in bringing a handful of anthropologists into direct contact with some of the major institutionalized patterns of American society which directly affected native Americans. It provided methodological and theoretical approaches whereby the processes of culture contact and social change could be more fully understood within the context of the crisis of colonialism. But applied anthropology as a distinct branch of anthropology had not yet emerged. Important foundations were laid, but it was not until 1941 that the climate of scholarly opinion brought the early precursors of applied anthropology together to form the Society for Applied Anthropology, in order to give voice to the professional goals of those concerned with specific problems of consequence to living peoples and the relevance of anthropology for policies and programs which affected them.

The Birth of Applied Anthropology

World War II marked a major turning point in the development of anthropological concern for contemporary human problems. Ever since the mid-1930s, anthropology had been undergoing a differentiation of specializations within the field. By the time the United States entered the war in 1941, subdisciplines within the field of anthropology had emerged. Ethnology had become clearly defined as the study of the living cultures of people, in contrast to archaeology, which dealt with the study of cultures which are now extinct, and physical anthropology, which was concerned with the study of humans as one of many mammalian species. Moreover, ethnologists had begun to give attention not only to "primitive" peoples who lived outside the range of "civilization" but also to cultures in transition and complex societies. Their aim and interests had become aligned with those in other social sciences, and cooperative efforts between anthropology, psychology, and sociology were well established. Anthropology was envisaged by some as the nucleus of a new Science of Man which would be "broad enough in its scope to include all aspects of human existence" and to ascertain "the processes and continuities involved in the phenomena with which it deals with a view to the prediction of events and ultimately to their control" (Linton 1945:17).

While John Collier had hired a few anthropologists during the depression years, the crisis of war provided unprecedented opportunities for anthropologists to participate in efforts related to war activities. During and following the war, spectacular technological advances such as the transformation of modern agriculture to the point where it could potentially feed the world, the threat of nuclear warfare, and heightened American involvement in world affairs, all contributed to an optimistic belief that many of mankind's perennial problems could be solved. The spirit of the time is well articulated in a book, *The Science of Man in the World Crisis,* edited by Ralph Linton in 1945. The book brought together articles by prominent anthropologists and other social scientists who discussed the application of their scholarly work to world problems in such areas as population, race and minority relations, the control of natural resources, international relations, and the adjustment of indigenous peoples to modernization and colonial administration. It was a report from the "frontiers" of research which aimed to bring knowledge from the social sciences into the cognizance of other scientists and planners.

This period set the stage for our own, and an understanding of the responses of anthropologists to the new conditions of American life imposed by the war and its aftermath is essential if we are to appreciate later developments in applied anthropology (Mead 1964a:13–15; Mead and Metraux 1965). It was an era in which America moved from an isolationist position to one of intense involvement in international affairs. Economic development, improved public health, the spread of democratic institutions, and sufficient food for everyone were believed to be attainable goals. Together with others, a number of anthropologists dedicated themselves to the reconstruction of the world in ways that would prevent the reappearance of the virulent racism of Nazi Germany and the nuclear holocaust which inevitably would follow should World War III ever begin. While the war-related activities of anthropologists are too numerous to describe fully here, a summary of some of the more significant ones will provide an understanding of the diversities of contributions made by anthropologists and the ways in which the experiences of the war years contributed to the birth of applied anthropology.

As early as 1939, a small Committee for National Morale was organized to consider the ways in which anthropology and psychology could be applied to the improvement of national morale during wartime. Committee members included Gregory Bateson, Eliot Chapple, Lawrence K. Frank, and Margaret Mead. Bateson (1935) had been one of the earliest to call attention to the systematic aspects of relationships whereby conflicts were inevitably escalated, a process he called "schismogenesis." Chapple (1942) was a pioneer of interaction analysis in industry. Frank had instigated the Lynds' study of Middletown (1939), one of the earliest studies of an American community, and Dollard's work at Yale, which led to his study (1937) of race relations in the American South. Mead had returned to New York after a brief trip to Bali. After seventeen years of work among "primitive" contemporary people, she "came home to a world on the brink of war, convinced that the next task was to apply what we knew, as best we could, to the problems of our own society" (Mead 1942a:3).

The Committee began to develop methods for interviewing highly educated members of other cultures about their own lives (Mead 1972a). The purpose was to elicit data on basic theories relevant to a better understanding of cultural differences germane to the problems of building and sustaining morale during wartime. The problem was an important one. Ignorance of cultural differences obscured an understanding of the actions of alien peoples, and misconstrued information exacerbated tensions among allies as well as between allies and enemies.

In 1940, M. L. Wilson, director of extension work in the Department of Agriculture, became chairman of a federal task force charged with coordinating the nutrition programs of all federal agencies for the imminent war effort. In the same year, the Committee on

Food Habits was formed by the National Research Council in an effort to mobilize scientific contributions for this effort. The Committee met once a month for two days, and leaders of the food programs in Washington, economists, and community organizers, together with anthropologists, addressed the problems introduced by Dr. Wilson (Montgomery and Bennett 1979:128–132). Ruth Benedict, Allison Davis, W. Lloyd Warner, and Margaret Mead were the anthropological participants (Mead 1964b). Out of their work came "The Problem of Changing Food Habits" and a "Manual for the Study of Food Habits" in 1943 and 1945, respectively (National Research Council).

The bombing of Pearl Harbor in December of 1941 and the entry of the United States into the war interrupted the academic and research activities of most anthropologists. One of the first to go to Washington was Geoffrey Gorer, who joined the Office of War Information. He was soon followed by Ruth Benedict. By 1943, anthropologists in and out of government included Clyde Kluckhohn, Margaret Mead, Ruth Benedict, Rhoda Metreaux, Gregory Bateson, Gorer and others who had joined in the study of "culture at a distance" or national character studies of parties to the conflict (Mead 1953a; Mead and Metreaux 1965). One result was the recommendation by Gorer, in a memorandum prepared for the Committee for National Morale in 1942, that the surrender and occupation terms for Japan be different from those to be imposed upon Nazi Germany. It was felt that faith in the Emperor and the divine way of life he symbolized indicated that abolition of the prewar government in Japan would only guarantee strong resistance. This recommendation was adopted. When the end of the war came in 1945, the emperor was not deposed but instead personally issued the surrender terms to his people (Mead, personal communication).

One of the domestic tragedies of World War II was the evacuation and relocation of 110,000 West Coast Japanese-Americans. Their impoundment in camps located in inland areas of the West remains today as one of the most dramatic examples of the violation of civil rights in our nation's history (Tateishi 1984). The human distress this mass incarceration caused was made even more acute by administrative traditions and policies which failed to bring Japanese-Americans into responsible policy-making positions in the governing of the War Relocation Centers. John Collier, who was still Commissioner of Indian Affairs at this time, recognized the importance of documenting and analyzing what was happening to both the evacuees and the administrators in this situation. He conceived the idea of establishing a Bureau of Sociological Research at the Poston center, for which the Bureau of Indian Affairs had initial responsibility. During the early summer of 1942, Alexander H. Leighton went to Poston as director of the new bureau and initiated research to help solve the administrative and human problems there. Edward H. Spicer worked with Leighton in developing research for this purpose.

At this time, John Embree had already joined the Washington staff of the War Relocation Authority (WRA) as an advisor on Japanese culture, and Solon T. Kimball had begun to assist in the organization of community government in the various relocation centers. Subsequently, after riots had occurred at the Poston and Manzanar centers in late 1942, it became clear that better understanding of the cultural aspects of Japanese behavior was needed. A decision was made to establish a Community Analysis Section under the direction of John H. Provinse, who was Chief of Community Services for WRA at that time. In early 1943, Spicer went to Washington as head of the Community Analysis Section. Katherine Luomala, Asael T. Hansen, Marvin K. Opler, and Gordon Brown were among the anthropologists who were hired to undertake community analysis of the centers, to trace the outcome of administrative policy, and to evaluate the human and social consequences of policy for the evacuees (Arensberg 1942; Brown 1945; Embree 1943; Leighton 1945; Provinse and Kimball 1946; Spicer 1946; 1979; Kimball 1946; Luomala 1947; Spicer et al. 1969). Their studies complemented those of anthropologists working on Indian reservations which had been described earlier. They reaffirmed the importance of examining the culture of those governed within the context of administrative policy and the society which was expressed by it. (For contrasting studies of the camps and the resettlement process, see Thomas and Nishimoto 1946; Thomas 1952; and Wax 1971:59–174.)

During the war years, anthropologists became intensively engaged in training officers for military government duties overseas. At Columbia University, for example, a School of Military Government and Administration for the United States Navy was formed. The curriculum included courses in languages, history, government, and ethnography of countries in the Pacific and Asia itself. Ralph Linton was involved in the school from its beginning and taught classes. The teaching of anthropology was expanded by the addition of John Whiting and George P. Murdock, both of whom were naval officers at the time, and by anthropologically trained linguists who taught unwritten languages through informant techniques (Linton and Wagley 1971:61). Similarly, the School of Naval Administration at Stanford relied heavily upon anthropologists as advisers in preparing navy personnel for work in Micronesia (Kennard and Macgregor 1953:837). After the war, under the Coordinated Investigation of Micronesian Anthropology Project, forty-two scientists, of whom thirty-five were anthropologists, carried on basic research of Micronesian peoples between 1947 and 1949. This work was sponsored and partially financed by the navy during its civil administration of the United States Trust Territory of the Pacific Islands. In 1945, the navy proposed that an anthropologist be appointed to the Trust headquarters and three others to district staffs. This number was increased to six in 1950. In these positions, anthropologists worked as advisers to administrators and research specialists who provided analyses which could be used in policy implementation (Barnett 1956; Fischer 1979).

Under the United States Scientific and Cultural Cooperation Program, the Smithsonian Institution established the Institute of Social Anthropology in 1943. This Institute worked in collaboration with the Institute of Inter-American Affairs, which had been founded in 1942 as part of the Good Neighbor Policy between the United States and Latin America. Anthropologists were sent to Latin American countries to train students there in anthropology and to work with local anthropologists and students in making community studies and undertaking research related to United States technical assistance programs (Kennard and Macgregor 1953:839, Foster 1979). A series of important studies about Latin American cultures resulted (Beals 1945; Foster 1948; Gillin 1947; Wagley 1941, 1949).

Beginning in 1942, the Institute of Inter-American Affairs initiated cooperative developmental programs with Latin American governments in the fields of public health, agriculture, and education. However, it was nearly a decade before the government sought anthropological advice in evaluating or administering these programs. During the early 1950s, the United States Public Health Service undertook a major six-month evaluation of the cooperative health work.

Five of the Smithsonian anthropologists became members of the team which examined the social and cultural problems encountered when new medical and health practices were brought into traditional communities. The public health programs were not working as well as expected, and administrators wanted to know why efforts in sanitation, health education, control of disease, and preventive medicine were failing. The evaluations of the Institute anthropologists were included in reports detailing progress, and resulted in modifications in planning and programming for the future (Oberg and Rios 1955; Oberg 1956; Foster 1969).

The work of anthropologists in the Committee for National Morale, the National Research Committee on Food Habits, the Office of War Information, the War Relocation Authority, the training of military officers, the United States Trust Territory of the Pacific Islands, and the Institute of Social Anthropology, all provide significant examples of the governmental employment of anthropologists in matters related to domestic and foreign policy during and after World War II. The use of anthropologically based scientific research in policy formulation and implementation reflected the maturation of anthropology to a point which permitted anthropological contributions to be made. In addition, there was a core group of distinguished anthropologists who accepted the public policy role of anthropology and were concerned with the applied implications of anthropology for an America which was emerging as a world power but had little knowledge of, or experience with, many of the peoples among whom it would find itself increasingly involved in both war and peace in the years to come.

The war crystallized efforts of the precursors of applied anthropology to utilize scientific procedures in the study and amelioration of contemporary problems. It was within this context that the Society for Applied Anthropology was founded at Harvard in 1941. Informal discussions about forming a society began early in 1940 and intensified after the annual meeting of the American Anthropological Association in December of that year. There a session entitled "Anthropology and Modern Life" had included papers by Eliot Chapple and John Provinse, who had both argued strongly that anthropology should be used in the solution of administrative problems within public and private institutions. There was sufficient favorable response to this session that strategies for establishing a new society began to be developed by Chapple, Derwood Lockard, Frederick L. W. Richardson, and Douglas Oliver (Kelly 1981).

The following four honorary founders were chosen and agreed to lend their support to the society: M. L. Wilson, director of Extension Services of the Department of Agriculture; John D. Black, professor of agricultural economics at Harvard; Alfred V. Kidder, director of the Carnegie Institution Division of Historical Research in Cambridge, Massachusetts; and Clarence Pickett, executive secretary of the American Friends Service Committee. In February, letters were mailed to several anthropologists across the nation to solicit their support and to seek their comments (Kelly 1981).

The Society was incorporated in April of 1941 with Eliot Chapple named as president. The first meeting was held on May 2 and 3, and the papers read included C. M. Arensberg, "Application of Anthropology to Industry"; E. D. Chapple, "Organization Problems in Industry"; R. S. Harris, "Scientific Diet"; M. L. Wilson, "Work of Food Habits Committee, Department of Agriculture"; D. L. Oliver, "The Problem of Changing Food Habits"; C. P. Loomis, "Administrative Problems of Resettlement Community"; F. L. W. Richardson, "Rehabilitation vs. Resettlement"; R. Underhill, "Anthropology in the Indian Service"; F. Rainey, "Native Economy and Survival in Arctic Alaska"; L. Thompson, "Anthropology in the British Colonial Service"; J. Gillin, "Work of the Committee on Latin American Anthropology"; M. Field, "Behavioural Factors in Mental Health Disease"; W. F. Whyte, "The Social Role of the Settlement House"; M. Mead, "Anthropology and the Social Workers"; G. Bateson, "National Morale and the Social Sciences," and R. Benedict, "Personality and Culture" (Kelly 1981).

Clearly, this was a new kind of anthropology that did not find expression in existing professional journals. At the meeting, George P. Murdock moved that a journal devoted to applied anthropology be established, and, with the approval of the fifty-six members present, *Applied Anthropology*—later to be renamed *Human Organization*—was founded. During the next several years, the articles which appeared in the journal provided evidence that a variety of human problems drew the attention of scientists devoted to the aims of the society—"the principles controlling the relations of human beings to one another . . . and the wide application of these principles to practical problems." The major problem areas investigated at the time were Social Psychiatry and Health Services, Rehabilitation and Community Development, Administered Peoples, and Industrial Relations (Arensberg 1947:2–7).

Most American anthropologists at that time were not involved in the work of the Society. Nonetheless, many who professed little interest in policy research or program development were affected by the events which had given rise to the Society. Beginning in the mid-1940s, there was a discernible shift from the study of ancient societies and past cultures to the study of contemporary ones. This new focus on the present necessarily entailed attention to problems of social and cultural change among living peoples. As Mead (1946a:13) has observed, the evolutionary theories of culture as professed by Leslie White (1943, 1959b) did not spark much interest at the time they were formulated. Even Julian Steward (1955), who had contributed an important reconceptualization of classical evolutionary theory, applied his research tools to the contemporary people of Puerto Rico (1956). Charles Wagley (1941, 1949, 1953) devoted his skills to analyzing the changes which were transforming the economies and societies of Guatemalan and Amazonian peoples, and Sol Tax (1942, 1951) began his work on ethnic and economic relations in Guatemala. Morton Fried (1953) and Martin Yang (1945) studied cultural change in Chinese society. Edward Spicer (1940, 1954) concentrated upon the modern Yaqui, both in their homeland and in migrant communities in the United States. Robert Redfield (1950) initiated the Yucatan Project, building upon earlier work with Villa Rojas (Redfield and Villa Rojas 1934), and focused upon the relationship of Mayan peasants to the urban civilization of which they were a part (Hansen 1976; Singer 1976). Numerous other examples could be cited, but it is clear from the above that the conditions of the 1940s and the leadership of Warner, Mead, Malinowski, and other precursors had redirected American anthropology. Contemporary plantation laborers, peasant farmers, and urban laborers, who were quickly becoming the majority of the world's people, were now the subject of study.

Empirical studies were accompanied by a series of theoretical and methodological statements addressed to contemporary societies and cultures. Steward (1950) pointed to the possibility of a comparative sociology of the modern peoples of the world. Arensberg (1955), Wagley and Harris (1955), Wolf (1955), and others proposed theoretical schemes for a much needed taxonomy of contemporary new world societies and subcultures. Arensberg and Kimball (1965) proposed that the community be considered as the basic unit of analysis and minimal sample for the study of primitive, peasant, plantation, and metropolitan societies of the world. Redfield (1955) formalized his concept of the folk-urban continuum, and with Singer (Redfield and Singer 1954) proposed a theory of the development of civilization.

The transformation of anthropology and the birth of applied anthropology were completed by the 1950s. The inductive empiricism of Boas, the systematic study of ongoing cultures by Malinowski, Radcliffe-Brown, Mead, and Warner, interaction analysis as an empirical method for discovery of behavioral patterns and definition of social units, and the holistic method of problem identification and study were all now firmly established. The optimism which followed the war about the possibilities for ameliorating social problems throughout the world as well as in the United States, together with the knowledge that anthropologists had made positive contributions to policy and program implementation, created an atmosphere in which applied anthropology could grow.

The Postwar Period: Retreat from the Challenge

Following World War II, the discipline and profession of anthropology expanded on an unprecedented scale. This expansion was part of the phenomenal growth of higher education during the late 1950s and the 1960s and the general burst of scientific endeavor in the United States after the Russian launching of Sputnik in 1957. Returning veterans eager to get on with their civilian careers, and subsequently, the products of the wartime baby boom, filled lecture halls to overflowing. Old departments were enlarged, and new departments were created where none had existed previously. In 1947–48, anthropology bachelor's, master's, and doctoral degrees numbered 139, 26, and 24 respectively. In striking contrast, these totaled an impressive 6,008, 1,078, and 445 respectively in 1975–76 (American Anthropological Association 1976b). Research monies flowed from both governmental and private foundation sources, and were available as never before to support anthropological training and research.

There were several results of this florescence. They include energetic efforts to discover new facts and theories through specialization, the rise of new subdisciplines to research particular variables, the forging of new links to other disciplines and professions, and a consequent fragmentation of the field of anthropology as a whole. In addition, the great increase in governmental expenditures for research and postsecondary education affected the nature and direction of academic research and teaching in ways that were heretofore unknown. The manpower shortage in academe during much of the postwar period meant that attention was almost exclusively given to the training of anthropologists for college and university positions. There was an exodus of anthropologists from government jobs as the war ended and academic opportunities beckoned. Most importantly for our discussion here, the concern of anthropologists with the applied uses of their findings declined as they turned to abstract problems.

The evolutionary theories of Morgan, Spencer, Tylor, White, and Steward were revived, and issues such as Morgan's concept of "ethnical stages" of evolution, Lowie's notion of "incorporeal property," and the like became foci of heated polemics (Harris 1968; Posposil 1963). The origins of cross-cousin marriage as interpreted by Lévi-Strauss (1969) arose as a major issue in college classrooms and evoked scholarly debate (Homans and Schneider 1955). Major advances were made in linguistics (Hymes 1964, 1972) and stimulated the creation of structuralism, cognitive anthropology, and componential analysis (Goodenough 1956; Lévi-Strauss 1963; Tyler 1969). The hope of achieving greater exactitude through the use of statistical models stimulated some to further distributional studies of cultural traits (Naroll and Sipes 1973). Important work took place in general systems theory, which was focused on man's role in the physical and biotic environment (Rappaport 1968; Vayda 1969). The biological basis of social life received fresh attention in behavioral anthropology (Chapple 1970). Van Gennep's 1908 formulation of rites of passage was given new significance by Turner (1969).

Concern with abstract problems during this period elicited fruitful insights which in many ways recast classical anthropology. Most anthropologists were primarily attracted to these traditional problems and disdained collaborative activities with those outside of academic circles who were concerned with practical problems of public policy and programs. Even in areas such as economics and development problems, abstract anthropologists ignored the data and theory of postcolonial, ongoing, economic change in favor of classical problems (Dobyns 1971). Paradoxically, though the number of studies of modern peoples multiplied, fewer anthropologists sought practical uses for this newly gained knowledge. As Mead (1975a:15) reports, in reference to anthropologists who were asked to teach Peace Corps volunteers going to Nigeria in the 1960s:

Most of them had not done any thinking about the wider scene for ten years; they did not think about broader issues. . . . So what did they do? They have a course on primitive rites among the Ibo or initiation ceremonies of the Yoruba. And Nigerian students who had come over here to study international affairs picketed the course and protested. Our anthropologists were absolutely myopic and did not take anything into account except nice little bits of ethnology. . . . As anthropologists withdrew from the world scene, they more or less withdrew from anything having to do with government. . . . They went into deciding how many cross-cousins could dance on the head of a pin.

The withdrawal of American anthropologists from the relevant problems of the world scene was not unanimous. In 1952, for example, Allan Holmberg and his associates at Cornell University, in collaboration with the Peruvian Indian Institute, embarked on a five-year experimental program of induced technical and social change in Vicos, which was directed toward the problem of transforming a highly dependent manor system into a productive modern self-governing community adapted to the modern Peruvian State. The Cornell-Peru Project still stands as a landmark endeavor to blend social science knowledge with action (Holmberg 1958; Holmberg et al. 1962; Dobyns, Doughty, and Laswell 1971; Doughty essay 19).

Though earlier opposed to applied anthropology, Sol Tax began to advocate an action anthropology to cope with the situation of the Fox Indians in the 1950s. Viewing the Fox as trapped in a political, social, and economic situation which prevented them from acting in their own self-interest, Tax and his students began to provide and suggest opportunities for such things as crafts and scholarships which allowed economic alternatives whereby the Fox could implement new goals (Tax 1958; Peattie 1958; Gearing 1970).

Many other anthropologists made significant contributions to applied work in areas such as the practical problems encountered in technical and economic development (Niehoff 1966; Spicer 1952; Mead 1953b and 1956b; Goodenough 1963; Erasmus 1961; Foster 1962; Arensberg and Niehoff 1964); improvement of health and health care delivery (Paul 1955; Niehoff 1966; Kimball and Pearsall 1954; Foster 1952; Caudill 1953); and education and child-rearing (Kimball 1960; Spindler 1955 and 1963; Macgregor 1946).

Developments in both medical and educational anthropology attracted sufficient interest and activities among anthropologists that the Society for Medical Anthropology was founded in 1967 and the Council on Anthropology and Education in 1968. Yet, even in these organizations and in the Society for Applied Anthropology itself, interest in abstract problems was high in comparison with applied problems. Governmental and other patrons of applied anthropology frequently complained—and with some justification—that applied anthropologists were unable to relate their work to the political realities and operational problems that agencies were confronted with or to conform to existing administrative requirements. Anthropologists, on the other hand, complained—with similar justification—that their findings were often ignored in the formulation of official policy.

Contemporary difficulties in relating anthropology to practical problems have been exacerbated by the emergence of a vastly expanded and centralized federal governmental structure. Warner (1962:30) has documented the growth of centralized administration in Washington, noting that of the thirty largest independent administrative and regulatory agencies in existence in the 1960s, twelve appeared between 1920 and 1940, and eleven more between 1940 and 1960. During the Civil War, there were 36,000 civilian employees in the entire Executive Branch and only 950 in the War Department. By 1940, the number had risen to over 1,000,000 in the Executive Branch and more than 250,000 in the War Department. By 1960, over 2,500,000 civilians worked in the Executive Branch, and Defense (formerly War) Department civilian employees numbered over 1,000,000. The power and influence of these giant agencies continues to be enormous.

For example, the Pentagon, unlike the earlier Department of War, is a permanent military establishment which can affect the entire range of economic, social, and ideological behavior of our society. It can create entire industries and support major portions of others. It offers to millions the opportunities to achieve the upward mobility of American mythology. The ideological symbols at its command can direct the attention of the vast majority of Americans to an obscure pinpoint on the global map of its interests and convince many that the pinpoint is an essential element of national destiny. Its immense number of personnel represents a constant bleeding of national wealth, which in time of crisis becomes an arterial lesion.

While the provenance of activity and the absolute amounts of power differ between bureaus and departments, the scale of the bureaucracy is similar in education, health, agriculture, and most of the fields in which applied research is undertaken. Decision-making in these vast corporate hierarchies seems at times mysterious, but Mulhauser (1975) has provided a useful summary to some of the reasons the holistic, systematic, and comparative perspective of anthropologists is often incompatible with bureaucratic perspectives.

The policy maker wants immediate action in reaction to troubles which arise, and in his or her view the complexity of a situation must be ignored in favor of *ad hoc* compromises within a bureaucratic agency. Moreover, fractionation of tasks within and between agencies means that questions are never phrased holistically; short-run solutions are sought in a continuing process of negotiation between the involved agencies, legislative committees and staffs, interest groups, and so on. Despite the numbers of employees in any given agency, since no single unit handles a problem by itself, staff shortages result from work overloads. As Mulhauser's (1975:313) personal experience indicates, lengthy consideration of scientific data can hardly be a factor:

In the Congressional subcommittee where I worked, the four professionals on the staff were involved in new or renewal legislation and administrative overseeing in the following areas: child abuse, nutrition and employment of the elderly, vocational rehabilitation, educational research, support for museums and libraries, the National Endowment for the Arts and Humanities, education for the handicapped, comprehensive child development, environmental and drug-abuse education, educational technology, accreditation of schools and state agencies for the blind, regulation of state social service agencies, a national institute for film, and still more.

Mulhauser concludes that the only way scientists can be heard amidst these pressures of time, work overlap and overload, is through "politically viable levers of action." Individuals and organized groups in and out of government who are receptive to anthropological theory and data must exist in order for information to flow effectively from research scientists to policy makers. When this occurs, as in the flow of information regarding surrender terms for the Japanese during the war or the case of potential epidemics today, the massive bureaus and agencies respond quickly. When such levers of action do not exist, the information flow is blocked.

During the crisis of World War II, vital links between anthropological research and policy applications existed, but as the crisis subsided the linkage was broken. Mead (1957a:13–14) describes it:

> We only do applied anthropology if somebody is going to apply it. We have to have a consumer. What happened in World War II is that we had, in every government agency, people who were prepared to use what those of us who were outside or in another agency were producing. We organized that. We assembled a group of people, prepared them, and sent them to Washington, where they were put into government agencies. . . .
>
> When the end of the war came, of course everybody was a little tired and anxious to go home. There was still a fair number of people in Washington who were willing to go on and work in this field. A great deal of the very best work was done right after the war. Then came the Joseph McCarthy era and the Korean War, when everybody inside the government who could have used the new material or insights that anthropologists could have produced went home or got fired. By 1952, there was no one in the government to ask for information of the sort anthropologists would have provided or to use it if it had been provided. We began to have boners of the kind that were not made in World War II.

A major indication of the break is that, according to the U.S. Civil Service Commission, there were only 55 full-time anthropologists employed by the government as of October 31, 1973. At the same time, in startling contrast, there were 4,638 economists, 2,492 psychologists, 2,200 psychiatrists, 69 sociologists, and 48 archeologists (Maday 1977:89).

The growth and proliferation of government agencies, the severe lack of skilled anthropologists within them, and the retreat of most anthropologists to departmental and disciplinary cocoons combined in the mid-1960s to create a situation of extreme distrust of the federal government on the part of anthropologists and heated debates about the ethical responsibilities of anthropologists engaged in applied work.

Within the profession, two events were particularly instrumental in precipitating these attitudes. The first was Project Camelot, a proposal sponsored by the Office of Research Development in the United States Army and oriented toward Latin America. The aim was to utilize social science data and analysis "to predict and influence politically significant aspects of social change in the developing nations of the world" (Horowitz 1974:5). The second was the involvement of anthropologists in research sponsored by the Department of Defense and the Agency for International Development in Southeast Asia, especially Thailand. The details of these debates and the issues entailed have been described elsewhere and will not be repeated here (Belshaw 1976:255–274; Beals 1969; Sjoberg 1967; Horowitz 1965 and 1974; Jones 1971; Wolf and Jorgenson 1970).

For our purpose, the important contribution of the controversies is that they revealed a basic lack of understanding of the nature of social scientific research in powerful governmental agencies and naiveté on the part of both governmental officials and social scientists. They also raised ethical issues inherent in applied work. In these instances, at least, it became clear that social scientists were being used merely as technicians who would supply information to governmental patrons who already had formulated prior assumptions about the nature of the problems to be investigated and the policies to be defended. The outrage expressed by social scientists reflected not only a reaction against the reduction of the social scientist to a technician who collects and processes data, but also raised a genuine doubt about the purposes for which the data were to be used.

If the quality of social research, its methods, theory, analytical techniques, and data collection procedures are to be determined by governmental patrons who are untrained in methods of scientific inquiry, unknowledgeable about the types of research needed to advance theory, and perhaps even unsympathetic to scientific development, there can be no applied *science*. Moreover, there can be no anthropology worthy of the name, if the social purpose of a project is accepted as an excuse for relaxing the criteria by which data and theory are judged for scientific reliability, accuracy, cohesiveness, and completeness, and a consideration of the potential consequences of the research for human beings.

The ethical crisis of these years produced debate, but few commentators agreed about the proper "applications" of anthropology.

Some took the position that application consisted in teaching or telling powerless people how to achieve power (Stavenhagen 1971) while others concluded that only the people who were being studied could teach the anthropologist proper applications of research results (Hessler and New 1972), ignoring the fact that such people are often ill-informed about forces affecting their lives (Gonzalez 1972). Still others concluded that the applied anthropologist must concede scientific definition of problems and research techniques to an employer, ignoring the lesson of Project Camelot (Clinton 1975). There were those, also, who argued that some form of individual commitment to the political beliefs of the people studied was the essential element of anthropology (Jacobs 1974), while a few claimed there could be no research during troubled times and the best an anthropologist could do would be to cook meals or gather firewood for a chosen faction (Talbert 1974). But by far the most common response was avoidance of the issues and retreat into abstract problems and academic career building.

Applied Anthropology Today

Those who became anthropologists during the decades immediately after World War II tended to take the expansion of academic departments and professional anthropology for granted. The abnormal period of rapid growth in higher education at this time created an acute need for teachers of anthropology to staff new departments and to expand older departments that were under pressure to serve increased numbers of students. Of necessity, primary attention was given to building departments. For example, in November 1958, a Ph.D. Curricula Conference was held in Washington, D.C., to recommend guidelines for graduate education (Foster 1958). Two years later, in 1960–61, a special Education Resources in Anthropology project, supported by the National Science Foundation, was undertaken by the Department of Anthropology at Berkeley. This project sponsored ten symposia throughout the country to discuss the teaching of anthropology in all of the subfields of the discipline, including applied anthropology, and the teaching of professional students in the fields of education, public health, law, and government. The papers presented were published by the American Anthropological Association, together with an extensive list of teaching resources (Mandelbaum, Lasker, and Albert 1963a; 1963b).

A paper prepared for one of the symposia by Fred Eggan (1963) succinctly expressed the tenor of this period by stating that "current prospects for expansion in anthropology suggest that we do not need to worry about an overproduction of Ph.D.s for some time to come." In less than a decade, the time for concern had arrived. An historic downward shift in birthrates, the accelerated departmental growth of the post-World War II years, and the overwhelming orientation of anthropology departments toward training students for college teaching careers created a situation in which higher education institutions could no longer absorb all of the Ph.D. graduates they were producing. Equally important, very few of the new anthropologists were trained for work in institutions other than the university.

Today professional anthropology, which began in the museums and private universities, then moved during the 1930s and 1940s into other institutions of society and expanded significantly into the public universities and colleges during the 1950s and 1960s, has now entered a fourth stage of development. In this stage, as during the 1930s and 1940s, applied anthropology is playing a central role not only in the United States but in other parts of the world as well. This is so partly because the demand for trained anthropologists beyond the university has never been greater, and partly because professional anthropology has trained many new anthropologists for work outside the academy. Moreover, recent nonacademically employed Ph.D.s often express greater satisfaction with their salaries and work than do the academically employed (Whitney 1985). New professional associations, significant changes in publications, the rise of graduate training programs in applied anthropology, and the increased specialization of the field itself express clearly the response of the profession to the new demands being placed upon it.

PROFESSIONAL ASSOCIATIONS AND PUBLICATIONS

In 1974 a Society of Professional Anthropologists was founded in Tucson, Arizona. Comprised of 180 members, SOPA began as a local regional group of professional anthropologists employed in nonacademic settings. The establishment of the Washington Association of Professional Anthropologists, based in Washington, D.C., and other regional groups quickly followed. Finally, a National Association for the Practice of Anthropology was formed as a unit of the American Anthropological Association in 1984 and currently has 600 members.

A major reason for the founding of special associations for practitioners has been the fact that traditional anthropological associations historically have shown little interest in meeting the professional needs of anthropologists who are employed outside of the academy. It is only recently, for example, that the American Anthropological Association has made an effort to compile a directory of practicing anthropologists (American Anthropological Association 1981; see also National Association for the Practice of Anthropology 1986) or to regularly include book reviews and articles on topics related to applied anthropology in the *American Anthropologist* and the *Newsletter* of the Association. Belated recognition of the contributions of applied anthropology in the past came in 1979 when the Association published *The Uses of Anthropology,* edited by Walter Goldschmidt.

Even the Society for Applied Anthropology neglected the career interests of practitioners during the halcyon days of academic expansion when most applied anthropologists joined the academy. In 1978, however, the Society began to publish *Practicing Anthropology,* a publication largely devoted to the career interests of the nonacademically employed. In the same year, the Society joined the Society of Practicing Anthropologists in cosponsoring the Documentation in Applied Anthropology Project at the University of Kentucky. Under the leadership of John van Willigen, this project addresses the problem of collecting and organizing an archive of the written materials produced by practicing anthropologists in the course of their work. In the past, these types of documents have had very little circulation among specialists or become fugitive due to the lack of adequate publication outlets for them in anthropoligical journals, the restrictions on the release of data to the public domain by national and international firms and organizations, and the reduced incentives to publish among anthropologists in careers where productivity is not measured by publication. A recent major bibliographic chronology of the development of applied anthropology is partially based on this archive (van Willigen 1980).

Similar developments are occurring in Great Britain. As more traditional sources of employment and research funds have dried up, British anthropologists have increased their interest in applied research and work opportunities. In 1981, for example, the Royal Anthropological Institute was an active cosponsor of the Society for Applied Anthropology's 41st Annual Meeting which was held in Edinburgh. This meeting brought together a critical mass of people interested in establishing a British-based applied anthropology group, and a steering committee to get this underway was formed (Eades 1981). In October of 1981, the Group for Anthropology in Policy and Practice (GAPP) was formally established. GAPP currently sponsors a newsletter, meetings, and workshops on topics related to applied anthropology and the nonacademic careers of social anthropologists (RAIN 47:13–14, December 1981; Stirling 1983).

In Britain also professional publications devote increased space to applied anthropology. Most notably, RAIN *(Royal Anthropological Institute News)* has regularly presented articles and listed news events pertinent to applied work in recent years. Most recently, special attention has been given to urban anthropology *(RAIN* 52:4–10, October 1982), social and community work *(RAIN* 63:2–15, August 1984), and to the question of expanding job opportunities for social anthropologists (Stirling 1982, 1983). Beginning in 1985, *RAIN* was incorporated into a new periodical, *Anthropology Today,* which is specifically oriented toward public and topical issues and other professions. A major purpose is to create public awareness of the work done within the discipline today (Benthall and Houtman 1985). The first four issues of this new publishing venture included several articles specifically dealing with applied anthropology (D'Souza 1985; Mair 1985; Hill 1985; Benthall 1985; MacCormack 1985; Helman 1985).

On this side of the Atlantic, discussion about the formation of a Canadian national organization for applied anthropology began in 1976, largely at the instigation of John Price at York University. A Society of Applied Anthropology in Canada (SAAC) was formally organized in 1981 with thirty-four professionals and ten students as members. The SAAC regularly publishes a newsletter, holds an annual meeting, and performs other services for its members. Local chapters of SAAC exist in Winnipeg and Quebec (Price 1985).

GRADUATE TRAINING

In several universities of the United States, graduate programs are being restructured so as to meet better the needs of students who wish to prepare themselves for nonacademic employment. A recently published *Guide to Training Programs in the Applications of Anthropology* lists twenty-eight universities where specialized training is available at the graduate level (van Willigen 1985). Other programs undoubtedly exist.

In the past, the training of anthropologists has largely emphasized the Ph.D. But many positions outside of the academy do not require a doctoral degree. As a consequence, some departments are giving emphasis to the training of students in applied anthropology at the master's degree level (van Willigin 1985; Leacock, Gonzalez and Kushner 1974). The University of Maryland (College Park), for example, offers a professional degree, the Master of Applied Anthropology. The program emphasis is on the utilization and mediation of anthropological knowledge in settings that require practical problem solving. At Harvard University, the Social Anthropology Wing of the department offers a special one-year program leading to the Master of Arts degree for persons with a demonstrable commitment to work in the fields of social change and development, medicine, and law. At the doctoral level, several departments, not to mention recent Ph.D. graduates, are exploring ways of combining doctoral training in anthropology with degree programs in other fields such as public health, urban and regional planning, agronomy, and nursing.

Recently, the American Anthropological Association and the Society for Applied Anthropology have sponsored jointly a series of *Training Manuals in Applied Anthropology* under the senior editorship of William L. Partridge. The first four of these, one on development anthropology (Partridge 1984), the second on medical anthropology (Hill 1985), the third on policy ethnography (van Willigen and DeWalt 1985), and the fourth on nutritional anthropology (Quandt and Rittenbaugh 1986) have been published. Volumes on educational anthropology and on management and administration are planned for the future.

SPECIALIZATION

Just as the field of anthropology has become increasingly specialized, so also has the subfield of applied anthropology. As Erve Chambers

(1985) and John van Willigen (1986) have recently noted, applied anthropologists today generally require special skills and expert knowledge in one or more areas of topical interest, and these often correspond to particular areas of public concern and policy. New areas of applied interest continually arise, often as a result of governmental and private agency funding addressed to particular social problems or events which bring new problems to the forefront of public attention. For this reason, it is impossible to list all of the areas which will engage applied anthropologists in the future nor even all of those which interest them today.

In the mid-1980s the most prominent areas of applied specialization are in the fields of medicine and health, education, overseas development work, cultural resource management, social impact assessment, corporate and industrial relations, and urban and regional planning. Anthropologists who work in these fields are likely to be trained in sociocultural anthropology. Some fields, however, include anthropologists trained in other major subfields of the disciplines. For example, significant contributions are being made to medical anthropology by biological anthropologists, to educational anthropology by linguists, to cultural resource management by archaeologists, and so on.

The specialization of applied anthropologists in one or more of the four traditional subfields of the discipline and in a topical area germane to applied work reflects the fact that contemporary institutions themselves are diverse and highly specialized in their structural, symbolic, and organizational characteristics. Modern institutions vary as much as the publics or clients whom they serve, the mix of products, functions, or services that they deliver to clients, and the environments in which they exist and which they seek to influence and transform. They vary also in the arrangement of their segments into divisions, departments, boards, and committees, the combinations of managers, professionals, staff and other personnel that inhabit them, the mythologies they create to perpetuate, change, or expand their activities, and the periodicity and patterns of organizational behavior which knit together and articulate their segments, clients, products, and symbols into rational systems. Anthropologists ignore these variations and specializations in modern institutions at their peril.

A Look Ahead

The essays brought together in this volume attest to the diversity and increasingly specialized nature of contemporary applied anthropology. They reveal that the vital essence of applied anthropology is the scientific analysis of the nature of human problems amidst changing technological, environmental, and social conditions. The nature of human problems is best discovered through the empirical study of the interplay between their macrocosmic context and the microcosmic contexts in which human beings live out their daily lives. Macrocosmic technological, economic, political, and social changes today link the microcosmic units of human behavior and interaction to regional, national, and multinational organizational structures in extraordinarily complex ways. As a consequence, peoples all over the world are confronting rapidly changing conditions which demand innovative adaptive strategies so as to change organizational systems which take the welfare of human beings into account. The application of a holistic view to the understanding of human problems, and the analysis of social systems in terms of their interdependence are unique contributions which can be made by applied anthropologists to the new types of problems that confront all of us. The essays to follow describe the types of contributions that can be made and the rewards and difficulties of making them.

The remainder of this volume is divided into three parts. Part I brings together contributors who have advanced theory through their applied work, thereby demonstrating the significance of the continuing dialogue between theory and practice. Theory is abstraction from empirical evidence serving the purpose of illuminating regularities and complex patterns, and demonstrating relationships which may be obscure. The testing of the validity of theoretical abstractions through empirical research is neither new nor unique to applied anthropology. But the creation of theory out of analysis of human problems is worthy of special attention, for this is at the heart of applied anthropology. Constant modification of the conditions of human life in which contemporary problems are given shape and meaning demands that theory be built out of analysis of primary data in specific settings. Change in contemporary societies is multilineal, and relationships among variables are predicated on numerous contingencies and alternatives. Adequate theory must be based on empirical evidence, and subsequently tested in application where the consequences of theoretical assumptions can be observed. If we would understand cultures as organic, changing entities which are part and product of the adaptive strength of our species, rather than as constructs composed of categories manipulated in the minds of abstract theoreticians, the dialogue between theory and practice described by the contributors should guide our efforts.

Part II reports the experiences of anthropologists who have taken actions based on analysis of situations in the roles of researcher, employee, advocate, administrator, consultant, evaluator, and expert witness. In each essay, we learn something of the obstacles to effective action found in specific institutional settings: development programs, government agencies, Indian reservations, universities, schools, hospitals, and courtrooms. Moreover, we learn that application does not necessarily proceed according to rigid steps, nor can we devise a cookbook formula that certifies that success will be forthcoming. The empirical nature of anthropological analysis precludes any such uniformity. For the constraints on application are the product of institutional goals, procedures, and organizations, the conditions in which institutionalized groups interact with one another, and the situational strategies utilized by actors in these groups to achieve goals, manipulate procedures, and shape the organization. These vary between settings, among groups, and over time. The analysis of these variations is a necessary first step in the process of devising appropriate actions. Beyond that, the applied anthropologist must devise situational strategies for taking action. Like the actions of other participants in the institution, these strategies must be varied, multiplex, and tailored to the institutional setting.

Part III examines some of the areas of application which come under the rubric of policy studies. As Kimball points out, policy recommendations must stem from scientific research just as in the case of other kinds of action. In the areas explored here, we are discovering both limitations and opportunities for the uses of applied anthropological research which lie in the political, economic, social, and cultural environments in which policy decisions are made. Administrators trained to think in the logico-deductive models of engineering have difficulty understanding more complex contingency-alternative models derived from natural science (Northrup 1953). The strictures of time, personnel shortage, and overload favor the use of familiar binary logics. Nevertheless, anthropologists who are sensitive to this fact work hard to learn the language and concerns of policy makers and examine carefully the several levels at which policies are made and modified. By bringing policy formulation into the realm of empirical analysis, applied anthropologists often discover creative ways to become engaged in the policy process itself.

Students of anthropology and professional anthropologists who are planning careers in applied anthropology require training in the dialogue between application and theory construction, the practice of anthropology in modern institutions and the communities they impact, and the critique and production of public policy. This volume cannot and does not cover all fields of endeavor in which applied anthropologists contribute to theory and practice, but it explicitly provides a guide to these three major areas.

Part I

The Dialogue Between Theory and Application

Like applied scientists in all fields of science, applied anthropologists systematically use theory in formulating problems for study and in developing new knowledge in the course of their work on practical problems. The contributed essays of Part I describe specific instances of the ways in which the dialogue between theory and application develops in nonacademic work settings. They provide glimpses into what is entailed in the interweaving of discoveries made about processes of human organization, adaptation, and change into both theoretical and practical concerns.

Together, the essays in Part I demonstrate that theory and application must be closely linked if either is to have any validity or impact. Application is the testing of theory. In the absence of such testing, theories in anthropology persist only as a consequence of data that are deductively generated and tailored to fit them. In contrast, application is necessarily inductive. It is the product of practicing anthropology within specific institutional and community contexts. It is these contexts which provide the settings for theoretical propositions, the formulation and implementation of actions based on theory, and the extraction and analysis of data that evaluate the outcomes of the actions taken and the validity of the theory on which they were based.

The essays presented here are limited to the dialogue between theory and application as it has emerged in the fields of what are today called development, educational, and industrial anthropology. Beginning in the late 1920s, these fields were among the first to attract visible groups of social and cultural anthropologists who were concerned with the application of anthropological research methods to practical problems. Some of these early pioneers are still active in the field today, and they can review the diachronic development of their work over a period of more than fifty years. The articles by Arensberg, Richardson, and Whyte represent reports of this nature and reveal the changes that occur in the theoretical formulations of applied anthropologists over time. The articles by Goodenough, Hill-Burnett, Cohen, Scudder, and Partridge are reports from applied anthropologists who have built on past theoretical contributions but who bring new perspectives into the field as a consequence of their own research and new theoretical perspectives in anthropology generally.

2

THEORETICAL CONTRIBUTIONS OF INDUSTRIAL AND DEVELOPMENT STUDIES

Conrad M. Arensberg

Too often those who write about complex societies and the institutions within them assume that they are the same or in the process of becoming so. They argue that such factors as scale, industrialization, economic development, technology, and mass communications operate so as to standardize and homogenize family structures, settlement patterns, community forms and functions, and other expressions of cultural patterns. In his review of the theoretical contributions of industrial and development anthropology, Conrad M. Arensberg presents a quite different point of view.

Arensberg's central theme is that complex social systems, founded in multiple asymmetrical relationships among members, are as varied and unique as the cultural traditions from which they evolve. Empirical evidence of applied and other anthropologists reveal that the structure of social interaction results in a variety of elaborate, coordinate patterns of initiation and response. There are cultural variations in these interactional sequences which are found in the variety of institutionalized hierarchical relationships which comprise complex societies. These variations may be observed in the domains of religion, politics, economics,

Conrad M. Arensberg (Ph.D., Harvard) is professor emeritus at Columbia University. He is a social anthropologist who has done research in the areas of industrial and community studies, and in both economic and applied anthropology. His fieldwork has been in the United States, rural Ireland, Germany, and India. He has served as a consultant and researcher with the United States Departments of Agriculture, Interior, and State, the Rockefeller Foundation, UNESCO, the University of Munster, Germany, and the Instutute for the Social Sciences in Cologne, Germany. He was a founder of the Society for Applied Anthropology, president of the Society during 1945–1946, and editor of its journal from 1946 to 1951. He was president of the American Anthropological Association during 1980–1981.

and other settings, and in the decision-making patterns of ongoing social life. Within American culture, the significance of these distinctive patterned interactional sequences in asymmetrical relationships is evident in hierarchical organizations as diverse as schools, prisons, hospitals, churches, communities, and governments.

The situations in which applied anthropologists normally work usually involve social change within the context of hierarchical structures. Successful planning, administration, intervention, advocacy, evaluation, and other applied activities flow from the discovery of effective actions in such settings. The elaborate ballet of behavioral sequences which Arensberg describes are the content in which novel behaviors are accepted or rejected. We learn from applied anthropology that change cannot be coerced, programmed, or legislated. Rather, it comes about when new behaviors are "naturalized" by all parties to the institutionalized hierarchical relationships and when the new pattern is incorporated into the interactional sequences considered proper, ethical, right, and rewarding by powerless and powerful alike.

MUCH HAS BEEN written about the practical successes and failures of applied anthropology. Equally important, though less well known, are its contributions to behavioral, social, and cultural anthropological theories. Here I discuss such feedback as it has already appeared in two substantive fields, and the possibilities for applying it to solve an insistent problem in social science theory: the nature of decision making in the context of hierarchical organization and leadership. This problem is not only insistent in the modern world of ever-increasing organizational complexity, but it is also central to anthropology's perennial concern with cultural evolution and institutional growth. In the two fields I shall report on, the use of anthropology has led to discoveries which show the ineluctable force of the emergence of regular social processes from personal and interpersonal behaviors and their assumption of hierarchic form. But a report of the feedback of field experience would be incomplete without an example of one of the many resultant theoretical advances. In this essay, I have chosen to present the advance into a processual understanding of the dynamics of communication, social interaction, and coordination in hierarchic decision making. Other examples closer to historical anthropological concerns, such as the evolution of other organizational forms (e.g., monarchy, civil-religious "cargo" systems, "hydraulic empires," etc.) are left for later work.[1]

This essay, then, will report on two fields and one extension of theory emanating from both of them. The first field is that of industrial behavior and relations. There, an early "industrial anthropology" worked beside industrial sociology and social psychology in "human relations" and "organizational behavior" in researches in factories, hospitals, and businesses (Mayo 1940; Roethlisberger and Dickson 1939; Barnard 1938; Richardson 1961). The second is the field of transcultural transfer of innovations, or, as more recently described, "development research" and development project "evaluation." In this field, anthropology's effort has become known as "development anthropology" (Cochrane 1971; Rubin 1961).

As mentioned in the editors' introductory essay, industrial anthropology took the science into small groups and personal networks within large institutions. Anthropology's methods of natural history observation, inductive generalization from participant observation and open-ended interviews, and its use of sociometric measures of interaction among live human beings in real events, lately expanded into network and event analysis, made new and telling contributions (Arensberg and Kimball 1965; Chapple 1970; Horsfall and Arensberg 1949; Guest 1962; Boissevain and Mitchell 1973). Fieldwork penetration of the relatively autonomous "informal" groups and networks of the diverse institutional personnel (workers, unionists, managers, engineers; doctors, nurses, patients, and so on) and cultural awareness of their differences gave scope for anthropology's special skills.

The field of development also provided useful employment of anthropological method and experience. It plunged anthropologists into working with the human subjects of current social and cultural change. As spectators of the "natural" worldwide transformations overtaking traditional cultures everywhere, anthropologists were pulled into direct observation of the planned local and "induced" social and cultural change involved in the political and economic modernizations of our time. They were especially close to the cultural innovations and the transfers of technology visited upon the recipients of the planned and programmed projects of regional and community de-

---

1. For application of processual and systems analysis to the problems of the emergence of shamanism, prophetic leadership, and the state, see Arensberg, 1981, 1982. For parallel observation, see Richardson's essay in this volume.

velopment that marked national and international modernization efforts around the world and reached again and again into the very
countrysides in which anthropologists worked.

Anthropology shared observation of development with the other
social sciences: economics, sociology, and political science. From
the 1930s up to the present, they have all turned to the world scene
and the developing countries beyond metropolitan societies. But anthropology's vantage point was unique. Its experience with grass-
roots cultures and its fieldwork outside national capitals and project
planning headquarters gave it a special advantage.

The fortunate position of anthropology in the study of development was a concomitant of its evolutionary trends. First, fieldwork
expanded out from tribal and antiquarian into community and village
studies. Attention turned from the "primitive" (preliterate) to the
peasant and "post-peasant" worlds and to comparisons of the other
great urban civilizations with the European one in which anthropology already had crystallized. Second, the science awoke, with new
fossil evidence, to the huge antiquity of Man. It rediscovered human
evolution, adaptive ecology, comparative mammalian and human eth-
ology, and "sociobiology." It turned back again to concern with the
emergence of successive stages of culture and the levels of complexity of behavior in men and animals. It came to accept empirical but
controlled cross-cultural comparisons based on the worldwide evidence, compiled now in such compendia as the Human Relations
Area File and the World Ethnographic Atlas. Documenting questions
as to what was various and what was universal in the cultures of
mankind, it could again ask evolutionary and nomothetic questions.
What are the lawful processes of change? After the end of peasantry
(Mendras 1970; Franklin 1969), what next?

These trends propelled anthropology into a confrontation with
the two kinds of modern culture change already cited, "the natural"
(adaptive and evolutionary) and the "induced" (planned). Appraisal
of change and development became inescapable. New experience called
for reexamination of older theories of culture contact and culture
growth, to be tested now in the interaction between the culture bear-
ers of the new ways and those of the old.

Developers' projects and the reactions of those served by them
were lively theatres of that interaction. The former came to be called
"change agents" and "donors" by the analysts, though they stoutly

called themselves "experts"; the latter came to be called "donees." The observed dramas taking place between these two sides called for further theory of the processes of change itself and the roles of individual and groups in behavior, attitude, social organization, and cultural values in change and contact situations.

Experience with industry had already discovered workplaces to be exactly such dramas of human relations, clashes of motives, adjustments of interests to larger institutional pressures and in wider economic and technical trends. Now old places of residence and subsistence in planned and project-engulfed villages became new stages of similar dramas of contact, power and pressure, and change. The feedback into theory that rose (and continues to rise) from watching these dramas will occupy us here.

The Feedback from Industrial and Organizational Studies[2]

Critics of anthropological research into industrial shops and business and hospital organizations during the 1930s and 1940s often state that the observation undertaken was only small group research. They hold that the study of small closed groups was too limited to yield results which could readily be transferable to larger settings of human social behavior and culture. Yet, we did not think of ourselves at that time as doing small group study. Instead, we treated observations of human beings in offices and workshops as studies in a laboratory of rapid social and cultural change where general processes of human organization and cultural interaction might be explored, for both grand trends and the dynamisms of relatively closed social systems.

The laboratory was not a setting of controlled experiment; we ourselves did not impose the changes we watched. Rather, it was a field of direct observation which provided a comparative microcosm of rapidly changing human events. These showed many variations in social organization and in cultural understandings and misunderstandings; they also showed misunderstandings which were analogous to

2. This section paraphrases sections of "Discussion" of C. Stewart Sheppard, "The Role of Anthropology in Business Administration" (Arensberg 1975).

larger movements outside. It was a laboratory of palpably and continually shifting parameters of human action and motivation—shifting from organizational plan to plan, from production drive to drive, from machine-process innovation to innovation, and from incentive scheme or interest negotiation to new scheme and new negotiation. In this respect, the early in-plant industrial and organizational research setting was similar to the changing tribal, village, and slum settings of contemporary studies of social and cultural change and modernization. To the extent that current anthropology is moving from studies of static social structure to newer treatments of social and cultural change, and is also working its way through the delineations of social strategies and emergent processes in social and cultural life, it is largely due to the experience gained in the early years of applied anthropology. It was then that the science first turned professional attention to scenes in American business, community, and institutional life.

In the case of both earlier industrial-interaction studies at home and modern studies of personal networks or development processes abroad, more is to be learned than the immediately useful practicalities for the businessman or national developer. In the industrial studies, there was more to be recorded and understood than the rooting of motivation for workshop morale and productivity in the informal organization. Likewise, in the current peasant and urban-immigrant studies, there is more to be learned about agricultural modernization than the dangers of wiping out peasant-villagers' traditional cultural supports. In both cases, there are the dynamics of human systems to be unraveled.

During the 1930s and 1940s, it was discovered that industrial unrest, dissatisfaction, and alienation on the job in factory or office were much like the current anomie, resistance to innovation, and conflict in agrarian countrysides among contemporary ex-peasants torn between pressures of the new market and planning entrepreneurs and their own remaining (or newly lost) peasant life and local subsistence. The problems of industry were not to be cured simply by an easy, purely local revival of informal organization among workers or by solely personal collective or community securities. As with the once closed peasant villages, now disrupted and torn by modern agrotechnics and world market demands, the workrooms and the offices studied were only relatively closable at best. They were remarkably sensitive and reactive to processes derived from managerial purposes and business imperatives, from engineering strictures and controls, and from the vagaries of economic and political worlds far outside the workroom but still influencing factory and business as larger wholes.

The informal organization of the work place, like the peasant securities of an earlier agrarian day, was protective and responsive. It reflected workers' universal human needs and fluctuated according to the pressures of the business institution and current culture. Teamwork and team support bolstered workers against their isolation and disciplined containment, the impersonal and arbitrary controls of standardized production, and the atomizing incentive pay schemes of the day. Nevertheless, teamwork efficacy fluctuated according to the extent that it provided workers with mediating remoter relationships, through informal and formal grievance reporting and workload adjustments in shop and in union representation. The informal organization gave workers both a work life with workmates and a voice in the larger organization which embraced all the levels of business personnel—supervisors, managers, engineers, and so on. Hence, social science discovered in that early anthropological fieldwork of modern culture not only some psychology of industrial morale, incentive, and productivity (or alienation and impersonalization, if you prefer) but also important dynamics of large-scale human organization.

The lesson of the workroom studies went far beyond the mere managerial practicalities of learning that "human relations" support of workers made better producers and happier employees. This trivial though salutary reading of the evidence eventually discredited the movement of social science study of work behavior. However, the more significant lesson was that, if workers were to be more productive and committed ("less alienated"), some initiative and responsible spontaneity must be returned to them; some initiative of theirs must be channeled into the larger, hierarchical social system of the factory, the business, and the corporation. Today, events such as the revolt against the assembly-line pressures in the Lordstown plant of Chevrolet have showed us a new generation of better educated factory workers who are no longer passive under the old disciplines of factory work. There is also the current recasting at Volvo in Sweden of the assembly line itself into teams, each completing a car of its own, from frame to fittings. With such examples before us, the lesson of local initiative is revived once more.

The lesson is an old one, presented from many disciplines—

history, politics, and our own cultural anthropology and sociology. Culture as shared meaning and organization as ordered behavior, together leading to cooperative result, are not merely planned and commanded; they are always partially spontaneous, responsive, both self-realized and socially sanctioned and inspired. Even in the hierarchical settings of the larger-scaled organizations of our present world, the rank and file are evolving a morale and organization of their own. There always will be a grapevine, at least, and usually more. Shared feeling and organization among workers can work either for or against their hierarchs, their pace-setters, and direction-givers. The "for" or "against" felt by workers depends inevitably on both their immediate satisfactions and their more extended participations.

Social science has still more than this to learn about large-scale organization and its dynamics, not only in general terms but specifically about business and the corporation in our civilization. Such knowledge is needed both at the rank and file level of workers and consumers, alienated or committed, and at higher levels. We need more insight into the dynamics of large-scale business organization for many reasons: for managing it; for teaching management to manage it; for efficiency; for taming business organizations for human use and social responsibilities; and for coming to terms with the powerful force and the steady growth shown by large-scale business organizations in national and international life.

Even in the early studies, the track of organizational dynamics led from a concern with the morale, motivation, and productivity of the worker on the assembly line or in the records office to interest in the broader relationships among the levels and kinds of personnel. Each of these often had, and continues to have, its own professional subcultural tradition. Moreover, each level and kind of personnel was cross-tied to the others. In order to trace relationships among diverse groups and through hierarchical ties in those settings, it is necessary to reveal the dynamics of grievances and of shop representational systems with their links to better productivity and freer participation. It is equally necessary to trace the connections from department to department, from specialty to specialty, or from profession to profession in the staff-line contacts, as well as in the other complexities of the organizational activity of modern multiplex bureaucracies and "plural societies." Large-scale hierarchical organization perforce builds structure putting persons of diverse traditions into harness together.

A way must be found to identify, and to reconcile if not satisfy, such diverse and opposed traditions.

The way was pointed out long ago. Veblen, for one, marked it in his *Engineers and the Price System* (1921). He was the first to study the clash of values and traditions in a single power system (manufacturing) and to foreshadow the concept of the "segmentary opposition." Segmentary opposition is a staple of anthropological study of lineages, plural societies, caste systems, and the ethnic mosaics of the stratified diversities in complex civilization. Veblen accurately observed that the engineers of the artisan tradition, valuing efficiency and serviceability in products, did not always see eye to eye with the businessman of merchant and countinghouse tradition who was moved by profitability, quick turnover, and "planned obsolescence" (a later word).

More recently, we have had further studies which tell of clash and differences of value and custom in the professions and of the difficulties of accommodation between scientist and businessman. As corporations have increasingly taken over occupations, they have come to dominate the once lone inventor's work with teams and laboratories of their own. They have pushed technology forward by harnessing scientists to their businesses, just as they have harnessed designers, publicists, salesmen, and artist-advertisers. The recruitment and engulfment of nonbusiness occupations into the corporation, in its search for newer lines of profit and for wider and more stable coordinate and conglomerate diversity, show no sign of abatement.

Scientists, we learn in particular from Livingston and Milberg (1957), Marcson (1960), and others, have a tradition of their own which differs from that of the engineer and the businessman. They are restive under fixed-period budgets and programmed results; they need freer wheeling to follow up unexpected openings. They are more responsive to collegial review and to publication notice than to superiors' program audits and balance sheets. Organizational tinkering is required for them to find a place in corporation and department plans.

We need to watch such acculturations and to follow plural societies as they unite various internal traditions both in our own and in other cultures. Ours is an age in which private or public bureaucratic corporations continually increase in size, complexity, and spread, as one dominant new social form within our own nation and between nations, whether as native enterprises or as multinationals. We need to observe these developments in order to teach and train the business and organizational personnel of our age, to balance their connections with the unincluded classes, and to gain scientific understanding of the signal cases that corporations present of the worldwide cultural fusings and the modernizing institutional evolutions which our age unfolds. It is both of anthropological interest and of use to business and administration to record the acclimatization in the outer world of business and the corporation which were originally social inventions of northwest Europe.

James Abegglen (1958), student and successor of W. Lloyd Warner, first explored the unexpected evolution in Japan after World War II. There, the factory organized machines and labor very much like, or even better than, European models. However, hiring practices, employee/employee relationships, and corporate lifelong careers were ordered in quite different ways from the European and Anglo-Saxon model which emerged from a medieval past of hiring fairs, short-term employment contracts, and layoffs for slack seasons between market sales. The cultural backgrounds of British industrialization were such ubiquitous concomitants of industrial enterprise that economists in our own country thought them indispensible to it. Yet the Japanese evolution, with a feudal past and an earlier imperial and Tokugawa centralization, retained quite other hiring practices and market-competitive interfirm relationships. The Japanese did not hire "at the gate," but rather for life; they did not "lay off" but instead they fed and nurtured firm-bound workers even through the ruin of World War II; they mounted research and operations research and development in pools of technicians and scientists who were permanently employed in their own corporations but temporarily pooled with others until the job was done, at which time they were sent home. As another anthropologist, Nakane (1970), later found, the factory and the firm in Japan replicate the *ie,* or kindreds of their family system, rather than the mobile small families of ours.

There are similar preliminary and instructive lessons from the experience of the corporation and its European and American cohesions of custom and practice in Brazil, the Middle East, India, and the Chinese Overseas (Nanyang) World of South and Island Asia. The evidence reveals that rationalized production—the machine, the assembly line, automation, production, and market planning, basic techniques of civilization and of business enterprise—managed, developed, and elaborated by our businessmen and our corporations, all need rethinking. We learn that large-scale organization can be analyzed, parts and processes separated, and institutions understood beyond traditional and untested acceptance of them. For example, the Chinese of Singapore and Hong Kong do very well with both nepotism and industry. The businesses of the private sector of India continue to grow, not by abandoning the caste system but by naturalizing it in part and moving it inside the factory walls and the office space. The Brazilian great families, *parentelas,* move from the fazendas of earlier years to incorporating as family corporations. The Arabs and the Greeks enter world commerce again without western stewardship ideals and impersonal relationships but as authoritative families and undissolved lineages.

In summary, the evidence mounts, from older as well as newer social science, that it is important for both practical life and the active professions such as business, the social sciences, and cultural anthropology, that study of business and the corporation not fall away but be carried onward. It is clear, too, that anthropological study of business, like that of the workroom, is not trivial piecemeal observation. Science always looks for the general in the particular, the great in the small, as well as the small in the great. The same attention to both observation and inference is still needed before our view of modern processes in our civilization, ones in which our lives are caught, firms into useful and generalizing science.

The Feedback from Studies of Transcultural Transfer of Innovations[3]

The second field in which applied anthropology has made major contributions to anthropological theory is that of "development." In particular, event analysis has had considerable and fruitful use during recent decades. Event analysis is a technique for the analysis of ongoing cultural and social process and is associated with the names of

3. This section reprints, with permission and modification, the text of Conrad M. Arensberg (1967), "Upgrading Peasant Agriculture: Is Tradition the Snag?"

Solon T. Kimball and myself. I review its use in the applied anthropology of development projects and give attention to its part in the identification of a common process which unfolds in a minimal sequence structure of interpersonal relations and is capable of modeling and thus of explaining the successful and unsuccessful transfer of skills between people of a "donor" culture and those of another "donee" culture.

I call the process of directed social change to be reported here the Reciprocal Accommodation Process.[4] It is built on older theories of culture contact and generalized from the accumulated experience of projects of planned innovation for the transfer of the skills, tools, seeds, and other items of modern technology to peoples all over the world. The Reciprocal Accommodation Process seems capable of predicting the outcome of these transfer efforts from the sequence of interpersonal events through which the transferred item of culture is proffered, received, and incorporated. Modeling the transactions between donors and donees in successful and unsuccessful transfers reveals more than an adaptive strategy for donor and donee (cf. current social anthropological analyses of participants in many political or economic structures). It suggests the existence of a specific sequence or flow of adaptive actions in and between the members of the donor and donee groups who are in contact with each other. Without the specific occurrence of this sequence and flow of actions, successful transfer fails. In other words, transfer seems to depend upon the unfolding of a social process, and progress can be made toward delin-

4. This model of successful incorporation of skills transferred from one culture to another through planned projects of social change arose in the time of the development efforts running from Point Four and the Community Development movement down to the Green Revolution. I have previously (Arensberg 1967) made a limited statement about the Reciprocal Accommodation Process model. I have also alluded to it elsewhere as follows:

"Whether in work productivity, role maintenance, or acceptance of innovations, as in factory workrooms or hospital offices or peasant villages in transfer of technique efforts, documented and analyzed by William Whyte, Frederick Richardson, Conrad Arensberg, Solon Kimball, Robert Guest, these covariances (between interpersonal equilibria and performances) were demonstrated during the heyday of "in-plant research," "human research," "human relations research," and "applied anthropology" of the 1950s" (Arensberg 1972:7).

The data on the acceptance or the rejection of transfers of skills have already appeared in a factorial correlation exploration in the work of Arthur Niehoff (1966). But a codification of the process by which the factors combine to move a project of directed social change has not yet been presented. The model has been used to good effect in a doctoral thesis, generalizing East African development data (Campbell 1971).

eating its exact form and rate of development. Before turning to the details, I will discuss some common assumptions that are often made about the introduction of new agricultural technologies in the developing world.

Prevailing opinion has it that agriculture in the newly emerging Third World will continue to limp and stumble so long as its backbone is the peasant. Everything is wrong with peasants, or so it is said. Their values and customs frustrate acceptance of necessary technical innovations; their religious observances block progress; their motives and purposes are out of step with the needs of a nation for modernity.

Some plans call for sweeping aside peasants and the impediments of their ways, values, and beliefs, and turning them as quickly as possible into more amenable kinds of persons and members of society: commercial farmers, salaried rural proletarians, or members of a commune that is both agricultural and industrial. Other schemes would clear them off to cities, just as the enclosure movement during the eighteenth century once cleared the land in Great Britain; or as the Negro in the southern United States is "tractored out" into northward, city-bound emigration; or as the serrano leaves Andean Peru for Lima and makes room for cattle in the high valleys. These efforts look for other chemical, mechanical, and agronomic food makers, and they assert the futility of establishing continuity with, or building upon, the ancient rural pattern of subsistence farming now dominant in most "have-not nations." They fail to take into account either the realities of the present world, especially of the developing nations, or the current record of successes in transforming the peasantry into farmers capable of expanding food production in the crowded nations over and beyond the advance in population growth.

Today, it is clear that the developing nations have both vast numbers of peasants in their increasing populations (the proportion is over half) and lagging food production. Moreover, plans for clearing out the peasants or for proletarianizing them on the land are not associated with past notable increases in food production. On the contrary, both historically and in the present, it has been shown that peasants have greatly increased productivity without having to abandon either all of their customs or all of their lands—their base for being.

European countries, such as Denmark, and Asian ones, such as first Japan and now Taiwan, have pushed forward with their peasantries undissolved. Old ways have not been obliterated but rather have been productively combined with new ones. Even the spectacular American agricultural revolution of the twentieth century did not move directly from folk subsistence to chemurigical manufacture on the land but instead it traveled through decades of upgrading family farming. American scientific advance and its movement to agricultural engineering on a corporate scale, with corporate capitalization, came very late. It came after and not before industralization and the transformation of the peasantry.

As with us, perhaps so with others. Perhaps an increase in food production in the developing world must come from a peasantry that slowly learns to combine entrenched customs and generations-old local know-how with new scientific knowledge. The application of science to new conditions of climate, terrain, and endemic disease may turn out to be a two-way process, a dialogue of research at the farm and village level, reminiscent of the earlier similar dialogue in industry, where shop practice preceded engineering advance, and scientists codified what the skilled artisan already knew.

The tradition-tested peasants of the underdeveloped world have long coped with the practical and special local realities of desert, tropics, and jungle which agronomic science has barely begun to explore despite its knowledge of European and American conditions. In the developed world, a thousand years of peasant experience lie behind current scientific agriculture, refined and distilled from the best practices of peasants long forgotten and superseded. In the developing world, the dialogue has just begun.

Far from being only unreasoned resistance, peasant custom may embody economies and techniques that today's scientists and planners can either adapt to their purposes or ignore at their peril. Many a project has introduced fine new herds into a village to replace scrawny ones, only to have the animals die the next time drought or disease struck the area. Many economies of scale in farming have failed to promote production and have eventually destroyed incentive, because they were introduced before the management skill needed to cope with them had been grafted onto the old inventory of traditional techniques.

The proposition that durable progress in agriculture depends on blending peasant know-how with scientific techniques is, therefore, not idly posed. It is based on a knowledge of successes and failures of a few projects of technical innovation that can be fully evaluated and on the insights that scholars are gaining into the true histories of agricultural progress in both western and nonwestern countries. The details are given below.

GENERALIZATION ABOUT INNOVATION

It is remarkable that so little generalization of the experience of technical assistance and other efforts directed at the transfer of know-how from one culture to another has been undertaken. In a summary of international technical assistance evaluation, Cyril Belshaw reported in 1966 that there is no continuous development of ideas, that very few attempts at evaluation have been coordinated, and that no bibliography of evaluation reports yet exists. Evaluation efforts of international and bilateral aid agencies are often made without cross-contact, and the agencies even appear to lose track of what they themselves have done before. Knowledge of the process of transfer in technical assistance, even in agriculture, where new methods, seeds, and other innovations are central, is minimal and the growth of technique and conceptualization slow.

In summarizing initial research on the experience of technical experts of the United Nations, AID, and others, Belshaw (1966:22) states that the "contribution of technical assistance to overall development cannot be judged finally without some fairly specific assumptions about the strategy of development in the circumstances of the country." If technical assistance is to win enduring acceptance and contribute to further growth, it must mesh with the preexisting wants of the people of the recipient country and not merely with government plans and aspirations for them. Aid must supplement indigenous resources rather than merely replace them; it must be "institution building," as the current phrase aptly describes it, but the building has to be done on the existing base, not as new edifices on a *tabula rasa*. New techniques and new institutions cannot be effective engines of development unless they are naturalized and interlinked with older, more established practices. This naturalization takes time, effort, and habituation to the local scene. What is needed is the training of local trainers who will take over and complete the process of interlacing the old and the new.

The experience of "development" anthropology corroborates and expands these conclusions, which are drawn from the few evaluations of technical assistance now extant. In recent years, both anthropologists and developers have evaluated programs and projects of directed innovation, technical assistance, and planned development. They have looked at these both as observers from the outside and as partial participants. At times, they have been asked to look into the real impact and the true fate of the programs or projects designed for their human subjects; more often they have come upon the scene by chance, gathering data on ways of life about to disappear under modernization.

As ersatz locals, anthropologists have had a different vantage point from that of the technical expert, the economist, or indeed any other developer, even the public health expert and the epidemiologist. They have lived in the village, learned the local language, and participated in the institutions of village and peasant and tribal life as part of their professional commitment to fieldwork; in many cases, they have been on the scene before, during, or after such projects. They have seen the planning office goals for these projects, or the home office reports, and they have observed their real impact on the people themselves, their acceptance or rejection by village families, and their contribution—enduring or ephemeral—to local knowledge and resources.

The projects of planners and innovators, whether in agriculture, medicine, or any other professional domain, are of interest to the anthropologist, not only because they affect for good or ill the lives of villagers, but because they are modern instances of an age-old dynamic of culture trait, or bit of human knowledge, and the receivers of the same. What the village does with the bit of transmitted lore, or what the villagers do in reaction to the innovators and their pressure, is grist for the anthropologist's mill as scientist of culture. The growth of civilization has always proceeded by just such transfer and reworkings of cultural material as villagers now undertake before the anthropologist's eyes. There is as much to learn from the new transfers that carry penicillin or hybrid corn or birth control to the village as from the older ones such as writing from the Egyptians to the Phoenicians, or gunpowder and paper money from the Mongols to the Europeans, or Christianity and metallurgy from the Spaniards to the Indians, or tobacco, chocolate, and the fateful potato from the Indians back to Europe.

To learn the process by which cultures change when acted upon by outside forces, and for the purposes of agency and project planners and directors who want to know more of the successes and failures of their innovations, anthropologists have compiled cases so as to draw comparative conclusions from them. The compilation is not easy. Equally difficult is the empirical distillation of the factors responsible for the success or failure in transmitting techniques, the process of contact and transmission, and the reworking and adapting by which one outcome or the other develops.

Compilation, assessment, and identification of process and final effect require a long, continuous, and thorough record. This record must document the needs and problems before the project, the plans and their implementation during the project, and the response of the recipients to the innovation and to the innovators. It must also include the details of how the local people worked out the "bugs," with or without the help of the innovators; how they fitted the amended technique into the other knowledge, resources, habits, and concurrent changes of their way of life; and finally, after the project, the ways in which the technique was incorporated into their culture—something that comes only when the receivers can pass the technique on to their neighbors and their children, in short, among themselves.

Such complete records, rare but usable, disclose, with event analysis and reduction to flows of interpersonal action between donor and donee personnel, a Reciprocal Accommodation Process in successful transfer. This process, a dialogue of donor and donee which grows to include them both in a common social structure, is the successful process of transfer. Unless it unfolds to follow the order of events described below, it seems that acceptance of innovation does not occur.

Arthur Niehoff (1964, 1966) has compiled 203 histories of efforts to introduce new techniques into peasant communities of developing countries. By means of factorial analysis, he established the primary variables leading either to success or to failure in the case histories. Using these variables, I have analyzed the processual structures of the events of the cases, sequenced the occurrences of the factors Niehoff finds significant, and modeled the flows of social interaction among the donor and donee personnel and in the two-way communication between them. I believe I have discovered in each case of transfer the same process at work, unfolding to acceptance ("success"), aborting to abandonment ("failure") where impeded or derailed.

In no case were peasants and others not yet modernized willing to give up their accustomed way of life, with its traditional techniques, merely on the promise of technical or economic advantage. In every case of success, there was a continuing dialogue of initiative and reaction between innovator and recipient, which moved forward until the new techniques became an integral part of the lives of the people.

In a feedback of experiences to theory, the cases validated the cherished maxims of experienced developers. A self-declared conscious need, they say, is better than imposed betterment; enlisting local leadership and self-help is better than paternalism; concrete and specific demonstration is better than proof in theory and tables; follow-up, feedback, and continuing attention are better than quick solutions; immediately perceived benefits and tangible gains in crop, health, convenience, or security are more effective than are vague long-term gains; peasants prove ready to innovate when they can personally experience any improvement they themselves can value, etc. Such maxims are hard-won half-truths which social science can reorder and verify.

It is clear, moreover, that these experts' maxims, now grossly empirical, can be generalized. They are examples of the theoretically statable process that I have named the Reciprocal Accommodation Process. The process, generalizing the experts' maxims of project experience, is the same kind of flow of initiative and localization of plans that can sometimes run upward from workers in the shops and production lines of industry, through worker participation and their unions into the decisions of managers and top brass. In industry this upward flow, though often too small, is the two-way communication necessary to create motivated and constructive hierarchical relationships as already attested in the literature of the industrial experience cited earlier. My (1972) social-interactional processual analysis gives a common minimal-sequence model of that same flow in development—another human and equally hierarchical setting.

As already noted, innovations presented in culture contacts, especially in settings of differential power and expertise, do not win acceptance on their merits alone. Both in industry and development, they are accepted or rejected on the basis of a social process of two-way communication. Nor are they accepted at once and exactly as initially presented. Reworking, localization, removal of the "bugs" are all part of the process of the mutual accommodation of donors and donees and the building of a new social system inclusive of the representatives of the two cultures.

The history of cultural innovations especially documents the failure of donors and developers when they do not respond to the peasants' reworking and naturalizing of their plans. They fail when they do not help the peasants, at peasant request, to remove unforeseen obstacles to their plans and when they do not continue to rework, on their side, the necessary adjustments to local experience the peasants know and face, as they, the donors and developers, do not. On the other hand, donors succeed when they do so respond and help donees to their pay-off.

This mutual accommodation is a social process. It is a sequence of human interactions that must unfold to have its result. In other words, accepted, successful change or "development" is a synergetic outcome of donor and donee actions moving themselves and one another in a proper order, a systematic process and a predictable result. As such, it can take its place in social science and in anthropology with other theories of system, process, decision, and hierarchy that are coming to be proffered (Goodenough 1963; Haskell 1972).

MECHANISMS OF AGRICULTURAL ADVANCE

The science of anthropology, then, with its evolution-long view of past cultural, economic, and social changes (both historical and archeological) and its processual analysis of human interactive sequences, has something to say about the most effective mechanisms of agricultural progress.

If the problem is to raise food production in the developing world, anthropology, and perhaps even the other social sciences as well, would bet on the present rural inhabitants of the villages of the tropics, the desert, and the mountain terrains. These people currently support (or nearly support) themselves and their city-based fellow nationals. Anthropologists would vote for upgrading these inhabitants *in situ*, both as the most practical course and as the historically correct one to pursue. They would argue that the absence of research into innovation and the agronomic realities of local terrain and climate is the bottleneck or the missing ingredient, as it were, rather than the paucity of fertilizer or new seeds.

John P. Lewis (1964) has argued that, historically and realistically, scientific advances in agriculture are the most difficult to achieve and come last because such advances must be made in the face of incredible diversities of microclimates, microsoils, and microtechnical supports—the very conditions that make it difficult to transfer techniques from the successful to the less successful. He uses the experience of Japan, Taiwan, and India to show that success is based not on paternalism and central direction but upon peasant naturalization of new information. He notes that new science meets real competition: the fact that peasants now have subsistence security, but little more, and no margin for error or experiment. This rigorous competition must be won not in the laboratory but in the village itself. The high-yielding rices of Japan do not yet produce equally well in tropical, semi-drought-ridden India; the tractors of America are too big and heavy for German field plots or South Asian rice fields. Fertilizers are needed, but so are new inventions and ways of getting them into farmers' hands.

John W. Mellor (1962) develops a different but parallel reasoning from history. He appeals to wide experience in the developing world and the comparative history of agricultural economics. He uses the instructive histories of the United States, Denmark, Japan, Greece, and Taiwan—countries that have been successful in making big advances in food production. He says:

A commonly recommended alternative to the evolutionary process of training the mass of farmers to make their own decisions is to institute a form of large-scale farming using specialized management. Unfortunately, economies of scale in farming do not continue . . . as in other industries, particularly if labor is cheap and the opportunity cost . . . of large-scale machinery is relatively high. (1962:712)

Regarding research and education of peasants, along with the provision of necessary agricultural inputs, Mellor concludes that increased productivity, especially a Rostovian take-off into full development and great increase, depends less on any one input than on a complementarity among several modern inputs. "In practically all underdeveloped countries," he states, "there has been continuous conscious effort by government . . . some of the nontraditional factors of production have been made available in a quantity out of proportion to other complements . . . additional amounts . . . may have very low short-run returns, while a small addition of others would provide extremely large [ones]." He goes on to cite developments in Denmark, Japan, and Taiwan, and the early phases of American growth (through the "agricultural extension" service of American land-grant colleges and other local stations) to show that: (1) a very small number of missing inputs curtails advance in many countries; (2) these missing inputs are by no means the same from region to region; and (3) there are substantial short-run returns when the missing inputs are plugged in (1962:714).

Mellor then gives an evolutionary, history-tested phasing of agricultural development that encompasses but does not bypass the upgrading of the peasants. This phasing strikes the anthropologist as promising real success, because it reflects the true process of culture contact, culture change, and the steps necessary to the successful transfer of the techniques we have already discussed. His comparative analysis of the sequence of stages America and Denmark went through some time ago, that Japan has just passed through, that Taiwan is already in, and that India perhaps has just barely entered, is especially instructive. Phase I is a "stagnant phase," in which production increase, if any, is achieved largely from increased application of traditional inputs—more sweat and labor from an expanding, traditional population. This phase can only lead to change if the preconditions for advance evolve—namely, changes in land tenure and in political power. These changes are not in themselves sufficient conditions, but they create a "decision-making environment in which farmers accept the possibility of personal gain from improvements" (Mellor 1962:712).

Phase II is the crucial stage: agriculture is still a large proportion of the economy, capital is scarce, new land is limited, and machines are too costly. Traditional forms of labor, land, and capital are abundant but as yet relatively unproductive. Only the peasants with larger holdings have any security. Increase is likely to be achieved through the growing acceptance of even a few technical changes in perhaps only a few areas of the country. These include insecticides, rodent controls, farm-to-market roads, seeds, fertilizers—in short, some of the innovations that our projects have striven to transfer. Later, a larger number of further changes builds on these: land consolidation, marketing facilities, storage, credit, and other institutions succeed the initial, recognizable gains that have been experienced. Once more, it is research and the transfer process that are the bottlenecks. To quote Mellor again: "The requisite research in this phase is of the applied type often involving no more than regionally decentralized comparative testing of variability in traditional [cultural] practices. The major input . . . is personnel of the level of training that can be provided in large quantity in a . . . few years' time" (1962:714). If Phase II is successfully passed, the result is a dynamic process of continuing increase.

Phase III is the final emergence of chemurgical, scientific agriculture, the factories-in-the-field. Japan, after ninety years of intensive development, is just entering it. We ourselves went fully into it only in the 1930s, long after our industrialization. Mellor, like the anthropologists, believes that evolution moves through its own phases and has its own laws. Perhaps upgrading the peasants before industrializing them is just such a law. If the developing world is to grow the food it must have, this is the route it may be compelled to take.

New Models of Behavior, Social Process Leadership, and Hierarchy

Finally, let us consider the feedback of industrial and development anthropology into theories of organization and organizational behavior itself. What does the theory of process necessary for successful change and rewarding hierarchical relationships have to say about organization and about the behavior of the individuals involved in it?

The feedback from applied anthropological research into the theory of organizational behavior and innovation process has led to new models of interpersonal interaction, social process, emergent structure, and, most widely, to a new look at organization and hierarchy theory. The experience of the two fields of applied anthropology just reviewed has also illuminated current theories of leadership, organization, and social hierarchy from interactional and behavioral anthropology (Arensberg 1972; Collins and Collins 1973).

William Foote Whyte, a fellow contributor to this book, reminds us that in recent years we have seen a boom in organizational and interorganizational studies. He points out that ''we have come to recognize that civilizations advance through increasing division of labor and specialization, which means, among other things, the creation of more and more organizations to perform specialized functions.'' He calls for a better meshing of individual and shared human problems as they are experienced within organizations by the individuals manning them and those they serve. Our knowledge of organization as social process and cultural form must be improved if we are to develop the ''organizational forms and strategies that coordinate specialized services and resources (that) people need. This means particularly studying the coordination and cooperation among organizations, or, more generally, interorganizational relations.'' This is, of course, a modern problem of biology as well, where organization also takes hierarchical form. In addition, it is an aspect of general systems theory and what Herbert Simon (1973) has recently called an intersystems interlocking ''cross-coupling'' of hierarchies.

Whyte feels that, while organization and hierarchy and the cross-coupling of organizations are fields of rapidly growing inquiry, we have as yet no theoretical framework adequate to deal with the phenomena. I hope here to suggest some aspects of more adequate theory and I am glad to see that Whyte himself, along with Leonard Sayles, Chapple and Coon, Kimball and I, and still other anthropologists, applied or not, have provided pieces of that theory. Indeed, applied anthropology of earlier years now provides specific pieces of theory directly applicable to the problem. One of these pieces is worth reviewing here. It is a behavioral, social-interactional, sequential-process model of leadership of ''decision making'' in large-scale hierarchies.

LEADERSHIP AND "DECISION-MAKING" THEORY

There are excellent summaries of current inquiry into decision making from social psychology, political science, and writings on administration. Their only omission is that class of studies of ongoing organization and the leadership and decision making within organizations made by observational methods. They completely omit studies made by fieldwork and natural history (''ethological'') methods. These studies come into social science from social and cultural anthropology, where leadership is treated from the point of view of leaders as diverse as shamans, chiefs, sheikhs, and prophets, and from applied anthropology (and small group sociology), which seeks out natural and informal leaders, culture-brokers, and community influentials.

The nonanthropological studies of leadership, organization, and administration provide formal deductive models, schemata and tables of organization, generalizing observations, historical summaries and biographies, and even some laboratory experiments. They treat decisions as part of organizational behavior in a general and often static way. The natural place of decisions in the flow of organizational events in which they are only one kind of action is not precisely explored. Excellent as they are for their purpose, these studies abstract the matter of decision processes out of context. The "process" is studied for itself, but not for its relations or functions within the overall context of organizational activity.

Suggestions for a different look at decisioning are to be found where naturalistic and participant-observational studies have been made. These can be found in the tradition of the field-worker in anthropology or the applied anthropologist who comes into a factory, project, or tribe with no prior knowledge of what is going on or what he or she shall find. Anthropologists in these situations treat organizational and institutional behavior whole, making comparisons not only from people to people but from organization to organization—for example, from business, to church, to army, or to Algonquin village. They follow, as best they can, the canons of depicting a culture as an integrated whole system of observed behaviors and of placing that culture in the spectral range of the crosscultural variation of all mankind, and of placing a culture's subsystems in a spectral, comparative range.

The anthropologist thus places the acts of decision making leaders—whether chiefs or high priests or generals or businessmen—in the full context of the other behaviors and activities of the persons they decide for and among. Hence, naturalistic studies of ongoing situations treat decision making as one regular kind of action which is less an art or a skill than a necessary and regular role which most persons—once their awe of the responsibility and honor which surrounds decisioning is overcome—could well be taught to fill. It is a natural role, and has become a regular part of organizational life. As such, it is to be understood as a data processing and data checking function where education and science may, indeed must, be part of the individual decision maker's equipment. But leadership is also, and importantly, a regular procedure of social action which is related to the other kinds of action which make up organization. And like them, it is capable of being ultimately reduced to technique.

It is possible to remove the mystery from decision making: by treating it as one kind of action among many in a human social system; and by following it as a sequence of interpersonal actions having a natural place among like sequences of actions carried out by other personnel. This approach requires that organizations be viewed as a field of persons among whom the actions of the events in the life of the organization or social system flow in several directions or lines of persons (and their offices) which can be observationally recorded and statistically compared. By doing so, it is possible to establish a naturalistic matrix of contacts and relationships among the personnel and to define and separate activities of every organizational function, leadership included, in terms of the involvement with and initiatives upon other personnel. Functions can be stated not so much in terms of what is done as in terms of with whom and at what rate of interpersonal contacts such functions are done. Decision making, like the other activities in this interpersonal mapping of the human events of organization, becomes an activity clearly defined in context and quantifiable in the relative directions and frequencies of contacts in which it occurs. It is comparable and contrastable with the other activities of the human system.

By quantifying them in context, decisions can be related to various occurrences of human relations and company activity within an organization, as well as to the balance sheet of sales and purchases outside it. When we perfect techniques for reducing the events of action within organization to a ledger of flows and pressures of action and interaction among the personnel, the possibility arises that the rightness or wrongness of one or several decisions can eventually be checked against the human track record of timely interactions performed or necessary actions missed, as well as the record of dollars and cents.

Treating decisions in context, as they are made in the ongoing flow of human action and interaction making up the life of a group, company, or other institution, means that they must be viewed not merely as judgments of persons, however bold or skilled, but also as events which have a necessary fit, in time occurrence, within a matrix of other events. Looked at as an element of a pattern of action, even the most abstract model of decision making takes on new dimensions. The model one must use is no longer limited to the decisions themselves or to the data-gathering, shifting, and testing processes which the decider himself goes through. Necessary as these processes are, decisions are also events in a field of interpersonal action within an ongoing organization. Their field and their place in it take abstract minimal form as Diagram 1 shows.

Diagram 1 Simple Decisioning: Pair and Set Events

(The structure of action)

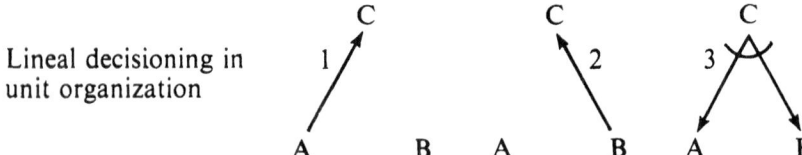

Lineal decisioning in unit organization

In minimal definitional terms of social action, a decision arises when three events occur in order over time and involve a unit organization of three persons in a set of relationships uniting them all. The relationships entail all three persons acting upon one another within a field of common experience and concern and within limits of custom, consent, and right, though not necessarily for a common goal. The sequence is as follows:

Act 1. A pair event in which A informs, etc., C, who delays response and does not immediately initiate new action.
Act 2. A pair event in which B informs, etc., C, who delays as above.
Act 3. A set event in which C responds or acts, having collated information, etc. C originates a new action in which B and A respond alike, together, or in coordination or unison. (The ligature of the arrows from C to A and B indicates this "set event" of joint response.)

A system of leadership in decision making arises in minimal terms when a repetitive sequence of some frequency (at least greater than events of alternate form and sequence) arises in which decisioning repeats itself among the same personnel, in the same order of their interpersonal action upon one another, with the same alternation of pair events and set events (dyadic and triadic relationships). The comparative regularity establishes roles: leadership in C, follower-ships in A and B (Diagram 2).

Diagram 2

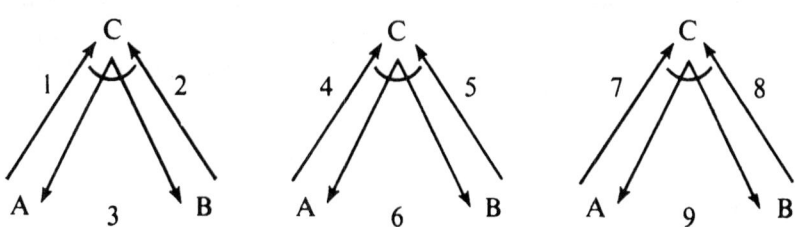

We thus have three decisions in nine consecutive interpersonal acts (interactions) and a system of action; a unit organization with decision-making attributes and leadership/followership roles has emerged. A, B, and C now cooperate, but in a structured way reflect-ing decision-making or leadership. Each act, relationship, role, and decision has measurable, comparable, predictable relative frequencies of occurrence, operational definition, and interdependent qualifica-tion.

Organizational decisioning in organizations having line organi-zation, hierarchical form, and pyramidal form merely combines through levels and linked units such acts and events of decisioning into fur-ther concatenated sequences and orders of progression. It thus estab-lishes—again in operational definition—lines or flows of action in interpersonal and intergroup relationships through the entire organi-zational population (Diagram 3).

Diagram 3 Complex or Organizational Decisioning: Flows of Action

(The structure of organizational action and decision)

Hierarchical decision making
in linked units, making up
pyramidal or hierarchical
organization

Units: triangles

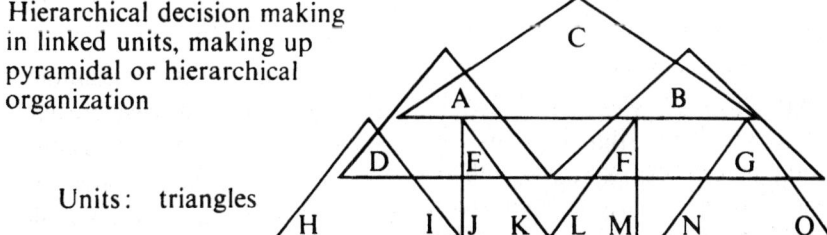

For example, CAD H is such a flow of action, of common direction, in direction and levels of progression comparable to CBG O. Both are operationally definable "line authority," as chains of pair events, comparable again to set events A/HIJK or C/DEFG in direction but not in level, definable likewise as "line action." Similar operational definitions, which are measurable, quantifiable, and comparable, can express all and any other parts or elements of organization and the decisions taken within it.

Each combined sequence has its own frequency of the occurrence of events flowing down it ("commands") or up it ("reports"). One can matrix these, of course, or otherwise summarize them as rates (acts per time periods), and so on. A model of hierarchical decisioning as a down-flow among other sequences of action can be sketched as in Diagram 4.

In other words, decision making is one flow of action among many in an ongoing organization. We are treating here only internal decisions—those that involve authority or "down-the-line action." Other decisions involve adjustment of the whole to the outside, for example, in interaction of the personnel at various levels with customers, the community, the state, suppliers, competitors, and so on. But internal processes can be treated apart from external interactions and relations and relationship. The internal decisions, such as have been modeled here, are not only judgments about such things as data, actions, and resources. Naturalistically seen as behavior in context, they are also steps or acts, where the actor-decider does the next thing required in the drama of continuing the balance of organizational relationships comprised of the interactions of the personnel of organization in their many flows.

When Barnard (1938:194) tells us, as we are told here again, that the decision-making art lies in "not deciding questions that are not now pertinent, in not deciding prematurely, in not making decisions that cannot be made effective [which the next fellow won't act out], and in not making decisions that others should make," he is telling us what the above diagrams tell us: There is an elaborate, necessary, closely timed minuet—a stately dance of many coordinate persons, of exquisite choreography, of figures now individual and now in unison. This choreography is what we lamely call "organization." This choreography, this rhythm may be under the baton of

Diagram 4 Decisioning as Down-Flow among Other Sequences of Action

Hierarchical decisioning in
the matrix of organization
relationships as flows of
actions among all personnel
in the various directions of
most frequent occurrence

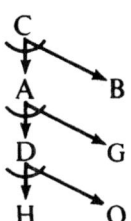

Note the flows: 1. C A D H etc. "down the line."

2. H   O "the flow of work."

3. O   H "against or out of the
flow of work," i.e.,
Informal Organization.

4. H D A C "up the line" (reporting)
"in channels."

5. O G B $\begin{smallmatrix}C\\A\end{smallmatrix}$ either

    a. staff-line ("advice").

    b. grievance, etc. "out
of channels, up."

Decisions: Note that only the barred arrow events, the down-the-line
flow, are treated as decisions.

All these flows: down-the-line (authority, decisions), the flow of work,
up-the-line reporting, informal organization, staff-line action, and
grievance channel, have their rates of occurrence. Any full picture of
decisions and their effects must set them in the ongoing streams of
these flows.

the "manager," C, our top decider and our captain, but he can only
lead or, failing to lead, rearrange again.

Good decisions, then, are not only those which show the right
science of materials, the market, the economic cycle, or other skills
that have nothing to do with management or organization *per se*.
Rather, they are those that act out the right steps and lead the right

rhythm in organization itself, based on a sure knowledge of what organization is and what makes people work in it. We are only now just beginning to incorporate this knowledge of organization, people, and their orchestration into the social and psychological sciences of today. The experience of applied anthropology will continue to feed back into the mastery of this knowledge.

3

MULTICULTURALISM AS THE NORMAL HUMAN EXPERIENCE

Ward H. Goodenough

Understanding of the structure of action between individuals requires analysis of the ongoing behavior of the actors themselves rather than the aggregate categories of statistical data. This theme, already discussed by Arensberg, is further elaborated by Ward H. Goodenough. The elaborate patterns of initiation and response highlighted by Arensberg are here approached from the standpoint of patterns of cognition and individual perception. These cognitive "microcultures" attach ideas of what is good, proper, satisfying, and the like, to patterns of interaction. They constitute varied expectations among the people of complex societies.

The differential social power which is characteristic of asymmetrical relationships has the effect of legitimizing or denying the validity of cognitive perceptions. Powerful and powerless alike display contrasting microcultures which act as barriers to communication insofar as they are exclusive or singular in nature. Multiculturalism is the normal experience of most individuals in the world today, for they are perforce drawn into the microcultures of administrators, physicians, teachers, and others who have power over them. Skill in multicultural situations is thus a basic requirement of life in modern societies, especially for the powerless.

Ward H. Goodenough (Ph.D., Yale) is university professor of anthropology at the University of Pennsylvania. His fieldwork has been in Micronesia and Melanesia, with a primary focus on the theory of culture change and linguistics. Dr. Goodenough has been especially interested in community development. He was president of the Society for Applied Anthropology from 1963 to 1964.

This essay was presented in substantially its present form as a paper at the seventy-fourth Annual Meeting of the American Anthropological Association, in the symposium entitled "Toward a Definition of Multiculturalism in Education." It is reproduced by permission of the American Anthropological Association from *Anthropology and Education Quarterly* (1976), 7(4):4–6. Not for further reproduction.

An important question raised by Goodenough is whether the narrowly trained and highly specialized professional has sufficient normal life experiences to permit the development of interactional skills in multicultural situations. To the extent that enforced isolation and administrative layers separate professionals from each other and from those they serve, the work of the applied anthropologist can be extremely important in the "naturalization" processes of new behaviors described by Arensberg.

THE VIEW OF culture and the individual which I present here is one I have arrived at in the context of thinking about the contributions anthropology can make to programs for social and cultural change (Goodenough 1963). A major problem in the course of all such programs is the emotional investment of individual persons in preserving or changing existing customs and institutions. Why is the same individual distressed at one kind of change and unconcerned about another? Why do individuals in the same community differ so markedly in their feelings about the same situations? Why do some segments of a population, for example, express little interest in having their children learn to read and write, while other segments are distressed that their children are not learning to read and write better? Applied anthropology's recognition of the crucial importance of wants and felt needs—of the role of motivation—in social and cultural process inevitably forces theory to come to terms with how individual, purposeful, human beings relate to that process.

Anthropologists traditionally have acted on the assumption that most societies are not multicultural, that for each society there is one culture. They have seen multicultural societies as developing only in the wake of urbanism, economic specialization, social stratification, and conquest states.

The view of culture as characterizing societies or subsocieties as wholes is appropriate to problems that involve comparing societies as organized human systems or that call for the classification of societies according to one or another taxonomic scheme. For these purposes, minor cultural differences from household to household, such as reported from the Navajo by Roberts (1951), or even from village to village, can often be conveniently ignored. But such a macroview of culture, if I may call it that, is inappropriate for the theory of culture, for any theory of something necessarily considers the processes of which that something is a product and which account for the way it changes over time. If, by culture, we have reference to the understandings about things and the expectations of one another that the members of a society seem to share, then a theory of culture requires us to consider the processes by which the individual members arrive at such sharing. In this regard, the differences among individuals, their misunderstandings, the different ways of doing things from family to family and village to village, all become noteworthy.

When we look at process, then, we no longer look at societies only as wholes but at individual people as learners of culture in the context of social interaction, as they pursue their various interests and try to deal with their various problems of living—problems that involve the necessity of choosing among conflicting goals, competing wants, and long-range as against short-range concerns. From the standpoint of process, multiculturalism is no longer a feature of complex societies alone; it is to be found in simple societies as well. To say this is not to gainsay that multiculturalism plays an increasingly prominent role in the affairs of complex societies, but that the difference between complex and simple societies in this regard is one of degree and not of kind.

Anthropologists have always properly insisted that culture is learned. From the learner's point of view, the problem is to learn what the expectations are in terms of which others act. The understanding arrived at regarding the expectations of one's parents is applied to other adults. In the absence of feedback to the contrary, one assumes that these others have the same expectations as one's parents. Thus, one comes to attribute concepts, beliefs, and principles of action uniformly to a set of other people, finding that for one's own practical purposes, one can successfully do so. What is thus attributed to that set of others becomes the culture of that set. I use the word "culture" advisedly here, for in anthropological practice the culture of any society is made up of the concepts, beliefs, and principles of action and organization that an ethnographer has found could be attributed successfully to the members of that society in the context of his dealings with them.

From this point of view, the sharing of culture by the members of a group is a matter of attribution. The apparent validity of this attribution is measured by its practical utility for dealing effectively with members of the group in situations in which one deals with them. The process is that of stereotyping. The very limited purposes and situations in which a plantation manager in the Solomon Islands interacts with his Melanesian workers may result in very crude stereotyping of them by him and of him by them, stereotyping that serves its very limited purposes but is found entirely wanting when the bases for interaction are expanded. There is a difference between this kind of limited stereotyping and the kind that occurs in ethnography. Good ethnography requires us to test the adequacy of our stereotypes within the full range of contexts in which the people to whom we attribute them deal with one another. By direct participation, if we can, and by various forms of vicarious participation, we test our stereotypes, in the same way the society's members individually test the adequacy of their own individual stereotypes of their fellow members.

What does all this have to do with multiculturalism? In the learning process, people inevitably find that they cannot generalize the same expectations to everyone. Children learn that the expectations of their parents and other adults are not the same in many respects as the expectations of their playmates. They find that the expectations of their mother and father's sister are different, and so on. There are different role-expectations that go with different social relationships and different social situations. Each of these different expectations constitutes a different culture to be learned. Because such cultures are situation-bound and thus ordered with respect to other situation-bound cultures, we may choose to think of them as subcultures or microcultures, reserving the term "culture" for the larger, ordered system of which these are a part; in this sense, culture ceases to refer to a generic phenomenon of study and refers instead only to some level of organization of that phenomenon. From a theoretical viewpoint, the process of learning a society's culture or macroculture, as I would rather call it, is one of learning a number of different or partially different microcultures and their subcultural variants and how to discern the situations in which they are appropriate and the kinds of others to whom to attribute them.

All human beings, then, live in what for them is a multicultural world in which they are aware of different sets of others to whom different cultural attributions must be made, and of different contexts in which the different cultures of which they are aware are expected to be operative. Their competence in any one of these is indicated by their ability to interact effectively in its terms with others who are acknowledged as already competent. Everyone develops varying degrees of multicultural competence in relation to at least some microcultures. Moreover, intersocietal contacts make at least some people minimally competent in some aspects of different macrocultures. The range of cultural diversity increases in complex societies, where multicultural competence at the macrocultural as well as the microcultural level may play an important role in the conduct of affairs and in differential access to privilege and power. I shall come back to this in a moment.

Before I do, I wish to summarize what I have been implying in the foregoing discussion of culture by observing that it is analytically and conceptually useful to distinguish among the following: (1) culture as a phenomenon, arising out of learning in the context of interaction, the expectations people attribute to others; in this regard akin to G. H. Mead's (1934:152–163) concept of the "generalized other"; (2) the specific micro- or macrocultures individuals attribute to specific sets of others as the ones that are appropriately operative in social situations; (3) the range of variance in what the individual members of an interaction network or group attribute to the membership of the network or group as the group's culture; (4) the number of such interaction networks and groups in a social unit under consideration, the degree to which they overlap in membership or come together in larger networks or groups, and the subject matter with respect to which they function as networks or groups; and (5) the total range of knowledge of, and competence in, various microcultures and macrocultures that is possessed by the members of a given social unit, whether or not they are appropriately operative in interactions within that unit, and that compose what can be called the "cultural pool" or "reservoir" of the membership of that unit (Goodenough 1971:41–44).

Several of those considerations are of obvious interest for the study of process and change. What, for example, are the specific processes by which the variance in cultural attributions individuals make to their networks or group (3) is kept within workable bounds? Whatever these processes are, they clearly have to do with the rates and kinds of interaction that take place among members of the network or group. Of interest, too, are the processes by which elements in a group's cultural pool (5) achieve or lose status as part of a specific microculture that is expected to be operative in some context (2). Also of interest are the processes that increase or reduce the number of networks or groups within a society (4) and that affect the extent of overlap in their memberships. All of these processes involve people pursuing their various and competing interests, a consideration that brings us back to privilege and power.

Real social power, as distinct from jural authority, is a function of two variables. One is the extent and intensity of people's wants, and the other is the extent to which people are in a position to facilitate or impede the gratification of one another's wants. If nothing matters to me, even whether I live or die or whether I am free of pain or not, then no one is in a position to affect my behavior, and no one has any social power in relation to me. If, on the other hand, others are unable to gratify any of their wants without my cooperation, then I have enormous power in relation to them. In no human society is real social power evenly distributed. The greater dependency of the young, the old, the sick, and the infirm on others for the gratification of their wants and the relative lack of dependency of others on them, guarantee unequal power relationships everywhere. Such inequalities are compounded by individual differences in knowledge and skills and in physical and personal attractiveness. The cultural definition of jural relationships and the different rights and duties that attach to different social identities in their dealings with one another inevitably reflect these inequalities in real power, and also reflect the kinds of trade-offs that people in their past dealings have been able to achieve as the basis for present cultural expectations.

Among the resources to which access is of paramount importance in power relationships are the various microcultures that make up a macrocultural system. Growth in the number of specialized skills and bodies of knowledge creates more power in the social system to be distributed and managed and increases the consequent possibilities for inequalities in power. The amount of power in a social field of relationships, it appears, increases directly as the complexity of the field increases, and its management becomes a problem of increasing importance and difficulty for the people involved.

Even in the relatively uncomplicated societies of Melanesia and Micronesia, with which I am personally familiar, control of specialized forms of knowledge is perceived as a source of social power generally and of political power in particular. Validation of claims to land and political office rests on a public display of a kind of knowledge that only those in line of succession are given access to. For those not in line of succession to aspire to such knowledge is to presume to something they are not entitled to. I suspect that it was no accident that in 1964, in the little community of Romonum on Truk in Micronesia, all four of the government salaried positions under the American administration (medical assistant, local judge, and principal and teacher in the local school) were monopolized by the highest ranking men in the two chiefly lineages. Even more significant was the fact that only the children of chiefly rank had qualified for education beyond the elementary level, in accordance with an apparently impartially administered examination system. Access to the kinds of alien cultural knowledge and skills which the schools afforded seems to have been perceived in the same way as access to important forms of traditional knowledge, i.e., as appropriate for persons of high social rank only, and inappropriate for those without such rank. I do not think that this was a matter of which people were necessarily conscious; rather, it resulted largely from what each individual felt somehow to be appropriate to his or her own sense of social self.[1]

If the management of social power involves, among other things, the manipulation of access to knowledge and skills, the obvious targets of such manipulation are the conditions necessary for acquiring knowledge and skills. These may be briefly summarized as: (1) mental and physical aptitudes needed to develop the indicated skills and to acquire the necessary level of comprehension; (2) a perception of self and self-goals that make developing the skills and acquiring the comprehension seem appropriate or desirable; (3) freedom from emotional blocks in relation to the skills and knowledge in question (partly related to 2 above); and (4) access to situations in which there is opportunity to rehearse the skills and work at getting the knowledge, as well as opportunity to acquire helpful feedback (guidance), until the desired proficiency is achieved.

In complex societies, the many microcultures and even macrocultures they comprise are inevitably the subject matter of social and political manipulation. Access to the cultures and subcultures in which

1. In the years since these observations were made, children of commoners have begun to succeed in school.

competence must be demonstrated in order to establish eligibility for positions of privilege becomes a major matter to which social organization is geared and is at the same time a prime target for political maneuvering. The social rules that serve to control such access, usually multiple and mutually reinforcing, become a prime target for reform in times of change, with accompanying changes in personal aspirations. Today, we are witnessing this phenomenon in connection with the concerns with women's liberation and education for minorities.

The problems of multiculturalism, then, arise as aspects of the processes I have been discussing, as does human concern with them. Multiculturalism is present to some degree in every human society. Differential access to and knowledge of the various microcultures in macrocultural systems is a significant aspect of power relationships in all societies. As multiculturalism becomes more pronounced and elaborated and the field of power becomes greater with increasing social complexity, multiculturalism becomes an ever more important consideration in the management of power relationships. As such, it also becomes an increasingly serious problem in the politics, education, and other institutions which are the instruments by which people control access to more specialized microcultures and to the power and privilege they confer.

In conclusion, practical considerations both in social action and in social theory continually invite us to deal with our fellow humans as aggregates rather than as individuals. The practical necessity to do so helps account for the stereotyping process of which the important phenomenon we call culture is a consequence. But practical considerations should not lure us into the false expedient of forgetting to look for relevant individual and small group differences. Nor should we allow our ideals for our fellow human beings lead us to forget the stuff of which social power is made and to forget that in pursuing those ideals we are seeking to alter or reinforce existing distributions of power. The arena of education is no exception. The design and implementation of learning programs in a world in which multiculturalism is the natural condition requires that these considerations have our close attention.

4

THE ELUSIVE NATURE OF COOPERATION AND LEADERSHIP: DISCOVERING A PRIMITIVE PROCESS THAT REGULATES HUMAN BEHAVIOR

Frederick L. W. Richardson

Differential social power is characteristic of all societies, and conflict between superiors and subordinates has been documented throughout history. At the same time, human survival and productivity require cooperative relationships between superiors and subordinates. What are the processes whereby these adversary relationships are transformed into mutual collaboration?

Here Frederick L. W. Richardson summarizes several decades of applied anthropological research into this basic and critical question. From the work of applied anthropologists in industry, we have learned that interactional sequences of behavior between managers and workers are a key factor in productivity. The early discoveries of applied anthropologists about the nature of superior-subordinate relationships in factories and other institutions must be augmented in light of what we know about the significance of the cognitive patterns described by Goodenough. Richardson adds still another dimension to these behavioral subtleties based on the work of those who have discovered the

Frederick L. W. Richardson (Ph.D., Harvard) is professor emeritus of business administration in the Colgate Darden Graduate School of Business Administration at the University of Virginia. Dr. Richardson has worked as research associate in the Harvard Business School and the Labor and Management Center of Yale University, and was professor of business administration at the University of Pittsburgh. He has been a consultant in the area of organizational improvement and human problems in organization for American business corporations, the United States Department of Agriculture, and the Massachusetts General Hospital. He has written extensively about human organization in industrial and other work settings. He was one of the founders of the Society for Applied Anthropology and served as president from 1952 to 1953.

importance of sensory and nonintellectual processes in interactional behavior among humans and other mammals.

In contemporary, complex societies, specialization usually results in people who are either intellectually intelligent or behaviorally intelligent. Successful leadership today, however, requires a comprehensive intelligence which encompasses both dimensions of organizational life. Thus, Richardson echoes Goodenough in calling for novel learning experiences so that leaders and others may become better able to respond to the interactional patterns of the diverse groups and individuals in contemporary competitive hierarchical structures.

THIS ESSAY PRESENTS the results of several decades of trial and error in the systematic study of work organizations to comprehend how to help members transform adversary or rebellious actions into productive collaboration. The work began in the mid-1920s, and by the late 1920s several anthropologists and psychologists had been recruited for pioneer, long-term projects to develop a new profession concerned with worker problems and later focusing on administration and leadership, especially that of business management. Up until that time, the problem of how to run an organization to ensure the cooperation of members had consistently eluded intellectual comprehension.

These pioneer projects were financed for over a decade by grants to the Harvard Business School for research directed by Elton Mayo, one of the earliest psychologists working in industry. Mayo collaborated closely with a number of anthropologists, especially with W. Lloyd Warner. The projects also served as a training ground for several professionals who later continued to make important contributions to the field.

During this pioneering period, two different but complementary general strategies and methods were launched and developed. One was the individual interviewing of informants away from their jobs with a special emphasis on their personal concerns; the other was the observation and recording of what workers did while with their coworkers both on the job and occasionally in experimental situations.

The former was used and developed by psychologists, and the major results were reported by Mayo (1940 and 1945) and Roethlisberger and Dickson (1939). Observation, in contrast, was principally developed by anthropologists. In particular, W. Lloyd Warner promoted the generalized method of participant observation (Roethlisberger and Dickson 1939:389), and Eliot D. Chapple introduced and developed a method of precise quantitative recording. In turn, Chapple and Arensberg (1940) emphasized that the social and psychobiological study of man must be based not on verbal symbols of what persons say they do or feel, but rather on visible and audible behavioral data that can be unambiguously and clearly defined. Contrary to the conviction overwhelmingly prevalent at the time, these researchers believed that the painstaking and laborious effort such observations required would in the end provide the foundation for a science of human behavior that no analysis of the spoken word could obtain.

This essay focuses on major contributions to our understanding of transforming adversary into collaborative relationships resulting from primary reliance on observation, with special attention to the contributions made by four different observational strategies. These strategies represent different methods used to discover and evaluate the critical variables by which people induce one another to cooperate and, in particular, to identify the leadership traits responsible for doing so. The first strategy, participant observation, is the well-recognized and essential method that provides researchers with a general understanding and firsthand familiarity with situations. The second, more technical and focused strategy of identifying and quantifying critical variables, necessarily follows from the first. As will be presently described, this second strategy has made possible the identification of an interactional process that apparently induces participants to cooperate.

The third and fourth strategies, the historical and ethological, provide comparative evidence from human and animal societies that strongly corroborates the interactional discoveries revealed by the second strategy. In summary, the evidence to be presented below shows that cooperation—and the leadership skill that induces it—is primarily neither verbal nor intellectual but rather a reciprocal process between and among interacting persons that involves, for example, the rhythmic interplay of actions and inactions and the decibel level and tone of vocal sounds.[1]

---

1. See Guest (1962) for a particularly revealing and readable account, clearly differentiating skilled from inferior management.

Strategy 1: Participant Observation

In industrial settings, participant observation is the application of the same approach used by more traditional anthropologists. Extreme care must be taken to become as unobtrusive as possible in order to minimally disturb the normal activities of the subjects as they go about their daily affairs. The method requires being present, wherever one is allowed, when the subjects are engaging in their daily routines, and the observation and recording of what takes place. One must be prepared to act intuitively by paying particular attention to unusual or problem situations. As a field technique, participant observation holds an important place among other methodological strategies, for it provides an absolutely essential means of acquiring first-hand familiarity with situations that are otherwise puzzling when more restrictive methods are used.

In industrial situations, some major discoveries resulting from participant observation, or combinations of interview and observation, have included: the importance of informal relationships as they influence cooperation for or against management (Roethlisberger and Dickson 1939); determining the dependence of sentiments on behavior (Richardson 1961); and recognizing job boredom and technological factors that strongly influence relationships (Walker 1962; Woodward 1965; Richardson and Walker 1948). In addition, participant observers have repeatedly described feuding and adversary activities, a subject which will be elaborated on below.

The Western Electric and Harvard Studies focused professional attention on the human problems of business and industry during a period when national attention was focused on these and related problems due to the depression of the 1930s. It was a period of great worker-management unrest, with government intervention providing unions with considerable legitimate power and, hence, a period of intensive labor organizing. During this time, intellectuals and sympathizers, personally unfamiliar with labor–management problems, began to penetrate industrial sanctuaries and to associate with and listen to the plights of working–class people.

To gain firsthand familiarity with worker-management relationships, whether unionized or not, required either the introduction of scholarly spies as workers into management's controlled territory, or

the winning of approval from both labor and management protagonists to allow free access for and cooperation with an ob-
server/interviewer. This latter step was difficult to achieve. Labor–
management controversy was high, and considerable skills and tact
were required to maintain objective neutrality and to be constantly
alert against "playing favorites" by associating more with the members of one group rather than with another. Consequently, only a few
dozen scholarly observers succeeded during the 1930s and 1940s (and
rarely in serious conflict situations) in gaining acceptance and remaining for long periods of time within company-controlled buildings and
territory. Several who did succeed, however, were anthropologists or
those working closely with them. They included Burleigh Gardner,
William F. Whyte, Melville Dalton, Conrad Arensberg, and myself.

Although these observer/interviewers gathered information in many
work places not actually in open conflict, subtle kinds of suppressed
hostility were evident everywhere. There was chronic feuding between company men struggling to get workers to increase their output, while at the same time workers were cleverly and covertly re-
sisting these maneuvers (Whyte 1955). Management's principle weapon
was to establish a minimum level of output, reward those who met
or exceeded it, and punish those who failed. During this continual
feuding, on the one hand to raise and on the other hand to withhold
production, skirmishes between labor and company men were daily
affairs, as were their partisan discussions of feuding and counter-
ploys. When any union member's partisanship weakened, he or she
was soon set upon to be forcibly reconverted by fellow workers. Supervisory and company men had similar experiences if the dominant
"hard-line" members of management felt the former were "soft" on
workers.

Unionized workers developed great skill in misleading company
men, especially those establishing output standards. Through a system of warning signals, these workers slowed their pace whenever
company men sallied forth with clipboard, pencil, paper, and stop-
watch. More importantly, they rarely revealed to company men the
shortcut methods they had devised to increase their daily output. Those
who kept these treasured secrets to themselves were able to complete
their daily quota of work in a fraction of the official time designated.
Thereafter, if not too evident, they idled their time away by visiting
and talking with their co-workers, organizing gambling pools, and

disciplining rate-busters when necessary. Now and then, they occasionally even used remote corners of the shop for sleeping and clandestine rendezvous.

Simultaneously, in company offices, a superintendent might be bawling out a foreman for practicing the "soft" human relationship skills he had learned in an academic seminar. In a conference room, an aggressive, young, well-dressed, college-trained engineer, aspiring to high position, might be giving a pep talk to older and simply dressed working class foremen, demanding that they push for high production goals, assert their management prerogatives, and punish slackers, and finally finishing off with warnings against sabotage, troublemakers, and Communist infiltration.

Numerous studies revealed that however obvious hostility is to both parties during conflicts and feuds, many persons, particularly dominant ones, are often unaware of the frustration, annoyance, and anger they sometimes generate in others simply by their inadvertently obtuse or superior manner. Such a manner on the part of an organizational superior unconsciously provokes antiproductive responses among subordinates that are often far more automatic than conscious. Thus, supervisory relationships are closely related to the output of work groups.

When a superintendent or plant manager cockily strides about taking over in a curt and uncompromising manner, the response of his subordinate managers is usually to let him do so while they themselves withdraw from active supervision (Richardson 1961:69; 1965:17–19). Should the superintendent actively rebuff his subordinate managers as problems build up, he can further provoke them to angry rebellion. In contrast, there are supervisors who feel they must know every last detail, and in doing so they frustrate and annoy their subordinates through persistent quizzing and long-winded discussion. Even more destructive to cooperative endeavors are authoritative individuals who devote much time to fraternizing with some while ignoring others, and who busily walk around and glance about checking on those they distrust.

It is one thing to be deliberately hostile toward an enemy and even sometimes to be forceful, if not a bit hostile, toward intimates and companions to ensure an even sharing of privilege and chores. But why do organizational superiors so often unconsciously annoy and alienate their subordinates and thereby diminish their productivity? A second observational strategy, to be elaborated upon below, has made possible the discovery of numerous behavioral subtleties by which interacting persons often unknowingly please or alienate each other.

Strategy 2: Identifying and Quantifying Critical Variables

As previously mentioned, the two anthropologists, Chapple and Arensberg (1940), set themselves the task of precisely defining what they determined would be critical behavioral units to observe, record, and quantify.

By the late 1930s, they had identified and defined two distinct classes of units. One was rather simple, namely, a *contact* or the period during which two or more persons first interacted, beginning when they greeted or acknowledged each other, and ending when they parted, ceased to interact, or were joined by one or more others. The other is a more elemental and complex unit that makes it possible to describe within seconds and fractions of a second the timing of the sounds and the motions by which, for example, conversants attract each other's attention and indicate that they respond. As the tempo of interchange is often rapid with nods, eye glances, and "hums" following in rapid succession, many subtleties are often missed by simple pencil and paper recording. To attain the necessary split-second accuracy requires special recording equipment. In addition, a specialized computer technology is required to analyze the deluge of quantified data.

These two methods of counting and timing—one simple and rough, the other complex and detailed—have yielded important quantified results clearly identifying leadership traits which an analysis of language has never revealed.

INTERACTION AND PRODUCTIVITY

Considering first the simple pencil and paper method of recording and quantifying contact units only, one of the important advances has been a further simplification that made it possible to predict the work performance of groups by recording only the supervisor's contacts which lasted one minute or longer. The usefulness of this simplified method was demonstrated in the early 1960s after I conducted a systematic study of nearly thirty design engineering sections in a large electronic laboratory (Richardson 1965; Richardson and White 1965). For a two- to four-week period, managers recorded all their contacts at work which were one minute or longer in duration. The findings provided a means for clearly differentiating high from mediocre and poorly performing groups. It was discovered, for example, that the managers of the high-production sections practiced what might be called *contact moderation*. This term is best defined as the balance between the extremes of interaction, between too much and too little, between contacts too numerous and too few, or too long and too short in duration. This "golden mean" would characteristically vary from situation to situation. The managers studied tended to devote not less than one-half nor more than three-quarters of their time to contacts with others. They also distributed their time among subordinates without favoring some and ignoring others. Moreover, the average length of their contacts was neither long-winded nor curt; the number per day was not less than fifteen nor more than thirty; and they did not resort to excessive proportions of group versus pair discussion. A rank ordering of the sections by the quality and quantity of work completed within allotted time periods was compared with a ranking of section managers according to the degree to which they conformed to the above mentioned interactional moderation or golden mean; there was more than a 90 percent correspondence.

By using a special electronic device and computer called an interaction chronograph, elemental interactional units within a contact were counted and timed accurately to fractions of a second (Chapple 1949). Using this equipment, Chapple and his associates were able to specify personality traits far too subtle to be revealed through interview data. To reach such conclusions with minimum recordings, Chapple (1953b) devised an experimental stress interview by subjecting his subjects on the one hand to a standardized manner of interrupting and on the other to the contrary stress of a uniform bland manner of nonresponsiveness.

The systematic use of this quantitative and experimental method soon yielded all kinds of unsuspected results. It became possible, for example, to establish that different interactional tempos are associated with different kinds of selling, such as retailing inexpensive and familiar items in contrast to the bulk selling of more expensive ones (Chapple and Donald 1947; Norman 1954; Chapple 1970:278–281, 284–285). It was also possible to detail the different tempos required, for example, a pattern of interjections of shorter duration for the first than the second, and the degree to which a salesperson should attempt to take over or keep silent and let the customer contemplate and ask questions.

In a similar fashion, Chapple (Chapple 1970:282–283; Chapple and Donald 1946) has compared low- and high-level supervisors and managers. He found that those in supervisory positions tend to have a higher activity rate (e.g., more talkative than silent), greater dominance (i.e., holding the floor despite interruptions), and greater interactional flexibility (more adaptive in varying the length of their talking and listening depending on such things as the idiosyncracies of other persons or on the situation). Additionally, it was determined that higher-level persons are less temperamental or "flappable." They do not react emotionally to a series of persistent stess-provoking interruptions or prolonged silences introduced by the interviewer. In contrast to their subordinates, they over- or underreact less to excessive talking or silence by more persistently maintaining their normal rhythm despite the stress introduced by others.

INTERACTION AND VERBAL DISCUSSION

Supervisors or salespersons are judged not only on their ability to influence the productivity and purchasing of things but on their skill in verbal discussion. On the one hand, they must have skill to take over, control, and persuade, and on the other they must be able to learn from others and encourage them to inform, critique, and suggest. Interactional recordings provide a surprisingly useful, simple, and revealing method of judging these skills.

To make this possible, a simple paper and pencil recording method of intermediate exactitiude between the two mentioned above was devised to count and time to five-second accuracy all utterances or "talks" during a conversation or meeting. This method proved useful for evaluating a community resettlement program with the purpose of developing leadership and initiative among the so-called homesteaders (Richardson 1941:47–51). It provided, for example, one concrete piece of contrary evidence. Based on a systematic recording of seven management-homesteader meetings during a nine-month period, the few members of management consistently appropriated about 30 percent of the talks, while no single or small group of homesteaders increased their talking percentage.

To improve an understanding of committee skills and chairmen, and those of a moderator-chairman in particular, I organized a series of five-person, twenty-minute, experimental committee meetings using students as subjects. A study of about twenty such committees (Richardson et al. 1972) revealed major interactional distinctions between good, poor, and mediocre committees, as judged by the number of ideas generated or the development of a practical plan. In the poorest committees, for example, considerable time, 50 percent or more than in the other committees, was consumed by monologues of one minute or longer, or "duologues" (the same two persons monopolizing at least two consecutive minutes). The poor committees were not mediated by active chairmen skillfully using their initiative and pregrogative to encourage the reticent and to silence the garrulous.

In addition to committee discussion, leadership skills are critically important in two-person dialogues. A study was conducted of an able surgeon in a teaching hospital who revealed a number of interactional traits that he regularly practiced (Richardson 1966:166–171). One was his control of conversations by continuing to talk despite interruption. However, with appropriate persons and times, this assertiveness was balanced by a parallel ability to listen more than he talked. He also displayed considerable skill in what might be called composing a conversation from beginning to end with a well-structured internal sequence. When reassuring patients, for example, he commonly talked twice as much as he listened at the beginning and end, but in the midst of the discussion, he reversed the proportion. When advising and persuading on one occasion, his pattern was more or less the reverse: when seeking information, his percentage of talking time progressively lessened from the beginning to almost the end.

Close familiarity with dozens of leaders and hundreds of their followers has revealed that in contrast to the poorer leaders having too much or too little contact, the better leaders won over their followers through a more moderate pattern of contacts. The more highly placed and successful leaders exhibited numerous interactional subtleties, such as greater flexibility in adapting their conversational tempo to others, and in controlling discussion by skillfully timing and directing their interruptions at appropriate persons.

Strategy 3: An Historical Approach to Superior-Subordinate Disassociation and Involvement

Firsthand familiarity with a number of work organizations repeatedly revealed that poor performance, conflict, and troublesome superior-subordinate relationships were often associated with leaders who had, for example, little or at best erratic contact with their subordinates (Richardson 1961: chapter 15; Richardson and Walker 1948: chapters 2 and 3) or a similar degree of contact neglect between members from two different but closely interdependent groups such as test and production (Sayles 1964: chapter 8). To check this general observation which had been reinforced by considerable quantitative evidence, I undertook a survey of the literature of past and present organizations—particularly large states and business organizations. This survey not only corroborated the above generalization, but also revealed several independently evolved institutional practices designed to promote a closer acquaintance between superior and subordinates. Some of these are briefly mentioned below.

ANCIENT PRACTICES

It should first be emphasized that the long history of mankind amply documents superior-subordinate dissension, particularly in large states and class societies with minimal social mobility. Consider the struggles of peoples against enforced subservience, the striving of subordinates for more advantageous positions, and the violence which accompanies the rise and fall of rulers and dynasties, particularly in large states and empires. Those states that succeeded in converting strangers or enemies into working associates and cooperative subordinates gained competitive advantages over those less able to do so. Some of the practices which developed for this purpose have a long history.

One is trade, which, in contrast to military conquest and forced subjugation, provided a relatively peaceful means of meeting and penetrating into alien societies. A second is the development of an increasing number and kind of services and help that professionals supply to complete strangers or large numbers of persons they barely know. A third is joint consultation and negotiation among the leaders and representatives of constituent units to reach agreements essential for de-escalating a natural feuding and rivalry. With the emergence of large states, this latter practice required the shuttling back and forth by high level intermediaries between the capital and the provinces.

Thus, in pre-nineteenth-century Great Britain and Japan, the ruling provincial lords regularly alternated their residence between the capital center and their local territories in contrast to the metropolis-bound lords of Russia and France. In no small measure may the revolutions of the latter two nations be due to the nearly full-time metropolitan or palace involvement by their provincial elite and the growing estrangement from peasants, tenants, and serfs. As a comparable adaptation, large American industrial corporations, in recent decades, have reversed the practice of executives exclusively residing at the company center and occasionally commuting outward to confer with plant superintendents and low-level supervisors at local factories. Instead, some of the executives have replaced the local superintendents as plant managers, and now usually reside near the branch plants. Only occasionally do they visit the more distant home office.

In addition, there is a more recent means of forcing members of the elite to take greater cognizance of common people. This has increasingly come about, beginning with the Industrial Revolution, in response to the accelerating rate of discovery and invention by many persons of humble background who, in the recent past, have often been without much formal education. As a consequence, these inventive commoners were sought after, financed, and employed by persons of means, thus, in these instances, weakening interclass avoidance and status taboos. It should be noted, however, that while the Industrial Revolution may have forced a greater interaction between the elite and some commoners, it did not obliterate class distinctions or the actual wealth and power of the elite. On the contrary, the system frequently became more autocratic and the jobs of the workers even more rigidly proscribed.

The above practices provide means for unfamiliar persons to become better acquainted, and often lessen fears and uncertainties inherent in strangeness. By acquiring a familiarity, many not only came to accept one another, but also developed an actual liking or a cooperative and productive working relationship. With the progressive enlargement of business and other organizations during the past century, the difficulty of transforming superiors and subordinates, or rivals and strangers, into productive collaborators has continued to present a constant challenge and has given rise to numerous corrective programs. Let us now consider the practices that have developed in industrial settings in an attempt to overcome these difficulties.

ENCOURAGING INTERACTIONAL INVOLVEMENT

Over the past six decades, there has been a succession of practices providing means by which the members of an organization may become better acquainted and devote more attention to one another, while at the same time possibly even improving their productive output. These practices include the famous Hawthorne experiments in the Western Electric Company, T (training) groups (Bradford et al. 1964), organizational development (Huse 1975), and the more recent emphasis on management by objectives (MBO) (Raia 1974). Often, the ostensible purpose may be directed toward a specific concern such as MBO, which focuses on objectives, or Sensitivity Training, which emphasizes self-awareness, but the implementation of all these programs necessarily results in the relevant persons becoming better acquainted. Similar in nature are a number of programs conceived to encourage subordinates to make specific suggestions for improving company performance and, if improved, to implement suitable innovations. Such examples include the much-copied Coordination-by-Committees practices by General Motors (Sloan 1964: chapter 7), the Multiple Management plan, or Junior Board of Directors (Craf 1958), first developed in the McCormick Spice Company, and the Scanlon Plan (Lesieur 1958), whereby workers actively participated in foreman and management discussions.

   In addition to those programs focusing on some particular detail, there have been numerous generalized programs such as a series of changes in IBM's Endicott plant to bring about closer relationships between workers and foremen. There, foremen were urged to spend as much time as possible away from their desk, maintaining contact with and assisting rather than "bossing" their men as well as with all other plant personnel. To this end, foremen were provided with clerical assistants, and the number of workers reporting to each was greatly reduced (in one department from sixty-five to twenty-seven) despite a doubling in the size of the department (Richardson and Walker 1948:20–23).

EXECUTIVE COURTING

Some of these ancient and modern practices have involved more than a formal attempt to get better acquainted. Instead, the controlling executives require of their managers, administrators, or ruling lords, a major commitment to win subordinate loyalty. The IBM plan is a good case in point, as is the Multiple Management plan in which top executives court younger and lower-level managers, and the Scanlon plan in which managers, foremen, and workers regularly discuss production problems and where workers have a significant financial share in the enterprise. In some instances, company executives, in competition with labor leaders, have succeeded in winning over worker loyalty to such an extent that workers have no active desire to affiliate with labor unions.

Historically, taking the effort to court previous enemies and rivals is probably as ancient as civilization. A famous example is Alexander the Great, who took extraordinary means to win over the leaders of those he conquered, as did William the Conqueror to win over the English. George Washington demonstrated superior skill and tact in getting the colonial, and later the state, representatives to work together for a unified central government.

The expansion of organizations and their competitive survival requires that unfamiliar members acquire increasing understanding through closer acquaintance. It seems only natural, therefore, to infer a close connection, as did Homans (1950:110–117) between interaction, liking, and companionship. I would add cooperation also.

Strategy 4: An Ethological Approach:
Comparative Human and Animal Behavior[2]

The truism that friends cooperate with each other more than with strangers and that the latter are often indifferent or hostile is apparently contradicted by the kindness that many exhibit to strangers, such as to the weak and the handicapped, or at the time of an accident or death. During dangerous situations, such as wars, fires, and floods, persons sometimes even help rivals and enemies. On all such occasions, for those who proffer their help, there are others who harm, loot, and kill. The proposition is therefore presented that among friendly companions, cooperation is more automatically mutual or reciprocally programmed and, hence, less subject to chance or will. Among strangers, in contrast, cooperation and help depend more on conscious volition or on the personal needs, learned habits, and peculiarities of each individual.

That cooperation or reciprocal helping is far more reliable and usual among friendly companions than among strangers and enemies, slowly rose in my consciousness when I was repeatedly confronted by nearly identical intergroup difficulties. In one familiar work situation after another, I was forced to consider why problems and poor performance were commonplace among interdependent groups whose members were more or less segregated, who rarely intermingled, and who apparently often avoided each other.

Considerable experience in industrial firms, hospitals, and other organizations had led me to believe that conflict and cooperation were often attributable to imprecise causes. One of the examples that made this intuitive insight more precise was a carefully recorded situation which provided dramatic evidence concerning two rival and antagonistic cliques in a small department whose members remained exclusively segregated during the two daily ten-minute rest periods. One group, under the direction of management's designated leader, cooperated to withhold production, while the other group resented such behavior. A third group of workers within the same department formed a friendship group, as opposed to a clique, evidenced by the fact that during rest periods their members sometimes mixed with those of the

2. See Richardson (1975) for fuller discussion of the material presented in this and the following section.

112 Frederick L. W. Richardson

two exclusive cliques and maintained satisfactory relations with members of each. Members had the greatest contact within their own closed clique where they were regularly friendly and exchanged favors with each other. They had a moderate degree of contact, greeting and conversing with members of the open friendship group, but with much less if any exchange of favors. Between rival clique members, contact was both hostile and limited.

The distinctions in intergroup contact were documented with considerable precision by quantitatively recording who was interacting with whom during rest periods. These data helped formulate an hypothesis that the greater the contact, the greater the exchange of favors; conversely, less contact is associated with less favoring and with greater potential for hostile exchange.

To test the hypothesis that gradations in contact and degrees of friendly to hostile exchange are closely related, a preliminary research was made of simple human societies, by perusing anthropological monographs. Three strongly supportive instances were found and no contradictory ones. However, most monographs neither contained the relevant information nor reported it in sufficient detail. Hence, this approach has not been further pursued. Strong corroboration, however, emerged unexpectedly from seemingly peripheral and unrelated evidence regarding other social mammals.

From numerous studies of bands of monkeys, apes, lions, wolves, prairie dogs, zebras, and others, it became evident that the close connection between gradations in contact and degrees of friendly to hostile exchange can be extended to apply widely to adult mammals living in child-rearing family groups (Richardson 1975:326–328). Commonly, if not universally, the adult members within a family group have considerable contact, are usually friendly together, and come to each other's assistance, whereas they are collectively indifferent or hostile toward nonmembers and strangers of their own species. Within a group or close community of members, the most regularly associating companions collaborate more closely for their mutual advantage than they do with other members (Van Lawick-Goodall 1971: note "friendship" and "alliances" in index; Eaton 1976). Morever, many of these families and genera of mammals emerged tens of millions of years ago and presumably evolved cooperative relationships automatically binding interacting individuals to one another long before the emergence of Man and his much enlarged outer brain.

INTERACTIONALLY PLEASING

In contemplating this mutual assistance that characterizes cooperation, consider three other kinds of reciprocal behavior that companions commonly exhibit—and particularly human companions. One is imitation, each to a degree copying the other; and the second and third, both related to the first, are that companions are usually relaxed in each other's presence and, as judged by their facial expressions, for example, they often indicate a mutual contentment, amusement, or pleasure. The proposition last mentioned is that the critical consideration is the contentment or pleasure they reciprocally induce in each other.

Consider the wealth of evidence that led to the so-called Learning Theory, and the recent applied programs in Behavior Modification, for which the critical consideration is that for both humans and other mammals a sensing of pleasure induced by a reward is an essential accompaniment to behavorial change. From this thesis it can be further assumed that to transform hostile subordinates into productive collaborators requires that such subordinates somehow derive pleasure therefrom. The more specific propositon is that the most successful leaders, in addition to material rewards, possess the interactional skill to induce more intangible ones.

It is recognized that effective leaders are often able to alter the moods of their subordinates in ways that spur them to greater effort. Sometimes the latter also derive greater satisfaction therefrom, which they in turn somehow reciprocally convey in ways their leaders also find pleasing. What are these intangible ''rewards'' that persons sense as mutually satisfying, and what are their inexplicit counter-parts that alienate and annoy?

TOUCH, WARMTH, SOUND, AND DISTANCE

Four of the most basic means by which humans and all mammals induce emotion in one another are through touch, warmth, sound, and distance. In contrast to such hostile displays as striking, kicking, and biting, nonhuman mammals groom, nuzzle, and lick, while humans, for example, embrace and hold hands. When cold or chilled, individuals huddle, each warming the other.

Regarding sound, loud rasping noises frighten, displease, and agitate all humans and animals that hear them, while soft melodious tones generally calm and please. Moreover, as so clearly described by Hall (1966), the intervening distance that separates interacting individuals, whether human or animal, is critical in causing them to be agitated or at ease. To be too close or too distant are both commonly displeasing, whereas a satisfying distance lies somewhere in between. The specific distances involved vary from society to society, subgroup to subgroup, and from one kind of situation to another.

RHYTHM

Less recognized than sound and distance as a means of inducing emotion between individuals is the importance of interactional rhythm. Consider first the daily or yearly periodicity of meeting, convening, and parting—the frequency and length of time that persons contact or avoid others. We all, for example, sense the annoyance or anger of those who are curt, who snub, or avoid, and that such behavior commonly induces displeasure in those toward whom it is directed. In contrast, a mix of short and long contacts, at an appropriate frequency, with initiative more evenly shared (referred to above as contact moderation) is usually indicative of cooperative persons and friendly companions. Not only do persons perform better work for those who achieve this contact moderation or golden mean (Richardson 1965:7, 11–14), but, judging by their facial expressions and manner, they also derive greater pleasure therefrom.

Consider next during a contact, the alternation of talking and silence or motions and nonmotions while, for example, two persons interact or converse. Such interchanges vary widely depending on the degree to which one individual yields to another, with both taking turns talking and listening, or whether both talk at once or remain simultaneously silent. Chapple (1970: 45–48, 73–76) has repeatedly pointed out that it is pleasureable for persons when the actions and sounds of one synchronously mesh with the inactions and silences of the other. The evidence for these claims becomes apparent once noted, yet, although most experienced persons may intuitively sense such interconnections, the human mind is apparently so constructed that such interactional, nonverbal insights do not reguarly rise to consciousness. As regards unpleasant sensations regularly induced by asynchronous conversing, Chapple (1970:76) writes:

Think how hard it is for a naturally "outgoing," "social," "friendly" person to try to keep from being exasperated by a stone-faced, unresponsive partner who appears to ignore each effort to strike up a conversation. Consider the bore who persists in telling you all the minutiae of his daily life until your every will to indicate attention by a smile or other signal becomes paralyzed to immobility.

In contrast to the above, the next time you see friends enjoying each other, observe them and note the scarcity and brevity of their interruptions and double silences. Kendon has apparently systematically established that synchronous interchange is far more frequent among close friends and compatible couples than among strangers interacting for the first time (Kendon 1963). Chapple and Lindemann (1941) have similarly demonstrated that with an interviewer, "normal" persons have a much higher frequency of synchronization than mental patients. These close interconnections between interaction and emotion are not merely limited to man but occur widely among animals and may even be universal for mammals. Thus, in fighting situations, two contestants simultaneously, and hence asynchronously, strike at each other, in contrast to the synchronously alternating give-and-take characteristics of courting, chasing, grooming, and many kinds of play.

LANGUAGE, HUMOR, AND LISTENING

In addition to the reciprocal impact that touch, warmth, sound, distance, and alternating rhythms of action-inaction have on emotions and feelings, humor is another and virtually unique human trait that instantaneously triggers changes in mood. Humor is distinctive in that it is tied closely to language, whereas the nonverbal interactional traits are not. As Koestler (1967) has elaborated, incongruous contrasts provide the sparks that repeatedly ignite humor or laughter—not only incongruous behavior but also incongruity in verbal content. Hence, it is nearly always amusing to hear children seriously conversing in a grown-up manner, hilarious to listen to Charlie Chaplin scream and sputter while imitating Hitler, or Danny Kaye rapidly jabbering nonsense in imitation of foreigners talking.

Unlike sound, distance, body contact, and rhythm, all of which can reciprocally trigger among participants a wide gamut of negative to positive emotions—from anger to fear to fondness and love—most humor, by inducing pleasurable feelings, foster the latter. In the form of ridicule, however, humor usually pleases some while belittling others, if not actually at times inducing hostile retaliation. However, humor usually fulfills a very special need to offset the innumerably annoying and sly ways humans use their much extolled languages and intelligence to gain personal advantage and discredit others without appearing to do so. Without humor to lighten their moods, the daily strain from unresponsive, overzealous, boring, and rude persons— not to mention their own failings—might be too great a burden for humans to bear.

In addition to humor, another means by which persons relieve emotional disturbance (although sometimes transferring it to others) is the practice of actively accusing and complaining to persons who obligingly and understandingly listen. In fact, a formal interviewing program, with professionals privately listening to workers' concerns and complaints, was for a long period of time once institutionalized in a large corporation (Dickson and Roethlisberger 1966).

When antagonistically relieving anger, frustration, or fear by destroying and harming, there is no place for humor or quiet attentive listening. Only for those who attain a degree of companionability does it become possible to listen and joke. Instead of intensifying belligerence, the various nonverbal, "intangible," peaceful means cited above interactionally serve to de-escalate conflict and have the potential to transform feuding into pleasing and productive collaboration.

The Evolution and Circumvention of Interactional Order

COOPERATIVE EVOLUTION

To continue surviving, the members of a species have been improving their cooperative strategies since the beginning of life by evolving increasingly complex practices that attract others of their own kind. Thus, countless eons ago, mating developed as a critical strategy for all but the simplest species; the feeding and care of the young became universal among mammals and birds perhaps 200 million years ago; and *lifelong* cooperation with group members, for example, excluding outsiders, evolved more recently among a small minority of mammals and birds. Such critical collaborative functions are to important to leave to chance, and hence means have evolved which strongly attract individuals to one another and induce in them a near automatic capability to perform the programmed collaboration required.

These functions of mating, rearing young, excluding outsiders, and the like are all similar in that individuals behaviorally attract one another in ways that induce in each a peaceful and apparently pleasurable internal sensation or mood as an essential prelude in the programming of the collaborative behavior. For the critical function of mating, as well as for social insects communally rearing their young, cooperation is usually more or less rigidly programmed through smell or biochemical emanations (pheromones), from one individual to numerous others or, as in social insects, from mouth to mouth interchange of an apparently communal fluid. In contrast, among mammals and birds, for the rearing of young and calming of adults, gentle touching and bodily warmth or tactile stimulation are widely characteristic. Among humans, in addition to the above, familiarity resulting from sufficient interaction, both visible and audible synchronous interchange, and contact moderation have apparently evolved to become the most common means by which adults mutually induce and maintain their companionship and collaboration.

In the evolution from amphibians to primitive long-living mammals to man, there have been an increasing frequency and duration of interaction to the point that organizational leaders and managers, for example, devote from about one-half to nine-tenths of their working day interacting with others (Richardson 1965: 11; Burns, 1954; Mintzburg 1973; Stewart 1967). Such interactional stimulation, and in particular pleasurable interchange, has reached the point that it has apparently become essential for human health and well-being. This has been repeatedly demonstrated by studies of neglected or lone-living versus gregarious persons.

One famous study demonstrated that infants, regularly fondled, handled, and played with, in addition to being dutifully fed, clothed, and cleaned, were much healthier than those who were given only formal health care (Spitz 1945, 1946). These infants were far more prone to illness, and some even died. It is well recognized, similarly, that following the death of one member of an old couple, the other often dies soon thereafter. Finally, suicide rates have frequently been closely associated with loneliness, as many studies of rooming house districts in large cities have shown in the recent past (Zorbaugh 1929; Sainsbury 1955) and studies of isolated young people are currently demonstrating. There is also the old revealing statistical study from France showing that suicide rates increased as family size declined (Halbwachs 1930).

PRODUCTIVE COOPERATION

With regard to an increasing comprehension of human cooperation, particularly among superiors and subordinates, I suggest that the most significant discovery during the past few decades has been the identification of this unsuspected interactional-sensory and nonintellectual process. The following four-stage sequence is proposed as an approximate description:

First, moment-to-moment alternations of action-inaction and sound-silence sequences among interacting persons stimulate the lower brain which, second, triggers electrical signals that travel along the nerve network, rapidly permeating the entire body, and also hormonal secretions that move more slowly, activating usually a particular organ or a more restricted part of the body. This highly complex physiological process is internally sensed in ways that words imperfectly convey, but which can be impressionistically described as ranging between pleasure and displeasure or from high euphoria on one extreme to fear, anger, or violence on the other.

Third, in varying degrees, this internal physiological state in turn induces or inhibits work effort whereby "superiors" frequently stimulate their subordinates in ways the latter often find pleasing (although with some occasional fear and deference). Some such mix apparently tends to induce cooperative inclinations that often predispose members to work hard in contrast to a greater mix of displeasing ways that alienate and repel. This mix, in turn, predisposes members to withhold their productive effort, if not to engage in counterproductive or retaliatory exchanges that, fourth, determine the work output, productivity, or performance of an individual or group and, over time, their degree of well-being and health.

This alternating, interactional rhythm and pattern provide to participants a nonthinking automatic means of reciprocally regulating each other. As presented above, it is common among humans and other mammals that participants who induce in each other mutual feelings of pleasure become thereby automatically predisposed to cooperate. It was, in addition, proposed that for human beings the commonest behavioral means by which groups of individuals become mutually stimulated to cooperate include (1) familiarity or becoming acquainted through sufficient interaction, (2) synchronous interchange, and (3) contact moderation—in addition to some degree of deference and fear. It was further proposed that gradations of cooperation were more or less directly determined by the degree to which the interacting individuals pleasurably and reciprocally stimulated each other. Thus, for example, the less the acquaintance, synchrony, and moderation, the less pleasing to the participants, and the less their inclinations to cooperate.

THE INTERACTIONAL AND SENSORY PROCESS OF RECIPROCAL CONTROL

Within a group or community of familiar individuals, relationships are not always peaceful, as members usually from time to time fight briefly, for example, over mates or simply who yields to whom. What, then, other than inhibitions from companionability, are the additional means by which members limit the intensity of such confrontations?

Among vertebrates, including humans, one common means is for the loser to defer, withdraw, or both, which usually more or less automatically causes the victor to desist (Lorenz 1966). When deferring, it is common also for the loser not only to avoid any appearance of threatening, by, for instance, lowering or cowering, but also by exposing a vulnerable part of the body as does a wolf by presenting his neck to the victor. Moreover, once having escalated a confrontation to a state of vicious hostility, two such rivals usually thereafter keep a safe distance (Lorenz 1966:215).

In addition to these largely automatic reactions is the fact that rival members of the same species, age, and sex are usually closely matched in fighting ability and thus each is more or less equally capable of inflicting pain on the other. As a result, there exists within a group reciprocal means by which members interactionally limit their fighting in addition to the aforementioned interactional-sensory means of inducing greater or less cooperation.

This reciprocal, self-regulating, interactional-sensory process, moreover, is primarily controlled not by man's outer and newly developed thinking brain but by his inner and lower brain (Chapple 1970:63–67), otherwise referred to as the old mammalian brain or limbic system which, when compared to that of apes and monkeys, has remained relatively unchanged (MacLean 1968). It is this ancient, inner, lower, and interactionally stimulated mammalian brain that primarily controls the emotions, as contrasted to man's newly developed outer brain or cerebral cortex that makes thinking, memory, and learning possible.

The fact that man's limbic system or old mammalian brain appears relatively unchanged, compared to that of apes and monkeys, strengthens the proposition that a similar self-regulating interactional process controls cooperation and hostility among human beings but obviously, because of the enormously developed outer, thinking brain, with less effectiveness than among other primates and mammals. It is proposed that the reason mankind's self-regulating process functions less well is because the superior endowments that the new outer brain makes possible—intelligence, technology, and language—provide unique means for circumventing these automatically programed stimuli and controls (Richardson 1975:328–334).

In the first place, technology, when monopolized by a few, circumvents competitive equality or parity in power, especially when it makes possible the killing or jailing of rivals, and hence eliminates the confrontations by which members of approximately equal dominance reciprocally limit each other. Secondly, when dominant members use their intelligence to subordinate more individuals than they can ever know, the restraining influences of companionship are also circumvented. Finally, as language makes possible indoctrination, conniving, and spying, and human memory prolongs hatreds, superiors and subordinates often polarize into implacable feuding classes and cliques, with the former refusing to desist and the latter giving only the pretense of deference.

That interactional stimulation provides a means by which participants may reciprocally control cooperation and rivalry strongly suggests that for humans, as well as for other family-dwelling mammals (and possibly birds also), this process results not from memory and learning only but also from some inborn predisposition. To a large extent, therefore, these cooperative, indifferent, and hostile responses appear to be triggered by some inborn nonrational process—some neuroglandular-sensory means more primeval and programmed than thinking and learned.

Interacting and Talking While Simultaneously Feeling, Sensing, and Thinking[3]

Relationships among people, as they engage in discourse, can thus be conceived as a highly complex behavioral-sensory and neurophysiological process. Communicatively, however, it can be conveniently conceived as a *dual* process: (1) interacting (the interplay of actions or sounds vs. inactions and silence), and (2) talking (verbal exchange). This duality is reinforced by the fact that not only humans but all mammals (and to a degree, reptiles also) are controlled by two vastly different but interdependent physiological or neuroglandular mental processes. One is intellectual and a late vertebrate development that makes possible the consideration of future actions in light of past experience. Among humans, this development is both intellectual and verbal. The other is a primordial, unthinking behavioral-sensory process concerned with immediate relationships with others. It is essential for health and well-being and a process upon which cooperation largely depends.

In our developed technological society, persons often tend to specialize in one or the other. Thus, thinking, scheming, and scholarly persons develop skill in the first-mentioned *intellectual-verbal* kind of intelligence, as evidenced by their IQ, articulating ability, or both; congenial, playful, polite, and considerate persons specialize in the second, or what might be called *behavioral* intelligence, as evidenced by their interactional manner. However, to be a successful

3. For a partially comparable presentation, see Johnson (1953).

leader of a competitive enterprise requires a *comprehensive* intelligence that specializes in neither but skillfully encompasses both. It is an unfortunate and worsening dilemma that, although leadership requires an all-inclusive, comprehensive intelligence—both behavioral and intellectual—our educational system focuses only on one.

5

DEVELOPING ANTHROPOLOGICAL KNOWLEDGE THROUGH APPLICATION

Jacquetta Hill-Burnett

The complexities of human organization and relationships in the institutions of contemporary societies require versatility not only on the part of managers and those they manage but also on the part of applied anthropologists. Jacquetta Hill-Burnett provides a perceptive glimpse into the theoretical and methodological versatility demanded of her as the director of a federally funded action research project which was designed to improve the intercultural educational processes of Puerto Rican youths in a midwestern urban school.

In this situation, the use of anthropological paradigms and knowledge continuously entailed the reformulation of the research design so that new knowledge could be developed and used in the school setting. The rigid hierarchical interaction of Puerto Rican students and their non-Hispanic teachers resulted in the intellectual comprehension of anthropologically based suggestions in ways that perpetuated stereotyped behavior between the two groups. Intergroup conflict inhibited the novel

Jacquetta Hill-Burnett (Ph.D. Columbia, Teachers College), is professor of psychological anthropology in the department of educational psychology and affiliate of the department of anthropology, University of Illinois (Champaign-Urbana).She has done field research in the United States, Puerto Rico, Australia, and among Hill Tribes of Northern Thailand. She is a past president of the Council on Anthropology and Education.

The research reported here was supported by Research Grant No. RD 2926 G 69 from the Division of Research and Demonstration Grants, Social and Rehabilitation Services, Department of Health, Education, and Welfare, Washington, D.C. The author also wishes to thank Delmos J. Jones for helpful criticisms and suggestions on revisions of an earlier draft of this paper.

behavioral learning experiences necessary for collaborative educational relationships.

While both teachers and pupils learned something about each other's behavior and the cognitive meanings associated with it, only a few individuals were able to adapt to the institutional setting. Those who did so displayed a behavioral intelligence which enabled them to decode the meanings of others' behavior and change their own behavior accordingly. This essay illustrates not only the subtleties of turning institutionalized conflict relationships into productive ones, but also the "worsening dilemma" posed by the fact that our educational system fails to focus on behavioral intelligence. By combining an ecological approach with behavioral and cognitive approaches to her collection and analysis of data, Hill-Burnett demonstrates the ways in which the exclusive emphasis of formal schooling on intellectual intelligence perpetuates the present disadvantaged position of minority groups in our society.

THERE IS A common stereotype that applied anthropology consists of the application of already established anthropological principles to some problematic situation raised by a client, or communicating anthropological perspectives to a client who then makes practical use of the information. This concept is misleading because it implies that knowledge development is complete before the knowledge is used (Clifton 1970:xi). It projects the overly narrow view that client relationships with anthropologists primarily result from clients seeking out anthropologists to consult about a problem.

The use of knowledge entails its further development, not simply by adding to it but through transforming its assumptions, categories, and paradigms. Knowledge is *tested* in use; when found wanting, it must be further developed or clarified. In the social sciences, where experimental controls for testing knowledge are available to only a limited degree, applied anthropology should be the testing cauldron for the forward edge of anthropological knowledge.

This essay presents a story within a story. The documents, as well as the findings, of a federally funded project to study intercultural processes and problems experienced by Puerto Rican youths in a midwestern city are used as evidence for the proposition that the use of anthropological knowledge continuously involves its further development. The proposals and discussion papers of the project, when carefully examined in temporal order, lend evidence to, or, in the idiom of Glaser and Strauss (1967), "ground," the view that applying knowledge entails not only adding to it but transforming assumptions, manipulating categories, shifting paradigms, and coming to grips with the human consequences of using given conceptual schemata.[1]

Problem and Setting

The general objective of the EPIC *(Estudio de Problemas Interculturales)* project was to study the intercultural process and problems in migration, education, and occupations of Puerto Rican youths in a large midwest urban center, and, based on this knowledge, to design and implement educational procedures and programs that would improve their chances of obtaining better jobs. The project began with the proposition that cultural factors and differences were one major source of the educational problems experienced by Puerto Rican youths in United States schools. The educational questions were studied in the seventh and eighth grades of a grammar school in which over 75 percent of the children came from Spanish-language dominant homes, while their teachers came from a range of other, mostly second generation east and southern European, backgrounds. A second set of questions asked how educational problems and cultural factors affected occupational socialization and access to occupations for Puerto Rican youths in an urban setting in the United States.

The household of a Puerto Rican youth was regarded as the domain and conservator of a characteristic Puerto Rican culture. At the same time, the school was viewed as the domain and conservator of the professional educators' version of a dominant and characteristic North American culture. Peer relationships were a third domain, potentially of great relevance to acculturation of youth, but their cultural characteristics were unknown and had to be discovered.

We selected for study the pupils in a sample of thirty egocentric

1. Space limitations do not allow complete documentation of the claims about conceptual statements and project decisions through quotations from the project papers. A fully documented account of the conceptual changes is available on request from the author. A report of research results is available in Burnett (1972, 1974b) and Hill-Burnett (1976).

networks which began with thirty egos who were chosen by stratified random samplings from the 1967–68 seventh grade of a large urban elementary school. By starting with seventh-graders, we could examine the effects of a difference in experience with school cultures. We included in the sample five girls and five boys who had attended Puerto Rican schools for at least five years of their school careers before coming to the city; five girls and five boys from Puerto Rican families who had spent all their school careers in this city's schools; and five non-Puerto Rican girls and five non-Puerto Rican boys. The last ten provided a "controlled" comparison for sorting out cultural factors from other factors that were endemic to the inner city: socioeconomic level, broken homes, and so on. It helped to keep us "honest" and self-critical about what might be attributed to poverty and urbanism rather than cultural difference (Burnett 1974b:24–32).

This methodological procedure allowed the identification of natural relational networks radiating out from the egos to three types of persons. We first established contact with a youth attending the school. We then established contact with that particular youth's parents so as to begin observations and interviews with them in their household about the course and conditions of their lives and their perceptions and interpretations of relations and events in the school. We next located the teacher or teachers who were in contact with each youth, and, through participant observers, described the course of school life. The researchers interviewed teachers and other professionals to learn their points of view on the problems, solutions, and irresolvable conditions that had bearing on the student's school life. Finally, we established contacts with the youth's friendship network and observed and interviewed his or her peers in nonschool as well as school contexts.

In the early project documents, the research problem was stated in ways that placed culture in a primary causal position. It was implied that doing something about culture difference would change educational circumstances for children. The methodological statements focused on behavior, action, and interaction (Burnett 1968a).[2] The cultural formulation of the school situation emphasized the idea of professional subcultures and defined the research setting as multicul-

2. The theoretical and methodological concepts were based on the theoretical and empirical work of Chapple and Arensberg (1940), Arensberg (1951), Arensberg and Kimball (1965), Chapple and Sayles (1961), Barker (1963), and Harris (1964).

tural. The situation was conceptualized as probably imbued with mis-understanding and conflict inevitably arising out of the disparity between the culture of students and that of teachers. We suggested that Puerto Rican children, many of whom migrate back and forth from island to mainland, may often experience further complication because of their contact with the culture of Puerto Rican Schools as well as "mainland" United States schools.[3]

The opening statement of the project proposal expressed our concern that the burden of adaptation was being placed on students and not on adult professionals. This concern was the basis for including research questions that might lead to developing better intercultural teaching (Burnett 1968a). Despite my initial propensity to think of the teachers in terms of their ethnic background, rather than in terms of a professional culture or "code" for behavior to which they were socialized, certain facts about their backgrounds and observations in the school led me to believe the professional culture was more dominant than the ethnic culture. To my surprise, perhaps because most teachers were second-generation ethnic, they were adamant assimilationists and advocates of the necessity for cultural and linguistic replacement if the children were to find economic and occupational success within their lifetimes.

We were dealing with views, attitudes, beliefs, and guides to action that were acquired and developed while they were studying in the professional teacher training institutions of the city (where the great majority of them were trained) and through their early apprenticeship during the first years of teaching in city schools. Initially, we saw their reactions as coming out of middle-class cultural origins, but closer examination of the facts indicated that this view was too simple. It did not fit the facts of their ethnically mixed and largely lower income backgrounds. Their version of "Anglo" middle-class culture was not necessarily learned from households practicing "middle-class culture" but was the version or "register" learned in a higher educational setting that prepared them for the work place.

The methodological sections show the focus on behavioral stream and interaction as the data base for formulating recommendations to school people regarding changes in behavior. The theoretical position was that behavior is primarily a function of organization or structure

---

3. This is not an annual migration; its regularity is tied to the mainland economic cycle and thus is recurrent but not regularly periodic.

in interactive relationships. For example, the first public report of the research presents a behavioral, interaction version of what later was to be described as "the joking relationship" and describes our methods for studying it in these terms:

our next step is to follow the network of those Puerto Rican boys . . . to their households and to events in that household in order to see whether the pattern of interaction and the procedural aspect of activities directed toward sanctioning and toward inhibiting violations of behavior rules seem to follow the same procedures as those we've seen in school. . . . If there is sharp contrast then we can pursue the question through interviews with informants concerning how these behavioral procedures and their differences affect them and strike them in emotion and in value terms. (Burnett 1968a:19)

It should be noted that the decision about similarity and contrast in the conduct of interactions was to be based on the researchers' own etic system (cognitive mapping) of distinctive features, not on the prior careful delineation of actors' categories and defining features. The data plan, in the early part of the research, was to locate contrast by using the researchers' cognitive mapping, and only then to turn to questions of affective and conceptual mapping by participants. In a subsequent project document, this behavioral emphasis was reflected in the claim that investigation of cultural conduct involved selecting a sample of events involving interacting persons rather than a sample of individuals (Burnett 1969:20, 1973).

Interviews were not precisely coordinated with the specific record of interaction (cf. Burnett 1969 with Burnett 1972). Deliberate attention to peoples' expression of perceptions and sentiment toward particular events was added as a result of a theoretical shift in the second year of the project. At that time, the idea of the "interview from a behavioral record" came with a later cognitive concern with "cultural mapping" (Burnett 1970).

As a result of our initial emphasis on interaction and behavior, we began the study with a strong bias which viewed intercultural teaching as more than curriculum materials, test performance, and grades. Rather, it had to do with regularities of behavior, initiation of actions, and responses to actions. Moreover, we had a strong bias toward treating as mere rationalization the claims that lack of competence in English explained everything. Yet, in the process of neglecting the curriculum content, test performance, and grades, and favoring instead the behavioral data, we found that our communication of results back to teachers had little meaning for them. While our observations of classrooms provided excellent opportunity to study the process of the structuring of patterns of social relations, the findings did not provide information that was useful in trying to respond to the cognitive, conceptual, and motivational kinds of questions teachers asked us to answer or to help them answer. Our data did not deal with the problems and failures that the school system defined as primary considerations. We were addressing issues and troubles that ranked low in the professional educator's hierarchy of things on which energy, time, and thought were to be expended. Because of this experience, we reexamined and reoriented our conceptual approach.

The Sociolinguistic Study

The teachers' explanations of intercultural problems became important to us in order to formulate specific hypotheses that could be tested,thus providing information relevant to teachers' belief and explanatory systems. The approach utilized the experience of full participants in the phenomenal context in which we were working, and subjected it, as well as our own explanations, to empirical test. It was our belief that by dealing with teachers' explanations, with the same regard and respect as we did our own, we would persuade them to consider other types of explanations should theirs not stand up well under empirical test. If they denied the adequacy of our empirical tests of their ideas, they might at least consider developmental plans based on other optional explanations, even if they did not entirely reject their own previous beliefs. Moreover, it would be easier to invent, create, or formulate an ameliorative plan that included measures which teachers themselves might act upon.

Since six of the seven eighth-grade teachers specified language, or Puerto Rican students' lack of ability to use the English language, as the main source of their problems (Burnett 1974b), we added a linguist to the staff. She addressed herself to the question of the role of language in the performance of students, and to some degree the judgments of those performances by teachers. She made a distinction between competence, the mastery of the rules underlying sentence construction (such as the passive rule), and language performance, the way in which the speaker uses the rules. She also studied what kind of English was spoken by whom, with whom, and where, in terms of linguistic distinction.

Loy, the linguist, reported that responses to her tests, along with evidence of fluency in interview situations, indicated that the Puerto Rican students participating in the study knew the underlying principles of English sentence formation. Students whom she interviewed were able to understand and produce novel sentences and to converse freely with her. She concluded:

The study of English capabilities and usage and attitude among Puerto Rican youth . . . indicates a strong trend exists toward native fluency and usage of English in nearly all domains. Although many Puerto Ricans speak standard English, many speak a dialect incorporating features of both the North American neighborhood dialect and Spanish. These findings suggest that educational problems encountered by Puerto Rican students cannot be assumed to be caused by lack of fluency in English, and that intensive or special programs to develop fluency in English as a second language, as distinguished from reading and writing skills, are not the sole answer to the students' problems. (Loy 1974:324–325)

Having dealt with the linguistic explanation for school failure, we still had to examine the teachers' other favored explanation. Poor performance and lack of success were often attributed to the youths' lack of desire to learn or to parental lack of interest in their child's education. The language attitude questionnaire effectively contradicted any explanation based on negative attitudes toward English (Loy 1974:322–323). The results from interviews with families by the participant observer team also contradicted the teachers' view of the Puerto Rican families as uninterested and unmotivated. When compared with non-Puerto Ricans in the same neighborhood, our sample Puerto Rican families were characterized by higher positive evaluation of education and stronger desire for the success of their children in school (Burnett 1974b:116–133).

This finding was communicated back to the teachers. They were more skeptical of this information than they were of the results of the language survey, perhaps because they felt more expert in judgments of behavior than in technical judgments of language.

Culture Explanations and Stereotyping

Just as the teachers' favored explanation of culture difference between home and school ran into difficulty, so also did the researchers' explanation. We discovered the ironic fact that using culture at the level of generalized group norms to explain "puzzling" student and parent behavior could support the stereotypes that feed into an ideology rationalizing subordination and discrimination. Even while the team focused on the interactive structure of social relations, the behavior, in keeping with a long tradition in anthropology, was still interpreted in customary terms. Knowledge of island cultural norms of Puerto Ricans was used to interpret and explain behaviors in the school. Since one member of the research team was a native of the island, and the director of the team had lived and worked there, this approach seemed legitimate.

While the behavioral data of the classroom were not interesting to the teachers, some teachers were interested in the team members' generalized cultural knowledge. Initially, the information seemed to encourage more positive attitudes toward Puerto Rican students. However, the use of generalized cultural knowledge about Puerto Ricans led to stereotyping and overgeneralized explanations of their behavior. Our knowledge input actually interfered with the process of individualized diagnosis, explanation, and instruction of Puerto Rican children in the classroom (cf. Leacock 1971, 1973).

Early in our work, we often presented the cultural point of view to teachers by reinterpreting in cultural terms student conduct that teachers described but interpreted as bizarre, strange, abnormal, or deviant. To illustrate, one teacher described the "odd" behavior of two Puerto Rican boys who fought in the shop class. It was not the fighting but the incident which precipitated the fight that puzzled her. Carlos was very attracted to Antonia, Mrs. Berger reported to me. And Carlos had begun to pursue Antonia's attention with notable ardor. In shop one day, as everyone was working on their lamp shades, Carlos, who was seated next to Antonia, engaged her in attentive, admiring conversation, when a messenger, Renaldo, Antonia's brother, walked in. As he started toward the teacher, he suddenly turned aside and physically attacked Carlos. After the teacher separated the combatants, Renaldo's only explanation for his action was that Carlos was talking with Antonia, who had been told by her parents not to talk with Carlos. In the eyes of the teachers, the physical attack was far too extreme for the explanation. We began to interpret the event in terms of Puerto Rican parental concern with the chaste reputation of their unmarried teenage daughters, and the role of brothers in guarding the reputation of the family. The family's reputation would be undermined should a daughter—like Antonia—compromise it by arousing suspicion about her proper conduct with a boy. Carlos was well known as a charming, sometimes ardent "ladies' man," but he was also a member of a street gang, the Latin Disciples. He was "danger" to a daughter's reputation.

Our good intentions were frustrated when the teachers fitted this perspective into the general stereotyped picture of amorous Latins and Don Juan exploits. It reinforced their notion that Puerto Rican parents cared only about their daughters' marital status rather than their schooling and future employment. This inference was not true; as we noted above, it was contradicted by our family interviews. It is an excellent example of how overgeneralization arises easily from knowledge *about* other peoples' culture, as contrasted with actual use of cultural knowledge in interaction.

Midstream in our work, we attempted to incorporate more refined cognitive data by adopting a more cognitively oriented theory of culture. This new framework guided us to a more situational view of culture and to an effort to collect cognitive as well as behavioral data on encounters and interactions.

We decided that the reason knowledge about culture was stereotyping was partially due to the overgeneralized way we had presented the descriptions. They did not include information on contingencies, variable conditions, and contextual constraints. Formulating descriptions at this more refined level would demand greater precision. We decided that preparation for intercultural teaching required teaching about culture more for use than for general familiarity. The decision to spell out relationships in such detail that one could probably teach them like a language would be taught, represented a second stage of our effort to persuade teachers to take culture into account when teaching children from culturally different backgrounds. We hoped to prepare teachers for intercultural teaching by persuading them to self-consciously learn "some culture."

We turned to the question of how to describe the culture of the

Puerto Rican youth, or of adults in situations where Puerto Rican culture dominated, so that teachers could use those rules and guides, or culture code, at least to decode student behavior and hopefully to encode their own behavior in Puerto Rican terms when the situation demanded it. The techniques for doing this were most clearly offered in theories of cognitive culture, or culture as knowledge. Although we came to this decision late in the project, we still were able to gather some information, following Goodenough's ideas of rethinking role and status (Goodenough 1969). Culture was viewed as standards for deciding what is, what can be, what to do about it, and how to go about it (Goodenough 1963:258, 1971). The conceptual formulation, however, emphasized the event context as well as the symbolic rule guides:

When I use the notion of *reference culture,* I have in mind a concept of culture that includes not only the activity level . . . , but also . . . the "rule-guides" that summarize the activities in terms of ordered elements. There are then two fundamental aspects of culture—culture at the symbolic level consisting of rules and standards. The other basic aspect of culture is behavioral in the form of action, feeling, interaction, material items, all in time and space. The latter might be called the concrete level. From the point of view of scientific description, it is essential to distinguish these two levels. The operation of a rule-guide at the phenomenal level requires that it be referred to . . . the behavioral and situational context. (Burnett 1970:5)

The data collection procedure, the interview from a behavioral record, was introduced to collect data in the required form (Burnett 1972; cf. Keesing 1970).

We tested the idea by singling out one relationship that had been associated with intraclassroom conflicts—the joking/teasing relationship between two identity "categories," Puerto Rican students and their teachers. Quite early in the project, the observational field data had reported frequent use of teasing and joking as a strategy used by teachers to relate with students in regularly occurring events: it was used in social control; it was used to reduce tension; and it was used as a way of being friendly and companionable with students. The occurrence of conflicts when the strategy was employed with Puerto Rican students suggested that it often was not interpreted in the same way by Puerto Ricans and teachers. My own knowledge of joking behavior in Puerto Rico suggested that the point at which teasing became malicious and baiting was different for Puerto Ricans than for American school teachers (Lauria 1964). Interviews with several Puerto Rican students about those episodes disclosed that they felt they were being "picked on."

To avoid stereotyping, we wanted to collect ideas on "rule-guides" in such a way as to take into account human variability with respect to models or rules. The recurrent regular episodes, or events, of classroom and school had to be investigated both for standard models and for individual model variations. Not all students reported the same reaction to similar levels of joking on the part of the teacher. There was sufficient individual variation to survey the range of variability.

We decided to include the joking relationship in a questionnaire so as to collect data from a large population of students about who could joke with whom. We would try to discover the range of variation as well as central tendencies in youths' views of this domain of rule-guides. Accordingly, we used questionnaires to ask eighth-grade students about the appropriateness or inappropriateness of joking and teasing between paired sets of social identities, such as male student and female teacher.

While the procedure was crude, it was a move in the direction of testing our notion of standard, and it offered an honest display of the differences among individuals that teachers might encounter. It could better reveal that cultural standards were subject to individual variation. We felt that individual variation might prove important to a teacher's plan of action in a given situation, thereby supporting an individualized approach in relating cultural experience to learning and teaching. In a sense, it was a step toward being realist, not academic and theoretical, about the nature of culture *in vivo*.

Briefly, the results suggested that the difference between island and mainland Puerto Rican standards for the joking relationship is a matter of a shift in referents of labels. To use North American coding, a Puerto Rican must change underlying principles of judging relationships as appropriate or inappropriate (Hill-Burnett 1976). Both the results of the questionnaires and our observations of the interactions of several Puerto Rican and other Latino boys in the top eighth-grade class suggested that some had learned to switch to North American coding of the meanings of the behaviors; other Puerto Rican boys in the same class had not developed code switching ability.

Yet, while the cognitive culture approach provided knowledge at a level which might be used more readily in interaction, the approach still placed the burden of changing institutional outcomes on those who suffered but had no means of redress. Even an improvement in the teachers' ability to encode and decode behavior in Puerto Rican terms would only relieve some of the symptoms of organizational impositions. *We had begun to recognize that not all cultural differences lead to conflict, and, further, that not all culturally based conflicts lead to educational problems for Puerto Rican youths.*

The Ecological Context
of Interaction and Code

Our continuing collection of participant observations in the school as an organizational context for behavior gradually led us to another theoretical perspective which did not contradict the results we had obtained regarding culture, but rather questioned our basic assumption that culture was a primary determinant in what happened in the students' lives. Questions were first raised by our observation that some conflicts attributable to culture difference did not make any difference in what happened to students in the educational process whereas other conflicts did. In part, the significance of the effect of culture difference was not that of culture difference *per se* but of what the difference was, whom it was with, and its organizational consequences. For example, teachers spoke of the greater propensity of Puerto Rican pupils to touch them during communications. The teachers' withdrawal response resulted in a feeling on the part of students that teachers were "cold." The behavior bothered many teachers, but it did not lead to negative consequences in the youths' placement in the organization of the school. The same seemed true of the teachers' response to Puerto Rican students' propensity to inquire about matters that some teachers defined as personal and private.

Because the conflicts over joking often fell in the realm of social control, they appeared to be more serious. This was not due to the culture pattern *per se* but rather to the close association of the conflict with the patterns of authority in the organizational setting. Their importance is clear when one assesses the educational consequence of frequent conflicts in this area. Conflict with respect to joking rules led to the placement of students in social groupings that had access to fewer educational resources, and to a generally denigrated reputation among both teachers and other students (a judgment that was openly communicated to the students by teachers). The judgment of youths by teachers was one key to the consequences of culture differences. If conflicts led to behaviors that drew the attention of other teachers, other students, or the assistant principals, negative consequences were likely to result. Circumstances that had to do with noise control were particularly important in the development of negative consequences. Conflicts that led to the social adjustment office or to complaints that brought someone from that office to the classroom were the kinds of events that led to reconsideration of the student's placement. From an educational point of view, abundance of resources depended on the class to which one was assigned. Judgments on performance were key acts of power that had significant organizational consequences for students' differential access to the limited resources of the school.

For example, a rank ordering of the eighth-grade classes according to reading scores led to the clustering in one class of students who spoke little English. At the same time, some of the students whose conduct was "disruptive" of classroom routine were also placed in that room. A new, inexperienced noncertified temporary male teacher, who was monolingual in English, was assigned to the class. Thus, if events led to a pupil being assigned to that room, there were clear consequences in terms of the educational resources that were available to him or her. There was obviously less opportunity for those who did not know how to converse in English to learn to do so from peers, who are a major source of English language learning, according to our own and other studies. With a monolingual teacher, a second consequence was that those who spoke only Spanish were learning very little subject matter content or none at all. Inexperienced teachers seemed ingenious in devising ways of transmitting information, but they lacked the organizational skill to deal with problems of social control.

As I studied this set of conditions, I was struck not so much by the pupils' deficiencies but by the weight and extent of the school's deficiencies and those of the educational system itself. From an ecological perspective, the school was a disadvantaged one, unable to call on the knowledge and skill needed to deal in a professional manner with the population of students it was supposed to serve. From this point of view, the school was maladapted to its student body.

In part, the internal allocation of resources was poor. Thus, funds were going to a program of Teaching English as a Second Language (TESL) which was not an irrational allocation in view of the school board's perspective that children were in transition to English language speaking and to North American "core" culture. But money was allocated *first* to the TESL component of the program rather than to bilingual teaching staff, although many teachers favored a priority allocation of funds for the latter. Some expenditure for bilingual teachers would have provided Spanish language instruction in course content, allowing students to continue to learn other subject matter while at the same time learning English.

The school existed in an environment; it was not autonomous. Even had the principal decided that bilingual instructional staff should have priority, staff changes were partially controlled by the teachers' union, so that special staff had to be hired with special funds. The funds themselves were often earmarked. Expenditure for TESL was specified; its use for bilingual staff was circumscribed. In the follow-up year of our project, when our sample of students had either gone on to high school or dropped out of school, our contacts with teachers in the school brought news that the funds for the TESL activity would be withdrawn. Hence, funds and resources were uncertain, and the decisions regarding resources were made by the central board. External events that were unpredictable and nonrecurrent often forced the local school to cope with a state of disequilibrium on the basis of limited resources.

In summary, uncertainty overshadowed implementation of ameliorative plans. The lack of autonomy was evident in the frequency with which external events transformed conditions for the operation of school programs. Uncertainty about reliable resources seriously interfered with organizational adaptation to the special conditions of the population within the school.

This ecological approach led us back to a more materialistic theoretical framework for developing perspectives on the original problem. Competence in language and culture had to be expressed in performance. Educational effects from judgments on those performances depended upon the organizational consequences for particular students' placement with respect to resources that maximized their chances for success. Even those resources were marginal, however, and their allocation was so greatly affected by external agents that local programs were a tenuous illusion.

Conclusion

The research project described above clearly displayed the complementary nature of the interaction and cognitive approaches. Used in the same context, the strengths and weaknesses of both approaches showed up with great clarity. Each type of data—the behavioral and the cognitive—is conceptually distinct, and different methodologies are used to collect the two types of theoretically relevant data. Yet, viewed in synthetic perspective, each points up the limits of formulations based on the other type of data. "Minding" and "behaving" are interacting phenomena which should be embraced in the same theory as coordinated dimensions of culture, if the theory is to be used for understanding organizational behavior.

While our attention to interactive behavior and then cultural codes of knowledge allowed us to describe processes and procedural effects, the more primary causes in the system could not be delineated by these means. This is not to argue that the framework of power and material resources is contradictory with the other frameworks; it is as complementary to them as they are to each other. All three—behavioral, cognitive, and ecological—systemics are essential to a theory that purports to guide research to the point where policy decisions can be derived from it.

When anthropologists address themselves to problems raised by colleagues within the context of scientific inquiry, it is possible to constrict and simplify a theoretical framework and focus so that the conceptual postures detailed above might appear to be three different positions on theoretical issues. In practice, they are not three ways of approaching the same thing but three complementary and essential ways of approaching sets of data which, when synthesized, offer a more complex and powerful framework of ideas. It is a better framework from the point of view of action and policy decisions.

Applied problems arise from the conduct of social affairs, where either anthropologists or others may encounter them and engage in seeking solutions for them. Basic research problems arise from the problem posing and resolving activities of disciplinary colleagues. Both basic and applied problem-solving processes benefit from each other. A system that maintains an openness to both types of problem formulation and the free flow of information between them is more likely to be a vital center for the growth and development of substantive knowledge. The special contribution of applied anthropology to building theory arises from the demand that theory be sufficiently complex to address the realities of processes, as well as to distinguish symptoms from causes and primary from secondary causes in the social world.

6

POLICY AND SOCIAL THEORY IN ANTHROPOLOGY

Ronald Cohen

In the previous essay, Hill-Burnett argues for the building of theory through the application of ethnographic techniques to practical problem solving. In this essay, Ronald Cohen argues in favor of the use of ethnographic techniques to construct social criticism. He directs our attention to popular social theories and the values that are embedded in their domains (belief systems or symbolic logics). Cohen is concerned particularly with those social theories that are used to justify, defend, assert, or challenge political policy in the field of international development.

The essay explores several social theories popular in the 1970s by categorizing them in terms of the logical systems from which they stem, and then examines their basis as belief systems which express a conflict/dialectical logic, an integrative/functional logic, or a cost/benefit logic. These logical systems and the values they reflect represent ready-made critiques of competing logical systems. Thus they serve to discount any genuine consideration of evidence that supports competing systems.

Cohen emphasizes that empirical evidence plays only a weak role

Ronald Cohen (Ph.D., Wisconsin) is professor of anthropology at the University of Florida. He has worked in Africa and the Canadian Arctic on a range of topics covering ethnography, methodology, and applied anthropology. He has held positions at the University of Toronto, McGill, Northwestern, and Ahmadu Bello University, Nigeria. His current research interests include the search for increased productivity in African farming systems, ethnicity and national unity, and the relation of war and peace to the evolution of the state. He served as a consultant on the Master Plan for the new capital city of Nigeria. He was the cofounder and first director of the Northwestern Program on Ethnography and Public Policy.

I wish to thank Robert A. Rubinstein for permission to reprint portions of this paper from my article "Approaches to Applied Anthropology," in R. A. Rubinstein and R. Pinxten, eds., *Epistemology and Process: Anthropological Views* (Ghent, Belgium: Communication and Cognition Books, 1984), pp. 7–34.

in mediating competition among these competing belief systems. He attributes this weakness to the influence of popular social theorists. Advocates of social theories rely heavily upon the presumption that the
policies derived from their theories benefit human communities. Cohen
calls for increased ethnographic attention to the documentation of the
real-world outcomes of competing social theories and the policies supported by them.

FOR THE FIRST century of its existence social anthropology has had
a basic science approach to the understanding of sociocultural variation and its evolution. The research agenda for this enterprise is autonomous, determined more by factors inside the discipline than by
those outside. The ideal arena for such "normal" sciencing are the
professional journals, meetings, and grant-giving bodies like the National Science Foundation, where standards are set and priorities created by the members of the discipline itself. Other agencies from
whom anthropologists have obtained funding, such as the National
Institutes of Mental Health or the foundations, might have more practical goals but in the past were staffed by people convinced that "basic" research into social life and cultural variation provided a foundation for the solution of practical problems.

Conditions have changed drastically. For a variety of reasons,
research directed toward improving social conditions is moving rapidly onto center stage. Even "basic" research efforts increasingly
reflect efforts to investigate applied issues rather than continuing former efforts and directions. This is correlated to job creation outside
academia and to a shift in the role of the social scientist from that of
outside observer who creates a scientific body of facts and theory to
that of participant in organized efforts to develop public and private
sector policy and to aid in the implementation process.

The change is deep and fundamental. It portends a paradigm
shift in the discipline whose effects are bound to change the problems, methods, and theories that characterize teaching and research.
Topics once thought central are giving way to new ones, each of
which can be traced directly to an applied focus or demand from
outside the discipline. Theory construction, indeed the very nature of
anthropological theory itself, is changing as this direction becomes
more dominant within the discipline.

The most important quality of this shift is a move from social science to a more inclusive critical stance which I call social theory (Cohen 1981). Social science refers to a body of propositions, questions, and methods whose primary goal is to explain social life using theory and systematic observations. Ideally the observations are logically related to theory although anthropology has a long tradition of inductive generalization based on the extraordinary ranges of variation among human experiences recorded by field workers. I use the term "social theory" in the philosophical and political sense in which the primary theoretical goal is that of prescribing and explaining social goals and arrangements for the achievement of human betterment. In this sense social theories are directed at societal needs and problems. The application of these theories to contemporary society generates critical propositions about the social arrangements, distribution of scarce resources, the goals, and the cultural expressions surrounding all of these societal features. Social theory is broader and more inclusive because it depends on social science findings and explanations for empirical relevance and the validity of its behavioral knowledge claims.

But the two are quite distinct. Social science sets out to observe and explain; social theory does so too, but it is evaluative and sets out to be so, while social science tries its best to be nonevaluative. Social theory adds a critical and normative dimension in which statements are made concerning why and how a society is failing to achieve its objectives, whether these are "good" objectives, and in what directions society should move in order to improve the lot of its population. Social theories are avowedly social scientific; they make assumptions and create propositions and explanations but they are critical-normative as well. As theories they seek to express dissatisfaction with what is; they are rooted in a profound and professionalized concern for the achievement of human betterment.

Social theories are in this sense more akin to some earlier ideological writings that claimed scientific validity. Marx and Engels wrote in this mold. They tried to explain society, its evolution, and various stages in that evolution. However, the theory was, and is, quite clearly prescriptive. Not only does it analyze and explain all of human history but it also judges, evaluates, and proclaims the morally appropriate pathway to a better life for the entire species. At the other extreme, *laissez faire* liberalism suggests an almost completely opposing view of human welfare and prescribes remedies for human ills quite abhorrent to serious Marxists. But these bodies of assumptions and propositions are not simply ideologies. Adherents cite them as theories, often as established scientific approaches. Researchers use them to explain their findings and to ask questions and design new research investigations. Social theory embodies both social science— what is this, and why is it so?—and ideology—given this explanation as true, where ought we to go and what is the most desirable pathway to the achievement of these ends?

Policy and Implementation

Using the argument so far, we can say that social theories are made into human action through the development of *policies* and their *implementation*. Policies are sets of guidelines that depict and order social goals and/or the means of achieving them. Once translated into action, social theory becomes one among a number of determinants for setting guidelines. Actual policy formation occurs in bureaucratic settings in which goals and decisions about them are made necessary by prevailing conditions, the social theoretic and personal value preferences of decision makers, and the political and economic determinants of decision outcomes. Policies change and conflict with one another, and those implementing policy must compete for scarce resources. In other words, policies express social theory within real-world settings where they interact with other determinants of decision outcomes.

In the literature, policies are treated as goals, programs, projects and even agencies and outputs that carry out policy decisions. Most of the writings in the field tend to analyze and classify policies in terms of their desired social theoretic effects (Salisbury 1970; Salisbury and Hienz 1970; Jenkins 1978). Well-known examples describe policy as "regulative," "self-regulative," "distributive" or "redistributive" (Jenkins 1978:99). Theory and analysis using this approach tend to concentrate on how to achieve certain ends. The ends themselves are not discussed. On the other hand, a few writers (e.g., Etzioni 1971) use policy research as the critical analysis of goals and their utility in terms of societal needs. Generalizing, we can say that some analysts see social theory reflected in policy and focus their attention on that aspect; others see implementation as the major manifestation of policy research making it behavioral and real rather than speculative. In the latter approach, theory describes how to get from here (contemporary conditions) to there (the desired objectives of policy) and the causal nexus that facilitates and restrains this process.

For purposes of analysis and theoretical clarity, goals, directions, and the formation of policy are better kept separate from the actual process of achieving or carrying out policy directives. This latter aspect we can call implementation. The process involves the attempt to forge desirable, policy-directed, future effects. The process assumes that those carrying out such directives know what will happen when they initiate change. This requires, ideally, a knowledge of all cause-effect relations in the implementation setting so that the innovations will produce predictable changes. Unfortunately, the best we can ever hope for is a better than random albeit still imperfect understanding of intervening causes. In other words, there is always a variable degree of uncertainty, and unintended consequences accompany even the best executed implementation.

Policy and implementation are separated here because they can and do vary independently. Policies have their own determinants which include social theory that is expressed in, and enacted by, policy. Implementation is a function of the social, political, economic, and cultural contexts in which policies are turned into action programs. For example, policies may change, but those implementing policy may decide to continue with older ones quietly subverting the innovation. Implementation is a function of the number of decision settings from point of initiation to actual sites of operation. The greater the number of points (offices and officials) involved in carrying out a policy the greater the likelihood of distortion (Pressman and Wildavsky 1973). In other words, each phenomenon, policy and implementation, responds to different sets of determinants even though together they form the core features of directed processes of change.

Parenthetically, the uncertainty involved especially in the implementation is the major reason why ethnographic techniques are so important in applied anthropology. Ethnography is based on the assumption that observable outcomes capable of intersubjective agreements (i.e., reliability) are the complex function of two domains of causality. First there are general principles governing the relations of entities that are situationally neutral or nomothetic. Secondly, and crucially, there are context specific, historically derived causes or ideographic determinants and explanations. These latter factors must be investigated in particular settings. They are posited most validly by experienced observers or by ethnographers or better still by a combination of both. Helping to implement a policy or evaluating what happened during implementation cannot be competently and accurately executed by applying only situationally neutral cause-effect relations. In other words, cross-culturally applicable social science theories and findings invariably fall short of providing clients with adequate understanding and evaluation of implementation. This is why experience in the context or situation being worked with is so important. Whether trained in ethnography or not, people with experience in particular social and organizational settings know a great deal about how and why things are done in their own context. Ethnography taps this knowledge through the systematic learning and recording of such understandings. Implementation takes place in the existential and messy realm of experience, not the systematic modeling of that world we construct in social science theories. Only methodologies that take into account both realms of causal relations provide adequate information to evaluate what did occur, or estimate more accurately what will happen when policies are implemented in specific contexts.

THE PLACE OF BASIC RESEARCH

In the best of all possible worlds, basic research should be closely attached to unknowns at each step of the process. Working backwards from outputs to inputs, this refers to implementation, policy formation, and social theory. Implementation requires that we understand what will happen once changes are introduced. This in turn means a better understanding of cause-effect relations. Thus basic research on social problems—crime, socialization, poverty, interethnic conflict, and so on, provides a growing body of data upon which to base both policy and implementation strategies. Uncertainties about the consequences of actual implementation strategies always remain.

Ongoing research increases the necessary knowledge base across specific contexts; ethnography fills the gap for particular instances.[1]

Research into policy formation processes provides understanding about what sorts of directions of change are feasible at any given time in the life of a society. Research into the American legislative process, for example, shows that even attempts to deal with the clearest moral issues, for instance, child abuse, run into conflicting interests, such as child protection vs. privacy, so that compromises must be made which weaken the original attempt to solve the problem (Dorothy Willner: personal communication). At present, in many third world countries civil rights are inadequately protected. Those interested in fostering such rights must know when it would be feasible to press for decisions and policies to protect individuals against the arbitrary use of power. (Here is a much needed research frontier!) Again, however, there are always uncertainties, and many outcomes are only knowable after the fact, after something has been done. Nevertheless, basic research can and should reduce the risks by increasing our knowledge of relevant relations that significantly affect the desired change.

The most important arena for research, that of social theory and the values, assumptions, and propositions that influence and lead to policy, are not part of any serious research tradition in anthropology. Nevertheless, they are the "givens," the assumptions of individuals, regimes, whole blocks of countries and regions of the world. They are essential and unquestioned. As a participant one doesn't, or mustn't, question the validity of social theories and policies at least in their heyday: Tanzanian socialism in the 1960s and 1970s, Keynsian economic policies during the New Deal, mistrust of multinational corporations in the Third World, the dominance of the cold war in East-West relations, the benefits of bilingualism in the Latino community, the benefits of separatism among Quebec radicals, the evils of counterrevolution in socialist countries, the necessity of apartheid to white South Africans, and so on *ad infinitum*. Such theories stem from deeply

1. At a more general epistemological level it is important to realize that ethnography is *not limited* to this very useful role of adopting and extending general theories to specific contexts. As a research strategy it performs this function efficiently and is, consequently, essential to applied work in real world settings. However, ethnography also stimulates inductive generalizations that are applicable, theoretically, across situations. It can therefore be used to amend, extend, or test existing theories, or even to create new ones. Indeed the history of social science is full of examples of ethnographic case studies which provided the basis for major theoretical innovations (Cohen 1984).

held value preferences. While in ascendency, they are part of the sociocultural landscape, guiding judgments, influencing decisions, setting the direction of programs, until failures and unresolved problems stimulate and support the emergence or acceptance of one or more alternative theories.

The above illustrations indicate that social theories and the policies they generate are similar to Kuhnian type paradigms. They come into fashion, run a course of normal productivity from which specific policy guidelines and implementation programs emerge and then run into difficulty, shortfalls, failures, and are replaced by competitors. While in their heyday, however, enormous support is garnered for one position over another. Adherents use the theory and its value hierarchy as a logic and a vocabulary of criticism for other policies and as justification for their own.

It is at this point that social science theories merge with social theories so that values both guide research and flow from the results. Underlying the theories are a few epistemological principles which determine what kind of social theory will develop. These differ significantly from one another in their assumed foreknowledge of the cost and benefits of large families of policy options and social theories. These assumptions then lead to quite different modes of analysis, different questions, and not surprisingly to quite different, often opposite, policy recommendations.

DOMAINS OF SOCIAL THEORY

I turn now to a consideration of closely related sets of assumptions that underlie social theories. These are not theories in and of themselves, but rather "domains" because each set supports and continues to spawn families of closely related theories. Thus Marxist class analysis and cultural materialism are closely related but different; so too are Keynsian and monetarist development theories (and policies!). These latter theories differ from one another but they are closer than either is to Marxist and cultural materialism ideas which in their turn are in the same general family of explanations.

Although I am still working to understand a large spectrum of such theories, it is clear that there are at least three distinct syndromes of assumptions that define differing domains. These are (1) the conflict/dialectical, (2) the integrative/functional, and (3) the cost-benefit modes of setting up theories and carrying out analyses. These modes of intellectual production cut across all sectors of policy formation and of judgments about them. They are applied to activities and enterprises of varying scale and levels of development, from small-scale communes to nation states and to industrialized as well as less industrialized nations. Because of my own interests I will, for the most part, restrict my illustrations to those of development, but this classification can be applied to all varieties of theorizing about policy and implementation.

The dialectical or conflict mode of analysis, sometimes termed "emancipatory" (Habermas 1971; Bernstein 1978), assumes that unequal power produces unequal benefits. Therefore the most important questions for analysis and the creation of social theory and policy are those that ask, who benefits? Benefits to the more powerful are assumed to deprive or "exploit" the welfare of the less powerful. Negative or disconfirming data are referred to as "trickle down" effects. Since distribution of benefits invariably involves the breakdown of quantity in inverse proportion to the size of the population served, it can easily be "shown" that any and all benefits are minor compared to those gained by the more powerful—who are fewer, and often larger in scale (e.g., a factory vs. a household) requiring larger amounts of resources to survive. The conflict/dialectician argues (quite logically) that given unequal benefits resulting from unequal power, then each side develops different interests that are in conflict. Failure to see this (or false consciousness) is seen as the hoodwinking of the exploited by those whose benefits and power are greater. Injustice may be legitimized but it must be sought out and exposed.

Development theorizing and policy options are easily derived. Since inequality produces conflict and the maintenance of their position by those who receive more, the situation (i.e., lack of development) will continue as long as the inequity persists. Development is therefore dependent upon the establishment and maintenance of as much equity as is feasible within an ordered society. Once social justice is seen as the fulcrum for successful development, social theories and policy are logically generated. Poorer nations are poor because others are rich (Rodney 1972). Richer farmers should be done away with before they form an interest group with enough power to maintain their position and prevent the bulk of the rural population from developing. As we know this was actually done in Tanzania during the 1970s (Hyden 1980), with somewhat disastrous results. Nevertheless the paradigm continues, and elsewhere others have come to the same conclusions (Heyer et al. 1981) with similar policies implied to those described by Hyden. Given the conflict/dialectic assumptions, other options are not possible if development is the goal even when their shortcomings are known.

The general principles have been used in innumerable projects in Third World countries—always governed by the same mode of analysis, the same social theory; wealth disparity impedes development because the gain of the few is at the loss of the many. Exacerbated by fears of neocolonial attempts to retain power and influence in ex-colonies and the almost unopposed preachment of dependency and world system theories in Third World universities (Court 1982:132), policy concerning outside investment has become xenophobic. Profits by foreign-based companies or multinationals is at the expense of insiders. Wealth extracted by investors is wealth lost rather than value added. Cash crops for export means less food crops for home consumption. And the remedy is written into the analysis; restriction on profits, especially the repatriation of profits by foreign investors is a logical requirement if development is to occur. More generally, equalization of outcomes through policies of regulation and redistribution is the cornerstone of social theory and the test of policy.

It is important to note here that these social theoretic ideas are the result of academicians like Frank (1969), Amin (1973), Rodney (1972), Wallerstein (1974), and a host of followers who turned their theories into a "normal" epistemology. From the late 1960s to the present, this reigning set of notions has been taught to thousands of future elite members of Third World countries (Court 1982:132). These students, now journalists, teachers, managers, and public servants of all varieties live in a world made comprehensible by the conflict/dialectical way of asking and answering questions. The original theorists (e.g., Frank 1969) who adapted Marx and Lenin's notions of imperialism to contemporary conditions and developed these ideas had no applied contracts with agencies yet their research has had enormous impact. Millions of lives have been very radically changed by the policies that flow out of their researches. Theoretical work directed toward social theory is applied science by its very nature, because it is the soil out of which policy is sown and grown.

The functionalist/integrationist approach to policy is almost the exact opposite of the conflict position. Whereas the conflict assumption starts with the notion that if X succeeds, Y in the same system must fail, because X's good fortune and power are at the expense of Y's, the integrationist says X and Y are functionally related. Therefore if X succeeds Y will benefit too, because the "system" has had X's success added to its storehouse of benefits. Being interrelated, such benefits will be distributed throughout the system, eventually, just as blood takes nutrient ingested at one point to all parts of the body once it has been digested.

But where blood is driven through the system by the heart, benefits (and costs) are distributed by the market mechanism. And these theorists assume that as long as actors have some discretionary capacity to choose amongst alternatives the market mechanism is *ipso facto* present, even in the most regulated, most controlled system. The market as a concept refers to the societal process by which information about value equivalences among desired goods and services is produced and disseminated through interaction and individual choices. These transactions become "market" information as people agree and disagree on the value equivalences of exchanges in response to the supply, demand, control, cultural prescriptions and proscriptions, etc., of their wants. In this sense it is neither capitalist, socialist, nor even economic. Rather it merely refers to, but doesn't explain, the enormously simple notion that people in a society have wants which they try to satisfy within their capacities, and in line with their values. Social theory, empirical research, and policy relevant to development can now be deduced. Betterment occurs when a few enterprising actors take advantage of opportunities and create more profitable productive units. These units employ others, and are emulated by others, absorb the "less efficient" units and the benefits spread throughout the population. Inequity, not equity, is the elixir of the better life. Thus a World Bank report (1981:67–68) describes how a changeover from public to private distribution of fertilizer in Bangladesh decreased the price, spread the use of fertilizer more widely and efficiently, created a new class of private wholesalers who managed procurement and distribution problems previously handled (badly) by government. Kuznets (1980:21) cited in another World Bank report, shows how the lowest levels of incomes in the poor countries increase faster and take up progressively more of the national wealth once overall per capita incomes go up over $700 per year. And

Hirschman (1981) marshalls facts and arguments to support the proposition that development *requires* a tolerance for inequity at its early stages.

The implication for policy is clear. Development *means* encouraging foreign investment, encouraging exports, increasing productivity. This in turn requires more complexity and therefore more stratification. In rural areas, for example, it means working with the more "progressive" farmers (called capitalists or kulaks by conflict theorists). Their success through improved technology creates wealth that is then distributed in jobs, spending, saving, and more internally generated investments. In some cases the entrepreneur is the state or a parastatal organization. The main notion persists. Increased wealth at one point in the system increases the capacity of the system as a whole and will have ramifying effects over time through the operation of the market, "historically doing best for those on the bottom of the economic pyramid" (Roche 1976:11).

And policies, projects, and programs are put into place guided by these assumptions, the most controversial of which is the notion that increased inequity of reward promises a long-term trend to widespread improvement for the population as a whole. In a few countries (such as Malawi, Kenya, Ivory Coast, and to a large extent Nigeria), government has espoused such "free market" ideas and allowed capital formation and productivity to be more important criteria than equity. The poor are still poor, the rich are getting richer. Conflict theorist critics say these societies are unstable and will become increasingly polarized and conflict-laden unless policies change so that the distribution of benefits is more rapid, equitable, and coerced by the state. Supporters say that productivity increases today will produce better standards of living for everyone tomorrow.

The saddest result of all this controversy is the wasted effort, the failed programs, and the increased suffering accomplished by those elites who blindly espouse one or the other of the positions. Another is the polemical style of the protagonists, especially conflict theorists. The latter often use emotional pejoratives as technical terms in an attempt to convince their readers by righteous moralizing as well as analyzing. Inequity seems so obviously unattractive in terms of social justice that there is no need to research it. Better therefore to condemn and move on to more "progressive" policies; ones that help stamp it out. Thus a recent collection on rural development in Africa

(Heyer et al. 1981) goes over case after case in which "who bene-fits" is the initial and most pervasive question guiding research. If the answer is only a few, the policy is a failure—or even worse, a conspiracy against the interests of the rural poor. Social theory pre-determines policy analysis. Thus, what one writer in the volume (Shepherd 1981) calls "an unmitigated disaster" referring to a rice-growing project that increased rice supplies in northern Ghana, could easily be interpreted as exactly the opposite by functionalist integra-tionists. And so it goes. Each set of writers, theorists, planners, pol-icy analysts, see the world through the tunneled vision of their own concepts and assumptions. Very few research projects designed to test one set of ideas versus the other are devised, or believed by the opposing side if carried out.

In my view, conflict writers tend to be more polemical. While functionalist research looks for data that test empirical predictions of theory, conflict writers seek situations that show how power and in-equity work to the detriment of the poor. Thus Wallace (1981) shows how large-scale irrigation works and mechanization are displacing poor farmers from the land in northern Nigeria. On the other hand, she does not consider the impact of these developments on overall food productivity and national level needs and omits research that contra-dicts her views.

Conflict theorists writing in the dependency-world system tradi-tion condemn cash cropping as part of the world market exploitation in which rich nations manipulate the poorer nations into producing for export, thus decreasing their own food supplies. Recent empirical tests of this idea by functionalist-integrationists indicate the reverse; cash cropping and food production are positively correlated in Africa (World Bank 1981:52). As far as I know, this research is not cited by conflict writers and unfortunately such crucial tests are few and far between. Instead, the real world and actual policy implementation is the testing ground so that the welfare of ordinary people, usually the most needy, is the price to be paid if our social theories deliver failures and crashed hopes because of their imperfections. Often as not, policy makers can shift goals claiming that program effects are policy accomplishments. Those at whom the policy was originally directed still lose. And too often the defective theories go on at least for the short run, supporting policy and perseverating its failures.

And when research shows a particular social theory to have some validity, it unfortunately doesn't mean that a law of nature has been discovered. Things change. It is impossible given our present knowledge to say whether the positive correlation between cash and food production in Africa will continue as it is, or where it is negative or likely to turn negative. More likely, it seems to me, such findings are *ceteris paribus* ones. At some point under new conditions, for example land scarcity instead of land surpluses, the conflict theorists will be able to say "Aha, we were right all the time"; the correlation is turning negative just as we always predicted it would. No social science is forever. And in policy/implementation, change is the avowed goal. This includes background and contextual features as well as unintended consequences. There is no way, therefore, that our knowledge can be made to remain constant in its applicability. This leads to the third approach to social theorizing and policy formation, that of cost-benefit analysis.

The cost-benefit approach involves looking at collectivities as sets of individuals and groups that seek to satisfy their interests within some form of evolving social order. They do so "economically," i.e., by maximizing. But activity always occurs within interaction which means some form of order or "social formation" in which interaction outcomes are nonrandom at the aggregate level, albeit that each individual interaction is governed by chance and necessity. Benefits and costs are empirical questions and it is assumed that neither the conflict position nor the functionalist one is valid for any length of time. What benefits A may indeed deprive B, and may worsen through time, or be ameliorated. Instead it is assumed that some values are held in common so that a basis for social ordering of scarce wants is present and some accounting of costs and benefits is possible.

I also make the Hayekian (see Machlup 1976:51) assumption that policy formation is based on an impossible condition which invalidates it before it is ever implemented. This is the idea that peoples' needs and wants as they themselves experience choices are based on billions of bits of information out of reach to policy makers. No matter how much coercion is exercised, each person has some degree of freedom in his reaction to policy (Hyden 1980). It is impossible to gauge precisely what is best until something is tried. This produces the information needed to improve or jettison a policy. Thus monitoring and iterative research are part of policy and its implementation.

No approach is perfect and many may even be unworkable. In the planning stage, therefore, the cost-benefit way of doing things assumes that if all possible options are considered, fewer mistakes will follow. Each option for enhancement (the goal of social theory and policy) leads to ramifyingly different programs of implementation. A tree diagram of options results because each choice point produces its own subset of options. The analysis then can consider the largest set of logically possible policies and programs. Each choice point must then be "tested" against a set of priorities or value criteria. Ultimately all options can then be ranked and one or just a small number are chosen. All dropped options can also be rationalized as not meeting some criteria of value sufficiently to be given further consideration, while those chosen meet all criteria better than others. The process can be repeated for programs in place so that readjustments can occur as implementation proceeds.

No logically possible program scores highest on all criteria. The winner(s) score low on some, but high on many, or on those considered most important. Failure to meet criteria at acceptable levels is a "cost"; meeting them well is a "benefit." The most beneficial is the program that promises (planning) or fulfills (implementation) most of the desired ends formulated by social theory. Nevertheless, the basic notion is very simple. If we have to decide whether to do A or not, the rule is: do A if the benefits exceed those of the next best alternative course of action. If we apply this rule to all possible choices, we shall generate the largest possible benefits, given the constraints within which we live (Layard, quoted in Stewart 1975:31).

Critics ask, predictably, whose benefits—which is, in my view, already set forth in the social theory and should therefore be clearly stipulated and carefully discussed and argued out beforehand. It is also claimed (Barnett 1981:309) that cost-benefit analysis comes from the (capitalist) theory of the firm which can be more easily managed than an open society. But this is already foreseen in the notion of uncertainty and iterative research which admits to such weakness and, it is hoped, corrects for it.

The main problem is that of social theory and the values it promulgates used as criteria when policies are being analyzed. For particular problem areas, the most sought after values are derived from the technical skills and theories of the practitioners. Criteria for a "good" city plan are given by city planning experts; on constitutions, by legal experts on such matters, etc. However, when such expertise fails, as is the case at present for psychiatry, public debate opens and values compete until some new criteria become more widely accepted. As already noted, intellectuals, social scientists, journalists, and artists play an important part in the process. As Hayek (1967) has noted, they are tremendously influential in setting priorities among values, and criticizing those that exist.

Many of the anticapitalist values of the twentieth century can be attributed to the reaction of intellectuals to nineteenth-century capitalism and its attendant evils. Anthropologists participated in such value creation when they preached against ethnocentricism in the 1930s and 1940s. Since then, however, they have not until very recently and with a few notable exceptions engaged in social criticism. It is time to get back into the fray. What should we strive for to enhance human life? Putting together our technical social science theories and findings, with our understanding of a pluralist humankind, anthropologists must begin to theorize and research basic issues of value and the relation of values to one another in real world conditions.

When and how should particular values have priorities over others? There really are very few options. Either we accept the value criteria handed down by existing social theoretic paradigms—with all their weaknesses and their failures to achieve the betterment they seek—or we must address these issues because valuational criteria are the foundation stones of applied social science. Certainly cost-benefit analysis cannot proceed without goals, and goals are simply values operationalized into concrete aspirations. And if we devote ourselves to such a task we will also, once again, join those who seek to influence the continuing debate that always goes on in a free society—that of setting priorities and criticizing directions. Social criticism and applied anthropology are inextricably intertwined, unless we decide to opt out. And that way lies sycophancy or dogmatism.

The Implications for Applied Anthropology

Summarizing the argument so far, we postulate that policy as an expression of social theory contains two nesting forms of explana-

tion. First there are theories about what factors can and should enhance the human experience. These theories are critical because they
express specific dissatisfactions with present circumstances and put
forward propositions stating how and why efforts must be directed
towards improvement. Social scientists, intellectuals, and political
leaders who carry out such work can become enormously influential
because others responsible for specific policy creation require theories
and explanations that rationalize the value priorities they use to develop and decide among policy options.

The "how" of social theory is a set of notions about causal
processes in human society which enables administrators to predict
how efforts can be made to get from the here-and-now to the there-
and-then. This is traditional social science and is the arena in which
most applied work is carried out. The "why" is an addition that turns
social science theorizing into social theory. It includes a set of ideas
that explains what is better, worse, good, better, and bad. It is therefore a critical theory of value applied to specific periods and problems
in the human condition. Although social science notions nest inside
social theories, they are independently variable. Social science can
serve as a basis for quite different and even contradictory social theories.

Contemporary policy analyses can be divided into three varieties, two of which make basic assumptions about betterment, and
one that does not. Conflict analysts assume equity to be the highest
value and thus seek through analysis and policy recommendations to
ferret out unequal outcomes so that they can be avoided. Although I
have not discussed it here, such theorists most often develop policies
that involve coercive regulation and redistribution to ensure equity of
result. Functionalist integrationists show a deep and ubiquitous concern for productivity and wealth creation. They assume that market
mechanisms will distribute benefits and they develop policies that
produce more material goods through improved technology. This starts
with innovators who benefit first. Thus inequity is their road to progress. Cost-benefit analysts leave questions of value open to discussion and development. Once some valuation schema is derived, a
rational and potentially changeable value hierarchy is used to assess
policy options and implementation programs.

All of this assumes that social science is and always will be
imperfect. No one seriously believes that we can predict outcomes

accurately enough to assume that planned outcomes will occur as set forth on the drawing board. Thus policies and programs must be monitored and evaluated iteratively. The proper place for applied social science is to be an integral part of the implementation process, such that social science serves the shortcomings of policy and as a self-correcting mechanism for the impossibility of perfectly predictable implementation. Experience with implementation and with policy creation, indeed with applied work in general, produces questions about the value preferences that influence choices in policy formation and programming. The social scientist must then criticize the social theories that underlie the value preferences and which led to these particular efforts. Value preferences are never written in stone. They must be analyzed in terms of changing conditions and needs. Social theory and the critical analysis of society are also the job of the applied scientist. The proper study of humankind is its improvement.

If we accept this challenge then much of what has, up to now, been seen as basic research must have some open and avowed social theoretic goals. In more precise terms, this means that empirical research must be directed at the real world effects of differing value hierarchies and ideological systems. What happens when differing value hierarchies are put into effect through policies meant to implement their ultimate goals? What is the proper place of incentives, persuasion, mobilization, centralized or local control, social differentiation and stratification in making for a "better" life? Are there situations in which inequity temporarily tolerated, as Hirschman (1981) suggests, will optimize collective well-being more rapidly and securely than any other mode of improvement? Economic and political anthropology, as well as working in development realms, is beginning to look at such issues. But we need an active research tradition that looks at the effects of social theory in practice. This will provide us with two important products. First we can evaluate how value criteria actually work out when tried in the real world and, even more importantly, we will develop a cumulative body of research on the cause-effect relations associated with the attempt to make value hierarchies into social formation and legitimized order.

Given the growing acceptance of these research directions, training and research methods in anthropology must develop to meet the needs of this agenda. Students must receive training in value analysis and in modern evaluation techniques. I have found that introducing applied students to philosophical materials on values and to political science analyses of ideology, as well as case studies of ideologies put into practice, gives them a set of categories and relationships to classify policies and underlying social theories. And to be competent, such training must examine as wide a range of such materials as possible. In a recent course, we covered the three positions discussed above and then had critical case analyses of capitalist and socialist policies as theory and practice.

Evaluation is a form of research method. Cost-benefit analysis in applied anthropology requires that we isolate the goals, the inputs, organizational processing and implementation, and the outputs of policy as it is implemented. To maintain our trustworthiness we need an ongoing self-critical analysis and experimentation with both quantitative and qualitative techniques that show how and why, and where, social theories in practice are never what they seemed when first envisaged. Implementation is a form of change that approaches the logical arrangement of a natural experiment. In this sense it is one of the most important means for creating and testing basic cause-effect knowledge claims. The fact that it is also in the area of hoped-for betterment means, again, that basic and applied research are inextricably tied together.

Finally, it is clear that as applied anthropology moves toward social theory and critical analysis, value hierarchies, ideologies, and valuation criteria must become research objects. The *a priori* belief in a pre-set order among value criteria that leads to uncritical ardor about what ought to be done to improve the human condition will, indeed must, give way to a more secular and scientific approach. Policy research leads directly to social theory and social theories must be subject to investigation, to testing, and reformulation—even to extinction. If we are to use anthropology for human betterment, we must train our students and ourselves to see betterment itself as a question—not a goal.

7

ORGANIZATIONAL BEHAVIOR RESEARCH— CHANGING STYLES OF RESEARCH AND ACTION

William Foote Whyte

The technological revolution of the modern world has been accompanied by the rise of organizational structures that are significantly different from those studied by applied anthropologists during the 1930s and 1940s. Contemporary organizational structures have considerably more specialized functions, and the task of coordinating their work so that people may receive services and products has become acute, especially in the deepening economic crisis of the United States.

William F. Whyte reviews the history of organizational behavior research and notes that the social-psychological questionnaire research of the 1950s has yielded little that is useful for understanding organizations as systems which relate people to technology, to resources, and to each other. This latter type of knowledge is required if new organizational models are to emerge in response to human needs.

Whyte underscores the unique contribution made by applied anthropologists who have adapted ethnographic methods to the task of diagnostic research. He analyzes specific instances in which he and others have diagnosed organizational ills. He then notes specific cases in which applied anthropologists have moved beyond the diagnosis of

William F. Whyte (Ph.D., Chicago) is professor emeritus of industrial and labor relations and sociology at Cornell University. He is currently active in applied research as Co-Director of Cornell's Programs for Employment and Workplace Systems. Over the years, he has worked in research and technical assistance in industry or rural development in the United States, Canada, Venezuela, Peru, Colombia, Costa Rica, Guatemala, Honduras, and Spain. He is a past president of the Society for Applied Anthropology, the Industrial Relations Research Association, and the American Sociological Association.

problems to actions that assist in the solution of problems. The latter type of work includes not only analysis of innovative solutions that have emerged in response to problems and their transference elsewhere, but also enlisting the subjects of research into the research process itself so as to improve the viability and validity of the solutions invented. Foreshadowing the major points made in several essays to follow, Whyte documents cases in which applied social research that includes research subjects as participants delivers up new social innovations *and* new scientific knowledge about modern organizational forms.

NOW THAT MORE than half a century has elapsed since the Western Electric research program was launched in 1927, we are in a good position to assess past trends and visualize future possibilities for a field of research increasingly called Organizational Behavior. While a beginning date for any field of study is necessarily arbitrary, it was the publication of the comprehensive report on the Western Electric program (Roethlisberger and Dickson 1939) which set off in the 1940s a rapid development of courses and research projects focusing upon the human problems of industry.

As reported in previous essays, anthropologists were a major force in the early development of this field. W. Lloyd Warner was a consultant to the Western Electric program and helped to shape the research methods used in the bank wiring room, a classic study of informal organization among workers. As part of the Yankee City study, Warner and Low (1947) published the first book examining a strike in social anthropological terms. In the first meeting of the Society for Applied Anthropology, Conrad M. Arensberg, Eliot D. Chapple, and F. L. W. Richardson, Jr., reported (for publication in the first two numbers of *Applied Anthropology*) upon their research in industry (1941 and 1942). In 1945 Burleigh B. Gardner published the first textbook on *Human Relations in Industry*. After working on Warner's Yankee City study (along with Kimball, Chapple, Arensberg, and others), Gardner moved into research with Western Electric and subsequently joined with Warner in 1943 to set up the Committee on Human Relations in Industry at the University of Chicago. In 1946, Warner and Gardner organized Social Research Inc. as a means of applying their expertise to help business organizations solve their human problems (Gardner 1976).

This strong beginning justified hopes that organizational studies would become a major field for applied anthropologists, yet in succeeding years very few anthropologists joined these pioneers. Furthermore, we were swamped by other social scientists, particularly the social psychologists, who entered industry in large numbers and developed theories that for many years enjoyed great popularity in management circles.

Now the tide of social psychological studies seems to be receding, leaving little in the way of solid contributions to show for the innumerable dollars and man hours of talented people expended in this style of research. As disillusionment grows over the fruits of this research approach, the stage is set for reformulation of research strategies and a new forward movement.

This is a critical period for us, since the history of recent failures in social research points to the need for an anthropological orientation to research and for the skills of the applied anthropologist. This new forward movement demands people with the ability to conceptualize human behavior into systems of interpersonal, intergroup, and interorganizational relations, to relate the structure and functioning of the organization to the structure and functioning of the community, and, finally, to integrate economic and technological with social data.

How the point of view and the methods and diagnostic skills of the applied anthropologist can be applied to this emerging new style of social research, I will discuss later. First, let us consider past failures which have led to the present reassessment and reformulation of the field of organizational behavior.

Fixation on Democratic Leadership

Behavioral science activities in this field were partly a reaction against the authoritarian and mechanistic views of management represented by Frederick W. Taylor (1911) and his followers in the school of "scientific management." Taylor and his associates had placed their emphasis almost exclusively upon formal organization structure, technology, material rewards, and the management methods required to operate a mechanistic system.

The Western Electric research led to the discovery of something which was then called "informal organization." Apparently, the behavior of workers did not correspond to the formal logics of management, but instead, workers tended to develop their own subculture and their own group solidarity in opposition to management.

Since we could not regard workers as being motivated exclusively by material interests, it seemed important to study the attitudes and beliefs of workers regarding their work situation. For the investigation of the subjective life of organization members, the questionnaire or survey, developed and popularized particularly during World War II, proved an invaluable method. Use of this method permitted collection of a large body of quantitative data that, with the rapid development of computers in recent years, has made possible an enormous volume of data analysis on how workers think and feel about their organization.

While early researchers in the field were examining the limitations of formal authority, social psychologists sought to discover patterns of more "democratic leadership." Many hoped to discover that "democratic leadership," when skillfully practiced, was not only superior from a humanistic standpoint but also led to greater productivity. Early studies along this line, particularly at the University of Michigan's Survey Research Center, did indeed seem to show this pattern, but later research there and elsewhere brought out such discrepant findings as to discredit the comforting view that democratic leadership or "participation management," as it was also called, necessarily resulted in greater productivity than more traditional styles of leadership. This produced a period of confusion and frustration, while the researchers searched for new hypotheses and new strategies of research.

While "participation management" was for many years the most popular doctrine in management training programs, the studies designed to support this general orientation were subject to several serious weaknesses. In the first place, this work was based exclusively upon the survey, which is a valuable instrument for some purposes, especially when combined with other research methods. However, when used alone, it does not enable us to cope with the complexities of organizational behavior. While the social psychologists wrote about the relationship between participative leadership behavior and worker attitudes, their conclusions, in fact, were based upon a legitimated fraud. I use the word "legitimated" to indicate that the manner of reporting the presumed relationship was widely practiced by eminent social psychologists and sociologists, even though it clearly had no scientific foundation. In effect, the writers were relating worker attitudes toward the supervisor (as measured by responses to a number of attitude items) with the supervisor's behavior *as perceived by the workers* (in their responses to items describing various aspects of supervisory behavior). The survey researchers simply inferred from worker perceptions how supervisors were behaving and had no independent observations or interviews to provide more acceptable evidence on supervisory behavior.

This line of research also involved the study of interpersonal relations in a structural and technological vacuum. Writers provided some sort of orientation regarding the technology and organizational structure within which the study was carried out, but this was simply background information. It was not utilized for the establishment of typologies or variables related to organization structure and technology, which might have impacts upon individual behavior and interpersonal relations. To be sure, the survey researchers did eventually discover differences in leadership styles of more successful supervisors (as rated by their superiors) in a production organization compared with a maintenance organization, but this revelation did not lead—as it should have—to an effort to arrive at generalizations regarding interpersonal behavior related to structure and technology.

Furthermore, the social psychologists were almost exclusively concerned with only one aspect of organization structure, the vertical or authority relationship between a worker and his boss, the foreman and his general foreman, and so on. Most of the writers along this line have been completely oblivious to horizontal relations (those between individuals at the same hierarchical level in different organizational units) or diagonal relations (those between two individuals at different hierarchical levels in two different organizational units where neither one has authority over the other). I do not mean to suggest that the work of all social psychologists is subject to these criticisms. I am simply describing the style of research most popular among social psychologists.

Re-Enter Structure and Technology

During the period of the popularity of "participation management," studies of human reactions to technology were not totally neglected. In fact, applied anthropologists Charles R. Walker, Robert Guest, and Arthur Turner (1952, 1956) carried out a series of studies of the impact of technology on worker attitudes and behavior. Nevertheless, these case studies of worker reactions to technology remained unrelated to research on managerial leadership—with one exception (Guest 1962). For leadership studies, the importance of structure and technology only came into focus later with the classic work of Joan Woodward (1965) in England. Seeking to check the relationship between types of technology and organization structure, she carried out an impressive examination of 100 firms. This enabled her to demonstrate that there were systematic differences in such aspects of structure as the span of control in different types of technology.

Woodward's work set off a burst of activity in which researchers concentrated attention on technology and formal organization structure and on the relations between these two factors. In a sense, the researchers were returning to the original field of interest of the scientific management school but with one basic difference. F. W. Taylor and his followers assumed there were principles of organizational structure that could and should be applied universally to any type of organization. Researchers now abandoned the search for the "one best way" to set up an organization and began examining the structural properties that tend to be related to particular types of technology.

The Woodward program also stimulated a number of macro-structural studies. Instead of concentrating on the analysis of a particular case, the researchers gathered comparative data on a large number of cases. While this has led to a discovery of some interesting quantitative relations among structural variables, the methodological problem of macro-organizational studies makes it impossible to glean data from a large number of organizations. Researchers must content themselves with items of information that can be readily picked up and that are reasonably objective in character. Then, while we may be encouraged to find correlations among a number of structural variables, generally the correlations are at such a low level that, however interesting they may be to theorists, they provide little guidance to the person of action. That is, a correlation of .30 may be statistically significant and of considerable interest to the theorist, and yet it accounts for less than 10 percent of the variance. This means that the consultant who uses these data can only report that if the organization is structured in line with the correlation found, there is a slightly better than 50–50 chance that the resulting structure will be more useful than competing models. Furthermore, while it is certainly of importance to learn more about the design of organization structures, the macrostructural approach leaves off at this problem, giving us little or no guidance on how to operate the structures that are indicated by the design.

Recent years have also seen a boom in interorganizational studies. We have come to recognize that civilizations advance through increasing division of labor and specialization, which means, among other things, the creation of a greater number of organizations to perform specialized functions. But human problems still tend to present themselves primarily in unspecialized form. Thus arises a lack of fit between human problems and the organizations created and developed to deal with those problems. If we are to deal more adequately with human problems in complex societies, we must provide new organizational forms and strategies that coordinate the specialized services and resources which people need. This means, particularly, studying the coordination and cooperation among organizations, or, more generally, interorganizational relations. While this is a field of rapidly growing activity, as yet we have developed no theoretical framework adequate to deal with the phenomena under study.

We are also coming to reevaluate the role of money and other material rewards in organizational behavior. The history of thought in our field seems to be marked by pendulum swings from one extreme to another. Thus, when the early human relations researchers discovered that the scientific management writers were wrong in treating money as the exclusive motivator of workers, we tended to swing to the other extreme, concentrating on other motivations and treating money as if it had little or no importance. We are now beginning to recognize that material rewards are indeed of great importance to organization members, but this recognition solves no theoretical or practical problems. It is important to know how decisions are made on the distribution of material rewards, how individuals and members of work groups feel their rewards compare with those of others doing work of comparable value, how grievances regarding inadequacies and inequities in the reward system are handled, and so on. In other words, economic rewards do not function by themselves but in the context of a social system, so that the impact of the particular reward can only be understood in its social context (Whyte 1955; Lawler 1973).

Toward a New Theoretical Framework

While we still seem to be in the period of tearing down old theoretical frameworks and the dust has not yet settled sufficiently to reveal the building blocks that can be used for the development of a new and more useful theoretical framework, I shall try to take a first tentative step toward construction by outlining what seem to me some of the main elements of the new research strategy. I shall illustrate these ideas from my studies of agricultural research and development (Whyte 1975; Whyte and Boynton 1983).

We must think and act in terms of social systems consisting of horizontal and diagonal as well as vertical relations. The study of diagonal and horizontal relations, of course, take us beyond the boundaries of a single organization into the exploration of interorganizational relations.

What aspects of these human relations do we study? While I continue to believe in focussing upon the observation and measurement of human interactions and activities, I now see these elements as embedded in a flow of resources within and among organizations. Though material resources are of obvious importance, I find it useful to concentrate upon the flow of *information*, which seems to me a resource of steadily growing importance as civilizations become more complex and specialized in their functions.

In the primitive tribe or small peasant community, the individual can acquire all of the information possessed by the adults of his or her community through growing up in the family, with perhaps the addition of a few years of schooling in the community. As civilizations advance, the individual finds that a steadily decreasing proportion of the information needed to orient him or her toward work and the world can be acquired in family and community and elementary school. As the bodies of information grow in volume and complexity, social and economic development comes to be largely a problem of acquiring, integrating and utilizing information.

Why speak of "information" rather than "knowledge?" Knowledge implies systematic bodies of validated data and relationships in particular disciplines. Information is a more inclusive term, covering not only formal knowledge but also where to go to find something out, who has done what and with what result, who has the money to support what project, and so on. By the use of the term, I do not mean to limit myself to *validated* information, and yet I find the common dichotomy between information and misinformation an oversimplification. The people who generate, transmit, or receive information develop ways of judging both the accuracy of the information and its relevance for their purposes. At some points information may be validated (or invalidated) through scientific tests; at other points it may be evaluated in terms of the reputation of the transmitter or in terms of the reactions of influential others in the social world of the receiver.

While the accuracy of information is important, we will concentrate here particularly upon the channels through which information flows—or should flow—for accelerated agricultural development. If the information does not reach the intended recipients, then, for their purposes, its quality is irrelevant. On the other hand, as we diagnose the gaps and blockages in information flows, we are necessarily dealing with factors creating distortions in transmission and misunderstandings in reception and indirectly focusing upon some of the influence affecting information quality.

If we begin where new scientific information is generated in research institutes and universities, we tend to visualize a one-way flow in research at these points and ending with the farmers. We need also to check on the flow in the reverse direction. Do farmers try to tell extension agents what they want and need? Do the agents respond? Do extension agents tell research people what kind of research projects and research reports would be especially useful to them? Do the researchers respond?

At the farmer end of the organizational system, it is a mistake—unfortunately quite a common one—to think in terms of the relations between the extension agent and individual farmers. The rural community has its own organization, with the relation of families to land providing the main structural elements. Rural areas differ greatly in degree of equality/inequality in land ownership, in the presence or absence of sharecroppers (and in the nature of their contractual relationship to the owners), in the degree of farm tenancy, in the use of full and part time farm labor, in the presence or absence of serfs who provide labor to large landowners in return for rights to cultivate their family plot, and so on. Intervention strategies must be adjusted to these structural conditions, and, under conditions of extreme inequality in landownership, land reform may be a necessary precondition to successful programs to improve the welfare of lower-class rural people.

Communities also differ in their structures of local government and in the capacity of local government to mobilize the citizens for improvement projects. The presence or absence of a farmers' cooperative also affects whether change agents should seek to work through an existing organization or whether the program they hope to develop will require building a new organization. The extension agent's success in promoting agricultural development will depend less upon skill in communicating with individual farmers than upon ability to comprehend the organizational structure of the community and to devise ways of linking the extension service effectively to that structure.

Reception of useful information is a necessary but not a sufficient condition for improving farmer productivity. At the local level, we need to examine the ways in which the flow of information is (or is not) coordinated with the flow of other resources (credit, fertilizer, insecticides, etc.) which poor farmers need. Similarly, for the organizations primarily concerned with the generation and transmission of information, those functions cannot be performed without the support of complementary human and physical resources which must be supplied by the administration of the organizations involved in these stages of the information flow process.

Diagnostic Research for Improvement of Organizational Systems

Crude as it is, the organizational systems framework presented here should enable the applied anthropologist to do in a short period of field work the kind of diagnostic research that is invaluable to the administrator or program planner. I use the term, "diagnostic research," to contrast with the stereotype of the traditional anthropological field study. We are accustomed to thinking of the social anthropologist as one who puts in a year or more doing a study of a primitive tribe or peasant community and then takes many months or years to write up his or her findings. If the objective of the anthropologist is to make an intensive and comprehensive study of the culture and social structure of tribe or community, then a year of field work is a short time indeed. But the administrator or program planner cannot afford to wait a year for the anthropologist to live with the organization before he or she reaches the point of saying anything useful about it.

If applied anthropologists have an organizational systems framework to guide them, they should not need the traditional long-term immersion before their analysis leads them to action implications. Consider, for example, the problem in agriculture of the relationship between the research and extension organizations and between extension and the farmers. There is no such thing as a good extension service without effective linkages to an agricultural research organization. A research organization may be rated good by tradition minded agricultural scientists if its scientists do "interesting work" and publish frequently in the best professional journals, but the farmers don't read the technical papers. Unless the research program is effectively linked with some sort of human service to bring the fruits of new knowledge to the farmers, and to bring the concerns of the farmers to the researchers, the organization's research output will serve only to enhance the professional standing of its scientists.

Given this necessary interdependency, it makes no sense for the researcher to undertake an intensive study of the research organization or of the extension organization. He or she can begin by asking: are the two organizations effectively linked together? If they are not (which is the case in at least nine out of ten developing countries), it should take only a few interviews with researchers, extension agents, and administrators to diagnose the general nature of the existing lack of coordination and absence of cooperative relations.

Of course, the preliminary diagnosis does not lead automatically to the solution to the problem. However, it does focus the researcher's attention upon a critical problem area and launches him or her on an exploration to discover the changes necessary to solve the problem.

From Diagnosis to Problem Solutions

In contrast to many other behavioral scientists, applied anthropologists do not look solely to changes in attitudes and styles of leadership for solutions to problems. They recognize that attitudes do not change in response to the consultant's recommendation but they do change, rather, in response to changes in organizational systems. They recognize that a leadership style should not be seen simply as the property of a leader but as a component in a total organizational system. Without denying the important roles played by individuals in key positions, they recognize that it is impractical to recommend a personality-changing program because adult personalities are exceedingly difficult to change, even under intensive psychotherapy. But they also recognize that individuals *behave* differently in response to changes in the organizational systems in which they participate. They therefore seek to discover the organizational changes required to bring about the desired behavioral changes.

Fortunately, we need not depend solely upon the imagination of the applied anthropologist for the design of new structures, roles, and social processes to solve social, economic and political problems. While most decision makers continue to define organizational problems in traditional ways and to seek in vain to solve them through actions guided by conventional wisdom, if we keep on searching we eventually find creative leaders who have defined their problems in new ways and have devised *social inventions* that appear to yield important benefits. That has been my experience both in studies of agricultural research and development and in research on the Mondragon cooperative complex in the Basque country of Spain (Whyte 1982).

Following this line of research, we first discover a social invention that appears to be worth studying. We then work out a systematic description of the nature of the social invention and seek to discover the theoretical basis of its operation. If further study yields solid evidence of the value of the social invention, we go on to assess its potential transferability to other cultures and organizational situations. This leads to a line of analysis for which our background knowledge of social anthropology and sociology should be particularly helpful.

To determine why the social invention works well, we need to examine it in the cultural, social, political, and economic context where we find it. If we hope to utilize the same social invention (or some adaptation of it) in another context, we must next analyze the potential fit between the imported social invention and the new context into which it must fit. Of course, any analysis of a potential fit must be to some degree speculative, but the applied anthropologist need not be alone in making this analysis. We can play useful roles in bringing social inventions to the attention of decision makers and then join with them in assessing the adaptations in the inventions themselves and the changes in the cultural, social, economic, and political context that may be required in order to achieve the hoped for results.

Up to this point, in focusing on social inventions, we have discussed their discovery and the social diagnosis necessary to determine if a given social invention may be applied with good results to a given situation and set of problems. That leaves open the question of what roles the subjects of the research should play in linking research to action.

Should the subjects of research serve only as materials for the study of the researcher, or should they be active participants in the research process? This question is seldom raised by those committed only to basic or pure research. That orientation provides for only two general models. In one, the researcher seeks to maintain detachment from the people he studies, so as not to influence their behavior. In the other mode (the social experiment), the researcher seeks to establish as much control as possible over the behavior of the subjects so as to be sure that the behavior then observed is produced by the experimental conditions. In neither mode do the subjects have anything to say about the research beyond allowing themselves to be studied.

It is only as we shift into applied social research that we open up possibilities for subject participation in the research process. However, that is not to say that applied social research always or even generally involves subject participation. I have found it useful to distinguish among types of applied social research in terms of the degree of subject participation (if any) in the research process. For convenience, I call these ASR-1, ASR-2, and ASR-3.

In ASR-1, the researcher acts as a professional expert who serves the client or client organization in providing information and ideas for action. In this mode, the subjects of the study may be interviewed by researchers, but they do not participate actively in the research process. (For a more extensive discussion of types of applied social research see Whyte 1984:163–191).

When the client organization is seeking to determine the facts regarding some problem situation, along with suggestions for action, ASR-1 is both legitimate and useful. Although it is most often used on behalf of "establishment" officials, this does not necessarily have to be the case. Many anthropologists have utilized ASR-1 on behalf of Indian tribes in land claims litigation.

ASR-1 is of little value to an organization whose leaders are undertaking to carry out a major process of organizational change. ASR-1 may be of some value in providing an initial diagnosis of the organizational situation before the change project is undertaken, but decision makers generally get little help in carrying out a complex change process when they are simply supplied with a diagnosis and recommendations for action. To play a more useful role, the researcher must be involved in the change process.

In ASR-2 the researcher plays an active role as consultant in the change process. When the researcher serves simultaneously as an organizational development consultant, the subjects of the study play a much more active role than in ASR-1, as they discuss with the researcher not only what their problems are but what they think ought to be done.

In complex hierarchical organizations ASR-2 can be very useful in overcoming blockages and distortions of communication, especially as it gives higher-level officials greater understanding of the situation and problems among rank-and-file workers and supervisors. However, this mode can be self-limiting unless it is extended (into ASR-3) so as to get the members of the organization at various levels talking with each other and listening to each other in ways that enable them to take control of the change process.

We have often found in situations of tension between union and management (even in cases where the research has been supported by management) that workers come to look upon the ASR-2 researcher as someone who can get management to listen to worker problems and ideas that they have been unable to bring effectively to management's attention. This experience is likely to be personally satisfying to the researcher-consultant, as he or she is able to please both the management people financing the research and workers and union leaders who are getting action that would otherwise be blocked. However, following the ASR-2 model may simply involve substituting worker and union leader dependence on the researcher for their dependence on management.

In ASR-3 the subjects of the study serve also as fellow participants in the research and as teachers of the researcher as well as his or her students. Work along these lines is still relatively new, but some of us have been moving independently in the same direction and are now finding that we are on a common path that should lead to more powerful and socially effective combinations of research and action.

The Norwegian Industrial Democracy Program provides a number of impressive examples of applied social research. Here I am following particularly Max Elden as he wrote about "Three Generations of Work-Democracy Experiments in Norway" (Elden 1979). In the first generation (1964–1967), the researcher served in the role of expert. Working under a labor-management committee, the researcher analyzed problems, recommended changes, managed the change process, and evaluated the results. In the second generation (1968-early 1970s), the researcher served as a consultant. He was more involved with workers, who participated in working out recommendations and also assumed some responsibility for implementing and evaluating. In the third generation (early 1970s onward), Elden describes the researcher as a "co-learner." Employee redesign teams work actively with the researcher to analyze their own organization to develop recommendations, to implement changes, and to evaluate results.

I had established my own categories before Elden's came to my attention, but I am encouraged to discover the close correspondence between ASR-1, ASR-2, and ASR-3 and his typology of three generations. We concentrate below on Norwegian third-generation cases.

One major project involved participatory action research to redesign Norwegian merchant ships. Here the officers and seamen participated actively with the research group headed by Einar Thorsrud in analyzing the changes in human resources and in the physical structure of the ship and in the design of jobs required to maintain Norway's merchant marine in a strong competitive position.

In a bank project, a committee of workers and management people guiding the bank's study worked with Max Elden to develop an interview guide that he used in interviews with workers and management people. The committee worked with Elden to analyze the interview material and then went on to develop a series of recommendations for change, which were subsequently implemented by management. Although the interviewing was done entirely by the researcher, Elden (personal correspondence) writes that "representatives from management and the employees determined both research design and most significantly the interpretation of the data that resulted from the interview round."

This project also led Elden toward an advance in conceptualization, as he distinguished "local theory" from formal behavioral science theory. Elden recognized the common error of social scientists to think that only they act in terms of theory. He found that the workers in the bank had their own "local theory" about what was going on and what kinds of behavior were effective. Of course, they did not describe this framework as a theory, but Elden found it essential in understanding the nature of the organization to discover local theory as expressed in the views of the workers. Furthermore, he found that there was not simply one local theory for the whole bank. Management people had their own local theory which overlapped to some extent with the workers' local theory but was quite distinct in other aspects. In order to help organizational members advance their process of change, he had to link his formal theory of organizational behavior with local theories prevailing in the organization.

My work at Cornell with students and professors has led us to our own style of participatory action research. For example, the Sky River Project in Alaska did not begin as research but evolved into this form as Timothy Kennedy based his doctoral thesis (1984) on his work with Eskimo communities over eleven years in Alaska.

In analyzing the roles of change agents (including himself), Kennedy distinguishes among three types: power broker, liberal advocate, and facilitator (or social animator). The power broker links the Eskimo community to the political and economic establishment by taking it upon himself to interpret the needs and interests of the Eskimos to outside powers and interpret the policies and programs of the establishment to the Eskimos. The liberal advocate seeks to deal with the political and economic establishment on a confrontational basis. He tries to organize the Eskimos so as to lead them in making demands for change.

From the outset, Kennedy was hostile to power brokers, seeing them simply as manipulators of the Eskimos in the interests of the establishment. Initially he found himself playing the liberal advocate role, but reflections on his own experience, and on what he learned about others playing this role, led him to recognize that, to the extent he was successful, the Eskimos substituted their dependence on him for their dependence on the white establishment.

This realization led Kennedy to search for ways in which he could build a pattern of interaction and communication in which Eskimos would have direct and effective impacts upon those who held political and economic power. He recognized that some politicians and some agency heads had a sincere interest in responding to Eskimo needs and interests but did not know how to go about establishing relationships where this was possible. He had witnessed a number of public hearings in which a politician or agency official would fly into town, meet with Eskimos, and invite them to voice their opinions and concerns. Always the real leaders of the community would remain silent while those few deviant individuals who did not really fit into the Eskimo community but had some experience with white people stepped forward to give their personal views. In some cases, Kennedy learned that such an individual might have what appeared to be a formal position of leadership, such as mayor, but was locally known by an Eskimo term that meant "play boss." In other words, he could play the role of boss to the white man but was not taken seriously by his fellow Eskimos.

To break down the communications barrier between the Eskimo villagers and public officials, with the support of the Office of Economic Opportunity, Kennedy went about putting modern technology at the service of the people. The technology in question involved vidcotaping and making brief sound movies on community problems.

Kennedy emphasizes that he should not be considered a filmmaker—though he did later serve as executive producer of "Challenge for Change" with the Canadian National Broadcasting Company. He was not making documentary films to enable Kennedy to interpret to outsiders what Eskimo life and problems were like. Rather, he was developing a methodology to get the Eskimos themselves to put their information and ideas on key problems on tape or film. The process began through group discussions in which the Eskimos would decide which problem they wanted to focus on first. Then they would choose one of their members to be interviewed on this problem. With his Eskimo assistant (who later took over leadership of the project) Kennedy would then interview the spokesperson at a time and place where he felt comfortable. Before the filmed or taped interview was to be shown outside the village, its contents had to be approved by the person interviewed and by his villagers as representing the kind of statement they would want outsiders to hear and see about their problems. If they objected to the videotape or film or to any part of it, Kennedy went back to do further videotaping or filming until they all had arrived at a product they would acknowledge as the true expression of their problems and views. When they had signed a statement to this effect and also a written permission that this tape or film be shown to particular public officials, Kennedy and his assistant then went to those officials to provide them with this direct communication from the Eskimo villagers.

Kennedy then invited the officials in question to make their reply on videotape or film, with the same editing rights that had been accorded the villagers. In other words he sought to make it clear that he was not an investigative reporter aiming to put officials on the spot. When the public officials had viewed their statements to the villagers and agreed that this was what they really wanted to say, Kennedy and his assistant would return to the villagers and show them the response.

This process stirred tremendous interest and activity among the Eskimos and among public officials and between the worlds of Eskimos and Whites. Kennedy had found Eskimo villages isolated from each other and separated also by considerable rivalries and misunderstandings. Now, as the videotapes or films from Emanok were shown in neighboring villages, the villagers there would say, in effect, "those people from Emanok are talking about the very same problems we have been experiencing." This recognition of common interests and concerns led to regional meetings of Eskimo villages and with government officials for the viewing of the tapes and films and for direct discussion of the views and problems they presented. As the process continued, Kennedy's Eskimo assistant took over the technology and the organizational methodology so this work could be continued after Kennedy left.

The Sky River Project produced important concrete results. Until the project began, it had been the government policy to fly Eskimo children who were determined to get a high school education to Indian schools in Oregon or Oklahoma. After the state educational officials had participated in the tape and filming process on this problem and in discussion with the Eskimos, Alaska embarked on a $140-million regional high school building program. In another case, the Rural Electrification Administration had been constructing underground cables to bring electricity to Eskimo villages. A videotape of Eskimos standing in the snow on both sides of a crevasse where the heaving of the permafrost had ruptured the cable led eventually to the abandonment of this impractical underground approach and a substitution of a decentralized system in which small generators in each village provided local service through overhead wires. In another instance, a videotape of sagging floors and ice on inside walls of houses built by the government for the Eskimos led to the discharge of the official responsible for this kind of housing program and toward a more realistic strategy for Eskimo housing.

With fellow students and professors at Cornell, since 1975, I have been involved in a series of studies of worker participation in private industry and of employee ownership. In some of these projects, we have been able to develop a participatory action research strategy. We made our first contact with Rath Packing Company in Waterloo, Iowa, when we heard that this major firm in its industry was to be shut down unless the employees were able to buy it. In May of 1979, when Professors Tove Hammer and Robert Stern went to Waterloo to explore the possibilities of including Rath in our research, the union leaders believed that they were likely to be able to raise the necessary money to purchase 60 percent of Rath stock and to gain initial control of the Board of Directors, but the union negotiating committee was about to accept a structure of ownership and control which our research had shown would inevitably lead sooner or later to ownership and control slipping away from workers. Chief Steward Charles Mueller had been reading some of the research reports I had sent to his local, and he urged Hammer and Stern to meet with the negotiating committee and talk them out of what they were about to do. Quite properly, they replied that they should not get involved in internal union matters, but they did offer to sit down with the negotiating committee and review our research findings. There followed an unusual and intense research seminar in which the professors refrained from making any recommendations but simply made clear the probable consequences of various forms of employee ownership. Before this seminar, Mueller was the only one holding out against nine members prepared to go the traditional route. After the seminar and the departure of the professors, the negotiating committee voted unanimously to insist upon an arrangement which was ultimately written into the employee stock ownership trust: 60 percent of the stock to be owned by workers but held for them in a trust. The trustees who would vote the majority of the stock and thus control the Board of Directors would then be elected by the workers on a one-worker-one-vote basis, thus plugging into an employee stock ownership plan the basic principle of a worker cooperative.

The employee buyout plans enabled the workers, through their union, to expand the six-man Board representing private interests with ten representatives of their own choosing. In addition to three workers in the main plant, they chose seven outsiders to provide the information and expertise they thought they would need. To her surprise, Tove Hammer was one of those chosen to represent the workers. She accepted the position on the understanding that she would serve as a participant observer, taking notes on the Board meetings and later using this material—within the limits of her fiduciary responsibilities—for research and eventual publication.

This was the first employee buyout in which workers, through their union, had secured control as well as ownership. Her position on the Board of Directors enabled Hammer to become a participant observer at the highest decision-making levels in a path-breaking case.

Since we did not believe that the hoped for gains in productivity through worker-management cooperation could be achieved simply through worker and union power exercised at the top level, six months before the buyout was achieved, Christopher Meek, Warner Woodworth, and I consulted with union and management leaders regarding setting up a cooperative problem-solving program at various levels from bottom to top of the organization. Now teaching at Brigham Young University, at the time Meek had been working with our Cornell program, in research and technical assistance with the Jamestown

Area Labor-Management Committee in Jamestown, New York, a highly effective community-based activity designed to bring leaders of labor and management together in community affairs and in in-plant cooperative projects. Woodworth, from Brigham Young University, had similar experiences consulting with unions and management in private industry elsewhere. From January 1980 through the summer of 1983, Meek and/or Woodworth spent two to three days a month in Waterloo, consulting with labor and management officials and guiding the development of the joint steering committee, the joint long-range planning committee at top levels, and the action research teams of workers and supervisors at the shop floor level. Through one eleven-month period, we were able to have a graduate student, Kate Squire, living in Waterloo and working with the action research teams while documenting their activities. Throughout our involvement with Rath, the union's chief steward and a member of middle management played the key roles in developing the cooperative problem-solving program.[1]

Unfortunately this story does not have a happy ending. When the workers took over officially in June 1980, Rath had gone through almost a decade of heavy financial losses and was in effect bankrupt. In spite of substantial financial sacrifices by the workers and the infusion of new loan money from the federal government, Rath finally was forced to shut down in 1985. However, at the time of the employee takeover, over 2,500 employees were working at Rath, and the buyout made it possible for 1,500 to 2,000 of them to keep their jobs for four years in spite of the fact that the takeover occurred just before the onset of the severest recession following World War II.

On the positive side, we can document approximately 20 percent increases in worker productivity, a cut of the absentee rate in half, and substantial savings in energy costs through the cooperative process. However, labor costs throughout this period accounted for only 15 to 20 percent of total costs, so that a 20 percent improvement in labor productivity yielded only a 3 to 4 percent gain in overall financial results. These savings were overwhelmed by the continuing drain

1. Our work with Rath, as with most of our other work over several years on employee ownership and labor-management cooperation in private industry, was financed largely by grants from the Center for Work and Mental Health of NIMH. The Blackhawk County Economic Development Committee provided support to finance most of the work of Meek and Woodworth in Waterloo, and the Ford Foundation provided further financial support on the research and documentation side.

of high-interest costs and inefficiencies in general management and marketing. In addition to providing us with rich data on the problems and processes of achieving a cooperative relationship between labor and management in production, we had to recognize that improvements in industrial relations will not save a company from bankruptcy if they are not accompanied by major improvements in general management, financing, and marketing. (For more detailed information on the Rath case, see Whyte et al. 1983.)

At about the same time of our involvement with Rath, Peter Lazes (also of Cornell) became involved as facilitator in the development of a quality of working life (QWL) program with Xerox Corporation and the Amalgamated Clothing and Textile Workers. The program developed steadily but slowly at first along conventional lines, as Lazes worked with workers, union leaders, and management officials in developing the cooperative problem-solving process. As in most such cases, in the early months of this program the action was limited to the shop floor level and the QWL groups were not allowed to discuss or study problems covered by the labor contract or by management prerogatives and policies.

The breakthrough came when Xerox management announced to the union that the company was going to have to shut down a department of 180 workers because management had found that it could purchase from vendors the components produced by this department at an annual saving of $3.2 million. Lazes proposed to the union leaders that they work with management to study the operation in question to determine whether it would be possible to reorganize the work and the technology so as to become competitive with the vendors, without sacrificing pay and jobs. Management people believed that it would be impossible to reach the objectives proposed by the union, but Xerox had enjoyed a generally good relationship with the union, so management was willing to give the proposal a try.

In most QWL programs, labor and management people meet at least monthly and sometimes as often as weekly for an hour or so to discuss problems and possible solutions. The Xerox project for saving the wire harness department went far beyond those time limits. The parties set up an eight-person study-action team, six hourly workers selected so as to cover the whole range of skills and experience in the department, and a line manager and an engineer. They then worked full time on the project for a six-month period. Furthermore, all restrictions as to questions they might ask and topics they might consider were removed. They were free to explore changes involving the labor contract and also involving management prerogatives and policies. They also were granted access to any and all information from management they needed to solve the problem, and they were supported to make three trips to vendor facilities to study how the competition was doing.

Lazes worked closely with the study-action team through this period but avoided any involvement in the technical or financial decisions. His role was one of participant observer, providing training in group processes and occasionally intervening to help the participants overcome blockages in their work.

At the end of the six-month period, the study-action team brought in a report proposing changes that were designed to cut costs by more than the $3.2 million target. The fundamental nature of the work of the team is indicated by the fact that one of the proposed savings involved a reduction in the divisional overhead charged against this department. Team members asked what they were getting from divisional headquarters to justify the overhead charges. The answers indicated that they were getting some services that they did not think they needed, other services they believed could be performed better within their own department, and still other services that were on paper but were not being performed. In other words, while saving the 180 jobs at the shop level without cutting pay and benefits, management also had to initiate a process of reexamining its policies and procedures regarding corporate overhead and staffing at the middle and higher management levels.

Following the success of the wire harness project (Lazes and Costanza, 1984), management and the union initiated four more study-action teams to concentrate on other problem areas where Xerox costs were substantially above those of vendors who could supply the same components. In other words, management was in the process of institutionalizing this form of participatory action research. Working with Lazes, Cornell graduate Leslie Rumpeltes has carried out field work in the wire harness department and in the four departments subsequently involved in the same process in order to provide detailed documentation of the process. Out of this participatory action research, therefore, is coming further knowledge about how to make U.S. companies more competitive nationally and internationally.

Let me conclude with this summary statement:

The basic researcher who carries out a social experiment in the field has opportunities to study that would not exist except for his or her intervention. However, since field experiments are very difficult to design and carry out, the literature reports few such cases. Especially in its ASR-3 form, applied social research offers much broader opportunities to study situations that would not exist except for the involvement of the researchers. Without such involvement, the changes described in the Norwegian Industrial Democracy Program, and the Sky River Project, and in the Rath Packing Company [and at Xerox] would not have taken place. While it does not allow the apparent scientific rigor of a well-executed experiment, participatory action research greatly extends the variety of situations available for study. At the same time ASR-3 advances knowledge for researchers, it greatly enriches learning opportunities for organization members who work with us in designing, implementing, and evaluating research. (Whyte 1984:191)

Conclusion

From the 1920s into the 1940s, social anthropologists were strongly involved in research leading to the creation of a new field of study, first known as "human relations in industry" and now more generally called "organizational behavior." In later years, studies of industrial organizations or government bureaucracies generally failed to appeal to those with doctorates in anthropology. However, now that even business executives are talking about "the culture of our organization," we may anticipate a reawakening of interest among social anthropologists, who should be able to provide practitioners with an understanding of the meaning of culture for organizational studies. In any case, the interdisciplinary spirit that led to the creation of the Society for Applied Anthropology has encouraged many of us with degrees in sociology (like myself) or other disciplines to continue working in this field under the banner of applied anthropology.

We began our work reacting against "scientific management," devoting much of our efforts to demonstrating what was *not* true in the basic assumptions of F. W. Taylor. Many of us then went on in a search for more democratic and participatory ways of managing an industrial organization. Eventually we came to recognize the futility of studying human relations in a technological and economic vacuum. This led us to cast aside the study of "social systems" in order to focus on "socio-technical systems." The need to integrate the economic as well as the technological with social systems led us to broaden still further the scope of our studies. We also saw a need to go beyond interdisciplinary collaboration among the social sciences in order to collaborate with engineers and management specialists in industry and with plant and animal scientists in rural studies.

In general, most applied anthropologists hold democratic values and are concerned with finding ways that workers and poor farmers can participate more effectively in shaping decisions affecting them. Finally, this has led some of us to recognize the importance of devising ways in which the people we study can participate in the research process as well as in the actions that flow from the research. Participatory action research is now only in the early stages of development, but it may one day become the predominant style of research among applied anthropologists in organizational studies. Through involving the people we study as active participants in the research process, we maximize our opportunities to learn from them and also their opportunities to learn from us.

8

OPPORTUNITIES, ISSUES, AND ACHIEVEMENTS IN DEVELOPMENT ANTHROPOLOGY SINCE THE MID-1960S: A PERSONAL VIEW

Thayer Scudder

The diagnostic research and social innovations discussed by Whyte are the product of several decades of anthropological and sociological research in modern bureaucratic organizational structures. In this essay, Thayer Schudder presents a personal case study of the practical and theoretical contributions that stem from long-term field research among people whose lives are changed drastically by these structures. Theory and practice are improved remarkably when they are grounded and interrelated one to the

Thayer Scudder (Ph.D., Harvard) is professor of anthropology at the California Institute of Technology and a founding director of the Institute for Development Anthropology. His major research interests include river basin and regional development, land settlement, compulsory community relocation, and long-term community studies. He has worked as an anthropologist in twenty-two countries of Africa, Asia, the Middle East and North America, including Zambia and Zimbabwe, where he has spent approximately four years researching the Gwenbe Tonga of the Middle Zambesi Valley. He has served as a consultant for the World Bank, various United Nations agencies, USAID, the Ford Foundation, the Navajo Nation, and the National Academy of Sciences. In 1984 he received the Solon T. Kimball Award for Public and Applied Anthropology of the American Anthropological Association.

This essay is a shortened version of my lecture, "Development Anthropology: Looking Ahead," which was sponsored by the Department of Anthropology at the University of California, Los Angeles, during the spring of 1985 as one of three Harry Hoijer Lectures on New Issues in Applied Anthropology. This lecture was published later in 1985 as part of the proceedings of the Harry Hoijer Lectures for 1985. I wish to thank Peter Hammond for inviting me to participate in the Hoijer series and for agreeing to the reprinting of an edited version of my lecture in this volume. I also wish to thank Michael Cernea and Elizabeth Eddy for their detailed critique of an earlier draft of this essay.

other in the inductive process of ethnographic research that addresses the long-term outcomes of programs and policies.

For nearly three decades, Scudder and Elizabeth Colson have been committed to field research among the Gwenbe-Tonga people who, as a consequence of the building of the Kariba dam and reservoir, were evacuated forcibly from their lands and homes and then resettled to new sites. The data based on this research yielded Scudder's theory of response to forced resettlement which has now been tested and refined in numerous other societies of the world. The accumulative data and theory have resulted in reliable predictions of the serious problems which accompany forced resettlement and the responses of communities to these problems. In turn, these predictions have enabled organizations and agencies to formulate programs of assistance to populations threatened with relocation and the need to reconstruct their lives. Finally, the data and theory have contributed to the formulation and eventual adoption of a resettlement policy by the World Bank which has improved its performance in this area of concern.

This case study reveals that sound anthropological research, combined with ethical commitment to use the results for the benefit of people, is a major key to effective application.

DEVELOPMENT ANTHROPOLOGY IS in flux, as befits a field that is dynamic and rapidly growing. At least two definitions are extant. The first, used by both critics and some practitioners, sees development anthropology as a nonfield. It is a conceptual frame of reference and as such it refers not so much to a type of research but to the motivations of the investigators and their sponsoring institutions. Not unified by topical emphases, a distinctive set of methodologies and theory, development anthropology is little more than the sum total of its practitioners who are individuals and institutions committed to drawing out and applying the policy implications of their own and other peoples' research. While that is a worthwhile goal, it has yet to lead to a distinct subfield which can be called development anthropology.

There is a lot of truth in the above characterization. At the moment most development anthropologists do constitute an aggregate of individuals who have yet to synthesize their methodologies and knowledge and demonstrate the distinctive features of their discipline. On the other hand, I think this is only a temporary phase in development anthropology. Within the next few years, I would expect development anthropologists to carve out an area of expertise dealing with a wide range of topics in a systematic way.

The emphasis will be on development interventions planned, implemented, and financed not just by national governments and international donors, but also by local governments and local level participatory action organizations. Though including rapid survey techniques, the methodology will emphasize detailed, longitudinal studies with investigators collecting minimum core data (a term coined by Scarlett Epstein) for comparative purposes. The focus on development interventions will have major implications for social science theory (see Arensberg, essay 2) if comparatively and longitudinally studied; for such interventions tend to speed up change in certain areas of human behavior, although they could be designed to have the opposite effect.

Where roughly similar interventions are replicated in different areas or in the same area at different points in time, the development anthropologist is presented with a quasilaboratory situation whereby the same experiment is repeated, though with different sets of actors. If we systematically study such interventions, we should be able to learn much more about the dynamics of human behavior—about thresholds of tolerance for very rapid rates of change, for example, and the need for continuity in institutions and value systems.

I accept both definitions of development anthropology for the moment, but in the future I expect development anthropologists will be identified more by the type of research done than by the application of research results. Granted the newness of the "field" and its current transitional state, however, this essay presents a range of examples of how development anthropologists are trying to influence policy formulation and implementation, as well as examples of current and ongoing research which I expect to have major theoretical implications. This research involves the customary hallmarks of research in social anthropology—that is, in-depth habitat and cultural knowledge—but the primary emphasis is on topical expertise. Examples include the dynamics of the cultural ecology and socioeconomics of pastoral systems in arid and semi-arid habitats; the socioeconomics of the settlement component of government-sponsored settlement schemes; and the responses of "development refugees" to compulsory relocation in connection with dam construction and other disruptive (though potentially beneficial over the longer term) development interventions.

Even if my assessment of potential contributions to science is overly optimistic, development anthropology is not going to go away. There are several reasons for this. First, though there are fluctuations, the trend is toward increasing use of anthropologists by multilateral and bilateral funding agencies, by foundations, by international research organizations like the Institute for Development Anthropology, and by some private voluntary organizations. Second, working for agencies of this nature enables anthropologists to work in countries and areas which unfortunately are less accessible—due to both financial and political constraints—to academic anthropologists. Although working for donor agencies involves a range of ethical issues, in my experience they do not offset the advantages of gaining access to the field and to documentation, and to having an opportunity to help local populations realize their expectations.

The discussion to follow draws on my own research and on my work with the World Bank and the United States Agency for International Development, those agencies being the main funders of my consultancies and AID being the main source of financial support for the Institute for Development Anthropology (of which I was one of three founding directors).[1] My anthropological career can be divided

1. The Institute for Development Anthropology (IDA) was founded in 1976 by David W. Brokensha, Michael M. Horowitz, and myself. It is a tax-exempt, independent, and nonprofit scientific research and educational organization. Headquartered in Binghamton, New York, the Institute has a resident staff of eleven, two full-time research associates on assignment in Niger, and a computerized roster of over 580 associates classified according to area, language, and topical expertise.

The Institute's main source of funds has been the United States Agency for International Development (AID). AID funding is provided in four ways. Of major importance is a Cooperative Agreement on Settlements and Resource Systems Analysis (SARSA), which IDA shares with Clark University and which has been renewed through fiscal year 1988. A second significant revenue source is a Rural Development Indefinite Quantity Contract (IQC) for the design and evaluation of rural development projects, awarded to IDA on the basis of competitive bidding. The other two routes for AID funding are AID-initiated financing of specific activities and self-directed policy studies proposed by IDA to the Agency. After AID, the Institute's most important sources of funds are the Food and Agriculture Organization of the UN and the World Bank.

To date IDA activities have taken place in twenty-eight countries in Africa, Asia, Latin America, the Middle East, and North America. Overseas activities include involvement in all stages of the project/program cycle including identification, appraisal, monitoring, midterm review, and evaluation. They also include self-directed research, completion of social institutional profiles of specific countries, and training of host country officials. As for "at home" activities, these include workshops on a range of topics, comparative evaluations of the development record as it relates to certain production systems (transhumant pastoralists and riverine fishing communities, for example) or

into two rather distinct phases. Between 1956 and 1963, my interests were primarily academic; thereafter I increasingly emphasized the policy implications of my own and others' research.

At the invitation of the Rhodes-Livingstone Institute (now the Institute for African Studies of the University of Zambia), Elizabeth Colson and I initiated in 1956 a long-term study of approximately 56,000 Gwembe Tonga who were soon to be forcibly relocated due to the construction of the Kariba Dam in the Middle Zambezi Valley. Kariba was a huge project—involving the largest loan that the World Bank had given to date and creating what was at the time the largest artificial reservoir in the world. Between the two of us, we have made twenty visits to the Valley, usually at one- to three-year intervals (the last visit being in 1983), spending at least eight years in the field over a twenty-nine-year period.

During those twenty-nine years, I also have had the opportunity to compare the experience of the Kariba relocatees with those of other "development refugees" in ten other countries in Africa, Asia, the Middle East, and North America, as well as to research a wider range of topics in another ten countries. While my interest in development anthropology began in the early 1960s, when several of us—including George Appell, Francisco Benet, and Robert Fernea—tried to start, unsuccessfully, a center or institute for development planning, 1964 was the turning point for me. That year, the World Bank hired me as its first anthropological consultant to participate in a major study of agricultural development in Tropical Africa. That assignment led to a merging of my academic and development work to the extent that today I often cannot distinguish between them.

While Colson's and my Kariba study remains primarily an academic one, it has provided me with many of the insights, ideas, and hypotheses that I have applied elsewhere in the tropics. And since 1967 our study periodically has had policy implications, especially after we were invited back to the south bank of Lake Kariba following Zimbabwe's Independence in 1980. There we have helped the University of Zimbabwe, under the auspices of the faculties of agriculture and social science, develop a research program to facilitate

types of development projects (such as land settlement schemes), and responses to requests for a wide variety of development-related information (see Scudder, forthcoming, for a more detailed history of the Institute for Development Anthropology).

the regional development of the Sebungwe portion of the Middle Zambezi Valley.

While it is becoming increasingly difficult for academic anthropologists to work in certain countries, this unfortunate trend has yet to have a serious impact on development anthropology. Indeed, as more agencies cautiously hire anthropologists, the opportunity to do research, and apply the results of that research, are increasing. In my own case, consultancies and development-related studies have definitely allowed me to work in areas, and to research topics, not equally available to academic anthropologists. Let me give some examples. As a consultant to the United Nations Development Programme, the Ford Foundation, and the United States Agency for International Development, I was able to make seven trips to the Central and Southern Sudan between 1976 and 1981, working in some areas that recently had been devastated by the seventeen-year civil war.

Support from the United States Agency of International Development for an unsolicited research proposal from the Institute for Development Anthropology enabled me to direct between 1979 and 1981 a global evaluation of land settlement schemes in the tropics and subtropics with special emphasis on the policy implications of state-of-the-art knowledge (Scudder 1981 and 1984b), and to commence in 1979 a program of annual monitoring (except for 1982) of Sri Lanka's Accelerated Mahaweli Project (Scudder and Wimaladharma 1985). More recently, support from the World Bank has involved William Partridge and me, through the Institute for Development Anthropology, in what we hope will be an ongoing assessment of the reservior relocation component of India's Sardar Sarovar and Narmada Sagar Projects in the states of Gujarat, Maharashtra, and Madhya Pradesh.

As a result of support from donor agencies and host countries, I have been able to undertake research and surveys during the past five years in a majority of the ten largest development projects currently under way in Asia, Africa, and the Middle East. A six billion dollar plus project, India's Sardar Sarovar will provide water for the world's largest irrigation scheme under single management, with over two million hectares to be eventually irrigated. Sri Lanka's Mahaweli Project, Indonesia's Transmigration Projects, Malaysia's Federal Land Development Projects, and the Sudan's Jonglei Canal, Rahad, and

New Halfa projects are also grandiose in scale, with my donor- and host- country-sponsored work allowing me a form of access that would not have been available to me as an academic. It is from such work that I wish to point out some of the theoretical, policy, and ethical issues and achievements associated with research in development anthropology.

Substantive Achievements and Issues with Theoretical Implications

Although this is a personal view with the examples that follow taken from my own areas of expertise, equally important examples could be added as from the study of pastoral systems, and the interface between riverine communities and pastoralists in arid and semi-arid communities where I believe we can now make generalizations with global applicability and major policy implications. Furthermore, I could provide additional examples from my own experience including predictable conflicts between centralized government parastatals and local farmer organizations; household, kin group, and community participation in the management of such natural resources as fisheries, irrigation waters, wildlife, and floral resources; and response of local communities to such windfall situations as the explosion in fish populations that follows the creation of artificial reservoirs in the tropics. In regard to each case, research in development anthropology has proceeded to the point that we can predict, with considerable accuracy I think, how local populations will respond to differential kinds of development agencies, programs, and opportunities.

ACHIEVEMENTS: THE DEMAND FOR DEVELOPMENT
AND THE DEVELOPMENT PROJECT CYCLE
The Demand for Development
    As social scientists increase their familiarity with local responses to development, it becomes increasingly clear that a majority of even the most isolated populations in the tropics, with the possible exception of some very isolated gatherer-hunters and bush fallow cultivators, desire greatly improved developmental services (especially for

the education of their children and the health care of all family members and livestock) and some disposable cash income. They want development, but on their own terms.[2]

This conclusion was brought home to me during recent travels among the Nuer and Dinka in the Central and Southern Sudan. In Nuer cattle camps I suspect there has been little change in the "atmosphere" since Evan-Pritchard's fieldwork in the 1930s. Among the Eastern Dinka, one of our visits coincided with a major ceremony which attracted Dinka and their cattle from many cattle camps. One early morning we watched as Dinka youths sprinted naked out of cattle camps in which dung fires for driving off mosquitoes still smoldered, singing the praise of their favorite oxen and simulating, with their arms as they ran, the animals' magnificently long and trained horns. Among the Western Dinka, we saw fields manured by staking-out cattle in a way identical to that described by Stubbs and Morrison before World War II (1938).

Clearly some things had not changed, especially the value placed on cattle. But other things had. To rebuild their herds after the seventeen-year civil war, Nuer were extensively involved in a range of market activities. Some were fishing the Sudd commercially, with profits invested not just in cattle but also in small shops which were springing up in the small administrative centers between Malakal and Bor. Others were working in the building construction industry in the Northern Sudan—both in Khartoum and on the major irrigation projects. Still others worked as agricultural labor on the mechanized rainfed sorghum lands of the Central Sudan. As for the Dinka, once they realized that old steers and cows were apt to perish en route, both Eastern and Western Dinka began driving prime beef long distances to urban markets (carefully picked and changed according to current prices), with profits invested in more cattle, in lorries to bring back building materials for cattle byres and homes in the timber-depleted uplands, and in stores and small eating establishments (as in Bor), with lineage organization often used as the mechanism for owning commercial enterprises.

2. While the majority of the Third World's citizens may desire development, as they define it, there are many obstacles to their participation in the development process. These include national and international policies (especially in relationship to terms of trade) and exploitation by rural, regional, and national elites. The capacity to control the future of that minority of people who do not desire development or who are unaware of other options is far worse (Goodland 1982).

The problem for these people was not development as such but the lack of the type of development opportunities and services (such as improved medical facilities for themselves and their cattle) that they wanted (Lako 1985). The same can be said for many tribal peoples in India, including the Bhils of Gujarat. In the more accessible villages in the Narmada Valley, for example, Sanskritization (Srinivas 1968) is proceeding rapidly (Joshi 1983), while some villagers are moving their families out of the hill country to the western plains and urban centers. Again the problem is not development as such but rather the failure of state and national agencies to plan *and implement* the type of projects and programs which people want.

The Development Project Cycle

Various social scientists, including the political scientist Chambers and the economist Nelson (1973), have emphasized the importance of studying development projects as "entities which change over time" (Chambers 1969:226). Chambers has concentrated on land settlement projects which, if they are to be successful, he believes must cause major transformations not just in production but also in institutional behavior and in the behavior of the settlers. By focusing on the participants—who as the main risk-takers should be the main beneficiaries of development—anthropologists have broadened our knowledge of the processes involved in, and the complexities and dynamics of, the different development stages. They have also broadened our knowledge of how the settler participants attempt to develop viable production systems and communities.

While most analysts deal with three stages, I have slowly evolved a five-stage framework for the comparative analysis of government-sponsored land settlement projects. In temporal order these are: (1) planning; (2) initial infrastructual development and settler recruitment; (3) transition; (4) economic and social development; and (5) handing over of responsibilities and incorporation of the settlement area into the political economy of the encompassing region.[3] The whole process takes at least a full generation. Handing over, for example, refers both to the handing over of management responsibility from a parastatal organization to line ministries, local government,

3. While I find a five-stage framework more useful for the analysis of settlement projects as projects, in other publications I have combined the first two stages in order to focus more attention on the beneficiaries (Scudder 1981, 1985).

and such settler participatory organizations as farmer and water user associations, and the handing over of management responsibility from the first generation of settlers to a second generation who may or may not be the descendents of the pioneers.

These five stages are derived from the analysis of successful settlement projects in different parts of the tropics, success being defined in terms of major multiplier effects, especially in regard to non-farm employment generation arising from the increased disposable income of large numbers of settler households. Contrary to the fears of two Latin American anthropologists (Bartolomé and Barabas 1984:5–9), passage of settler households through this series of stages need not lead to cultural homogeneity (or ethnocide, in their terminology). Indeed, the stage of economic and social development should be characterized by a resurgence of cultural identity such as Colson and I found among the resettled Gwembe Tonga between the mid-1960s and the mid-1970s, and I observed among Balinese settlers in Sulawesi in the late 1970s.

For anthropologists the last three stages are the most interesting, with the anthropological input greatest in the analysis of the transition stage that begins once households of future settlers decide to move or learn that they have been recruited, either voluntarily or involuntarily, to move. The interesting question here is how an aggregate of hundreds or thousands of pioneering households establish viable production systems and form new communities in a habitat that is unfamiliar to the majority. This is where the laboratory or experimental aspect of development anthropology comes into being for the researcher. In hundreds of settlement areas around the world, aggregates of households are attempting to form new communities in which to live more productive lives and raise their children. While community formation should be a topic of great interest to anthropologists, actually the relevant literature is not very voluminous, with much of the available material dealing with communes and other utopian-type communities (see, for example, Erasums 1985) or with forced community relocation (Hansen and Oliver-Smith 1982).

The study of forced community relocation in connection with such development projects as dams has been dominated by anthropologists. Here comparative analysis suggests that communities with strong ties to an area respond initially to relocation to an unfamiliar habitat in remarkably similar ways irrespective of cultural background or relocation policy. Presumably because of the stress in-volved (as measured by increases in morbidity and mortality rates, increased anxiety and uncertainty, and reduction in cultural inventory and in effectiveness of local leadership), forced relocatees adopt a risk- adverse stance in their new habitat. That is, the majority deal with stress by clinging to the familiar, by initially changing modes of production, institutions, and values as little as possible. If, in fact, there are no major exceptions to this generalization, and I am cur-rently aware of none, it is obviously of considerable theoretical inter-est and policy relevance.

I would like here, however, to extend these generalizations be-yond forced relocation and apply them, though in diluted form, to a much more common form of settlement—to spontaneous and govern-ment- selected settler households who move voluntarily to new habi-tats as literally millions of people are doing today, especially in the humid tropics of Latin America and Asia. From my own review of the literature I assume that the transition period is stressful also for the majority of these participants. Perhaps I am trying too hard to extend generalizations from the study of forced relocatees, but I do not think so. Even though they tend to move as household units, as opposed to communities in which everyone must move (including the sick and the elderly), voluntary settlers still have to adapt not just to a new physical and biotic environment, but also to new modes of production and to new knowledge systems. Furthermore, because they seldom move as communities, they also have to adapt to new neigh-bors. And on government-sponsored settlement schemes they have to adapt to a new management system which diminishes their options and freedom of action.

I assume, therefore, that stress is present and that stress partially explains why the majority of voluntary settlers also appear to be ad-verse to risk during the transition stage. They too tend to cling to the familiar, even to the extent of trying to introduce from their com-munities of origin inappropriate crops and production techniques, and housing forms. New networks for building homes and clearing land tend to be restricted to relatives or neighbors from the old habitat; otherwise households tend to operate independently, especially where surrounded by strangers. While Moran (1985) rightly points out the importance of labor constraints as an explanatory factor for initial emphasis on a subsistence mode of production, I think that the stress factor and risk adversity are also partially responsible for settlers' concern with subsistence. Like forced relocatees it would appear that establishing self-sufficiency and coming to "feel at home" in the new habitat are necessary conditions that must be met before the majority of settlers are willing to emphasize the cash cropping of edible crops or other market strategies, and to put their energy into community formation whereby discrete households are integrated into a wider social framework.

Even in the most successful settlement areas, the transition stage appears to last for at least two years, with three or ten years being a more common time period. That figure refers to the more successful settlements. The majority of land settlements are not successful in terms of multiplier effects, government goals, and settler well-being. No extraordinary stage of economic and social development follows, with many settlers either dropping out (or being forced out), or perpetuating a subsistence mode of production. If the settlement continues, it passes into the first stage of handing over and incorporation without ever undergoing the type of development associated with stage four.

Where economic development and social change does begin, it can happen for the majority with extraordinary speed—with settlers stressing subsistence one season and market oriented production strategies the next. A paradigm change is involved here with settlers rapidly shifting (when conditions are favorable) from a risk-adverse to a risk-taking stance, with risk-taking being greater than that undertaken by kin and neighbors who remain in the settlers' communities of origin. Since this generalization appears to apply to forced relocatees as well as voluntary settlers, presumably something more than the entrepreneurial and risk-taking propensities of the immigrants (versus nonimmigrants) is involved. That something may well be the improved opportunities that properly planned and implemented settlements can provide to settler households once the initial period of adpatation is behind them.

I find it fascinating that throughout the tropics a majority of settler households tend to follow the same series of investment strategies once the stage of economic and social development begins. Initial strategies emphasize land clearance and/or acquisition. Means of acquisition include sharecropping, leasing, and purchases. Settler households also stress education of children, increased cash cropping, and integration of livestock into the farming system. Especially in irrigated settlement shemes, as incomes go up more reliance is placed on hired labor with family labor reallocated to more economically productive, or socially approved, activities.

Intermediate investment strategies expand the family enterprise into nonfarm activities both within the household plot (which may or may not be separate from the main cropping area or areas) and the settlement area. In densely settled schemes, extra rooms may be added for rental purposes, while other small businesses operated from the homestead include tailoring, carpentry, teashops and stalls, and stores. Subsequently such businesses may be expanded into nearby settlement centers, while another common type of off-farm enterprise includes transport involving oxcarts, two- and four-wheel tractors, taxis, minibuses, and lorries. Later investment strategies focus increasingly on developing nonfarm enterprises both on and off the settlement. Off- the-settlement activities include urban real estate and business, with the more successful settlers at Abis in Egypt investing in Alexandria while Gezira (which is a mixed success story) settlers in the Sudan invest in North Khartoum businesses and transport between northern and southern cities.

As for household consumption, as disposable income goes up domestic housing is expanded and improved. Inside, a remarkably similar set of furnishings are acquired—including sets of sofas and padded chairs, glass-fronted cupboards showing tea/coffee sets and other family valuables, and tables and chairs. Walls are decorated with calendars, family photographs, and wall-clocks, while appliances include, in order of purchase, transistor radios, radio/cassette players, and television sets. Petromax pressure lamps replace wick lamps for illumination.

Where community formation is concerned, kinship and other networks between neighbors, co-ethnics, and members of the same religious sect are expanded in almost predictable ways. First come benevolent or welfare societies which cover funeral costs for member families. Next, community-wide groupings are formed to build churches, shrines, temples, or other religious structures. Indeed, community action to build a mosque or church is one indicator that the transition stage is about to, or actually has, come to an end. Such production oriented organizations as farmers associations, water user associations, and marketing cooperatives tend to follow, although there are of course exceptions to these generalizations. In terms of specific research, Chaiken's recent Ph.D. thesis (1983) shows nicely the importance of kinship during the earliest stages of spontaneous settlement on the west coast of Palawan in the Philippines while Eder's work (1982) on the east coast provides insights into community formation over a longer time span.

During this period of community formation, I have observed in a number of settlements what can almost be called a cultural renaissance involving both forced and voluntary settler communities. In the Gwembe Tonga case, some five years after resettlement in the Lusitu area below the dam, hunting shrines and other types of household shrine (such as I had not seen before resettlement in the 1950s) were reestablished. Funeral ritual also reemerged and over the years has become, if anything, more colorful. But the most impressive case of the resurgence of cultural symbolism that I have seen was among Balinese settlers (the large majority of whom were voluntary government- sponsored and spontaneous settlers) in Central Sulawesi. When I visited the Parigi area where Gloria Davis had previously done dissertation research (1976), many settlers clearly had entered stage four. Not only were disposable incomes up, but there was an amazing resurgence of Balinese ritual as exemplified by household and community shrines that Davis (oral communication) informed me were elaborate in comparison to their equivalent in Bali. These two examples show that government-induced economic development and cultural expression are not necessarily incompatible.

As Roberts (1975) and Moran (1981) have shown in Colombia and Brazil, respectively, over the years old lands systems of land tenure tend to be replicated in land settlement areas, although I wish to emphasize that similar degrees of social stratification and social inequity are not inevitable *if* the host population is incorporated within the settlement area, land survey and land titling is handled promptly, producer prices are equitable, efficient services exist for handling inputs and marketing, and credit is available at the right time on reasonable terms. The World Bank, in particular, is putting more emphasis on financing projects that include such features—Indonesia, Malaysia, and Colombia being cases in point.

A small number of other projects started back in the 1920s and the 1930s illustrate my point. In Sri Lanka, the Minneriya scheme commenced in the 1930s. Following up on samples used by an earlier investigation, Wimaladharma (oral communication) found in the early 1980s that over 95 percent of the settlers on this successful scheme were descended from the original pioneers. Another case is a major scheme initiated in Northern Parana, Brazil, by a land development company in the 1930s, a scheme which may well be the most successful in Latin America. There large numbers of small coffee holders were established on the land, with the development company using the income from land sales to build a railway, with local and regional towns, through the settlement zone. Rising disposable incomes gradually increased settler demand for a wide range of goods and services, with nonfarm employment increasing significantly and large towns growing up at certain locales along the railway (Katzman 1977). While it is true that the descendents of many of these settlers have lost their lands since the 1960s, this was due to the type of unexpected event—in this case in the form of crippling frosts (Margolis 1979)—that threatens all of us.

While rural elites, as in old lands, come to dominate settlement schemes in time, even their base can be broadened if water user associations, for example, are designed to give equal representation to bottom, middle, and top enders so that the latter are unable to use water to the detriment of those below them. It is this potential of land settlement to broaden the participatory base up to the point that beneficiaries include a majority of settlers that I find so attractive about the land settlement process, with examples coming from all major areas of the world—including Papua-New Guinea, Malaysia, and Peru. While researching the settlement component of such schemes is very interesting, and has theoretical importance for social science, the type of knowledge that I have just outlined also has major policy implications for designing, implementing, and managing improved settlement schemes (see Scudder 1981 and 1984b).

ISSUES

There are many major issues with global policy implications to which development anthropology could make a major contribution. In this section I would like to discuss briefly two issues. These are rapid social change and revitalization movements, and rapid economic downturn and community unraveling.

Rapid Social Change and Revitalization Movements

I believe that we have now a fairly good scientific understanding of some aspects of the settlement component of land development schemes, an understanding which already has had important policy implications. The same cannot be said of our understanding of the interrelationship between rapid social change and revitalization movements—a topic of tremendous theoretical interest and policy significance not just for Third World nations aspiring toward rapid change but also for the world as a whole.

In most of the countries in which I have worked recently, there are strong and growing fundamentalist religious movements. These involve not just Christianity, Islam, and Judaism but also Buddhism, Hinduism, and Sikhism. The impact within Islam stretches from the Pacific to the Atlantic, and includes not just Iran, Lebanon, and the Sudan, but also Malaysia, Pakistan, Egypt, and Nigeria (where even now, 1985, the Army and the local populace are involved in combating a fundamentalist cult in the northern part of the country). The impacts of this global trend in terms of communal strife are reported daily in the national and international press so that I need not give examples other than the less well known case that involves Buddhism.

Since 1979, I have been making annual visits, except for 1982, to Sri Lanka. In that potential paradise, there is now no doubt that some fundamentalist Buddhist priests and their supporters are a major force trying to discriminate against, evict, and eliminate Tamil-speaking Hindus and perhaps Tamil-speaking Moslems, with their activities spawning a countering guerrilla movement among Tamil-speaking youth which may or may not have a fundamentalistic religious component.

To what extent are these movements reactions to the rate at which national development programs, Westernization, and Americanization are occurring; to insensitivities to local ideologies and institutions; and to the sheer immensity of the impact of change since the end of World War II? Clearly, all the conditions are present for the emergence of revitalization movements, and clearly such movements are surfacing. What are their implications for those caught up within their ferment, for national governments and the world? These are important questions for all of us, and development anthropologists have been remiss in not paying more attention to researching the issues involved.

Following Wallace, I do not suggest that national development programs, Westernization, and Americanization need necessarily cause such revitalization movements (indeed, in Sri Lanka historical factors predating the present century are important). Nor have I suggested that such movements are incompatible with the aspirations of their followers for both change and continuity in the nature and quality of their lives. Revitalization movements can and have promoted constructive change for their followers. Wallace's analysis of the revitalization movement initiated by Handsome Lake among the Seneca Indians in the late eighteenth and early nineteenth centuries reveals that, developmentally, it was a "Successful Revitalization Movement" (1967:449). Following Wallace, the important question then becomes how can "the tremendous energies of the revitalization movement . . . be placed at the disposal of technical development," hence accelerating the rapidity with which "great progress can be made" (Wallace 1967:454).

Rapid Economic Downturn and Community Unraveling
    The second issue for discussion concerns the possible correlation between a significant economic downturn (following a period of rapid economic development) and community unraveling. My case material comes from several communities of Gwembe Tonga resettled in the Lusitu area below the Kariba dam. There a period of rapid development occurred between the mid-1960s and the mid-1970s, during which educational and occupational opportunities, disposable income, and living standards improved for the majority without major changes in the egalitarian quality of rural Gwembe society, in kinship, and in ideology. In other words, there appeared to be, both from the peoples' and from the anthropologist's point of view, a fairly advantageous balance between continuity and change. After 1974, however, there was a very rapid downturn in the Zambian economy—especially in the village sector of that economy (Scudder 1983, 1984a, 1985).

    In the 1980s I found the villagers in a miserable condition. Housing and overall living standards had deteriorated—and government services had virtually ceased to operate with the result that schools suffered from lack of maintenance, books and other supplies, and teacher morale; and clinics and veterinary offices from a lack of essential medical supplies such as measles vaccines and prophylactic and curative drugs to protect cattle from bovine trypanosomiasis. As a result morbidity and mortality rates for both people and livestock had gone up. In a several week period in 1982, for example, over twenty children in the surrounding villages died of measles and associated complications, while death of plow oxen was causing many people to revert back to hoe cultivation.

At the behavioral level, heavy beer drinking among men and some women continued even though disposable incomes had shrunk to the extent that money used for beer was unavailable for essential food for other members of the household. In the village that I know best, drinking appeared to have increased, with a majority of men in 1983 on what was colloquially called "daily service"—meaning that each day they sought out local beer halls where they remained until supplies were finished. Theft within and between villages had increased, as had assault, including murder, and suicide. Sorcery accusations and belief in sorcery as the major cause of personal and household misfortune had reached an all-time high, with drunken men screaming accusations at night from the edge of their homesteads at unnamed rivals whom they accused of killing their children and livestock.

Though livestock maiming was not a new pattern, irate cultivators in the past being apt to spear domestic stock found feeding untended in their fields, its intensity had increased. Dogs straying into a neighbor's homestead ran the risk of being scalded with boiling water, while fowl, small ruminants, and cattle ran the risk of being poisoned with insecticides. Rather than joining together to bring legitimate grievances before their government representatives, and to seek communal solutions to local problems, villagers were taking out their misery on each other. No one was free from the envy and jealousy of neighbors.

As Elizabeth Colson has pointed out to me, the downturn in these Lusitu villages most likely had been exacerbated by a number of situational factors including forced relocation in the 1950s, environmental degradation accelerated by that relocation, very rapid improvements in living standards between 1962 and 1974, and being caught up violently in the war for Zimbabwean Independence (the Lusitu being on the then Rhodesia-Zambia border). Possibly the community unraveling that I have just described was a situational response to an extreme situation. But discussions and communications (through the newsletter *Culture and Agriculture*) with colleagues who have done research elsewhere in Africa and the tropics during recent years, and with medieval historians at the California Institute of Technology, suggest that the Lusitu situation is far from unique. Anderson, for example, "associates a rise in 'black magic' and ethnic and community conflict with 'sudden and desperate economic reverses' " in a Malaysian example (quoted from Scudder 1984a). Conversations with colleagues during recent field trips suggest that similar associations may characterize an increasing but unknown proportion of low-income people in both India and Sri Lanka.

The situation, however, is obviously complicated and dynamic, with a wide range of current responses to different as well as similar factors showing that we still are far from a synthesizing theory. Nonetheless, I think we have identified at least two key variables. One is the rapidity of the downturn in relationship to the rapidity and nature of the preceding upturn. The other is the ability of the local society to regain its resiliency by returning to a domestic mode of production and a degree of sociocultural closure after the downturn occurs. Both variables have global significance today. While I think it is true that many peasant communities throughout the world improved their living standards and the quality of their lives during the 1960s and early 1970s, one can make a strong case that this period of rapid upturn began to level off in the mid-1970s, to be followed in many countries of Asia, the Middle East, Africa, and Latin America by a period of downturn. This I expect to continue so long as terms of trade remain unfavorable to Third World nations at the international level and rural-urban terms of trade remain unfavorable to peasant and other local communities at the national level, and so long as present rates of environmental degradation continue.

Ethical Issues and Possible Solutions

In this section I wish to discuss a major ethical issue which confronts development anthropologists, along with possible approaches to a solution. The latter will emphasize both conventional and nonconventional ways in which development anthropologists can influence policy formulation and implementation. As for the issue, it concerns whether or not anthropologists should be involved at all in the type of large-scale development fostered by such agencies as the World Bank and USAID.[4]

IS THE INVOLVEMENT OF DEVELOPMENT ANTHROPOLOGISTS WITH SUCH AGENCIES AS THE WORLD BANK AND USAID UNETHICAL?

Here I think the critical question is whether or not the recruitment of local and expatriate anthropologists by development agencies has the potential over the short, medium, and longer term of helping low-income populations raise their living standards and quality of life in a nonenvironmentally degrading way, and increase (through institution building and decentralization of fiscal resources) their ability to compete for scarce resources? Before this can be answered, the question needs to be broken down into two questions relating to the short and medium term, on the one hand, and to the long term, on the other. Over the short and medium term I think the evidence is overwhelming that the use of development anthropologists and other development social scientists not only increases the rate of return from development projects (Kottak, in Cernea, 1985), but also helps low-income populations increase disposable income and improve the quality of their lives.

On the other hand, I am uncertain as to whether current levels of development are sustainable over the longer term, especially if that development increases national dependency on international markets and local and regional dependency on national markets. If, in the case of some countries, they are not, then any development that incorporates local societies into a large political economy in such a way that they lose their resiliency when that political economy fails is probably undesirable. Yet even where development may not be sus-

---

4. I single these two agencies out for consideration only because I am most familiar with their operations. Though the nature of the answer would vary, the question could be asked just as well of other bilateral and multilateral donors and of host country agencies.

tainable, what are the options other than attempting to tailor development interventions to the needs, habitats, and cultures of local populations and their natural resource base? Granted accelerating environmental degradation, population increase, and *the fact that the majority of low income people wish to improve their living standards,* is there really any other option? Though we may have serious doubts, is there really any other approach to trying to help low-income populations raise their living standards in ways which are not environmentally degrading? Although there is a long way to go, and trends are downhill at the moment, at least voices arguing (both within and without development agencies) for a sustainable form of nondegrading development have never been greater than is presently the case. Development anthropology has an obligation to join the chorus and work with local populations, private voluntary organizations, national and other government agencies, and international donors toward viable futures.

Justification

I did not select the impacts of large-scale engineering projects on local people as a research topic—rather, that topic, through Elizabeth Colson, selected me. In 1956 she had been asked to return to Zambia—where previously she had been director of the Rhodes-Livingstone Institute and researcher among the Plateau Tonga—to study the Middle Zambezi Tonga before and after their relocation in connection with the Kariba Dam project. There was funding for two people, and Colson selected me as her coworker.

Our writings have been very critical of the negative impacts of the Kariba project on the relocatees (Colson 1971), and much of my writing since 1967 has attempted to generalize these negative impacts to large-scale river basin development projects throughout the tropics with special emphasis on the multidimensional stress associated with forced relocation (Scudder 1973, and Scudder and Colson 1982). So how is it that I can still justify working for the agencies that fund such projects?

The answer is relatively simple. In one form or another, large-scale engineering projects are very difficult to stop and have very little, if anything, to do with structural reforms in political economies at national and international levels. Let me elaborate. When the World Bank decided not to fund the Kossou Dam in the Ivory Coast, the

United States stepped in for political reasons with then Vice President Humphrey sent over as personal emissary to show the flag in a formerly French-dominated area. When the World Bank, under pressure from the United States, pulled out as a funder of the Aswan High Dam, the Russian government stepped in as a bilateral donor. Since that date the USSR has designed and planned implementation of some of the largest water resource development projects in the World.

In China, scientists are developing a complicated mathematical model to "optimize" the development of the lower basin of the Yellow River—a model that involves major water transfers which will have a tremendous impact, for better or worse, on local peoples and their habitat. Throughout the War for Zimbabwean Independence, the Central African Power Corporation, with joint membership from Rhodesia and Zambia, continued to meet regularly not just to run the Kariba Dam installations but also to consider future dams on the Zambezi. And throughout the Vietnam war, I have been told that the Mekong Secretariat, with representatives from all the member states, including North Vietnam, continued to plan the development of the Mekong Basin.

Currently a number of bilateral and multilateral donors (including the World Bank, UNDP, UNICEF, UK, Sweden, the FRG, Japan, the United States, and Saudi Arabia) are involved in funding Sri Lanka's Mahaweli Ganga Project. Saudi Arabia and other Gulf States are relatively recent funders of Third World development. But since the increase in petroleum prices over a decade ago, their cultural and developmental impact has been considerable. They are major funders of the International Fund for Agricultural Development, which carries out feasibility studies of, and provides funding for, projects designed for the rural poor. Gulf funds are especially apparent in the Islamic nations of West Africa, where Saudi assistance has funded new mosques in various capital cities, while Gulf assistance has contributed to dam construction along the Senegal and Niger Rivers.

The point is this: regardless of ideological stance and the nature of a nation's political economy, large-scale river basin development projects are going to continue. The option, therefore, is to stand on the sidelines complaining about their negative impacts but having relatively little effect on their number, location, design, and purpose, or to try to influence—both from within and, *where necessary, from without*—their planning, implementation and management in ways which incorporate local populations in project benefits in an environmentally sound way. That is what the Institute for Development Anthropology is trying to do.

We pick those development projects and countries which we believe have potential for low-income populations. Though such populations do not hire us, do not pay us, and more often than not do not know of our existence, we nonetheless see them as our clients. That means we try to expand project benefits to reach the local population in culturally relevant ways while also trying to minimize negative impacts.

While problems are associated with sponsorship by agencies such as USAID, I consider them to be more institutional and developmental than ideological. Generally speaking, we are not uncomfortable with our sponsors. As we noted in an interview for the *Anthropology Newsletter* (21[9]:4–5), "foreign economic assistance of no Northern industrial country is disinterested. . . . But it is a gross mistake to look on AID . . . as homogeneous; there are many AID officers who are genuinely committed to human rights, to income redistribution . . . , and to development from below." We try to work closely with such officers, to strengthen their hand by feeding them useful perspectives and information. Because we are not a profit-oriented consulting firm, we can and do reject invitations to participate in projects or to work in countries that make us uncomfortable.

That said, it is important to state that to date we have had little difficulty in finding worthwhile projects which are largely compatible with IDA goals. As national and multilateral funding agencies go, AID compares very favorably in regard to our major areas of concern. AID, for example, was one of the first development agencies to include social and environmental impact studies as part of their project planning process. AID was also a pioneer in institutionalizing the monitoring and evaluation of its projects and in directing them at low-income populations. The problems that we have are not so much with the goals of such agencies as AID and the World Bank as they relate to social and environmental soundness, to focusing assistance on the household and community level, and to local participation, but with the difficulties such agencies have in implementing those goals.

Within development agencies we attempt to work closely both with individuals who we believe are sympathetic with our views and are in a position to push them, and with those who are unsympathetic. It is the sympathetic who recruit us in the first place, and once recruited we try to help them influence their colleagues to place more emphasis on "people first" projects (Cernea 1985). A commonality of interests is not hard to find. IDA's relationship with Michael Cernea, Sociological Adviser to the World Bank, is a case in point. In 1977, Cernea asked Horowitz and myself to prepare separate papers for a series of seminars that he was organizing for Bank personnel on the relevance of sociological inputs in project planning (Cernea 1985 contains revised or rewritten versions of many of these papers).

My May 1977 paper on "Policy Implications of Compulsory Relocation in River Basin Development Projects" was more critical than supportive of the Bank's role to date. Some of the ideas in that paper, along with ideas generated by the research of Elizabeth Colson and others, were subsequently incorporated by David Butcher, Michael Cernea, and D. Rubin within the Bank's 1980 policy and procedural statement on Social Issues Associated with Involuntary Resettlement in Bank-Financed Projects. While I do not believe that this statement goes far enough (insufficient attention, for example, is paid to underemployed, landless relocatees), it goes well beyond the views of many Bank staff members, not to mention officials in other donor agencies and within host countries. As such, it is a major step forward. Furthermore, it has had a major impact on resettlement plans formulated by member countries of the Bank.

In a recent review, Cernea (oral communication) concluded that the policy and operational statement adopted by the Bank resulted in improved treatment of resettlement issues by a good number of national and local governments. Furthermore, he noted that projects using anthropologists and sociologists produced better resettlement plans. Currently the Bank and IDA are working closely with various Indian government agencies at the federal and state levels to formulate acceptable resettlement plans in connection with two very large river basin development projects in Gujarat, Madhya Pradesh, and Maharashtra, and to monitor the implementation of those plans.

Within AID we have worked closely with a number of officials with whom we share common concerns. While Alice Morton was largely responsible for pushing through the Agency our unsolicited proposal to make a global evaluation of land settlement schemes, subsequently several AID officials facilitated the distribution of the results of our completed evaluation. For example, the 1981 Executive

Summary was published by AID in 1984, with several thousand copies distributed around the world. IDA's more recent evaluation of the World Bank's experience with land settlement projects was initiated by the Bank's Office of Evaluation and Sociology Adviser.

In both land settlement evaluations, we argue that much more attention needs to be paid to the host and settler beneficiaries (especially to their net incomes and to the potential of disposable income to generate nonfarm employment) in relationship to such topics as infrastructure, production, and management. Hosts, we argue, should be given priority treatment, while development must be better integrated with environmental planning and natural resource management. We also argue that appraisal methodologies need to pay more attention to potential multiplier effects.

Critiques, of course, frequently do not influence policy, and even where they do, policy and the resulting plans are not necessarily implemented. Here constituency building outside development agencies may prove to be an effective mechanism to bring pressure to bear on developers to take their own guidelines and plans more seriously.

Constituency Building

A major problem facing development anthropologists is that all too frequently project goals and plans that we support are not implemented. Reasons for this situation vary. Such unexpected events as natural disasters or wars may preclude implementation or host country priorities may change following changes in government. Unfortunate as such circumstances may be, a more common occurrence is for the implementing agency to deemphasize plans and goals relating to the beneficiaries and their habitat—plans and goals with which development anthropologists are particularly concerned.

Such plans and goals include, for example, efforts to facilitate local participation, or to incorporate the host population within a settlement project, or to provide promised benefits to "development refugees" who must give up their land and homes to reservoir basins or other encroaching development projects. While governments may agree to such goals and plans because the donor agencies increasingly insist on them, after the loan agreement is signed and the funds begin to roll, the implementing agencies proceed with their own agenda in spite of loan agreements that contain mechanisms for protecting local populations and their resource base.

Failure of implementing agencies to observe loan covenants and their own official policies is a very serious and common problem. Though individuals within the donor agencies may be concerned, and supervisory missions may complain, very rarely do donors stop loan disbursements once a project is under way, especially if the major components of the project, like dam and irrigation construction, are proceeding at a "reasonable" pace.

In dealing with this problem I have developed a strategy that emphasizes four approaches. The first is to help build partial safeguards into the project plan in the form of required supervision, monitoring, and evaluation of what I consider to be key components. In connection with World Bank contracts, I have concluded that the Bank supervises most carefully those project components that it funds; hence where a project requires, for example, some residents to give up their land and homes it is important that sufficient Bank funds are involved for relocation purposes to ensure frequent supervision.

My second approach is to help build a training component into the project in hopes of sensitizing the relevant officials to the importance of involving local communities in project benefits.

The third approach is to collaborate closely with concerned individuals both within the donor agency and the host country who one can inform if implementation is faulty. In the case of host country colleagues, I have found during my recent work in Asia that these should be of two sorts—government officials with influence, and academics and private citizens (including agents for private voluntary organizations working with local communities) who have ready access to the project area.

The fourth approach is by far the most difficult. It involves formation of a strong constituency to bring pressure, including law suits, to bear on both the implementing and donor agencies. For that to be effective one has to have access to up-to-date information, hence the importance of monitoring, and one has to have access to people within (and where necessary, without) the funding and implementing agencies who can and will make use of that information. Such access is very difficult for one who is "outside of the system." On the other hand, if constituency building and pressure is too apparent and embarrassing to donors and implementing agencies, consultancies may be terminated, and the constituency builders may find themselves outside the system after all.

Whether or not development anthropologists become involved in such constituency building involves very difficult personal decisions. As time goes on, I personally find I am more willing to take the time and the risks involved in constituency building, which involves not just working with concerned local, national, and international nongovernmental organizations but also with concerned government officials and government agencies.

To summarize this section, I believe it is possible to work within the system, although the risk of merely providing "window dressing" to meet unpopular requirements for what USAID calls social soundness analysis is ever-present. Yet if my assessment is correct that most water management projects are going to go ahead in one form or another, then it is worth trying to make such projects more relevant to local populations and to improve their long-term environmental soundness. This can be done in a number of ways, including influencing the number, siting, and design of dams as well as their regulation, so that, for example, a regularized drawdown within the reservoir and a controlled flood below the dam increase benefits for local populations. And should it become clear during planning studies and personal involvement that a project's detrimental effect has been seriously underestimated for political and other reasons, it may be possible to stop it—although success in that regard probably requires constituency building, as was the case with the fight against Orme Dam in Arizona in which anthropologist Patricia Mariella was actively involved.

9

TOWARD A THEORY OF PRACTICE
William L. Partridge

Effective applications of the theoretical and practical insights won through anthropological research requires that practitioners make an ethical commitment to improve the bureaucratic institutions which impact upon humans and their communities. The preceding essays and those that follow attest to this commitment as it is being expressed by practicing anthropologists in many fields of endeavor. In this essay, William L. Partridge outlines a theory of practice that links theory to ethical and effective application in a variety of settings.

Partridge points out that ethical and effective practice becomes possible only when the anthropologist has empirically discovered and mastered the informal, unspoken, common-sense rationales for institutional activities. These are quite distinct from and hidden by the formal or objectively stated goals, rules, and policies of such institutions. The knowledge needed for ethical practice is discovered primarily through ethnographic observation and participation in the daily, seasonal, and yearly rounds of institutional activities in their symbolic and instrumental contexts. This type of knowledge is not accessible to outsiders any more than knowledge of the organization of Fulani pastoralists or Aymara agriculturalists is accessible to observers who fail to conduct eth-

This essay is an expanded version of a paper presented at the symposium "Collaborative Research and Theories of Social Change" for the American Anthropological Association annual meetings, Washington, D.C. in 1982. I am grateful to Sally Falk Moore for drawing attention to the practical implications of Bourdieu's problematic and to Robert Hackenberg for suggesting bibliographic materials relevant to the issues raised, and to Jean Schensul, Gwen Stern, Don Stull, Sally Falk Moore, Maxine Margolis, Antoinette Brown, Terri Leonard, Cynthia Woodsong, Steven Schensul, Robert Hackenberg, Ronald Cohen, Fred Erickson, and Elizabeth Eddy for critical comments on the first draft. None of these, of course, are responsible for the uses I have made of their suggestions. This essay is reproduced by permission of Sage Publications from *The American Behavioral Scientist* (1985), 29(2):139–163.

nographic research in the native language and natural setting of the people themselves. Practicing anthropologists are in a uniquely good position to contribute new knowledge about contemporary institutions and to use this knowledge as a basis for devising ethical and more effective actions for the improved performance of these institutions in meeting the needs of human communities.

CONTEMPORARY APPLIED ANTHROPOLOGY does not so much lack a theory of practice as it lacks a capacity to articulate it clearly against the background noise of abstract anthropology. In this chapter, I take a step in the direction of articulating it, but first it is important to recognize that theoretical discussion in anthropology as a whole is hampered by several problems which make any discussion of the theory of practice difficult. These problems are not unique to anthropology, and similar issues to those discussed in this essay have been raised in economics (Kvaloy 1984), sociology (Cernea 1985), and other social sciences.

In the heady days of academic hyperextension and university department building in the United States after World War II, the profession of anthropology lost much of its commitment to applied anthropology or the practice of the profession in the modern world that characterized the 1930s and 1940s (see essay 1). The theory of practice being developed in the earlier period, and upon which this essay is based, slipped out of the intellectual armamentarium of anthropology as almost all energies were thrown into the proliferation of theoretical taxa.

What passed for theoretical discussion in the 1960s and 1970s was an exercise in pidgeonholing and then disregarding theoretical issues and, more importantly, disregarding their significance for the practice of anthropology. During the 1960s and 1970s anthropologists who talked about symbols were labeled mentalists whose most profound stand was on their heads. Use of a systemic analytical framework elicited the category of the functionalist, who swims in a circle of self-lubricating cybernetic logic. Those who proposed interpretations emphasizing the social relations of production were classified as Marxists—or if ideology was mentioned somewhere in the first two sentences, as neo-Marxists. To express a similar emphasis in terms of energy balance was to be transfixed as a materialist. To study economic development was to risk being classed as serving the interests of multinational agents, but to emphasize the viability of proven cultural practice was to exploit exotica. Talking about structure and social process, particularly at the subcultural level, was to have blithely ignored the entire world system (of which this is the most infinitesimal bit). And when one attempted to incorporate elements of several of these approaches into a community study or ethnographic analysis, some colleagues attempted to force one into a declaration of allegiance to one camp or the other or branded one an air-head.

A related problem was the proliferation of theories without purpose. Theoretical debate during the 1960s and 1970s had all of the earmarks of the ontological successor to ethnographic butterfly collecting in the early twentieth century, but during these two decades the specimens crying out for recognition as taxa were called "theories." Their developers were gifted anthropologists whose contributions to the profession spanned a variety of substantive interests and analytical frameworks, but their followers usually had need for only one. Thus Geertz, who gave us one of the most sophisticated ecological analyses of a complex society to date (1963a) and who contributed theory in economic development (1963b), is forgotten while Geertz the symbolic anthropologist is followed (1973). Turner the structuralist (1957, 1969) is forgotten while Turner the symbolic anthropologist is remembered (1967, 1974). Harris's work in community studies (Harris 1971) and symbolic/structural constructions called "races" (Wagley & Harris 1958) are rarely mentioned, but Harris the cultural materialist (1968) is followed. White, who theorized about the superstructure of Pueblo Indian culture (1932 a,b, 1935, 1942), is forgotten but White the infrastructural determinist (1943) is remembered. Indeed, leading anthropologists of the period prior to the 1960s and 1970s were utilizing for explicit purposes a great variety of theoretical frameworks. By concentrating upon only one and closing ranks into discrete camps, whose primary purpose was academic career building for the camp followers, they gave little thought to the purposes of theory building.

Most importantly, as the application of theory in practice was ignored during the debates of the 1960s and 1970s, the profession as a whole neglected the dialogue between theory and practice that is at the heart of progress and creativity in the sciences and arts. The profession as a whole became increasingly oriented to the college and university setting, academic rather than practical matters, and teaching 18- to 24-year-old Americans as the only career of *bona fide* anthropologists. This institutional setting in which abstract anthropology thrived failed to demand a theory of practice from the discipline, by which anthropology could emerge as a politically effective and ethically relevant social science in other institutions of the modern world.

When practice was addressed, as sometimes occurred in the pages of *Human Organization,* its linkage to theory was not explicit. Practitioners spoke of advocacy, action anthropology, and applied anthropology in order to articulate rationales for purposeful participation in modern government, health, education, and other institutions of society beyond the university. Such discussions were often couched in ethical obligations to protect research participants (I prefer this word to "informants") from the onslaught of the normal functioning of such institutions (Jones 1971; Peterson 1974, essay 11; Jacobs 1974; Schensul 1974). The larger profession of anthropology for the most part failed to pay much attention to such efforts, and failed to address the problem of promoting practice which is articulated to an explicit theoretical framework. Wolf (1969) and Stavenhagen (1971), among others, called attention to this remarkable deficiency and urged the profession as a whole to direct attention to establishing the theoretical framework for politically effective and ethically relevant participation in the modern world.

Some of the generation that entered anthropology in the 1960s and 1970s have, therefore, concluded that anthropology is devoid of a theory of practice (Ortner 1984). Others who entered the profession during this period consciously combined both abstract and applied anthropology, and rediscovered an earlier anthropology of the 1930s and 1940s when practical action in the world was of interest to many professionals. The latter moved beyond anthropology and the taxonomic wars of the period to educate themselves in practical fields: they studied agriculture, nutrition, economics, biology, education, medicine, and so forth, sometimes encouraged by anthropologists, sometimes penalized. They are today in an excellent position to contribute to a new emphasis upon practicing anthropology.

Now that it is clear that the period of hyperextension of academe has ended, and that the profession has need for a theory of practice that will lead to an effective knowledge of and action in the modern world, it is understandable that interest in such a theory has grown. But I do not think it fruitful to attempt to discover the germ of that theory in the taxa established during the recent past; a longer historical perspective directs our attention to that creative period when anthropology first entered the modern world and before it retreated from the challenge. I will argue here that the theory of practice is central to an anthropology of the modern world, and that it is and has for some time been embodied in applied anthropology.

The Concept of Praxis

The Greek concept *praxis* in its ordinary English language meaning roughly corresponds to "action" or "doing" and is usually translated as "practice." But, as Bernstein (1971) points out, if one considers the meaning which Aristotle ascribed to it, the concept takes on a distinctive technical meaning missing from ordinary English usage. Aristotle used the term *praxis* to designate the sciences and arts that deal with the activities characteristic of human ethical and political life. He made the distinction I will emphasize here between *theoria* and *praxis*. The former signifies those theories and activities of the sciences and arts that are concerned with knowledge for "its own sake." The latter, however, is theory and activity in those sciences and arts that are concerned with doing something, where the end embodied in the activity is not primarily the production of an artifact (e.g., creating knowledge *per se*), but rather the performance of the activity in a certain way—performing the activity in an ethically responsible and politically effective way (i.e., creating knowledge that is instrumental to ethical and political ends).

Praxis in this context signifies the theories and activities that affect human ethical and political behavior in social life. Such theories and activities contrast with other theories and activities that are not involved with or relevant to ethical and political behavior in social life. It would not be accurate or illuminating, on the other hand, to distort Artistotle's notion of *theoria* to mean merely contemplation; this connotes a passive activity level. Rather, *theoria* is a way of knowing about the world that involves strenuous, disciplined activity, much of it devoted to avoiding worldly activity, as is done in a nunnery, monastery, or college. Since I have spent no time in monasteries or nunneries, but have spent some time in colleges and universities, I will utilize the latter example.

While the goal of *theoria* is knowledge for "its own sake," we should recognize that knowledge of this kind is only partly valued for this reason. It is also of instrumental, pragmatic value to persons whose rank, income, and power within academic institutions depend upon transmission of specialized kinds of knowledge. Outside of this interactional context the knowledge may or may not be known, pragmatically useful, or ethically relevant to anyone or any group; nor are these supposed to be important to its existence and status as knowledge for "its own sake." On the other hand, it is impossible to ignore the fact that knowledge generated for "its own sake" is often of interest to the Department of Defense, Standard Oil Company of California, the City Government of Atlanta, Georgia, and other taxpayers, donors, and contractors that provide funds to and buy services from colleges and universities. Transmission of such knowledge to the public domain through publication or other ways is the normal practice of *theoria;* the wise among us "publish or perish" as the saying goes.

This type of knowledge is judged as such by being the product of agreed upon methods that reduce all facts to those identified by the methods as "relevant." By definition, knowledge is comprised of such facts without regard to ethical choice and political efficacy. In the mythology of this "its own sake" kind of knowledge, the practitioner is free to explore and contribute new knowledge as interest and opportunity allow. Conceptually, accepted theory and method constrict both interest and opportunity to those facts which are valuable. Pragmatically, knowledge based in such fact is valued as property, an instrument possessed by the practitioner of *theoria:* it is the currency, the only legitimate tender in which bartering over identity, membership, promotion, tenure, income, space, typing services, and the like takes place (or ought to, at least). Theoria is, therefore, theory and practice of a *kind of knowledge.*

Theoria is also a method for knowing about the world. Without referents in ethical and political processes of the world, which is to say evolving or changing only in reference to itself, *theoria* lurches forward rather as Kuhn (1962) has described scientific advancement. This is because the world is perceived as an object which can be manipulated intellectually. The world, in other words, is a collection of facts made intelligible (objectified) only by *theoria*. Facts not judged to be factors because they are not in accordance with accepted theory and practice, or what Kuhn called the "paradigm," are not acknowledged or incorporated into *theoria*. (They accumulate and persist as infamous "grey literature".) Yet, ethical and political process external to *theoria* constantly creates new conditions and new environments in which the accumulated but unknown, unwanted, unrecognized, unintelligible facts may force dramatic "paradigmatic shifts" in order to encompass the previously excluded. Thus, the practioner of *theoria* knows about the political and ethical processes of the world in an objective form only, not by taking action, or more accurately, *inter*acting in the world in such a way as to reveal such processes. It can be noted parenthetically that *theoria* derives from the same Greek and Latin roots as "theater," in which observers react but do not accept responsibility for acting in the spectacles which engage actors, according to the Oxford English Dictionary.

Our common-sense notion of practice in English fails to convey clearly the meaning of *praxis*. The term *practice* in English connotes the mundane, everyday, bread-and-butter activity in which the practical man gets on with the business of living, largely unconcerned with theory or even opposed to theory and the intellectualism it represents. Yet nothing could be further from the meaning of *praxis:* it is a way of knowing which embodies ethical and political theory *and* practice as processes of social life, including intellectual life. The practitioner of *praxis* is engaged in an interaction between theory and activity in the real world, an interaction through which social life is lived in such a way that the practitioner is compelled to make ethical and political decisions that matter. This is possible precisely because the practitioner of *praxis* is embedded in the social reality to which the theory of *praxis* has reference, and in order to continue being so embedded must continually, constantly adjust both theory and activity. *Praxis* is a *kind of knowledge* of the world which compels ethical and political decisions; it is an ongoing interaction with the world in which the results or outcomes of those decisions shape the nature of the *praxis* which is achieved.

Because social life requires that decisions must be taken, *praxis* is in part subjective; it is grounded in decisions taken by actors, not by spectators, who must live with the consequences. This requires a distinct method of thinking about the world. In contrast to the binary logic which characterizes *theoria,* a dialogue in which the only relevant components are inherited theory and practice, the practitioner of *praxis* is engaged in a multiplex interaction in which social reality, as it is lived concretely and on the ground, so to speak, throws up innumerable contingencies. Each of these contingencies has the potential to transform the relationship between theory and practice as they are related to one another at that particular point in time and space. This is the case because *praxis* represents that multiplex interaction between objective knowledge of the world, subjective experience with the world, and emergent social reality. *Praxis,* then, is also a method or way of knowing the world.

Bourdieu (1977) has addressed this Aristotelian problematic in terms of the contrast between the "theory of theory" and the "theory of practice," although he derives it from Marx's *Theses on Feuerback:*

The principal defect of all materialism up to now . . . is that the external object, reality, the sensible world, is grasped in the form of *an object or an intuition;* but not as *concrete human activity,* as *practice,* in a subjective way. This is why the active aspect was developed by idealism, in opposition to materialism—but only in an abstract way, since idealism naturally does not know real concrete activity as such. (Emphasis in original, quoted in Bourdieu 1977:vii)

Using the ethnographic case of the Kabylia during the Algerian war, Bourdieu focuses his attention upon the contradictions inherent in ethnology as a scientific practice. His reflections on the theory of practice, however, are addressed wholly to the manner in which scholarly activities take place, the way in which academic discourse is structured by the objective and subjective components of practice, and the place of academics in social reproduction. This is to say that Bourdieu is concerned primarily with mediating an academic contradiction or paradox, one derived from ethnologic *theoria.* On the one hand (objective) culture is held to be determined by conditions of existence, and in turn determines human behavior. On the other hand, the ethnologist experiences (subjective) culture as ongoing change, adjustment, improvisation, approximation, negotiation, trade-off, struggle, conflict, revolt, and creative action. His theory of practice is elaborated to resolve this paradox confronted by the ethnologist. I will return to the details of Bourdieu's theory below.

At this point I merely emphasize that Bourdieu's effort is not intended to understand *praxis* as it relates to the way people behave in the world, "as concrete human activity." Rather, his effort attempts to resolve a particularly knotty intellectual problem for social theorists. He attempts to mediate a conflict derived from *theoria* through the use of *praxis*. The much broader issue has to do with the way people (who are generally not ethnologists) live in a culture and society, perceive that society and culture, and perceive what they are doing and acting upon. The "theory of practice" which concerns us here is theory which can explicate concrete human activity as it is lived and perceived by actors (including ourselves) who are part of ethical and political process, as are all humans living in society.

Object and Subject Elements of Practice

A theory of practice is concerned with the kinds of theory that operate in the world and the activities within which they are embodied. The focus is on the relationships between what people actually do and the theories that people construct about what they do. Practice consists in a tension between objective knowledge of the world that is operant in a given time and space, and the subjective experience of the world in ongoing human activity. Anthropologists can readily understand the objective element of practice, for it corresponds to certain of our theories of culture, and one in particular.

Human memories are individually and collectively selective, and some anthropologists, in their efforts to comprehend human behavior, use the term culture to refer to this selective construction of reality. For the culture of a social group is not merely past or prelude or precedent. It is both less and more than the popular notion of culture as "heritage." It is less because in no sense does the totality of past experience persist into the present, and it is more because the past is reconstructed continually to serve the needs of the present and in this artificially cohesive, rational form it is made more potent. Through the conscious construction of a culture, legitimacy is established, claims are justified, identities are secured, and boundaries are asserted. This does not mean that there exists any objectively correlative or causal relationship between some particular cluster of selected elements and contemporary activity. In fact, such contradictions as are inherent in the ongoing construction of culture are the grist of alternative constructions, revisions, challenges, and contending assertions for legitimacy. These contradictions are ultimately resolved through the exercise of power.

Bateson (1935a), in his classic study of *Naven,* was the first modern anthropologist to posit the nature of culture as the product of social forces involving manipulation, negotiation, barter, cooptation, dispute, and conflict between dynamic social groups. He observed and carefully recorded the conflicting constructions of genealogical rights to land and labor resources, genealogies carried about in the heads of the old men who could remember filial and affinal relations back several generations. Powerful old men, those with numerous descendants and dependents, were locked in ritual combat over the "correct" construction of past relationships, the outcome of which was either negotiation of a temporary agreement or escalated conflict. More recently Bailey (1969), Parkin (1972), Smith (1974), and Moore (1975) have developed this model of social process in which groups with manifestly antagonistic interests shape, or more exactly, frame a culture to strengthen and assert those interests. In this view, culture is not a driving, determinate force as much as it is a product of ongoing social interaction. It is only one resource, upon which actors draw in an ever-present process of recasting, reinterpreting, reinventing, and revising culture so that it conforms to the needs of social practice then emerging.

The result of this ever-present process of revision is the objective element of practice, and it exists as the product of prior social actions. Practical activity, then, is the generative act of cultural construction. That a culture or objective knowledge seems to have an integral, cohesive unity at any given point in time is an illusion which all of us as culture-bearing humans willingly perpetuate. In fact, no such integrity can be claimed for objective knowledge. Yet as Turner (1969) and Myerhoff (1978) have noted, social life and social reproduction is everywhere carefully circumscribed by public and private ritual enactments that are designed to reinforce conviction in cohesive, enduring, unquestionable cultural truths where none may exist.

Culture in this articulated, logical, orthodox, and codified form is objectified and made powerful for social actors through ritual enactments. It is not the case that social actors "learn" a culture through such ritual performances and high ceremonial displays. This objective knowledge component of practice is already known, already part of the cultural scene, and social actors are only to be convinced once more of the "obvious" in Rappaport's (1974) sense. Repetitive displays of the obvious, the objective and the object, in which actors are supposed to become conditioned to a particular version of social reproduction, helps keep at bay the nagging realization that whatever coherence, stability, or authority is perceived to exist is the product of our own rational construct. It also helps to keep at bay the realization that the orthodox, the legal, and the rational are all merely temporary negotiated settlements among contending social groups, which could change tomorrow. And, of course, it is of immediate practical benefit to any dominant individual or social group to present its particular culture as an immutable, timeless knowledge stretching deep into the past, a seamless whole reproduced once again for the benefit of those present. Yet do not all social groups so posture themselves?

The subjective element of social practice escapes social expression and social reproduction in the same codified, artificially cohesive, abstract, and orthodox form as objective knowledge. This is so because subjective experience can never attain the level of ordinary discourse—it can never be articulated in advance of the activity in which it is embodied, for it is the product of activity and interaction with objects in the world. As such, subjective experience constitutes a pattern of perceptions and actions that normally remain beyond the grasp of deliberate construction; they cannot be made explicit *ex ante*. Nor can they be deliberately constructed *ex post* into abstractions, discursive symbolic logics, and orthodoxies without transformation into objects. Yet to say that subjective experience remains beyond the grasp of objective knowledge is not to say it is unpatterned. As Lévi-Strauss (1969) argued, subjective experience is structured by "unconscious" pattern and series reflected in streams of ongoing activity. Because subjective experiences are not normally objectified, but are largely unconscious, they are extremely powerful determinants of perception and action in the world. Indeed, subjective behavioral patterns are the essential bedrock we might call common sense or habit, over which objective knowledge accumulates, erodes, and weathers as contending social groups grapple to build newer configurations of orthodoxy upon them.

Bourdieu (1977:83) speaks of these implicit patterns of subjective experience as *habitus* or habits of practical mastery. Subjective experience entails mastery of the unspoken, nondiscursive, nonobjective yet essential rationale that lies behind the practical experience. Social actors are habituated to the rationale of any particular activity through successive experience, through exposure to order and series, through mastery of the pattern of steps entailed in action upon the objects of the world. The habits of practical mastery or the underlying, unspoken organizational rationale for human activity in the world is what we mean by the subjective component of practice. Subjective knowledge, then, entails mastery of the unspoken yet essential rationale which lies behind patterned experience: "what is essential *goes without saying, because it comes without saying*" (Bourdieu 1977:167, emphasis in original). Moreover, the essential order and organization of practical mastery are not perceived by actors as arbitrary, or the product of successive habituating experiences, but as natural and self-evident. Subjective experience is a pattern of organization which can be learned but not taught; it is habituation to an unspoken rationale, inarticulate yet compelling because it is embodied in social interaction.

As an illustration, one can recall Marx's (1967:178–181) example of the master artisan. A woodcarver "knows" objectively before blade ever touches wood what the finished product will look like. He can "see" it in the timber that lies untouched before him; even the details of grain, hue, and texture conform to the nature of the finished product he projects. These are visible and real to him. The artisan experiences lengthy apprenticeship, and because he has seen the emergence of that finished product from similar timbers many times before, he has a clear objective knowledge of what will emerge from the timber lying in front of him now. Yet it is physically impossible to carve the product that he can so clearly visualize, for as he works the piece it becomes apparent that this material has a distinct grain, or an interesting and challenging swirl he could hardly have foreseen just a moment ago. This constitutes his subjective knowledge, which is not the experience of having crafted such objects before or having known analagous timbers, but stems from the process of working with all manner of surprising properties hidden within this specific timber. Subjective knowledge is delivered up by the craftsman's actions and transforms the objective perception through which the action was framed in the first place. What emerges conforms neither to a logic that pertains to all things of like code or category in the world, nor is it the product of particularistic features unique to this specific thing in the world. It represents both. Practice is the negotiation between objective knowledge and subjective knowledge. Each is transformed by the other in action, and so wedded they constitute the generative process of culture building.

While one is of less value without the other, the theory of practice asserts the primacy of subjective experience in the formation of objective knowledge.[1] Practice is temporally prior to objectification, and subjective knowledge acquired in practice returns to transform objective relationships, as Sahlins (1981:50) has pointed out. The theoretical assertion of the priority of the subjective experience in shaping culture, in distinct contrast to the determinant role of culture in dictating behavior, is precisely the intellectual foundation upon which applied anthropology in the United States was constructed in the 1930s and 1940s.

---

1. Cohen pointed out in the discussion following the initial presentation of this essay that, contrary to my assertion, "theory of theory" is quite important in influencing practical behavior and prior to it. The example mentioned by Cohen was Andre Gunder Frank, and one can also imagine a similar claim being made for Karl Marx or Adam Smith. This view fails to come to grips with the thesis of this essay, and sidetracks the argument into the "great man" notion of history. Frank represents a recent expression of a deeply seated liberal and Marxist critique in Latin America regarding center-periphery relationships, which grew strongest following the (subjective) experience of disappearing export markets for raw materials in the Great Depression (Preston 1982). Articulated elegantly by Raul Prebish in the 1940s, but reflected in the anti-imperialist writings of Latin Americans for decades, center-periphery theory provided legitimization for a single-minded concentration upon rapid industrialization already in progress and part of government policy throughout Latin America in the 1940s long before Andre Gunder Frank popularized it in English. Second, it should not be forgotten that the theory espoused by Marx bears little relationship to the behavior of those who adopt his name in order to create a revolutionary charter legitimizing actions more deeply rooted in Russian, Chinese, or other political economies and histories. This was indeed the whole point of Rosa Luxemburg's (1961) famous critique of Leninism—it was related to Marx's theory rather as the teaching of Jesus Christ is related to the actions of that famous Christian Ronald Reagan in Central America.

Theory of Practice in Applied Anthropology

A theory of practice in anthropology finds its roots in early applied anthropology in what was then called "interaction analysis," as developed by Chapple and Arensberg (1940), who were influenced directly by Warner, Radcliffe-Brown, Bateson, Malinowski, and Mead as well as by the physiologist Lawrence Henderson, the social psychologist Elton Mayo, and the psychiatrist Erich Lindemann (see Chapple 1953; Richardson essay 4 and 1979). They viewed humans as biologically functioning organisms totally dependent upon social groups for survival. In this view, humans, in order to survive, are temporally conditioned from infancy onward to change their behaviors, adapting their patterns of activity in response to fluctuating conditions in environmental stimuli. Humans make these adjustments as responses to changes in light, temperature, and the actions of other animals. The synchronization of interaction with other humans is of the most interest, given the primacy of social groupings in human origins, persistence, and development.

The extraordinarily long period of infant and child dependency in humans directs attention to enculturation processes which go on independent of intellectual, moral, or symbolic communication between human organisms. Adaptation at the outset is achieved, therefore, primarily through adjustment of interaction rates, frequencies, duration, and intensities to the organizational pattern set up by other actors who comprise the social group. The most significant of these are the two sexes and three generations which constitute the principal vehicle of cultural transmission, the community of families (however defined) whose inter- and intrafamilial habits of interaction establish the range and variation of the organization field as then constituted. Before the first symbol (which will later exert powerful influence) is even susceptible of cognitive perception, the offspring has mastered the interaction sequence, series and pattern of initiation and response, the steps leading to positive and negative feedback derived from coordination of activity within that sequence, and the emotional satisfaction or frustration that is the outcome. The sex, age, and status interactional hierarchy of all human groups is expressed in an emotion-laden organizational rationale, the inarticulated, perhaps unconscious habits involving the coordinated activity of its members. Or as Arensberg (essay 2) describes it:

There is an elaborate, necessary, closely timed minuet—a stately dance of many coordinated persons, an exquisite choreography, of figures now individual and now in unison. This choreography is what we lamely call "organization."

Inspired with this insight, applied anthropologists have pursued this organizational rationale for several decades. The studies of the patterns of work interaction sequences at the Hawthorne plant of the Western Electric Company in Chicago, designed and directed by Warner, provided the first opportunity to delineate such an organizational rationale, through close observation and recording of visible and audible behavior *in situ* and *in vivo*. The empirical results were widely interpreted as the discovery of an "informal" system of social organization, of habitual interaction sequences, that lay underneath the formal social structures consciously designed and manipulated by humans (Roethlisberger and Dickson 1939). It was an important distinction, one encapsulated succinctly by Goodenough (essay 3): "Real social power, as distinct from jural authority" resides in such organizational rationales.

Warner and his colleagues (Warner and Lunt 1941; Warner and Srole 1945; Warner and Low 1947) extended the studies from small work units to entire communities in the Yankee City project, and here again delineated a complex organizational rationale entailing dozens of "informal" interactional networks comprising voluntary associations which underlay and in many instances undercut the formal social class and corporate structure of the community. Indeed, it was this elemental organizational rationale which permitted the formal structure to work; when disarticulation occurred between the two, the conflicts demonstrated the real social power of the former. The same point, the relationship between the objectively constituted symbolic-structural order we call social structure, and the informal, inarticulate, and perhaps subconcious behavioral process we call social organization was pursued in cross-cultural studies as well: in Ireland (Arensberg and Kimball 1938), in small towns of the United States south (Davis, Gardner and Gardner 1941), in an Italian neighborhood (Whyte 1943), among the Navajo Indians (Kimball and Provinse 1942;

Kimball 1946, 1979), and in United States hospital-clinical settings (Chapple and Lindemann 1941).

These researchers and others pointed the direction to an understanding of how social systems change due to the discontinuities, conflicts, and incongruities that exist between organizational rationales and the social structures grown out of them or imposed upon them. Indeed, the conflict between emerging labor unions and management in the United States in the 1930s probably stimulated the initial advances in an atmosphere marked by red-baiting, scapegoating, violent beatings, goon squad assassinations, and intimidation of workers in industrial plants by police and judiciary. The applied anthropologists were among the first social scientists to study the industrial workplace firsthand, and use their findings to devise and implement alternatives to the violent conflict. The theories, methods, and findings were equally applicable in the colonial setting and in development programs, where the conflicts between indigenous structure and organization and superimposed colonial structures were dramatically apparent (Kimball 1946, 1979; Arensberg 1942, 1967, essay 2; Whyte 1975; Spicer 1979).

From the foregoing it is clear that the distinction between the formal, symbolic/structural order of human social life and the informal, behavioral process called the organizational rationale together provide a rather explicit framework for the theory of practice discussed above. *Praxis* consists precisely in this tense negotiation between the actor's objective knowledge of the world and his or her subjective experience in the world. And the latter is, in our theory of practice, the generative force whereby the former is constructed, adapted, and changed. The objective component of practice, then, corresponds readily to the applied anthropologist's concept of the symbolic/structural order. The subjective component of practice is that subjective organizational rationale in which actors are habituated.

Finally, in order to complete this analysis, an important issue remains to be addressed. This is the process(es) whereby interactional rationales or the subjective component of practice feed back to and transform formal, symbolic/structural order or the objective component. To do this we should return to those anthropologists who, like early applied anthropologists, posit the nature of culture as the product of social manipulations, negotiations, barter, cooptation, improvisation, and conflict between social units.

The beginnings of such thinking can be traced to Bateson's (1935b) theory of schismogenesis, whereby conflict is escalated through antagonistic groups working at cross-purposes. Out of this conflict the symbolic/structural is transformed and reinterpreted to fit the needs of the factions with little regard for the integrity of the established order. In British social anthropology Gluckman (1955) and Turner (1957) also addressed hierarchical conflict, but Firth (1951) was the first in Britain to formally distinguish social organization from social structure and point to the inherent conflict between them. Yet Firth, like Gluckman and Turner, seems to feel that the constraints and incentives embodied in social structure add up to a deterministic influence upon social actors; and organization as discussed here is seen as a pragmatic end-around-play when structural constraints prove inconvenient. Or in Turner's (1969) model, it is "anti-structure," more defined by what it is not than what it is, as well as its confinement to ritual "time in and out of time." Bailey's (1969) more dynamic framework identifies normative or objective rules and pragmatic, behavioral strategies which contend in such situations of conflict and negotiation. Bailey places greatest emphasis upon the exercise of differential social power, understandably since the analysis is based in the caste system of the Indian subcontinent, seeming to indicate the priority of structural constraints and incentives. Yet, it seems clear that all coordinated activity among humans is not the product of coercive social power.

Parkin (1972) traces the negotiations and manipulations among contending social groups in a situation where a pragmatic organizational rationale evolved quickly to create a set of competing constraints and incentives to those embodied in the symbolic/structural order; the organizational changes, producing as they did a new interactional pattern, dictate the transformation of the old symbolic/structural order. Parkin's analysis indicates that as the pragmatic organizational patterns change, social actors feel no particular need to retain intact a symbolic/structural order ill-suited to the new conditions, and they experiment freely with little regard for the integrity of the old order.

The most fruitful theoretical model developed which advances our understanding of practice and pragmatics is provided by Moore (1975) and her concept of "indeterminacy in culture." As with Bateson, Moore postulates an enduring symbolic/structural order only as an outcome of ongoing practical activity. She assumes that that which is fixed in social reality is that which is continually reasserted, renewed, and recreated by social units whose interests are served by order; similarly, disorder or the transformation of the previously fixed into a new form is the product of the ongoing activities of social units whose interests are served by change. This conceptualization of culture as indeterminate prior to the actions which challenge it or change it and those that assert it and attempt to renew it places pragmatic practice in its proper relation to symbolic/structural order, as the generative force of cultural persistence and transformation alike. This emphasis is also complemented by Smith (1974), whose recent work on corporate group formation and dynamics upsets previous notions of fixity based in symbolic/structural control of property, coercive force, or cognitive consensus. Smith argues that collective activity is the operational and formative factor in corporate group emergence, persistence, and transformation, in contrast to the thinking of Maine, Weber, and Durkheim, which focused exclusively upon the symbolic/structural features of such groups. Finally, in a not unrelated development in economics, Hirschman (1984) has stressed practical participation in group action as the generative force of social and cultural change.

While Bourdieu (1977) refines for us the concept of a nondiscursive *habitus*, in which we can see a definite link to habitual interaction patterns emphasized by applied anthropologists, his use of the concept to mediate the paradox of determinant culture and ongoing forces for change limits the use of the theory of practice. Its potential is much more significant if, with Moore (1975), we dispense entirely with the problematic in which culture is determinate of the behavior of social groups and actors, recognizing that such order as exists is in fact continually and constantly created by the pragmatic practice of contending social groups and actors. The theory of practice, then, emerges as the analytical framework within which we assert the priority of the organizational rational or *habitus* to account for both the decisioning-negotiating processes leading to symbolic/structural continuity and the decisioning-negotiating processes leading to symbolic/structural transformation.

The Ethics of Practice

I began this essay by emphasizing the difficulty of articulating the theory of practice which has been developed in applied anthropology against the background noise of abstract anthropology or *theoria*. The theory of practice demands and depends upon the engagement of anthropologists in the world of pragmatic, practical human activity if it is to advance the state of our knowledge of the world and, equally important, if it is to empower anthropologists for ethically and politically efficacious action. The two objectives are coincident and mutually instrumental within the theory of practice—as they are separate and attenuated within the theory of theory—because the theory of practice is both a kind of knowledge and a method for gaining that knowledge that makes possible ethical and politically effective action.

Habits of practical mastery, it is asserted by our theory, underlie all formal symbolic/structural cultural systems. Whether hamlet or corporate board room, village faction or bureaucratic department, community organization or international organization, the rationale or logic which informally organizes the elaborate choreography of action and reaction remains undiscussed, inarticulate, and imperceptible to the outsider. It is not accessible to objective instrumentation; interviews, content analysis, symbolic analysis, and statistical refinements of these will invariably turn up the objective structure and symbolic logics which defend and display it. It is only by direct observation and recording of sequences of visible and audible behavior that the subjective rationale of the particular organization being studied can be discovered. When this challenge is accepted, the rewards are quite compelling.

For one example, Allan Hoben (1980, 1982), convinced that bureaucratic behavior was probably as rational as peasant behavior, undertook an analysis of the organizational rationale in the United States Agency for International Development (USAID). He was able to do so only as a practitioner working in the bureaucracy, for only in this fashion would he have been exposed to that which "goes without saying." Anthropologists have been working for USAID for several decades, but almost consistently as outsiders, and none attempted to make systematic sense of the often contradictory, usually confusing, and too frequently counterproductive series of USAID actions and explanations for them. By concentrating his observations upon the verbal and nonverbal interactions among personnel, the flow of work, and the decisioning process, Hoben was able to map out the organizational rationale, the *habitus* which governs ongoing behavior among these development professionals. This, more than the symbolic/structural aspect of the bureau expressed in mountains of printed paper, provides our first ethnographic glimpse of the nation's largest development organization.

Equally important, it is only when armed with an understanding of the organizational rationale that one could possibly know how to be effective in USAID, that is, to know the manner in which ethical and political decisions are to be taken, the timing of such decisions in the project cycle, how and to whom to raise them, ways to buttress a position, ways to argue against a contrary position, and so forth. (For economists, Judith Tendler [1975] did the same thing. Hoben's and Tendler's analyses are quite congruent, although Tendler is a bit more optimistic, probably because of the greater influence economists now enjoy in the bureau.)

Of course there are other examples of practitioners who are contributing to our knowledge of the modern world through anthropological analysis, and empowering themselves and others to take more effective action in the world. The list includes many colleagues, and I mention Allan Hoben in particular only because of the absurdity of the example: a host of anthropologists, many of whom have been ethically and politically effective, have dealt with USAID for decades yet not shared with the profession the basic research results upon which, our theory of practice tells us, efficacy depends. As more anthropologists enter practitioner roles, and to the extent they are committed to a theory of practice, we can expect our practical knowledge and capacities for effective action will increase (Partridge 1984; Van Willigen and Dewalt 1985).

In turn, our theory of practice demands an *ethics of action* embedded in the Aristotelian notion of *praxis*. This is an ethics that evolves from and in concert with practical activity. It is not a "code" of ethics that guides human activity uniformly in war and peace, famine and affluence, hamlet and corporate board room, college classroom and government bureaucracy (see Adams 1981). Rather, it is an ethics of responsibility within an organizational context, within the world of value dilemmas that matter, and moral ambiguities stemming from contradictions in social and political process which have genuine consequences. It is an ethics based in commitment to socially responsible science. This commitment requires that the practitioner employ the best professional tools available that are appropriate to the task. It requires a pragmatic strategy based in practical knowledge so that there is a *good chance of being ethically and politically effective*. It demands a commitment to human rights; the most fundamental is the right to full development of the human biological and social potential as this is culturally defined. It requires *a commitment beyond narrow professionalism to take action* once analysis indicates a course of action, which is part of one's responsibility in the institutional context to provide excellent work. It demands a commitment to professional integrity, such that one is free to describe and analyze empirical realities of human social life and/or to find ways around the scientific and pragmatic constraints of preexisting policy, administrative procedure, or contemporary fashion. Finally, it demands a willingness to accept moral responsibility for the consequences of one's actions, which implies all of the above. One of those consequences is undoubtedly the prospect pointed up by Dobyns (essay 16) of anthropologists taking different sides of a practical issue.

This ethics of action contrasts vividly with the *ethics of noninvolvement*, which fits hand-in-glove with abstract anthropology, the way of knowing about the world called *theoria*, or the theory of theory (Berreman 1980). The latter explicitly condemns scientific work in the public and private sectors outside the university as polluting and views the involvement of anthropologists in the institutions of the modern world as prostitution. It candidly argues for abstract anthropology as a kind of social criticism—a noncommitted, nonparticipatory series of pronouncements as to the state of the world and its multitudinous organizational entities. This is the ethics of a sidelines field judge, which for *theoria* raises political and social impotency to a level of moral exemplum.[2]

2. Most anthropologists give little thought to the ethics of action, which is not surprising given lack of interest in practice. Critics of practicing anthropologists generally believe it is sufficient to simply raise the ethics question by observing that practitioners accept money for their work, thus introducing the possibility that such work is controlled by an employer. Such critics generally do not provide evidence to support the suspicions raised, and through which all practitioners are tarred with the same brush. Such sweeping and undocumented statements should be mistrusted, much the same as one should

This kind of thinking represents, if you ignore its self-justifying functions, an attempt to express the concern of *theoria* practitioners with practical issues, some of which are profound concerns indeed. Such expressive "concern behavior" if done well can briefly raise public awareness. But as Hansen and Oliver-Smith (1982:6) point out in the case of dislocated people,

After the cameras and reporters have departed, and the attention of the mass audiences everywhere has turned to other events and areas in this world of instant but fleeting imagery, the uprooted and resettling people remain to cope with the old and new problems of their lives.

Statements of professional concern, while of passing interest, have no long-lasting impact where impact is needed most, in order to actually do something effective where "people remain to cope."

It should be clear from the foregoing that if we direct our research focus to the institutions of the modern world to which the theory of practice leads we move well beyond what is normally known as "policy research." As Rein (1971, 1976) observes, value-critical research that addresses the ideological or "social theory" basis of public policy can be helpful to the extent that it leads to alternative ways to conceptualize problems to which policy is directed, ways that are critical of the conceptualizations of policy makers. What such writers mean by "policy" and "policy research" is sometimes ambiguous. (The vague political pronouncements of presidents? Broad mandates provided by division or bureau directors? Specific directives issued by department managers? The program guidelines developed by technical staff? The statements made by field staff?) Nevertheless, wherever such ideological stances might be found, it is clear that critically focused research on symbolic logics alone is limited to only the objective side of practice. While this makes for satisfying criticism, without an equally strong focus upon the subjective ratio-

dismiss a claim that all anthropology academics accept money from sources which have a great deal to gain by the inability of the profession to take action through which theories might be tested in the real world. Nor is guilt by association a valid basis for ethical criticism of practitioners; if that were the case, then we would suspect the department at the University of California, Berkeley, ethically culpable of failing to develop critical anthropological action in defense of native Americans because of its early association with the Hearst family money (Thoresen 1975). This would be as unfairly abstracted out of context as is the facile indictment of all practitioners who work for the United States government, casting them as bureaucratic lackies that agree with all the government does.

nale underlying policy such critiques do not result in new knowledge and suggest no effective or ethical action leading to either change or continuity. Anthropologists and other social scientists most often become involved in "policy research" only at the evaluation end of policy, the point when outcomes are to be measured. If new knowledge and effective and ethical action is an objective of research, then, as Cernea (1984) observed, this is the wrong end at which to enter the process. If we remain forever ensconced at the tail-end of that process, we will be effectively prevented from developing information and action plans whereby such processes are either changed or perpetuated.

Anthropology based in a theory of practice and an associated ethics of action can reach fruition only in the institutional context of activity in the modern world which is eschewed by theory of theory specialists. Each anthropological entry into the institutions of the modern world holds the potential for creating new objective knowledge of the world and new strategies for action by "concerned staff," provided our theory of practice guides the practitioner to delineate ethnographically and empirically the subjective rationales embodied in commonsense institutional *habitus* as the vehicle to both new knowledge and action. In short, those anthropologists whose locus of scientific work and ethical responsibility is found within institutional contexts as diverse as community, national and international voluntary organizations, administrative and service agencies of government, private and public sector industries, international business, health and development organizations, and a host of others, those we call applied anthropologists, are in the best possible position to contribute to the advancement of our profession toward new knowledge and action.

Part II

PRACTICING ANTHROPOLOGY

By definition, practicing anthropologists are concerned with the human aspects of the many technological and social changes which are endemic to the world today. Their work entails the ability to understand and work effectively within the interactional matrix that develops when the policies and programs of complex modern institutions impact upon human communities and individuals.

The work roles of practicing anthropologists vary considerably. Nevertheless, their work usually entails taking steps to lead, influence, or facilitate adaptive changes among those who are the recipients of institutional policies and programs or among the professionals who strive to modify and implement policies and programs that will better serve recipient groups. Practicing anthropologists often work with both of these groups simultaneously, and those who do so commonly refer to themselves as "culture-brokers."

The practice of anthropology entails much more than the production of classical ethnographic descriptions of communities and instituations. Rather, it requires the analysis of organizational behavior, the delineation of theoretical and ethical guidelines for policies and programs to modify behavior, the development of programmatic strategies to initiate and implement change, and follow-up activities that monitor and evaluate the outcomes of these strategies.

The contributors to this section describe these and other aspects of practicing anthropology in a variety of settings which include hospitals, universities, courtrooms, development agencies, schools, and tribal governments. Like all anthropological field reports, these essays are limited to the observations made by particular persons in specific career situations. Even so, they tell us much about practicing anthropology and reveal clearly that anthropologists who work outside of the academy must themselves adapt to new and "strange" situations which require that they work as peers with other professionals who have not been trained in anthropology. Anthropological theory and assumptions are continually tested in these new situations as they are put to use and further developed in the analysis of problems and the search for their solutions. In addition, anthropologists themselves are tested as they interact within social systems which they do not control or dominate. Thus, a high premium is placed not only on theoretical contributions but also on behavioral ones. The personal reports of the contributors to Part II bring the subtleties of what is entailed into view.

10

THE "PRODUCTION"
OF A SOCIAL METHODOLOGY

Michael M. Cernea

Perhaps the most ubiquitous challenge in social science is the call for the participation of beneficiaries in the planning and design of programs intended to help them. Yet, as Michael Cernea points out in this essay, the social sciences are woefully underdeveloped in terms of their capacity to provide concrete, systematic, and tested methodologies whereby people can be involved meaningfully as participants in such activities. This essay presents an analysis of the PIDER development project in Mexico, which made a serious attempt to address this problem. The Mexican government established the project in order to achieve development goals by facilitating the participation of the benefiting rural communities in investment planning.

Cernea documents the processual steps by which the social scientists who worked on this project systematically evolved a social meth-

Michael M. Cernea (D. Phil., University of Bucharest) is the sociology advisor of the World Bank, Washington, D.C. He has taught sociology in several universities in the United States and Europe. He has been a fellow of the Center for Advanced Studies in the Behavioral Sciences at Stanford and of the Netherlands Institute for Advanced Studies in the Social Sciences at Wassenaar, Holland. He joined the World Bank in 1974 as its first sociologist and has worked there since in operational research and advisory positions. His major research areas are rural development, the sociology of agriculture, family sociology, cooperatives and farmer organizations, rural communities, participation, and agricultural extension. He has carried out applied and operational sociological work in Algeria, India, Mauritius, Mexico, Romania, Senegal, and Tanzania.

During the years since I started to follow the development of the PIDER program in Mexico, many individuals have contributed to my knowedge and understanding of it. Among my colleagues in Mexico, I would like to thank in particular Marcos Arellanos, Victor Chagoya, Jorge Echenique, Jamie Mariscal, Antonio Monzon, Rudolfo Stavenhagen, and Arturo Warman. I also acknowledge valuable comments from D. Lindheim, A. Schumacher, N. Uphoff, and three anonymous readers.

odology to implement project objectives. He emphasizes the chronology of actions taken to develop the methodology of community participation and discusses the institutional, cognitive, and cultural barriers that had to be overcome. The important elements of this process included a conceptual framework that required local information and action as well as outside expert opinion in order to reach project goals; a series of activities and events that involved local people and outside experts in debate about technical issues; the sustained support of high-level leadership within the agency that initiated the conceptual framework and supported the activities; and continued support over the long period of experimentation, adjustment, and learning that was needed to develop and institutionalize participatory methods. The example of PIDER is one that can be extended to many other contexts where action-research is needed to develop innovative social methodologies for the implementation of program objectives.

AN OLD AND wise adage says that the way to the truth is as important as the truth itself. In other words, it tells us that the process is as important as the end-product. With this in mind, this essay analyzes the research *process* that led to a product of applied sociology and anthropology. Since space here is limited, I will analyze the type of social science craftmanship that was mobilized to generate this final product rather than describe the final product itself.[1]

The product in question is a methodology for building the participation of beneficiaries into the process of planning community investments. This methodology was prepared by a team of social researchers in Mexico in an effort to model the process of investment selection and implementation, and to redirect the work of the agencies involved in deciding upon investments and executing them. By analyzing the work process of this team, we may distill some lessons of experience in the epistemology of action-oriented research.

Applied social science must redefine its own epistemology, which is at least partly different from the general epistemology of basic

1. The actual "product," namely the set of principles, approaches, and procedures which together represent a methodology for community participation in local investments in Mexico is described in great detail in a number of manuals and guidelines (see bibliography), as well as in the World Bank Staff Working Paper No. 598, entitled "A Social Methodology for Community Participation in Local Investments: The Experience of Mexico's PIDER Program," on which this paper draws.

anthropological research. The analysis undertaken here will focus on two aspects of this epistemology; first, the definition of one specific product of applied social research, which I call "methodology for social action"; second, the characteristics of the "production" process capable of generating such a social methodology. Identifying this type of product and the ways to create it may allow for easier replication elsewhere.

A Social Science Product: Methodologies for Social Action

Sociology and anthropology have endeavored primarily to describe and explain past or existing social structures rather than to look toward the future and plan for purposeful change. However, the calling of social sciences is not only to analyze and explain, but also to help transform the *status quo*. Findings about the past should be distilled into methodologies for further action. If analytical social diagnoses are accompanied by proposals for problem solving, policy makers and practitioners are more likely to respect and apply them. Such proposals should offer more than a solemn pronouncement: "thou shalt. . . ." If recommended solutions are sound and acceptable, they should be developed and articulated as full-fledged methodologies for social action. Methodologies of this nature show *how to* achieve a certain development. Rather than rehashing endlessly what the policy objectives should be, they spell out in detail how to take processual steps for translating objectives into reality.

One need not belittle the importance of contributions to the definition of policies and objectives in order to recognize that the overdue debt of anthropology and sociology in terms of methodologies for action is considerably greater than their debt in terms of policy statements. The perennial requests of social scientists for opportunities to contribute to policy making will remain hollow and inconsistent if their contributions to policy formulation are not supported by sociologically designed operational strategies to translate policies into real life.

Applied social research results in end-products which are often different from the standard end-products of mainstream sociological and anthropological research (Freeman and Rossi, 1984). There are major differences not only between the products of fundamental sociological/anthropological research, on the one hand, and those of applied social research, on the other, but also among the different products of applied social research itself. These various types of "products" are all valid and needed. For instance, a resettlement plan for a community displaced by a reservoir lake is a different "product" from the ethnographic monograph of this village community; a methodology for organizing pastoralists into pastoral associations with range management functions is a different "product" from an anthropological analysis of the structure and function of spontaneous pastoral social organizations; a theory on kinship systems is a different social science "product" from an *ex-post facto* impact evaluation study, and so on. The differences between these products (be they epistemological, substantive, or only in the terminology used) should be understood clearly in order to facilitate their production process by social scientists engaged in applied developmental work.

My argument is that methodologies for social action are a specific type of product of applied social science. Ideally, these methodologies codify existing social experiences, sociological theoretical knowledge, and empirical findings into new sets of procedures for modeling human activities in order to achieve defined objectives. These methodologies may be regarded as "social technologies" or a part of what is often called "human engineering," "sociotechniques," or "social engineering" (Barnes 1980; First 1981; Rossi and Whyte 1983); they represent a specific body of know-how suitable for guiding the actions of human groups and institutions.

The significance of recognizing that *social methodologies are necessary* for building the "software" of development interventions and programs transcends the particular case that will be discussed below. While many technologies are available for the "hardware" components of development projects, this is usually not the case for the institutional components and the sociocultural parts of these projects. Although methodologies for software development are crucial for project success, these are not generally available in a conceptualized and operationalized form; development assistance agencies have not joined with social scientists in efforts to elaborate them. As Korten (1980) has observed, "rarely is the social scientist called on to help an organization build a capacity to actually *use* social science knowledge and data in ways that would contribute directly to improving performance.''

The scarcity of social methodologies for developing the ''software'' of development interventions is doubly counterproductive; it leaves the operational questions unanswered, and it leaves plenty of room for amateurism, incompetence, and improvisation. This scarcity is invoked by planners or managers as an excuse for neglecting the institutional and sociocultural variables, and it accounts for failures in many development interventions.

The scarcity of social methodologies is an indicator also of the underdevelopment of development sociology and anthropology. The idiosyncratic contribution of individual sociologists or anthropologists to development projects may be very valuable, but it remains a piecemeal, particularistic contribution if it is the occasional product of an individual rather than the translation of a sociological methodology (Cernea 1985). Quite often, development agencies must rely excessively on a social scientist's personal aptitudes and on the accident of his or her flair in the field, rather than on a systematized disciplinary approach. The intuition and *ad hoc* judgment of the individual sociologist or social anthropologist may be critical for a development program and ultimately may contribute to disciplinary development as well, but it is essential in the long term to replace ''ad-hocism'' with a systematic body of sociological know-how that is readily transferable and usable in operational work. Unless systematic methodologies are developed, behavioral sciences connected with development will advance only slowly. It is therefore essential to aim deliberately toward working out such social methodologies as valid endproducts of applied social research. I turn now to a presentation and discussion of a case example in which social methodologies of this nature were developed.

From Simple Advocacy to Methodology —A Case Example

The case used to illustrate the above points is the PIDER program in Mexico, under which a model for farmers' participation in local investment planning was designed, tested, and introduced. PIDER ("Programa Integral para el Desarollo Rural"—"Integrated Program for Rural Development") was established in Mexico in the early 1970s and has continued since that time. It is a major program for financing a broad range of small investments at the community level in low-income, underdeveloped rural areas. The purpose is to increase the productive capacities and improve the social infrastructure of these communities. Under PIDER, Mexico spent by the end of 1984 more than two billion United States dollars in 139 PIDER microregions with about 9,000 communities. At the Mexican Government's request, the World Bank supported the PIDER program through three massive loans in 1975, 1977, and 1981 for three projects (PIDER I, II, III), which were, in fact, slices of the overall program.

In a way, PIDER is unique in that the enormous financial resources it controls have not been invested in a handful of huge and very costly projects, but in several thousand small projects tailored to the needs and size of small villages or of subgroups within these communities. Located within the Federal Secretariat of Programming and Budgeting (SPP), PIDER does not dispense these investments itself but operates as a program that involves technical line agencies in a coordinated administrative-financial mechanism for channeling investment funds to specific small rural projects. Investments are made, for example, for small-scale irrigation systems, soil conservation projects, fruit tree plantations, rural roads, fish ponds, livestock units, rural health units, schools, potable water systems, village electrification, and so on. For this reason, it is crucial to ensure that intended beneficiaries actually participate in selecting—among the infinite number of possible local investments—those which have high priority, make better use of local resources, and address the most urgent local needs.

The priority-setting task cannot be entrusted to planners alone. Early in PIDER history it became obvious that planners lacked the requisite local knowledge to make these choices wisely. Participation of the beneficiaries in these decisions appeared as the only avenue to pursue; this was not solely for political or ideological reasons but primarily for greater efficiency and for reasons of an economic and technical nature. As Jorge Echenique, who played an important role from the outset in designing PIDER's participatory approach, observed correctly:

There is a tendency for rural development programs, PIDER included, to proclaim farmer participation, organization, and self-management. . . . But these goals are never actually defined or explained in detail. . . . As a result, this approach often goes no further than the pronouncement stage, and is not reflected or put into practice during the course of the program. The official agencies, whose inertia is evident, mostly act along their old hidebound traditional lines, defining what is to be done, how it is to be done, and who is to benefit, without having any specific knowledge of the real social and cultural context in which they are operating. Limited to a superficial view of the natural environment and resources, they entertain the naive conviction that the aspirations and needs of the rural population match their own institutional priorities, and continue to dwell in the blissful certainty that the peasants know nothing of technology, projects, and serious things of that kind. (Echenique 1979)

Against many odds, PIDER took the course of actually working out a social methodology able to elicit the involvement of farmers and the mobilization of their knowledge and material resources. The particular social action for which a methodology was developed was the planning and implementation of local investments. The objective became to make planners, executing agencies, and beneficiaries contribute to planning and implementation in a joint "participatory" manner.

The saddening results of many top-down, paternalistic, and unsustainable interventions are well known. "Participation" has become more or less a code word in development policies and programs; it has become fashionable, not only for politicians but also for planners, technocrats, and economists to promise or claim loyalty to participatory approaches. Yet the rhetoric of intent is still far ahead of the design for purposeful action. Despite high-pitched claims, participation in many rural development programs is more myth than reality. The test-question—"how participatory is 'participatory' development?" (Castillo 1983)—is fully warranted and must be asked incessantly.

No decree can introduce farmers' participation in the design of investment programs overnight. No participatory approach can evolve simply in a sanitized executive office, away from the communities for which it is destined, and then be imposed from on high. No design of a participatory procedure can be perfect and workable on the first attempt. Although these observations would seem self-evident, the designs of many rural development programs testify to the contrary. They simply proclaim participation as a goal, assume that once proclaimed it will happen by fiat, and lamentably fail because they have not taken the *processual* steps for translating the proclaimed participation into actual practice. Development sociologists and anthropologists share responsibility for this persisting discrepancy; they themselves have been more vocal about the need for participation than about the social techniques for achieving it.

Sociological advocacy for participation is not of great use if the operational and pragmatic questions asked by lay practitioners are not answered by social scientists. Such questions, *inter alia*, are: "How do we increase participation? What are the costs? . . . What are the contextual factors which make success more or less probable? How do we address problems such as class stratification and different class interests within villages. How do we link village demands with vertically integrated implementing agencies that have diverse budgets and policies? What is needed is not only the willingness to do participatory projects, but a tool kit of concepts and examples on how to proceed" (Davis 1981). This is precisely what social scientists, not to mention laymen, must know to determine whether participatory projects are feasible and how they should be accomplished.

The operational maturity of social sciences in prescribing participatory development is to be measured not just by their advocacy effort but by their capability to offer guiding models for action. As noted earlier, development practitioners *expect* sociologists and anthropologists who theorize about participation to transform their ideology into an applicable social engineering of participation.

Within the PIDER program in Mexico, the need for such a methodology was proven by experience. The conventional investment and programming system for rural communities in Mexico was unambiguously top-down: certain authorities or agencies first decided to carry out a project and notified the community later. Therefore, PIDER management decided in 1974 that a new set of procedures for identifying priority needs and optimal investments at the community level was necessary. PIDER mandated the Research Center for Rural Development (CIDER—Centro de Investigacion para el Desarollo Rural) to prepare such a methodology.

The preparation process was expected to be an effort in action-research rather than a desk-bound exercise. The goal was to develop and test empirically a set of approaches and procedures, to be eventually articulated in an *overall methodology* that would replace the top-down imposition of investment decisions with a system of planning from the bottom up.

THE CHARACTERISTICS AND CHRONOLOGY OF METHODOLOGY GENERATION

In retrospect, we can identify at least eight *key characteristics* of the process through which this social methodology was generated, as follows: (1) the presence of professional researchers; (2) multidisciplinary approach; (3) action-research orientation; (4) close linkage with a development program/organization; (5) sociological understanding of the groups and processes affected; (6) use of social experiments; (7) built-in learning mechanisms, with frequent returns to the drawing board; and (8) institutionalization of the resulting methodology. These characteristics will be examined further. The chronological chart (Table 1) that follows summarizes the main stages and junctures of the process.

Little knowledge was available at the outset for achieving PIDER's aim of the "organized participation of the local population" in investment planning. The very setting of this goal was a courageous social and political step. It confronted the lack of prior experience, the opposition of vested interest groups, and the stifling routines of entrenched bureaucracies.

In setting out to achieve this task, CIDER established a work group of professional researchers with a multidisciplinary mix of skills: social anthropology, economics, sociology, agronomy.[2] This working group was given the necessary opportunity and authority to design new methods of mobilizing local communities and to test out the devised procedures during the actual investment planning operations in several microregions.

In turn, the central CIDER-PIDER working group helped establish several *local* multidisciplinary teams (consisting of sociologists, economists, planners, and technical experts) that embarked on performing social engineering work at the microregional level. The researchers were thus in the propitious position of being linked to an

2. The core members of this central team were Jorge Echenique, Marcos Arellanos, Victor Chagoya, Antonio Monzon, and Alfonso Cano.

Table 1 Chronology of the Preparation, Testing, Application, Revision, and Retesting of the Guidelines for Participatory Programming

Period	Stage of work	Who did the work	Areas of testing or application
1975 Aug–Sept	Design (preparation of first methodology)	CIDER/PIDER staff	
1975 Oct–Dec	Field-testing	CIDER/PIDER staff	Mazahua (Edo. de Mexico)
1976 Jan–March	Field-testing	CIDER staff	Tejupilco (Edo. de Mexico); Ensenada (Baja California Norte) and other micro-regions (for annual reprogramming)
1976 April	Revision & Training Seminars (for PIDER's technicians) on Programming	CIDER staff CIDER, PIDER, and State staff	Headquarters; Baja California Sur; Sur de Yucatan; Hecelchacan (Camp); Sur de Nuevo Leon
1976 Oct–Dec	Revision & document preparation (PIDER's programming methodology)	CIDER/PIDER	Headquarters
1977 Feb–June	Application & training seminars (in different regions for PIDER and agency technicians)	CIDER/PIDER and State staff	Oriente de Morelos Poniente de Morelos
1977 July–Oct	Revision and document preparation (new document on programming)	CIDER/PIDER	Headquarters
1978 Feb–April	Application	CIDER/PIDER	Sur de Yucatan
1978 June–Oct	Partial application (of CIDER's methodology on PRODERITH/S.A.R.H. Regions)	CIDER	Ostuta (Oaxaca) Huixtla (Chiapas) Tixcancal (Yucatan)
1979 Feb–Dec	Application (including the entire plan for Zacatecas)	CIDER/PIDER and State staff	Chatina (Oaxaca); Valparaiso, Norte, Sombrerete, Pinos, Fresnillo, Jalpa (Zacatecas)
1980 Jan–Feb	Revision & document preparation (new Manual)[a]	CIDER/PIDER and coordinator	Headquarters

Date	Activity	Actors	Notes
			Costa Chica (Guerrero), Tlaltenango and Valparaiso (Zacatecas), Sur and Litoral Norte (Yucatan)
1981	Application (for full-scale programming)	SPP and agencies' staff	Additional 9 microregions financed under the PIDER III Project.
1981 April	National Seminar on PIDER	SPP Fed. and State staff	Reviewed national experience with PIDER, including participatory methodology for transfer of certain responsibilities to state level
1982 March	Issuance of Methodological Guidelines of the Support Program for Rural Community Participation (PAPCO) (focused on information and motivation)	SPP/PIDER	Application in several microregions
1982 May	Issuance of 2 manuals (on the socioeconomic analysis of rural communities and on the formulation of productive project)	SPP/PIDER	
1982 June	Issuance of manual on PAPCO (revision of March '82 guidelines)	SPP/PIDER	
1982 July	Issuance of manual (on procedures for programming-budgeting in PIDER)	SPP/PIDER	
1982 Aug–Sept	Issuance of 2 manuals (on project implementation monitoring and evaluation)	SPP/PIDER	

[a] "Manual de procedimientos para la programacion de inversiones publicas para el desarrollo rural" (Mexico, D.F.: SSP and CIDER, January 1980).

actual development program and to its agencies at the central and local level; they were enabled to work from "within," to learn from immediate observation of the ongoing processes and to obtain a multiplier effect by constantly interacting with the personnel of the action agencies.

The preparation of the participatory methodology was launched as action-oriented research. It continued over a period of several years through a series of actual social experiments in which the intermediate "products" were recurrently subjected to real-life tests. Because the same researchers did both the design and the implementation of the new procedures, they were able to avoid the trappings of a purist academic or utopian social experiment, to learn from field difficulties, and to enhance the practicality of the proposed methodology.

Reviewing the main stages and moments of this process, as reflected in the chronological chart (Table 1), one grasps the image of an incessant "dialogue" between work at the drawing board, field testing, and actual application. In fact, the back-and-forth cycle was even longer than the table suggests: from design to field testing, from testing back to the drawing board, then again to testing in the field and redesigning, then on to *training* of staff to apply the new design on a larger scale. And so the back-and-forth process continued creatively.

Designing-Testing-Learning-Revising

As noted in Table 1, the design of the participatory methodology started in 1975, and its practical testing began in the Mazahua microregion (Mexico State) in the fall of 1975. The process involved meetings at the community level, village diagnostic assessments, and other procedures. With some corrections, the initial programming design continued to be tested during the first quarter of 1976 in a larger area consisting of eight microregions: Tejupilco (Mexico State), East Morelos (Morelos State), Ensenada (Northern Baja California), and Chol, Cintapala, Zoque, Lacandona, and Bellavista (Chiapas). These tests were carried out either as the original programming of investments for a given microregion or as part of the annual exercise for reprogramming allocations made previously.

Based on these experiments, the first guidelines were drastically modified, and a more down-to-earth document was prepared. At that point, and at PIDER's request, CIDER also organized a *training pro-*

gram to start educating PIDER personnel generally about the principles and procedures of the emerging participatory methodology.

It is not my purpose here to reconstruct and describe each one of these initial or intermediate methodologies, which were provisional when they were drafted and therefore needed a succession of revisions. Rather, the intent is to emphasize the *process* of working out a methodology through trial and error, through iterative approximations and sequences of refinements.

Following two more rounds of testing and refinement of the participation-eliciting methodology (in 1976 in South Yucatan, Hecelchacan, and other microregions, and in 1977 in the Western and Eastern Morelos microregions) new recommendations were readied and applied in early 1978 through actual planning exercises in limited areas. The difference between simply "testing" and "application" was that the latter was done as part of the regular annual programming exercise, and its results were incorporated into the investment plan. Not only CIDER/PIDER staff, but many other line and technical agencies were involved. The methodology emerging from these repeated rounds was not just the output of a few imaginative minds, but the result of confronting the issues in practice and of repeated fine tunings at the drawing board.

The social experiments were difficult and complex. Different lessons were derived from microregions with varied social settings and different institutions. Messages from the field tests were often contradictory and unclear. New tests were necessary. Successfully tested principles had to be solidified in clear prescriptions, while the areas of uncertainty had to be gradually narrowed down. Firm normative prescriptions had to be built in *together with* overall flexibility, so as to allow room for local differences in applying the guidelines. The entire sequence was a social *learning process* for developing an approach based on lessons from experience.

During the designing, testing, and refining of these procedures, PIDER and CIDER continuously stressed the linkage between the *sociological* and the *technical* sides of the planning process. Participatory planning was intended to mean more than collecting a "shopping bag" of community proposals and accepting them without sound review. Understanding the sociology of the given community, its power and economic structures, was important but not enough. The social engineers of the participatory approach soon learned that a careful technical-economic scrutiny and justification of each proposal was also required. Social engineering had to go hand in hand with, and not substitute for, the technical engineering and financial soundness analysis.

This awareness led to a significant correction, by redirecting part of the efforts toward the production of analytical instruments for assessing the technical and economic soundness of local investment proposals.[3] These were necessary because the proposals emerging from communities often contained nothing more than an attractive idea, without backup technical information and economic justification. Therefore, PIDER has gradually developed instruments and standard forms for the technical and economic justifications of grass-roots proposed projects standard checklists for investment analysis, and identification guidelines for assessing the engineering requirements of projects. The use of these instruments enhanced the quality of micro-project preparation, particularly their economic and technical justification.

Another correction of the overall approach was the late but increasing recognition of the need for promoting participation not only in planning investments, but also in the implementation and monitoring of the works financed by PIDER. This modification was triggered by the 1978 mid-term evaluation of the PIDER I project, which uncovered, *inter alia,* many disastrous cases of waste of resources (Cernea 1979). These, it was felt, could have been prevented or mitigated through involvement of beneficiaries in the *execution* of the local projects and in the *monitoring* of the work performed by private contractors and technical agencies financed by PIDER. Unfortunately, a full-fledged effort to prepare a methodology for participation in project execution and monitoring (as had been done earlier for programming) was not initiated immediately after the mid-term evaluation. However, the new understanding stimulated some attempts to work out solutions, which produced results three to four years later.

3. The simultaneity in preparing both types of "instruments"—social and technico-economic—was in fact an adequate response to two fallacies often present in the arguments in favor of or against participation—the "populist" fallacy and the "paternalistic" fallacy. As has been correctly argued, the populist fallacy that the rural majority always "knows better" than the technical personnel and has sufficient skills to bring about development by itself is as erroneous as the paternalistic fallacy that the bureaucracy knows best and can do alone all that is needed for development (Uphoff and Esman 1974).

A further phase in testing the participatory programming methodology was the decision to apply it, for the first time in 1979, to an entire state—Zacatecas—for preparing the *overall* state investment plan (see CIDER 1979; Plan Estatal 1979). Compared with applying the new procedures only in selected microregions, the challenges involved in this effort and the staff resources required were of a larger magnitude than any prior testing. Altogether, diagnostic work at the grass-roots level was carried out in over 1,050 village communities in Zacatecas, and nearly 200 staff of different agencies were involved. The state plan was a result of using the participatory methodology for the first time across the board for an entire state.

One other observation that comes out from the chronology in Table 1 relates to the discontinuities that interrupted, and sometimes disrupted, the continuous process of producing and testing the methodology. To understand Table 1 better, one should know that the period of 1980 (second half) and 1981 was a time of important administrative changes in SPP/PIDER that affected the institutional arrangements for promoting participation. Major decisions to decentralize PIDER were made in 1981. These entailed the strengthening of SPP/PIDER staff at the state level, including more specific responsibilities for organizing participation and the creation of several new "support" departments in SPP headquarters to assist the participation promotion programs carried out at the state level. Also in 1981, the relationship between PIDER's management and CIDER became somewhat tense, and CIDER ceased to be involved in the further refinement or application of the participatory methodology. Although the pre-1981 experience was carried out further in the new organizational setting, there were unfortunate interruptions that caused losses of accumulated lessons. The subsequent, repeated reorganizations of PIDER also had some undesired, disruptive effects on the implementation of the participatory approach.

THE CONCEPTUAL FRAMEWORK

Backtracking a bit from the chronology of the "production process" described above, it is worth noting briefly some of the salient characteristics underlying the work during these years. The entire action-research process started with a preliminary formulation of a conceptual framework, a "philosophy" that defined the orientation toward achieving participation in investment planning and implementation. The "what" and "why" of participation were conceptualized before addressing the "how."

Under this framework, community development was regarded in PIDER as the result of combined efforts of the community itself and of government agencies at all levels: municipal, state, and federal. The sociological framework adopted for producing the methodology of participatory planning was based on an analysis of the social forces or groups involved in, or excluded from, the process of investment planning, on a critical social analysis of prior experiences with community planning, and on an evaluation of the institutions and bureaucratic agencies involved and the changes they would need to implement. The participatory methodology was intended to mobilize latent *local* resources more successfully than is done (if at all) by bureaucratic planning and to avoid unilateral decisions (and entailed errors) made by the agencies' technical staff who fail to consult community members or local authorities.

Thus, PIDER/CIDER pointed out that promoting community involvement is not an end in itself: it is essentially a means, along with other components of the program, for mobilizing local resources to achieve development. With local involvement, program activities cease to be solely external initiatives and become projects that tend to be incorporated into the life of the community as part of its own processes. In addition, community cooperation and resource mobilization for building infrastructure enables public funds to go further and to benefit a larger number of people.

One basic principle formulated by CIDER/PIDER was that the development plan should reflect the "self-definition of interests" by the beneficiary peasants. Recognizing peasants' own definition of their interests and "felt needs" is crucial for securing their participation. Therefore investments in each regional program must support proposals put forward by local peasant populations themselves. Although expert technical knowledge for identifying development potential is indispensable, PIDER took the position that officials do not automatically have a better perspective on peasants' problems than peasants have themselves; nor are they necessarily the best exponents of farmers' interests. The experts and officials fulfill their role as agents of change when they assist the peasants in becoming more aware of what the technical options for their own development are.

An objective pursued during the elaboration of the methodology for participation was to introduce the farmers' perspective into the process of planning local investments. The difficulty and novelty of this approach was to make the planners see development needs and opportunities with "farmers' eyes," rather than limit themselves to remote technical and financial assessments. By "the farmers' perspective" on a given investment, the authors of the methodology meant the evaluation that the farmers *themselves* make of a proposed project, in light of their own past experiences, resources, and current needs. This evaluation often differs from the experts' image.

However, peasant communities themselves are not monolithic and the "farmers' perspective" is not homogeneous. Therefore, provisions were built into PIDER's approach to ensure that village social stratification is recognized, and that the interests and priorities of various community subgroups (for example, irrigated or nonirrigated farmers, landless peasants, youth, women) are reflected as much as possible in the scheduling of priority investments. Again, the sociological concept underlying the recognition of the farmers' perspective is the principle of self-definition of needs.

The farmers see aspects which the remote experts may not perceive, as suggested by the following example. During a conventional investment programming exercise, the technical planning staff mockingly rejected a "crazy" written request from a village where the farmers proposed that a dance hall be constructed. A CIDER team then decided to visit the ejido which had proposed that unsuitable expenditure. It found that many of the farmers in the village were musicians and that their reputation was so good that on Sundays and holidays inhabitants of surrounding areas came to dance on improvised, open-air grounds. Most of the ejido members felt that a dance hall would be the best means of attracting more visitors, of selling local products, and thus of bringing in revenues and generating employment. In terms of rural development, as the team commented afterwards, "we wondered whether the application for a dance hall was not more justifiable than many of the 'white elephants' included by the experts in PIDER programming."

PATTERNS FOR FIELD TEAMWORK

The essential instrument for understanding the farmers' perspective in the field assessment was the community diagnosis. In the conceptual framework of the CIDER team, field assessment is a comprehensive term under which several activities have to be carried out. These include data collection regarding existing population, infrastructure, and resources in the microregion, assessment of past programs, selection of communities eligible for the program, study and diagnosis of each selected locality, meetings with local groups, selection of investment proposals, and preparation of an assessment report and of the proposed strategy.

The work of the planners' team in the communities is central to the participatory methodology. It is not possible to describe here the very detailed, culturally and socially sensitive sets of guidelines developed for the planners' fieldwork as an integral part of the overall methodology. But the general pattern is summarized in Table 2.

What this "pattern" strives to achieve is to bring together the planners and the communities to share information, to identify existing potential and needs, and to cooperate in defining the development priorities and approaches. For the planners, this is an action-oriented study and the way to learn the farmers' perspective. The planners are explicitly expected both to *learn* from the local population and *inform* the population about their technical assessments of the local opportunities for development investments. Community readiness to contribute to the investments for various projects (for instance, through labor, cash, or other contributions) is also assessed during the village diagnosis.

It is not surprising that the investment requests made by the peasants during this public analysis are often different from the solutions proposed by the experts. For instance, in the microregion Baja California Sur, the Ministry's livestock experts responded to the farmers' requests for breeding cattle by recommending the purchase of Swiss cattle. The farmers, however, had proposed Zebu cattle. The experts argued that a cross of Swiss and the local Chinampo cattle would be an excellent solution for meat and dairy yields. The villagers nevertheless insisted on Zebu, and during the meeting an interminable discussion ensued, ending only after one determined farmer described his past experience. He had purchased two Swiss breeders out of his own funds following the recommendation of the experts. However, one cow died during the first dry season; he had to keep the other in his home due to its poor physical condition. Looking into the causes, the farmer observed that during the dry season the animals had to eat the topmost leaves off the bushes, and to walk enor-

Table 2 Pattern for Field Teamwork

Activity	Purposes	Carried out by
1. General informational meeting	a. To announce the purposes of program preparation to the village population at large b. To talk with small groups and/or individuals and to identify informants c. To identify natural leaders in the different community strata d. To ask the authorities for census data (on 2.c. below)	Field team in cooperation with village population
2. Locality study	To ascertain, in general terms: a. The status of the existing general infrastructure and technologies (technical packages being used) b. The available potential resources and those to be rehabilitated c. The existent social groups and their salient features (first approximation) d. The village power structure	Part of the field team (division of work)
3. General programming meeting	To ascertain: a. The estimated production targets b. The approximate credit, input and other needs c. The investment proposal(s) and the social group making it (them) d. The ranking of the investment proposals	Part of the field team
4. Follow-up of the locality study	a. To check the technical feasibility of the proposals in the field b. To check the social acceptability and feasibility of proposals through talks with individuals and/or groups	Part of the field team

mous distances to find water, even drinking seawater at times. The Swiss cattle, with their short legs, could not get food and water in this way, but the Zebu, with their long legs, were able to reach the highest branches, even helped the other cattle to get food, and could also travel to the most distant watering points. This ended the discussion.

TRANSLATION INTO FORMAL ORGANIZATIONAL NORMS

By the early 1980s the process of designing-testing-learning-revising the methodology was virtually completed. The essential lessons had been accumulated and the methodology for participatory investment programming had already become an instrument reliable enough for widespread application. The time had come to move ahead from experimenting to institutionalizing, from testing approaches to prescribing procedures. In other words, the experience accumulated and the several generations of draft guidelines had to be synthesized into a formal methodology with normative authority for mandatory application in PIDER.

This happened with the issuance, early in 1980, of a SPP Manual for Programming containing the strategy and the detailed procedures that had emerged from the previous several years of testing (SPP 1980). This Manual was made the norm for immediately programming PIDER III areas. Numerous training seminars were organized for staff at various levels and in different regions to familiarize them with the Manual. Four states (Sinaloa, Guerrero, Zacatecas, and Yucatan) included for financing under the World Bank-assisted PIDER III project were required to use the methodology prescribed by the Manual. Investments in the first eight microregions were programmed according to this methodology in 1980 and in early 1981. This did not mean that the methodology was closed to further improvements, but rather that it was regarded as an instrument perfected enough to be introduced as the formal norm throughout the entire PIDER.

The path toward this "final" methodology was not devoid of conflicts. Besides the difficulties inherent in the mechanics of testing, there were institutional and political obstacles to overcome. At various levels in one or another agency, the bureaucracy reacted with a mix of support and reluctance, sometimes opposing the new approach openly, at other times paying it lip service while in practice sidestepping it. Even within PIDER, the acceptance by staff and managers evolved only gradually and not monolithically. In fact, at every stage that a new, revised methodology was readied, it had to be cleared formally before further application.

The team responsible for testing and refining the methodology was basically a group of applied social researchers, but those who had to approve and enforce its implementation were managers, administrators, and politicians. The views of these groups sometimes clashed. The managers often felt pressed by time and execution deadlines; they were concerned that the application of the participatory model might lengthen the planning process or entail excessive costs and staff resources. Various management teams that succeeded each other at the helm of PIDER over the years were not convinced equally that the improvements resulting from the participatory procedure would justify the greater efforts involved in planning. In turn, various line agencies at the local level recognized rhetorically that a participatory methodology was needed, but did not necessarily apply the proposed procedures in earnest.

The sociologists and anthropologists involved in changing the new methodology derived strength during this process from their increasing immersion in the technical and social-change practicalities of investment identification and planning, as well as from the ultimate support given by SPP/PIDER's senior management. This support and commitment was instrumental in keeping the social experiment going and in triggering some reorientation within the line agencies as well.

STAFF FOR IMPLEMENTING THE NEW METHODOLOGY

The production process of a social methodology is not complete without an *organizational mechanism* and the *staffing resources* able to implement it. It should not be assumed that a new approach can simply be superimposed over the existing administrative-bureaucratic organization to make the latter function differently. Reorganization is required in one degree or another; this implies some reallocation of staff resources, redefinition of functions and responsibilities, building in of learning mechanisms, and rearrangements of linkages between different units of the administration to establish the work-patterns necessary for carrying out the methodology. Korten (1980) and Uphoff (1985) define such processes as a "bureaucratic reorientation." Without such reorganization a new participatory methodology would remain a simple utopian notion, and business as usual would continue.

Although major reorganizations have happened in SPP and PIDER during the period from late 1980 to the beginning of 1983, only some of them were related to the implementation of the participatory methodology. Political reasons contributed to triggering others. Particularly relevant to setting up the mechanism for participation was the decentralization process launched in 1981 when increased authority was assigned to state governments. This decentralization was a necessary complement to promoting participation because the maintenance of tight central management control over each microregion in PIDER was no longer consonant with progress in vesting expanded rights in the local communities.

The mechanism instituted through decentralization for carrying out PIDER with increased involvement of beneficiaries called for the establishment of Subregional Rural Development Committees for each of the PIDER microregions and the assignment of additional staff to act as "support groups" (Grupos de Apoyo) to inform communities about PIDER and to make socioeconomic analyses and diagnostic assessments of project communities through direct work with their populations. This represented a significant step in institution building for participatory development and a substantial enhancement of staff resources mandated to interact directly with the local communities.

At the same time, and while essential functions were devolved from the center to the periphery, SPP considered it necessary to set up a more elaborate structure for providing support and assistance to the states in implementing their new responsibilities. Four support programs were established and staffed in SPP headquarters. These were the programs for (1) supporting participation of rural communities (PAPCO), (2) socioeconomic analysis of the rural community, (3) supporting the formulation of productive projects, and (4) the monitoring, execution, control, and evaluation of project implementation. These four central programs were mandated to carry on the effort for developing methodologies, guidelines, and manuals for their specific areas, to be used in all states.

The institutionalization of these methodological concerns in SPP/PIDER headquarters has provided additional structure and focus.

In short time, a flurry of "Lineamentos Metodologicos" (methodological guidelines) and "Manuales" were prepared and issued, elaborating further on the "how-to" aspects of the social technology for community participation. Particularly interesting is the "Manual for the Support Program for Rural Community Participation." The program is abbreviated as PAPCO (see SPP 1982c). This Manual sets forth the strategy for "information and motivation"—in other words, the approach to explaining to communities and agency staff the objectives and investment means of PIDER. At almost the same time, two other manuals were prepared and published on the socioeconomic analysis of communities and on the formulation of productive projects for local communities (SPP 1982a; 1982b). Also a revised manual on procedures for programming and budgeting in PIDER was issued in July 1982, summarizing both the justification of the participatory approach and the procedures for carrying it out. Before the 1982 year was over, two other manuals on project monitoring and on execution control were published (SPP 1982d; SPP 1982e; SPP 1982f). Each one, in varying degrees, specified ways in which the communities could and should be involved, not just in *identifying* programming investments, but also in *project implementation and monitoring.*

To sum up, the process of producing a methodology for community participation in investment programming continued in PIDER from 1975 up to 1983. Building upon previous efforts and experiences, the years 1981–84 saw an extension of previous concerns for participation in the *programming* of investments to other forms of participation, and the establishment of organizational and staffing instruments in support of the participatory methodology. In the process, prior errors have been corrected. The institutional memory of PIDER has been crystalized in guidelines and manuals, although a large part of this experience has been lost because of the high turnover in staff and managers. The new managers often do not identify themselves with the guidelines that preceded them, and the participatory orientation is threatened or undermined.

Some Lessons on Generating
a Social Methodology

The reader should recall that this essay does not attempt to describe the actual methodology for organizing participation (as it is formulated in various manuals; see the bibliography), or to demonstrate the benefits achieved by applying this methodology to the selection and execution of local investments (see Cernea 1983). Rather, my purpose is to analyze and derive lessons about *why* and *how* the learning path that CIDER/PIDER have followed has resulted in a modeling of the process of identifying, selecting, and executing local investments with people participation, and in a pragmatic methodology for actually doing it. These lessons are instructive for social researchers and development practitioners interested in creating propitious circumstances for replicating similar efforts elsewhere, and I summarize them below.

First, there was a set of facilitating circumstances that proved crucial for setting the climate and taking the organizational road toward working out a participatory methodology. These circumstances include the following: agency awareness of failure, meaning the unmitigated recognition of the ineffectiveness of prior programming procedures, and consensus on need for change; establishment of a multidisciplinary (basically social science) working group, with a shared conceptual framework, to design the new approach through sustained effort over a long period of time; support from the top echelons of the government agency (SPP); willingness to experiment in the field, to make mistakes, and to learn from them; recognition that innovative social engineering needs time and patient "laboratory" action-research before being ready for large scale generalization.

The core component of the entire process was a sustained action-research effort. The researchers were concerned with modeling the social process of local investment planning and implementation for applied purposes. The primary three functions for which action research can be used were pursued: action research was used as a social research tool, as a training tool, and as a management tool (Lenton 1981).

Further, several conclusions about sound social engineering can be derived from the entire process. Although not any one of them is necessarily a novelty to applied researchers, the approaches involved are far from being unanimously accepted. In light of this, it is relevant to note that the PIDER/CIDER experience strongly supports the following conclusions:

The elaboration of a social methodology requires the joint effort and integrated skills of professional *researchers* and development *practitioners;* they must design for "software" together.

Social engineering requires real-life *social experiments,* as opposed to the ivory-tower concoction of schemes; the model for participation of project beneficiaries is not simply a brainchild, but a pattern of social organization for development action. The establishment of this pattern requires patient set-up and observation of these experiments, learning from errors, and repeated returns to the drawing board.

Training is critical in social engineering because even partial, mid-way results have to be communicated to, and learned by the client audience; ongoing training builds up the constituency and receptivity for the products of the social engineering effort.

Sustained political commitment in support of the social engineering approach is necessary for going the distance and fighting off entrenched bureaucratic and vested-interest obstacles.

Normative institutionalization of participation has to follow after the experimental period is completed.

Organizational and staffing rearrangements must accompany the social engineering effort; no new methodology can be effective, viable, and sustainable without allocating the organizational and administrative resources it requires.

The process described above, impressive as it is in terms of continuity of efforts and quality of results, should not be regarded as the only way of "producing" a methodology for a certain type of social action. Moreover, it should not be idealized, because it had its own weaknesses, some of which have been pointed out here. Nevertheless, it is one of the relatively few cases in which a team of applied social researchers worked with continuity over a period of several years to produce a methodology for participation, rather than a simple advocacy and loud pronouncements; a methodology designed carefully and based on social analysis and social experiments, rather than improvised hastily with more enthusiasm than meticulous social design.

The "production" experience described here is one that needs to be replicated by other applied researchers, with adequate adjustment to their areas, if we are to develop more adequate theories and methodologies useful for purposive development activities.

11

THE CHANGING ROLE OF AN APPLIED ANTHROPOLOGIST

John H. Peterson, Jr.

As Cernea observed in the previous essay, practical social innovations are the product of learning experiences that engage practitioners and human communities in long-term interaction. In this essay, John H. Peterson describes the continuous process of change and adaptation experienced by the practitioner as he or she works with a human community. New situations present unique learning opportunities, and the practitioner's role changes in response to accumulated experience and in relation to the changing needs and capabilities of the community served.

For several years, Peterson has worked with and for the Mississipi Choctaws. Over time, the working relationships have changed significantly in response to changes that have occurred among the Choctaws and in Peterson's own professional development. At the outset, he articulates the uncertainties felt by many who accept the commitment to undertake practical work and fear that their choice will jeopardize their professional status with those who choose more academic career pat-

John H. Peterson, Jr. (Ph.D., Georgia) is director of the Cobb Institute of Archaeology and professor of anthropology at Mississippi State University. His fieldwork has been among the Mississippi Choctaw. He has done applied work as chief planner for the Choctaw Tribal Government, as project director for water resource development and information dissemination in northeast Mississippi, and in bilingual education among the Choctaw. He has been a Congressional fellow of the American Anthropological Association and a consultant to the National Science Foundation, the Brookings Institute, the United States Army Corps of Engineers, the Mississippi Band of Choctaw Indians, the Library of Congress, the National Academy of Sciences, and several educational institutions.

The basis for this chapter can be found in a series of papers: Peterson (1973a; 1973b; 1974a; 1974b) which describe my changing role with the Choctaw Tribe. Detailed descriptions of the Mississippi Choctaws can be found in Peterson (1970a; 1970b; 1972); Peterson, Spencer and Kim (1974); and Thompson and Peterson (1975).

terns. When Peterson first began to work among the Choctaws, he did not know that they would continue the work of educating him as an applied anthropologist and that he had much to learn. This essay describes this learning experience and the contributions that practicing anthropology can make to the professional development of the anthropologist.

Today, sixteen years after his initial decision to become a tribal employee, Peterson has the satisfaction of knowing that the collaborative and changing relationships he has had with the tribe have indeed contributed to the development of the Choctaw community. The best evidence is that the Choctaw people now fill the roles and perform the functions that he once was employed to carry out on their behalf.

THE ESSAY DESCRIBES the changing relationship between one anthropologist and one client group, the Mississippi Choctaws. During the past sixteen years, my role as an anthropologist changed from that of a neophyte fieldworker to a middle-aged administrator at a nearby university. My positions with the client group included working as an externally funded fieldworker, unpaid friend, paid consultant, full-time tribal employee, subcontractor on tribal programs, and appointed member of the Choctaw Heritage Council. The client group changed from an Indian tribe just beginning to question the complete authority of the almost totally white-staffed Choctaw Agency, a branch of the Bureau of Indian Affairs (BIA), to an aggressive tribal government with major tribally owned industrial enterprises and an Indian-directed Choctaw Agency. Under the circumstances, my role as anthropologist shifted in accordance with my own knowledge and capabilities, the needs of the Choctaws with whom I was working, and their knowledge and capabilities for utilizing my anthropological skills and talents.

The approximately 6,000 Mississippi Choctaws live in seven small reservation communities scattered across a seven-county area centered in east central Mississippi. They are the descendants of those who resisted both the general Indian removal from the Southeast in the early 1800s and a later removal effort in 1903. These Choctaws were not legally recognized as an Indian tribe until 1918, when the Choctaw Agency was established. The Agency bought land in the areas of existing population concentration, thereby creating the seven separate reservation communities of today. Although medical and educational services were provided from the very beginning, the Choctaw Agency has been underfunded throughout its history. As a result, the educational level remained extremely low until the past decade. There was little out-migration, and the population remained primarily Choctaw-speaking. A tribal council was not established until 1945, and most issues on the reservation continued to be determined by the Choctaw Agency.

I first visited the Mississippi Choctaw reservation in 1967 when preparing to undertake fieldwork for my dissertation. I was accompanied by Professor Wilfrid C. Bailey, who had previously assisted the Choctaw Agency in carrying out a total tribal survey in 1962. I originally intended to focus my research on the Choctaw schools. I had hoped to enter the field supported by the GI bill and a small research grant from the University of Georgia.

The Agency superintendent strongly discouraged me from attempting a school study because a major new program in the schools had recently caused some disruption. He felt that another outsider would only exacerbate the situation and increase the confusion. Instead, he proposed a new tribal survey along the lines previously carried out by Professor Bailey. If I were willing to complete a questionnaire, train and direct interviewers, and analyze and prepare a final report, the Choctaw Agency would supply ten people to undertake the survey. Under the circumstances, this seemed to be a good alternative to my original plan. So I returned to the University of Georgia to complete my academic work there, and to draft a questionnaire. I returned to the reservation at the end of the spring term, 1968.

Anthropological Field-Worker

Arrangements were made for me to share office space in the Branch of Social Services of the BIA in Philadelphia, Mississippi, which is located seven to fifteen miles from the three reservations in the county and much further from the remaining reservations located in nearby counties. The location was ideal for the purposes of working with agency interviewers, checking interview forms for accuracy, and comparing interview data with other available data. Further, since interviewers were selected from many different branches of the Agency, including social services, home economics, employment assistance, credit, and education, I had an excellent opportunity to rapidly gain an impression of the Choctaw people and the Agency programs for them. As a result, I soon developed a degree of insight into the various BIA programs as well as into individual employees.

Through daily interaction with BIA employees within their own offices, I observed the vast range of attitudes toward the Choctaws associated with different programs, and between individuals on the same program. Within the BIA structure, there was a general dichotomy between those who perceived themselves as working for the Choctaws and those who perceived themselves as working for the BIA. Although the local distinction was never made in these terms, the "hard-liners" took a literal letter-of-the-regulation attitude and described others as "soft on Indians." In contrast, those who perceived their jobs as working on behalf of the Choctaws viewed the "hard-liners" as legalistic bureaucrats.

As the months passed, I began to feel that I was buried under a mound of questionnaries. Nevertheless, I took pride in the fact that I was avoiding the conflict between the "hard-liners" and the "soft-liners." I felt I was carrying out the ideal role of the applied anthropologist by finding a balance point between my own research interests, the interests of the client group, the Choctaws, and the interests of the service agency, the BIA.

Because I worked with the personnel and in the offices of the Choctaw Agency. I was often perceived by others as an Agency employee. Even those who knew differently classified me as working with the Agency rather than as an independent researcher, since the task of supervising the survey occupied most of my time during Agency working hours. This was no great disadvantage in terms of meeting the Choctaw people, however, since most community activities took place at night in the form of intercommunity ball games in the summer, school related activities during the winter, and church activities throughout the year. As the year passed, I came to know many of the Choctaw people personally; nevertheless most Choctaws continued to perceive me as an Agency employee.

There was little reason for the Choctaws to assume that I was not an Agency employee. With the exception of two candidates for master's degrees who had undertaken brief periods of summer research, there had been no major anthropological field research among the Choctaws for almost thirty years. Indeed, one of my aims was to create a role of anthropological researcher working on behalf of the Choctaw people. For this reason, I periodically reported on the progress of the survey to the tribal chairman, as well as to the superintendent of the Choctaw Agency. The tribal chairman, Mr. Emmett York, was supportive of my work. Thus, although the majority of the Choctaw people did not know of my work, I believed the role of independent researcher was being accepted by the Indian leaders with whom I had direct contact.

UNANTICIPATED CONFLICT OVER RESEARCH DATA

In the closing days of my fieldwork, this illusion was rudely shattered. Robert Benn, the housing officer of the Choctaw Agency, was preparing a proposal for a federal housing program and was able to use the questionnaires to determine the number of potentially eligible families. I was pleased with this development; it underscored my assumption that the survey results would be of benefit to the Choctaw people. Shortly thereafter, a private company, under contract to the BIA, for relocation training, also requested use of the raw data and offered secretarial assistance for cross-checking the validity of questionnaire information. The head of the Choctaw Community Action Agency also offered secretarial help for this purpose. Both organizations were interested in using the raw data for the preparation of refunding or supplementary funding proposals for their respective programs. It seemed like a good idea to me. It would save time, make the data available sooner, and hopefully result in expanded programs for the Choctaw people.

My positive feelings about the above requests were not shared by the leaders of the Choctaw Agency. They informed me that data collected by personnel of the Choctaw Agency belonged to the Agency, and that I should not have entered into such discussions without their prior approval. Suddenly, satisfaction about my role as an applied anthropologist who worked in the interests of both the Choctaw people and the agencies serving them fell apart. I was forced to recognize that only my previous insignificance, in terms of the forces operating on the Choctaw reservation, had protected me from the conflict which now engulfed me. The potential importance of my work did not become evident until the questionnaires were used to support the Choctaw Agency's housing effort. It was after this event that other organizations on the reservation expressed interest in the survey and the analysis of the data for their own purposes.

I had been keenly aware of the conflicting attitudes toward the Choctaws and their needs among the different branches of the Choctaw Agency. I belatedly understood the existence of potential conflict among all agencies working on the Choctaw reservation. I was informed that since the bulk of the effort behind the tribal survey had been furnished by the Choctaw Agency, the decision for the release of the data must be made by the Agency. At this point, I feared that nine months of work would go down the drain. However, an agreement was reached that no data would be released to any individual or group prior to completion of a published report. This compromise insured that the data would become public property, thus safeguarding my need for use of the data as well as the needs of other organizations working on the Choctaw reservation.

From hindsight, I realize that part of the dispute over the data was due to my naïveté and failure to make detailed written agreements concerning the project prior to undertaking the task of directing the survey. At the same time, the direct experience with this problem of ownership of research data provided me with a more graphic education about the problems of applied anthropology than I would have otherwise obtained.

Ironically, I had been trying for many months to disassociate myself in the minds of tribal officials from employees of the Choctaw Agency. When they came to understand that I was an independent researcher. I found that in fact I was not. My only choice was to return to the private firm and the Choctaw Community Action Program and explain why I could not accept the offer of help on the survey, and to promise that I would get the material into print as rapidly as possible so that it would be available to everyone. Although this decision was accepted with relatively good grace, I felt that I had let the tribe down. This situation was to affect my choice of a job in the year following the completion of my fieldwork.

Academic Anthropologist

With my fieldwork drawing to a close, I began looking for an academic position. While I was being interviewed by several universities outside the state, I was asked if I would be interested in a potential position with the Choctaw Agency. I was told that I could be assigned to complete the survey. The salary was higher than that which had been offered by universities and, given my financial situation, I was tempted to accept the offer. But the tribal chairman, with whom I discussed the matter, stated bluntly that if I accepted the position, I would be on the other side of the fence, and we could no longer be friends. Moreover, my major professor emphasized the importance of completing the dissertation and beginning publication if I wished to be an anthropologist.

Since I had just spent several years studying to be an anthropologist and felt obligated to the Choctaw Tribe, I decided to take a university position. Because I had over 500 household surveys to analyze, support for data analysis was a primary consideration. Only nearby Mississippi State University could provide both released time and funds for code clerks and data analysis; so in July 1969, I accepted my first academic appointment there as a full-time researcher with the Social Science Research Center.

When I began my work at Mississippi State, I believed that the conflict I had experienced could be resolved by getting my data into print quickly so that it would be equally accessible to all parties, and my obligations as an objective scholar would be fulfilled. Within a year, I completed both a research report and my dissertation. I was gratified to find that my published data were found useful by both the Choctaw Tribe and the Bureau of Indian Affairs. I was almost convinced that my earlier questioning of the role of the applied anthropologist was premature and resulted largely from my inexperience.

TECHNICAL ASSISTANCE TO THE TRIBE

Upon the completion of the research report, I began to receive requests for assistance from the Choctaw Agency, the Choctaw Tribe, and the Choctaw Community Action Agency, headed by Phillip Martin, a Mississippi Choctaw. At first, these requests were primarily for specific socioeconomic or historical data needed for program planning or funding requests. In giving this technical assistance, there was never any question of consultant fees or research potential. I was not working as an outside consultant; rather I was simply helping my neighbors and friends. For example, I was asked by the Branch of Employment Assistance of the Choctaw Agency to reanalyze the Choctaw population and employment data to fit the data categories required by the BIA semiannual manpower report. At the request of the tribal chairman, I worked with HUD planners to provide data to meet the needs of the Choctaw Planning Commission.

A broader range of requests came from the Choctaw Community Action Program, and I gradually became involved in considerable technical writing which went beyond simple data analysis. This expanded role was not a new development. Even during my initial fieldwork, I had prepared a critique of a proposed Indian village development proposal at the request of the tribal chairman and the Choctaw Agency. The difference now was primarily in terms of increasing frequency and scope of these later requests.

The technical assistance I provided was quite different from my earlier role as an independent researcher who I hoped was contributing to both the Choctaw Agency and Choctaw Tribe. The new role was essentially one of technical assistance in the preparation of what might be called background briefs such as proposals, position papers, and correspondence supporting a Choctaw position. The word "advocate" has sometimes been used to describe this role, but the term is misleading in that the tribal leaders were completely capable of personally presenting their own cases and in outlining the scope and content of the written material they wished me to prepare. My task was to translate their ideas into a written form acceptable to agency officials and elected representatives, and to provide detailed supporting data. One of the primary factors in the increasing number of requests for my help was my willingness to offer such support without formal recognition that I had given it.

As time passed, I became involved in projects which went beyond the socioeconomic or historical data I had under my control. Hence, I was dependent upon being furnished information which would not normally have been available to me but was now provided. My access to information was given with the understanding that I would use it to document the case in hand. I made no attempt to keep notes on either the data or the discussions of the direction which the draft material should take. I believed it would be unethical to utilize information, given to me in confidence for a specific task, as data for possible future academic publications.

With the election of Phillip Martin as tribal chairman in 1971, my involvement rapidly increased. Under Martin's direction, the tribal government was restricted by the 1971 Tribal Council (Mississippi Band of Choctaw Indians 1972–1973). Community Action programs and tribal programs were consolidated, and the Tribal Council adopted the goal of an expanded effort in self-development and self-determination. Unlike the previous tribal administration, the 1971–1973 tribal administration established a Tribal Planning Center. As a result, rather than working alone, I found myself working on assignments with other consultants or members of the tribal planning staff. In most of these efforts, the fact that I was an anthropologist was not as important as whether I could provide the needed technical assistance. Rather than preparing initial drafts of documents for tribal leaders which were then reviewed by others, I myself reviewed documents prepared by full-time tribal employees and suggested revision. Thus my role had changed from that of technical writer to a technical adviser. As a technical writer, I had worked on specific issues, proposals, or documents. With the consolidation of tribal programs, these individual efforts became less important than the contribution they made to the overriding cause of Choctaw self-development. I began to understand the importance of every action becoming part of an expanded effort at tribal self-government under the direction of the Tribal Council.

UNANTICIPATED CONFLICT OVER TIME COMMITMENT

As my activities increased, I began to experience some conflict with my position in the university. From the beginning, my university appointment had been predominantly in research, with only one-fourth to one-half of my time spent in teaching. In my academic role, I was continuing typical work as an applied anthropologist. In simple terms, my salary at the university partially depended on my ability to secure funds for applied research projects. But, the more I assisted the tribe, the less time I had to invest in securing funds for my own university-based work. As I assisted both the tribe and other branches of the university in developing programs for the Choctaws, senior faculty members within my own department began to ask questions about the potential benefit of my activities for the department. As a junior non-tenured faculty member, these questions were a cause of concern to me. Fortunately by the spring of 1972, funds were secured for a joint university–tribal effort in the field of education, which allowed me to work with the Tribe under a subcontract, in ways which more nearly approximated my other efforts in applied anthropology.

Full-Time Tribal Employee

Before the above program became operational, the tribal chairman requested that I take a leave of absence from the university to become chief of the Choctaw Planning Center. This request caused me to seriously consider my role as an applied anthropologist. By means of the subcontract, I had hoped to reduce the pressure on me by becoming a university-based researcher working on a funded research project with the Tribe. Yet, now I was being asked to become a full-time tribal employee for a year. I worried about my status within the profession. As a young anthropologist, how would a year of nonproductivity, in an academic sense, affect my career? A future factor in my consideration was the growing conflict between the Choctaw Agency and the Tribal Council as the latter continued to press for expanded self-government on the reservation. Members of the Council were actively advocating the replacement of the Agency superintendent. I was still agonizing over my decision when I was warned by Choctaw Agency personnel who were unfavorable to the tribal government, that a petition was being prepared for recall of the tribal chairman. Even if this move was unsuccessful, it was doubtful that there would be sufficient funds to permit the tribe to employ me. At this point, my position in anthropology seemed to be less important than my willingness to respond to a request to support Choctaw efforts and to trust the tribal government to provide the financial assistance to enable me to do so.

I have elsewhere described some of the general orientations and skills which were required in my position as chief of the Tribal Planning Center (Peterson 1974b). It is more difficult to describe the change that this position brought about in my relationship with the tribe. The title of chief of the Planning Center created humor, especially among Choctaw friends who would remark, "Now we have a white man chief." A solution to this problem occurred when an older Choctaw brought me a newspaper clipping which described my appointment. The headline stated "Anthropologist Appointed Tribal Aide." I was told, "John, now I know what you are doing."

Titles such as chief of the Planning Center or chief planner indicated someone in authority who was responsible for telling others what to do. On the other hand, several positions on the reservation utilized people as "aides" such as teacher aides, nurses' aides, and social service aides. I used this description of "tribal aide," as a mental orientation to my job. This approach was also taken by the tribal chairman when he introduced me and other new employees at a series of community meetings. He simply stated that he had asked me to leave the university for a year and come down and "help out."

The difficulty in undertaking my new assignment was the identification of exactly whom I was to help out. When based at the university, I undertook efforts which I believed were helpful to the tribe generally. When I had been previously requested to carry out a specific assignment, I worked on a single program or with a specific group. But as a full-time employee of the tribe, I had to fit into the structure of an existing tribal government. Although I understood the need for the overall goal of increasing tribal self-government, there were multiple relationships to be established with many individuals and groups.

The Planning Center was organized to provide technical assistance to the Tribal Council as the governing body of the Tribe. The Council was composed of sixteen members representing seven distinct reservation communities. The chairman of the Council was employed as the full-time top administrative officer of the Tribe and charged with implementing the decisions of the full Council. As a result, the Planning Center worked directly under the tribal chairman. The work of the Center was intended to assist the chairman in the implementation of policy decisions decided upon by the Tribal Council as a whole.

It would be simplistic to state that members of the Planning Center could assist the entire Tribe by carrying out the direct instructions of the tribal chairman. Any active tribal chairman is far too busy to be able to give detailed daily instructions to his staff. In the case of Choctaw tribal chairman, Phillip Martin, this involved some twenty-two separate program directors. He also served as the official spokesman of the Tribe in negotiations and program coordination with state agencies, various federal agencies, and related agencies on the reservations, such as the Choctaw Agency and the Public Health Service. This resulted in extensive travel on behalf of the specific tribe and of Indians in general. Finally, a tribal chairman is an elected official whose door must be open to all tribal members.

In summary, members of the Planning Center worked under the broad direction of the tribal chairman to implement the policy decisions of the Tribal Council. They were forced to learn to anticipate the desired means for carrying out these broad instructions and were subject to the approval of the tribal chairman and Council. One consequence of this situation was that the Planning Center was potentially subject to the same diversity of interests as those to which the chairman had to respond. In discussing my potential employment with the Tribal Planning Center, the tribal chairman made clear that one of my specific responsibilities was to maintain a balance between these diverse pressures.

At the time of my employment, there were two polar viewpoints expressed by individuals within the Planning Center. The first of these viewed the Center as accountable solely to the tribal chairman. When carried to an extreme, this perspective led to a lack of communication with other Council members, the Choctaw population, and representatives of other agencies. The negative aspect of this position was that it tended to result in a definition of the Center as an elitist group of non-Choctaws who planned actions for the Choctaw reservation without sufficient input from the Choctaw people. More positively, this position clearly removed planners from policy or political decisions and reserved these for the Tribal Council.

In contrast to those who held the above position, others believed that true implementation of increased self-government on the reservation demanded close interaction between reservation planners, all Council members, and a broad base of community members. The positive aspect of this view was a broader understanding of policy alternatives by both Choctaw officials and planners. The negative aspect was that planners became involved in policy decisions which were the legal responsibility of the Tribal Council. My charge was to insure that the Planning Center achieved a degree of balance between these two alternatives. I was employed not so much because my judgment in this context was superior to that of other planners, but because I had the necessary background and knowledge to understand the various alternatives.

The second charge I received at the time of my appointment was to effect liaison with the BIA and other agencies. Other planners within the Planning Center were young men committed to the common cause of Indian self-government, but with divergent views about the best ways of implementing this goal. Because of their youth and enthusiasm, they tended to take a combative attitude toward the Bureau of Indian Affairs. The tribal chairman made it clear that, despite the political and policy conflicts between the Tribal Council and officials of the Choctaw Agency, it was my responsibility to establish amicable working relationships between tribal and Agency personnel at the program level so that effective delivery and coordination of services could be maintained while political and policy issues were being resovled. This was easier for me than for other tribal planners since I had been working with many Choctaw Agency employees for several years.

My new position had an important effect on my relationship with the Tribe. I was now a tribal employee, answerable directly to the tribal government, and working daily with many members of the Tribe, but especially with tribal program personnel and elected tribal officials. Some of these were older people whom I had met in the past, while others were younger individuals whom I had first met when they were college students. Whereas my doctoral field work had located me in the offices of the Choctaw Agency and labeled me as working for the Agency, I was now labeled as working for the Tribe. Even today, when I meet Choctaws, I am asked, "Didn't you once work for the Tribe?" It is a quite different relationship from that of student field worker or part-time technical assistant, and one that I cherish.

At the end of my leave of absence, I returned to Mississippi State University on sabbatical leave. I had hoped to devote much of my time to writing about my recent experience on the reservation, but this was not to be the case. First, I had to devote considerable time to technical assistance as other people began to take up the work I had left uncompleted on the reservation. Second, a new relationship had developed between Mississippi State University and the Choctaw Tribe during my leave of absence.

Previously, since entrance examinations at the university had blocked admission of more than one or two Choctaw students, the remainder usually went to college in other states. During my year on the reservation, meetings between tribal and university officials resulted in entrance requirements for Choctaws, which recognized their problems with the English language. This increased degree of cooperation enabled the Choctaw Tribe to secure funding for an Indian teacher training project which they subcontracted to Mississippi State University. Through this project and a related one, eighteen Choctaw students enrolled in a university which had formerly not recognized their existence (Martin, Peterson, and Peterson 1975:1–9). Some of these students had been fellow employees the preceding year, and considerable time was required in assisting them to adjust to the university. It was also necessary to help faculty become accustomed to having Choctaw students. The success in this first year led to an expansion of cooperative university-tribal efforts which included, in addition to the Indian teacher training program, a bilingual program, an educational evaluation project, and a manpower survey to replicate my earlier survey. I was the principal investigator for the university phase of most of these programs and was looking forward to a second attempt to establish my role as an applied anthropologist, this time under contract from the Tribe. Unfortunately, the scope of my activities was limited, this time by a request from the university rather than the Tribe.

University Administrator
and Program Coordinator

Anthropology was scheduled to become a separate department during the same year that the above contracts were to be carried out. The coordinator of anthropology, who had laid the groundwork for establishing the department, resigned to accept another position. At the request of university officials, I assumed the headship of the new department in addition to my research commitments. Thus, I had to hire other people to carry out the research I had intended to do my-self. I became more a research supervisor and administrator than re-searcher.

Even worse was the conflict between my position as contractor to the Tribe and my responsibility as a university administrator. In the past, I had been somewhat critical of the university's response to tribal needs. Now, I experienced firsthand the problems created by the limitations of funds and personnel in an academic department and the need to insure that work carried out for the Tribe did not exhaust available resources. My discussions with tribal officials seemed to be limited to contracts, finances, and personnel. The conflict between my role as director of some of the Indian programs and as head of an academic department became apparent. I could not give sufficient time to the department, and was unable to provide any assistance to the Tribe beyond contract obligations.

ACADEMIC ANTHROPOLOGIST AGAIN

In preparing for academic year 1975–76, both the university and tribal administrators agreed that Indian programs in the university should be carried out by people with a full-time commitment to each and that I should devote full time to university teaching and administra-tion. In 1976 I was already somewhat nostalgic when I ended this essay by observing that both I and the young Choctaw professionals with whom I had worked had moved to leadership positions in our respective bureaucracies:

most of us have become "established." We are no longer on the outside saying, "Why doesn't the university, or the Tribe, or the Agency do some-thing about this?" We are now experiencing the limitations of the bureau-cracies in which we work. We spend more time on budgets, personnel ac-tions, and committees than on discussions of what we really believe should be done. . . .

There is an attractiveness in my past role of full-time tribal employee. There was great freedom in the lack of organizational responsibility which enabled me to work with the full energy and dedication of youth attempting to un-derstand and change social system without preoccupation with either bureau-cratic or ivory tower concerns.

While my involvement with the Choctaws has been less intense in recent years, it is now (1985) sixteen years since I arrived at the

Choctaw reservation for one year of anthropological fieldwork. This additional passage of time permits me to add a brief report on a remarkable tribal success story, and to reflect upon what has now become a long term involvement with the Choctaws.

When I returned to full-time university employment in 1975, the Choctaw tribal government had already demonstrated significant change. At the end of my first period of fieldwork in 1969, Tribal Chairman Emmett York indicated that he wished he could offer me a job, but the Tribe lacked the necessary resources. Under Tribal Chairman Phillip Martin, I was the first academic professional to be hired under the expanded tribal programs. By 1975, three Ph.D.s and three individuals who had completed Ph.D. course work were on the tribal payroll. Thus the more general technical assistance I had given earlier was less needed because the tribal government had employed a full-time technical staff.

My relationship with the Tribe was also temporarily altered by political developments. As part of the effort to strengthen the tribal government, the Tribe had adopted a new constitution providing for a directly elected tribal chief with a four-year term. In the first election for this office in 1975, the tribal chairman under whom I had worked was defeated. The new chief was a man whom I had known for some time, but for whom I had never worked directly. I had naively assumed that I could continue working with the new chief as I had with the two past tribal chairmen. But while I had perceived my role as nonpolitical, it soon became apparent that others had perceived me as a supporter of the former chief. From hindsight, it is obvious that a close working relationship with a political leader could not avoid having political consequences. I remained friendly with the new chief, but he did not call me for assistance. However, I remained involved in two long-standing court cases.

In the first of these cases, I assisted Choctaw lawyers with historical research related to a challenge to the legal existence of the Choctaw Tribe in Mississippi. This case was ultimately decided in favor of the Choctaws by the United States Supreme Court in 1978. Historical evidence I produced was used in final oral argument before the court. I also assisted the Lawyer's Committee for Civil Rights under the Law with historical research in a challenge to racial bias in Mississippi history books, and served as an expert witness before the United States District Court for Northern Mississippi in 1979. This case was also favorably decided, resulting in state adoption of a text-book which describes more realistically the historical role of the Choctaws and blacks in Mississippi history.

Soon after these cases were decided, Mr. Martin was elected as Chief in 1979 with a primary goal of economic development. Even before assuming this office, he was active in negotiations to establish an automotive electrical parts assembly plant on the reservation. A former tribal employee, who had completed a Ph.D. in economics, joined the Mississippi State University staff in 1978 to become the primary university contact with the tribal government. Between 1979 and 1985, the Choctaws' industry grew to include four automotive electrical assembly plants, and a greeting-card assembly plant. With over 700 industrial jobs being added on the reservation during a time of general economic decline, the Choctaw efforts at self-development began to achieve national notice. A national educational television program highlighted tribal development and their progress was described in an article in *Reader's Digest* (Michelmore 1984:2–6).

The Choctaws had achieved not only an effective tribal government, but a strong and complex tribally owned industrial enterprise. With Mr. Martin back in office, my role with the tribe has increased, but remains minor compared with the current scope of activities. As a broadly trained applied anthropologist, I had been of most assistance to the tribe when they were just beginning to develop a structured tribal government, and when their effort had been primarily in the area of human services. By the time I left tribal employment these activities were staffed by highly qualified permanent tribal employees. The new thrust in tribal economic development required special skills in financial and economic planning which I do not possess.

As the one hundred and fiftieth anniversary of the original treaty of Choctaw removal approached, a new role for me developed. As the Choctaws responded with public and scholarly presentations, Chief Martin and the Tribal Council recognized that it was appropriate to provide more support for cultural preservation. The Tribal Council established a Choctaw Heritage Council and a Choctaw Museum and Archives in 1981. As an appointed member of the Heritage Council, my work with the Choctaws over the past four years has more nearly resembled traditional anthropological interests of ethnohistory and cultural preservation. Within the past year, I have also participated with tribal leaders in economic development symposiums at both the annual meetings of the Society for Applied Anthropology and at programs funded by the Federal Government. These have provided a basis for mutual reflection upon the role of an anthropologist with the Choctaws.

In Retrospect

From the perspective of the past sixteen years, the most useful research I accomplished for the Choctaws was the complete socioeconomic and demographic surveys of the Tribe (Peterson 1970a, 1974) and the assistance I gave for later surveys by the tribe. A recent monograph on *Long-Term Field Research in Social Anthropology* (Foster, Scudder, Colson, Kemper 1979:332–334) emphasizes the importance of the collection of a set of basic core demographic data against which to measure future change. But most long-term studies (or, in my case, a long term relationship) appear to be largely accidents of circumstance. Where there is no anticipation of future continued study, there is little motivation for the laborious effort which must go into the collection of such survey data. The value of good base-line data on an entire tribal group is often unrecognized in applied programs. Collection of such data is frequently beyond the resources of a tribal government or of specific programs or research projects. While collection of the core data was probably my greatest single contribution to the Choctaws, my ability to utilize these data for specific purposes was a major factor in establishing a long-term relationship. Fifteen years after the publication of the first socioeconomic study, tribal planners and industrial developers still emphasize the importance of this base study in current activities. It has provided a documentation for the great strides made in improving all aspects of Choctaw life. The striking improvements made in general educational levels through adult education and related training programs is of particular interest to industrial prospects who are interested in how a population will respond to training for modern technological jobs.

Foster, *et al.* (1979:344) are correct in indicating that long-term involvement leads to more of an "Action or Advocacy" stance. In my case an initial decision to collect a body of useful data for tribal planning resulted in the development of both a long-term relationship and an advocacy stance. The Choctaw experience has contributed more than any other activity to my professional growth, and this relationship still remains the most valuable personal reward I have from my career in anthropology.

12

LEARNING TO BE AN ANTHROPOLOGIST AND REMAINING "NATIVE"

Beatrice Medicine

Both Cernea and Peterson have reported that the role of the practicing anthropologist entails working amidst institutional restraints and groups with conflicting interests and goals. For native Americans and other minorities, these restraints and divergent demands are experienced in a highly personal way. Beatrice Medicine vividly describes her experiences of learning to be an anthropologist while still remaining a native American.

Medicine's identity as a Sioux creates problems of professional identity as an anthropologist when colleagues persist in using her as an informant. Her identity as an anthropologist opens the door to similar exploitation by the Sioux, who view her as a counselor and a liaison to agencies outside the reservation community. As an advocate of Sioux interests, Medicine is especially concerned with this latter role.

While Medicine is not a tribal employee, as was Peterson, her professional status results in demands for her specialized knowledge and skills. These demands are often emotionally stressful. Her advocate role requires commitment to her people as a whole in the face of segments

Beatrice Medicine (Ph.D., Wisconson—Madison) is associate professor of anthropology at California State University, Northridge. She is currently on leave and is professor of anthropology and director of the Native Studies program at the University of Calgary, Canada. She is actively engaged in fieldwork among numerous Indian groups in Canada and the United States. Her teaching career began in three schools sponsored by the United States Indian Service—Haskell Institute; United Pueblos Agency; and Flandreau, South Dakota. She has taught anthropology at the University of British Columbia, the University of Montana, the University of Washington, the University of South Dakota, Dartmouth College, and Stanford University. Her research interests are in the areas of bilingual education, women's studies, native belief systems, and alcoholism. Her work as an advocate for native issues stems from a strong commitment to indigenous peoples and the application of anthropological knowledge to policy decisions and legal affairs.

and factions which press for diverse and special interests. The hierarchical relationships between governmental and other service agencies and the human communities which receive the policies and programs designed by the dominant society create formidable tasks for her role as a culture broker.

I AM A part of the people of my concern and research interests. Sometimes they teasingly sing Floyd Westerman's (1969) song "Here Comes the Anthro" when I attend Indian conferences. The ambiguities inherent in these two roles of being an "Anthro" while at the same time remaining a "Native" need amplification. They speak to the very heart of "being" and "doing" in anthropology. My desire to be an anthropologist has been my undoing and my rebirth in a very personal way, but this topic is outside the scope of this contribution.

Recently, many students—particularly native Americans—have been dazzled by Vine Deloria Jr.'s scathing attack on "Anthros," as we are called by most native Americans. His article, which first appeared in *Playboy* (August 1969), has since been reprinted in many anthropological works. Besides serving as a "sweat bath" to purge anthropologists of their guilt feelings, it has become a rallying cry for Indian militants and tribal peoples alike. Many native peoples have articulated their discontent with the exploitative adventures of "Anthros" in the American Indian field. (See, for example, a symposium entitled *Anthropology and the American Indian,* held in San Diego at the 1970 annual meeting of the American Anthropological Association, and published by the Indian Historian Press, 1973.) However, native readers seemingly do not go beyond page 100 of Deloria's manifesto entitled *Custer Died For Your Sins.* Later, he states: "This book has been the hardest on those people in whom I place the greatest amount of hope for the future—Congress, the anthropologists, and the churches" (1969:275). Since the churches and Congress have eroded my faith in the institutions of the dominant society, I shall focus on anthropology. It is, after all, the source of my livelihood.

"Anthropologist" as a role designation has been traditionally meaningful to American Indians or, as we have recently been glossed,

"Native Americans." In the early days of American anthropology, we were seen as "vanishing Americans." Thus, students of Boas collected data on Plains Indian reservations and Northwest Coast villages in order to recapture "memory cultures" which reflected the "golden days" of natives whose aboriginal culture was denigrated and whose future was seen as oblivion or civilization. Many feel that American anthropology was built upon the backs of natives (De-Laguna 1960:792), but the contributions of American Indians to the discipline has never been fully assessed. (Recently, Panday [1972] has detailed the interactions of "Anthros" and natives at Zuni pueblo.)

Initially, it was Franz Boas' interest in folklore, linguistics, and other aspects of culture which led him to seek and train indigenous persons who seemed especially responsive to viewing their own cultures. Among the tribes of the American Midwest, there were persons such as Francis LaFlesche, an Omaha, and William Jones, a Mesquakie (Fox), who worked in the discipline. The latter died on a field trip to the Philippines while working among the Ilongots.

Nevertheless, the role of informant as anthropological reporter creates qualms among natives who contemplate becoming anthropologists, and it is not surprising that early contributions by Native Americans were primarily in texts on the native languages and in folklore and mythology. A pertinent observation is made by a black anthropologist:

In the same spirit that Boas encouraged natives to become anthropologists, he also encouraged women because they could collect information on female behavior more easily than a male anthropologist. This attitude strongly implied that native and female anthropologists are seen as potential "tools" to be used to provide important information to the "real" white male anthropologist. (Jones 1970:252)

The late Ed Dozier, Pueblo anthropologist, once commented that many native Americans "went into anthropology as a means of helping their people." This suggests strong interest in the application of anthropological knowledge and is tied to the native idea of education, no matter in what field, as a means of alleviating problems and providing self-help among native groups. It may also reflect the dominant white society's designation of "*the* Indian Problem." Moreover, anthropologists are the educated persons with whom most Indians are familiar, and they justify their data collection to us on the basis that "we want to write down your history and culture so that your grand-children will know something about it."

The "personal communication" aspect of anthropological reporting upset me when I began reading interpretations and analyses of us (Lakota/Dakota: Sioux), based upon E. Deloria's "field notes," "personal communications," and "personal conversations," in such works as Mirsky (1937) and Goldfrank (1943). Later, I realized that these and similar excellent studies based on others' field notes were common and acceptable in the discipline. Nevertheless, native populations are wary of others' interpretations of their behavior, even when they are dealing with "one of their own." An added native concern is that areas of living will be presented which they do not want revealed.

In all anthropological investigations, mutual trust and understanding must be built carefully and sensitively. As with any human relationship, reciprocity, responsiveness, and responsibility are essential. I myself learned this lesson early during an intensive year I spent in a southwestern pueblo noted for its conservatism. There I learned to eat hot, spicy foods and to leave the pueblo along with the non-native teachers on special ceremonial occasions. I learned, too, that I would never write about this pueblo.

The pueblo experience affirmed the importance of segmentation for survival. An elder of the sacred and secret realm always spoke to me in his native language, as he held my hand and put a turquoise ring on my finger during each visit to his home. Later, I saw him in his trader role in the southwestern city and heard him converse in excellent English. I rushed home to tell my son's father, "Mr. Z speaks English!" Little did I realize that I was being tested. Was I native or white-oriented? Was I informer or friend?

While resident in the pueblo, my research interest in child-training methods was fulfilled. I established strong ties with the people and maintained visiting patterns and exchanges of gifts. However, my input into the village was minimal, consisting mainly of writing letters, purchasing materials, doing odd chores, and interpreting educational policies. With respect to the last activity, this was my first experience in a Bureau of Indian Affairs "day school." It was my unhappy chore to explain to Pueblo parents why their kindergarten children could recite "Dick and Jane" stories by rote, even though they did not understand a simple question in English. Theories of social change and social organization made my year tolerable as far as the school structure was concerned. I hope that I was a means of explaining the rigid educational system to the pueblo people, who knew precisely what skills they wanted their children to have—mathematics and "enough English to get by." Their belief system, however, was a secret never to be divulged; I still heed this directive when a pueblo student asks me not to discuss pueblo religion in my classes.

Being a native female delineated areas of investigation which were closed to me. This was aggravated by my prolonged infertility. Conversation or gossip about such matters as deviant sexual practices, abortions, and pregnancy taboos was immediately terminated when I appeared at female gatherings. It was only after ten years of marriage and producing a male child (!) that I was included in "womanly" spheres. Until then, I was referred to as "Little Bea." The cultural constrictions of working within my own group caused me to reexamine value configurations, sex roles, Indian-white relationships, and socialization practices by spending most of my time with the children. Some persons in my *tiospaya* (extended kin group) said I "spoiled" (i.e., "catered to") children. But by treating children as people, I was only acting in the way I myself had been socialized.

In the contemporary era, the concepts of acculturation or culture change, cultural transmission, role-modeling, bicultural and bilingual education, cultural brokerage, and others are highlighted in anthropological research. For me, these concepts have become personal and concrete during years of learning to be an anthropologist while remaining a native. My learning began in childhood and continues in the present.

Early Learning

Of significance to many of us Lakota people was Ella Deloria, a daughter of a Santee Dakota Episcopal missionary who worked among the Hunkpapa and Sihasapa (Blackfeet) bands of the Teton (Western) Sioux who were placed on Standing Rock reservation. She and other native Americans and Canadians came within the orbit of Boas, with whom she coauthored a book on Dakota grammar (Boas and Deloria 1941). Her other work included further linguistic, folklore, and kinship studies (Deloria 1944).

As a child, I observed Aunt Ella asking questions, taking notes and photographs and, according to my mother, "finding out how the Indians lived." Even in those days, the divisions of intragroup polarities of "mixed-blood" and "full-blood" were operative. Because my father was a "full-blood," he was a good source of linguistic and other information. Very often, questions were transferred through my mother. The division of Lakota souls into various Christian denominations, though arbitrarily assigned, could not obviate kin loyalties and expectancies. I am certain that Aunt Ella forgave "poor Anna" (my mother) for marrying a "full-blood" and a "Catholic."

Aunt Ella's participation in a world far removed from Standing Rock reservation where she lectured "about Lakota" presented a model which I found attractive. Much later, I attended a lecture by a physical anthropologist (now deceased) who asked, "Will all the persons in the room who have shovel-shaped incisors please indicate?" This experience and being used as an informant (together with a Swedish student) in a "Personality and Culture" course raised many questions in my mind about becoming an anthropologist. Would it be possible to retain dignity as a native while operating in roles other than informant? Would anthropological training alienate me from my people? Would it affect marriage? Aunt Ella had never married. Lakota ideals for women included marriage and children. I knew my father did not believe in what he later termed "cross-cultural" marriages.

In retrospect, I am pleased that my father was sufficiently farsighted to enroll his children as full-bloods. It has made my life and acceptance on reservations and reserves easier. I am also appreciative that my father took me to tribal council meetings when I was young. It was in this context that I was remembered and asked to translate for a Lakota male elder who was a non-English speaker in the Wounded Knee Trials of 1974. Such was socialization for modes of Lakota adaptation and persistence and the demanding and expected behavior of a native ("Anthro"—and female, at that!)

During my early life, I was cognizant of living in a society which was different from the one in which I would eventually interact. Many natives have to learn to assess cross-cultural cues and circumstances as techniques for accommodations and adaptations. Although we were trained for adaptation in the superordinate society, the ideals of expected behavior or responsibility and commitment of the native society were constantly held before us. Being Lakota was seen as the most essential aspect of living. It was from this cultural base that strong individual autonomy was fostered and an equally strong orientation to the group's welfare and interest was instilled.

Early in my college experience, I was asked to read treaties and Bureau of Indian Affairs (BIA) policy directives, and to write letters involving pony claims for elderly people on my reservation. Later, while doing fieldwork on Pine Ridge reservation, I was asked to edit an elder Oglala male's collection of Lakota folktales which began with "And a Hearty *Hou Kola* (Hello, friend) to you all!" He was collecting these for a well-known female "Anthro." As I congratulated him on his excellent collection, he said, "I got them from a book put out by the Bureau of American Ethnology and changed them here and there." This raised issues of ethical consideration which were unimportant at that time, but it also indicated that many native societies had access to previously published data.

At the time, I was not too concerned with his approach. I had already seen anthropologists offering old clothes to natives in exchange for art objects, and I had witnessed courting behavior on the part of male anthropologists with young Indian women. On the other hand, I had seen the equally horrendous scene of a large, aggressive Lakota woman forcing a thin, young, intimidated archeologist to dance with her and buy beer in a border-town tavern.

My brother felt sorry for the archeologist and allowed his crew to camp in our "front yard." In the Northern Plains, rapport between archeologists and the local Indian group has been generally good. Many archeologists have maintained contacts with the tribes. Their domain of investigation differs from that of ethnographers and social anthropologists, and they were more aware of my place in the social system and did not use me as a source of information. They also heeded the advice of my father (then a tribal council chairman) who, after feeding them buffalo steaks, said, "All we want from you guys is a good report." (It is the lack of good reporting back to the tribes under investigation which has evoked the ire and discontent of so many.)

The same young archeologist witnessed border-town "justice"

when one of my kinsmen was beaten by the police while in jail for intoxication. His attempt to intervene in the city court was negated as he was threatened with contempt of court. This need for intervention frequently presents itself to anthropologists. Working with powerless people has its heartaches and times of despair.

For me, these relatively common "advocate" involvements with police made later appearances in court in support of native women (one arrested for shooting her child's molester) somewhat less emotional. With increased articulation and age, by the time I testified in the case upholding our 1868 Sioux Treaty, I was classified as an "expert witness" (Jacobs 1975). I thought I was upholding family tradition and honor. My great grandfather, Sitting Crow, was a signer for the Sihasapa (Blackfeet) band of the Teton. He had signed in good faith. My father had been involved in treaty rights and other government obligations, and tribal attempts to enforce them. Nonetheless, the Wounded Knee Legal Defense and Offense Committee, which was concerned with the dismissal of the occupiers of Wounded Knee hamlet, apparently expressed some hesitation in my court appearance. I was not seen as an overt supporter of the American Indian Movement (AIM).

Looking like a "native" has been advantageous in my work. Although I have what Nancy Lurie (personal conversation 1973) has described as a "universal field face," which has often led me to be classified as northern Chinese, Japanese, and Filipino, my main research has been with the natives of North America.

The Teacher Role

Early in my career, I was assigned the teacher role by the majority of tribal peoples. Not having attended a Bureau of Indian Affairs or a parochial boarding school, my decision was to teach in one. I went with a baccalaureate degree to Haskell Institute, which Ed Dozier has referred to as "the Harvard of the Indian Service." There I encountered bureaucracy more concentrated than on reservations and the complete institutionalization of native students. To be fair, there is tremendous *esprit de corps* among graduates of this former business college, now a junior college. "Haskell Clubs" are common throughout the country. Many graduates feel sorry for those of us who never attended its hallowed halls.

At Haskell I first encountered differential evaluation. "For after all," I was told, "you did not spend ten years at an isolated school on some reservation but came here right from graduation." This merited me a rating of "good" rather than "excellent" teacher. I resigned. However, the teacher image still predominates, for the "professor" role is currently in the forefront of my activities.

Parents and others assume that I have information regarding aspects of career opportunities for students. They are continually reassured that educational activity on a post-high-school level is not necessarily alienating when they see me participating in "pow-wows" and "give-aways" on Standing Rock and other reservations. My current role also involves advisement and support to native and other minority students enrolled in colleges and universities.

A major request made of me is the distribution of anthropological sources to various tribes or native organizations for specific, usually legal, cases. This is a continuing process, as is the dissemination of knowledge about private and governmental sources of funding which can be utilized by these groups. The monitoring of proposals, without jeopardizing one's position as a reader of them, entails a constant weighing of benefits to both tribal groups and educational agencies. Extremely delicate situations are created when cousins and other relatives call for special considerations. Reliance on "old Lakota values" such as integrity is a healthy and understandable resolution for all concerned.

There are other requests of a general nature. These include native persons seeking genealogical information, and nonnative students writing at the request of their anthropology professors. Two examples from letters in my files are as follows: "What we need is a list of Sitting Bull's nine wives and a list of his many sons and daughters. . . ." "I want to work on an Indian reservation—preferably for money—this summer. Can you give me information?" There are constant requests for information about the treatment of foster or adopted Indian children, e.g., "This child was fine until he went home to the reservation when he was thirteen. Now we can't do anything with him. Do you think his family gave him drugs—peyote— or something?" I am certain that requests of the kind described here are the lot of many natives, not only in anthropology but in other professions as well. Fortunately, having worked as a psychiatric social worker with Metis and native persons in Canada, I am able to use my training in psychological anthropology in meeting them.

Work among natives, however, is difficult when they view anthropological reports about their tribes as unreliable. Susie Yellow Tail (Crow) defines ethnographies as "Indian joke books." There is no noticeable reliance or reference to many of the earlier ethnographic sources, especially linguistic and ethnohistorical studies. Many tribes are writing their own tribal histories in an attempt to present their experiences from their own unique point of view. Native Americans often believe that most anthropologists enter an indigenous social system with a theoretical framework and collect and report data in support of this prior formulation.

I have attempted a concerted effort to let people know the focus of my own investigations. Among the Lakota on Standing Rock, it is customary for "pow-wow committees" from various communities to ask visiting returnees to the reservations to address such gatherings of people. I have found this an ideal way to present interpretations of research in an acceptable manner. There is response and reaction to the speech-maker and members of my *tiospaya* (extended family). It is also an accepted means of conforming to tribal expectations. Many of us have been criticized by persons in governmental agencies, such as the United States Public Health Service and Bureau of Indian Affairs, who see our statements as ego-centered accounts of our activities in the "outside world." They fail to understand that this modern form of "coup-counting" is viewed by most community members as a means of modeling and enhancing Lakota values and conforming to expected behavior in contemporary reservation culture. It is a valuable outlet for letting the people know what will be written and for obtaining their assessment of it.

Many native enclaves today are aware of the large amounts of money poured into the funding of research on such topics as Indian education. Statements such as the following:

The Indian teachers, then, seem to be characterized as a group with close contacts to the Indian communities and firm Anglo orientations for themselves and in their view on the role of the school. (Fuchs and Havighurst 1972:197)

cause Indian education committees of tribal and community councils to request that this and other studies (e.g., *An Even Chance*) be presented in terms which they can more readily understand. Native enclaves are aware of the large amounts of money poured into the funding of such research. In their minds, natives involved as token researchers and validators tend to confirm their negative views of anthropological researchers. To explain without being patronizing is a skill to be learned, as is the need to be charmingly combative in certain anthropological arenas.

The translation of research terminology into an English vernacular which native parents and students can comprehend is a formidable task which "target populations" take for granted. This is not to disparage the intellect of tribal peoples, but rather to acknowledge their estimate of anthropological research and indicate their preoccupation with the many daily tasks of reservation life. It speaks to the need for less jargon in anthropological reporting. The increasing number of native college graduates who return to reservations or urban Indian centers and survival schools seldom utilize these studies at all. Their concern is the development of curricular materials which are more pertinent to their own and their students' needs.

One of the most successful educational endeavors in which I have worked was with the Sarcee tribe living on the outskirts of Calgary. I had already become involved in the social aspects—"pow-wow" and "give-away" events—before I began working there as a teacher-counselor. The aim of the Indian Affairs Branch of Canada was to enroll and keep Sarcee students in the public and parochial schools of Calgary, for there was the usual high dropout rate.

I visited every home on the reserve and became acquainted with the parents and grandparents. Fortunately for me, the chief was married to a Dakota female from Manitoba, and a pseudo-kin relationship was initiated by them. My goal was to enroll students in a kindergarten in the city and to hire a local native man to drive students into the city. This was accomplished, and the man now has a fleet of school buses which transport all Sarcee students to city schools. Although he says, "I am still driving buses," he is also Band chief. Today a Sarcee college graduate is also working in native education, and many of the young people are involved in tribal affairs.

During this time, some of my white Canadian friends and I worked to establish an Urban Indian Center in Calgary. Some of these white friends have continued their work with urban groups and one has received a degree in anthropology. Many of these individuals, who are both native and Canadian, are involved in national Indian educational associations in the United States. A truly binational interest in native education and native issues (National Indian Education Association, North American Bilingual Education Association, and, more recently, the North American Indian Women's Association) seems to be emerging. Much of this involvement is attributable to the growing self-determination and articulation of native peoples in North America. The thrust of commitment has gone beyond the mere networks of "pow-wow circuits" and kinship ties.

One aspect of concern and meaningful education for native students has proven counterproductive to my own professional development. Additionally, I cannot seem to cast off the indispensable mother role. (I once overheard my son telling his friend, "You've heard of Jewish mothers; Sioux-ish mothers are worse.") Native pressure to take fellowships and jobs to ensure continued occupancy by native peoples is great. Although I have, since 1969, spent two years in "my own area" of Montana and South Dakota, I have frequently moved to areas where Indian students have expressed interest or initiated action in hiring me. A common accusation, especially in California, is, "Why aren't you working with your own people?" This is an indication, it seems to me, of a growing tribalism with its incipient and, in some cases, strong ethnocentrism. As far as moving so often is concerned, I jokingly refer to the former nomadism of my people. More recently, I have utilized a Pan-Indian joke: "Sioux are just like empty beer cans, you find them everywhere."

Increasingly, native students who have been in my classes are fulfilling my expectations. Many have entered into occupations with tribal groups and educational endeavors. They are, hopefully, negating my fears of untrained Indian educators replacing uncaring and, in some cases, badly trained white educators. A number of these students, who have absorbed anthropological theories and research methods, are working in areas of concern to our peoples. An interesting dilemma exists. Many tribal councils often "resolve" a problem with a statement: "We need a study on this." Yet, it is in the areas of research and writing that the lack of skills is most evident in the training of native college graduates. White "ghost writers" are too prevalent!

Affirmative action policies in institutions of higher learning raise other problems. Administrators are seeking names of native Americans to fill these slots. An onerous aspect of this recruitment is the validation of self-ascribed natives, whom I have termed "woodwork" Indians, who emerge to fill the slots of the momentarily "in" people ("Indians" and other minorities). This poses critical questions. How does one deal with a person who claims to be one-sixteenth or one-thirty second Indian ancestry (usually Cherokee)? What is a cultural native versus a native of convenience? We know that there are many blacks who, either through intermarriage or miscegenation, fit into a similar category. A more recent anomaly is the use of the gloss "Native American" by Samoans and Hawaiians in the quest for federal funds. These and related issues create real problems for the native anthropologist. Does one set up a registry for "Red-bloods"?

Even more challenging dilemmas result from requests which native intellectuals make upon anthropologists. One example came from an Oglala (Sioux) law graduate who requested that I present evidence that the Native Americans originated in the New World. (What temptation for a native American Piltdown "plant"!) Concerns of this nature have even greater future repercussions because of the current rejection of the "Bering Straits Migration theory" advocated by some tribal leaders. Many tribal peoples are as committed to their origin and creation statements as any other people. "What do you think of the story told by the anthropologists that we all came across the Bering Straits?" was the question asked of me by a Navajo teenager in 1960.

Issues based on Indians' tribal sovereignty, water, and treaty rights, will make the future interface of anthropologists and natives a vital concern for those of us committed to a changing profession. This is especially evident in the use of the latter in the "contrived cultures" of native militants.

"Traditionality" is often seen today as a selective mechanism which includes persons whose rhetorical "right-on-ness" negates tribal heritage, oratorical wisdom, and concerted action which have sustained the nativeness of the group. "Identity-questing" assumes a new perspective and reflects generations of superimposed policies of change. It is tragic to view some individuals who do not know their own unique tribal heritage amid the vast cultural heritages of native North America. Thus, respect for elders is eroded in the exploitation of native medicine men and translation of native prayers into slogans.

However, a common denominator is that we native Americans are varied hues in a bronzed and battered native world and present uneven views of tribal traditions.

More importantly, our sheer survival has hinged upon a flexible ability to segment, synthesize, and act in changing situations. While this should be understood and respected by anthropologists and others, a lack of sensitivity and perception has been a main tragedy of comprehending native life. There is often a unidimensional aspect of power. The indigenous society is seen as a target population for manipulation and change with little or no attempt to understand the textured and realigning configurations of persons and ideas, through time, which have allowed for native persistence. For me, the categories of constituency are meaningless because my identity rests as a constituent of a viable native group. Advocacy is constant and resides with the powerless peoples. Involvement is ongoing, demanding, and debilitating emotionally, economically, and educationally.

To me, the most important aspect of applied work is the delineation of social forces which impinge upon indigenous societies and the ways that these affect each distinctive group. Social change and how it is understood and acted upon by native Americans is the crux of anthropological understanding. It is through the role of cultural broker that the lack of insight and understanding of a more powerful social order may be mediated. The fact of living in social situations of administered human relations, where decisions affecting the present and future of native Americans are controlled by external power components, is understandable and workable with anthropological concepts. In educational aspects especially, it has been imperative to reinterpret and to flesh out the parameters of methods and techniques of change in terms which are meaningful to native aggregates. Moreover, it is important that persons on both the receiving and applying levels understand the nature of factions in these societies. For native societies, the labels "Progressive" and "Traditionalist" have many different meanings.

The "full blood"/"breed" constellations have been correlated with both "traditionalists" and "progressives" in some Lakota reservations. This division of allegiances to old values and affinity toward "feathering one's own nest" at the expense of the other group are basic to understanding factions on contemporary reservations. Recently, the "progressives" or "featherers" have begun to harken back to "traditionality" which is operationally part of the reservation political arena.

The politics of social capital and power are elements which are forever present in native social systems. They have served as vehicles for differential adjustment to the dominant culture. To the anthropologist from the native enclave, kin affiliation is often within both spheres of social structure, necessitating a constant reassessment of power and emotional alliances. Surges of disaffection and disenchantment have to be isolated and put in proper perspective as a prelude to action.

There are events with simple and fulfilling moments, such as sitting around a campfire visiting with friends and kin "waiting for the coffee to boil" or watching Lakota children "playing cowboy" in the bright moonlight. On other occasions, listening to the Sioux National Anthem and then "dancing the drum out" in the cold dawn of a Northern Plains summer have become memories which sustain me in university settings, governmental "advisory' boards, or anthropological "tribal rites" (annual meetings) where we hear new interpretations and speculations about our native life-styles. Being home and doing fieldwork recall Al Ortiz' significant statement: "I initially went into anthropology because it was one field in which I could read about and deal with Indians all of the time and still make a living" (in *Anthropology and the American Indian* 1973:86).

I know I went into anthropology to try to make living more fulfilling for Indians and to deal with "others" by attempts to apply anthropology to Indians and "others" in meaningful ways.

13

ADMINISTRATIVE ORIENTATIONS FROM ANTHROPOLOGY: THOUGHTS OF A COLLEGE PRESIDENT

Paul A. Miller

Writing from the perspective of a long career as an administrator/anthropologist, Paul Miller describes the contribution of anthropology to his past responsibilities and duties as president of the Rochester Institute of Technology. Administrative actions and decisions require analysis of both the macrocosmic and microcosmic contexts of institutional relationships and the interplay between them. In examining the macrocosmic context of higher education today, Miller notes the historic tension between preserving and adding to knowledge and the function of channeling knowledge into use. The discipline of anthropology itself is confronted with this tension.

Miller exemplifies an anthropologist who has chosen to use anthropological training for the purpose of better understanding and coping with the daily demands of administrative work. Yet, he is not only a participant but also an observer of the social system of higher education. He reveals the need for administrative leaders to encompass both the intellectual and behavioral intelligence earlier described by Richardson. In addition, the essay is a testimony to the fact that the administrator/anthropologist can continue to make a contribution to the storehouse of knowledge. He tells us much about contemporary developments in

Paul A. Miller (Ph.D., Michigan State) is president emeritus and professor, College of Liberal Arts, at the Rochester Institute of Technology. Initiating his career as a county agricultural agent, he proceeded to such posts as professor of sociology and provost at Michigan State University, president of West Virginia University, assistant secretary in the United States department of Health, Education, and Welfare (1966–1968), and distinguished professor of education and director of university planning studies at the University of North Carolina, Charlotte. He is currently engaged in research related to comparative science policy.

higher education which need to be more fully understood by students, professors, and others who work within it.

APPLIED ANTHROPOLOGY HELPS the college president to place a particular institution or class of institutions within the overall drama of historic context: how institutions are formed, how they adapt to social need and pressure, and how they fall into obsolescence. Anthropology, dealing as it does with the interwoven beliefs and values which give meaning to social activities, tries to understand the functions of social activities as they, patterned together, shape the lives of those who perform them. The anthropologist as educational administrator asks how the functions of education interweave and overlap with other institutions and organizations. This raises the further question of how the school or college in microcosm influences and is influenced by the beliefs and values of its members and the cultural forces which are linked to and patterned with it.

Anthropology helps the academic administrator to gain the perspective of the wide horizon. No other discipline can do this better if both understanding and the basis to act administratively are required. This larger view enables the administrator/anthropologist to understand how social need and pressure determine the nature of educational institutions, why new ones come into being, serve for a period as prototypes, then recede to a less illustrious place as other academic forms emerge.

In the United States, the anthropologist is drawn especially to the successive prototypes which have arisen to meet the evolving demands for education. At least three distinct American prototypes responded to such demands. Each adapted to change, yet other prototypes succeeded them. Responding to claims for suffrage and equal opportunity, the state universities were formed. A rebellious rural majority wanted something more—a pressure that helped create the land-grant colleges in 1862, which mixed subjects in agriculture and engineering with those in philosophy and literature (Miller 1973). As the public school movement gained momentum, social demand created new offshoots, notably the normal school academies, which later became the teachers colleges. This overall public educational system grew for nearly a century, but it was unprepared for the upheaval in the meaning of higher education which emerged in the single generation which knew the Great Depression, the technology of World War II, and the Soviet sputnik.

From this more modern context sprang the community college, perhaps the major academic form thus far in the twentieth century. The land-grant college made it fashionable to teach students how to work and live along with how to think. The community college emerged to do the same thing, but to do more of it—to serve more people, to meet the needs of the whole community, and to demonstrate the relationship of education to social and economic growth.

With such an historic succession as an example, applied anthropology helps the administrator to learn how prototypes adapt to new social needs, yet not so quickly that the force and haste of social pressure create new forms. For example, the land-grant college helped transform agricultural efficiency. But, as unneeded rural workers flee to urban centers, these colleges find it difficult to adjust to urban society, and voices are raised for the need of an "urban-grant" university (Johnson 1964; Watchman 1974:242–247). Teachers colleges helped to fashion staff, evaluate, and support the public schools. However, having weakened their local ties by emulating the more classic university, they have been unable to respond to the crisis of the urban school as a prime center of social disintegration in American life. Meanwhile, nontraditional education—the provision of external degrees, open universities, classrooms without walls, and the learning system which the electronic revolution has helped the whole community to become—creates doubt that community colleges will adapt rapidly enough to fulfill the aims for which they were invented. Perhaps a new prototype is now in the making!

As applied anthropology helps the administrator gain the perspective of the wide horizon, it also clarifies the college as a closely interwoven web of mutual and reciprocating relationships: in short, a natural community. The unity of such relationships becomes important to the administrator/anthropologist. It brings integrity to the institution and helps reveal how the various client groups—students, faculty, donors, employers, public officials—may influence each other. An interest in the college as a community, with its accompanying tendencies to localize and decentralize, will focus the fundamental concern of the administrator/anthropologist on the response to the growing tendency for external agencies to centralize the guidance of the university system.

For example, as democratization of higher education has sped forward in the United States, a new administrative class has arisen for guiding the larger and more complex institution by creating more and stronger measures of executive direction. The new academic managers have perfected formal managerial techniques. They specialize in the cultivation of clients and donors, invent interlocking links with state and federal governments, as well as with new planning agencies, become the customary and sometimes the only link between students, faculty, and trustees, influence the agenda of governance, and tend to strengthen vertical as against lateral channels of communication.

Another related example is the mushrooming of multi-institutional systems and consortia. The growth of federal financing of colleges and universities, which increased almost sixfold in the 1960s alone, ushered in a newly forged link to the federal government, together with a widespread orientation to research. It opened the way for a myriad of other formal arrangements, such as state systems of higher education, which have moved the location of planning and decision away from the inner life of the college as a community and toward the outer public life of society. The administrator/anthropologist is both concerned and curious about how such ties to the public world, and the manner of their management by the new administrative class, complicate the location of education as it is continuously absorbed into a bureaucratized society (Trow 1973, 1969:181–202).

The anthropologist's view is shaped by the basic concept of culture. While other disciplines may emphasize social conduct, belief, language, human artifact, and skill, the anthropologist focuses upon how such aspects of life are interwoven and patterned into a whole. Anthropology asserts that culture touches every part of human life—the visible, the invisible, the biological, the intellectual, the moral; that culture does not change nor can it be changed by addressing it part by part; that it is not possible to understand the life of mankind, nor any part of it, without a larger understanding of the culture in which that life, whether of a person or of society, is embedded (Hall 1976:22–35). In the instance of the school or college, the anthropologist's interest turns to the institution as a microcosm and how it links to and is influenced by the shape and direction of the more macrocosmic aspects of culture. The administrator/anthropologist seeks to know how the educational community links its efforts to the projects of the larger cultural and societal order.

This interest in the interplay of microcosmic and macrocosmic projects becomes the centerpiece of the academic administrator, whose way of looking at higher education is anthropological in nature. These two aspects, under the cultural view, eventually fall together. As they do, the administrator finds in their relationships a way of viewing the academy in the holistic sense which is so characteristic of the anthropological method (Fallers 1974). Moreover, this method embodies interests which veer to lateral rather than vertical channels of communication, and to the ties between small and large systems. There is an emphasis upon working effectively within a given system of interpersonal relationships.

It may be possible to understand the macrocosmic (a cultural) context and the microcosmic (also a cultural) institution. But what does one do about it, as administrator or leader? The study of a particular field seems eventually to yield a cluster of values and techniques—a way of thinking that actually suggests a procedure for acting on the basis of it. In the realm of personal outlook and style of acting, one finds that applied anthropology offers much that is worthwhile.

The Macrocosmic Context of Higher Education

The specifics of administrative/anthropological actions within the microcosm of institution occur within the macrocosmic context of higher education today. Underlying the entire cultural context of higher education for more than seven hundred years is the fact that it institutionalizes and sustains two opposing ideas of Western thought and experience—the first, knowledge viewed as an end in itself, an intellectual challenge in its acquisition; and, second, knowledge seen as the solution to social problems. The academic center confronts, as do all of its component parts, including the discipline of anthropology itself, the tension between preserving and adding to knowledge and the function of channeling this knowledge into use, whether by teaching or in other acts of dissemination. Distinctive organizations within academic structures rise to sponsor these functions: in general, the disciplines for the first and the professional schools for the second. For example, the secondary position assigned by the early English university to the professions reenforced its faculties of arts to resist the inclusion of science in the curriculum. Likewise, the autonomy and prestige of the German professoriate placed the delights over the utilities of science. Conversely, part-time doctors, lawyers, and other professionals in Scotland facilitated an early interest in the practical applications of knowledge (Ashby 1959:6). This historic conflict in two basic intellectual functions sustains to this day a tension between general and specific studies and between the purely intellectual and the practical. Perhaps even more important is the historical suggestion of mankind's two different interests in the mode of observing the natural and human worlds—the one emphasizing intellectual adventure and enhancement of the person; the other, more active and short term, adding to social enhancement.

The slowness of change within the academic enterprise has been in one sense the basis of its durability. For it is therein able to tolerate two quite dissimilar functions—that which hoards knowledge and is personal in its use, and that which shares knowledge and is social (Ashby 1959:69–70). The university adapts slowly and imperfectly. The process invites and includes the creation of new institutions. Due in part to such durability, colleges and universities provide in their everyday activity a quite remarkable product. Through their academic channels, they send people to society who have been exposed to what is known about science, technology, the arts, and administration. Through their technical channels, they provide skills, ideas, and products which have come to bear fundamentally upon industry, agriculture, health, education, and communication. These channels function without much conscious design. But when "missions" are established, when limited projects are devised in response to special social needs and pressures, the accommodation tends to become more slow and incomplete (Moravcsik and Ziman 1975:699–724).

The traditional reverence of the United States for higher education's product has been strengthened by an ethic which saw higher learning as a chief avenue of personal advancement. The industrial revolution reenforced this belief and molded the culture to a concept of progress aimed at scientific–technological advance and material success. Educational institutions have managed to touch, influence, and be influenced by that culture in ways never before achieved. Yet disquieting cues forwarn that these points of contact are now blurred. Beset by swift change and new pressures of an interdependent world, both society and education are less sure of themselves today. Societal goals of technological and material advance are becoming more clouded, complex and filled with unexpected outcomes. Educational institutions are strained between the need to respond to new socioeconomic realities and their desire to be the embodiment of an active culture in a nation that many feel is floundering for lack of a cultural/ethical identity. During the very rise in size and prominence of higher education, the shared values which bind the social context have seemed to unravel and disintegrate (Blau 1974:615–635). Concern over the social costs of material progress is evident, but the search for new briefs, legitimacies, and purposes seems sporadic and incoherent. Question after question arises. To what extent are the disatisfactions with education related to broader failures to find new meanings and legitimacies? Has so much been expected of education that it is blamed for conditions quite beyond its control? Is education being asked to assume the roles of other social institutions and programs which have failed?

In the modern period, higher education has been characterized by a pronounced shift from the historic preparation of leaders from the elite classes to the training of great numbers of managers and technologists. From elitism to mass education to universal access has been the nature of an epochal transition (Trow 1973:6–7). While elite forms served to enhance the intellect and character of the few, the new mass forms respond to the many who demand access to educational opportunity. The rapid growth in higher education which resulted in the industrial countries has become the major element in the social context of higher education today.

This significant change shows how the cultural imperatives of the macrocosmic level of society may come to dominate projects at the microcosmic level. This influence changes the nature of institutions; it alters the very meaning of daily (the truly microcosmic) life and work and production. For example, early capitalism in America built upon an enormous resolve to achieve and produce, which drew upon the core values of self-discipline, objectivity, and rationality. These values were incorporated into the aims of mass education. In the later stages of secular capitalism, economic production grew more specialized in more complex work places (with attendant separations of production centers from family and community). The basis of employment shifted from a tie to austerity and achievement and toward the idea of work and production as a means to acquire goods, services, and possessions: in short, to achieve affluence and to consume. A heightened devotion to pleasure, to hedonism, was introduced (Etzioni 1972:2–11). These shifts were accompanied by growing interests for acquiring the knowledge, skill, and status necessary, initially, to produce, and then to produce in order to consume. Education swung inexorably to honoring these qualities, and academic institutions assumed the major task of sorting and credentialling human talent so that it could be more rapidly and efficiently allocated.

This evolution sped onward and apace with the democratization of culture. Human skill and economics became inextricably linked. Then the experience of World War II ignited the unprecedented move to technologize society and to democratize education. Pressured by such social need, higher education exploded along a sharply rising curve of growth. The institutions themselves became bureaucratized. As the doors opened to the mass desire to share in culture and technology, and as knowledge was demanded for direct use in community and society, the obligations of the academy multiplied. Nearly all the historic functions have seemed useful and have been carried forward to the new day—professional training from Bologna, the nurturing of gentlemen from Oxford, the conduct of research from Berlin, the grooming of technologists from Zurich (Ashby 1959:68).

Along this way, curriculum became more flexible and varied. Teaching of skill and application grew more rapidly than the teaching of theory and concept. Old differences between secondary schooling and college receded, so that attending the latter became more of a continuation of experience already in process. Educational standards became more varied as they responded to differing interests and capabilities of students. Standards also differed in response to the ranking and other characteristics of fields of study. Consensus over standards weakened as the mass approach grew. The old idea that the professoriate is the very heart of the college was seriously eroded.

These shifts indicate that mass education has now arrived at a watershed of academic history of no less enormity than those of earlier times. Comment about this watershed has dominated the discussion and planning of higher education for nearly a decade. Some have come to hold the "view that the Golden Age of higher education lies more in the past than in the future" (Carnegie Commission 1973:7). The monumental studies of the Carnegie Commission on Higher Education have examined, analyzed, and measured higher education. They describe new problems of politicization, the unwillingness of the public to transfer income from other sectors to higher education, the lagging productivity of academic people, and the almost certain decrease in numbers of conventional students in the next twenty years. These features of the "crisis of confidence" which now envelops the academic world suggest that the hypotheses which seemed implicit in earlier watersheds—the overriding power of the social context, the split in basic educative functions, and the slowness of prototype forms to respond—will be much in evidence for the balance of this century.

The administrator/anthropologist searches behind these profiles for new shifts in values and beliefs about higher education. The search leads back to the cultural context that surrounds the work, production, and achievement that went far in underwriting the transition from elite to mass education: first, the shift from production in relation to personal austerity and, second, achievement in relation to consumption and possession. Now it is possible to detect a third era, one that would justify work and production as a prime source of personal enjoyment (Bell 1976:37). This new era, defined not alone, as supposed, by young people, subscribes to work and production but does not view the success that comes from them as the primary measure of life. These new values rise to challenge clusters of values which have shaped both American society and its institutions of higher education.

First, there is the stronger hold that personal pleasure has taken upon life in general, and the hedonistic element contained within the new demand that success in life is measured by enjoyment and self-understanding rather than by work for individual achievement, and production (Yankelovich 1974; Gottlieb 1974:541). Second, research and observations indicate that younger people fear economic disaster less than their elders. They may worry over the lack of personal fulfillment, but worry less about economic catastrophe. Third, there is what some term the new psychology of entitlement: that society has achieved such a level of technology and material means that each person has earned the right to a job that gives satisfaction, to participate in the decisions that affect that job, to a secure old age, and to have major health care provided. Moreover, this view holds that it is natural for people, once they have food, shelter, and safety, to pursue self-development. Fourth, the challenge made of the impersonal by the personal also questions the rationality upon which modern efficiency and science are founded. Whether in the distrust of management (as when some educators find efficiency and learning antagonistic, for example), in the views of the counterculture or occasionally within the environmental movement, efficiency is here and there alleged to be exploitative and inimical to future society (Etzioni 1972:5).

As an overview, one may say that the first third of the present century gave rapid rise to modernism in the arts, literature, and science. The middle third employed mass education to democratize the fruits of this modernism by disseminating it into the common culture. The final third of the century looms as a period of confusion, tension, and uncertain reform of colleges and universities; for they confront the conflict between the rational use of knowledge and a resistance to the modernism which such use has been dispersed to achieve. One must wonder what new prototypes may now be conceived to answer the question: having moved from cultivating character to training and certifying the uses of technique, where will the liberated autonomous person be educated (Lasch 1975)?

The Microcosmic Context of Higher Education

What values and skills evolve from anthropology to guide the administrator within complex organizations? What values and skills help one to achieve consensus about goals and objectives? How does the administrator/anthropologist think of and comprehend the academic institution as a whole?

Anthropology encourages the administrator to seek the boundaries of the institution, whether ecological or functional. Of similar interest will be the zones of tension, how well personal and institutional goals mesh, and where incentives reside and how they function. The administrator/anthropologist is motivated to think of the institution as a whole. Applying anthropology helps the administrator to face three ways at once: to groups which provide resources and support; to the institution itself; and to those for whom its product is intended. Anthropology becomes directly useful when one must deal with connections and with relationships and the values and symbols which sustain them.

How these questions and principles assist the administrator will doubtlessly vary from person to person; however, they tend to instill the following values about how one conducts overall administrative tasks in the university, especially those of the university president. They do not stand alone nor do they represent all that is possible from the study of anthropology. Further, they doubtlessly spring also from the trial and error and the successes and defeats which characterize any administrative career and outlook.

One such value encourages the administrator/anthropologist to improve the unity among the several disciplines which compose the college or university. This value is fed by a concern for the gulf between the issues of society, which grow more interdependent, and the nature of knowledge, which grows more specialized. Thus, the disintegration of shared values in the larger world, and the evident despair of matching specialized solutions with generalized problems, both relate to the academic manner of separating rather than fusing the many categories of knowledge. Moreover, the old historic tension—knowledge for its own sake or for use—is everywhere evident. The academic form continues to be absorbed into technological society, as it has come to depend upon the linkages of its mission to state and federal governments and as the shift continues from cultivating citizens to training technologists. Accordingly, academics have been led to perhaps overstated premises of certainty and precision. They tend also to isolation, suspicion, and distrust between the disciplines, especially when enrollment growth and resources are jeopardized. They have been only partially capable of responding usefully to those grievous issues of the modern world—e.g., food, energy, pollution, population, human settlements—which persist at the intersections of the boundaries among disciplines.

Anthropology helps an administrator to look below the surface of the college or university in order to see how its missions and the location of knowledge may be brought into harmony. Related ways

of planning must be found, as well as the manner of allocating resources, securing personnel, and adapting organization. The anthropologist will search for integrative ideas and will help them rise
alongside of the customary compartments. Such themes may respond
to real problems, as when the agricultural colleges once placed departments geared to segments of industry next to disciplinary departments in order to focus both the natural and social sciences upon
actual problems of farm production and marketing. Themes dealing
with communications and environment, or with technology and values may arise in such professional schools as engineering and archi-
tecture, in order to attempt fusions of scientific and humanistic values. Or more general and linking disciplines may emerge, as happened
in biophysics and biochemistry, as well as in the *bauhaus* conception
of building a bridge between art and technology.

     A second value that emerges from the theory of culture into the
guidance of institutions is that which strengthens the administrator's
desire to seek outcomes from interpersonal relationships rather than
from formal rules of organization. To be sure, such values and skills
will conflict from time to time with the seeming necessity of position
and authority. But an anthropological accent remains upon those shared
beliefs and symbols which reflect the self-consciousness of the institution as a community, to include those usages and ways of thinking
and doing which are reflective of culture. This interest calls on one
to know how people feel about their part in the institution, to be
concerned for their personal growth, to know why they may become
alienated. This valuing of interpersonal meanings will lead to interests in informal and lateral communications, their special good sense
and durability, over those formal and vertical channels which carry
the official messages of guidances and response (Gouldner 1959).

     Two examples serve this concern for the meaning of interper-
sonal relations. Both illustrate that one of the great influences which
anthropology brings to the administrator is that it reminds over and
over again that compiling a useful ethnography of the campus results
from direct involvement rather than from the reconstruction of official
memoranda and interpretation. The first refers to how the administra-
tor/anthropologist will be concerned with the imcompleteness of the
formal environment for schooling. Applying anthropological insights
turns such a person to the "third world" of the campus—the informal
experiences along human developmental lines—and how they link up

with classroom and residential activities (Panel on Youth 1974). For example, anthropological interests will point out the need for more and continuous studies of incoming new students, about varied human developmental stages and potentials, and further reviews as students proceed with and depart from college careers. Such interests are not without strain, for they challenge the conventional meaning of the educative process. They call also for alternative learning environments, an activity which tradition insists is solely the province of the faculty. But anthropology leads the administrator to ask: "Is there a campus culture, and what is its meaning for student growth?"

The second example refers to the embarrassing lack of academic interest in adult development. This is especially the case when faculty growth itself is held back by the failure to relate learning to adult growth and development. Informed research on adult development of faculty is rare. An anthropological view will detect the anomaly between what appears as a natural web of intellectual relationships amongst faculty and the presence of frequent isolated and narrowed life cycles and styles among many of them. The isolation of the classroom model, the privacy of much research and scholarship, disciplinary loyalties which run to specialties rather than within institutions, success defined by peers—all combine with the decay of mentoring roles (as among departmental chairman and deans) to yield an incomplete climate for potential growth, especially for those at midcareer (Hodgkinson 1974:263–274). Anthropology helps one to examine and improve the mentoring function (who are the helpmate/advisors?) and to devise projects and personnel policies to increase variety and change. Since lines of status and power tend to confine the administrator to the center, the field orientation of the anthropologist nevertheless insists that attempts must be made to overcome it. Anthropology suggests that one may do so by interacting informally in the faculty precinct, by gaining firsthand information about campus events and personalities, and by working at the grassroots, and in person to reconcile policy and rumors of policy.

The third administrative value which emerges from the study of anthropology suggests a preference for a course of studies to be learner-centered rather than dominated by the authority of teacher and subject matter. This value points to another incompleteness of higher education: the reluctance of most colleges and universities to devise inventive ways to conduct the educative process, as they are more apt to do in scholarship. At the national or other macrocosmic levels, higher education has engaged in projects that were truly transforming, but the mode of transmitting knowledge to students has changed very little. The university has not seriously studied its own educational role; its abdication to the professional schools of education merely weakened the overall concern with innovative research and development on the subject of human learning itself. A basic challenge results therefrom for the administrator/anthropologist—overcoming the inherent limitations to fostering independence of students whose college participation should help them make a mature transition to adulthood.

Anthropology gives to administrators a view about transmissions of ideas between cultures and cross-cultural influences, whether in small or large societies. Anthropology reveals how important out-of-school instruction is, especially the informal learning that occurs in family and other intimate groups. The administrator/anthropologist will try, therefore, to lead in ways that reduce the tendency of the academic form to narrow (and sometimes trivialize) the classroom model. Such leadership will introduce concepts and practices about how people learn from the tension between the isolated and sometimes exclusive assumptions of the single institution and those stimulants and media of culture which condition not only the learners but the institutions themselves. Surely anthropology, perhaps more than other fields of study, reminds the administrator that a single institution is but a fractional and humble part of the total educative process in the society.

The fourth value which emerges from the influence of anthropology gives the administrator a concern for strengthening the "natural-system" model of organization in contrast to a more "rational-legal" model (Gouldner 1959:404–405). That anthropology would influence one in this manner roots somehow in a basic tenet of the field—to study the manner of life of people—and the humanism which emerges from the responsibilities of such study. It is a short distance from there to a sympathetic and even ethical concern that the lives of people properly change indigenously rather than by the direct intervention of others (Thompson 1970; Hymes 1969). To be sure, the administrator must strive to reconcile the natural and rational models, for both are present. But the underlying interest which draws the anthropologist to observe the meaning of group life creates a desire to see that such a community is sustained and strengthened. When choices have to be made, they tend to be made on that side. Genuine role conflicts and personal ambiguities will result from these actions to balance the natural and rational systems as one acts on the basis of formal authority on the one hand and tries to sustain informal community on the other hand (James 1971:223–228). There is no better example of how these choices occur than by what happens to an administrative posture in issues of academic governance.

Complex, slow to change, and generally imitative of a widespread model, overall academic governance—who joins in the definition of goals, the allocation of resources, and the creation of policies—is perhaps the most complicated and elusive problem to test the application of anthropology in the administration of a larger college and university. Great pressures to reform academic governance have followed the rise of an academic managerial class and the shift from elite to mass higher education. Academic constituencies feel, on the whole, that they have lost power. Hopes that greater participation might generate more power have been disappointed. Meanwhile, institutions continue to juggle three different, sometimes contradictory, forms: the ancient idea of the "collegial" or self-governing community; the corporate model of formal and hierarchical levels of decision-making; the organization of the university as a companion to the professional systems of society, e.g., engineering, medicine, business, law, education, social work, and agriculture. It is characteristic of American academic institutions that they accomodate to all three forms; it is better done than many expect or believe.

At the heart of institutional governance rests the critical question of who, and by what terms, takes part in the process of allocating resources. Governance remains but an exercise until the question arises over who has knowledge of and access to the process of making a budget. It is here that both the "rational-legal" and the "natural" systems come into play and not infrequently into conflict. The key decision involved here, both for the present and for its precedence for the future, involves how much financial knowledge should be shared broadside with the institutional community as a whole. The administrator, an agent of the fiduciary body, will reserve final determination; but this is the "rational-legal" claim at work and will not normally satisfy the "natural" community's desire to be aware and involved. This example brings to view the manner in which anthropology induces loyalty to the natural community. One may expect the administrator/anthropologist to move on the side of open disclosure of financial knowledge. For here, there is in test the question of what is the most durable component of the leader's authority: competence as perceived by the community or power as defined by statute.

Thus, the administrator/anthropologist will likely respond to such problems by an interest in the *process* of governance in contrast to its *structure*. Anthropological exposure creates a posture that advocates administrative decentralization, task-oriented coalitions, and problem-solving styles. However, strengthening the natural system may increase the institution's resilience and endurance but weaken its capacity for sensitive adjustment and invention. Indeed, perhaps the chief problem of the applied anthropological view for the administrator is the conflict between helping to sustain a decentralized community with its own natural ecology within a formal bureaucratic medium which demands, under its sponsors and charters, that accountability for institutional results be defined and accepted.

Summary

The manner in which anthropology influences and sharpens certain basic values for the administrator cultivates distinctive styles and outlooks for the conduct of administration in the corporate society.

Such an administrator is likely to exhibit a mood of detachment from the administrative process. The related tasks will in all likelihood be viewed as necessary and important to organizational life, objects of professional study in their own right rather than objects of power and status. Such a practitioner will want to understand prestige and its symbols; hence they will likely offer no unreal inducements. This mood fosters an interest in being intellectually and physically mobile in the institution. It provides a positive regard for all the specialized talents of higher education which, in the end, must be integrated.

A related aspect of style will be a mood of dispensability, a view of administration that defines each task as the choosing of courses within shifting purposes. This mood requires one to be able to understand and restrain personal identities, tensions, and private expectations. Certainly the holistic character of anthropology, its overall interest in the activities, patterns, and symbols in human groups, will soon reveal that administration can be at best but a means of dealing with conflict and consensus, and that only continuous compromises for the common good will attain the goal. Each administrative choice, in the face of the always uneasy tension between rational and nonrational forces, can be the final one; hence, a steadfast mood of dispensability.

Another aspect of style is an accent on consultation. Academic people of exceedingly specialized talents function with a mix of both manifest and latent identities, as is illustrated in the conventional suspicion of faculty for elective and representative forms of governance. To move from conflict through consultation to consensus requires more than casual skill with helping members of the institution to free themselves from the outlooks of their own compartments and to assume both the role and the outlooks which others have. However, the administrator/anthropologist does after all practice administration, and sometimes even the most mundane of its functions cannot be avoided. Real skill is required in knowing when and where consultation must cease and a sequence of actions begin. Organizational ends tend to break down into an often elaborate means–ends scheme, with each step at once an end and a means to still another. Deciding what this sequence will be like, who will and should be involved, how much time the sequence should take, and what groups in and out of the institution may help or retard its flow, are all questions for which administrators must find answers. They cannot be answered with assurance unless the executive mind is able to systematically comprehend the institution as a whole and the general terms of who gives and who receives from its presence (its "support-recipient" situation).

But nobody can sort very clearly those forces which together shape both personal outlook and style. Family and social origins, the nature of schooling, the kind of organization, even the not-so-subtle differences between line and staff duty—all these and more are ingested into the strain which the corporate society asks all administrators to pay. One does little better in trying to note those uses of anthropology which seem to alter administrative behavior. But when the measure is taken of complex corporate life, and what administrators can and are expected to do is placed against that measure, the influence of anthropology will likely stand on the side of the following elements.

Anthropology leads one to grasp the wholeness of a situation, to get at the kinds and diversities of human patterns as well as the values which sustain them and the symbols which communicate them. This is a competence for sensing first and knowing later that less is happening than is possible. Certainly in a time when the specialization of technological society obscures the ties between people, acts, and events, the uses of anthropology point to administration which is reasonably at home with social complexity.

Anthropology further leads its students into expanding awareness of the interdependence among groups. For example, the connection between the myriad of projects at the working and living level of society and those projects of larger societal systems (as in the relation of a university to Washington, to the international community, or to a state planning agency) sharpens understanding of invention, change, stability, transmission, and reaction. Such an administrator veers unhesitantly to the study of social change, of how it evolves and from where, and of who is implicated in its impact and resolution. All administration in the corporate society works to diffuse and utilize knowledge and skill, a core value indeed. Thus, the uses of anthropology help the administrator to identify, understand, and practice at the crucial interfaces of this flow in technological civilization.

Anthropology strives to discover the core values of groups—families, communities, universities, corporations, societies. It is a search for how the group perceives its own world—all those intimately possessed values and concepts about social order, of the proper way by which people of different classes may function together, of the meaning of personal identity, of the self and how it is defined, and of how best to organize space, direction, and time. The anthropologist learns how people in groups come to grips with all the ambiguities of their own perceptions, thus giving a glimpse of how universal the condition and the study of humans are. Is it surprising that an administrator prepared in this way would have sympathy for those whom he or she has come partially to know, and understand that their chance to build new forms beyond where they are belongs to them and not to those who would intervene? We may safely say that we need more, not fewer, of those administrators who hold affection for people in whose service they have been called to administer.

14

PRACTICING MEDICAL ANTHROPOLOGY: CLINICAL STRATEGIES FOR WORK IN THE HOSPITAL

Thomas M. Johnson

I n essay 13, Paul Miller described the administrator/anthropologist role in terms of articulating the divergent groups and social processes in a university. Based on their own experience, many readers of this volume will accept readily the identification of faculty, students, alumni, and other constituencies as distinct groups in the institutional settings of higher education. This essay reveals the nature of practice in a very different type of institution which is conceptualized as a "clinical" setting by those who work in it or pass briefly through it. Modern medical and health care institutions are set apart from other bureaucracies by the assumption of this clinical relationship between professionals and their clients. This assumption is based on the perception of health care professionals that their work entails treatment of an individual—the patient. This perception is reinforced by formal precept and other symbols; in fact, those in the health professions usually do deal with a specific pregnancy, a particular surgery case, the recovery or death of a person with an identity, a case history, a name.

Thomas M. Johnson (Ph.D., Florida) is assistant professor of anthropology at Southern Methodist University and clinical assistant professor of psychiatry at the University of Texas Health Sciences Center in Dallas. As an applied medical anthropologist who has worked for a decade in community mental health and medical school settings, he has emphasized teaching in clinical settings, including supervision of medical students in obstetrics and gynecology, internal medicine, and psychiatry. He has conducted research on strategies to reduce pain in burn care, the process of medical education, physician-patient interaction, and high-risk obstetrics. He has been a member of the education committee of the Association for the Behavioral Sciences and Medical Education. He is currently the editor of the *Medical Anthropology Quarterly*.

As a practicing anthropologist, however, Thomas M. Johnson perceives in so-called "clinical" settings an elaborate latticework of asymmetrical and symmetrical social relations that organize categories of individual patients and types of professionals into structured and patterned interactions. This organizational system is not normally noticed, discussed, or examined by the actors within it. Through observation, participation, and analysis, Johnson is able to articulate these interactions which are usually taken for granted but not articulated by health professionals. Johnson conceptualizes the system of human organization that fits obstensibly idiosyncratic individual behavior into a social context that gives it meaning. This technique of placing the individual within the pattern, anchoring the idiosyncratic within its meaningful context, and of finding the order within apparent disorder is a key contribution of the applied medical anthropologist who takes both patients *and* health care specialists as his or her "clinical" clients.

THIS ESSAY DESCRIBES and discusses my experiences as a clinically applied medical anthropologist in hospital settings. The term *clinical* has sparked debate among medical anthropologists, and has raised the spectre of conflict with other professionals traditionally viewed as comprising the helping professions. Before turning to my own clinical activities in hospitals, I examine the concept of clinical anthropology and its historical roots.[1] In this essay, I also suggest that applied work in Western medical systems may be inherently and unavoidably clinical.

The Concept of Clinical Anthropology

Major interest in the concept of clinical anthropology dates from the 1980 "Open Forum" on the subject in the *Medical Anthropology*

---

1. It is a measure of the maturity of applied medical anthropology in the 1980s that no single essay can adequately review all of the activities of applied medical anthropologists, or discuss in detail the theoretical underpinnings of such work. Even the most recent publications in applied medical anthropology (Hill 1985; Chrisman and Maretzki 1982; Shimkin and Golde 1983) do not attempt exhaustive reviews of the many perspectives of the discipline which have been the focus of books, articles, and symposia at national meetings.

Newsletter (now *Medical Anthropology Quarterly*), the official publication of the Society for Medical Anthropology (M.A.N. 1980).
There, several applied medical anthropologists presented their views
about the nature of clinical anthropology. The most radical view calls
for the formation of a subdiscipline of "therapeutic anthropology"
within medical anthropology (Shiloh 1978; 1980). This view notes
that many problems which cause patients to seek care from mental
health professionals stem from cultural rather than intrapsychic processes; it advocates that in these cases therapy should be conducted
by specialists in culture rather than in psychology. Anthropologists
specifically trained in counseling skills would treat patients, after certification and licensure procedures similar to those of traditional mental health practitioners.

The movement toward a clinical anthropology has deeper roots
in the history of anthropology, however. For example, after completing analytic training himself, Alfred Kroeber started practicing analysis at the Stanford Clinic in 1918. Subsequently, he opened an office
in San Francisco where he saw patients several days a week until
sometime in 1922 (Kroeber 1970:104–106). Moreover, Margaret
Mead's work has been remembered as inherently clinical in that she
operated with the clinician's notion of "disciplined subjectivity," the
bringing of one's subjective response to a field setting into consciousness so that it becomes part of the available data to be considered
(Bateson, M. 1980:272). Mead (1952:343) viewed anthropological
research as a "clinical skill," with emphasis on good listening, sensitivity to nuances, and extracting of patterns from data. During the
1960s, Tax (1964:237) employed a medical metaphor when he wrote,
"The anthropologist who undertakes [clinical activity] . . . takes unusual burdens and risks. Like a physician, he takes the problems of
the community as his own. He can never be wholly successful and
must take some of the blame. Stakes are high and the game dangerous." For Tax, action anthropology of whatever variety is clinical: it
involves close and continued collaboration with subjects, empiricism
with trial-and-error corrections, use of *ad hoc* interventions, and
learning from the *process* of intervention (quoted in Barnett 1980).

Thus, the roots of a clinical anthropology are firmly grounded in
the history of anthropology. They include interest in the relationship
between culture and behavior (including definitions of normality,
causation, and appropriate treatment), cultural influences on the ill-

ness experience such as on pain perception and symptom expression (Zborowski 1969; Zola 1966), human relations in health contexts (Bateson, G. 1972; Alexander 1977), public health and community organization (Paul 1955), and community psychiatry (Weidman et al. 1978; Murphy and Leighton 1965).[2] There is also precedent for understanding hospitals as sociocultural systems (Goffman 1970; Caudill 1958).

Unlike their predecessors, however, contemporary clinical anthropologists receive specific training in applied medical anthropology, rather than becoming involved in the medical arena as a serendipitous, accidental, temporary, or unexpected career shift. This development reflects the growth of an applied focus in anthropology generally, the recognition of Western medicine as a legitimate field for anthropological inquiry, increased public criticism of medicine, changes in funding for the training of anthropologists, and decreased opportunities for academic employment.

Borrowing from medical sociology (Straus 1957), anthropologists have begun to differentiate between anthropology *of* and anthropology *in* medicine, with many moving to apply anthropological theory and method to the solution of practical problems in health care. Medical anthropologists *in* medicine have assumed roles as teachers in medical and allied health schools, as researchers and evaluators in health care settings, and as consultants with traditional knowledge of cultural and ethnic influences on health behavior. The greatest impetus to the development of clinical anthropology has been provided by anthropologists who are also trained, certified, and/or licensed in another recognized clinical specialty (e.g., nursing, family therapy, medicine, social work, public health) and who, therefore, have a professional mandate from outside of anthropology to engage in "participant interference" in clinical settings.

As increased numbers of medical anthropologists have begun to *intervene* in clinical settings, the concept of clinical anthropology has become more salient. First used in approximately 1979, the term has been variously defined as "objective and personally detached," "therapeutic," "involving clients or patients," or as "taking place in clinical settings." Some employ the term to distinguish anthropologists who do ethnomedical research in Western, as opposed to non-

2. The best review of the entire issue of clinical anthropology and the discipline is the Introduction in Chrisman and Maretzki (1982).

Western cultures, and to label medical anthropologists who are employed in health science schools as distinct from those in academic anthropology departments. The terms "therapeutic" and "clinical" anthropology are sometimes used synonymously, to refer to anthropologists directly engaged in therapy with patients or clients; others use the term merely to describe those who work in settings designed to provide care to people who are ill or in need of some type of professional medical assistance. Most recently, the term "clinically applied anthropology" has been proposed to differentiate the majority of applied medical anthropologists who teach, conduct research, or serve as clinical *consultants* with no legal, ethical, or supervisory basis to intervene in patient care, from those who are especially credentialed in *both* anthropology and a clinical discipline (Chrisman and Maretzki 1982). Defined in this way, applied anthropologists do not treat patients as might clinical or therapeutic anthropologists, but use their specialized data, theories, and methods to clarify specific clinical issues for a nonanthropological audience of health professionals.

My belief is that "clinical" is an appellation revealing as much about one's own professional attitudes toward the people one is studying as it is an artifact of professional credentials. If one is committed to improving health in individuals and optimal functioning in health care systems and works directly in settings where people seek and provide care, such work may be termed clinical. Strong motivation on the part of some medical anthropologists to intervene actively in the personal and professional lives of others is part of the clinical anthropology equation. Active intervention of this nature has been viewed suspiciously from both within and outside of the discipline; it needs to be monitored constantly by those who are so motivated.

Anthropologists who work successfully in health care delivery settings may also discover that being clinical is an expectation as much imposed by the setting as insisted upon by the anthropologist. Health care providers assume that participants are either patients (or their significant others) or practitioners involved in patient care, and there is an expectation that anyone who is not a patient should be therapeutic or instrumental in the healing mission. Anthropologists who enter hospitals with the sole intent of doing research inevitably find themselves interacting with practitioners or patient/research subjects in the midst of difficult life crises, and are expected to assist in the clinical mission, either through the generation of immediately relevant research results, or by gathering incidental data about patients which can assist in patient care (Barnett 1985).

Some therapeutic functions of a clinical anthropology may be an integral but largely unrecognized feature of *any* ethnographic work in one's own culture. Because of the implicitly shared world view between ethnographer and informant from the same cultural background, as well as common life-experiences, it is easier to project one's feelings, fantasies, and frailties. Ethnographers who are unaware of the increased likelihood of transference and countretransference in relationships with informants from a similar cultural background lose a valuable source of data about both informants and themselves. Traditional ethnographers in these settings who feel guilty for taking information from informants without giving something in return should be reassured by an understanding of the therapeutic power of catharsis, an often unintended and latent clinical function of the ethnographic interview, in which the relationship is the gift.

Work in the Hospital: Systemic Diagnosis

By describing some of my work in the hospital setting, I shall demonstrate that a narrow, Western medical model of clinical activity has been unwittingly accepted by many anthropologists. Emphasis on the dyadic nature of clinical activity minimizes the importance and efficacy of public health and other community health activities, particularly in non-Western settings. It also fails to recognize the legitimate therapeutic functions of medical anthropologists whose clinical interventions are directed at the level of social systems, such as a hospital ward, clinic, or other setting in which patients are but one element of the social milieu (cf. Schwartzman et al. 1984).

In hospitals, individual patients are usually seen as the sole objects of clinical activity by health professionals, whose training predisposes them to individualistic treatment modalities with emphasis on patient-practitioner dyads. Yet anthropologists have long known that variables beyond the biopsychological reality of any given patient profoundly affect both illness and the delivery of health care. "Unhealthy" work environments for health care practitioners result in less than optimal care for patients, and the reduction of role strain and other noxious conditions for staff will likely be therapeutic for patients. Complicating the hospital milieu is the fact that each patient brings into the hospital a culturally derived baggage of health beliefs and treatment expectations which may or may not be congruent with those of health professionals. Moreover, family members often become involved in the care of patients as third parties in the therapeutic endeavor; their presence is a source of both support and stress for practitioners. Moreover, hospitals are businesses, subject to the vagaries of economic trends and administered by professionals who are divorced from day-to-day treatment activities.

Any hospital or clinic can be studied as a social system or community: a corpus of interdependent and interacting subsystems (such as nursing, dietary, social work, physical plant maintenance) with external connections to the larger community (political, economic, religious, etc.). Dysfunction at any level of the system can have pathological consequences for patients. Applied medical anthropologists working in hospital and clinic settings have begun to develop skills necessary for diagnosing and treating at this systemic, organizational level. These skills are not ordinarily taught to either anthropologists or health professionals, but they are as critical for dealing with systemic dysfunction as are the stethoscope or ophthalmoscope for the biomedical clinician. Such skills are true grist for a clinical anthropology dedicated to accurate diagnosis and therapeutic intervention in cases of organizational distress and to creation of environments which function maximally to meet the psychosocial needs of patients and practitioners.

My own work in hospitals espouses a systemic approach, an approach which has been endorsed only recently by some consultation-liaison psychiatrists (Miller 1973a, 1973b; Tarnow and Gutstein 1983; Hertzman 1984). In my current work, on a consultation-liaison psychiatry service of a major teaching hospital, I am a member of a team of psychiatrists, psychiatry residents, and medical students, whose function is to respond to other specialists' requests for assistance in the care of hospitalized patients (Johnson 1985).[3] These consultation

3. This specific hospital work is not the type of work many anthropologists choose to engage in, but the types of general methods employed should serve a diversity of

requests result when patients have problems which are traditionally in the psychiatric domain (e.g., drug overdose, suicide attempt, history of psychiatric treatment), and when hospitalized patients deviate from expected behavior, such as experiencing "too much pain," appearing overly anxious or depressed, reacting with hostility or anger, or complaining of physical problems which are viewed as psychosomatic. However, requests of this nature arise also from problems in patient-practitioner relationships and the displacement of intrastaff conflict onto patients. In addition, requests may result from systemic confusion related to ethnic differences in beliefs and behavior among patients whose cultural backgrounds differ radically from those of the professionals caring for them. In short, patient problems are not solely the result of disease processes; they emanate also from systemic dysfunction in the hospital.

IDENTIFYING THE LOCUS OF SYSTEMIC DISTRESS

When our consultation team receives a request to see a patient on another service, the psychiatrists tend to gather data from the patient, the patient's chart, and others in the setting with the intent of diagnosing what is "wrong" with the patient. From a clinical anthropological perspective, however, consultation requests are potential symptoms of organizational stress, and I take each request as an opportunity to diagnose an entire ward or hospital service.[4]

As with any system, a hospital has rules and regulations which operate to homeostatically maintain its basic structure and functioning. Rules and regulations, such as visiting hours or who is given staff privileges, serve to maintain the hospital's corporate identity as a special place to take care of sick people, and to maintain the professional identities of staff. Threats to systemic and personal identities may be both external and internal. The major internal threat to organizational identity is changing membership due to staff turnover, ex-

applied medical anthropologists working as patient representatives, organizational development consultants, administrators, clinical researchers, program evaluators, and in other roles.

4. I first heard many of these ideas articulated in a Psychiatry Grand Rounds presentation by Dr. Jay Tarnow. Subsequent conversations and reading of his article (Tarnow and Gutstein 1982) have contributed greatly to my ability to discuss this aspect of my work. This article should be required reading for medical anthropologists who work or study in hospitals.

pansion, medical students' rotating services, and so on. Staff turn-over prohibits the slow elaboration and internalization of rules and procedures, as well as mechanisms for building flexibility into the hospital's functioning; instead, it encourages rigid reliance on simple rules and regulations that can be internalized quickly. The major external threat is the constant invasion of the hospital system by patients and their families who have health beliefs and treatment expectations which differ from those of practitioners.

Despite the need for continuity and stability, the hospital system must adapt constantly to changing internal conditions and external challenges. The hospital's ability to change is determined by the relative flexibility of its internal structure. Too rigid a structure results in staff regimentation, demoralization, and inability to adapt to the special needs of individual patients. Yet the complete absence of internal structure and rules would cause a hospital to become dysfunctional—to have an "identity crisis."

Health professionals help to create and are influenced by the hospital's "identity," and generally function best in a work environment which is relatively flexible and conflict-free. Although professionals may themselves exhibit symptoms relating to a stressful work milieu ("burnout"), symptoms of organizational stress are manifested frequently as patient problems resulting in requests for psychiatric assistance. My activities attempt to pinpoint places in the hospital system where there is role strain, "burnout," role conflict, poor teamwork, inadequate information flow, and similar problems. This type of distress may be directly related to the care of a patient identified in a formal consultation request, but often it stems from general problems in the hospital system. Conflicts at all levels in hospitals tend to be displaced onto patients, who occupy the paradoxical position of being the most marginal members of the community in terms of tenure, but the central concern of everyone else in the system.

As noted above, consultation requests can be generated by intrastaff conflict. For example, when nursing supervisors "crack down" on floor nurses for taking too long on lunch breaks, floor nurses may respond by enforcing the "letter of the law" in visiting hours because they know irate family members will complain to supervisory nurses. Family members may then be subject to formal visiting rules, regardless of the condition of the patients, who then become depressed, angry, or regressed, leading their physicians to request psychiatric assistance. Similarly, if an attending physician admits a patient by telephone in the middle of the night and does not provide his over-worked resident with enough guidance about what "admission labs" to run, the patient may get too many diagnostic procedures, and they may be done during the night when the patient could be sleeping. Sleep deprivation may then lead to delerium in the patient, again leading to a "psych consult." Overworked physicians and nurses may ask psychiatry to order unnecessary sleeping medication for patients who prefer to stay up past the eleven o'clock shift change, or they may become frustrated and seek psychiatric consultations for patients whose problems result more from failure to be adequately informed about treatment decisions than from depression or confusion.

When physicians from several different services treat patients with complex problems, there are often disagreements about treat-ment strategies or incompatible recommendations. Specialists may concentrate on their own areas of expertise, losing sight of the par-allel work of others or of the patient's overall condition. The resultant treatment plans can be uncoordinated and confusing. Confusion on the part of patients, family members, or staff then results in anger and complaints to nursing staff and poor communication with and among physicians, another example of systemic dysfunction which may result in a "pysch consult."

Nurses and physicians also displace their disagreements onto pa-tients. Nurses, who cannot directly question the decisions of physi-cians (Stein, L. 1967), may use a more roundabout way to register displeasure with the manner in which physicians are handling a case. If they feel that physicians are not paying enough attention to their concerns about a patient, nurses may raise questions of a psychoso-cial nature, an area of patient care in which they perceive themselves to be better trained. In such cases, nurses may ask for a "consult" from psychiatry on a particular patient as a way of asserting the im-portance of their domain and subtly communicating their contention that physicians are not treating the patient adequately. A consultation psychiatry team which responds by focusing solely on the patient misses the underlying impetus for the request.

Patients themselves may unwittingly contribute to system con-flict by being hostile or demanding, emotions and behaviors which most health professionals attribute to illness and stoically overlook on an overt level, but may react to unconsciously. This patient behavior is often appropriate, given the compromised interpersonal functioning that accompanies illness, the frustration resulting from the sequelae of institutionalization (e.g. forced dependency, conflicting expectations, inadequate information flow), and the incongruity of lay and professional health beliefs. But control of emotions toward patients is a major issue in hospital systems: health care professionals are socialized strongly to display "affective neutrality," but most prefer patients who are cooperative and curable.

In short, patients of practitioners who request a psychiatric consultation are not the only ones who need to be investigated. Just as a thorough physical examination of a patient includes investigation of all organ systems to assist in diagnosis, systemic diagnosis in the hospital demands investigation of all the subsystems involved in patient care. A physician usually signs the consult request which formally asks for psychiatric assistance, but the impetus may come from a nurse, dietician, medical student, hospital chaplain, social worker, or even patients themselves. Knowledge of the locus of consultation requests is a highly significant datum in the differential diagnosis of systemic distress. Many systemic conflicts in the hospital are unconscious or repressed, with the etiology of the discomfort felt by those in the system not accessible directly to its members. Knowing something of the rate of consultation requests from a given hospital ward is important information: deviations from baseline in the frequency of requests may be an early warning sign of systemic distress.

EXPLANATORY MODELS AND CLINICAL REALITY

As in traditional community study, an anthropologist working in the hospital views that setting as a functioning community, and individuals within the setting relativistically. Some members are fairly permanent (e.g., physicians and nurses) and some visit and stay only briefly (e.g., patients and their families), but the expectations and concerns of each must be seen as equally legitimate and systematically explored. Each person has a unique view of the "clinical reality" which needs to be explored and compared.

One useful technique used to better understand diverse perspectives in medical settings is the explanatory model (EM) paradigm (Kleinman et al. 1978; Katon and Kleinman 1980; Johnson and Kleinman 1984). Briefly, the EM approach holds that all patients have culturally derived health beliefs which lead to elaborate interpretations of any symptoms. By asking key questions, health practitioners can better understand the meaning of symptoms, as well as the expectations for treatment of their patients. They can then tailor their approach to increase "compliance" with medical advice. In the past, the EM technique has been applied almost exclusively to patients' perspectives, particularly those from different cultural backgrounds, with the intent of helping practitioners better understand them.

My own practice has been to assert that all actors in the system have perspectives which need to be systematically explored. The EM approach, more broadly applied, becomes a first step in diagnosis of the ward system. Rather than first interviewing the identified hospitalized patient, I initially interview the practitioner who signed the consultation request in order to clarify the nature of the request. This informal interview helps our team to better diagnose the source(s) of the consult, to know better how the consultee feels affectively about the patient, what the consultee feels is the etiology, pathophysiology, severity, and prognosis of the patient's problem, and the nature of the assistance requested from psychiatry. I gather similar EM data from all involved in the care of the patient. Just as the application of the EM paradigm allows a practitioner to tailor the treatment recommendations to fit patient expectations, so also the expansion of the paradigm to include the expectations of the consultant and others allows us to better meet the expectations of *all* members of the ward system.

BEING THERAPEUTIC IN CLINICAL ANTHROPOLOGY

By systematically elucidating beliefs about a patient's problem from all members of the hospital system, an anthropologist can broker the interactions between various health professionals and patients, with the goal of increasing congruence, efficacy of care, and satisfaction on the part of both patients and those who treat them. Sensitivity to the pernicious effects of bureaucratization on the flexibility and openness of hospital subsystems, and upon effective teamwork in patient care activities, enables a clinical anthropologist to be in a position to do specific "systems therapy." An approach I have found useful is that of health team development (Rubin, Plovnik, and Fry 1975). Although it is designed to be employed overtly in structured workshops, I have used this approach covertly to increase effective team-work (especially in multidisciplinary teams) by systematically encouraging clarity of goals, roles, and procedures by which group decisions are made.

The team development approach holds that conflicts in health systems result not from clashes of personalities but from lack of clarity about basic goals, reciprocal roles, and procedures for allocating responsibility in making decisions. This fact is not recognized readily by most actors in the system, who commonly attribute their problems to the "bullheadedness," "laziness," or other personality attributes of coworkers and assume that they all share the same basic goals and have congruent role expectations. Fortunately, most teamwork problems do not stem from personality problems, but rather express individuals' lack of clarity about system goals and roles.

My first step is to encourage agreement about goals. Individual health care workers have a hierarchy of goals and personal expectations for their work that is based on both internal and external demands which color the way work is viewed and the priorities given to specific activities. Internal demands reflect personal attitudes, values, or beliefs about the nature of the work to be done such as "to keep people from dying" or "to make as much money as possible." External demands, on the other hand, are forces outside the individual such as family claims on time, the pressure of bill collectors, or the professional expectations of colleagues.

Systemic problems arise when health care team members have different goals and priorities but are unable to verbalize the source of disagreement. Numerous examples could be cited, but a particularly poignant example occurs frequently in burn units when a severely burned patient is admitted. When nurses, who are more experienced than the surgery residents who admit patients, know that a particular patient will likely die because of the severity of the burns, they often have as their goal "keeping the patient as comfortable as possible and letting him (or her) die peacefully." Residents, on the other hand, have as their goal "keeping the patient alive at all costs." This goal leads them to order many procedures and demand more nursing time, thereby forcing nurses to work extra hard on a patient who they believe ought to die, and to feel guilty because they are unable to spend more time with patients "who really need them." Without examining the sources of these divergent treatment goals, which are rooted in both professional ideologies and pragmatic concerns, nurses feel that physicians are "arrogant" and "like to play God," while physicians feel that the nurses are "lazy and not really dedicated to saving lives."

In cases of goal conflict, my role is to help staff share their demand systems (by both verbalizing and listening better), and choose one of two strategies: if conflicting goals are related to internal demands, the preferred strategy is to negotiate and compromise and the secondary strategy is to quit or get fired; if they are related to external demands, the preferred strategy is to join together to change the system and the secondary strategy is to cope. It is surprising how frequently personnel *assume* that they have common goals, and how much easier it is, after sharing their respective demand systems, to see why priorities for patient care are not always shared for reasons other than personality quirks.

Many hospital practitioners feel that it is unprofessional to share demand systems, particularly if they are external (e.g., "I just can't work an extra shift because my husband wants me at home!"), but are more comfortable with sharing internal demands (attitudes, values, etc.), particularly when they relate to professional ethics (e.g., "I don't believe in ever 'letting someone die'!" or "Nurses are not supposed to be subservient to physicians . . . and I refuse to take orders like that!"). Goal conflicts caused by internal demands, however, are frequently more difficult because they demand negotiation and compromise of personal values. External demand conflicts, which are resolved either by system change or simply coping, more frequently result in the "banding together" of a health care team as all suffer together or work cooperatively to find a solution to a shared problem in the hospital environment.

Next to conflicting goals, the second most common cause of poor teamwork in hospitals is "just not being able to work with that person." Inability to work together effectively is also often attributed to personality traits, but is actually caused by role conflict, ambiguity, strain, and overload. These occur for a variety of reasons, but they have a pernicious influence on the interaction of individuals who must work together in order to carry out patient care effectively. A common symptom of role conflict is the phrase "it's not my job" or the statement "if he would just do his job we would all be better off!"

Many people do not recognize that roles involve at least two people and instead believe that, if they "have their own act to-gether," good patient care will result. Patient care activities do not work in reality the way they do "on paper": a nurse will call in sick and leave a ward short-handed, a patient's condition may worsen un-expectedly, or procedures may have to be altered for any number of reasons. These and other challenges to teamwork require flexible for-mal work roles and personal negotiation of mutual role expectations between interdependent coworkers to meet changing situations.

Although many roles in hospitals are negotiated informally by trial and error, through "role modeling," or by covert conditioning which shapes a coworker's behavior, my interaction encourages the sending and receiving of overt role messages. Role messages are statements between collaborating health professionals which indicate how each would like the other to perform in their reciprocal activi-ties. I try to help those in the system to make their messages behav-iorally specific, linked to shared goals, and reciprocal. For example, role clarity and agreement will not likely occur if one nurse says about her coworker: "if only she would be more friendly" or "if only she wouldn't be so lazy!" Instead, I might suggest that she say to her coworker: "In order for us to help these patients (goal link-age), I need you to help me by filling out these papers each day when we first get to work (behavioral specificity). If you can do that, I shall be happy to help you with your other work (reciprocity)." The second person can then make his or her expectations known, again with behavioral specificity and tied to goals that both share.

My methods for systems therapy with health professionals are both overt and covert. In a formal, weekly support group that I facil-itate for burn unit nurses, I frequently ask them to discuss the goals which underlie a particular course of action, and help broker the dis-cussions aimed at compromise or mutual understanding. In a more covert fashion, when one nurse confides to me that she thinks another nurse is "just lazy," I suggest that conflicting goals may be respon-sible and suggest examples. When health practitioners complain to me that they "can't get [one of their colleagues] to do a procedure in a certain way" or to otherwise perform differently, I may suggest a behaviorally specific, goal-directed role message to try. If a group of health practitioners is having difficulty with a patient problem, I may overtly ask for goal clarity, and broker negotiation of roles, or I may listen carefully for areas of agreement and simply suggest a course of action which I recognize will be acceptable to all, thereby covertly pointing out those areas where team agreement is already present but unrecognized.

INSTITUTIONAL ANALYSIS

The ethos (sometimes referred to by industrial psychologists as the organizational "personality") which accompanies the structure and functioning of any organization has profound effects on those who associate with it. Conflict is endemic in most hospitals, in part because the bureaucratic tendency to reduce variability and flexibility is challenged constantly by the need to treat every patient individually. In terms of personal satisfaction and sense of therapeutic efficacy, the approach to this and related problems that I have found to be most provocative has been termed "being the institutional analyst."[5] Unlike an organizational development consultant who gives time and task-specific feedback to those in the organization who hire him, the institutional analyst learns as much as possible about the "personality" of the organization and helps the organization to change by facilitating awareness of problem areas.

Institutional analysis requires careful listening to spontaneous comments of organization members and to their answers to nondirective questions. It also requires access to all parts of the institution. Being a member of a consultation psychiatric team is helpful in this regard because it encourages interaction with patients and staff on a variety of wards. Being an anthropologist is also important because I am able to do participant-observation apart from the formal consultation activities of the Department of Psychiatry.[6] As an anthropolo-

5. I am indebted to Dr. Lorna Amarasingham Rhodes, of the Department of Anthropology at the University of Washington in Seattle, for suggesting the term "institutional analyst" in a paper she read at the annual meetings of the American Anthropological Association in 1983 (although I use the term here in a manner she did not originally intend). For years I sought an appropriate metaphor to capture both the substance and style of this aspect of my clinical work in the hospital. It is a type of work which has never, to my knowledge, been written about before in the anthropological literature; I was also unaware that other colleagues were consciously engaged in quiet "systems therapy" in the course of their work. Dr. Rhodes has clearly done this work well, but more importantly, has taken the time to reflect on her work in a way which has brought more focus to my own professional identity and contributed immeasurably to this chapter. Her original paper, with modifications, is due to be published in *Ethos*.

6. In fact, institutional analysis may be a psychiatric metaphor for fairly traditional anthropological investigation of the ideological aspects of organizational culture, which seeks to describe the ethos or world view of the hospital.

gist, I remain marginal: I have no authority over those with whom I interact and am not viewed as a threat or cut off from access to information.[7] Freedom of movement and access permits a breadth of vision that is impossible for those with traditionally defined roles. Potentially, I can understand more about the "personality" of the institution than can its more entrenched members.

However, data gathering from hospital professionals must be done carefully. In organizational settings where there is role strain and ambiguity, status differentials, and a high affective load such as that created by sickness, there is a high probability of hypersensitivity to criticism and high levels of defensiveness. Thus, questions intended to elicit data about patient problems must convey a sense of neutrality. Maintaining objectivity and neutrality about Western medical systems is difficult for most anthropologists, who tend to condemn physicians while overly identifying with patients (Stein, H. 1980). But "taking sides" with one group or another in the system, and particularly with patients, is a temptation which must be avoided. Premature advocacy for the position of any group is counterproductive; maintenance of status-role ambiguity is crucial; and it is imperative that conclusions not be reached nor blame assigned prematurely. Physicians usually believe that social scientists are uncritical patient advocates, and this motivation tends to be attributed even if it is not present.

"Keeping a finger on the pulse of the organization" is an important methodological metaphor for another essential aspect of this type of clinical ethnography, but one which cannot be accomplished adequately through formal consultation activities alone. I spend considerable time "lurking"[8] on the wards. I listen to nurses and others talking in the cafeteria, read personnel notices on bulletin boards, peruse minutes of staff meetings, read nurses' notes in charts, make rounds with residents and medical students, and facilitate a support

7. A more thorough treatment of this important point is included in a paper by Hazel Weidman (1982:203), who has steadfastly refused to be "promoted" from a staff to a line position in her department, feeling that such a position would "compartmentalize" and "channel activities tangentially." She prefers to "put the mission ahead of the position."

8. This technique, and many of my perspectives on hospitals as organizations were taught to me by Dr. Carol Taylor, of the University of Florida. Her book on hospitals (Taylor 1969) provides important theoretical underpinnings for my type of clinical anthropology.

group for nurses in the burn unit. My purpose is to understand system goals, organizational structures, role relations, supervisory styles, communication dynamics, reward systems, power loci, and use of time and space in each relevant subsystem of the hospital. I assess processing by the system, including the manner in which anything (patients, staff, supplies, information, etc.) enters and leaves the system, and the internal and external feedback loops which allow the unit of diagnostic interest (e.g., a ward) to adjust to changing conditions in its internal or external structure and functioning. The data collected in this way help to define sources of support and stress for staff in the hospital environment.

These characteristics of hospitals need to be understood, apart from any specific patient-care issue. Hospitals in which there is participatory decision-making by staff and administration have a different quality from those which are rigidly hierarchical. In the burn unit, for example, I noted a memorandum to the staff which was signed "the Management": a datum which spoke volumes about the impersonal supervisory style in that unit. In contrast, another unit had a "communication book" in the staff lounge, with personal, handwritten notes back and forth between staff and administration, as well as between staff nurses, suggesting alterations in procedures, reminding others about policy or upcoming continuing education programs, and commending others for particularly noteworthy patient-care contributions. Knowledge of these characteristics makes it possible to better pinpoint the cause(s) of patient problems, and to better predict problems in their care. It is valuable data, too, for the clinical anthropologist who desires to help create a more healthy work environment.

The focus of my assessment of organizational "personality" is the relative flexibility and openness of the system because these traits are characteristic of healthy systems. Patient care in most hospitals requires ongoing, effective teamwork by professionals from a variety of disciplines. Within each professional subgroup, there are multiple levels of staff who have different statuses and roles. The processing of patients through this complex organizational system demands careful coordination between subsystems and flexibility of roles within each subsystem. In a burn unit, for example, rigid role differentiation between RNs, LPNs, "burn techs," and nursing supervisors inevitably leads to suboptimal patient care (e.g., unnecessary delay or waiting between system processing tasks such as bathing and feeding, or dressing changes and physical therapy), role conflict, and nursing stress. It leads also to poor communication within the system, an emphasis on power and manipulative behavior, inefficient use of space and time, and practices which are not modified to meet changing conditions in the system or in its patients. Lack of flexibility has deleterious effects on both patient care and staff morale.

In hospitals, as in other bureaucracies, the most efficient, innovative, and satisfying work is accomplished not by the "formal" system, but through a parallel "informal" system which exists because of the willingness of some members of the organization to flout rules, bend regulations, try new procedures, step outside their job descriptions, work extra hours, and otherwise compromise in the service of increasing system flexibility. My work entails understanding the formal bureaucratic structure and function of the hospital, and constantly comparing this *ideal* "anatomy" and "physiology" with the *actual*. Systemic sickness occurs when the formal bureaucratic system, with its rigid, "obsessional-neurotic" tendencies, overwhelms the informal system. These system conflicts are expressed in individuals by symptoms such as authoritarian supervisory styles, staff apathy, hostility toward supervisors, absenteeism, indifference to patient and coworker needs, and other symptoms of "burnout."

At one level, the organizational personality is a "collective unconscious"—the hospital's view of itself that influences employees and their work. For example, the hospital in which I work is both a county hospital which treats a high percentage of indigent patients and a medical school teaching hospital. In comparison with other hospitals in the city, there is a negative organizational self-image. The hospital is not held in particular esteem by its employees, jokes are told by staff about the hospital and its patients, and there is a sense of being constantly underfunded and understaffed. A sense of deprivation influences staff, who feel exploited, but the fact that so many patients are viewed as getting "free care" leads to an institutional ethos that patients do not have to be catered to because they are already receiving a favor by being admitted. Although unrecognized by staff, this aspect of the organization influences patient care.

On another level, I am concerned about the "basic personality" of the staff. All staff members in the hospital are influenced to some degree by the organizational culture, sometimes in ways unrecognized. After starting work in the hospital, enculturation leads to internalization of the organizational ethos or world view which causes staff members to react, often subconsciously, to patients and others in the work setting in characteristic ways (e.g., with apathy, cynicism, dogmatism).

Each staff member also has idiosyncratic feelings about professional activities, which are frequently troubling and often unrecognized, and with which I can help in the course of normal ethnographic data gathering. Merely being there and quietly trying to understand the complete picture of what is going on can be therapeutic; it facilitates a free exploration and modification of feelings toward the hospital work environment by staff. I walk around the wards visiting with staff, letting them talk about whatever is on their mind, and listen actively. My consultations occur in staff lounges, in hallways, or even at the bedside of a just-deceased patient. At times I will make a statement ("It must be difficult to work under these circumstances . . .") or ask a general question ("What's it like to work here?") to both facilitate staff expression of troubling feelings and increase my understanding of the hospital. Most staff *assume* that I am supportive, a kind of transference which betrays their needs to be cared for as individuals. The fact that I am encouraged in my work from many levels, including hospital administration, says much the same about the hospital.

Staff members often reveal "horrible" or "forbidden" thoughts to me, such as the wish that a particular patient would die, feelings that their hospital is a repugnant place to work, or the fantasy that a particularly difficult supervisor is killed. By merely listening, I facilitate the bringing of such conflict-laden, unconscious thoughts into the conscious; by being nonjudgmental I allow them to be acknowledged by the individual. It is only when staff members can accept these parts of themselves which they normally repress or deny that they have the freedom to change them. It is only when a large number of staff alter their view of the hospital as an organization, or when the hospital undergoes major institutional changes, that the "organizational personality" changes.

Crucial to my analytic approach is the use of silence. In classic psychoanalysis, silence is used to allow the uncovering of unconscious material—to prevent, for example, the blocking of instinctual drives by the superego. In the hospital, as in the analysand, one part of the organizational hierarchy (e.g., administration) could use any injudicious, premature interpretations by the anthropologist/analyst to repress others (e.g., staff). Therefore, I do not often "take sides" and I never gossip. The institutional analyst does not make the patient change, but rather, provides a vehicle for bringing unconscious conflicts into consciousness, so that individuals (or the hospital as a whole) can safely consider alternative courses of action or attitudes, or work with less anxiety and self-recrimination. It is difficult always to know who is the patient in these analytic activities, because there is a fine line between the collective and the individual unconscious. My current practice is to view the hospital as the patient, but treat at the level of the individual staff member or the ward. It is hoped that as individuals and wards feel better about their work through institutional analysis, the hospital itself will be more healthy.

For my brand of clinical anthropology, both quiet analytic work and overt data gathering from health professionals involve the use of empathy: adopting a therapeutic approach which assumes that staff are as much afflicted with an organizational disease which they may unwittingly pass on to patients as they are the cause of distress. For example, when gathering information about a particular "problem patient" from staff, I attempt to elicit staff feelings toward the patient. Phrases like, "This must be a very difficult patient . . ." or "It must be frustrating to try to work with this case . . ." convey both a willingness to hear staff frustration or anger and to be sympathetic, as well as the sense of neutrality and relativity mentioned earlier. It acknowledges the legitimacy of feeling "stressed out" by forces beyond personal control, and the human tendency to displace anger and frustration onto others, or otherwise deal inadequately with such feelings. It invites catharsis, the open expression of emotions which, in itself, can be therapeutic. It taps into the commonly held belief among health professionals that no one really cares about their problems and that resolution of staff problems must be sacrificed in the service of resolving those of their patients. This common ethos is in part responsible for the fact that health professionals are a class of individuals who need but receive very little mental health care. By "witnessing" (Bosk 1985) for clinicians in this manner, a medical anthropologist provides the same solace as do clinicians for patients: listening to pain and problems confirms that the suffering is real and allows the sufferer to begin to deal with it.

Most importantly, a therapeutic approach toward staff allows for simultaneous data-gathering and rapport-building, the former essential for good theoretical anthropology as well as for accurate diagnosis of problems in the system, and the latter a key ingredient for later design of approaches to treat systemic distress. It facilitates the discovery of incongruous views of patient problems which serve to impede effective teamwork; it enables comparison of professional and patient explanatory models of problems which allows for effective brokering of disparate perspectives as a part of "treatment"; it is a mechanism for "keeping a finger on the pulse of the organization," which promotes understanding of the many variables in the hospital unrelated to patient problems which influence patient care; and it lets me feel that I am contributing to an enhanced quality of life for both patients and the practitioners who treat them.

But Is It Anthropology?

There is a strong applied tradition among medical anthropologists, but the debate about the legitimacy of the type of clinical anthropology described above continues to rage and will not be resolved soon. Many will continue to question the implications of such work in the hospital, and some already question whether or not it is anthropology. My conscious use of medical, and specifically psychiatric, metaphors may contribute to confusion in this regard. Moreover, some of the techniques I use are employed also by those from other professional disciplines who have historically had a service mandate in hospitals.

My view is that the approach described here is uniquely anthropological because it requires an ability to juxtapose, if not integrate, the several different cultural "pieces" in the hospital. At the core of my clinical work is an understanding of the hospital as a cultural system, and a constant learning about that system through participant observation. However, anthropological work within hospitals must be practical and perceived as providing a service. For this reason, even while engaged in ethnographic research, I seize opportunities to help health practitioners to perceive and solve patient-care problems in new ways. My empathy with patients and staff is now based upon the knowledge gained about medical culture from long-term field-work in hospitals which extends over more than a decade. The "clinical ethnography" approach which I find useful is not primarily intended to be therapeutic on the individual level. I use psychological skills acquired through specialized training, but I know full well that health care professionals tend to suffer from the assumption that the locus of problems is psychological and that patients in the hospital are isolated individuals. My type of ethnography attempts to work *through* individuals to develop treatment strategies at the systemic level.

I view my primary role as that of teacher and consultant, and I advocate strongly the transmittal of clinically efficacious anthropological skills to health practitioners. I help others to themselves become clinical ethnographers and institutional analysts rather than compete with them. Despite differences in theoretical models, clinical anthropologists, psychiatrists, other physicians, and those in allied health professions typically share a wish to define and solve the "right" problems in patient care, although the presence of inevitable "red herring" symptoms[9] in patients may conveniently become the focus of attention when the "right" problems are actually located in the health care system and its practitioners. A good clinical anthropologist joins in a *shared* effort to define the scope and boundary of a patient's symptom, and we help our medical colleagues best when we demonstrate that we are all trying to accomplish the same thing. I practice anthropology as described here primarily because practitioners in the health field currently do not. This leaves a niche in hospitals and medical education which, although there are a few consultation-liaison psychiatrists involved, remains largely open. My goal is to discover methods and generate theoretical perspectives which

9. The concept of "red herring" symptoms belongs to Dr. Howard Stein, a medical anthropologist/medical educator in the Department of Family Medicine at the University of Oklahoma College of Medicine who practices the same type of clinical anthropology as presented here, but in an outpatient clinic rather than a hospital setting (Stein 1985). The term refers to a tendency for practitioners to focus on a particular topic or symptom to avoid discussing a different topic or symptom which is actually more important for the patient, but which is more personally anxiety-provoking. Examples of red herring symptoms are focusing on weight loss or tumor growth in a terminally ill patient to avoid the issue of dying, or turning attention to a cultural issue in a particular patient's care to avoid discussion of his iatrogenic hepatitis. I am indebted to Dr. Stein, not only for the concept of red herring symptoms, but also for his thoughtful comments on an initial draft of this chapter and for our ongoing dialogue on clinical anthropology, which has been most helpful in clarifying my own thinking on the subject.

will be incorporated into the roles of health professionals. I forth-rightly try to make the hospital a better place in which to work and be treated, an endeavor which offers the promise of simultaneous expansion of the discipline of anthropology and expression of care for others.

15

THE ETHNOGRAPHIC EVALUATOR

David M. Fetterman

Ethnographic data collection and analysis is the bedrock upon which anthropology contributes to the solution of practical problems. This theme is a major one in this volume, but in this essay David M. Fetterman relates this contribution of anthropology to the practical world of educational policy and program evaluation research. He makes the important point that, during the past several years, evaluation research specialists have recognized the limited usefulness of research designs that rely solely on the use of variables that are quantifiable (cf. Whyte in essay 7).

Fetterman places ethnography in the context of practice by clearly

David M. Fetterman (Ph.D., Stanford) is a medical and educational anthropologist who is currently an administrator and assistant professor of education at Stanford University. He has conducted fieldwork in Israel and the United States. He has engaged in national and state educational policy studies related to dropouts and pushouts, gifted children, and migrant children. He recently received the President's Award from the Evaluation Research Society for his contribution to the use of ethnography in evaluation research and the Praxis Publication Award from the Washington Association of Professional Anthropologists. He is currently cochairperson of the Ethnographic Approaches to Evaluation Committee of the American Anthropological Association.

I am indebted to many other risk-takers who helped to shape my own role as an ethnographic evaluator. I thank Pertti J. Pelto for grounding me firmly in anthropological theory and the ethnographic method. I am grateful for the guidance of my mentor, George D. Spindler. His intelligence and friendship made my scholarly rites of passage challenging and enlightening. I appreciate also his encouragement to work in this brave new world. Lee J. Cronbach's critical eye sharpened my focus and helped me to hit my target squarely in addressing national- and state-level policy matters. NIE sponsorship of ethnographically informed work contributed to an educational research environment conducive to the application of ethnographic concepts and techniques. G. Keston Tallmage was one of the early risk-takers in hiring an ethnographic evaluator. I also appreciate the supportive attitude and assistance of Elizabeth M. Eddy and Deborah S. Waxman toward this new venture.

This essay was especially prepared for this volume, but it is printed also in Fetterman and Pitman (1986). It is reproduced here by permission of Sage Publications.

demarking its limits. The practical task of evaluation demands that the practitioner go beyond these techniques and the data they yield in order to produce a judgment or recommendation based on analysis of alternative courses of action. In situations of this nature, the analytical skills of the ethnographer are clearly tested in a highly charged political atmosphere. Those who cannot conduct analyses of their own, formulate judgments and recommendations, and assert and defend them, are soon washed out. In practicing anthropology, the data are never the sole objective. Moreover, the job is not finished when the data have been collected and analyzed; the data are merely the foundation upon which decisions and courses of action are constructed, proposed, and sustained.

ANTHROPOLOGISTS HAVE PLANTED deep roots in the soil of educational evaluation. They have been able to generate useful insights and effective solutions to contemporary social problems. This contribution has gained them a measure of acceptance and popularity in educational evaluation. They have offered evaluators a new paradigm, a new way of looking at educational innovations, and new methods of data collection and analysis. Moreover, they have diffused a cultural interpretation of behaviors and events within educational research.

Ethnographic educational evaluators have contributed to theory, theory testing, and practice in the course of their studies. They are characterized by their ability to step analytically beyond description to judgment. These judgments are made within the highly politicized environment of education. Ethnographic evaluators must adapt to this niche if they are to be effective. Finally, the work of ethnographic evaluators is reflexive. They contribute to practice, specifically to the development of design, data collection, and analysis in ethnography. They contribute to both anthropology and education; revitalizing one and expanding the horizons of the other.

Cultural Broker

The ethnographic evaluator is a cultural broker. He or she communicates cultural knowledge across disciplinary boundaries. The ethnographic evaluator's contribution can be understood more fully by examining the nature and character of this change agent's role in practice. The cultural broker is bicultural and must be a hybrid to be effective. In essence, evaluators must be able to speak and think in two different languages and to articulate the conceptual concerns of contrasting cultures; they are interdisciplinary ground-breakers.

During culture contact, assimilation and acculturation occur. The new environment consists of conflicting world views and work settings, and ethnographic evaluators adapt to it in a variety of ways. This context, with its accompanying incentives and constraints, shapes the ethnographic work. The ethnographic evaluator is also a human being. Tracing the life cycle of this academic entrepreneur gives depth as well as breadth to our understanding of the role of this cultural risk taker.

BICULTURAL

As noted above, the educational ethnographic evaluator is an educational anthropologist and as such is bicultural, like most applied anthropologists. Educational anthropologists work within the two very different worlds of education and anthropology. Luminaries in the field such as Mead, Spindler, Kimball, and Eddy among others have worked effectively with educators and established the foundation upon which the ethnographic evaluator works. Nevertheless, the cultural chasm between anthropology and education periodically erupts in conflict. Evaluation is one of the areas in which conflict still exists.

Educational evaluators and anthropologists experienced severe cognitive dissonance in the early days of their union. In the late 1960s and 1970s educational anthropologists and educational evaluators were concerned with different topics. Educational evaluators focused typically on such professional topics as teaching, curriculum, and administration, while educational anthropologists were preoccupied with such topics as culture, religion, social structure, and human organization. Moreover, as these differences in topic preferences suggest, these two fields represented different ways of thinking about the world.

Conflict, misunderstanding, and miscommunication resulted from poorly communicated expectations of each other's performance. A rapprochement between educational evaluators and anthropologists has grown as their respective cultural values are being made more explicit and as an interest has developed in pursuing more topics of mutual concern. Anthropologists increasingly are focusing on new topics of interest to educational evaluators. They study these new topics, however, from their unique cultural perspective. The classroom is viewed as part of a larger sociocultural system. This perspective focuses attention on the processes of schooling, teaching, learning, cultural transmission, and social change. To function within these two worlds, educational anthropologists must learn the rules dictated by each. These rules govern speech, dress, and both public and private behavior. They must be able to translate what they see into a format useful to educators, and yet communicate with academic anthropologists in their own language as well. This often requires linguistic competence as code switchers when working with mixed groups.

HYBRID

The ethnographic educational evaluator is not only bicultural, but he or she is also a hybrid. The label ethnographic evaluator suggests a contradiction in terms to some scholars. How can an anthropologist be nonjudgmental and judgmental at the same time? The question provides a handle by means of which we can clarify the role of the ethnographic evaluator.

First, it is a myth that anthropologists are completely nonjudgmental. The selection of a topic itself reflects built-in biases. The process of collecting data requires discrimination and judgment. Analysis and the manner in which findings are skillfully crafted and communicated reveal explicit and implicit biases. The aim, however, is to assume a nonjudgmental orientation toward different cultural practices. Ideally, value judgments are not made about marriage practices such as polygamy, gender-favored inheritance patterns, the lifestyle of a merchant or beggar, or personal hygiene practices. Both traditional ethnographers and ethnographic evaluators attempt to adopt this posture throughout a study and to make explicit their more conscious and obvious biases. A nonjudgmental orientation and an evaluative approach are not mutually exclusive. Evaluation simply represents another level of analysis. The evaluator can assess the functions and adaptations of a system, program, or policy without making a value judgment about the cultural practice *per se*.

The major difference between the traditional ethnographer and the ethnographic evaluator is that the traditional ethnographer *concludes* the study with a description of the culture, while an ethnographic evaluator *begins* the evaluative segment of the study with a description of the culture. The ethnographic evaluator describes what is going on and then makes a qualitative leap beyond description to the explicit appraisal and assessment of the cultural system in terms of its own cultural norms. As an ethnographer and an ethnographic evaluator, I have found explicit assessment to be a more honest and useful approach to the study of human beings.

Ethnographers, in practice, are continually making assessments regarding the nature of the people and the system under study. Ethnographic evaluators simply bring this subconscious, and often subliminal, process to the surface of conscious expression. Moreover, participants and clients in educational research have learned to expect feedback as part of their daily lives. Holding back one's assessments upsets a delicate balance of reciprocity and mutual expectations. Educators perceive evaluation in a positive manner. They understand the role and recognize the evaluator's work as a useful contribution to the group. The typical ethnographic endeavor by comparison seems less relevant and inadequately reciprocal, almost exploitive, in nature.

ASSIMILATION AND ACCULTURATION

Basically, the key to understanding the label ethnographic evaluator can be found in a simple grammatical analysis of the term. The word ethnographic is an adjective, characterizing an anthropological type of evaluator. Whether this means an anthropologist is walking around in an evaluator's moccasins or an evaluator is walking around wearing an anthropological lens is simply a function of who is doing the study. Each individual finds what Aristotle called a "natural resting spot" from which to see the world. The ethnographic evaluator's selection of a resting spot determines how he or she will conduct the study. The traditional ethnographer will not survive in an interdisciplinary environment requiring flexibility, adaptation, and innovation. The poorly trained ethnographer will not be able to differentiate between adaptation, mutation, and mutilation. The well-trained ethnographic evaluator is able to apply anthropological theory, concepts, and methods to new areas in new ways without compromising the integrity of the endeavor. In addition, a competent ethnographic evaluator, like a seasoned researcher, recognizes his or her limitations. We cannot be experts in all matters. The secure ethnographic evaluator recognizes that it is as important to know when one does not know the answer or even the right questions, as it is to know whom to ask for assistance. The insecure ethnographer who enters educational evaluation is likely to overcompensate by applying rigid standards to a situation requiring a novel approach. On the other end of the spectrum, there are some insecure ethnographers who become elite acculturationists. They may deny or disparage their own methodological heritage and assume a highly stylized version of the dominant evaluation culture. Finally, there are a number of individuals who begin as ethnographic evaluators and, if they remain in the profession at all, are fully assimilated into the dominant culture. They either identify themselves simply as evaluators or fade into the woodwork.

Contrasting World Views and Work Settings

We are all products of our environment, and it is necessary to analyze our environment to identify how we have come to select our own way of looking at the world, our own natural resting spot. Ethnographic evaluators function within three conflicting world views: academe, the research corporation, and the federal bureaucracy. The manner in which ethnographic evaluators identify with and cope with these competing versions of reality determines the nature of the home or prison they construct for themselves. A particular source of difficulty for many lies in the transition process from academe to the world of contract research. A brief discussion of these world views will serve to identify the variables that shape the character of the ethnographic evaluator and in turn the quality of his or her work.

ACADEME
The university environment has traditionally represented "home base" for most anthropologists. Anthropologists and other social scientists

operating within the academic sphere are socialized to place a high value on autonomy and independence in their research endeavors (Clinton 1976). Universities provide a supportive context for the pursuit of these aims, preventing the more obvious vested interests and biases of external agencies from contaminating research. Academe is able to pursue this course because the economic support system for research is based primarily on grants. Most grants provide academics with a relatively small fiscal budget and a lengthy period of time for investigation, in contrast to contracts which usually provide larger budgets and less time. In addition, academics typically specify the problem and formulate the study design.

Sponsors of grants within academe are more flexible than the contract monitors or sponsors of research in the corporation. They are typically more generous in their consideration of research design and implementation modifications than are contract sponsors. This is a function of the sponsors' differing environments, a topic which will be discussed below. Anthropologists in academe conduct exploratory, traditionally long-term studies and are provided considerable flexibility in terms of time and focus. An academic orientation collides head on with the demands of work in the "outside world" of contract research. It is a contradiction or "culture shock" that all applied anthropologists must face eventually.

The academic orientation is enhanced by additional scholastic trappings. The university environment fosters the development of the lone scholar. The promotion and tenure of an individual in this setting is dependent on a personal publication record, as well as other economic and political factors in the academic department. The hackneyed formula "publish or perish" still applies to modern university-based scholarship. In the humanities and social sciences, including anthropology, interdisciplinary research is praised but atypical; it is considered a marginal contribution to one's professional development. In addition, co-authored works or works with multiple authorship are viewed less favorably than publications representing the efforts of one person. Graduate students are socialized to accept these fundamental tenets of the academic world view. Unfortunately, many elements of this world view clash with the values guiding the worlds of educational evaluation and the federal bureaucracy. The ethnographic evaluator is most likely to confront these new worlds for the first time within an office in a research corporation.

THE RESEARCH CORPORATION

The ethnographic evaluator entering the research corporation is confronted immediately with a different set of values and research paradigms. Traditional educational researchers dominate evaluation research corporations. They have been socialized by graduate training to accept the educational research establishment's orthodox credo. This view is characterized by the experimental, quantitative approach to research. Campbell and Stanley (1963) and Riecken et al. (1974) are among the most widely recognized proponents of this approach. Campbell and Stanley have traditionally viewed the experiment as follows:

the only means for settling disputes regarding educational practice, as the only way of verifying educational improvements, and as the only way of establishing a cumulative tradition in which improvements can be introduced without the danger of a faddish discard of old wisdom in favor of inferior novelties.(1963:2)

Educational researchers employing alternative methods or perspectives have been, until very recently, regarded as operating outside the mainstream of "acceptable" educational research. An overemphasis on the importance of the design has led to a situation in which the methodological tail wags the proverbial research dog. Researchers have often allowed specific tools to dictate the way research is conducted, rather than first identifying the research questions and then selecting the appropriate methods to respond to them. This is partially a function of federal dictates.

Fundamentally, the confrontation between the ethnographic evaluator and the traditional research corporation employee is paradigmatic in nature. My own first days in a research corporation were marked by loud arguments with the president of the company. I would argue about the low validity of his approach and he would argue about the low reliability of mine. The ritual hazing was rooted in our paradigmatic differences, in phenomenology and logical positivism. In time, this phase passed. Once the tribal chief was convinced of the utility of the ethnographic approach, others in the office followed, albeit cautiously and reluctantly. In some cases, ethnographic evaluators are too quick to follow the path of least resistance and accept without question assertions and untested assumptions. In such cases, both parties are denied an opportunity to learn from each other on basic paradigmatic levels—questioning basic assumptions about how we view the world.

The research corporation has another significant difference from "home base." The evaluation corporation is fundamentally a business which is primarily concerned with producing a reputable research product, advancing the state of the art, and making a profit. (In nonprofit organizations the profit is referred to as the "margin".) It stays in business by bidding for proposals in which the problem, and often the research design, has been defined in advance. "Independently the agencies push out tentacles, brandishing separate RFP's [requests for proposals]. Firms on the other side of the chasm send out tentacles in response and, as on the Sistine ceiling, a spark leaps across" (Cronbach et al. 1980a:463). The contracting process itself shapes the evaluation as Keith Baker has discussed:

Many applied research administrators push for such a detailed specification of the problem and research design that the only important question left for the contractor is how much it will cost to carry out the agency's plan. The agency, knowing what it wants done and how it wants it done, is looking for a skilled staff to carry out its needs, not somebody else's desires. . . .

The agency's desire to maximize control over the research, to make sure its problems get addressed the way the agency thinks [they] should be addressed, is precisely the reason why it uses contracts rather than grants. The important feature of a contract is that it maximizes the agency's control. (1975:210)

The RFP is very important in the research process. It fixes the outline and many of the details of the study's methodology as well as specifying the problem to be studied. The RFP will generally define the population to be studied, sample sizes, and whether the study will be experimental, post-hoc interviews, or pre- and post-field observations. The RFP may even specify the instruments to be used and the type of statistical analysis to be employed. In general, the two areas where the RFP leaves greatest discretion to the proposer is in the instrument content (the specific items) and data analysis. Note again that the RFP is prepared by the agency. The people who ultimately do the work have no involvement in many of the basic decisions of the research process. (1975:213–214)

There is room for negotiation but the above pattern encourages the adoption of research proposals and designs without sufficient scrutiny. The day-to-day operations of the research corporation described by Cronbach et al. where there are plenty of "mouths to feed,'' provides an insight into the research corporation's behavior in this regard.

Life in the contracting firm is dominated by the scramble for contracts. At every turn new money must be won to keep a staff in place. However, only large and experienced organizations can successfully solicit and manage large evaluations. A stack of blue chips is required merely to enter the bidding. The competitor must have a sophisticated business office for preparing proposals and keeping track of expenses. A public-relations staff stands by, ready to protect the flanks of a politically sensitive study. Computer facilities have to be extensive and up-to-date. Professional managers are needed to keep activities on schedule. And behind the scenes the firm's Washington representative keeps in touch with those who will be commissioning evaluations. Albert (quoted in Biderman & Sharp, 1972, p. 49) commented cynically that good research directors are far less necessary to a firm's success than are intelligence agents able to pick up early word on bidding opportunities. But the firm does what it can to maintain a staff of professionals qualified to plan, collect, and interpret data.

Some firms offer services of many kinds, in many program areas. Once well established, a diversified firm can take the ups and downs of fortune more easily than a specialized firm. But even the largest firm shivers during a budget freeze, and it goes into a spasm of readjustment when it wins an unusually large contract. A narrow specialty makes an organization highly sensitive to the funding priorities of agencies. Over and over the same tale is told. A firm waxes as federal interest in its specialty grows. It welds together a team with complementary skills. The team accumulates special knowledge of the social problem. Then support disappears, the team splits up, and a capable organization is lost (Abt, 1979, p. 50). (Cronbach et al. 1980b:329)

Excessive protests regarding the study's design jeopardize the corporation's chances of winning a contract. This business orientation promotes compromises which may contribute to the overall pattern of misused designs. In addition, corporation researchers look at present sponsors as potential future sponsors, and are therefore more likely to adopt research proposals and designs without sufficient scrutiny. Most successful proposals are characterized by the quantitative designs which reflect the dominant culture of the educational research establishment, the research corporation, and the federal bureaucracy.

THE FEDERAL BUREAUCRACY

A brief examination of the federal agencies' real world constraints and views provides a rationale for the research corporation's perspective and behavior.[1] One of the primary responsibilities of the federal sponsor is to produce the most credible and socially relevant research (Holcomb 1974) dictated by Congressional mandate. Policy research, in contrast to basic research, represents another significant facet of the federal bureaucratic perspective.

[Policy research in juxtaposition to basic research] is much less abstract, much more closely tied to particular actions to be undertaken or avoided. While basic [research] aims chiefly to uncover truth, policy research seeks to aid in the solution of fundamental problems and in the advancement of major programs. (Etzioni 1971)

Policy research seeks immediate action in response to a troubled situation such as unemployment, a high dropout rate, and so on. It attacks a discrete facet of the situation to "avoid turf problems." Decisions are made in a context of accommodation rather than command (von Neuman and Morganstern 1953). Policy is more a process of drifting toward a decision than a Platonic pattern of a single commander handing down decisions affecting the entire social sphere (see March and Olsen 1976). There is, according to Mulhauser (1975:311) "no search for a comprehensive understanding of the problem's nature or origin." Glennan (1972) pointed out that significant go/no-go decisions are rare in policy. Cronbach et al. (1980b:287) add to the picture the fact that "Policy makers do weigh alternatives that have incommensurable outcomes—reduced-crime versus community-harmony, say, or children's shoes-versus-Army boots." The ever-present time pressure requires immediate identification of politically viable "levers of action." Often, Mulhauser (1975:311) points out: "The action taken is a minor variation on what was done the last time something like this came up."

Federal agencies are constrained also by the responsibility for providing timely input for policy makers. As Coward (1976:14) points out, "Evaluation data presented after a policy decision has been made

---

1. The perspective of federal government policy makers is clearly presented in the literature by Mulhauser (1975), Coward (1976), Holcomb (1974), Etzioni (1971), von Neuman and Morganstern (1953), March and Olsen (1976), Acland (1979), Cronbach et al. (1980b), Rich (in Weiss, 1977), Elisburg (1977), Lindblom and Cohen (1979), Baker (1975), and others.

can have little impact on the decision.'' The role of evaluation itself is limited in the policy arena. It is used, according to Rich (in Weiss 1977:200), in ''groups and clusters'' as one piece of evidence or data in the larger fundamentally political equation (Acland 1979). Cronbach et al. (1980b:294) point out that ''What impresses a research expert obsessed with method may not impress someone who sees the larger picture.'' Elisburg similarly places the Congressional role of evaluation into perspective:

It cannot be stressed too strenuously that scientific program evaluation is itself evaluated by the Congress in terms of its utility to promote the effectiveness and precision of legislative judgments in a political milieu. (1977:67–68)

Furthermore, according to Cronbach et al.,

Knowing this week's score does not tell the coach how to prepare for next week's game. The information that an intervention had satisfactory or unsatisfactory outcomes is of little use by itself; users of the study need to know what led to success or failure. Only with that information can the conditions that worked be replicated, or modified sufficiently in the next trial to get better results.(1980b:251)

In addition, federal agencies must maximize their returns in efforts with limited fiscal resources. Combining scarce resources with pressures of accountability produces a climate of interagency rivalry over those resources and thus the need to employ the maximization model (McClelland & Winter 1969). The maximization model suggests ''that human beings everywhere tend to choose the personal action they they feel will gain them the greatest benefit (or avoid the greatest loss) with the smallest expenditure of resources'' (Bee 1974:198). (See Bailey 1960; Barth 1963, 1966, 1967; Erasmus, 1961; Kunkel, 1970.)

These fundamental constraints shape the agencies' perspective and enable them to adapt successfully to the federal environment. The federal agencies' survival literally depends on an adequate understanding of, adherence to, and manipulation of these norms. The fluidity of funding from year to year, political fluctuations and alliances, career-building concerns, and the acquisition-maintenance of power games all contribute to the political instability of the bureaucratic hierarchy and federal perspective. ''The political process has a lifestyle and morality of its own—a lifestyle and morality that evaluators have to respect if they are to be of use" (Lindblom & Cohen 1979, as paraphrased by Cronbach et al. 1980b:349).

The demands for data, according to strict guidelines and time-tables, are generated from this environment. Knowledge is power, and information is required at prespecified periods to assist in the federal decision-making process which entails the assessment of the relative merits of competing programs. Coward (1976:14) warns: "Agencies place themselves in highly vulnerable positions if they sponsor a research effort that is unable to provide data under constraints imposed by policy deadlines." The inability to address these concerns in this fashion may leave an agency "out in the cold," with little or no future funding. These constraints and the socialization of federal bureaucrats according to the canons of the traditional educational establishment have guided the federal government into the pattern of traditionally associating the most credible and timely research with the experimental design, regardless of the task at hand. The federal climate of inflexible deadlines, interagency rivalry, and scarce resources shapes the behavior of its primary client—the research corporation. Research corporations respond to their sponsors with a watchful eye toward future funding. Overspending and ignoring deadlines does not sit well with sponsors whose very survival is dependent upon the delivery of information to policy makers at a fixed time. Ethnographers who enter this environment very quickly sink or swim.

These three conflicting world views are logical expressions of their respective environments. Unfortunately, graduate training rarely prepares anthropologists for this culture shock. A conversion process is required when moving from one environment to the next. In fact, academic training compounds the difficulties encountered in this transition. Ethnographers trained in the academic sphere must learn to readjust many ingrained patterns of behavior as they enter a new field; these include accepting rather than generating a problem to be researched (although you select the RFP of interest) and working in multidisciplinary teams. These alternatives should be regarded as real but superficial concerns in the adaptation process.

The way an ethnographic evaluator functions is shaped by the influences and pressures discussed above. In combination with the individual personality and training of the ethnographer, these pressures determine whether a traditionalist, a moderate, or a completely coopted posture will be adopted. The tensions produced by the reinforcing world views of the educational research establishment, the research corporation, and the federal bureaucracy have been reduced in recent years by more open discussion of these problems (Fetterman 1982; 1984b). In addition, at least on the paradigmatic level, some of the leading proponents of the educational research establishment have expressed a change of heart in their attitudes toward qualitative research. Campbell, for example, has written in "an extreme oscillation away from [his] earlier dogmatic disparagement of case studies as follows:

We should recognize that participants and observers have been evaluating program innovations for centuries without the benefit of quantification or scientific method. This is the common-sense knowing which our scientific evidence should build upon and go beyond, not replace. But it is usually neglected in quantitative evaluations, unless a few supporting anecdotes haphazardly collected are included. Under the epistemology I advocate, one should attempt to systematically tap all the qualitative common sense program critiques and evaluations that have been generated among the program staff, program clients and their families, and community observers. While quantitative procedures such as questionnaires and rating scales will often be introduced at this stage for reasons of convenience in collecting and summarizing, non-quantitative methods of collection and compiling should also be considered, such as hierarchically organized discussion groups. Where such evaluations are contrary to the quantitative results, the quantitative results should be regarded as suspect until the reasons for the discrepancy are well understood. Neither is infallible, of course. but for many of us, what needs to be emphasized is that the quantitative results may be as mistaken as the qualitative. (1979:52–53)

This position is symbolic of a much larger change taking place in the field of educational evaluation. It is a silent scientific revolution.

Increasingly, evaluators are turning away from quantitative designs and toward the acceptance and use of qualitative concepts and techniques in educational evaluation. *Qualitative and Quantitative Methods in Evaluation Research* (Cook and Reichardt 1979) opened a new door on the discussion of qualitative methods in evaluation. *Ethnography in Educational Evaluation* (Fetterman 1984a) focused the discussion on ethnography, specifically the role of ethnographic techniques and a cultural interpretation in educational evaluation. This collection contributed to this shift in professional allegiances by presenting a series of systematically rigorous ethnographic studies that have worked. The change is reflected also in graduate school curricula throughout the country. Qualitative course sequences are becoming common features of graduate training for educators. This shift in professional allegiances has been somewhat turbulent, but the change has served to raise the methodological consciousness of evaluators and to ease the tensions endemic to this enterprise.

The Life Cycle of the Ethnographic Evaluator

The above cultural and paradigmatic backdrop of the ethnographic evaluator is important, but a more revealing picture can be seen by tracing the development of an ethnographic evaluator. This development is closely tied to the cyclical process of contract research, a pattern which characterizes not only the inception and growth of a particular project, but of the researcher's career as well.

CONCEPTION
The life cycle of both researcher and project begins with conception, writing a proposal for funding. This lays the foundation and sets the tone of the study. Experienced ethnographic evaluators have learned to take charge during this critical phase of the life cycle. This is the period in which to establish the budget: to provide for field-workers, equipment, and time to think, analyze the data, and write up the findings. The time devoted to planning and designing the ethnographic component of the evaluation is well spent. The proposal reflects the creativity of the ethnographic evaluator or the degree of assimilation to the mainstream of evaluation design.

BIRTH
The next stage is birth, receiving a contract to begin the study. This is an occasion for celebration—champagne, Brie, chocolate cake, and popcorn. Jokes are told, moments of desperation are remembered, such as the time a photocopying machine broke down hours before a deadline. Moments of high tension are relived, as when one corpora-

tion learns that a competitor has found a "ringer" or has supplied misinformation. The formal celebration usually lasts for only an hour or less (in proportion to the size of the contract) but the atmosphere remains highly charged for weeks. The president or project directors are quick to remind researchers of the tasks remaining on ongoing work and everyone settles back into work. By the same token, when a large contract has been lost to a competitor, there is a subtle form of mourning that shrouds the atmosphere. Eventually, this somber mood is eased by some form of comic relief or work on another proposal or a current project.

Immediately following the receipt of a contract, it is necessary to receive routine check-ups. Meetings are scheduled immediately with the sponsor to reaffirm what was promised and agreed to in the proposal. Most surprises are mitigated if caught early. Periodically, however, gross misunderstanding occurs between contractors and their sponsors even in the early stages. In one case, I won a contract that was explicitly ethnographic in design. One week after the award, the sponsors demanded a change to a closed questionnaire approach with both the questions and the choice of interview subjects under their control. They wanted us to provide compliance information about each of the programs during the course of the study and to increase the number of sites visited without altering the funding. As an ethnographic evaluator and project director, I found it necessary to take a firm stance against this mutilation of methodology, ethics, and fiscal administration. In this instance, we convinced the sponsors of the untenable ethical and fiscal problems their alterations imposed. Unfortunately, we were unable to come to a satisfactory solution to the radical methodological alterations imposed on the study after the fact. The proposed ethnographic methods and concepts were selected by the sponsors over those of such major competitors as ETS (Educational Testing Service). Their subsequent flip-flop in orientation appears, in retrospect, to have been in part a power play to establish their control over the study. This case has entered litigation and is being argued on methodological-contractual grounds.

CHILDHOOD

Assuming a healthy birth, the ethnographic evaluator enters his or her formative years. This period involves identifying key actors and informants in the project, making detailed schedules, appointments, and other plans. Letters and phone calls are used to arrange for entrance into the field. During this period, first impressions dominate interactions. The more common errors that may cause irreparable damage to a working relationship involve the formalities of contract research. It is critical, for example, to recognize and respect protocol. Educational settings are governed by hierarchical relations. Permission from the superintendent must be granted before permission from a principal is proposed. The impact of protocol on one's ability to gain access to documents and people should not be underestimated. Respecting protocol can create a halo effect; ignoring protocol can place obstacles in the ethnographer's path throughout the entire study.

ADOLESCENCE

Conducting field work is much like entering and re-entering adolescence. The field worker must learn a new language, new rituals, and a wealth of new cultural information. This period is marked by tremendous excitement, frustration, and confusion. The ethnographic evaluator exposes him or herself to personal and professional turmoil as a part of the experience. One of my first site visits for a research corporation that had never heard of an ethnographer prior to my hiring is highly illustrative. I had convinced them of the utility of the approach and had made successful arguments for doubling the budget of the ethnographic evaluation section of the study to accommodate field work and equipment. I was therefore under considerable pressure either to show them a few interesting insights provided by using ethnographic evaluation or at least to come back with some basic information in hand.

I collected a mountain of material during the first two weeks, from interviews, observation, and documents. I sketched a few informal networks and felt that I had accomplished a lot in a very short time. On what was to have been the last day of the site visit, a student befriended me. He was tall and weighed over two hundred pounds. After a few hours of conversation about his life and the neighborhood, he decided to show me around. He introduced me to a number of the characters who run the street life. It was getting hot and he knew I was from California so he brought me to a health food store for a cold drink and a snack. We went in and my new friend winked at the owner of the store and told him to give me a granola bar with some natural soda. I said thanks and reached out my hand for the granola bar and felt something else under the bar. It was a nickel bag of marijuana.

I looked at the owner, then I looked at my friend. I didn't want to show any form of disapproval or ingratitude but this was not exactly what I had in mind when I agreed to play the role of guest, visitor, and friend. A moment later, I heard steps in perfect stride. I looked over to the front window and I saw two policemen walking by, looking right in the window. My hand was still in the air with the mixed contents for all to see. My heart dropped to the floor.

My first thought was "I'm going to get busted. How am I going to explain this to my colleagues at the research corporation?" They were already skeptical about ethnography. How was I going to explain to them why I was studying the community outside the school program? Fortunately, the police disappeared as quickly as they had appeared. I asked my friend what had just transpired. He explained to me that they were paid off regularly and would bother you only if they needed money or if an owner had not made his contribution. After picking myself up emotionally and finishing the tour of the neighborhood, I went back to my hotel room and furiously wrote up the event. I later used it in one of my governmental reports to describe the neighborhood context of these students. This provided a context for assessing the relative success of an educational program that had tremendous competition for the students' attention. The incident was useful also in showing me that my informant was both proud of his cultural knowledge ("knowing where to cop dope") and yet capable of experimenting with a conventional lifestyle by entering the educational program under study. This experience reveals some of the benefits of living and working in a natural setting, as well as the role of serendipity in field work (see Fetterman 1984c).

During this period the ethnographic evaluator begins to gather the strands of information which will form the fabric of his or her understanding of the culture. The ability to gather this information relies on an early recognition of the formal and informal power brokers within a community and school. Establishing contacts with clergymen, politicians, local business people, police, and gang leaders opened doors to me throughout my national study of dropouts, potential dropouts, and pushouts. The ethnographic evaluator must keep one foot on either side of the ethnographic-evaluation line. As an ethnographer, he or she must remain nonjudgmental and maintain confidentiality. Identifying with one side or the other will close important lines of communication and allow access to only half the story. On the other hand, one must remind informants that as an evaluator, one is assessing the functional or dysfunctional qualities of the program or situation. On an administrative level this role is generally understood; however, sometimes things go wrong. Generally, a constructive orientation can be conveyed by playing the role of a management consultant informing administration of positive and negative elements of their system with the aim of improving the system's operation. On a student level, all that is necessary is to be honest about the two halves of one's role—part student trying to understand how the system works and part professional evaluator trying to come up with recommendations to improve the school program. Adolescent students possess a psychological "radar" which tells them if someone is being honest. If they sense dishonesty or insincerity, they can undermine the value of any study.

One of the dangers of this period is miscalculation about the appropriate degree of reciprocity required. Ethnographic evaluators can become easy targets for informants who feed them the information they think the evaluators want to hear and then collect the rewards for that information. Another problem that can emerge is field-work paralysis. Ethnographic evaluators, like conventional ethnographers, attempt to remain as unobtrusive as possible. Unfortunately, this can be carried to an extreme. I have observed cases where my own staff felt unable to collect any information for fear of disrupting the system. They overdramatized the sensitivities of their prospective informants and withdrew from any data collection. After I convinced one of them to break the ice with a few nonthreatening questions, he realized that he had projected his own concerns on the informant and that the system was not quite as delicate as he had assumed. In a second case, the individual had to be replaced.

A similar danger occurs when a fieldworker goes native. In one case, a staff member felt so strongly affiliated with the group under study that he decided to join them and leave his data collection responsibilities behind. In such a situation, the cost to the study and the sponsors, and to the credibility of coworkers, can be devastating. Ethnography is a personal science and individuals must make personal decisions about how they are going to live their lives, even in the middle of a study. Careful consideration should go into the decision to enter any role that may have competing obligations and responsibilities. Ethnographic evaluators should err on the side of professionalism and responsibility; a large number of individuals rely on their data, ranging from the sponsors to the students in the programs being evaluated.

ADULTHOOD

The ethnographic evaluator reaches adulthood when he or she has gained acceptance into the community or school under study. Acceptance improves the quality of data by opening up new levels of previously undisclosed symbols and cultural knowledge. Within the research corporation, adulthood for the ethnographic evaluator is knowing when to wear an ethnographer's cap and when to wear an evaluator's suit. This may sound simple, but in fact it is not time-bound or purely situationally directed. An ethnographic evaluator is always collecting information throughout the study—in the streets and in plush conference rooms in Washington, D.C. Similarly, the ethnographic evaluator continually appraises how well the system works, whether it is the system of administering funds for the program or of classroom instruction. The key to being an adult ethnographic evaluator is, first, knowing when to allow one approach to dominate one's mode of operation, and second, knowing how to present oneself for the right audiences.

There is a delicate balance between collecting enough information and making an assessment. Additional information will always be informative. There is, however, a law of diminishing returns in any endeavor. There are also many time pressures such as sponsor deadlines and proposal writing for the next project. Judgments must be made to allow the next stage of the study to begin. The ethnographic evaluator must constantly guard against making assessments prematurely. At the same time he or she must be able to get at the heart of an issue and often make best guesses about the fate of a school.

I encountered a difficult decision of this nature several years ago, involving the fate of one of the educational programs for dropouts (discussed earlier). The sponsors were unhappy with the progress of a particular program and did not want to wait for the results of the study, which was only one-third complete at the time. They informed us that they were ready to make a go or no-go decision regarding continued funding of the program. They asked for our assessment of the program before all the data were collected, analyzed, synthesized, and reported. We objected to being put in this position, and informed them that we would not be a part of such a travesty. The sponsors explained to us that based on their perception of the program's progress it did not warrant additional funding. The phone call ended with this ultimatum: we could either provide insights into the program or maintain our ethical stance. If we chose the latter course of action, the sponsors would act on the information they had (or didn't have) in hand. They gave us two and half hours to think about it before calling us back.

We sat there stunned, irritated, and unsure. We discussed the matter for about fifteen minutes. We went over the reasons for not disclosing any information about the program. Then a few pragmatic arguments were made for providing our opinions to the sponsors. Reluctantly, we decided that some input would be better than no input, given the present circumstances. Unfortunately, we didn't have much data to go on. The traditional evaluators had only some of the pretests. The scores were terrible, which was expected because they were received prior to treatment in the program. I went through my precoded, preanalyzed field notes and found a few points that could be interpreted in favor of the program and a few against. In sum, we pooled our information together and took our best guess. We believed that the program merited further funding and further consideration.

The ethnographic data were useful on two levels. First, they documented when the sponsors had collected their information and what they collected. Thus, I was able to explain that the reason they didn't see any students around during their visit was because it was during the middle of the summer and it was at 4:30 P.M. (after regular school hours). Second, the attendance data did look bad. The average attendance level was less than sixty percent. I simply offered the observation that it depends on one's perspective. The sponsors were comparing this program's attendance figure with local school attendance reports of seventy to seventy-five percent average daily attendance. I explained that, given this comparison, the program did not look too good; however, this was comparing apples with oranges.

The students in this program were not the same as the average student in the regular school; in fact, they were systematically different from the average student. These were students who dropped out of the neighborhood schools—they were the regular nonattendees. In addition, assessments of this nature are determined according to some baseline. Once again, the assumed baseline for comparison was the local high school. I provided a sense of proportion and context to the discussion by explaining that in this case the local school baseline was not appropriate. The accurate baseline to use was zero percent attendance because these students were dropouts. This made fifty-five percent attendance look suprisingly good. These arguments, in conjunction with additional anecdotes, saved the program.

In a more pristine ethnographic endeavor, it is unlikely that these pressures would have surfaced. External pressures are a routine part of applied anthropology—particularly ethnographic educational evaluation. In this case, it was crucial that the ethnographic data be used as appropriately as possible; but the information had to be presented in the form of an evaluator's appraisal of program progress. An ethnographic evaluator should have enough experience with the educational and evaluation subcultures to know how to act or how to get around conforming to educational and evaluation norms in an appropriate (nondisruptive and nonobtrusive) manner. An inability to adapt in these situations manifests a mind-set that may have deleterious effects as the study unfolds.

Similarly, at advisory panel or professional association meetings or in the classroom, it is important to know when to argue as an evaluator and when it is imperative that you be a participant-observer. In advisory panel meetings, a ritual common to evaluations where experts sit in judgment of the progress of the study, an ethnographic evaluator must be prepared to be a player in the politics of emergent vested interests. This role requires an adept evaluator or politician, to maintain the integrity of the study, defend its progress, and mold it in the right direction. During the same meeting, as ethnographer, he or she presents descriptions, patterns, and preliminary findings for discussion. This is easy to do at separate association meetings where the audience is more homogeneous. Periodically, however, the presentation draws a mixed crowd, as with the advisory panel, and it is incumbant upon the ethnographic evaluator to become a cognitive code switcher. This requires the ability to think in two conceptual frameworks simultaneously—addressing concerns of reliability and validity (from a logical positivist's perspective), and at the same time insuring a phenomenologically based study.

MARRIAGE
Marriage is an interlocking of fates and a commitment to meet mutual emotional, social, and fiscal responsibilities. For the ethnographic evaluator, this involves making a long-term commitment to working in an interdisciplinary team in a policy research context. The benefits of this union are rewarding. Financially, the field can be extremely lucrative. The opportunities to travel are plentiful and the opportunity to conduct policy research at the cutting edge is enviable. In addition, the experience of sharing your interests and insights with scholars with a different, if not conflicting, world view is profound. This commitment, however, should not be entered into lightly.

Team members come to depend on the stability of this relationship in writing proposals, conducting the research, and writing reports. A creative and financial interdependency evolves in an interdisciplinary team setting. Leaving the team or dismantling it, like a divorce, can be costly for everyone. Staff no longer have the financial and emotional security that is taken for granted. Peers lose the synergistic effect of working together and learning from each other. Superiors have a role in the organization that may have legal as well as social and emotional overtones. The ripple effect runs all the way from the sponsor to staff to the students involved in the study.

FAMILY
The ethnographic evaluator's family includes not only the interdisciplinary team, but the network of colleagues in the field as well. They serve as a quality control to maintain methodological rigor. Experiments and innovations are required when working as an ethnographic evaluator. Working at the cutting edge of research is an exhilarating but unsettling experience. There is no place with a greater need for judiciously imposed quality controls. Effective ethnographic evaluators use members of the team to test their ideas. They solicit opinions from scholars from different disciplines to determine if a specific adaptation will address methodological concerns across disciplines. This

is particularly important when attempting to combine ethnographic, survey, and experimental or quasi-experimental designs in the same evaluation study.

Similarly, a network of ethnographic evaluation colleagues can be used to test the appropriateness of novel methodological innovations, e.g., projective techniques, short-term multi-site fieldwork schedules, and so on. This network is established and maintained by telephone, correspondence, professional meetings, scholarly literature, and computer communications. The Bitnet (Because Its Time), EARN (European Academic Research Network), and ARPANET (Advanced Research Projects Agency) systems facilitate communication. These systems link over 1,400 computer nodes together, connecting universities and research facilities throughout the world, ranging from the City University of New York to Stanford University in California and from the Ecole Centrale de Paris to Hebrew University in Israel. Brief messages, letters, and manuscripts are shared through an electronic mail system. This type of network provides feedback that can be measured in nanoseconds (Fetterman 1985b).

RETIREMENT

The ethnographic evaluator lives a relatively fast-paced life on a project. When projects end, the ethnographic evaluator must be able to wrap up his or her work and move on. Ethnographic evaluators immerse themselves in the field, like conventional ethnographers. This long-term personal involvement can make it difficult to recognize when participant-observation has ended. The ethnographic evaluator has a responsibility to his team, the network of coresearchers, to disengage from his or her segment of the study at the appropriate time. This often involves beginning the disengagement process before all the findings have been reported and the money is spent.

The ethnographic evaluator's talents may be needed elsewhere in the corporation. New proposals need to be written all the time, ideally before the team runs out of money, if continuity and quality is to be maintained. In addition, coresearchers often need the ethnographic information to help them interpret their own segments of the study. They cannot wait for a self-indulgent ethnographer to dawdle with the delivery of his or her findings. In some cases, retirement for the ethnographic evaluator may involve recognizing when it is time to enter a new phase of his career. A career change or advancement, such as making the transition from ethnographic evaluator to administer, is a form of retirement.

LAST RITES

There is a final stage for some ethnographic educational evaluators, and that is recognizing when to leave the profession entirely. Methodological sloppiness, job burnout, and a significant shift in disciplinary interests mark the point at which it is time to shift gears and leave ethnographic pursuits to the next generation. A lack of commitment to this enterprise has devastating effects on the quality of the profession and, in turn, on how it is perceived by the outside world. In addition, ethnographic educational evaluation is a highly demanding profession personally. Conducting ethnographic evaluations places the ethnographic evaluator in a schedule where he or she is on the road and away from home for months. The insecurity of federal funding, the pressures of proposal competition to support staff members, arguments with sponsors regarding deadlines and methodological designs, and arguments with colleagues in the process of creating a new field can take their toll. Not knowing when to completely disengage can be lethal—mentally and physically.

Conclusion

The promise of this new branch within anthropology and education has come to fruition in evaluation and policy settings. Ethnographic educational evaluation has addressed the needs of children ranging from the disenfranchised dropout (Fetterman 1981b) to the envied and neglected gifted child (Fetterman 1984a; Fetterman in press c). Topics range from improving parental involvement (Smith and Robbins 1984) to mainstreaming the hearing impaired (Hemwall 1984). Ethnographic educational evaluation is what ethnographers do in the process of adapting ethnography to educational evaluation. Ethnographic evaluators have increased our understanding of educational issues and the processes of cultural transmission. They have broken down myths and misperceptions about anthropology—demythologizing the qualitative-quantitative dichotomy. They have offered a contextualized, nonjudgmental, holistic perspective to educational problems. Moreover, they have been able to generate policy and programmatic recommendations for change and improvement. In the process of contributing to evaluation and policy research, ethnographic educational evaluation has been reflexive. This new hybrid has made contributions back to anthropology and education in the areas of ethics (Fetterman in press a; 1984c; 1981a), theory (Fetterman in press b; Fetterman and Pitman 1986; Goetz and LeCompte 1984; Pitman and Dobbert 1986; Simon 1986; Studstill 1986), methodology (Chesterfield 1986; Fetterman 1984b, 1985a; LeCompte and Goetz 1984; Maxwell 1986; Messerschmidt 1984; Firestone and Herriott 1984; Goldberg 1984; Wolcott 1984), and politics (Ferrell and Compton 1986; Marotto 1986). In the process of coping and adapting to the strange new land of ethnographic educational evaluation, the ethnographic evaluator has become a part of the intellectual landscape of educational evaluation and educational anthropology, and indeed of anthropology as a whole.

16

TAKING THE WITNESS STAND

Henry F. Dobyns

I n complex societies, conflicts between groups or individuals are increasingly resolved through formal litigation procedures. Contemporary American society is especially litigious. The courts and quasilegal bodies are playing a greatly expanded role in settling the claims of citizens who feel that they have been victims of injustice, malpractice, fraud, or other actions which impinge upon their civil rights. One result of this development has been a growing demand for expert witnesses who can testify for one side or the other on the basis of specialized professional knowledge.

Henry F. Dobyns describes this role as he and others have experienced it in native American claims cases. Although the role is episodic, it is extremely demanding in terms of the time, energy, and resources required to prepare for a case. There is little in the training of anthropologists to prepare them for such work, which typically entails the confrontation of anthropologists with each other on opposite sides of the issues involved. Other difficulties arise due to the expectations of clients and the important implications for future relationships with plaintiffs or defendants as a result of court testimony. In litigation of this type,

Henry F. Dobyns (Ph.D., Cornell) is consultant to the Gila River Indian Community. He has directed and carried out research in Peru, Ecuador, Bolivia, Colombia, Venezuela, and Mexico in Latin America; and among the Northeastern Pai, Northern Piman, Apache and Kaibab Paiute Indians, Spanish-Americans, and Anglo-Americans in the United States. He has taught anthropology at Cornell, the University of Kentucky, Prescott College, the University of Wisconsin (Parkside), and the University of Florida. He has been a consultant to the Peace Corps, the Organization of American States, and domestic corporations. He has testified as an expert witness before the United States Indian Claims Commission and Claims Court.

Numerous expert witnesses contributed to this analysis by evaluating earlier drafts and sharing their experiences. They include R. C. Euler, P. H. Ezell, C. H. Fairbanks, B. L. Fontana, W. R. Jacobs, T. F. King, N. O. Lurie, M. E. Opler, O. C. Stewart, H. H. Tanner, W. H. Unrau, and attorney A. S. Cox.

**the macroculture and the microculture come together in a unique man-
ner, and the expert witness role offers unusual opportunities to affect
the way in which problems are defined and solved in the interplay between them.**

DAMAGE AWARDS RUNNING into millions of dollars have
stemmed in part from anthropologists and historians testifying as experts before the United States Indian Claims Commission. Native
Americans have been kept out of prison when state courts accepted
expert anthropological testimony about the Native American Church.
Testifying, therefore, meets Lantis' (1945:20; Lurie 1955:357) criterion of true applied social science: the practical application of research findings on behalf of a group of people. Because more social
scientists are likely to become expert witnesses in the future, this
essay undertakes some analysis of this role.

Numerous anthropologists and historians have already taken the
stand as experts before various federal and state courts as well as the
Indian Claims Commission. Their experiences provide useful guidance for future anthropological expert witnesses in these and other
types of litigation.

That more social scientists will play the expert witness role is
certain. Federal and state legislation now requires that environmental,
social, and cultural impacts of proposed governmental projects be
assessed beforehand. Consequently, archeologists and other anthropologists are at present busy writing environmental impact statements, predicting how highways and other projects will affect existing resources. Litigation is already occurring over environmental impact
issues. Such litigation will involve many professionals of various disciplines, who prepare the necessary statements and also serve as expert witnesses in court proceedings. In fact, one archeologist has already paved the way for future litigation by testifying in a case in
which he himself was one of the plaintiffs.

As long as the nation pursues a policy that recognizes the value
of cultural diversity, anthropologists and historians will be responsible, because of their specific expertise, for becoming involved in litigation generated by conflicts between culturally diverse groups. Anthropologists are also testifying as experts in cases involving native

American treaty rights that have been violated by state fish and game managers or by corporate leaseholders. And in view of the increasing public awareness of these problems, tribes will need expert testimony as they litigate to compel faithful observance of treaties.

One reason for analyzing the expert witness role is its relative periodicity. Foster (1969:49) considered all applied anthropology to occur as part-time activity by persons otherwise engaged during most of their careers. Taking the witness stand certainly is episodic. Testimony can become necessary over a period of many years. For example, I appeared as a witness for the Gila River Indian Community in a 1974 water right hearing seventeen years after testifying for the Hualapai Tribe in a 1957 land loss hearing. Social scientists appearing as expert witnesses seem to average two such assignments during their career. Only about 14 percent of those who have been expert witnesses spent five or more years on research leading to testimony, with 3 percent spending ten years or more.

Such periodicity of role performance means that an expert witness can train for the role to only a limited extent. One may gain some experience testifying before legislative committees or regulatory commissions. Whether these bodies allow cross-examination of witnesses or not, the expert who is testifying inevitably learns formal testimony procedures and at least some role constraints.[1] Nevertheless, most of the socialization for the expert witness role must perforce be anticipatory. Thus, this essay is designed to guide the future expert witness.

Recruitment

The nature of topics upon which social anthropologists can testify as experts tends to channel the process of expert recruitment. Omer C. Stewart's (1961a:18; 1970:4) frequent testimony as an expert on the Native American Church is an excellent example of this. His expertise stems from both participant observation in peyote ceremonies—

---

1. Archeologist Thomas F. King (Wilke, King, and Hammond 1975) found such less formal testimony before other public bodies helpful preparation for expert testimony in federal court.

good ethnography—and careful tracing of the diffusion of this denomination among tribesmen—good ethnohistory. In other words, an expert witness must in fact be expert on some aspect of the subject of litigation. For, "the good faith, scholarly conventionality, and academic correctness" of anyone offered as an expert is likely to be challenged (Lurie 1957:68). This means that a nonacademic person with firsthand knowledge gained from several years of research with a particular group may be better qualified to testify about that group than would an ethnologist who has made only a brief survey of the population (Lurie 1955:358).

Because anthropologists and historians conduct research with people, the recruitment process at times incorporates a measure of ideological sorting. Historian Wilbur R. Jacobs and anthropologist Bea Medicine testified in 1974 in United States District Court in Nebraska concerning what Sioux chiefs meant when they signed the 1968 Treaty of Laramie with the United States. They appeared as expert witnesses for the defense in cases arising out of native American occupation of Wounded Knee, South Dakota, in 1973. Jacobs' (1950, 1954, 1972, 1974) published works establish him as expert on native American government relations, particularly Indian treaties. Yet, these same works also identify him as a revisionist historian who has used extensive interdisciplinary and comparative data to challenge Anglo-American elitist interpretations and stereotypes. That general scholarly status and his concern for the welfare of contemporary Indians "preselected" him, by creating defense attorney expectation that his expert opinions would fit into a defense theory of a particular case. Jacobs clarified his views to defense attorneys before testifying, pointing out that he would willingly testify on historical evidence and interpretations, but that he did not agree with many of the actions of native American defendants or some of the policies of the American Indian Movement (AIM). Jacobs has indicated that the prosecuting attorneys followed the same practice in obtaining sympathetic witnesses.

Medicine's expertise on Sioux oral tradition stems in part from her ascribed status as a Pine Ridge Sioux and in part from her achieved status as anthropologist. That unique combination also "preselected" her as a suitable defense witness.

During the past twenty-five years that the Indian Claims Commission has been in existence, such sorting has been clearly perceptible. Attorneys representing Indian plaintiffs have often recruited anthropologists and historians convinced of the merit of native American claims before research on specific cases began.[2] Attorneys employed by the U.S. Department of Justice to defend the government have been able to recruit experts from the same disciplines who opposed Indian recovery of damages.

Basic motivations of the latter individuals are understandably difficult to determine. Nonetheless, the moccasin telegraph (Witt 1968:71; Rachlin 1968:107) has compiled and disseminated information culled from public pronouncements and private utterances. Those who listen to the moccasin telegraph hear that some experts opposed the Indian Claims Commission Act and its goal of recompensing Indian groups for unjust and unconscionable loss of resources. So they enthusiastically testified for the defendant. On the other hand, the moccasin telegraph also says that others took the witness stand for the defendant from professional motives, insuring that defendant's expert testimony was scientifically unbiased. Their premise was that testifying would serve the goals of both science and justice. Much less ideologically, some experts take the stand simply as an opportunity to earn money.

The specificity of anthropological and historical research significantly influences recruitment of experts. The research activity of the social scientist with any given group of people rather narrowly defines his or her expertise. In other words, the researcher's personal and professional relationships with the people whom he or she studies are often crucial to his or her recruitment. Thus, the chairman of the Papago Tribal Council initially recommended the author to attorneys representing his tribe before the Indian Claims Commission. Typically, recruitment rests partly upon one's professional stature. Toward the end of his long career, the late A. L. Kroeber tremendously impressed attorneys with cases before the Indian Claims Commission. In other words, recruitment also rests upon litigant and attorney perception of qualifications. Thus, Thayer Scudder testified in Hopi-Navajo litigation as an expert on forced relocation rather than as an expert on either ethnic group.

---

2. One demographer has accused all anthropologists of pro-Indian bias (Petersen 1975). "Preselection" clearly occurred in Indian Claims Commission litigation (Lurie 1956:261).

Expert-Expert Confrontation

Once an expert witness is recruited, he or she faces a set of role demands that are often quite outside previous professional experience. Anthropologists prefer to perceive themselves as working within a *gemeinschaft* discipline. They are, therefore, typically startled by the adversary proceedings of litigation, a *gesselschaft* situation. Both sides can and very often do retain experts to testify on the same issues. The Indian Claims Commission Act of 1946 authorized the Commission to establish a research division (Lurie 1955:360; 1957:59; 1970:5), but the attorneys appointed to it did not elect to do so. Commissioner John T. Vance (1969:335–336) proposed activating the research unit to expedite decisions, but his colleagues continued to rely on traditional adversary suits instead.

Adversary proceedings are actually scientifically positive, because they generate checks on the quality of each expert's research product. The direct hearing room confrontation has proved even more effective than has customary "scrutiny" of findings by scholarly colleagues with no personal practical responsibility. Certainly, such confrontation between social scientists testifying for opposing sides generates greater methodological sophistication in the interpretation of many kinds of evidence than anthropologists customarily employed prior to the appearances of many of them before the Indian Claims Commission.

The courtroom confrontation sometimes contains elements of the same kind of drama as that depicted by fictional television programs. The circumstances produce more than face-to-face confrontation between two social scientists. Adversary proceedings pit a team of attorneys, historians, or other experts who supply attorneys with questions to ask during cross-examination against each expert, a tactic that frequently is most effective in revealing "inaccuracies and/or slipshod research methods," as one who knows phrased it.[3]

Cross-examination constitutes the core of adversary proceedings. In fact, the Indian Claims Commission has in recent years insisted that expert direct testimony be offered in written form. During cross-

3. Stewart (1961b) cites numerous instances of "works listed in bibliography not cited in report"; reference to works not describing Southern Paiutes, the litigants; secondary works by popular writers; and unevaluated scholarly works.

examination, attorneys put questions, but these are typically suggested by experts. Since the attorney usually lacks comparable acquaintance with the expert's scientific field, it is the expert who, in
all likelihood, will recognize any inaccuracies, omissions or distortions in the report or testimony of another expert in the same field.
Thus, an expert witness may provide indispensable material to the
lawyer who is cross-examining an opposing expert witness. This phase
of expert-witness/attorney cooperation can and has mercilessly exposed unscientific research. The expert suggesting questions to the
cross-examining attorney is limited only by his own knowledge and
skill in data storage and retrieval under time constraints. Inevitably,
the very merciless quality of cross-examination makes it unpalatable
to many potential expert witnesses.

One dynamic of the involvement of anthropologists as expert
witnesses before the Indian Claims Commission has been the reluctance of commission members to accept at face value the testimony
of native Americans belonging to plaintiff groups. The commission-
ers preferred to have Indian testimony evaluated by experts accustomed to analyzing such statements before admitting it as legal evidence (Lurie 1955:359; 1957:50–60). Consequently, the Commission
even considered archeological evidence of aboriginal land use and
occupancy (Dobyns 1974).

Since the passage of the National Environmental Protection Act,
prehistoric remains have also become a resource at issue in litigation.
Because of the passage of so many years since the United States
seizure of Indian resources, and because of memory loss and destruction of physical evidence, the quality of available data often parallels
that in industrial product liability litigation. The process, therefore,
occasionally becomes ''a sophisticated guessing game'' because of
the imperfect nature of evidence (Piehler et al. 1974:1092). Nevertheless, the adversary procedure and standards of proof observed by
courts tend to demand from social scientists an unusual quality of
data collection and its analysis. The prospect of involvement in litigation as the pawn of a federal agency and its attorneys has been
known to frighten an archeologist away from a research contract he
would happily sign under other, more propitious circumstances.

The role strain generated in many anthropologists who testified
before the Indian Claims Commission led some of them to conclude

that adversary proceedings are "patently unpleasant to most of the experts" (Manners 1974:18).

Attorney/Expert Relations

Actually, adversary proceedings are not in and of themselves necessarily unpleasant for an expert witness. Some social scientists consistently enjoy serving in that role. Personality differences affect one's emotional response to stress during a hearing. Verbal and well-prepared experts welcome the challenge of turning cross-examination into an opportunity for creative testimony,

Intensity of commitment to an abstract goal of scientific truth also affects one's witness-stand reactions. Those with a strong commitment to such truth can exult in cross-examination which exposes inadequate preparation or conceptualization on the part of presumed experts. The social scientist considering this applied role should, in a word, keep in mind the Harry Truman dictum: Those who can't stand the heat should stay out of this particular kitchen.

Yet personality and goals of the expert provide only partial keys to successful performance of the witness role. Technical and legal researchers have analyzed the conduct of litigation over corporate liability for manufactured product malfunction (Piehler et al. 1974:1091). They have concluded that attorney/expert relations really determine whether an expert carries out his testimonial role with enjoyment or degradation. This is also true of social scientists as expert witnesses.

A complicating factor is that people as well as artifacts provide social scientists with data. The influence of counsel upon clients such as Indian tribal council members compounds the role of a social scientist expert witness, compared to that of a technician dealing only with artifacts. Manufactured goods pose problems such as the preservation of crucial physical evidence until it can be studied. Attorney influence over clients upon whom the social scientist depends for data adds complications for the latter far beyond those of destruction of physical evidence or natural memory loss in any human group. What some anthropologists find unpleasant in adversary proceedings stems

from attorney/client/expert relationships which depend on how lawyers define their own roles, and how they influence their clients.

INFORMANT BIAS

This component of role strain for the expert witness was quickly and
explicitly recognized by some anthropologists employed to testify before the Indian Claims Commission. Desirous of continuing research
among specific peoples, they anticipated being unable to convince
informants that the latter should provide them with future data (Lurie
1956:262–263). Manners (1974:132) relates his role strain when Ha-
vasupai individuals did not wish him to interview them. Manners
(1974:140–143) also inveighed against "New Yorkerish" behavior
of attorneys because a Paiute informant handed him the business card
of an attorney whom the Paiute reported had told him not to talk to
anyone without consulting said lawyer first.

Because litigation is an adversary proceeding, the expert witness
role often throws this specific kind of role strain upon the anthropologist. Cases docketed by the Indian Claims Commission or involving
treaty provisions frequently require experts for both an Indian plaintiff and a government defendant to interview native Americans. Generally the latter show a firm grasp of the necessity for adversary proceedings, and they cooperate with social scientists retained by the
governmental agency as well as those retained by their own counsel.
Nonetheless, at least some anthropologists retained by the Department of Justice have felt impelled to present to potential informants
a somewhat stronger statement of benefits to be gained from cooperating with the government's expert than was really true. Some experts whose personal value structure led them to object to the entire
concept of awarding damages to surviving Indians for historic unfair
and unconscionable dealings with their ancestors by representatives
of the United States government, became especially odious to Indians
for their self-serving claims of this nature.

This pattern of conduct, plus the involvement of such social scientists in litigation upon which millions of dollars depend, accounts
in part for Indian skepticism about anthropologists expressed in recent years. Vine Deloria, Jr. (1969) has eloquently phrased the view
that anthropologists are powerful and exploit Indians. Admittedly,

some anthropologists have wielded, albeit indirectly, considerable power as expert witnesses. Some of them have even exploited that temporary role in order to facilitate their own data collection.

Being experienced and wise in the ways of Anglo-Americans, most Indians do not overgeneralize in the Deloria style. Nonetheless, many of them recognize the inconsistency of the social scientist's role in eliciting statements in order to testify as an expert on behalf of the adversary of their own group. Consequently, such Indians tend to identify social scientists who testify as experts for plaintiffs before the Indian Claims Commission or courts as ethical. They also tend to stereotype those testifying as experts for defendants in litigation initiated by Indians, after obtaining Indian cooperation in collecting data, as unethical.

Whether or not Indians formally cooperate with the social scientist they consider unethical, their perception of such behavior cannot help but affect their enthusiasm in collaborating with such a person. This throws significant role strain on the social scientist. Litigation which necessitates taking a firm stand appears to be on the increase. Historian William E. Unrau already has testified in 1974 in a U.S. District Court as an expert on Kaw history, in litigation over which faction constituted the legal government of the group. Ethnohistorians, specializing as have Jacobs, Unrau, and Medicine, may well find themselves called upon to play the expert witness role in similar litigation. Under such circumstances, whenever both sides introduce expert testimony, those taking the stand on either side must anticipate lessened access to informants with vested interests on the opposite side. That implies diminished expertise both as witness and as researcher. Such applied social science will, in other words, redefine the research role.

If attorneys influence their clients' behavior toward expert witnesses who must elicit statements from them, those attorneys even more directly structure expert witness roles. Lurie (1956:265–266) hinted at role differences between attorneys when she noted that the lawyer who propounds the questions asked of an expert witness governs the "selectivity of data." I maintain that courtroom confrontations do not strike experts as unpleasant because these are adversary proceedings. Instead, rewarding or punishing confrontations are defined long before an actual hearing by attorney/expert relations. I perceive attorneys who utilize expert witnesses as falling into at least two distinct types.[4]

LITIGATION DIRECTORS AND TEAM-LEADERS

One type of attorney has been clearly identified in other litigation. Lawyers representing either plaintiff or defendant in product liability litigation typically view themselves as the main "directors of the litigation" (Piehler et al. 1974:1091). As a result, the attorney tends to relegate an expert to a "service position." In other words, the attorney may not even explore the subject of the litigation with an expert, and clearly develops his or her own theory of the case. This kind of lawyer expects the expert to fill in evidentiary gaps in the attorney's theory. It is my belief that many attorneys in Indian Claims Commission hearings or in similar cases in federal courts closely resemble those in product liability litigation.

Possessing the power to impose their own definition of the role-set (Merton 1957:372), such attorneys do so without being aware of counterproductive consequences. These attorneys typically do not realize how ill-trained they are in gathering and analyzing oral and written evidence pertinent to issues litigated by special groups such as Indians. In one extreme instance, an attorney neglected to inform an expert what another expert testifying for the same client was preparing until the day the hearing began. Consequently, the error-filled report of the second witness "nearly threw me for a total loss" reports the witness who was taken by surprise.

The litigation-director attorney rarely educates an expert witness as to the legal criteria involved in a case before channeling the expert witness into a subordinate role. The witness therefore, may take the stand unaware of how the lawyer might employ legal discovery procedures to facilitate arriving at the truth. The expert may not know how the attorney could at least try to redefine by motions the court-established parameters of the litigation.

A minority of attorneys recognize some of the pitfalls involved in playing a litigation director role, and play more of a team-leader role. In Merton's (1957:374–376) terms, these lawyers strive to make

4. The following discussion assumes attorneys to be technically competent. Green (1975:1, 4) reports increasing concern among judges whether many attorneys admitted to the bar are in fact competent.

their activities visible to the expert instead of insulating themselves from observation. Such an attorney spends much time deliberately consulting experts in order to find out what theories the experts can contribute to a case under active litigation. Lurie (1957:69; 1970:6–7) noted that some anthropologists persuaded attorneys to amend the very petitions upon which cases were based. Stewart and Morris E. Opler report, in personal communications, uniform success in persuading attorneys to alter dates-of-taking, exclusive use-and-occupancy areas, etc.

During hearings, team-leader attorneys frame questions that enable an expert to present his or her opinion clearly and fully during direct testimony. This tactic helps the experts avoid the strain of having to try to cram their expertise and data into a framework artificially restricted by a lawyer's theory of a case developed without adequate input from the expert. Such a witness finds an astute attorney of this type most rewarding to work with.

Because a hearing is an adversary proceeding, opposing counsel's function is to impute testimony by witnesses for the other side, if he can possibly so do. The attorney who has experts testify for a client also relies upon these experts to suggest cross-examination questions that will expose any serious defect in opposing expert testimony. Two specific traits of litigation director style attorneys compound the role strain inevitably induced in social scientists by the basic adversary proceeding to which they are subjected.

The litigation director forces experts to try to fit their opinion and information into an attorney-framed case theory which has been formulated without adequate consultation. This often exposes the expert to brutal cross-examination by opposing counsel which is "personally degrading" as well as extremely frustrating. The litigation director also displays the role attribute of seeking an expert opinion stated with the highest possible degree of certainty (Piehler et al. 1974:1092). The litigation director who succeeds too well in persuading an expert to disregard those limitations inherent in his or her formulation of an opinion exposes that expert to the embarassment of cross-examination which backs him or her steadily away from "absolutism."

The team-leader attorney, in contrast, elicits from an expert only direct testimony which can be absolutely defended on cross-examination. The team-leader lawyer does so, first of all, by framing a case-theory that adequately takes into account the expert's theory and data. Next, the team-leader recognizes, from prior disposition or consultation with the expert, the inherent limitations in the expert's opinion. The lawyer then presses the expert for an expression of certitude commensurate with the data and no more. This enables the expert to answer cross-examination without having to maintain inflated claims—other than those of his own making. Indeed, the team-leader attorney lays a basis for the expert to strengthen his or her opinion during cross-examination.

Research Time

One serious constraint sometimes built into the expert witness role is preparation time too brief to allow for adequate research into the litigated issues. For example, even I have suffered from severe role strain generated by having less time to investigate a question than I thought necessary. I have also watched the agony of a witness being cross-examined upon testimony that revealed totally inadequate preparation time. Again, this aspect of the expert witness's role frequently appears in product liability litigation, when a technical expert enters a case too late to allow adequate investigation (Piehler et al. 1974:1091).

A team-leader style attorney endeavors to avoid placing an expert witness under this handicap. Yet, even the best intentioned lawyer may not understand the complexity of the research operations required in a given case. Nor will the attorney always be able to predict correctly when a given case may come to trial. For the social scientist working part-time as an expert witness while teaching at an academic institution or otherwise engaged, full preparation for testimony may prove difficult.

A social scientist's problem in preparing for testimony often stems from inadequate compensation rather than from a true lack of time. The social scientist may have two to four years to prepare for a specific hearing, yet he or she may not be able to do so adequately because he or she cannot devote full time to the project. Lacking adequate case-preparation funds, or not realizing the inordinate amount of time required for thorough research, or being downright unethical (Shipek 1974:2), the party to the litigation pays the expert too little, with the result that the expert witness lacks funds to pay for time taken from his other duties. Academicians employed by public institutions which expect them to render public or community service, more than occasionally find themselves in the time/money bind when conducting such research unless they receive released time from other duties.

Social scientists and technologists suffer from two handicapping expert witness role stereotypes among attorneys when compensation is settled. One role perception derives from physicians and similar experts whose "research" can be carried out in a few hours or days, instead of months or even years. Attorneys in large legal firms which devoted years to preparing cases before the Indian Claims Commission have earned fees running into hundreds of thousands of dollars. Yet, they regard social scientists as "instant" experts, not recognizing that truly competent testimony also requires great expenditures. A second role perception of social scientists views them as partisans willing to donate their expertise to a cause. "Patsies" seems a more accurate label.

Conclusions

A few morals drawn from this consideration of attorney relations vis-à-vis experts and clients may aid future social scientist expert witnesses. First, the social scientist needs sufficient sophistication in terms of hearing procedure to know that the burden of proof falls upon a plaintiff. A defendant has only to raise doubts and pose questions, and often strives to confuse and obscure issues (Lurie 1956:271). Within that framework, an expert must anticipate greater role strain working for a litigation director type attorney than cooperating with a team-leader style lawyer. In other words, expert and attorney present the most effective case when both recognize the utility of a high degree of interaction between attorneys and experts at all stages of litigation (Piehler et al. 1974:1090).

Social scientists could well emulate land assessors, medical doctors, mathematicians, and technologists who testify in a professional capacity for plaintiff in one case to become defendant's expert in another (Lurie 1956:267). Those whose pursuit of truth is firmly embedded in their social personalities can enjoy the confrontations of experts during litigation. It can expose shortcomings of method, failures to consider all of the accumulated data, inaccuracies of execution, and faults of all kinds. Those whose ideological commitment to scientific truth is less than their commitment to a litigant can suffer personal degradation and severe role strain and feel that they have aged a decade during a single hearing. So can those whose methods or procedures are at fault—and perhaps even those who simply lacked sufficient time and money to prepare to testify.

Part III

PRACTICING ANTHROPOLOGY
AND PUBLIC POLICY

The dialogue between theory and application in practicing anthropology, and the roles and institutional settings in which practicing anthropologists work, bring them into direct contact with major issues in the field of public policy. In the past, even applied anthropologists seldom thought of themselves as policy scientists, and the influence of anthropologists on public policy has been limited. There are three major reasons for this situation: the nature of policy formulation and implementation as a continually changing political process with which anthropologists have little familiarity, the fact that mainstream anthropology largely ignored contemporary social problems, and the limited use of empirical data of any type in many policy decisions.

The growth of practicing anthropology in recent years has resulted in increased numbers of anthropologists who have become more directly involved in the formulation, implementation, and modification of public policy. In some cases, practicing anthropologists are hired specifically to work on the drafting of policy statements and legislation. More commonly, practicing anthropologists become engaged in policy issues as a byproduct of work activities which are greatly influenced by existing public policies. They are frequently initiated into policy analysis by their involvement in the empirical documentation and measurement of the outcome of social policies within the context of communities and institutions.

The essays in Part III describe several ways in which practicing anthropologists have participated in social policy analysis in the past and continue to do so in the present. They make clear that a strong commitment to empirical data and multidisciplinary analytic skills are essential for effective work in this area. They also underscore the fact that existing social policies often serve to perpetuate institutional and community interest groups which may be at odds with the interests of those who lack political skills and power. Practicing anthropologists who specialize in policy analysis will likely do battle with those who would prefer that the outcomes and impacts of their policies remain undocumented.

17

ANTHROPOLOGY AS A POLICY SCIENCE
Solon T. Kimball

The development of anthropology as a policy science will not be easy. It will require a greatly expanded research emphasis on contemporary complex societies and a vigorous development of applied anthropology so that data may be provided for the better understanding of the consequences of strategies used to achieve programmatic goals and to test theories of change. Research methodologies which produce only ethnographic description must yield to methodologies rooted in the natural sciences which allow a systemic analysis of communities, organizations, and processes within them.

Solon T. Kimball develops the above themes and describes the difference between policy recommendations based on empirical analysis and those based solely on one's own moral judgments. Pronouncements about policy issues do not necessarily constitute policy analysis. Unless such pronouncements are based on scientific methods of investigation, the policy statements of anthropologists are similar to those of any other citizen with an opinion.

THE USE OF social science as an instrument of public policy and programs is not new. Spokesmen from political science and econom-

The late Solon T. Kimball (Ph.D., Harvard) was graduate research professor emeritus at the University of Florida at the time of his death in 1982. During his life, he contributed widely to the fields of educational anthropology, theory and method, and applied anthropology. His fieldwork was in rural and urban Ireland and in United States communities. He had been a fellow of the Social Science Research Council and a Guggenheim Fellow. He had served as a consultant to the United States Departments of Agriculture and Interior, UNESCO, the Brazilian Center for Educational Research, the Peru Educational Development Project, and the Brazilian Fulbright Binational Commission. He was a past president of the American Ethnological Society, the Society for Applied Anthropology, and the Southern Anthropological Society.

ics, in particular, and to a lesser extent from sociology and psychology, have become involved during recent years in the discussion about the direction of our national life. The listing of such notables as Charles Beard, Charles Merriam, Adolph Berle, Jr., Harold Lasswell, Karl Menninger, John Galbraith, Milton Friedman, and Daniel Patrick Moynihan reminds us of their connection with public issues. That intervention by scholars is part of our Western heritage is attested to by such other illustrious names as Montesquieu, Auguste Comte, Jeremy Bentham, and John Stuart Mill. The efforts of these and others to influence the course of events is testimony to the application of systematic thought for public purposes.

The conspicuous absence of anthropologists from comparable involvement merits examination. The absence of applicable research interests may be judged partly responsible. Whereas major segments of political science and economics are directly linked with contemporary problems, the subject-matter interests of most anthropologists, in contrast, are with remote peoples or in the past. The trash heaps of ancient civilizations, the bones of ancestral primates, or the social-climbing feasts of isolated tribes may conceivably yield some cosmic truths, but they contribute little to explaining the price of beans. In truth, the expectation that such research findings might have some practical value has hardly been a consideration. Even so, some limited use has been made of anthropological findings during pre-World War II days in Dutch and British colonial rule. A few American anthropologists became involved with farm programs and Indian affairs during the New Deal and later in wartime activities and the administration of Trust Territories in the Pacific after World War II. In these and other instances, the anthropological contribution was nearly always of a technical sort.

Even so, a participation which only touched a small portion of the non-Western world and involved a bare handful of anthropologists aroused misgivings in the breasts of most anthropologists. Their aversion to engage actively in the world around them can be linked to deeply embedded views about the objectives of their discipline. Even during World War II, two spokesmen for the ivory tower tradition, Evans-Pritchard (1946:92–98) and Sol Tax (1945:21–23) argued cogently to retain the purity of scientific spirit and to reject involvement in practical problems.

A commitment to the search for "truth" as the overriding objective of anthropology has had certain consequences. First, there has been a willingness to accept the accumulation of knowledge as an intrinsic end in itself. Whenever some Babbitt queried the usefulness of a supposedly arcane fact, the response was likely to be a rejection of both the question and the Philistine world of the questioner. Second, most anthropologists confined their search for "truth" to nonliterate and peasant peoples and rejected outright the legitimacy of contemporary society as a field of study. This narrow focus provided no substantive base from which to comment on current issues, although that did not always deter such action. Third, the traditional scientific procedure of lengthy and often arduous field studies seemed to exacerbate in anthropologists the monastic tendency found among many scientists whose work is exclusively undertaken within the halls of academe. Lastly, it is not often that anthropologists have been invited to become involved in practical affairs. Those who are the managers of our society have habitually turned to soothsayers who carry the labels of economist, political scientist, sociologist, or psychologist.

Within anthropology, however, there are a few who have set a course counter to the traditional current. They have conducted research in contemporary society and have taken the lead in developing an applied science. The history of their activities and the specifics of their point of view and accomplishments are described in preceding essays. My purpose here is to explore the policy science potentials of anthropology—a topic which will be more fully elaborated in the essays to follow.

Anthropology and Public Policy

The growing maturity of social sciences in recent years has increased their value in the formulation and implementation of public policy. For example, the Roosevelt New Deal was the first national administration to extensively incorporate academics into the circle of policy makers and program planners. Receptivity to this professional wisdom has fluctuated under subsequent administrations, but has never been extinguished. The real issue, however, is not the source of policy, be it professors, politicians, or businessmen, but its conceptual origin. Harold Lasswell, the most consistent advocate of a social science contribution to policy makes the distinction between decisions based on theological, metaphysical, or other explanatory grounds and those derived from scientific evidence. He states that "the policy sciences study the process of deciding or choosing and evaluate the relevance of available knowledge for the solution of particular problems" (Lasswell 1968:181).

Any scientific discipline whose findings are directly applicable to the clarification of issues which determine a course of action may be deemed to be a policy science. This definition excludes physics, chemistry, and biology. Although the research findings on nuclear fission, insecticides, or the genetic code may have incredible implications for the future welfare, even survival, of mankind, these scientific disciplines cannot be counted as among the policy sciences. This does not prevent the practitioners of these sciences from becoming alarmed about the consequences of their discoveries and urging the adoption of policies that would control their uses, as indeed they have. Their statements, however, are based upon moral considerations rather than those of their objective findings, and this is the crucial factor which makes the difference.

The capability of the social sciences to make policy statements does not differ too markedly from the physical sciences with one important exception. Within anthropology, for example, most research is stimulated by academically posed questions. The result is all too often a flat, descriptive account topically organized around standard categories. If those who conduct such research were pressed to justify their activities, they would probably do so on the grounds that they add to the store of human knowledge and represent the scientific search for truth. Many would either deny or disavow any intent to solve practical problems since such a posture might contaminate their scientific neutrality.

Some anthropological research, however, lends itself to policy formulation. To mark the distinction between that which does and that which does not is more than a matter of either intent or use. More explicitly, the difference is a function of the theoretical perspective which guides the collection of data and their analysis. An ethnographic inventory of customs and groups is not enough. The researcher must have made observations of individuals engaged in events in the variety of situations characteristic of that group. From these data can be derived the detail of the systemic arrangements by which a specific group meets its problems. It is this type of knowledge which contains the answers for those who would seek to formulate policy.

Substantive knowledge derived from appropriate procedures for gathering data, theory based on natural systems analysis, and a concern for understanding the processes of change are all necessary ingredients of policy science. Practitioners in many professional fields are building programs based on implicit or explicit policy goals which run into difficulties because one or more of these aspects are inadequately incorporated. The deficiency is usually in the failure to see the problems in systemic terms or in understanding the processes of change. These two aspects are linked. For example, attempts by nutritionists to modify food habits have often foundered on inadequate data and theory. They do not reckon with the strong linkage between values, social context, and food patterning. The vitamin-packed menus they recommend may be esthetically, socially, and religiously objectionable. There has been a failure to identify the variables and to see their interconnections. This is in addition to the absence of the culture specifics on food behavior. Furthermore, innovative style must conform to cultural practice. The Madison Avenue technique that reaches the flotsam of the city streets may produce only bewilderment in the back country. Modifications of superficial practices should be left to the hucksters anyway since the important thing to know is whether or not it is possible to wring from the data powerful explanatory concepts such as Darwin's natural selection. Such principles provide the ultimate understandings of a natural universe.

But before anthropologists become too deeply enmeshed in the arena of policy science, it is essential that they make explicit to themselves any ideological commitment or operating assumptions they may hold. This problem is quite separate from the methodological one of data bias induced by the presence of the fieldworker in the social context being examined. Nor is it a question of the capability to attain an absolute neutrality or objectivity. It is primarily a problem of the basic premises of the discipline of anthropology, especially as they may be shaped by inherent cultural perspectives.

In recent years, discussion about scientific objectivity has led to a recognition that attainment of such purity is limited by the cultural tools of thought and language. This conclusion has been as salutary for science as the acceptance of organic evolution was for Western thought. Within these limitations then, and they are modest enough, there is nothing in the methodological stance of anthropology which should inhibit statements of the kind which specify that "under these conditions we may expect these consequences." Such an accomplishment is the *sine qua non* of an applied science.

Unfortunately, such a capability does not fully deliver us from the confusion of the intellectual forest. There are some premises of anthropology, derivative of scientific findings which, when combined with a humanistic perspective, inevitably limit some of the courses of action. Although these limitations do not subsume allegiance to any specific religious, political, social, cultural, or technological system, they do recognize that some conditions limit, if not prevent, the achievement of the human potential. No anthropologist could ethically subscribe to any policy which led to such a result.

It may be useful to restate the principles which govern here. The genetic programming of individual and species in the context of surrounding conditions includes the potential and sets the limits of the life-cycle of individual or group. Every known society carries a culture which brings its young into the full humanity of symbol-using social adults. Although the style and complexity of cultural details vary widely from society to society, there is no society which lacks the essential ingredients of cosmic explanations, stabilized social groupings, and technological devices. But not all societies extend in equal measure full access to the humanizing process. The deficiencies are a consequence either of traditional social arrangements (such as slavery) or the inadequacy of knowledge or resources. As example, endemic starvation or disease that misshapes the minds and bodies of its victims, or social practices that limit the capabilities or spirit of its members, may be judged as conditions harmful to the achievement of the human potential.

If we assign to this potential the stature of a natural right, then we cannot design or approve any course which inhibits its realization. As a basic humanistic principle, it becomes embedded in the perspective of anthropology. Such a commitment, however, does not link anthropology to any particular form of political organization, religious expression, or technological system. Only the naïve believe that a problem-free utopia is either achievable or desirable.

Perspectives within Anthropology

An uncritical acceptance of anthropological data as suitable for policy formulation would be unwise. Certain anthropological perspectives automatically orient research focus and findings because of the premises which they include. In order to identify implicit biases, it is necessary to identify the assumptions which influence the ordering and interpretation of data. For example, anthropologists whose activities are shaped by an ideological bias based on race, religion, or some form of political utopianism have already made commitments which may or may not have anything to do with the facts. As advocates, they exploit data to prove their position, rather than to acquire enlightenment. A number of avowed activists expressing political, radical, or sexist causes have surfaced during the past decade. However meritorious their intentions, their commitment brings into question their judiciousness in matters of policy science.

Presumably, mainstream anthropology should be free of such biases. However, close examination often reveals a shaping of the data due to both inadvertent and unconscious factors. For example, it is fully recognized that much of the detail of "female" culture is not available to the male ethnographer. In addition, many areas of behavior, such as child training, were once almost uniformly ignored until a belated awareness of their significance appeared. The recognition and gradual correction of deficiencies of this type are part of the growth of any science. Of greater concern, however, is the influence which a deeply held intellectual commitment will have on the direction of inquiry and uses of data. The effect of such a linkage is clearly illustrated in the career of Franz Boas who comingled the idealism of socialist democracy with late nineteenth-century scientific absolutism.

Boas took strong and often outrageous stands on public issues. Furthermore, he encouraged research in areas that were relevant to these issues, such as the condition of minorities. Notwithstanding his deep concern for achieving justice for the individual in contemporary society, he never became an applied anthropologist as we understand that term today. This step was neither necessary nor possible since he had already synthesized his science and his ideology. Thus his scientific findings confirmed his moral perspective about humans and humanity. These aspects of Boas' career are so illuminating of both the relatively unfavorable intellectual climate for applied anthropology under such conditions and the problem of public policy based on data rather than on personal views that some further examination of the details is merited.

There is no necessary connection between an American political party and anthropology. The late Fay Cooper-Cole, distinguished chairman of the department at the University of Chicago, was a stalwart Republican. Yet no one could ever say that he mixed his political views and his anthropology. But when an individual is commited to a political ideology, as was Boas, it may be difficult to disentangle the extent to which the scientific posture is influenced by political morality and *vice versa.* Some of his students see them as entwined.

Ruth Bunzel, in her introduction to the reissue of Boas' *Anthropology and Modern Life,* reports that:

Boas was educated in the tradition of liberal romanticism that produced Carl Schurz and the philosophical anarchists of the nineteenth century. He was the essential protestant; he valued autonomy above all things and respected the unique potentialities of each individual. He believed that man was a rational animal and could, with persistent effort, emancipate himself from superstitition and irrationality and lead a sane and reasonable life in a good society. (1962:6)

William S. Willis, Jr. added to the picture when he wrote: "Boas' political commitments can be traced to his German Jewish background and his family's response to the Revolution of 1848. Life in the United States intensified Boas' commitments, making them more explicit as he moved into the Socialist Party and finally toward the communist movement" (1975:309–310). Alexander Lesser also confirmed this activism when he wrote:

Boas spoke out boldly throughout his life against racism and race prejudice, against narrow nationalism and war, and for an internationalism based on the common interests of humanity. Boas believed that truth, widely shared through publications and education, can serve to liberate the mind from traditional confusion, error and prejudice. (1968:107)

For Boas, the subject areas and concepts of anthropology furnished the source of the ammunition for his battle on behalf of liberal ideas. Willis, (1975:309) who suggested "that the clash between politics and professionalism is the main key to Boas as a person and as a scientist," calls attention to the remarkable congruency between Boas' liberal ideas and anthropological interests. For example, Boas was committed to the concept of the psychic unity of mankind, a view which contradicts the assertions of the racists. His focus on linguistics and folklore was also connected to his political views. The former "revealed the complexity of all languages and the existence of identical processes of abstraction." The latter "as tradition provided an alternative to racist explanations for many real and alleged deficiencies of contemporary colored peoples" (Willis 1975:311).

Other dimensions of Boasian thought and political activity also connect with these aspects. The growth of culture through diffusion, for example, confirms that all people contribute to the growth of culture. Hence the attention given to historical reconstruction. Further substantiation in support of his views was provided by the conclusions he reached about mental processes. He saw cultures as the "beneficial environments in which human thought and feeling are structured and operate" (Lesser 1968:102).

Boas' views of the individual were summarized in *The Mind of Primitive Man* (1911). He believed that behavior is an expression of habits, not instincts. The human environment, not the biological inheritance, explains variation in behavior, hence culture, not race, is paramount. For Boas, ethnology became the study of the mental life of man and dealt with characteristic forms of thought (Willis 1975:310). An infusion of moral purpose looms large in his concern with folklore, language, and behavior, and the prevailing prejudice and superstition which rationality will dissipate through the spread of truth which liberates the mind (and implicitly changes behavior) from "traditional confusion, error and prejudice" (Lesser 1968:107). This intricate intermingling of a political-moral philosophy with a congruent scientific approach, helps to explain the quick defense by Boasians to criticism of him or to competing approaches such as that of functional social anthropology. The challenge was more than just a threat to the adequacy of a scientific approach; it was an assault upon an implicit but deeply entrenched utopian view of the universe.

It seems unnecessary and perhaps unproductive to attempt to determine whether Boas' public pronouncements should be counted as primarily reflecting his political views or his anthropological findings. They did both. More serious is the question of the extent to which his political views encased his anthropological ones. For example, he suffered no reluctance in making sweeping generalizations about cultural variability, human growth, and learning when he was attacking racial or other kinds of ethnocentric prejudice, yet he consistently cautioned against attempting to prematurely establish scientific laws. His crusade against prejudice (a mind-set), echoes openly in his emphasis on the mentalistic aspects of behavior to the near exclusion of the social. Boas found support within anthropological studies for his view of the direction which mankind should go. He was not concerned with nor did he leave as a legacy the use of anthropology as a policy science.

There is no intended condemnation in this examination of an avowedly great man. But there is need to make blade-edge sharp the distinction between advocacy and data based policy. Speaking out on public issues does not a policy scientist make.

Further Considerations

The essential conditions for the development of a policy science within anthropology have now been established. Briefly restated, the primary requirements are:

1. That natural systems analysis, rather than the prevalent flat ethnographic description, be utilized in describing and interpreting communities, organizations, and processes.

2. That research on contemporary societies be greatly expanded.

3. That a vigorous development of applied or non-academic anthropology continue in order to provide empirical data about the consequences of strategies in achieving program goals and to test theories of change.

4. That caution be exercised to prevent the ideological contamination of anthropological evidence and to recognize that pronouncements on public issues do not constitute public policy analysis.

Further discussion of the characteristics of a policy statement are still necessary, however. In the early phase of developing anthropology as a policy science, we cannot be too cautious in our attempts to define the problem. For example, the condemnation or approval of some situation or condition may carry policy implications but is not in itself a policy position. A resolution deploring hunger, disease, crime, or the unequal status of some sex or race cannot be considered as policy. It should be viewed as the public affirmation of a *position*. From this perspective, a position paper should be viewed as the formal statement of belief or program emanating from some ethical, political, or economic consideration. In a strict sense, these are policy statements only if they are based on evidence drawn from systems analysis. I shall sharpen this point in a moment.

We must also be wary of slogans. These ringing phrases are bait for the innocent and may appear to be either truths or basic policy but are in reality verbal traps. Such ringing phrases as "educate the whole child," "families that pray together stay together," or "make the world safe for democracy" have all the appeal of a siren's call but eventually turn out to be only temporary rallying cries. However, slogans may be connected with programs and policies as is true of those cited above.

Indication of specific areas where anthropological data are of significance will perhaps assist in further clarification. For example, local authorities are sometimes faced with the necessity of responding to changed conditions in their communities. Important areas often include the social services, education, health, and welfare; land use; traffic management; public safety; and recreation. Programs which emerge from consideration of these problems may be viewed as reflecting the diverse interests of a community. The national government faces many of the same problems on a much larger scale, but there are also some which are distinctively national such as policies about food, resource use, population, technological developments, defense, and international relations.

Anthropologists have seldom been invited nor have they shown much interest in participating in the activities which determine policies at either local or national levels. Where participation has occurred, their contribution has largely been as applied technicians. They report cultural practices of social groups that are expected to influence reception of a program. I maintain that the anthropological contribution can be much broader than heretofore accepted. Its contextual emphasis adds meaning to data beyond that supplied by other disciplines. Furthermore, from applied anthropology we learn about the procedures through which policy and program are formulated.

Even a brief examination of some specific topic such as food reveals both the complexity of the problem and the powerful contribution of anthropology. We can also learn how remote, perhaps even harmful, are such slogans as "Feed the World's Hungry." I select food as my example both because of its importance and because it has been an area of concern to me (Kimball 1974a).

The economic policy of the Department of Agriculture of the United States Government has for some years been derived from the theory that the "natural" economic laws of the marketplace determine type, quantity, and price of agricultural product. The logic argues that if the price of a commodity is high due to demand, the causative limited supply will encourage greater production since farmers are motivated by the principle of self-interest to make money. The resulting increased production brings a decline in prices. Thus, the self-interest of the producer serves the self-interest of the consumer. The dynamics of the marketplace, to which many agricultural economists subscribe, assumes a universal motive of self-interest which, combined with a postulated law of supply and demand, regulates price and production and results in profit or loss. These concepts provide the perspective which has shaped the recent policy and program of the American government toward food production. Would the justifying concepts have been changed if the policy had been one of using food for world domination? Or let us suppose that policy was based on principles of reciprocity and status as exemplified in distribution of the meat of newly killed animals among the Bushmen; the exchange of ceremonial bracelets and necklaces in the Kula ring of the Trobriand Islands, or the giveaway Potlach feasts of the Kwakiutl. It is obvious that principles other than those of the marketplace govern the exchange of goods in these situations. Furthermore, these illustrations clearly demonstrate the connection between perspective and policy.

The important principle to be remembered is that basic conceptualization guides the selection, organization, and analysis of data, and shapes policy and programs. The simple conceptualizations of traditional ethnographic descriptions provide inventories of cultural items but are inadequate for policy purposes. Instead, it is the systemic approach of the natural history method that proves productive. For example, if we focus on the behavior surrounding food, we search out the specifics and connections among the variables of macro-system including environment, technology, organization, customs, beliefs, and population. From the analysis emerges three contrasting food-chains or cycles of food production and consumption associated with foraging, agrarian, and corporate cultures. Food data, thus conceptualized, provides the basis for both policy and program (Kimball 1974b).

The comparative approach of anthropology readily establishes its superiority for this type of problem. Each one of the three major types of food cycles is connected with a distinctive organizational and valuational system. "Foragers" live in camps as members of band-type communities. "Agrarianists" live in households in open or closed sedentary communities. The "corporate" system or organizational linkages characterizes our own and other contemporary societies.

Migratory hunter-gatherers link all members of the band, in all phases of the production-consumption cycle. In agrarian societies, the production-consumption cycle is sex differentiated and centers in household and field. Activities are sequenced but with usually regular involvement of kinsmen and neighbors at such times as harvest and festivities. In corporate society, institutions and households are centers of consumption. The food chain becomes greatly extended and organizationally complex, and there is a sharp demarcation of personnel involved in the multiple steps of production and consumption. There is no necessary connection between the food producer and the consumer.

From this conceptually structured base, it is now possible to extend the systemic detail for any specified situation in order to describe how groups organize in cooperative tasks; enumerate the cultural practices which surround the uses of food; adduce the symbols, values, and sanctions associated with a worldview; and provide examples of the process by which modifications occur. Through such knowledge, we can identify the situations where a land tenure system drains off increased production instead of expanding the diet of the poor as the intervenors anticipated; or how a status system regulates production; or how cosmologies may inhibit innovation. More significantly, the systemic approach identifies the basic process (the food chain) and its system variations (foragers, agrarianists, corporate) which organize essential knowledge for both policy and program. By definition, policy which is systemically based is contingent, provides for alternatives, and includes self-correcting mechanisms to incorporate new data or changes in conditions. Its formulation must also involve those who are affected by programs which emanate from policy.

Conclusion

This broad overview should help us to understand the ramifications of the uses of anthropology for influencing the course of human affairs. If the distinctions which separate the roles of anthropologist as citizen, as applied technician, and as policy scientist are kept clear, there should be no difficulty in understanding the operations associated with each. The anthropologist as citizen can take sides on such crucial issues as world peace, energy conservation, environmental protection, women's liberation, abortion, or dozens of other matters which evoke diverse sentiments. Nor does there seem to be any special talent needed by those who declare for honesty, responsibility, and decency.

Although no special certification is required to take sides on public issues, there are situations where specific anthropological skills are needed. Possession of factual knowledge is a requirement for one who testifies in an Indian Land Claims case. Applied anthropologists require a broad range of competency. They use theory, as well as fact, and utilize their principles of process to develop sequential courses of action. Competencies essential for the anthropologist as policy scientist are even more rigorous and extensive. Those qualities already listed include freedom from ideological bias, a research interest in contemporary society, the empirical experience of applied anthropology, and natural systems analysis. The ultimate distinction, however, is a function of the analytical process. The policy scientist, unlike others, derives his formulations by asking questions which subsume knowledge of the dynamics of systems; the resulting propositions are consequences of the interplay between organized data and the method of analysis. They are statements of contingencies, not probabilities, about potential courses of action. The discussion of food policy exemplifies the point.

The time is ripe for qualified members of the profession to become involved in policy formulation. With the continued growth of competence in organizational dynamics and in professional and topical fields such as education and health, those anthropologists who have been concerned with contemporary society hold relevant knowledge of immense value for projecting future goals and programs. Our knowledge of the ongoing processes of community should also have prepared us to recognize that policy making must also be an ongoing and adapting process. Future prospects do indeed seem bright for anthropologists to become engaged as scientists with conceptual and research tools which can illuminate many of the problems which vex policy makers today. The way is already being paved by those who have begun to rethink anthropology in terms of the modern world and our society. A sampling of current efforts as they relate to policy may be found in those essays which immediately follow. These reveal not only the need for the anthropological contribution but also some of the barriers which must be overcome if that branch of anthropology known as applied or development anthropology is to fully emerge as a policy science.

18

ETHNICITY, PUBLIC POLICY, AND ANTHROPOLOGISTS

George L. Hicks
and Mark J. Handler

The orientation of Americans toward the present and the future often results in each generation confronting contemporary social problems as if they were appearing for the first time. What is true of Americans generally is also true of American anthropologists in particular. This ahistoricism means that we are often unaware of the lessons of the past and assume that there are no past guideposts for present actions.

George L. Hicks and Mark J. Handler present an historical review of the relationships between anthropologists and public policies with respect to ethnicity. Using the case studies of native Americans, immigrants, and black Americans as examples, they demonstrate the failure and success of anthropologists in influencing the major policies which have affected these groups. Present issues and concerns about ethnicity are then discussed within the context of historical developments of ideas in the discipline of anthropology and the meaning of ethnicity in American life.

From Hicks and Handler, we learn a great deal about the complexities entailed in studying our own society and the problems of separating our roles as researchers from our roles as well-intentioned citizens.

George L. Hicks (Ph.D., Illinois) is associate professor of anthropology at Brown University. He has specialized in the study of American Indians, utopian communities, Southern Appalachian communities, and the Azore Islands from the perspective of interethnic relations. Mark J. Handler is a Ph.D. candidate at Brown University, who has done fieldwork in interethnic relations in rural Saskatchewan and the Azore Islands.

ANTHROPOLOGY, WE ARE told, is besieged by crisis on several fronts. As a child of imperialism, it is guilty of the sins of the fathers. Our principal areas of research, mostly in the Third World, no longer welcome us. Acknowledging the weaknesses of traditional functionalism, we are bereft of theoretical paradigms. Whatever problems the discipline faces, the sense of crisis is largely nourished by inattention to history. The ahistoricism that we share with fellow Americans leads us to experience the events and ideas of our society and discipline as unique. Thus, we have recently *discovered* ethnic populations in our midst and declared the "melting pot" a misleading fable, thereby demonstrating a lapse of memory about the debates over immigration restriction in the 1920s that involved debunking that same melting pot. Our response has been similar to the issues of relevant research, academic freedom, ethics, and espionage. It is not that we deny a parallel between the Thailand controversy and Boas' public attack on the espionage activities of anthropologists in World War I. It is simply that we know little of these events and, in a world so rapidly changing, assume that the past offers few guideposts for the present. It is not that anthropology has no problems but that those we have appear as crises which not only overwhelm us, but keep returning because we forever face them for the first time. As a corrective to this ahistoricism, this essay begins with the past.

Of all the social problems subjected to public policy concern and social scientific investigation in twentieth-century America, none received more attention than those of the Indian, the immigrant, and the Negro. These three cases provide ample opportunity for examining the interplay of anthropology and public policy in dealing with ethnicity. While each has its own unique history in America, in some ways they are different facets of a single phenomenon. Each presented similar difficulties from the policy makers' perspective: poverty, mortality, deviance, crime, the potential of revolt or rebellion. Beyond their definition as social problems, Indians, immigrants, and Negroes share experiences that reflect fundamental contradictions in American society: between pluralism and homogeneity, between equality and individualism.

The role of social science has been twofold. At the level of social problems, findings of social scientists justified attempts and refusals to design and implement amelioration programs. On the ideological level, social science theories of human nature, treatments of race and culture, and descriptions of Indians, immigrants, and Negroes have explained and challenged explanations of the contradiction between the situation of these groups and the claims of American ideology. Ralph Ellison's (1966:292) observation on the place of Negro studies in the 1870s applies to the cases considered here: "Here was a science whose role . . . was to reconcile the practical morality of American capitalism with the ideal morality of the American Creed." As objects of exploitation and as prime examples of the killing power of social fictions, "niggers," "redskins," "wops," and so on, have always confronted anthropology with the issue of interrelations between power and symbolism. But these issues are only now beginning to draw our attention (for an interesting example, see Cohen 1974).

These themes are taken up here. Following the historical review, we discuss the political strategy of cultural nationalism and the development of public policy that supports ethnic pluralism.

Case 1: American Indians

An embarrassment of riches faces the student of anthropology and public policy in the case of American Indians. No other ethnic category has been subject to such elaborate and shifting policy, and the discipline of anthropology in the United States has been largely shaped by its involvement with North American Indians. In no other case have anthropologists had equivalent opportunities to influence policy decisions.

After an initial period, from 1754 to 1871, of public policy culminating in large-scale efforts to concentrate the Indian population in the lands west of the Mississippi River, federal policy fluctuated between trying to retain and incorporate them into the body politic and attempts to preserve them in isolation.

In the last half of the nineteenth century, educated Indians and sympathetic whites concluded that the "reservation system *per se,* . . . [was] responsible for impeding Indians in their course toward 'civilization' " (Lurie 1968:70–71). The General Allotment Act of 1887 (Dawes Act), authorizing a system of individual tracts for Indian householders and sale of surplus land to non-Indian interests, was promoted as a reform measure (Haas 1957:13), Forty-five years after the Act, two-thirds of Indian lands belonged to non-Indians, leaving 90,000 Indians without land ownership (Haas 1957:15). Enforcement of the Act was marked by "forced acculturation," with a major effort launched by the Bureau of Indian Affairs (BIA) to destroy the last vestiges of distinctive Indian cultural traditions.

Significant new policies toward American Indians did not emerge until after the inauguration of President Roosevelt in 1933, when there was a radical change of direction in federal policy (Tyler 1964:51–60). John Collier, commissioner of Indian Affairs from 1933 to 1945, administered the new policies, particularly the Indian Reorganization Act (IRA) of 1934, that sought to promote cultural diversity and tribal self-government, while at the same time retaining federal supervision. Within a few years, Collier was in difficulty with Congress, which apparently had not anticipated so far-ranging an implementation of its various acts. But Collier's interpretation could hardly have had a more favorable political climate than the Great Depression: encouraging Indians to stay on the reservations reduced their potential strain on state and local government in a period of severe economic distress (Tyler 1964:62).

Although there is a great deal of statistical evidence that Collier's programs were successful in reducing high mortality rates, landlessness, and extreme poverty among American Indians, basic antagonism to special Indian status and concern for the future of Indian resources led to repeated attacks from Congress and others, and as a result, Collier resigned in 1945. Within a few years, his policies were dismantled.

With the end of World War II, during which 65,000 Indians left their reservations for military service and defense work, public opinion opposed special status and work projects. The emphasis of policy was to relocate Indians to urban centers and terminate their reservations and federal supervision. The Senate's *Survey of Conditions of the Indians of the United States,* begun in 1928 and ending with over 23,000 pages in its final report in 1944, called for the "liquidation of the Indian Bureau" (Tyler 1964:91–92). The House of Representatives' Mundt Report of 1947 called for off-reservation boarding schools, voluntary relocation programs, and individual ownership of independent, family-sized farms—a return to the policy of the Dawes

Act of 1887. The Indian Claims Commission Act of 1946 established a means for settlement of claims as a necessary step toward breaking down Indian dependence on the federal government and terminating reservations.

Criticism of the postwar termination policy began even before its enactment. The effect of wholesale termination would be, as Collier said in 1943, to "create a permanently dispossessed and impoverished group that either would live on the dole or would become one more sore spot in the body politic" (quoted in Tyler 1964:109). The practicality of the policy was not debated. Rather, the issues were ideological: civil rights, democratic ideals, equality. Although the statement of congressional demand for termination was not repudiated, the movement lost its momentum in the 1950s. Soon thereafter, Indians were affected by the new programs of the 1960s aimed at the poor in general.

ANTHROPOLOGY AND INDIAN AFFAIRS

Founded in 1878 originally as part of the Smithsonian Institution, the Bureau of American Ethnology (BAE) was, until 1910, the major sponsor of ethnographic research in the United States. A major argument for the founding of the bureau was that it would provide scientific information for the administration of Indian affairs. The first head of the bureau, J. W. Powell, set out the bureau's policy orientation in his first Annual Report in 1881 as an effort "to produce results that would be of practical value in the administration of Indian affairs" (quoted in Barnett 1956:3). It is striking that the two areas for special research attention, emphasized by Powell—Indian progress and the causes and remedies of culture conflict—are precisely those in which anthropologists had little to say when, fifty years later, they were called upon to advise the Collier administration.

During the 1930s, anthropologists were drawn into federal research on Indian problems requiring administrative decisions. The IRA called for tribal constitutions and modifications of economic and social conditions on those reservations choosing to reorganize under its provisions. To provide information for these programs, anthropologists were hired by the BIA. In other developments, the BIA education division contracted with anthropologists to provide bilingual texts and other materials for use in Indian education. These were needed for Collier's new program of fostering Indian identity and cultural distinctiveness. Other anthropologists engaged in making surveys and conducting problem-oriented research for the Human Development Unit of the Technical Cooperation group of the Soil Conservation Service. Seventy-five to eighty studies were made between 1936 and 1946 for use in making administrative decisions (Nash 1973:26).

With few exceptions (Nash 1973:26), anthropologists knowledgeable about the BIA (e.g., Steward 1969; Nash 1973) conclude that anthropological activity had little impact on policy. For example, the massive interdisciplinary Indian Personality and Administration project directed by Laura Thompson was explicitly established to provide policy recommendations, yet Kluckhohn and Hackenberg found that "six years after the termination of the Thompson project, the Indian Service has apparently taken no action on recommendations it contains" (1954:33). Even more telling, twenty years later Nash could still detect no impact of the Thompson studies (1973:27).

Several factors limited the impact of research on policy. Statutory deadlines for tribal adoption of self-government sometimes forced action before research was completed (Barnett 1956:37). Anthropologists' inexperience in dealing with administrators played a part (*Anthropology and the American Indian* 1973:32). More importantly, anthropologists in the 1930s were "unequipped with relevant knowledge" (Steward 1969:3). Finally, Collier was guided by his own ideas about Indians and administration. "Even if anthropology had a body of theory about modernization it would not have been permitted to use it; for the utopian dream of preserving 'Indianhood' was unassailable" (Steward 1969:15).

At times, anthropologists have had more than an advisory or research role in Indian policy. In the late 1940s, a professional anthropologist, John Provinse, was assistant commissioner, and from 1962 to 1965 two others headed the Bureau of Indian Affairs: Phileo Nash as commissioner and James Officer as assistant commissioner. From his experience as commissioner, Nash suggests that research was not "very action-related" in the BIA "because the fundamental decisions that affect the lives of the people touched by the Bureau . . . are not made by free agents . . . because every one of these decisions is made while looking simultaneously in two directions . . . to look to the tribal leaders on one side and to the appropriating committees of Congress on the other" (Nash 1973:28–29).

Within Congress, anthropological work was often opposed. For example, Steward (1969:4) reports that the federal government, prior to the Collier administration, "had impeded ethnographic research, which had been directed toward recording aboriginal cultures which Federal policy was attempting to eliminate." Even Collier's support did not quell opposition. Research went on "in spite of a growing hostility in Congress toward anthropological investigations; indeed, in spite of Congress' attempted prohibition of them" (Thompson 1956:521; see, for details, *Anthropology and the American Indian* 1973:32–33). Complementing Congressional displeasure was opposition from within the discipline itself. Kroeber doubted that anthropologists could retain their independence in research when they were employed by a government agency. Indeed, the results were few (Beals 1969:52).

ANTHROPOLOGICAL DIRECTIONS AND INDIAN POLICY

Until World War II, American anthropology's research interests, methods, and theories were primarily developed in its relation with North American Indians. The major approach of the first generation of academically trained American anthropologists was the use of key informants in an effort to reconstruct "aboriginal" Indian culture. Operating with the ideals of "the tribal isolate," "the primitive," and the melting pot assumption that minorities were due for inevitable acculturation, anthropologists were professionally blind to contemporary conditions among American Indians. By implicitly suggesting that Indians had no culture worth maintaining, this orientation supported a policy of forced acculturation. Nevertheless, government officials objected to ethnographic recording of cultures they were trying to eliminate.

New research interests, particularly culture and personality and acculturation, emerged in the 1930s. Acculturation studies tied directly to American Indians shifted the focus of research to ethnographically "contaminated" and nonisolated Indians who had previously been ignored. Anthropologists now sought to delimit the processes of change and adaptation subsequent to European contact; acculturation as an appropriate subject was formally recognized with the 1936 *Memorandum* by Redfield, Linton, and Herskovits. While the shift in anthropological perspective appears to have coincided with the New

Deal, Margaret Mead's pioneering *The Changing Culture of an Indian Tribe* (1966) marked anthropology's first venture into "reservation sociology."

Both anthropology and policy apparently responded to common influences, such as the social circumstances of the Great Depression, and policy affected anthropology through the funding of research. Yet, the study of acculturation was only partly consistent with the goals of the Indian New Deal. The focus of acculturation studies on present conditions of American Indians was congruent with Collier's ideas. Just as the Boasians recorded the past at a time when the BIA tried to destroy Indian traditions, students of acculturation emphasized culture change while the BIA tried to minimize it.

INDIAN POLICY AND "AMERICAN" VALUES

No consistent development marks federal policy toward American Indians (Zimmerman 1957:39). A common element in all policies, however, has been the belief that the Indian problem was environmental and cultural rather than genetic and racial; this, as we shall see, was not the case with Negroes or immigrants.

Shifts in Indian policy reflect fundamental contradictions and alternatives in American ideology, particularly those conveniently labeled as *individualism, free enterprise, equality,* and *freedom*. Individualism and free enterprise support assimilation of Indians as individuals and oppose the BIA (because it is restrictive of individual freedom), federal trusteeship (because it restricts free enterprise), and tribal organization (because it appears contrary to individualism).

Equality is often equated with uniformity, and in Indian policy it stands in opposition to special status and distinctive culture. Yet the American concept of freedom supports individual and local community autonomy and toleration of difference. In the history of Indian policy, these latter values have been invoked less often than the others. Equality of opportunity as part of the national ideal justifies federal supervision and special services as a means of balancing the accumulated disadvantages of Indians. These basic contradictions in American ideology are increasingly evident in current federal policy for minority groups in general.

Although there is some broad correspondence between the selection of one or another of these alternatives and changes in national socioeconomic conditions—termination and allotment during prosperous times, cultural distinctiveness in the Depression—simple economic determinism fails as a satisfactory argument. Changes in anthropological perspectives and research interests have coincided with policy changes, partly due to government influence in research funding and partly because both policy makers and anthropologists hold some common assumptions and are subject to similar social conditions. One might have expected, given anthropologists' expertise about American Indians, a great deal of influence to flow from anthropology to national policy. It is nevertheless an inescapable conclusion that anthropology has had little effect.

Case 2: Immigrants to the United States

For the first time in American history, immigration policy was fundamentally altered with legislation passed between 1921 and 1929. Open immigration was radically restricted by sharply discriminatory nationality quotas that reflect racist doctrines of Nordic superiority by favoring northern Europeans over people from southern and eastern Europe. (In the first quarter of this century, what are now referred to as nationalities were also classified as races. In addition, Europeans were subdivided into Nordic, Alpine, or Mediterranean races.)

During most of the nineteenth century, immigration to America was actively encouraged by the federal government. Strong sentiment for restriction appeared with the racist nativism of the late 1880s. At that time, the volume of immigration was less troubling than the ethnic composition of the immigrants. Both concerns were satisfied by legislation of the 1920s: total immigration was reduced by 76 percent, with a disproportionate ratio affecting those from southern and eastern Europe. Italian immigrants fell by 87 percent, Russians by 99.9 percent, but Germans declined by only 58 percent.

With the Immigration Act of 1965, national origins and other discriminatory bases for quotas were eliminated, and the door was opened for a new immigration drastically changed in ethnic composition. From 1965 to 1975, the number of immigrants averaged 380,000 per year. Once again, the countries of southern and eastern Europe are the leading donor nations, along with Asia: in 1974, the first three

European countries sending immigrants were Italy, Portugal, and Greece. In recent years, there has been a shift to non-European donors: from 1881 to 1920, Europeans constituted 88 percent of the immigrants, while between 1966 and 1977 they accounted for only 28 percent!

IMMIGRATION POLICY AND LEGISLATION

Immigration involves several policy issues. Some concern the status of aliens: grounds for deportation, economic rights (for example, head taxes, occupational restrictions), and naturalization requirements. But the fundamental issue is open versus restricted immigration and the basis of restriction.

American immigration legislation is largely a series of successive steps in a tightening pattern of restriction. In 1882, convicts, lunatics, idiots, and those likely to become public charges were barred. An attempt to curtail the importation of contract labor (previously *supported* by federal law in the 1860s) was passed in 1885. The Immigration Act of 1891 brought immigration, for the first time, wholly under federal control.

The first general restriction law was passed in 1917. It required that all immigrants (with a few exceptions) be able to read some language. First proposed in 1887, the literacy test was the focus of the restrictionist campaign and was from the beginning intended as a respectable way to discriminate against newcomers from southern and eastern Europe, where illiteracy rates were highest. Presidents Cleveland, Taft, and Wilson vetoed literacy bills in 1895, 1913, and 1915, but Wilson's veto of the 1917 version was overridden. This act also excluded "persons of constitutional psychopathic inferiority" (a eugenics concept), vagrants, chronic alcoholics, alien radicals, and Hindus and East Indians.

In the post-World War I period, the literacy test proved ineffective in checking immigration, and temporary nationality quotas were established by law in 1921. The Johnson-Read (National Origins) Act established permanent policy in 1924 by setting quotas at 150,000. Each country's quota was to equal the proportion of people from that country (by birth or descent) in the total United States population in 1920. After two postponements, the national origins quota system took effect in 1929.

OPPOSITION TO IMMIGRATION

Business and labor are the most readily identifiable interest groups whose efforts affected immigration policy in this period. During the 1860s and 1870s, business groups actively promoted immigration, arguing that it provided positive benefits by increasing the number of workers and consumers in an expanding economy. By the late 1880s, after such highly publicized anarchist incidents as that in Haymarket Square, business leaders turned against immigrants and identified them as the source of radicalism and labor unrest. With the economic depression of 1893–97, this negative attitude hardened. But the economic boom of the early 1900s brought new demands for unskilled immigrant labor to tend the new semi-automatic machines. From about 1905, big business opposed literacy tests and quota restrictions while supporting Americanization programs.

Labor opposed immigration more consistently. Industrial labor, in direct competition with immigrants, was involved in all the anti-immigration moves in the nineteenth century. Although they earlier distinguished between voluntary immigration and that induced by contract labor supporting the former, organized labor had by 1906 abandoned the distinction and called for restriction of immigration. Immigrants were used to break strikes and undercut wage demands, and labor's support of restriction culminated in 1918 with the American Federation of Labor's demand for a two-year suspension of immigration.

Labor and business do not exhaust the list of pressure groups involved. The Immigration Restriction League, for example, was founded by "practical-minded intellectuals from well-to-do, long-established families steeped in Boston ways and Boston ideas" (Higham 1974:102. Their opposition to the influx of new immigrants was founded in *nativism*—"intense opposition to an internal minority on the ground of its foreign (e.g., 'un-American') connections . . . a zeal to destroy the enemies of a distinctively American way of life" (Higham 1974:4). Although nativism has been present in all periods of our history, it apparently erupted with special strength during times of national crisis. In these crises, Higham contends that "confidence in the homogeneity of American culture broke down. In desperate efforts to rebuild national unity, men rallied against symbols of foreignness that were appropriate to their predicament" (Higham 1974: preface).

Of the three recurrent themes in American nativism—anti-Catholic, antiradical, and racial nativism—it was racial nativism, phrased in anthropological terms, that underlay the restriction of immigration from 1910 to 1924. The influence of racial nativism began with the identification of the national genius as Anglo-Saxon, a notion imported from England and achieving wide currency in the 1840s.

As the different immigrants of the late nineteenth century—Italians, Slavs, Jews, and others from eastern and southern Europe—captured attention, only their lack of an Anglo-Saxon identity appeared as a common trait. To define the special threat of these immigrants, a system of racial classification distinguished clear-cut racial types among Europeans, and established an affinity between the old Americans, presumed to be Anglo-Saxon in descent, and northern Europeans.

Two currents of European thought reached America at the turn of the century and were combined into a scientific racism that found ready use in the arguments for restriction of immigration. Based in the new science of heredity, the eugenics movement gained great popularity after 1910 and appealed to both nativists and progressives. Eugenics was a scientific challenge to the regnant environmentalism: an individual's most important traits derived from heredity and were not subject to environmental modification. Hence, immigration restriction was necessary to protect the American population. Although the eugenicists' hereditary determinism called for screening defectives, it was silent on racial categories.

The second European contribution to American racial nativism came from physical anthropology.

In the end the race-thinkers had to look to anthropology to round out a naturalistic nativism. Anthropology alone could classify the peoples of Europe into hereditary types that would distinguish the new immigration from older Americans; it alone might arrange these races in a hierarchy of merit and thereby prove the irremediable inferiority of the newcomers; and anthropology would have to collaborate with genetics to show wherein a mixture of races physically weakens the stronger. (Higham 1974:153)

This kind of physical anthropology, nonexistent in America, was imported from Europe, where it had become well developed by the late 1800s. The assumptions and findings of this new science were developed in America by nonanthropologists. Although William Ripley, an economist (originally trained in anthropology at Harvard), in his

1899 *The Races of Europe,* adopted the anthropometrically based European racial classification—Teutonic, Alpine, and Mediterranean—it was the dilletante naturalist, Madison Grant, who provided the classic formulation of racial nativism. Blending racial classification, biological determinism, and rabid nativism, his *The Passing of the Great Race* first appeared in 1916 and was to have its real impact in the 1920s.

The scale of immigration in the decades after 1890 was too great for anyone to maintain the faith in the natural assimilative power of American institutions that had marked earlier nineteenth-century attitudes. For nativist and reformer, the twentieth century alternative to restriction was directed assimilation—in short, Americanization.

Americanization as an ideology and program was born in the 1890s from the efforts of two very different groups: the settlement house program of social integration and the hereditary patriotic organizations. The former aimed to Americanize immigrants only in the most general way, by attempts at what we might today call "Community development." The patriotic societies, however, had specific notions that adult immigrants should be taught loyalty to their new nation. After 1915, the goal of Americanization was, for liberals and progressives, no longer immigrant welfare but the breaking of Old World ties and speedy, thorough naturalization. The major Americanization organization of the political progressives, the Committee for Immigrants in America, changed its slogan "Many Peoples, But One Nation" to "America First."

With the end of World War I, fear of the foreign-born continued, with "Bolshevism" replacing Germany as the national enemy. Political radicalism and labor turmoil were, as in the 1880s, attributed to the foreign-born; Americanization became the means to fight this foreign menace. With the end of the Red Scare in 1920, the Americanization movement collapsed. It did not, however, carry nativism into oblivion.

MOVES TOWARD RESTRICTION

With tolerance for ethnic minorities exhausted and Americanization in disrepute, restriction seemed the only solution to a problem of growing dimensions. Scientific racism gained its widest acceptance at this time. The Ku Klux Klan, reborn in 1915, spread to the north in 1921, Tom Watson won a Senate seat with an anti-Catholic campaign, and Henry Ford emerged as a leader of anti-Semitism. In this xenophobic climate, Madison Grant's *The Passing of the Great Race* achieved the popularity it had failed to receive at the time of its publication in 1916. Grant's vision left no room for Americanization: the science of eugenics had destroyed the "pathetic and fatuous belief in the efficacy of American institutions and environment to reverse or obliterate immemorial hereditary tendencies" (quoted in Baltzell 1964:97–98). Madison Grant "taught the American people to . . . identify themselves as Nordics, and to regard any mixture with [Mediterraneans or Alpines] . . . as a destructive process of 'mongrelization' " (Higham 1974:271–272).

FRANZ BOAS AND THE IMMIGRANT QUESTION

Racial nativists' claims couched the restriction debate in anthropological terms, and the leading anthropologist of the period, Franz Boas, responded. As mentioned in essays 1 and 17, Boas was a strong advocate of rigorous empirical standards. His research was nonetheless deeply committed. His humanistic values influenced his choice of research topic, and he sought to make the political implications of his findings explicit. Boas' perspective—combining liberal ideas about "equality of opportunity, education, political and intellectual liberty, the rejection of dogma, and the search for scientific truth" (Stocking 1968:149)—was a fusion of scientific and political elements. In America, he was not only an egalitarian socialist; he was an immigrant and a Jew. While he worked actively in the cause of Negro civil rights, most of Boas' research on race was concerned with European immigrants.

Boas never denied the operation of biological processes, including heredity, but insisted that they were subject to environmental modification, and that culture, not biology, accounted for observed patterns of human behavior. Summarizing Boas' contribution, Stocking (1968:264) writes: "The whole thrust of his thought was in fact to distinguish the concepts of race and culture, to separate biological and cultural heredity, to focus attention on cultural process, to free the concept of culture from its heritage of evolutionary and racial assumption."

All of Boas' thinking on race was relevant to the immigration question, but he made one direct contribution to the debate. His report *Changes in Bodily Form of Descendants of Immigrants* appeared in 1910 as one of the forty-two volumes issued by the United States Immigration Commission, an agency established as a result of the 1907 Immigration Act, to investigate the effects of immigration. From 1908 to 1910, Boas obtained body measurements of 18,000 persons: East European Jews, Bohemians, Neapolitans, and Sicilians, all living in New York City at the time. He made direct comparisons between children and their parents and between the American data and available European measurements.

While consistent with his earlier research in showing environmental influences on rates of growth, the immigrant study yielded unexpected results. With other anthropologists of the time, Boas considered cephalic index as a stable, hereditary trait and expected "that the headform of the [children of] imigrants would remain the same." Instead, he discovered "far-reaching change in type" of each immigrant group which varied directly with the "time elapsed between the arrival of the mother and the birth of the child." He concluded that this change could "only be explained as due directly to the influence of environment" and that "all the evidence is now in favor of a great plasticity of human types" (quoted in Stocking 1968:178). Given that the changes in headform tended toward a common intermediate form, Boas provided a reasonable conclusion in respect to the restriction of immigration: "all fear of an unfavorable influence of South European immigrants upon the body of our people should be dismissed" (quoted in Stocking 1968:180).

Boas' study had no discernible effect on the Commission's recommendations, which were restrictionist in favoring a literacy test, but it gave the environmentalist position the kind of scientific authority that eugenics provided for the racial nativists.

IMMIGRATION AND THE OTHER ANTHROPOLOGY

Anthropologists carried out few studies of American ethnic groups until long after immigration had been restricted by law. Searching the literature, Spiro (1955:1241) found only two anthropologists who called for immigration research in the early 1920s: "Wissler (1920) and Jenks (1921) perceived the immigrants of their day as threats to American culture . . . and urged that anthropology take a 'paramount' role in their 'Americanization.' " The positions of Jenks and Wissler illustrate the non-Boasian anthropological response to immigration. Wissler declared immigrants "a menace to our own culture and national existence" (1920:9–10).

Albert Ernest Jenks was professor of anthropology and director of the Americanization Training Course at the University of Minnesota. The Americanization program, established in 1919, was directed to "the training of Americanization leaders to hasten the assimilation of the various peoples in America toward the highest common standards and ideas of America practicable for each generation" (Jenks 1921:241). Leaders from the course served in local governments, civic organizations, churches, and schools. As the following passage makes clear, Jenks's anthropology was distinctly not Boasian: "It is commonly supposed to be true that their differences are only 'skin deep,' but biologists know that ethnic groups differ beneath the skin . . . there is scientific reason to speak of different 'breeds' of people whose differing physical characteristics are today due to the factors of heredity resident in the reproductive germ cells" (Jenks 1921:242).

There is no doubt that Boas' refutation of racism reached an ever wider audience after the publication of his book, *The Mind of Primitive Man* in 1911. Simultaneously, however, Jenks was training teachers, and he exemplifies an anthropological viewpoint consistent with the assumptions of the eugenicists and restrictionists. His position blended theoretical genetic determinism and practical environmentalism. Education, he proposed, is the means to Americanize the different "breeds" with their innate dispositions. When the Americanization movement crumbled, such viewpoints provided the scientific rationale for discriminatory restriction.

Unlike the long-forgotten Albert Jenks, Clark Wissler is an important figure in the history of American anthropology, and he had considerable influence in government circles at the time of the debate over restriction. The non-Boasian position on race and immigration cannot be dismissed as an idiosyncratic aberration of marginal anthropologists. Its central location is well illustrated in the relation between cultural anthropology and the National Research Council from 1916 through the 1920s. The following account is drawn from Stocking (1968).

Organized in 1916 as part of the national preparedness campaign, the National Research Council created a committee on anthropology in an effort to apply science to the war effort. The committee's major concern was physical anthropology. There were few professional physical anthropologists in the United States, and Boas, despite his qualifications, was excluded from the committee because of his outspoken opposition to the war and his personal enmity with key figures in government science. The Council's director appointed Charles Davenport, the eugenics leader, and Madison Grant to the committee. Davenport took control, and those involved in the committee included "other anthropological writers who argued the existence of hierarchical racial differences" (Stocking 1968:288).

During this period, biologists and other scientists resisted the claim of cultural anthropology to being a science. A close link between this resistance and the nativists of the eugenics movement was significant for immigration policy. A major opponent of anthropology's claim was the Galton Society, a group organized in 1918 by Davenport for the study of "racial anthropology." Its membership included prominent foundation heads and government scientists. Another member of the Galton Society was Clark Wissler.

A postwar reorganization of the National Research Council included the creation of a Division of Anthropology and Psychology. Initial efforts to exclude Boas from the new Division resulted in a compromise agreement by which representatives were chosen by the American Anthropological Association. Wissler, nominated by Boas, was elected president of the Association in 1918 and in the 1920s served as chairman of the Council's new anthropology and psychology division.

Conflict between Boasians and the "Washington School" heightened, and at the December 1919 meeting of the American Anthropological Association, Boas was censured, stripped of his office in the organization, and pressured into resigning from the National Research Council. Ostensibly, this action was taken because of a letter he had written to *The Nation*, attacking four unnamed anthropologists for "prostituting science by using it as a cover for their activities as spies."

By late 1923, Boas had regained his power in the Association and towards the end of the decade was able to influence Research Council policy. Yet the key years in immigration restriction were precisely those when Boas was ostracized. Through sympathetic congressional committee chairmen, Madison Grant and the eugenicists influenced the framing of legislation. In May 1921, the first quota system became law, and three years later the National Origins bill was enacted. Thus, it was the anthropology of Madison Grant, not Franz Boas, that underlay immigration legislation.

If, in the early 1920s, cultural anthropology had little influence on racism, the reverse was not the case. Stocking suggests that the postwar reaction against cultural anthropology, with its demand for broadening anthropological interest beyond American Indians and for emphasizing biological factors, "was related to the national outburst of nativism" and "mediated in part by the institutional channels established under the peacetime Research Council; this externally conditioned reaction had a definite impact on the research orientations and to some extent on the theoretical assumptions of important cultural anthropologists" (Stocking 1968:297).

Boasian anthropology, together with liberal and progressive thought in general, suffered a setback in the 1920s. Most of the darker manifestations of this era (the Palmer Raids, the rise of the Ku Klux Klan) faded and disappeared by the end of the decade, but restrictive and discriminatory immigration laws remained in force until 1965. An entire generation would pass, unique in American history, when immigrants would not be a significant factor in American life. For cultural anthropology, the adversity was only temporary. By the mid-1930s, the culture concept (and the concomitant rejection of genetic determinism) was accepted in all the social sciences.

Case 3: Black Americans

Although the immigrant and Indian problems had a moral component and definitions and solutions were set largely by prevailing ideological assumptions, they were seen as pragmatic problems requiring concrete programs and policies. But the Negro problem was preeminently moral (Myrdal 1944). For most of this century, national policy toward Black Americans has been a policy of neglect, of maintaining the *status quo*. That *status quo*—pervasive inequality of conditions and opportunity of blacks in America—called into question the nation's egalitarian ideals.

After the Compromise of 1877, marking the withdrawal of active Northern interest in the Negro, the federal government's stance was noninterference in the development of the Jim Crow system (Woodward 1957). Large-scale black migration to northern cities, from 1914 until the Great Depression set in, once again brought the Negro problem to national attention. Policy, however, changed little. There were some ameliorative measures taken by presidential orders: Roosevelt barred discrimination in much of the federal government and in industries with government contracts; Truman abolished segregation in the armed forces. The Supreme Court, beginning with decisions in 1946 and culminating in the school desegregation orders of 1954 and 1955, reversed its 1896 approval of the Jim Crow system. Until the congressional acts and "affirmative action" programs of the 1960s and 1970s, however, there was no positive policy towards blacks.

During the first quarter of this century, anthropology's relevance for the Negro problem lay in its attack on scientific racism. After the mid-1920s, scientific racism had been discredited; the culture concept was dominant in anthropology and spreading to the other social sciences. We shall now therefore consider the elaboration of the culture concept as it related to blacks.

BOAS AND THE NEGRO PROBLEM

As citizen and anthropologist, Boas was actively involved in the cause of Negro rights. Closely associated with W. E. B. DuBois, he was founder in 1910 of the NAACP. In public lectures, newspapers, and magazines, he argued for Negro equality. It was at this time that his widely read refutation of racism, *The Mind of Primitive Man*, was published.

Boas' discussion of the Negro problem came from two directions. First, as he had in the case of immigrants, he distinguished race and culture. He statistically demonstrated that variation within the "races" was greater than that between them, and argued that an individual's racial identity, therefore, could not predict his cultural capacity. This was his contribution from physical anthropology. From ethnographic evidence, he marked another path. Pointing to the complexity of African cultures, he argued that these African achievements demonstrated Negro cultural competence. This provided the theme for his 1906 Commencement Address at Atlanta University.

to those who stoutly maintain a material inferiority of the Negro race and who would dampen your ardor by their claims, you must confidently reply that the burden of proof rests with them, that the past history of your race does not sustain their statement, but rather gives you encouragement. . . . say that you have set out to recover for the colored people the strength that was their own before they set foot on the shores of this continent. (quoted in Herskovits 1953:111)

ANTHROPOLOGICAL APPROACHES TO BLACK AMERICA

Three approaches can be distinguished. The first two, diametrically opposed on the question of distinctive Afro-American culture, are developments of Boas' thought. The third, community studies in the South, is independent of Boas. Only the denial of distinctive culture received general acceptance in the discipline; it was this view of blacks that precluded ethnographic research.

1. *Cultural stripping and Negro acculturation.* While his explanation of Negro traits was unequivocally environmental rather than genetic, Boas did not completely extend the assumptions of cultural relativity to his treatment of these traits. Contending that American Negro traits can be explained by history and social status, he wrote:

The tearing-away from the African soil and the consequent complete loss of the old standards of life, which were replaced by the dependency of slavery and by all it entailed, followed by a period of disorganization and by a severe economic struggle against heavy odds, are sufficient to explain the inferiority of the status of the race, without falling back upon the theory of hereditary inferiority. (1911:240)

The total loss of African traditions is a notion repeated in the writings of Boas' students, such as Benedict (1947:86–87) and the early Herskovits. Boas and his students, however, did not view American blacks as "decultured" but as fully acculturated: their culture was American, identical to (or a variant of) the culture of white Americans. As Szwed notes, "the overlapping statistics of the physical features of the two races together with overlapping scores on intelligence tests may have led Boas to infer that blacks as a group simply 'overlapped' white American culture, if only imperfectly" (1972:157).

2. *Study of Negro folklore and Afro-American culture.* Willis (1975) has documented a less well-known aspect of Boas' involve-

ment with black Americans, his support for the study of black folklore. His efforts ranged from an early (1903) unsuccessful attempt to
have Negroes included in the scope of the Bureau of American Ethnology, through a partial success in arousing interest in Negro folklore on the part of the American Folklore Society, to supervising the
principal students of black folklore. Quoting from Boas' letters and
articles, Willis indicates that the motivation behind these efforts was
to undermine the notion of white supremacy by documenting black
achievements (1975:313).

Elsie Clews Parsons was the first of Boas' students to work in
this area and became his principal colleague in the study of black
folklore. Other students of Afro-America, trained by Boas, include
Arthur Fauset, Zora Neale Hurston, Martha Beckwith, and Melville
Herskovits (Willis 1975; Whitten and Szwed 1970). Among these,
Herskovits did most to develop the study of Afro-American culture.
He systematically elaborated Boas' suggestion of African survivals in
American Negro culture, doing so on the basis of extensive fieldwork
and communicating to a wide audience.

Herskovits' thought closely reflects that of his mentor, but what
were unresolved oppositions in Boas appear as successive developments in Herskovits. His early work was anthropometric; his position
on race was identical to Boas and he at first shared the Boas-Benedict
assumption of complete Negro acculturation. Beginning after his research in Surinam (1928–29) and developing during years of fieldwork in Haiti, Trinidad, Brazil, and West Africa, Herskovits rejected
this early view and argued that persisting Africanisms were the basis
of distinctive Afro-American cultures. To counter racist use of these
findings, he stressed the validity of such cultural differences and
somewhat mischievously noted "that American whites had unknowingly absorbed a great deal of African culture" (Szwed 1972:165).
His mature position appeared in 1941 with the publication of *The
Myth of the Negro Past*. His purpose in this book was to make available "a foundation of scientific fact concerning the ancestral cultures
of Africa and the survivals of Africanisms in the New World" that
would promote confidence among Negroes by providing "an appreciation" of their past. The dissemination of "such a body of fact,
solidly grounded," would perhaps change attitudes about Negro capabilities "and thus contribute to a lessening of interracial tensions"
(1941:32). Boas had set forth the same goals thirty years earlier.

3. *Community studies and the southern "caste" system.* The third anthropological approach can be represented by Powdermaker's *After Freedom* (1939) and Davis, Gardner, and Gardner's *Deep South* (1941). These and similar studies focused on social structure and social control, analyzing black-white relations as a caste system supported by an ideology of race.

Many studies conducted in the 1930s and 1940s by social scientists fall under this heading. While the study of American Negroes was for many years dominated by the influence of Robert E. Park and the "Chicago school" of American sociology, W. Lloyd Warner, an anthropologist, was also a prime mover. The results of research range from *Black Metropolis* (Drake and Cayton 1945), a study of Negroes in Chicago, to the project at the University of North Carolina, directed by anthropologist John Gillin, entitled "Field Studies in the Modern Culture of the South" (Lewis 1955, Morland 1958, and Rubin 1951).

Cooperative effort in the funding, direction, and execution of a number of studies is evident. Lewis' study, one of several in the project directed by Gillin, was submitted as a dissertation at the University of Chicago (Lewis 1955:xi). When Powdermaker began planning her fieldwork in Mississippi, she was a researcher at Yale University's Institute of Human Relations, the same institutional base used by John Dollard, a social psychologist, for his research in Mississippi (Dollard 1937). Later, Dollard collaborated with Allison Davis, a coauthor of *Deep South,* in writing *Children of Bondage* (Davis and Dollard 1940). Financial support for many of the studies was provided by the federal Works Progress Administration and the private Julius Rosenwald Fund (see Drake and Cayton 1945:vii; Davis, Gardner and Gardner 1941:xii; Morland 1958:xi). Taken together, these studies provided a massive documentation of inequality and the disadvantaged position of the Negro in American life. Nevertheless, their impact on policy-making came only in the Supreme Court decision of 1954 when some of them were used as supporting evidence for the Court's opinion.

THE NEW ORTHODOXY

While most anthropologists continued to concentrate their research on American Indians and, to a lesser extent, upon nonliterate peoples in other countries, few of them followed the leads of Davis, Gillin, Warner, and Powdermaker in research on American communities and black Americans. The assumption of Negro acculturation dominated anthropology, and, without a distinctive culture, blacks held little professional interest for those who defined anthropology as the study of non-Western peoples. A concern for the political implications of the two Boas-derived positions on African survivals or full accultur- ation must have been a factor in this lack of interest. Ethnographic research revealing distinctive Afro-American culture could be used by the two anti-integrationist forces: white supremacists could argue that Negroes were nonassimilable, and black separatists (like Marcus Garvey) could bolster their nationalistic claims.

Other reasons for this tendency of anthropology to ignore black Americans have been suggested (see, for example, Mintz 1970; Wil- lis 1970, 1975). John Szwed summarizes various explanations:

The "impure," "acculturated" nature of American blacks made them poor subjects for a cultural anthropology originally bent on reconstructing the ethnographic past of isolated societies. . . . Afro-Americans were geo- graphically too close and of too low status for professional prestige in Amer- ican society . . . field work among lower-class Afro-Americans lacks the exoticism that so appeals to anthropologists. (1972:155)

On the first point, Willis has objected that no American Indian tribe was truly unacultured when studied and thus "anthropologists had the option of ignoring white cultural influence on Negroes as they did with Indians" (1970:35–36). It may be that most anthropologists at the time *believed* there were still Indian "memory cultures" to be recorded but that those of blacks had long disappeared. The fact re- mains that when, in the 1930s, there was a turn from ethnographic salvage to studies of acculturation, when cultural purity ceased to be a fieldwork requisite, the "acculturated" Negro was still largely ig- nored.

Defending anthropology's sharpening boundaries and avoiding competition with other disciplines also played a part in leaving the Negro to sociology and history. Powdermaker indicates as much in describing the reaction of Robert Lowie when he heard of her plans to go into the Deep South. Lowie, she says, "wrote me that although a study in Mississippi might be interesting, I should not go too far in the direction of modern communities. After all, anthropologists were then supposed to limit their studies to primitive peoples'' (Powdermaker 1966:133).

ENTER THE SOCIOLOGISTS

With the northward migration and new black protest after World War I, what had been a ''Southern problem'' since the Compromise of 1877 became once more a national problem. Sociology responded, with the cooperation of a few anthropologists.

From the end of the war through the 1930s, the Chicago sociologists were preeminent in the study of American Negroes and race relations. Their abiding interest was urban social problems, and Chicago served as a natural laboratory for the investigation of social pathology. Park and his students—principally E. Franklin Frazier—studied the Negro largely as a social problem. Their approach included the use of statistical surveys to demonstrate personal and social disorganization, an emphasis on pathology aptly labeled the ''pejorative tradition'' (Valentine 1968).

Park and Frazier developed their approach when scientific racism had been discredited, and the culture concept was supreme in their work. In explaining pathology, they did not invoke innate racial factors, as had a previous generation of sociologists, but, instead, they enlarged on the lead offered by Boas to shape a cultural explanation. If in previous hands American Negroes had been racially inadequate, they were now painted as culturally inadequate (Frazier 1939). The Park-Frazier approach was sympathetic to the plight of blacks: they were portrayed as victims suffering from deculturation or a pathological culture, the result of slavery and its aftermath.

What are some of the implications of this viewpoint? Both anthropological and sociological approaches rejected genetic factors. By identifying environmental causes for the Negro problem, the Park-Frazier view held out the possibility of change. There are, however, differences between the anthropological and sociological positions. Boas was a militant integrationist, associated with DuBois and the NAACP. He argued that there were neither racial nor cultural differences between blacks and whites in the United States. Park, on the other hand, was a moderate, supporting Booker T. Washington's accommodationism. Park's model of race relations postulated the *status quo* as a natural stage in a developmental cycle: race prejudice would eventually disappear.

Only in the 1960s, when the federal government began to act in regard to blacks, did the policy implications of these positions become manifest (in, for example, Moynihan's recommendation of "benign neglect"). Until then, these ideas served to justify the *status quo* and encouraged, if they were noticed at all, a policy of inaction.

In the immigrant case, the absence of a developed American physical anthropology enabled nonanthropologists to distort the concept of race into doctrines of Nordic superiority. In parallel fashion, anthropologists with few exceptions abandoned the study of Afro-Americans to nonanthropologists, and the result was a distortion of the culture concept. "Witness the wide popularity of the notion of 'cultural deprivation' among politicians, educators, and social workers by which . . . material poverty is grossly confused with ideological poverty, culture now being given a remarkably restricted definition" (Szwed 1972:162). On the interpretation of low test scores by Negroes as cultural deprivation rather than as a result of low incentive, Murray says:

By ignoring the most fundamental definitions of anthropology . . . the contemporary American social science technician substitutes academic subject matter for culture. He then misrepresents deficiencies in formal technical training as cultural deprivation. (1973:110)

Overview: Indians, Immigrants, and Blacks

It should now be clear that similar policy alternatives were present in each of the three cases. A choice between homogeneity and pluralism appears in the case of American Indians (forced acculturation versus quasi-autonomy under the Indian Reorganization Act), immigrants (Americanization versus cultural diversity), and blacks (special educational programs versus cultural nationalism). These similarities express the possibilities inherent in American national ideology.

A comparison of these cases uncovers differences as well. For example, the late nineteenth century and post-World War II periods saw changes in policies toward Indians and blacks. In the 1950s, Indian "termination" and court decisions reversing the "separate but equal" doctrine, both aimed at ending special status and drawing blacks and Indians out of isolation. In contrast, the compromise of 1877 "got the government out of the Negro business" just as Allotment aimed to get it out of the Indian business. Allotment, however, looked to integration of Indians, while the Compromise, confirmed by the *Plessy v. Ferguson* decision (1896), abandoned blacks to Jim Crow segregation (Woodward 1957). Thus, a policy intending to end Indian special status occurred at a time when blacks were subjected to a special, inferior status.[1]

Anthropology, however limited its immediate impact on policy decisions, has been influential by establishing a *cultural* rather than a *racial* view in ethnic affairs. The policy interpretation of this environmentalist victory has promoted education as the solution to minority problems, cultural homogeneity as an attainable possibility, and, contrary to the intentions of the theorists, has blamed ethnic minorities for the inequities they suffer.

We have seen a strong tendency toward the conformance of anthropological views with the dominant ideology and policy in American society, at least in portraying "vanishing" Indians, "melting" immigrants (or, in the 1920s, racially inferior ones), and "deculturated" Negroes. Anthropology has also passively served the *status quo* by ignoring the political situation of the groups it studied.

Understanding the relationships of American anthropology and American society requires careful historical research, for which Stocking's work provides an excellent start. It is too simple to shrug off anthropology's relationships with public policy as an exercise in *post hoc* rationalization or a reflection of popular ideas. Efforts like

1. Editors' note: The "special status" of native Americans is a legal status stemming from treaty rights to land, water, timber, mineral and other resources and protected by the wardship of the Federal government. The end result of termination of the reservations, as in the earlier Allotment movement, is to open up these resources to non-Indians. Thus, independence and freedom from government control and protection can be understood as fundamentally consistent with the desires of non-Indian economic interests which are always well represented in Congress. Black Americans and white ethnics as groups enjoy no such resource base or problematical legal status, which may explain the lag between the growth of the ideologies of freedom for native Americans and freedom for Black Americans and immigrants. As the energy crisis deepens we can expect that the fuel resources on western reservations will play a role in an intensified movement to end the "special status" of Indians and promote Indian freedom and independence.

those of Wolf (1972), while provocative as programmatic statements for studying the history of American anthropology, surely overstate the ease and directness with which anthropology has responded to changes in American life. Anthropology's connection with public policy might be understood better by a comparison with the relationships of British and French colonial policies to the anthropology of those countries. This kind of comparison is necessary if the putative relationship of imperialism and anthropology is to be more than empty polemics (see Kaplan 1974:835).

The New Ethnicity

Half a decade after the "deliberate speed" in desegregation ordered by the Supreme Court in 1955, the movement toward integration of schools had become a slow, tortuous process. With the inauguration of President Kennedy, who was committed to active measures toward equality for American blacks, and the sit-ins and bus boycotts of the early 1960s, a veritable revolution in civil rights began. Led by black activists and supported by white political liberals, pressure mounted for new, broad legislation. Kennedy's early executive orders, extending those promulgated under Presidents Roosevelt and Truman, signaled a "new deal" for black Americans. After Kennedy's assassination, President Johnson led Congress in producing the historic civil rights act of 1964 and 1965.

Neither the Civil Rights Act of 1964 nor the Voting Rights Act of 1965 provided for more than legal equality, and agitation continued for means to insure that black Americans would gain some degree of economic and political parity with whites as well. Once again, cultural nationalism, with its rallying cry of "Black is Beautiful," became attractive as a political strategy. The situation was much like that in many developing nations. Political action was stimulated by the difference between expectation and accomplishment (Makielski 1973:3), with ethnicity as an important principle of organization (for an example from the Third World, see Cohen 1969).

In the long hot urban summers of the late 1960s, it appeared that the frustration of black people had found a new and dangerous expression: violence. The response was to sharpen the definition of black urban ghettos as "problem areas," and to simultaneously contain and prevent violence while setting up programs of improved job opportunities and training. Continued agitation for political and economic power highlighted the disparity between legal equality and the failure of black Americans to achieve substantive equality during this time.

The social conflict of the 1960s, conducted at first with the tactics of nonviolence expressed by Dr. Martin Luther King and later by the less broadly based efforts of groups committed to violent tactics, seemed to many citizens a unique and unwarranted response to conditions that were gradually improving. Yet, in making their dissatisfaction louder and their demands more strident, argues Makielski (1973:135), blacks were following an American tradition. Further, it is held that, for "relatively powerless groups," conflict—at least below the level of rioting—is an effective political strategy (Rodgers and Bullock 1972:215).

"Affirmative action," a phrase first used by President Kennedy in 1961, had now become a keystone of federal policy. As federal guidelines developed, affirmative action replaced the older idea of equal opportunity in an effort to achieve economic parity for American minorities. While the Civil Rights Act of 1964 aimed to set American blacks free at last, the language of the legislation stated the prohibitions more broadly. Title VII of the Act, for example, forbade discrimination in employment "because of such individual's color, religion, sex, or national origin."

"The greatest inroads on discrimination have followed paths blazed by black activists" (Rodgers and Bullock 1972:174).

White ethnics have been moving from a traditionally defensive and protective stance to an offensive and assertive one. Their encounters with black progress have been one of the primary causes for their assertion, another being their emergence into the middle class, . . . [and] their recent alienation from American institutions and way of life. They feel neglected and forgotten. (Weed 1973:45)

As the federal and state governments increasingly made allocations of public monies contingent upon ethnic criteria, with special training and educational programs established for some but not all ethnic categories, the voices of those who felt "neglected and forgotten" grew louder. Native Americans, too, adopted strategies of cultural nationalism. The social divisiveness that appeared imminent in this varied chorus was quickly grasped by some social scientists and remarked upon for its pessimistic potential. Horowitz (1976:73), for example, labeled ethnicity as "a measure of disintegration in the American sociopolitical system."

Nathan Glazer sees the use of ethnic criteria by the national government as a distinct turn in a new direction. The attempt to provide substantive equality for American blacks, he contends, "turned into an effort to redress the inequality of all deprived groups" (Glazer 1975:31). This hope of making blacks the equal of other Americans "raised the question of who *are* the other Americans? How many of them can define their own group as *also* deprived?" (Glazer 1975:31).

Whether or not one agrees with Glazer's primary thesis that we have mistakenly slipped into "affirmative discrimination," public policy established in the decade of the 1960s laid the foundation for a sharpened pluralistic society. Glazer's opposition to current policy is based partly on his view that, in the United States, ethnicity is entirely voluntary, and "is part of the burden of freedom of all modern men who must choose what they are to be" (Glazer, 1975:69). While there are numerous instances of voluntary ethnicity (see Hicks and Leis 1977 for case studies), there are still situations in which one is involuntarily treated as belonging to one or another ethnic category. Under some circumstances, at least, it appears that ethnicity is still a "stigmatic emblem" (De Vos and Romanucci-Ross 1975:389).

ANTHROPOLOGY AND THE "GREAT SOCIETY"

It has been widely assumed in social science literature, including studies produced by anthropologists, that there is a single, relatively homogeneous "American culture." Frequently referred to as "the standard American culture" (Mead 1955b:185), this monolithic creation is taken as the measure of various ethnic groups and deviants. This notion of *an* American culture has not, of course, included native Americans nor, except as variants, black Americans. That American anthropologists participate in the general consensus about an American culture can perhaps be laid to their dual role when they observe aspects of life in the United States as citizens and observers. Our inability to "come to terms with Afro-American life," as John Szwed suspects, "is merely a special case of a much larger problem" (1972:174). The larger problem hinges on our blind insistence that there is *an* American culture.

In the realm of ethnic studies, this view emerges as a refusal to consider white Protestants as an ethnic category. As Ulf Hannerz sees it, white Protestants "seem not to be considered an ethnic group at all; they are non-ethnic 'real Americans' " (1974:46). This is, he suggests, an attitude "tainted . . . with white Protestant ethnocentrism" (1974:46). In this aspect of the notion of an "American mainstream," we come perilously close to a reformulation of the foundation for Americanization programs designed to standardize immigrants into Americans.

Jules Henry, in remarking on de Tocqueville's observations about the America of the 1830s, was struck with the accuracy of the portrait for contemporary life (Henry 1973). Henry was, of course, referring to the aspects of de Tocqueville's work that show sameness and conformity among Americans. But de Tocqueville was too accurate an ethnographer to miss the other side of American life. His view of the relations among American Indians, Negroes, and Euro-Americans resembles in language and import the formulation Furnivall (1948) made of a plural society. De Tocqueville (1945:344) noted that "fortune has brought [the three 'races'] together on the same soil, where, although they are mixed, they do not amalgamate, and each race fulfills its destiny apart."

In anthropology, two reflections of the unitary culture view of the United States deserve special note. One is the somewhat outdated idea that, in the interests of effective professional training and greater objectivity, American anthropologists should not study America. While excellent investigations of American life have been made by anthropologists, the prevailing idea has been that such studies should not constitute one's major specialty. If one looks at the United States, at least the Euro-American part of it, as sharing a single culture, it is consistent to advise students not to study their "own cultural traditions." But if one sees America as diverse in cultural traditions, as constituting for some purposes a single society within which there are numerous cultural traditions, the admonition becomes less convincing. In recent years, this traditional view has been reversed in a resolution adopted by the American Anthropological Association which encourages more investigations in the United States.

Another important expression of the unitary view of America was perhaps best stated, although in exaggerated form, by W. Lloyd Warner in his foreword to the reissue of *Democracy in Jonesville:*

Borrowing from the Gospel of John, we can say that Jonesville is in all Americans and all Americans are in Jonesville, for he that dwelleth in America dwelleth in Jonesville, and Jonesville in him.

To study Jonesville is to study America; it is a laboratory, a clinic, a field of study for finding out what we are as a people and for learning why we think and feel and do the things we do. (1964:ix)

Long before Warner's restatement about Jonesville, however, anthropologists were cautioning each other to attend to the diversity of American life (Mason 1955), and to avoid mistaking the part for the whole (Steward 1950:20–94; Wolf 1956; Casagrande 1959). Seeing in a single community, or even in a series of communities, the outlines of the entire nation—whether the United States or any other nation—was repeatedly criticized.

But the unitary view of American culture remained and is a salient feature of the "culture of poverty" advocates, particularly Oscar Lewis. First enunciated by him in 1959, the idea that there exist "cultures of poverty" received extended treatment in his study of Puerto Ricans in San Juan and New York. Lewis specifically noted that "the term 'subculture of poverty' is technically more accurate," and he used "culture of poverty." for convenience (1966a:xliii). The "culture of poverty" was frequently used to describe the lives of particular ethnic groups and neighborhoods. It was another way of labeling ways of living that appeared deviant from the "American mainstream."

Anthropologists have properly criticized sociological pronouncements that find urban black families enmeshed in "a tangle of pathology" (Moynihan 1965:47) or characterize the kinship behavior of Southern Appalachian people as "neurotic emotional entanglements" (Ball 1971:75). Yet, we betray the same tendency to conceive of the entire United States as encompassing a single cultural pattern by describing variations as "deviant" or "subcultural." Deviant from what? If subcultural, what constitutes the culture they are variants of? Wallace's (1961) demonstration of the *necessity* for nonsharing of certain elements of culture should caution us to expect our own society to be as problematic as others with respect to what is shared, by whom, and to what extent.

One of the most interesting features of the relationships between anthropology and public policy in the recent past has been the alacrity with which policy makers took up the idea of a "culture of poverty." It was broadcast in a number of simplified and popularized versions and is credited with much influence on national policy (Valentine 1971:193). The massive War on Poverty mounted by the federal government in the 1960s was based, according to Gladwin, "upon a definition of poverty as a way of life" (Gladwin 1967:26). The entire series of programs—VISTA, Job Corps, Head Start, and so on—aimed at changing attitudes, beliefs, and values, rather than on redistributing wealth and power. Lewis had indicated that poverty was probably easier to change than the *culture* of poverty, federal programs went for the tough goal: cultural retraining.

Anthropologists' conceptions of a unitary or mainstream culture for the United States were congruent with the assumptions that underlay these federal programs. The phrase "pockets of poverty" recognized poverty as a localized blight on an otherwise healthy and homogeneous cultural body. Subcultures of poverty, usually found in ethnic neighborhoods (Valentine 1968:125), were problems to be solved, deviants to be reconditioned and incorporated into standard American life. An alternative to the opinion that Lewis' "culture of poverty" idea was influential in itself is the suggestion that it served as a focal point for a view of the United states and its problems that was shared by government policy makers and many anthropologists.

As the anthropological study of the United States became more acceptable as a professional specialty, a new perspective emerged. With some exceptions (e.g., DeVos and Romanucci-Ross 1975), ethnicity came to be seen as not necessarily stigmatic, and heavy criticism of the "culture of poverty" idea made it less persuasive as an explanatory mechanism. Studies of black Americans treated them less as social problems than as distinctive cutural categories within American society. Linguistically, they were found to be different in very basic ways (Labov 1968). In Liebow's *Tally's Corner* (1967), Hannerz's *Soulside* (1969), and Stack's *All Our Kin* (1974), blacks are portrayed as acting rationally, given the constraints placed on their behavior. A new militancy among Native Americans led to greater appreciation of them as more than simply remnants from a disturbing imperialistic past. As litigation to reclaim tribal lands proceeded, a new recognition of Indians as citizens demanding their rights took hold, at least in some segments of society.

Increasingly, the United States is now acceptable as a professional area for anthropological investigation; larger numbers of anthropologists strike out to mine this rich but formerly devalued lode. The changing perspective on anthropological study of the United States is partly derived from the social and cultural milieu in which the anthropologist is simultaneously researcher and citizen. Those roles being more sharply recognized and distinguished, the path is opened for scholarly study as distinct from citizen partisanship.

Conclusions

From this review of policy and anthropology and their relationship, several points emerge clearly and provide material for constructing guides for the future. The difficulty of bringing an anthropological perspective to bear on the problems of our own society, and in defining those problems, should not be underestimated.

If our goal is to contribute to the making of policy as anthropologists, our most productive course is to treat the United States as we have treated other societies. In doing so, we can produce descriptions and analyses of value to both anthropology and policy makers. From this perspective, the anthropologist could:

1. *Explicate the logic and consequences of public policy.* Rather than stand on the sidelines or steadfastly take up partisan positions, anthropologists should be equipped by their training to undertake a dispassionate analysis of the implications of proposed public policy, and that which is operative at present. As an example, let us consider current federal policy toward minorities. Anthropologists might examine the consequences of the federal definition of minority people, and draw out the implications for particular regions where minorities not officially recognized constitute a significant proportion of the local population. Policies toward minorities appear to have tendencies

in two directions: toward insuring the maintenance of procedural equality (a policy of nondiscrimination) and toward bringing about substantive equality. The latter is operative in busing schoolchildren to achieve ethnic balance, in instituting programs of bilingual education, in establishing quotas for hiring and firing in federal contract work, and so forth. These two tendencies are sometimes congruent with each other—as in the affirmative action programs—and sometimes in conflict. There is a potential conflict, too, between busing schoolchildren and maintaining bilingual education: the achievement of appropriate ethnic balance could lead to distributing throughout an entire school system those most likely to benefit from bilingual classroom instruction. The well-known characteristic, whether by choice or not, for immigrants from the same country to belong to the same residential neighborhood seems to carry little weight in policy making. Strident calls for community control of local schools merely reveal another kind of partisanship. A cool-headed, ethnographically sound analysis could be more useful for policy and theory.

2. *Investigate the relationships between ideology and practice.* A task we have long been carrying out elsewhere, this kind of study of ethnic policy is strongly needed. Glazer's contention, for example, that the nation is violating its sacred ideals of individual equality by the use of affirmative action programs deserves close attention (Glazer 1975). This apparent discrepancy between ideology and practice is at issue in a number of legal arenas. The California Supreme Court, for example, ruled in late 1976 that a medical school's policy of reserving a number of places for minority students in its entering class was unconstitutional (California 1976). What are the consequences of a policy of "reverse discrimination" for other aspects of American life? Should such a policy be limited to a particular period of time? Anthropologists are fit by training and outlook to examine these kinds of policy issues.

3. *Bring cross-cultural perspectives to bear on policy-related problems.* The application of public policy on ethnicity will doubtless increase the pluralistic features of American life. Anthropologists, in investigating such issues, can draw on an extensive body of data and theory developed in the Caribbean, Africa, and Southeast Asia. If the United States is headed toward either structural or cultural pluralism,

then the experts in this kind of society are anthropologists. Just as we have performed as expert witnesses in the Indian land claims cases, we may also be called upon in the near future to play the same role in ethnic conflicts. If cultural differences become the criterion for such issues as federal aid, anthropologists are the obvious scholarly spokesmen.

In exploring for ourselves a larger role in public policy, the calm advice of Belshaw is appropriate as a conclusion:

The social scientist, then, should be reasonably modest in his claims; he should not go as far as many of my colleagues who say, for example, that since we don't know everything perhaps we know nothing, and that we should not use our knowledge as the basis for advice, since it is bound to be incomplete. Our responsibility, if we decide to enter this world, is to use our knowledge, give our advice, generate ideas, but never pretend that they have the kind of authority that can be provided in certain circumstances, in other fields, by physicists or engineers. (Belshaw 1976:275)

And if a deaf ear is all the response we get for our advice, take heart, for we are, historically speaking, in good company.

19

VICOS: SUCCESS, REJECTION, AND REDISCOVERY OF A CLASSIC PROGRAM

Paul L. Doughty

Opportunities for practitioners of anthropology and the other social sciences to contribute directly to the creation of public policy are rare. The opportunity to formulate and implement public policy on the basis of anthropological perspectives is even more rare. In this essay, Paul L. Doughty examines the Vicos case, in which anthropologists accepted responsibility for public policies intended to empower a Peruvian community to achieve equitable development and justice. The Vicos project is mentioned frequently in the literature, but it is seldom studied in the depth required to permit informed and accurate lessons to be drawn from the extensive experience

Paul L. Doughty (Ph.D., Cornell) is professor of anthropology and Latin American studies at the University of Florida. He is a cultural anthropologist who has worked in rural development and disaster relief programs in Mexico, El Salvador, Guatemala, and Peru and in other projects in the United States. He has been consultant and program evaluator for the InterAmerican Foundation, Brookings Institution, USAID, and the Peruvian government. He was a founder of the *Latin American Research Review* and the Latin American Studies Association, of which he was president in 1974. He is an active teacher and consultant in the fields of applied anthropology and development policy issues.

It is appropriate that, after three and a half decades since project inception, Allan R. Holmberg, Mario C. Vazquez, and Carlos Monge Medrano be remembered as the pioneers they were in applied anthropology. This paper is dedicated to their achievement. I wish to thank them in retrospect and the others who contributed to my understanding of these events. First, to Polly French Doughty for her companionship and steadfast collegial support; to Urbano Sanchez, Hilario Gonzalez, Enrique Gonzalez, and the late Rosa Gonzalez and Celso Leon; to Rodomiro Vasquez Giraldo, Henry Dobyns, the late José Sabogal Wiesse, William P. Mangin, William Stein, and Anthony Oliver-Smith. The critiques and comments of Allan Burns, Michael Evans, Stephen Schensul, William VanDiveer, Barbara Lynch, and the late Solon T. Kimball are also much appreciated on those portions of this essay presented at the Society for Applied Anthropology and the American Anthropological Association meetings in 1982.

accumulated by those who were engaged actively in this social experiment.

By any measure of development outcome (e.g., equitable and improved household income, increased productivity, educational advancement and literacy, health conditions, political justice), the experiment at Vicos was a successful one. In large measure, this was due to the ethical commitment made by Allan Holmberg and his students to long-term action research, a commitment embodied in Holmberg's phrase "participant intervention," which connotes responsibility for one's actions. Equally important was the adoption of a learning experience approach to development, the commitment to empower local people to make decisions, based on their own knowledge and experience, that would modify the innovations proposed or introduced by outside experts.

The reader will glean several lessons from Doughty's essay. Perhaps the most alarming one is the realization that, despite massive documentation of the positive achievements of the Vicos project, development professionals (including many anthropologists) remain ignorant of Vicos or distort the documentation of success. Does this mean that the lessons of Vicos represent a threat to the contemporary roles of development professionals and anthropologists in the Third World? The essay raises the unsettling query: under what circumstances do these professionals prefer failed development projects to successful ones?

TWENTY YEARS AFTER the official end of the Cornell-Peru project in 1966, the fate of the Vicos community remains a matter of strong interest and debate among anthropologists and in international development circles.[1] This curiosity is fired by a recent passion for the evaluation of effectiveness and impacts of development policies, assistance programs, and technological change, and a renewed interest in addressing the "basic needs" of the rural poor throughout the world. Despite widespread recognition of the project, its purposes and effects have often been miscontrued or even discounted. What relevance does the Vicos experience have for today's concerns?

1. For basic descriptions of Vicos and the project, readers may refer to Vazquez (1952), Holmberg (1960), and Dobyns, Doughty, and Lasswell (1971). Important specialized aspects of the project are found in Holmberg and Dobyns (1969) and Stein (1971, 1972b, 1985). Recent "independent" summaries of aspects are found in Himes (1981) and Lynch (1982). Detailed administrative descriptions and bibliographies are those of Dobyns and Vazquez (1964) and Wood (1975), although the latter contains some misconceptions (Doughty 1977).

Vicos and the Cornell-Peru Project

Hacienda Vicos was a manor located in the high Andean valley known as the Callejón de Huaylas in the Department of Ancash, Peru. Its vast terrain covered the uplands above the small district capitol of Marcará, ranging in altitude from 2,900 meters to the great snow-peaks of the Cordillera Blanca at 6,000 meters. Most of Vicos' 18,230 hectares (43,750 acres) is rough wasteland, with about 15 percent suitable for pasture and 8 percent for cultivation. In 1952, there were 1,785 persons living as manor serfs there, who were rented along with the rest of the property to an absentee landlord who assumed usufruct of the estate and its people for five ten-year periods, for about $600 a year. Vicos was the largest of the fifty-six such properties owned by the Beneficient Society, which used this rental income to operate the regional welfare hospital in the departmental capitol at Huaraz, fifty kilometers to the south.

The operation of Hacienda Vicos followed Andean customs for the management of estates: the serfs resided and worked there at the discretion of the landlord, enjoying limited use of a subsistence plot and pasturage in exchange for their labor as field hands or in any other assignment deemed appropriate for three days a week (Vazquez 1952, 1961). Vicos was considered the archetypical hacienda for the region: its people wore quaint, colonial-style homespuns and were 99 percent illiterate. The Quechua-speaking Vicosinos ("people of Vicos")[2] were living in a state of endemic starvation on 76 percent of recommended daily intakes of calories and proteins (Alers 1971:122).

Having surveyed the area in 1948, and seen the results of a year-long study of the manor, Allan R. Holmberg of Cornell University, in collaboration with Peruvian colleagues Carlos Monge Medrano and Mario C. Vazquez Varela, outlined a program of planned social and economic change for the hacienda (Holmberg 1952a, 1952b). Under this plan, Cornell University was to rent the estate, assuming the current landlord's unwanted lease. In Holmberg's words,

Broadly speaking . . . it was hoped to conduct . . . experimental research on the processes of modernization now on the march in so many parts of

2. In Quechua, they call themselves Wikusinukuna, with the same meaning. The terms are used interchangeably at Vicos, or Wikus. The Hispanicized terms Vicos and Vicosinos are predominant, however.

the world . . . [and to] assist the communinty to shift for itself from a position of relative dependence and submission in a highly restricted and provincial world to a position of relative independence and freedom within the larger framework of Peruvian national life. (1955:23)

This set the CPP (Cornell-Peru Project) into action for a fourteen-year period, from 1952 to 1966. During this time it became the most famous effort in applied anthropology, judging by the numerous citations which continue to occur some two decades after the end of the project (cf. Thompson 1976; Paige 1975; Stewart 1973; Plog and Bates 1976; Woods 1975; Pelto and Pelto 1979; Keesing 1979; Aceves 1978; Long and Roberts 1978; Yambert 1980; Marzal 1981; Alland 1981; Stein 1985; Chambers 1985). Interest in the project has never waned.[3] Yet, the Vicos program remains a curious phenomenon in anthropology, standing as a still rare example of anthropologists directing the planning and application of their theory and findings to the amelioration of felt needs among a research population. Not the least of the ways in which the project was exceptional was in the visceral reaction both for and against it which began early and continues to the present among anthropologists and others.[4]

Prelude and Background

Beginning in December 1951, the CPP constituted a pioneering effort for which there was little anthropological precedent or other definitive model to follow. From the start, Vicos was an experiment, or "pilot project," in the jargon of the time.[5] In the post-World War II era,

3. Annually I answer several letters from students and other correspondents who wish to know about it, an experience common to others who were connected with the project.

4. An example of just how controversial the project remains was brought home in a personal way. In 1982 a National Science Foundation proposal of mine was negatively evaluated by someone who felt that my previous association (1959–64) with the Vicos project permanently sullied my ability to conduct research, and said so in the review! Several major critiques have appeared (Mangin 1979; Himes 1981; Kohler 1981; Lynch 1981) and others are on the way (William VanderVeer and J. Fernando Sanchez, personal communications). Others have attempted to "reinterpret" aspects of the CPP to accommodate current perspectives (Stein 1985; Babb 1985).

5. Since then it has become a "model," "prototype," and finally, a "paradigm." It was part of a grand design, conceived by the Cornell Department of Sociology and Anthro-

modern United States foreign aid programs had their start around the world, largely forged by two themes: the humanistic, idealistic values of people who wanted to aid the nonindustrial world to modernize as a positive measure to achieve peaceful change (Doughty 1985); and the desire to respond to the "communist" influences outlined by cold war theorists. While the latter played no orienting role at Vicos, the former did. Many in the Western, industrialized societies felt strongly that they had much to offer the rest of the world—the question was how and what. Lewis (1951:448) raised the question in the concluding sentence of *Tepotzlán:*

They also have a greater desire to attend school, to eat better, to dress better, and to spend more. . . . It was clear that, for the most part, they have taken on only the more superficial aspects and values of modern life. Can western civilization offer them no more?

The newly promulgated Universal Declaration of Human Rights was a call to action and a philosophy which underwrote programs. When asked if anthropologists should intervene as he was doing in Vicos, Holmberg customarily responded that it was the failure to place our knowledge at the service of humanity which was unethical. To remain acquiescent in the face of manifest human need and deprivation and not use one's professional skills to address the situation was anathema to Holmberg, Monge and Vazquez, and thus to the spirit of the project. Science as a methodology must be supplemented by cultural values as a guide to applied policy and action. In Holmberg's words,

we took a value stand . . . we were concerned with helping the Vicosinos to transform the hacienda on which they lived in a dependent and submissive state into a "just, peaceable, morally and intellectually progressive commuity of . . . responsible men and women." While, of course, no such value position can be justified scientifically, we—and many Vicosinos— believe these to be good and desirable ends. Actually, beyond a clear statement of one's position, little further need be said about the value problem. (1955:25)

A new and vigorous literature (cf. Mead 1953b; Spicer 1952; Ruopp 1953) quickly emerged as new programs formed throughout the world.

pology, to study worldwide sociocultural change in the United States (southwest), India, Southeast Asia (Thailand), and Peru. Allan R. Holmberg came to Cornell to participate in this ambitious anthropological venture after having received his Ph.D. from Yale and after two years of work in Peru for the Smithsonian and San Marcos University.

The Mexican government, for example, in conjunction with UNESCO, began its program at the Centro Regional de Educacion Fundamental de America Latina (CREFAL) in the Tarascan area of Michoacan (UNESCO 1953) as a center for the training of international community development personnel to engage in what was then called "fundamental education."[6] Cornell's worldwide program and that at Vicos must be regarded as part of that broad attempt to improve the status of disadvantaged peoples.

The theoretical and conceptual underpinning of the project was also firmly in step with the times: wholism, functionalism, acculturation, personality and culture, values, and community study ideas were deeply embedded in the project's research and development approach. The exhaustive theoretical synthesis recently (at the time) put forth by Homer Barnett (1953) also contributed to Holmberg's thinking on the processes of innovation and cultural change. By way of example, the methods employed at Vicos were based on anthropological participant approaches. As "agents of change" both anthropologist and technician lived in the place of work on the presumption that by so doing, one would learn more and be able to act with more comprehension and effect.

In Latin America as elsewhere, both then and now, such an approach is somewhat of a novelty. For "experts" of significance actually to "rub elbows" with the world's peasantries for more than a few days was (and is) commonly thought to be a waste of the expert's valuable time. The applied aspect of anthropological participation was more than the classic "participant observation" technique so often debated as a biasing element in anthropological study. The anthropologist became a conscious agent of acculturation and change. Holmberg coined the term "participant intervention" to distinguish this modification of the usual role (Holmberg 1955).

The program at Vicos also operated from a different structural focus. Although the CPP was officially headquartered in the Ministry of Labor and Indian Affairs in Lima, the operational base was in Vicos. As the Vicos community government began to take on its

6. The Mexicans are hardly remembered as the pioneers they were in the community development field. Since the mid-1920s, they had operated field units called Rural Cultural Missions, designed to stimulate community development in socially and technologically integrated ways (Bonilla y Segura 1945). Similarily in India in the post-World War II period extensive efforts were being expended on "village level development" (Mayer 1958; Fraser 1968).

destined role, the decision-making process devolved upon it. The field director's position in the CPP became more of a consultant role and finally disapperared altogether, as planned.

The CPP avoided the Parkinsonian tendency to bureaucratize in the Peruvian tradition, coming into the paralyzing embrace of the primate city of Lima. Throughout its existence, the center of work and project power remained in Vicos. One of the first CPP acts was to reconstruct the hacienda buildings and build an apartment complex so that the permanent staff of school teachers and technical personnel could be induced to remain in the community for most of the week. This was important for two reasons. First, it would, if properly managed, enhance the acculturative change and give Vicosinos a greater opportunity for learning to deal with non-Indian Peruvians. Secondly, by remaining in the community rather than commuting, the schoolteachers and other personnel would presumably actually perform more of their assigned tasks, although the rural and Indian character of Vicos proved an uninteresting challenge to all of the medical doctors assigned to Nuclear School staff. As a result, the health programs at Vicos benefited only sporatically from medical input (see Montalvo 1967; Alers 1971:131–135).

Another major aspect of the CPP was that it rapidly became an important training program for the social sciences (anthropology, sociology, linguistics, agricultural economics, political science, law) as well as in other project-related fields (agronomy, nutrition, medicine, human biology, education) (Dobyns & Vazquez 1964).[7] The multidisciplinary aspect of the project was implicit from the start.

During much of this time, an average of eight schoolteachers, five staff of the ministerial programs, and three Cornell people regularly lived at Vicos. In addition there were many visiting experts, various politicians, and literally hundreds who arrived unannounced to "see the Vicos project."[8]

---

7. The CPP, by virtue of its agreement with the Peruvian government, was committed to working with Peruvian university students in appropriate fields for training purposes. Thus, all told, some thirty-four Peruvian and forty-two "North American" students conducted research projects of various types at Vicos. Additionally, some twenty-one postdoctoral researchers also conducted studies at Vicos. Most of these persons received some modest support from the project, especially in the form of board and room.

8. Contributing to this flow was one tourist guidebook which gratuitously suggested that on a morning's sidetrip to Vicos one could witness project activity (South American Handbook 1961:531).

All of this greatly affected the way in which the "team" oper-ated. The research material gathered by this steady stream of students was, in theory, added to a common data file, one copy of which was kept at Vicos, the other at Cornell. Only twenty-five of ninety-four potential contributors, however, actually did so (Wood 1975). This situation developed for various reasons, not the least of which was Holmberg's nonauthoritarian style, which placed responsibility for such things on the individual. Regardless, the archived field data is sub-stantial and a resource on permanent file at the Cornell Library (Wood 1975).

In the intellectual context of the times, the CPP was a pioneering attempt by a foreign university to be of service to the country of Peru (Adams & Cumberland 1960). Contrary to some assumptions (Morss et al. 1976) that the Vicos program was only a local effort with little outreach, it was regarded from the onset as having national import. Cornell signed an agreement in November 1951 with the Peruvian government which outlined its broad goals and Cornell's responsibil-ities (Artola del Pozo 1952; Monge 1952). In light of contemporary concerns about research ethics and procedure, the agreement now seems to have been well ahead of its time:

—Cornell and the Peruvian Indian Institute of the Ministry of Labor and Indian Affairs would jointly conduct the project in Marcara district where Vicos is, with Cornell supplying initial financing:

—The CPP would apply anthropological concepts towards resolving what was called "the Indian problem," under the direction of a social scientist and with all research subject to approval by the Institute;

—While foreigners would be assisted by the Institute, Cornell would pro-vide scholarship assistance and direction for Peruvian students and encour-age local university participation;

—Cornell would lend its knowledge and personnel for work in other areas of the country as requested. (Convenio 1952)

As bland as these stipulations and goals might appear, they marked a first in Peruvian history: a breakthrough in Peruvian government policy which heretofore had never been distinguished by its en-lightened qualities with repect to "Indian Affairs" (Davies 1974). The impoverished and oppressive socioeconomic milieu of Peruvian Indians in 1952 was well known (Mariategui 1971) and Holmberg,

Monge, and Vazquez were fully aware of the project's potential controversiality and importance.[9]

During the first decade on the Cornell side, funding was private in its entirety, amounting to $126,336 from portions of three grants from the Carnegie Corporation supporting Cornell's worldwide program, from 1952 through 1961 (Himes 1981:178). On the Peruvian end, funding came from regular ministerial budgets, principally Labor and Indian Affairs which paid for the Ancash Program personnel, Education which provided teachers, and Agriculture which provided extension service support. The general funding for the project, however, came from the Vicos community itself, which, after redeveloping the agricultural base, was not only able to fund construction of several buildings and other aspects of project activity but ultimately pay for hacienda land. Aside from regularly borrowing the movie projectors from the USIS and receiving United States backed assistance indirectly through the cooperative agricultural programs of the Peruvian Agriculture Ministry, there was virtually no U.S. government interest, support, or involvement in the CPP until the start of the Kennedy Administration.[10]

Project Action and Results

To mount this attack on Peru's legendary "Indian Problem," a frankly experimental approach was employed in the sense that no one in the country had attempted this type of effort previously. The "experimental approach" involved coordination of largely normal, ongoing Peruvian Ministerial efforts and expenditures, as noted above, with newly mobilizing community forces and resources to achieve a planned result. This was a simple but revolutionary concept in development

9. Just why the conservative Odria dictatorship would permit such a project to begin with was often conjectured by the CPP personnel, but plausible reasons or policy have never been identified.

10. This is misunderstood by some commentators who assume that the CPP was inspired and supported by the United States Alliance for Progress or other such assistance programs (cf. Wagley 1972; Yambert 1980:72).

strategy. Matters came down to getting the operative ministerial programs to work together, a target not struck with consistency (Himes
1981:171–176), but often enough to achieve the general goals. For
the Vicos community, it meant convincing people that they could
take control of the hacienda's affairs, deal with these agencies, become leaders of a representative community organization, and participate in changing their situation. The Vicos serfs were not all sure of
what might happen, nor did they understand in specific ways how the
changes they desired might come about, but they wanted to rid themselves of serfdom. Just six years prior to the start of the CPP, they
had requested the expropriation of the estate and had been refused.

To establish the economic foundation for a new community, the
inadequate food production and nutritional levels prevalent on the
hacienda had to be altered dramatically. This was done under the
direction of the project agronomist through the introduction of new
potato seed and planting techniques on the traditional hacienda lands.
Through careful extension work by all CPP personnel, the same practices were spread individually among Vicos farmers in conjunction
with a supervised credit program (Stein 1971; Holmberg and Dobyns
1969; Chueca 1962). The "hacienda" crop was sold in the national
marketplace with proceeds plowed back into the community. Individual farm families gained directly when their own land became more
productive.

The "mixed economy" which emerged freed Vicosinos so that
they could develop their own lands, family economies, and skills.
The former hacienda lands became the community land base for funding
collective endeavors and the future purchase of the estate. The subsistence plots of each family, more equitably adjusted under the new
regime, were worked as desired. Traditional hacienda work obligations were abolished. Instead, the people worked for the community
about three days per week or only when needed. Construction of the
school and project buildings provided a training ground for many
Vicosinos to gain new skills which would enable them to earn wages
beyond their farming incomes.

A new school replaced the old one which had but fourteen students and an indifferent teacher. This provided the opportunity for
learning the basic "three Rs" and a stage on which it could be proven
(contrary to popular local belief) that Vicosinos had the same intellectual capacities as other Peruvians. It would also become the most

important institutional relationship of the community to the nation (Vazquez 1965). A new basis for community organization replacing the "Patron" was gradually begun, with the ten zones of Vicos represented on a CPP-appointed council which made decisions. After about five years, this council evolved into an elected body, under a new community charter which had been worked out, and thenceforth operated the ex-hacienda and became its government.

Changes were introduced as in health, nutrition, adult education, and other areas as possibilities and interest permitted. On a day-to-day basis, events moved apace with normal Andean life, but the grassy plaza of the old hacienda soon was ringed by the new school building, an improved church, a clinic, the teachers' residence, and a storage building. The old reconditioned hacienda house was modified to suit community and project needs for a headquarters. In contrast to hacienda days, the Vicos plaza became increasingly identified with positive community life, and program activities spun outward from this nucleus into every sector of the estate whose population lived in dispersed clusters of houses scattered throughout the 3,700 acres of arable land, with no nucleated village center. As part of this strategy the project sought to stimulate the Vicosino sense of pride, self worth, and community solidarity in positive ways. To begin, the CPP abolished peonage at Vicos to facilitate development and as a key step in ending the personal denigration stemming from the disparagement of cultural "Indianness," which was a traditional aspect of Peruvian social values that underlay relations between highland Indians and the Spanish-speaking mestizo population (Stein 1972a; Doughty 1971a).

The execution of the Vicos project clearly aimed for a dramatic change in the social, political, and economic spheres of regional life that could not fail to have national repercussions (Holmberg 1960). A program designed to give power to serfs by elimination of the landlord, put the control of production and profits in the hands of the cooperatively organized producers, and promote literacy and political participation could hardly be viewed as anything less than revolutionary in the Peruvian ambience of 1952 which denied all such things to Indians.

As Eric Wolf (1969:290) demonstrated in his analysis of peasant wars, it is unlikely if not impossible for subordinated peasantries to muster the resources necessary to alter their condition unless they have access to some external power component. In this case, the

Vicosinos were able to achieve a change in their status because the CPP had legitimate power of its own, and because it had the ability to gain additional political leverage (Doughty 1971b.) The showdown with opposing vested interests turned on the CPP's effective use of political opportunity and provided a dramatic conclusion to project efforts (Mangin 1979; Dobyns, Doughty, and Lasswell 1971:57–60).

In 1960, Indian communities and hacienda serf populations in various highland areas were increasingly pressuring the government to take action on land reform. The government response was invariably hostile to these efforts, and on the adjacent hacienda of Huapra, Vicosinos and CPP personnel were witness to a police massacre of serfs who were attempting to construct a school "like Vicos." Mario Vazquez, the CPP field director, was harassed by police, and in the charged atmosphere of the valley, fear of violence was pervasive (Doughty 1985). Thus when the conservative Peruvian regime of Manual Prado and Pedro Beltrán continued to stall on their committment to sell the hacienda to the Vicosinos, pressures for action rose sharply.

After several attempts to influence the government to permit the sale and buy out the Beneficent Society interest, a fortuitous event occurred which broke the stalemate. Henry Dobyns, the CPP research coordinator, was advised that Edward Kennedy, the brother of the United States president, would soon visit Peru and needed to visit the highlands. Dobyns volunteered CPP services to brief Kennedy about Peru's rural and Indian problems. In the resulting visit to the Callejón de Huaylas and Vicos, Kennedy was convinced to request, upon his return to Lima, that Prado permit the sale of Vicos to its serfs as an act of "good faith," since Prime Minister Beltrán was at that time attempting to negotiate United States financial support for "studying" agrarian reform.[11] This effort provided the breakthrough needed.

11. The effort made by the writer and other CPP personnel, summer anthropology students, and the Vicos community to win Kennedy's understanding and support followed other lobbying efforts which had become part of the project strategy. Kennedy, like other invited dignitaries, was given a tour of the community, held a head-to-head meeting with the Vicos council for more than an hour, and was treated to a "pachmanca" (a highland barbecue). The fact that he was the United States president's brother weighed heavily with Peruvians. When Kennedy interviewed Prado the following day, his first point was to push for the sale of Vicos, according to both U.S. Chargé d'affaires Douglas Henderson and John Plank, a Harvard political scientist who accompanied him (personal communications). After much haggling with the Beneficient Society, in which the original value of the hacienda was more than doubled, the community agreed to pay two million soles: s/500,000 ($18,655) in cash from its farm profits,

Nevertheless, extensive lobbying and follow-through for an additional eleven months was required before the transaction was completed on July 13, 1962.

Today, visitors to Vicos are often surprised by what they do not find. Instead of a grid-pattern settlement of neatly plastered houses, the adobe homes of Vicos cluster in irregular patterns about the slopes, none appearing "prosperous" by regional mestizo standards. The bumpy dirt road uphill from the district capital of Marcará, is, like the pathways and trails, a stoney and winding affair. Field hands and shepherdesses tend their chores, acknowledging the stranger with but a glance. In the community plaza, few people are normally seen. While the women still retain much of their distinctive homespun dress, many men have adopted mestizo styles in varying degrees. The same is essentially the case with languages: Quechua remains the principal vehicle of communication at Vicos although Spanish is now spoken by a large number of bilingual persons, especially the young, who parade about to the accompaniment of their transistor radios. Coca is chewed by the men during work and at mealtimes. Heavy manual labor for both sexes is a requirement for existence. The old project buildings, now in disuse, are dilapidated from the 1970 earthquake, the clinic has been replaced by a new one, three additional school buildings have been built, including a kindergarden and secondary school, but the teachers' apartments are little used because most teachers now ride to Vicos daily on their motorcycles, small cars, or the bus.

Other signs of change have also appeared in the past ten years: at least three Vicos families own color TV sets, the growing "urban" center around the plaza has almost forty houses, and most of these have electricity. Nevertheless, there are few "monuments to progress" at Vicos. The place appears, in fact, very much like many other Quechua communities which lie along the high slopes of the Cordillera Blanca. Although Vicos has not transcended its surroundings in spectacular ways, it differs because of its long and special history. The legacy of the CPP experience still brings its impact: continuing attention of outsiders subjects the community to more scrutiny, analysis, and criticism than any other place in the Callejón

another half million in installments over a three- to four-year period, and a final million over twenty years. After the 1970 earthquake, which destroyed much of Ancash Department (although with minor damage in Vicos itself), the government canceled all such debts in the region in order to promote redevelopment. The result was that Vicos paid what had amounted to the original assessed value of the estate.

de Huaylas with the exception of the departmental capital. Vicos remains famous.

From 1963 onward, each Peruvian administration has attempted to place its own stamp on Vicos by adding to or detracting from the work of the preceding era. Thus, President Belaunde's "Cooperación Popular" program and Ministerial reorganization affected Vicos directly in the mid-1960s; the Velasco regime ordered the reorganization of the community in 1971 to conform with the new peasant community law,[12] and later, fraudulent projects were foisted on the trusting community by some former Peruvian Vicos program employees acting in the name of new bureaucracies of the 1970s. Clearly, one of the lessons of the CPP is that the subjects of exceptional projects, such as movie stars and the inhabitants of Yankee City and Middletown, will continue to attract the curious long after the significant moment has passed. Learning from the experience is another matter.

Assessments of the Vicos Project

Of the many areas on which "success" or "failure" might be judged, most critiques center around the following: cost, "true impact," politics and publicity, and applicability to other areas including theoretical and practical "lessons" learned. In contrast to academic and professional views, local opinion about the impact of the project has a different emphasis but is no less variable (Himes 1981:190–196) Local elites correctly identified the thrust of the project as being directed at the Indian serf population. That they resented losing control over the Vicosinos and feared project impact on neighboring areas is understandable. Such persons in the district, provincial, and departmental capitals held strong ethnoracial prejudicices about the Vicosinos and their regional counterparts and treated them as inferiors in every way.[13]

12. I was present at an open community meeting when new government ministerial representatives claimed that the CPP had deceived the community. These spokesmen were shouted down by the Vicosinos who defended the project and Holmberg and Vazquez specifically. Ironically, Mario Vazquez was then national director of Peasant Communities.

13. Common epithets and terms of reference used by mestizos toward the Vicosinos and others were "indios brutos," "salvajes," or "the animal closest to man" (Doughty 1971a).

Thus the CPP was deeply resented by many locally because it was expending its efforts on an "unworthy, subordinate, and unimportant" population instead of "decent" people like themselves. Holmberg recognized the importance of these attitudes and the negative character of social contact between the Vicosinos and the mestizo townspeople. Although he realized that many persons would never change their attitudes, he outlined plans (Holmberg 1956:4–5) to foster positive contacts beween the Vicosinos and local elites which were pursued by the CPP. His plan to monitor systematically such planned but "unpatterned voluntary contact" reflected the "research and development" approach which guided action. In retrospect, I think that it would have been well to follow through on these conflicts more than was done, to engender a more just society in the region. The resolution of intergroup tensions, well known from experience in United States race and ethnic relations at work at the time, was not and is not something to be left entirely to natural processes (cf. Williams 1947).[14]

The public relations portions of project activity were directed at meeting some of these problems. A continuous but sporadic flow of "news items" and popular articles appeared in Spanish and English language publications (cf. O'Hara 1953; Collier 1957; Harbord 1960; Curtis 1962; Zileri Gibson 1961). Because general public knowledge and support of the program depended to a significant degree on such accounts, the CPP made information available to such outlets whenever opportunities presented themselves. Visits to Vicos by various authorities served similar ends, were encouraged, and in the end were key factors as noted above.[15]

The response of anthropologists to the Vicos program has run the gamut from the highest praise to prodigal misunderstanding and complete denigration. Negative reactions to the CPP efforts assert: that anthropology (and anthropologists) should not become involved

14. Greater attention paid to this issue would have meant that, once the CPP folded its tents, the community might have had more and better regional allies and sympathizers in place, as opposed to resentful and powerful interests. The CPP was, nevertheless, unique in its attention to this social problem in the context of development program efforts which rarely address such issues at all.

15. It is therefore difficult to understand Cochrane's gratuitous attack on the popular dissemination of information about CPP work (Cochrane 1971:17), although it is a well-known pattern for disciplinary colleagues to disdain attempts at popularizing science findings and experience. In this instance, however, it was a singularly important contribution to the public's understanding and acceptance of the project, a "political" dimension of concern to any applied program.

in applied work; that the discipline has little to offer theoretically or methodologically in such matters; that the project was of little value despite its successes because it cannot be replicated (Carter 1972). Most of these detractions are exemplified in the following review:

Was it but a palliative attempt to induce change within the framework of a traditional and conservative society? Is the Vicos experiment transferable to other peasant groups? Did it serve as a demonstration of what planned change can achieve? . . . A flood of reports and publicity . . . drew . . . help from the Peruvian government and even from the United States (i.e., AID, the Peace Corps, and the National Farmer's Union . . .). How many community development programs have been able to count on such expert advice and public support? I think the authors . . . would agree that the conditions of the Vicos program could not be easily replicated. One would need a man with Holmberg's idealism, intelligence, and dedication; a group of talented and devoted students and associates; funds from various sources; and finally, as in a fairytale, the arrival of the White Knight (Edward Kennedy) to save the old homestead. . . . They view the Vicos program as relevant and "revolutionary." . . . Others might characterize the Vicos experiment as merely idealistic in its aims and paternal in its methods. (Wagley 1972:459)

Blatantly rhetorical critiques like this are sources of error and misinterpretation which may obviate any true assessment. Thus it must be noted that the Vicos project did operate in the context of a conservative Peruvian society (how else?) and attempted to introduce a small but highly sensitive change in its national views of land tenure and Indian and rural development policies. It was not intended to be, nor was it, "palliative." The "experiment" was transferable (cf. Dobyns, Monge, and Vazquez 1962; Nuñez del Prado and Whyte 1973:xiv–xxv) and did serve as a demonstration of planned change of international importance, as numerous citations reveal. Community development programs do count on expert support and advice, as any review of the pertinent literature indicates. Interestingly, only two of the programs cited by Wagley were involved at Vicos at all and those (Peace Corps and the National Farmer's Union) came after the Vicosinos had purchased their lands and the CPP work there was virtually finished. While Holmberg was an exceptional person, his qualities were not and are not unique: there are many who have motivated others—even academics—to action of an idealistic nature. And finally, the CPP ability to evoke external support, such as that of

Kennedy and others at crucial moments, was far from accidental, for the reasons noted above. Whether or not the CPP was "paternalistic" is debatable: that it was idealistic in its aims, is unquestionable.

Frequently, the project's applicability to other areas as a "model" for development and plan of action is raised. This must be seen on at least two levels. The first refers to the operational aspect of the project in the field as it was carried out, and the second, the conceptualization of the problem, its theoretical implications and scope. On the first, pragmatic level, the project was a "model of accomplishment" for some (Goodenough 1963:424) or stimulated an important advance which "may in the long run provide considerable payoff in terms both of more rational policy and better science," "a milestone" (Foster 1969:33–34). The CPP strategy of using holistic anthropological concepts and multidisciplinary inputs are viewed as positive examples for other project designs and work (Kohler 1981:137; Huizer 1969:163–165), and the enterprise is reckoned as having a catalytic effect in promoting constructive changes in the life conditions of Andean peoples (Adams 1967:97). Some, while viewing the Vicos project in a positive light, raise doubts as to its wider applicability because of the supposed "great cost" (Beals and Hoijer 1971:634; Marzal 1981:491).[16] Morss et al. add erroneous "data" to misinterpretation:

the project was never self-sufficient, and no attempt was ever made to make Vicos pay for the full costs of Cornell Staff members and other sources of outside technical assistance. Conservatively estimated, the price tag probably reached $.5 million. Nor can the project be considered replicable. It was initiated in response to a unique opportunity, its efforts were focused on a single community and it was implemented by competent anthropologists— human resources seldom available for rural development projects. In sum, the usefulness of Vicos as a model for other projects is quite limited. (Morss et al. 1976:428, 1–10)

Besides inventing a large "price tag" of whole cloth, Morss also introduces the idea that because Vicosinos did not pay "full" costs

16. The "great cost" to which these and other authors refer without noting any sources or facts amounted to about $10,500 a year of the Carnegie monies taken over the twelve active years of the project. Some individual students obtained separate scholarship funds, but most, such as myself, were funded from the Carnegie grants. Of course, the Ministerial expenses were part of their normal budgets (Mangin 1979). None of these expenditures singly or in total can be considered as "great" either at the time or at present. Indeed, an early evaluation of the project held that it was underfunded! (Adams and Cumberland 1960:187–196)

of the CPP, the project is invalid. As noted, Vicos paid a substantial portion of the program costs, including the purchase of the hacienda.[17] Morss' notion that the CPP was somehow not replicable because "competent anthropologists" ran it seems peculiar in view of anthropological interest in such work and availability of anthropologists for employment (Hoben 1982).[18]

For others, however, the CPP and the project at Vicos are seen through an even more distorted lens:

At Vicos the anthropologist apparently made all the major decisions. No competent administrator would himself deal with agricultural, legal, and educational matters since these are specialized subjects which require expert assessment and advice. (Cochrane 1971:18–19)

To the contrary, the CPP rested on an interdisciplinary approach from the very start, in terms of research and in terms of counsel to the community, relying at every turn on advice from agronomists, biomedical personnel, educationists, lawyers, and others associated with over a dozen Peruvian and international agencies.[19]

A second and more profound level of critique raises the issue of the overall meaning of the project to national policy and structures. Obviously, if Wolf's position noted above is correct (1969:290), then Vicos would either fail completely or, if it succeeded, have revolutionary implications. Paige as well as others (Long and Roberts 1979:299) see Vicos in this way:

While the Vicos experiment is usually portrayed as a model of moderate agrarian reform . . . it actually illustrates the limits of effective land reform in the absense of radical political change or peasant mass action. . . . What the Cornell project did conclusively illustrate . . . is that peasant culture does not inhibit change when restraining political forces have been elimi-

17. Indeed, Vicosinos strongly felt that as "slaves and peons" since 1595, they had already paid more than their share!

18. The ten-page article about Vicos in what purports to be a worldwide evaluation and analysis of rural development projects (Morss et al. 1976) funded by USAID, however, contains some twenty-five errors of fact or context knowledge. While the piece has several assessments I would judge to be correct, it stands as a textbook example of "quick and dirty research"—quite honestly described as having consisted of three days in the field.

19. The tactic of berating the findings or experience of others while advancing one's own is a fine expression of the "limited good" factor among the academic peasantry, but does little to build a cumulative body of social science knowledge on the subject of cultural change. Rather, it is a good case of academic "arribismo" ("upmanship") to use the late Carlos Delagado's apt Peruvian phrase (Delagado 1969:133–139).

nated. The Vicosinos were constrained not by the culture of poverty, but by repression . . . and the massive national social forces which hold that balance in place. (Paige 1975:175)

Holmberg, Monge, and Vazquez were acutely aware of this structural fact and designed the CPP as a first step in facing the demands of the situation (Holmberg 1960; Vazquez 1961). The opposition of the Prado-Beltrán government to the Vicosinos' purchase of the estate is testimony to the radical threat it posed to the system in place. The fact that the CPP was able to conduct its program against such odds seems even more remarkable today than it did to me then.

Benefitting from the Vicos Experience

The importance of the Vicos project not only in terms of its actual results but also in light of the ways in which others have responded is important. In the public sector, AID has funded three extensive reviews of the CPP: one, in 1965–67, included the entire Cornell Sociology-Anthropology Department research on Thailand and India as well as Peru (Dobyns et al. 1966, 1967a, 1967b). The second was an independent, contracted review of the project (Morss et al. 1976) and the third is a recent study based upon extensive research in the Vicos Project archive at Cornell (Lynch 1981). Morss does not cite the Dobyns et al. summary nor the early evaluation by Adams and Cumberland (1960) and Lynch originally did not cite Morss. Alas, the repetition does not lead to the advancement of ideas, although the lengthy summary by Lynch is on the whole comprehensive, sound, and fair. While she makes some use of Himes' excellent independent appraisal of the CPP's broader impacts in Peru (Himes 1972, 1981), Morss was unaware of its existence.

Morss and his colleagues conclude that the CPP did achieve its aims of aiding the establishment of an independent community, introducing farming improvements, and promoting literacy, and notes that "Cornell University did its job well" (Morss et al. 1976:426, 1–8). Lynch documents similar conclusions but in far greater detail and accuracy. She notes positive changes in Vicos' agriculture, integration into national society, well-being, sharing of power through elimination of the manor system and development of an open community government, greater realization of human dignity, and a number of other areas (Lynch 1981:131–141). Despite this, however, she concludes somewhat ironically that contemporary Vicos has not fulfilled its promise because of increased social differentiation (see also Babb 1985) and failure to develop industry, and because the educated youth tend to migrate. Because all of these features characterize the Peruvian highlands in general and this region in particular, it is hard to envision how Vicos alone might have transcended the pattern no matter what the CPP did two decades ago.

In the same vein, Mangin's ambivalent remarks generally argue that the project succeeded in the same areas outlined by Lynch, but he reaches the curious conclusion:

I have never been too pleased with the "applied" aspects of the project, but, since the late 1960s, a great many anthropologists have been castigating the profession for not having undertaken projects or action which would "benefit" the people studied and Holmberg certainly had that intention. I believe that if we had had more money and greater local resources we might have done *more* damage. The budget was never high and we were constantly forced to operate within the Peruvian system in such things as getting technical assistance from local agencies and teachers from the ministry. . . . The Vicos-Cornell project was one of many outside interventions in Indian local affairs and, unlike most, it is hard for me to see that the community is worse off for it. (Mangin 1979:82–83)

It is well documented that the CPP did achieve its major goals in the time frame of the program. It was a complex, pioneering project accomplished with a modest amount of money and within the range and availability of local resources—as planned, against enormous odds at the time. Whether overt or not, it had many widespread impacts both on the region and in the country (Dobyns, Monge, and Vazquez 1962; Himes 1981) and even in the national secondary school civics curriculum (Talavera 1961), which can be taken as either positive or negative aspects, depending upon one's viewpoint.

But then, what of the lessons for rural development work today? I am convinced that one of the reasons that the Vicos program fell into such disfavor in certain quarters, despite its agreed-upon successes, was that all community development efforts were rejected in the late 1960s. New theories which promised speedier development were proposed, processes which were supposed to modernize populations through instrumental investments on a large scale. The problem with community development was that it was seen as too "anthropological" (i.e., small-scale and unconnected to larger reality), an approach which demanded the personal investments of expert time and effort in the field, on a case-by-case basis. Whether true or not, development proponents soon turned to the "trickle-down" approaches, run by capital city bureaucrats who took their instructions and guidance from shifting cadres of international technicians and consultants. All of this was far removed from the living realities of the rural community so well known to those whose participation in the new forms of development strategy were minimal at best.

To accommodate this shift in program focus, efforts also moved away from the "integrated" development approach espoused in places like Vicos to "sectorial" efforts aimed at touching problems in the context of society's stratified nature. Sectors such as health, labor, agriculture, and education were to be largely treated in their own right and not as they intersected areas of community life. In this international swing in development planning, theory, and policy, the lessons and meaning of programs such as Vicos were easily dismissed as being too localized and idiosyncratic to be of modern use. Thus, a 1975 observer such as Morss could only see the Vicos project as having limited value to development issues (1976:428, 1–10).

In the search for "new" approaches to old developmental dilemmas the ideas of "community organization and rural development" are again being suggested (Korten 1980) for effective programs. Korten reaches the conclusion that what is required is "action based on capacity building," which is nothing less than the utilization of social science and "rural people" themselves in the active planning and execution of projects. He also recommends learning from past experience, which in light of Vicos and other community-level projects around the world in the past forty-five years is welcome.[20]

Another prescription for effective change and development programs calls for a "new directions" approach (Morss and Morss,

20. Curiously, this modern call for social science action contains but two references which predate 1971 in its otherwise extensive citations. Moreover, Korten's elaborate discussion and outline of the "learning process approach" bears a striking resemblance to Holmberg's description of his revolutionary idea of "participant intervention" (1955) and the "research and development approach" to change (1958).

1982:19–39, 91–105) which provides for the "basic needs" of the rural poor, employment opportunity and integrated development in operation and policy. The Vicos project, not only anticipated such an approach, but carried it out under concepts and plans which differ largely in name. With a strong sense of "déja vu," we turn to a summary of some of the larger "lessons" to be drawn from the CPP program at Vicos, with the hope that such may benefit the resurgent interest in integrated, community-based, participatory, rural development strategies.

Lessons

The applied anthropologist should be prepared to step into the roles of researcher, administrator, lobbyist, spokesperson, journalist, or activist as part of one's applied methodology. To "go public" one must be both convinced (and convincing) that such acts are in harmony with public and program interests, the professional knowledge on the issue, and one's own values. This requires conviction born of solid professional confidence and knowledge, a snag on which many anthropologists have long been caught as they sit on the stove's back burners, basting themselves in self doubt. The conservative anthropological response to "applications" has resembled one that would have been made by a committee consisting of Pontius Pilate and Chicken Little. It is immobilized by thoughts of cultural relativity, and insecure in a supposed absense of knowledge and theory at the level of behavioral laws (cf. Maquet 1970; Thompson 1965; Bonfil 1966). The result has been that many have deliberately denied anthropological authority in areas where it clearly exists, and have been theoretically modest to the point of virtually discounting its value or existence.[21]

Such were the reigning modes of disciplinary behavior during much of the era in which the CPP operated, and indeed, they touched

21. There are some notable exceptions to this statement, however. Historically, Malinowski, for one, did not hesitate to assert anthropological legitimacy and competence in policy science areas, drawing upon the basic principles of the discipline (Malinowski 1944). Margaret Mead's impact in this area is also obvious.

the operations of the project (cf. Mangin 1979:81–83). Thus, the CPP was "caught" *in flagrante delictu,* violating the conservative norms of contemporary anthropology. One "lesson" of the Vicos experience, then, as Barnett (1955:10–105) noted long ago, is that innovations which run counter to the received wisdom of the culture may not prosper until they gather support from the proper advocates or can be recognized in the context of cultural experience. Should the applied anthropological culture have now reached such a point, then we can anticipate the prospect of systematic learning from past experience entering not only applied anthropology, but other fields related to the management of human organization and change.

The original critique of "conservative" anthropology by Bonfil Batalla (1966) calls for anthropologists to direct their attention to the immediacy of change rather than an "evolutionary" time dimension. Cynical "nothing can be done" or "time cures all" theories of human problems simply do not respond to pressing demands or crises affecting Guatemalan villagers or the peoples of Sahelian Africa, nor those seeking redress of longstanding exploitation. Despite the urgency to get things done, serious programs of guided change cannot realistically hope for solutions under two-year budgets.

In this one small place, the CPP demonstrated that effective programs of socioeconomic change must be expected to endure several years to achieve goals which involve modifications in complex, organizational behaviors and/or commensurate alterations in cultural patterns. Given the fact that the CPP addressed problems that were several centuries in the making, one might argue that the Vicos work was rapid, even though it lasted through four Peruvian administrations and even more changes in agency policies. Personnel changed constantly, official interest waxed and waned, and was even hostile to project goals. Peruvian budgetary fluctuations and commitments were capricious. That the CPP endured for almost fifteen years (twelve years being primarily concerned with Vicos) was an administrative miracle, and probably key to its ultimate success in achieving its stated goals.

By contrast, in Peru as elsewhere in the world, normal government programs in such areas as "rural development" may barely survive for the full period of a biennial budget, a fact which must be comprehended as one of the principal deterrents to effective, planned change. The semi-autonomous, half private and half public character of the official CPP probably contributed significantly to the project's capacity to weather change, in effect outlasting fluctuations in public and private and funding agency interests, while persisting in its goals.[22] Thus, the Vicos case illustrates that the politico-bureaucratic thirst for conveniently fast results is the most unrealistic hope in planned change. This is not a popular conclusion.

Holistic theories of human life, in the organizational, community context which are widely accepted in anthropology, provide sound orienting premises on which to rest operational hypotheses. Such concepts, of course, emerge from broad, structural-functional social science theory (cf. Merton 1957; Holmberg 1969) and are, despite many criticisms, largely taken for granted today even by apparently "hostile paradigms." Proclivities to focus work in technologically dominated areas at the expense of difficult, larger social questions in virtually all contemporary development schemes make such perspectives invaluable to perfecting planned change. Yet, that the intimate relationship between technology and culture must be taken into account in development action is apparently one of the most difficult lessons to learn (Spicer 1952; Bernard and Pelto 1972; Farvar and Milton 1972), as recent analyses of technological "green revolution" impact reveals (Pearse 1980).

The "holistic" strategy of anthropology is not only relevant to such issues, but critical. The Vicos program brought issues of power, wealth, skill, respect, and enlightenment to the whole framework of development. Thus, when the home economist taught sewing to Vicos women, she not only imparted important technological skill, but also a sense of participation in the change process, the opportunity to gain new respect as possessors of modern skill, and the ability to add measureably to their families' and their own well being and wealth (Lasswell 1971:167–77; Doughty 1971a:209–213; Holmberg 1971:33–63).

The CPP showed that "research and development" are interrelated activities at both the project planning and execution levels and necessarily related throughout the life of the project. The need to act appropriately in the face of emergent contexts which may alter the premises of original assumptions, theory, and design is seen today as a critical aspect of program functions and "updating" (Korten 1980:18–

22. In the Vicos case, the principal funding came from the Carnegie Corporation, which remained steadfast in its support for the program.

22; Morss and Morss 1982:100; Hoben 1982:369–370). The important executive capacity is the ability to cycle ongoing research findings constantly through the operational system, as its indispensible fuel. For two major reasons it does little good to conduct evaluative research only after a project is over, when the deed is done: first, because as we have seen development agencies have historically ignored such evaluations, and second, because errors should be corrected as the program operates.

Directed change projects are not like scientific laboratory experiments which cannot be interrupted for fear of upsetting the design and ability to test the hypothesis. While planned change efforts do employ many scientific procedures, they require the acceptance of further responsibilities because the recipient population must live with program results. The responsibilities of developers to the "developed" is an ethical issue, and not simply a technical relationship. The CPP program "stayed with" the problems and did not forget them. This was true on both an institutional level as well as a personal one for CPP participants.

Perhaps the most difficult set of baseline conditions to be overcome or modified had to do with linking the abolishment of the repressive hacienda with amplified social and political participation in community life leading to effective empowerment. The circumstances were certainly daunting. The intricate patterning of the Vicos "culture of exploitation" was not to be easily altered by simple infusions of technique or the workings of a lone institution (Holmberg 1967). The way to break the repressive dependency and fear-bound traditions of Hacienda Vicos was through the empowerment and open participation of individuals in the Vicos community. Although this is hardly a novel discovery, the challenge to users of the integrated, holistic strategy like the one used at Vicos, or virtually any other social project, is to promote empowerment while avoiding the devastating growth of bureaucratic organisms which pretend to "coordinate" activity (Morss and Morss, 1982:99) but usurp a public's power and ability to participate.

On the other hand, the development program itself must learn to live with problems created by the participating community following its own interests. This is not readily acceptable to most bureaucracies, especially governmental ones fearing political embarrassment. The official program should be ready to accept community mistakes and use them to teach rather than castigate, a path frought with difficulties. The Vicos community committed several "blunders" both during and after the CPP period of action which some critics have hastened to categorize as the "failure" of the entire program. Developmental change, however, is not an immaculate process.

The difficulty of producing the systematic publication of findings in all aspects of the program was a deficiency noted by many persons. Although there were well over two hundred articles, reports, monographs, and books published about Vicos and the CPP, more findings might have been published by more of the participants. The use of this material is also limited in part because of its dispersal among numerous journals, books, and "fugitive reports," but then so is much of the analytical material on development (Hoben 1982:364).[23] Consequently it cannot be assumed that because reporting is done, lessons will be drawn and the state of the art advanced. Again, this is not only a problem of the Vicos project materials, but a characteristic malady of the development field in dealing with sociocultural variables (Tendler 1975).[24] The fact that AID has funded three mutually exclusive "evaluations" of the CPP over a fifteen-year period is indicative of the nonscientific state of the development field. The amnesia in which agencies operate with respect to prior knowledge and history is well known, but we must ask that it not remain that way, particularly among students of the process!

Fulfilling the Promise

As a contribution to applied anthropology and to Peru, the Vicos project should be remembered for what it accomplished: the success-

23. The recent assertion that the CPP failed to place its findings at the disposition of Peru (Marzal 1981:491) is unfounded. All thirty-two administrative reports were either filed with the Indian Institute as agreed and/or published by Peruvian journals and bulletins, over sixty papers in Spanish appeared in books and journals, and all the dissertations were given to the appropriate libraries. On the other hand, foreign language publications are inconvenient for many and indeed are often discounted academically in the United States. Although there have been several summary analyses of the Vicos program, they are often ignored or not regarded as acceptable because they are "official" (cf. Wagley 1972:459; Mangin 1979:70, 83).

24. The summary analyses cited here, for example, by Morss and Morss (1982), share few common references with Korten (1980) despite the fact that they coincide in many of their ideas, however differently labeled. In this light it is not surprising that the former, published in 1982, does not cite the latter, published in 1980.

ful completion of the first holistically designed, community development and land reform program, which upheld and enhanced the dignity, conditions of life, and citizen rights of impoverished Indian serfs against the weight of colonial tradition and the ultimate wishes of the elites. It was unabashedly a humanitarian program in pursuit of equity and justice for Vicosinos, and advocated this cause. As such, the CPP was always controversial in the context of academic anthropology. Nevertheless, the uneven reception of the CPP in applied anthropological circles suggests in retrospect a curious oedipal relationship of anthropologists to this applied grandparent, an intriguing phenomenon in a discipline struggling for responsible and mature roles in policy and action fields.

The Vicos experience demonstrated that anthropology has the theory, information, and method needed to make significant contributions to complex issues of social change and development. While it was heralded as "unique" and successful because anthropologists oriented the program and were in charge, it is exceptional for the same reasons today (Hoben 1982:361). Anthropologists as such are still predominantly academic players and have not assumed applied roles to any significant degree, although there may be cause for more optimism in this regard as their experience outside the academy grows. The Vicos case today signals the urgent need to provide for open, well-researched, and constructive use of past experience as well as the best use of our contemporary skills in the quest for future improvement in the equity and quality of human life.

20

APPLYING THE ANTHROPOLOGICAL
PERSPECTIVE TO SOCIAL POLICY

Robert H. Heighton, Jr.,
and Christy Heighton

Based on their experiences as employees of the Southern Regional Education Board, Robert and Christy Heighton consider specific contributions that anthropologists can make to deliberate social planning processes and their evaluation. They see the major contributions of anthropology in the discipline's breadth of view, theories of change, study of systemic relationships within the context of an organic whole, means of controlling for value judgments, and use of inductive reasoning. They note that the models and theoretical models of anthropology are only mirrors of reality which must be tested in applied situations.

The Heightons share the conviction of Kimball and other contributors to this volume that, if anthropologists are to contribute effectively to nonacademic roles and institutional settings, applied work and contributions will have to become as valued as academic ones. It is only as this occurs that anthropologists will be able to make significant contributions to social policy.

SOCIAL SCIENTISTS ARE increasingly involved in the formulation of social policy intended to improve the sociopsychological and phys-

Robert H. Heighton, Jr. (Ph.D., Hawaii) is an educational design specialist in the computer industry in California. He previously taught at the University of Florida, where he was also associate director of the Urban and Regional Development Center, and at Georgia State University. He has served as director of projects in mental health program evaluation and standard setting for the Southern Regional Education Board. His fieldwork has been in Hawaii, the Caribbean, rural and urban settings in the American South, and in state and federal health agencies.

Paula-Christy Heighton (B.A., Florida) is a professional author and former executive with a national youth agency.

ical environments of communities. Contemporary problems of population growth, environmental destruction, limited natural resources, food production and distribution, and technological change are all coming to a head in modern forms of urban settlement. Local urban or rural communities throughout the world provide the settings in which people engage in those activities which either worsen or improve the human physical and environmental dilemmas posed by rapid and uncontrolled growth amid a situation of limited resources. Using methods and findings of social research, policy scientists engage in the development and implementation of governmental actions directed towards the solution of these and related problems.

This essay examines social policy planning from the perspectives of sociocultural anthropology. Past contributions of anthropological theory to social policy planning have been largely limited to the concept of cultural relativity (Mann 1972:354). Thus, comparative cultural impacts related to early childhood experience are central to much of the social and educational planning thought that emerged during the 1960s. Planners are also aware of participant observation as a research method, although they seldom use it. However, basic concepts and methods of anthropology (e.g., the concept of culture, the community study method, the present-day concept of functionalism, holism, the natural history method, pluralism, and theories of innovation and change) have yet to contribute to social policy thought and practice.

Our purpose here is to examine the planning component of social policy in light of anthropological perspectives. We summarize some of the key concepts and issues in planning today, and suggest ways in which anthropologists may begin to meet the challenges posed by social policy planning. In discussing issues, we describe each one and then examine possible anthropological contributions to it.

Social Policy and Planning

The policy sciences study the process of deciding or choosing, and evaluate the relevance of available knowledge for the solution of particular problems. Rein (1971:297) outlined the scope of social policy as the "integration of values, the principles by which these values are translated into policies and programs, assessments of the outcomes of implementing these principles in terms of the values asserted, and the search for strategies of feasible change which promise a better fit between values, principles, and outcomes.'' Policy scientists use methods (e.g., economic, sociological, and quantitative) and findings of social research in the development and implementation of governmental actions intended to improve the sociopsychological and physical environments of communities and to meet their dependency needs.

The term *social policy* defies simple definition, and there are at least four different ways in which it is commonly used.[1] First, the term can be used as a *philosophical concept* which refers to the collective searching and actions of communities, organizations, and political agencies for solutions to mutual problems. A second definition views social policy as a *product* consisting of either documents or conclusions drawn by persons who are responsible for improving community living conditions and for the amelioration of social problems. A third definition emphasizes a fundamental *process* through which communities and agencies provide an element of stability (ordered change through time) and improve their social and physical environments by planning for desired future goals. Finally, social policy can be defined as a *framework for action*—as both the product and the process which, if clearly delineated, can serve as a guide for action to effect desirable changes in a community.

Five intellectual tasks involving planning are performed in social policy at varying levels of insight and understanding: clarification of goals; description of trends; analysis of conditions; projection of future developments; and invention, evaluation, and selection of alternatives (Lasswell 1968:181–182). In dealing with matters of social policy, there are no boundaries which divide problems into the disciplinary realms of economics, sociology, or psychology, because problems usually contain components that need to be addressed by several disciplines. Moreover, one cannot avoid working with a problem simply because it falls outside one's own field of knowledge. In principle, the anthropological perspective has always been one of dealing with a total cultural situation.

According to Lasswell (1968), as the globe shrinks into inter-

1. The discussion in this paragraph is based upon Freeman and Sherwood (1970:2–3).

dependence, relying more fully on science and technology, social policy will continue to gain significance. Interdependence implies that each participant and item in the social process is affected by the context in which it exists; the future structure of the context is in turn influenced by the changing pattern of detail. To work with this interdependence, we need information which is capable of providing rational guidance for attempts to maximize values (Lasswell 1968:184). Analyses of culture and personality have deepened and widened our relevant knowledge, but the examination of policy requires additional types of information about both economic and noneconomic factors, such as the following: educational and health facilities; the distribution of power in society; economic, social, and political stratification; institutions and attitudes; and intentionally induced policy measures designed to change one or several of these factors.

If anthropologists are to play a more active and vital part in social policy, they need to understand the practical operation of government so as to be better able to formulate policy questions, identify problems, produce information on problems, and provide specific situational information (Goodenough 1963). Anthropologists with this knowledge are in a better position to help policy makers examine and understand the daily interactions between the policy process and the systems of programmatic, systemic, and personal values which operate within it.

Social policy is essentially concerned with moral and ethical concepts. Thus, anthropologists who work as policy scientists must deal with two elements in decision making: selection of a set of alternatives to choose from; and selection of a set of preferences against which to rank the alternatives. Bauer and Gergen (1968) note that any optimized model for decision making is based upon a set of preferences (values) that indicate an optimal solution; however, there is no such thing as an optimal public policy, since the optimum varies according to political philosophies and cultural groups.

The value system in which a particular program originates and that evolves during program development influences both program goals and the means of attaining them. When programmatic values differ from those of the society at large, they may impede the optimal solution of the problem. In this situation, anthropologists can assist an administrator to specify program values, to discover the values of recipient populations, and perhaps to reconcile the two.

Because a program, with its associated value system, operates within a larger political system with its attendant values, administrators often need help in identifying what these political values are and who holds them. Anthropologists can help make explicit the values behind pertinent legislation and the possible compromises that can be reached among the political value systems of various power and pressure groups. Anthropologists also can help clarify intentional and unintentional vagueness in political value systems so that administrators can structure program priorities within the constraints of political reality. Policy makers themselves are influenced by hidden personal and professional values which affect their perspectives, priority setting, and interpretations of outcomes and their implications. Anthropologists can help administrators become sensitive to their own values and their resulting impact on actions so that these influences do not strongly distort policy decisions.

Traditionally, planning has been defined as a process of identifying alternatives, discussing the advantages and disadvantages of each, and then making a decision based on this information. Social planning involves the drawing up of plans for future action in regard to social institutions and resources (Madge 1968:125). The major distinction between traditional and newer schools of thought within the planning profession lies in the difference between a "rational" model and a "participatory" one. The rational model emphasizes planning as an intellectual activity divorced from its environment and considers the collection and analysis of facts as the major planning activity. The participatory model underscores the importance of planning as a political and social process carried out by, or in consultation with, those affected. These two previously distinct models are now merging under the rubric of social policy planning (Littlestone 1973:4, 9).

As a process, planning is neither plans nor forecasting. Plans outline a specific course of action, while forecasting is an attempt to predict future events. In contrast, planning is a dynamic series of guides to aid present decisions aimed at shaping the future to desired ends.

Evaluation is an integral part of the planning process, and must be mentioned in any complete discussion of planning. Full discussion of evaluation is beyond the scope of this chapter.[2] However, it is

2. For a more complete discussion, see Van Maanen (1973).

important to note that the cycle of planning and evaluation ideally operates in a continuous feedback pattern that modifies plans as a program "rolls" toward its goals. Thus, planning should be constantly reviewed and updated by evaluation throughout a project. This ideal situation has been described as follows:

evaluation begins during the planning phase of program development and usually involves such things as an analysis of the problem, the formulation of program goals and an appraisal of existing or alternative programs. Program implementation calls for another evaluation phase which, in turn, feeds back valuable information for the revision of plans and programs. This planning, implementing, and refining process to which evaluation is inherently connected may be repeated indefinitely until the goals are realized or discarded. Evaluation must be seen as an unfolding and cyclical process, for "good" programs may take years to develop. (Van Maanen 1973:12)

Evaluation of a program attempts to determine if it is meeting the goals set out in its plans. Theoretically, program evaluation is concerned with outcomes and impacts, but it also deals with the effort and activity designed to lead to desired outcomes. During the implementation of a program, evaluation monitors program operations for the purpose of providing information to planners and administrators which can be used for correcting procedures and revising objectives. Ideally, the evaluation process involves "determining the program components and operations requiring study, selecting the appropriate techniques for gathering data, and collecting, analyzing, and presenting the information in the most useful way for the administrator" (Heighton and McPheeters 1976:3).

There are two major categories of evaluation: formative and summative (Scriven 1972). Summative evaluation, which is usually conducted by evaluators not actually associated with a program, is supposed to determine whether a planned program is ameliorating a targeted social problem; it is related to decisions for program continuance or future program planning. Persons not familiar with evaluation generally consider summative evaluation to be the only or major type of evaluation.

The lesser known but more prevalent formative or "in-house" evaluation provides monitoring data for administrators during the life of the program. It appears to be more useful than summative evaluation because it provides specific information for immediate program correction and improvement. This type of evaluation can best be defined as "the process of making reasonable judgments in effort, adequacy, effectiveness, and efficiency based on systematic data collection and analysis that is integrated into management" (personal communication, Clifford C. Attkinsson).

Issues in Planning

The contemporary movement toward planning social policy has raised a number of significant questions related to the nature of social problems and the needs and expectations of both planning professionals and the public about the ways to reduce them. Fundamental changes are occurring that affect the ways social problems are defined and approached. During the past decade, numerous issues have emerged as matters of substantial debate among members of the planning profession. Three of these are discussed here: (1) the meaning of comprehensiveness; (2) the extent to which planning can and should entail democratic choices in contrast to authoritarian controls; and (3) the appropriate role for each level of planning.

COMPREHENSIVENESS

Planners have traditionally used the term "comprehensive" to mean a general plan that is "the finished official statement of a municipal legislative body which sets forth its major policies concerning desirable future physical development" (Black 1968:349). For some individuals in the planning profession, comprehensive means encompassing "all geographical parts of the community and all functional elements which bear on physical development" (Black 1968:349), while other planners argue that a comprehensive plan must encompass physical, social, economic, administrative, and fiscal elements (Kain 1970:221–223; Gans 1970:223–225).

Related to the definition of comprehensive is the question of the separation of physical and social planning. Traditionally, planners have been concerned with physical planning, which is based upon land use and physical design. The assumption has been that, if a good physical environment exists, social problems will be reduced in number or eliminated. Some planners have juxtaposed physical planning with social planning because of this assumption. The majority of planners consider these two distinctly different types of planning, although some (Gans 1970:223–225) are now calling for a union of the two to produce a humanistically oriented planning.

For anthropologists, the debates over the meaning of "comprehensive" and the question of the separation of physical and social planning are artificial. Planners who approach these questions from the holistic perspective of sociocultural anthropology would agree that there are no physical or social or economic problems, only problems composed of physical, social, and economic elements. The anthropological perspective would consider a plan comprehensive if it included all the important variables (human, social, environmental, economic, etc.) and the relationships among them that contribute to the definition and examination of the problem.

Studying cultural and statistical data in context by using the community study method (Arensberg and Kimball 1965), anthropologists learn that some interrelationships and subsystems are more important to the system than others and limit detailed study to these crucial areas. Planners who employ this method may avoid the problem of concentrating too much on unnecessary detail. Initially, the entire system should be studied as though one were looking in at it while standing outside in a larger system. Arensberg and Kimball state, "the most important point is not the exhaustion of detail, but the breadth of view" (1965:32).

The concepts of holism and community can also help planners to adopt a more useful form of the concept of functionalism than that which they generally use. Since the days of Radcliffe-Brown and Malinowski, this concept has evolved from the elemental definition of functions as reasons or purposes to mean the network of variable relationships between elements and patterns of a system, which cannot be understood without experiencing the culture in which they are found. The concept of community centers on these relationships as they are structured by the interaction of individuals, groups, functions, space and time in a community, and can be used to determine their contributions to group welfare and the extent to which modification in any element affects others.

Data derived from the community study method are often vital to building a context within which to place statistical data for interpretation, especially when multiple interpretations are possible. For example, planners may discover that a particular area has a large number of households with no resident adult male acting as head. These data could reflect a system of plural marriage in which co-wives reside separately and husbands live with one wife at a time, or a community organization in which all adult males reside together and apart from their wives and children, or a family form in which support for the household comes from kinsmen by blood, with no such position as resident husband, or the males may be migrant workers for long periods of time while their families remain in their home community. Thus, statistical data alone cannot describe a culture but require further investigation and additional cultural data in order to derive meaning (Valentine 1968:6–7).

In anthropological study, "the empirical fit between attitude and behavior, a belief and culture pattern, an institutional norm and a custom or sanction, is of more interest than the number of persons who express the attitude or practice the behavior on the average or other statistically representative quality of these things" (Arensberg and Kimball 1965:33). By studying cultural data and statistics in context through the community study method, anthropologists can add a living dimension to the planning process, which may help to improve the reception of plans and avoid accusations that planners are more concerned with figures and physical arrangements than with people (Fromm 1972:67–71).

AUTHORITARIAN CONTROL VERSUS DEMOCRATIC CHOICE

Planning seems to be boiling with issues, but the majority are symptoms and manifestations of the major issue of authoritarian control versus democratic choice, which reflects the American value of individualism and general distrust of governmental authority. In discussing this issue, we will examine the use of planning for change or maintenance of the *status quo*, ordering society, and elitism.

During the turmoil and fragmentation of the 1960s, various factions such as racial, ethnic, and radical political groups, struggling first for a voice in the process of governance and then control, began to see planning as a change mechanism to achieve their ends. Current turbulence in the planning profession is a symptom of the struggle to either change American society or preserve the *status quo*. Proponents of social change insist that in order to make substantial changes in American society, the nature of contemporary planning itself must first change. They maintain that modern planning has become change-resistant, because much of it is done by government and is designed to keep the country stable and calm. In an attempt to know every-thing in advance and to strictly control every outcome, planning ho-mogenizes the environment and leaves no room for unplanned change, unanticipated events, or changes other than those desired by the group in control, thereby replacing innovation with stability. Governments and other bureaucracies, rather than encouraging innovation at a time when we need new answers to old problems, attempt to stabilize the rate and type of change. However, historically significant change has always been unique and unpredictable, and often arose from innova-tion and instability (Grabow and Heskin 1973:108).

In attempting to order society, government sometimes uninten-tionally creates greater chaos. Although it is possible to create order in a subsystem while the rest of the system is in chaos, there comes a point when the more order one tries to introduce into a subsystem, the greater disorder one produces in the total system; the interdepend-ence of subsystems may cause a directed change in one to create unanticipated events in another. Further, government's attempt to create order, thereby decreasing the diversity that can cause conflicts, may reduce the flexibility of the system.

In nature, the survival of a community is correlated with the diversity of that community. When faced with a crisis, the diversified community has the flexibility to adapt to conditions that may cause the homogeneous community to die. Governments, with their pen-chant for ordering social and physical things, potentially create non-adaptive, homogenous human communities. Their policies may seek to continue the *status quo,* or perhaps attempt to move all social levels to a new order. In either case, the governmental role is usually prescriptive, and planners generally base their plans on what *will* be according to the government in power rather than on what *should* be. Far from serving the diverse sectors of society, some planners feel that their profession is increasingly beholden to one master, the gov-ernment (Barr 1972:155–159).

Traditionally, planners have served in advisory positions to gov-ernmental units and elites who have wanted particular social reforms implemented or scuttled. Because they have worked for power elites, planners are often viewed as members of these elites, an impression which some of them help foster. Some critics contend that planning is elitist because it separates planners from those for whom they plan; planning requires the use or manipulation *of* persons, nature, and the world; it foregoes meaningful relationships *with* them.

The anthropological perspective, using concepts such as culture, cultural relativism, the community study method, participant observation, pluralism, and theories of innovation and change, can offer some possible directions for the resolution of the controversy over authoritarian control and democratic choice. Charges of elitism in planning might be reduced if the concepts of cultural relativism, the natural history or inductive approach used in the community study method, and participant observation were used to sensitize planners to the sources of their biases and to keep them in contact with the citizens they serve. To guard against elitism, planners must understand the values and customs of diverse populations, the external values and influences at work in the larger culture within which these groups exist, and their own personal values.

Firsthand knowledge of the target population, gained through participant observation performed by planners or anthropologists, can provide baseline data; and the questioning of pressure groups and governmental units can help discover and specify the values that affect relationships between the target group and outsiders. By examining the values of their discipline, planners will become more sensitive to assumptions which may distort their perception. For example, if those for whom the planning is being done are conceived in terms of a deficiency model which defines them as "culturally disadvantaged," planning and action will likely be poor and inappropriate. The concept of "cultural disadvantage" is based on an assumption that everyone should be like middle class America (Howard 1970:169). On the other hand, extreme relativism can also be biased because it leads the planner to equate any recognition of differences with discrimination and to fail to consider differences when necessary.

The natural history or inductive method of reasoning makes no assumptions about the group under study, nor does it begin research with the intention of proving a specific hypothesis. It is not hampered, as the deductive approach occasionally is, by an incorrect model, but discerns the natural model of the community as the study proceeds. Its use can help planners avoid problems related to implicit biases because it does not start with value assumptions, but discovers the values of the community.

Acceptance of cultures as different rather than as better or worse, could lead planners to the acceptance of heterogeneity (also known as cultural pluralism) and away from the concept of the "melting pot," which assumes that all Americans want to lose their ethnic identity and conform to the stereotypic image of middle-class behavior and values. The anthropological concept of pluralism can be used to support the idea that uniformity is not a viable option but that heterogeneity can be a beneficial alternative, allowing diverse communities and/or cultures to work together creatively and still maintain their individual identities. Rubin (1961) has discussed how cultural groups which maintain separate identities on the local level cooperate with each other at higher levels. It is where diverse groups come together that heterogeneity produces its greatest flowering of creativity, as witnessed by the exhilaration in such cosmopolitan centers as San Francisco, Paris, and similar cities.

Heterogeneity, or the diversity of cultural pluralism, offers a community or culture a wide variety of adaptive possibilities in a time of rapid change. Anthropological concepts and theories of change can facilitate a general understanding of change and ease people's fear of it. Anthropologists working in developmental programs have produced theories and research methodologies dealing with the process of change that could be vitally important to planners and administrators (Smith and Fischer 1970:82). Some of these change concepts include the effects of urbanization, cultural borrowing and diffusion, acculturation and forced acculturation, innovation, and the influence of nonhuman factors such as environmental change. These theories are potentially useful in helping planners to guide change and to better understand how stability or maintenance of the *status quo* may lead to nonadaptive effects, as, for example, when ecological, social, or technological change has so altered the community's pattern of living that some or all of its current values and customs work against continued survival.

THE LEVELS OF PLANNING

Planning today exists in the national, regional, state, and local levels of government. We agree with Galloway (1941:29) that there should be three levels of planning: directive, administrative, and operative. At issue are the appropriate roles for each level and citizen participation. Ideally, policy making and guidance should be centered in Washington; administration should be decentralized in the states and regions; and operation should be localized. Thus, the farther the level of planning from the actual operations, the more generalized its activities. Detailed planning would be done only at the scene, where the planner could best understand peculiarities of local situations.

According to Perloff, local planning is generally concerned with aesthetics, engineering, land use, governmental procedures, social welfare, and the functioning and development of the community (Coke 1968:27). However, numerous localities lack viable planning departments and the financial or technical ability to plan for themselves. Furthermore, local areas have been so constrained by state, regional, and federal regulations that many have lost the ability to innovate and initiate (Rondinelli 1973:19).

In recent federal legislation such as that for the Urban Planning Assistance "701" Program and the Professional Standards Review Organizations, the National Health Planning and Resource Development Act of 1974, and the Community Mental Health Centers Amendments of 1975, the federal government has emphasized the participation of citizens in the allocation and uses of power. At present, when have-not blacks, Mexican-Americans, Puerto Ricans, Eskimos, native Americans, and whites try to act, they usually encounter elaborate ruses to reduce or eliminate their participation and influence.

Two examples from San Francisco point out what citizen participation in planning can accomplish. In the first, residents of Chinatown designed and proposed housing projects with a high number of occupants per square foot and with senior citizens near younger generations, in accordance with Chinese cultural values. The city initially turned down the proposal but accepted it when a large number of residents supported the plan. In the second example, black architects incorporated features congruent with black tradition in the United States by designing units with a shower and bath attached directly to a large living room that could be used to accommodate transient guests (Maruyama 1973:355).

However, some groups of citizens are unable to participate in the planning process because they do not share the necessary knowledge or technical sophistication. For these persons, advocacy planning is the only hope of representation. The advocate planner is their voice and represents their views to the decision makers. Advocate planners differ from most planners in their primary concern for low income or otherwise disadvantaged groups.

Some plans, such as those for environmental quality and transportation, must necessarily transcend local political boundaries and must therefore be handled on a state or regional basis. For example, comprehensive state planning is now under way in many states and is frequently accompanied by state-level activities involving supervision of local planning, coordination of local and intrastate regional planning, and occasionally, the institution of local planning.

Interstate regions are commonly composed of a group of states or parts of several states, which band together to work out a common problem or plan for a common resource or goal. Smaller intrastate regions may consist of several counties or municipalities. Thus, a river basin region may encompass all or parts of several states, while an environmental or sewage treatment problem may be common to several cities, towns, or counties. Acting alone, each could only partially solve the problem, but acting together, they can perhaps pool their resources to arrive at a better solution. In part, regional planning groups are a response to the impact of metropolitan growth on the rural areas, the need for resource and environmental planning, and the presence of regional needs such as transportation, and economic market areas.

The formation of regional planning organizations is frequently resisted by citizens who perceive regional bodies as one more layer of government in which they have no choice. Consequently, regional organizations are purposely limited in scope and advisory in activity. This problem will continue to haunt regional planning as federal pressure for planning increases and socioenvironmental problems worsen, unless the planning profession can educate the public so that they understand and participate in the planning process.

Regional planning has usually been based on political regions or physical-geographical ones having a common problem. We agree with Fisher (1969) that there is a need for more attention to human desires and patterns of living as compared to concern for land forms and political jurisdictions. In 1939, Howard W. Odum, a founder of the Department of City and Regional Planning at the University of North

Carolina, proposed that governmental policy should include programs of regional planning based on *cultural* regions. According to Odum:

a region has organic unity not only in its natural landscape, but in that cultural evolution in which the age-long quartette of elements are at work—namely, the land and the people, culturally conditioned through time and spatial relationships. Thus, Professor Aronovici defines regionalism as "the study of the relation of man to geographic areas, and the potentialities which this relation represents in terms of human welfare and progress. The history of tribes, nations and races is one long record of regional realism, in terms of expansion and contraction of regional boundaries (1964:156).

Because cultures, peoples, and nations grow from regional bases, it is impossible to understand or direct society except through a regional approach (Odum 1964:153). Regional delineations should take into consideration the organic human-culture regional areas, the geographical factors of situation and climate, the political factors of organization and control, and the technological aspects (Odum 1964:308–309).

Odum found that, in order for the characterization of one region to be useful in planning, it had to be contrasted to and compared with other regions in the nation. In this way, the regional approach could become a dynamic tool in the attempt to understand the living geography of a nation and the relation of each region to the whole; it could have a valuable application in the testing of proposed national policies on a regional scale.

National planning and regional planning generally go together, and ideally both should act to develop the concepts of constructive, farsighted management (Gillie 1967:9). The Appalachian Regional Development Program which was initiated by the United States Congress in 1965, the Tennessee Valley Authority, and the Mississippi and Ohio Valley Committees are examples of coordinated national and regional planning (Newman 1972; Odum 1964).

Various federal agencies have been engaged in planning for the economy, employment, international economic relations, social planning for public health, housing, education, recreation, manpower, social security, interstate migration, and rural and urban rehabilitation. A major part of the federal level's present involvement in planning consists of granting funds to state and local governments for transportation planning, urban beautification, urban planning and renewal, and economic development.

At present, federal planning policy is formulated and implemented by a multitude of middle-level bureaucratic offices with highly specialized personnel, information, technical expertise, and influence, each of which can carve spheres of dominion in policy implementation (Rondinelli 1973:15). Examples include the Model Cities program, antipoverty legislation (Donovan 1967), the Public Works and Economic Development Act (Rondinelli 1969), and Federal Highway Assistance (Morehouse 1969; Levin and Abend 1971).

Although federal level planning is currently fragmented into operative and policy setting roles, its ideal role is directive or guiding. In other words, the top level of social policy should be involved with comprehensive and coordinated policy making and the directions in which the country should move. The local governments should then implement the directives, with state and regional governments guiding and coordinating local efforts. In some instances, such as desegregation and energy planning, the federal level cannot simply be involved with policy making, but must also plan policy since the program must be implemented in all areas of the country.

When the federal level engages in planning and passes instructions to the states and local governments, the process is termed centralized and is described as planning from the top down. The public, states, and localities may or may not be given a chance to comment on the plans before they are implemented. Although this form of planning "for" a community may make the mechanics of planning more efficient, there is no proof that the result of the plan is better. Typically, the public views the entire process as dictatorial, elitist, and paternalistic. Advocates of community control criticize this approach for taking away the freedom of self-control. Many planners oppose the top down approach because it forces the profession to fight through a growing jungle of rules, regulations, standards, guidelines, and paperwork.

The decentralized process of planning from the bottom up, on the other hand, allows the community to make its own decisions and plans, while the planner handles the technical end of the process. Although this approach is more difficult to achieve because of the larger number of persons involved, plans are generally more readily accepted by community members who feel the plans are theirs. This closer touch with the community aids the development of plans which are more responsive to the problems, needs, and desires of community members.

Anthropologists can work as planners on all four levels of planning: national, regional, state, and local. At every level, however, they must remember that they are operating within a political system and must work within values which at times may run counter to their own. They must reconcile their values, the values of their discipline, and the values of the political system so that they can effectively fight within the system rather than flee from it. Anthropologists in planning must be committed to planning and must be willing to live on a battle line; they should realize they are going to win some of the issues and lose others.

Planning on a national scale offers opportunities for anthropologists in administrative and staff positions, particularly in the federal agencies of Health, Education and Welfare, and the Department of Housing and Urban Development, because national plans must recognize the human component. In 1934, the now-defunct National Planning Board said that the application of anthropology to national planning would have enormous significance if the study of man were used to obtain a clear view of the structure, interests, and activities of human beings, and that, in any plan concerning human activities, anthropology could contribute valuable insight on the conditions and states of mind of the people (National Planning Board 1934:52). While contributions to national policy have been and will continue to be important, anthropology's impact on this level will be necessarily limited because there are fewer jobs available than on regional, state, and local levels.

On the regional level, the community study method is potentially useful in planning because it can provide a living cultural snapshot of a relatively large geographical area by examining the relational systems, values, and customary behavior of people in time and space. The natural history, or inductive, approach of the community study method allows for the study of communities, relationships, systems, and subsystems, so that they may be compared and contrasted to discover what is typical and varying in the structure and process of a cultural region. This method of comparing and contrasting regions could be used to determine necessary regional modifications in national policy and to facilitate the use of regions as testing grounds for various proposed federal plans and policies.

On the state and local levels, there are opportunities for anthropologists to work closely with state and local officials and citizens in planning. In line with this they may effectively consult with state legislative staff in preparing legislation, or with local planners or officials in drafting new ordinances. Particularly in local planning, we see anthropologists' most important roles to be those of facilitating and initiating community planning efforts and training and consulting with community members.[3] For example, when we were involved in planning in a rural Florida county, we first had to convince community members and local officials that planning was necessary because state level planners and legislators were considering laws requiring local planning. A key aspect of convincing the persons involved was a knowledge of the community through firsthand observation and participation. During the planning process, we not only taught local officials and community members to plan for themselves, but we also continuously fed information to the county commission (the organization that was responsible for the plan), and held regular meetings with citizens.

When aiding a community to plan for itself, it is extremely important for anthropologists to remember that the primary planners are those in the community. Consequently, anthropologists should *not* make themselves indispensable. We have found that the most successful approach for anthropologists to take is that of the midwife, because people are usually wary of "experts."

As consultant planners on the community and state levels, anthropologists, through studying relational systems, can point out potential barriers such as racial or educational discrimination to citizen participation; can locate resources and the gatekeepers who control access to these resources in the system; and can identify the various groups within a system and help develop a plan that will include a voice for all. In promoting participation, anthropologists frequently will operate as mediators among community groups.

When acting as planning advocates, anthropologists may serve as cultural translators. Anthropologists have a long history of speaking up for "their" tribes or people, particularly in the South Pacific (Piddington 1970) and Latin America (Peattie 1968b), and more recently as advocates in the United States (Schensul 1974; Jacobs 1974).

---

3. For further discussion, see Peterson (1974b).

Anthropological skill in translating ideas and values cross-culturally will prove useful in pleading the cases of the disadvantaged before the power holders.

Conclusion

Anthropologists can make valid and valuable contributions working in policy analysis and planning, even though they, like other social scientists, sometimes have exaggerated doubts or make overly ambitious claims about their contributions to the solution of social problems. The perspectives of anthropology are particularly appropriate to combine with the skills of planning, because anthropology has what planning has always lacked: a greater connection with and understanding of the diversity of human wants expressed in the reality of life. We see anthropology's major contributions in the discipline's breadth of view, theories of change, study of systematic relationships in the context of an organic whole, means of controlling for value judgments, and use of inductive reasoning.

Anthropological research methods are usually broad, flexible, relatively unstructured, and based on the holistic perspective and the practice of continually testing data and hypotheses. In studying real life situations, each element or subsystem is placed within the context of its culture, and compared and contrasted with all other elements to gain a picture of the organic whole. This perspective allows anthropologists to view organizations and cultures as natural systems, and to recognize that problems of social policy planning may require the collaboration of several disciplines. While research for policy purposes often requires anthropologists to function as members of multidisciplinary teams, one of the major complaints of administrators is the general lack of teamwork skills among anthropologists. Mead (1973:5, 7) has pointed out that the last twenty-five years have been dominated by massive individual enterprises in the discipline which are notable for the style of the individual integrating intelligence but not for teamwork.

A key to the success of any endeavor is the inclusion of all pertinent data, but, rather than attempting an eclectic approach to collecting sociocultural data, anthropologists weigh the importance of each item within the system and then focus on the crucial ones. Systemic relationships can be elicited through the use of the community study method and other methods that emphasize induction and the discovery of the interrelationships of elements within the context of systems. The concept of systems proves valuable to anthropologists in action settings where a major part of their tasks as researchers and policy makers involves defining the boundaries of the system affected by a problem, determining the conceptual or theoretical levels on which the actors of the system are operating, and eliciting values through interaction patterns. However, anthropologists may need to communicate to nonanthropologists their understanding of systems, and facilitate communications among persons in various parts of the social policy process. Their ability to compare and contrast, by shifting levels of abstraction and conceptualization within and among systems, can allow them to act as facilitators and communicators, for example, between levels of government, between government and private interests, and among citizens, governmental representatives, and the private sector.

Nonetheless, since most plans and policies are intended to change the environment, citizens and some planning professionals may view anthropologists not as facilitators/translators, but as manipulators (Peattie 1968a). In one sense this is correct, since the power to conceptualize is the power to manipulate. Also, there are still some vestiges of paternalism among anthropologists, left over from the days of working in colonial administration. Perhaps if anthropologists approach action work with the attitude of the assisting midwife rather than the prescribing doctor, they can allay fears of manipulation and elitism.

The United States currently appears to be moving toward more planning, in an attempt to reduce conflict, improve efficiency, cut costs, and regulate society. Although planning may make American interactions and government more predictable, a healthy human society depends on the presence and stimulation of heterogeneity and some ongoing conflict. Anthropological research has demonstrated the viability of heterogeneity in human culture (Rubin 1961), and could be used to illustrate that too much concern with order may lead to an inability to adapt to change. Frequently, directed change is resisted either to vindicate the *status quo* or because of fear of the unknown.

Yet, once the processes of change are more fully understood, they often become something people can use rather than fear. Thus, anthropological theories and research methodologies dealing with the process of change can be vitally important to planners and administrators (Smith and Fischer 1970:82). Perhaps one of anthropology's greatest contributions is helping individuals to view change as growth and to understand its roots, processes, and outcomes.

The conditions which foster fruitful and productive change and cultural adaptations to change can be examined by using anthropological methods. Change can be planned to take place in one large jump, with consequently large unanticipated effects, or to occur incrementally through smaller changes directed to reach a goal over a period of time. Plans and policies are often best approached incrementally through achievable short and medium range goals that can be examined and understood before further change is planned, thus allowing the achievement of major goals through reaching successive subgoals. This organic approach to planned change uses the same method of thinking as Rothman, Erlich, and Teresa (1976) propose in their manual for planning social change.

The use of inductive reasoning in planning social policy and anthropology's means of controlling for value judgments are two further contributions of the discipline. Inductive reasoning allows the policy planner to explore situations and alternatives, unencumbered by preconceived models, and leaves him or her free to follow the natural logic and structure of a particular system. Cross-cultural knowledge and experience with value systems helps anthropologists to contribute to social policy planning in a number of areas: when there is a need to identify values which are to be satisfied; when a project implies that people will be making decisions and choices in the light of cultural values and cultural, economic, and social resources; when plans entail the interaction of individuals within a social structure or social organization and the ramifications of social networks for the passage of concepts, ideas, goods, and action; when it is necessary to analyze whether a strategy or project will have the desired effects upon the social system; when it is necessary to analyze the valuational and cultural components in the skill-resources available for development; and when it is necessary to evaluate the success of particular programs in light of their objectives (Belshaw 1972).

But, if anthropologists wish to have greater impact upon and apply their cross-cultural pool of knowledge to American institutions and policies, they must first change their popular image from that of a group of eccentrics working with bones and exotic cultures (Piddington 1970:128) to one of a practical profession which offers effective, comprehensive, sensitive, and workable solutions to current problems. As a beginning, they must realize that their models and theoretical constructs are not reality but only mirrors of reality which must be tested in applied situations. Anthropologists will have to learn to work within the constraints of American society and to make recommendations and accept responsibility for them. Finally, the discipline which concerns itself with the study of human beings must come to value applied contributions to human welfare as highly as it does academic contributions to the discipline. Then, perhaps anthropologists, with their holistic and dynamic approach to the understanding of peoples and the interactions of culture and biology, will take their place as important contributors to social policy.

21

SERVICE, DELIVERY, ADVOCACY, AND THE POLICY CYCLE

Michael V. Angrosino
and Linda M. Whiteford

In the previous essay, Heighton and Heighton discuss the contributions that practicing anthropologists can bring to the policy-planning process. In this essay, Michael Angrosino and Linda Whiteford examine policy formation and implementation as a social process. This process entails systematic interaction among policy makers, bureaucratic structures that carry out policy, and client populations to whom the policies are addressed. The classic model of policy analysis is the top-down model: policy decisions are passed from executive or manager to line agency personnel who transmit them to clients. In contrast, Angrosino and Whiteford propose a cyclical model which conforms more closely to their analysis of two case studies.

Michael V. Angrosino (Ph.D., North Carolina) is professor and chairperson of anthropology at the University of South Florida. He is a medical anthropologist whose research has been in the area of mental health policy, with an emphasis on problems of community adjustment among deinstitutionalized mentally retarded adults. He has also studied community-based substance-abuse programs. His fieldwork has been in the United States and the West Indies (Trinidad, Saba, Aruba, Surinam). He has worked as a consultant to community mental health centers and community-based retardation programs in Florida and has been an advisor to the Tennessee Department of Mental Health and Mental Retardation and to the National Association of State Mental Retardation Program Directors. He is currently an associate editor of *Human Organization* and a member of the Behavioral Sciences Advisory Council of the Association of Schools of Public Health.

Linda M. Whiteford (Ph.D., Wisconsin-Milwaukee; M.P.H., Texas) is associate professor of anthropology and medical anthropology track leader at the University of South Florida. She is a medical anthropologist who has done research on community advocacy and policy development, evaluation of the delivery of health services to the indigent, the politics of human reproduction, and family planning programs and policies. Her fieldwork has been in Mexico and the Southwestern and Southeastern United States.

The case studies presented in this essay, the Human Development Center and the Child Watch project in Tampa, Florida, demonstrate the processes by which new policy is developed in contrasting political and economic contexts. In each case, the line agency personnel were receptive to organized efforts of community advocacy groups that presented them with information and suggestions for policy modifications. Locally based practicing anthropologists were able to assist in the process of policy formation by collecting data and assisting participants in the conceptualization of problems related to policy issues at the macro-level.

Angrosino and Whiteford conclude with an analysis of policy making as a social process that is founded upon a feedback process between line agencies and client groups. In this process, innovative social policy arises as people raise issues about the consequences of existing social policy. In the cases described here, policy decisions were made that changed line agency performance, without the intervention of so-called "decision makers" at the executive or managerial level. Angrosino and Whiteford demonstrate that practicing anthropologists can have significant impact on policy at the local level. It is this level that provides the testing ground for national and state policies which must respond to local needs if they are to survive.

THIS ESSAY ASSUMES that the most critical issue in health policy *is* health policy. Regardless of specific problems which are the subjects of decision making, the underlying question is: how is policy *made* (i.e., authored, promoted, implemented, and evaluated)? This question is of particular relevance to applied social scientists who wish to contribute meaningfully to debates on substantive policy issues.

The relevance of this question has been amplified by recent trends

She has served as consultant to several local and regional health service agencies and to the Children's Defense Fund in Washington, D.C. The focus of her current research is on the political economy of health, exportation of high technology medical services, and ethical issues in human reproduction.

This essay was originally prepared for presentation in the Key Symposium entitled "Contemporary Health Policy Issues and Alternatives: An Applied Social Science Perspective," at the 1984 annual meeting of the Southern Anthropological Society in Atlanta, Georgia. The original version of the essay appears in the 1984 Proceedings of the Southern Anthropological Society published by the University of Georgia Press (Hill 1986). The essay is reprinted here by permission of the Southern Anthropological Society.

in our political system. These trends include the general conservatism of the Reagan Administration and Congress, increased skepticism about the value of many social programs developed during the half century which followed the depression of the 1930s, concern about the size and scope of the federal budget and deficit, the shift from categorical to block-grant funding, the emphasis (merely ideological or in practice) on local government support versus federal intervention in community service program delivery, the ideological or actual acceptance of the notions of volunteerism, and private-sector support for community programs (Champagne and Harpham 1984).

This political climate is likely to dominate health and human service policy for several years to come. One consequence is that standard assumptions about the policy process, as derived from the classic policy analysis literature, cannot be taken for granted. In the pages to follow, we describe briefly the classic model of policy analysis and introduce an alternative model. We then use this alternative model to examine two case studies in the field of health policy. These studies present instances in which policy developed at the initiative of a service agency or a local advocacy group. The first case, that of Opportunity House, predates the political climate of the 1980s. The second case, that of Child Watch, reflects post-1980 conservatism in social programs. The essay concludes with a comparison of the two cases and a consideration of how the lessons derived from these studies may be applied elsewhere by anthropologists working in the health field.

Models of the Policy Process

Traditional policy analysis assumes that policy flows downward, from legislators, administrators, or other elite groups (see Presthus 1974; Thompson 1981:252–282). Service agencies are treated as implementers of policy that carry out directives from on high, or respond to pressure from some designated service community; they are rarely viewed as creative partners in the process (Hargrove 1975). The very label ''agency'' connotes standing in for someone else. The literature suggests that agency staff often accept their uncreative lot in the delivery of health and human services. Moreover, the perceived marginality of their decision making position may be one factor in the development of a "burnout" syndrome among human service workers (Emener 1979).

Proponents of the classic model stress the innovative roles of legislative/executive bodies. They imply that the failure of policy to achieve stated goals is due to the foot-dragging of uncomprehending agency staffs. In the case of public programs, the staffs may form a kind of permanent bureaucracy that endures even as creative planners come and go. Having no stake in the game of shifting policy directives, agencies can be perceived easily as mere cogs in the wheels of the policy process. With the new emphasis on local initiatives, however, it seems clear that those most directly involved in service delivery will have to take a more active role if policy is to continue to evolve.

Public policy has been defined as "whatever governments choose to do or not to do" (Dye 1972:1). In other words, the making of policy requires a set of options from which a decision maker must select a course of action. The task of traditional policy analysis was to identify and clarify these options. While some social scientists have become decision makers themselves, as in C. Wright Mills' "philosopher king" analogy, most anthropologists interested in policy have played Mills' role of "adviser to the king" (1959:179–181). They have seen themselves as "knowledge transfer specialists" (Hobbs 1979) who research the scholarly literature on a given issue, translate it into everyday English, and present a set of clearcut recommendations to decision makers. This task is a worthy one, but it has caused us to lose sight of basic theoretical guideposts from our discipline.

The "knowledge transfer" approach often leads us to think of policy as deriving from a simple input-output process, such as one finds in the rationalist school of political science theory (Finsterbusch and Motz 1980:23–39; Frohock 1979). The problem with this model is that it neglects to place policy in its widest social and cultural context. It defines policy as an isolated process and an end in itself. Policy may be, in Dye's terms, a decision, and that decision may be based on the clarifying analyses of social scientists. But both decision makers and policy analysts are part of social networks. Because their policy decisions may affect society, there is a strong likelihood that they will have a ripple effect, stirring up as many new ideas and problems to be solved as solutions. Further, those affected by decisions should be viewed logically as offering their own input into decision making in the form of their response to policy. Even outright resistance is not a dead end but a creative response, insofar as it stimulates a reformulation of policy. Moreover, policy does not begin with reasoned input and end with a rational decision. Each time an issue is revisited, different people or institutions are likely to be involved in decision making.

For example, in 1946 Congress passed the Mental Health Act, which recognized some basic service needs of that era by providing for psychiatric and mental health research (Ozarin 1982). It also created the National Institute of Mental Health (NIMH), a centralized administrative agency to implement guidelines for training and research. But NIMH, by faithfully implementing the mandate for training and research, spawned a new generation of mental health professionals whose concerns were not with institutional psychiatry, but with community-based treatment. This shift of emphasis in service delivery was not entirely unintended by the framers of the Act, but neither was it a primary goal. Although NIMH was established to administer a few specific programs, by using its discretion about whom to fund and for what projects, NIMH in effect replaced Congress as the primary decision maker of mental health policy.

The standard model of legislation leading to the creation of an agency to implement policy must be broadened to include the evolution of the agency's own perception of its role and scope. In the case of NIMH, it seems safe to assume that the rise of a citizens' advocacy movement in mental health during the 1960s was stimulated by the pro-patient outlook fostered in the 1950s. It was this movement, rather than "policy analysis research" by congressional staffs, which impelled the President to appoint the Joint Commission on Mental Health and Illness in 1961. In turn, this Commission's investigations led to the Community Mental Health Centers Act of 1963 and the subsequent modern "revolution" in mental health practice (Wagenfeld and Jacobs 1982).

A more useful model for understanding the ever-expanding evolutionary sequence of policy formulation is represented by the *policy cycle* approach (May and Wildavsky 1978). Analysts in this school have identified the following eleven steps that move a mere "good idea" to the status of implemented policy (Jones 1984:27–28):

1. Perception/definition (What is the specific problem which needs to be addressed? Do I have a good idea as to how it should be addressed?)
2. Aggregation (Can I convince some other people that my idea is a good one?)
3. Organization (Can I form this group of concerned citizens into a body that can be effectively mobilized for action?)
4. Representation (Does our organization have access to decision makers? If not, how can such access be obtained and maintained?)
5. Agenda-setting (How can we convince the decision makers that the issue is one deserving priority attention?)
6. Formulation (Can workable, feasible solutions be devised?)
7. Legitimization (Can the solution of choice be supported by all the people needed to make it work?)
8. Budgeting (Can adequate funding be allocated to support this solution?)
9. Implementation (Can an appropriate agency be set up to carry out this mandate?)
10. Evaluation (Is the agency achieving its stated goals? Do gaps in service still exist? Why? Are they amenable to solution?)
11. Adjustment (Can the program be modified so as to deal with perceived gaps? Is additional programming necessary?)

This model makes clear that the making of decisions is only one small part of a much larger process which involves many more actors than the analyst and decision maker. Moreover, this process is cyclical in nature. Policy does not stop with implementation because the evaluation of implemented programs generates new information about unanticipated consequences that may require new policy solutions in the future.

In summary, the traditional model views policy as flowing downward from legislators, administrators, or other decision makers. Agencies are simply implementers of policy or, at worst, stumbling blocks to the realization of policy goals. Community advocates may make suggestions to decision makers, but their advice may or may not be factored into policy analysis. In the alternative model, policy is generated from those who implement policy or those affected by it as well as by high-level decision makers. Agencies may be creative identifiers of policy needs, legitimate repositories for justification of client need, and evaluators of existing services in close touch with and hence more responsive to the attitudes of clients or their advocates than those in centralized authority positions.

This cyclical model is strikingly congruent with traditional anthropological theory, specifically functionalism as presented by Malinowski in *A Scientific Theory of Culture* (1944). Malinowski's premise was that all human beings come equipped with basic needs which he did not label precisely, but which may be grouped under the rubric "nurturance." These needs are a consequence of the biological fact that human infants are born in a helpless condition. Their need for nurturance is the genesis of human social systems, for every society must create a set of "primary institutions" to satisfy these basic needs.

However, Malinowski recognized that no society is composed simply of primary institutions, for the latter create unintended problems of their own. Institutions which develop to meet these newly discerned needs are known as "secondary institutions." The process of need generation is not a static one, for institutions have the capacity to create new problems as they solve old ones. A living society is continuously in the process of generating needs. To put this concept somewhat differently, the culture engenders "striving sentiments" and a healthy society will evolve to help people achieve those perceived needs by modifying old institutions or even generating new ones (Leighton 1959:395–420).

Malinowski's functionalism is a matter of seeing beyond the need-satisfaction of any part of the social system in order to understand the way in which the generation of needs and the evolution of institutions form a complex whole. Society is thus a large, functionally integrated feedback loop, with a culture and value system to give meaning to that integration. The function of this system is to permit the continuing adaptation of society to its environment—an environment which society helps to modify, or even to create.

Without succumbing to a biological reductionism that some have detected in Malinowski's theory, one may argue that, from a functionalist perspective, the policy cycle itself is part of a social institution of governance. As such, it modifies and even helps to create the social environment and aids in community adaptation, at least in the short run. If so, we may move beyond the traditional model of analyst-and-decision-maker to a better understanding of policy as a social process.

One of the few anthropologists who has examined how modern societies organize to administer policy is A. F. C. Wallace, who has pointed out that modern industrial societies are characterized by the presence of "administrative structures" comprised of three social groups: owners (or those under whose auspices work is done); target populations or clienteles; and administrative organizations themselves (1971:1–2). The latter are defined as the "action groups" and they are "responsible *for* the clientele and responsible *to* the owners" (1971:2). The "action group" is the vehicle by which "owners" (such as the government) achieve their impact on the clientele. There is a tendency, as societies evolve toward greater complexity, for administrative structures to survive by a process of "insulation," the adaptation of an ethical principle that seeks to eliminate any personal factor in administration. The agency is supposed to be a value-neutral implementer of policy (1971:5).

However, Wallace believes that it is inherent in the nature of administrative structures for them to be engaged in an almost constant process of "aging and reorganization," composed of incremental changes in structures analogous to the process of his more famous revitalization model. This gradual process is necessitated by the tendency in administrative structures toward "corruption," by which he means "a kind of emotional or social entropy" (1971:7). On a more positive note, administrative structures need also to "respond to changes in the demands made on them by their owners or their target/clientele populations (1971:8).

Administrative structures, despite their tendency toward insulation and corruption, are part of a self-correcting and adaptable system. Our only point of departure from Wallace's view is in the attempt to demonstrate that impetus for change can arise from *within* the agency (or administrative structure), or advocates from the client community who mobilize in certain ways. The following case studies illustrate the assumption of an activist role on the part of structures that are not usually thought of as creative partners in policy-related decisions.

How Local Structures
Become Creative Partners
in the Policy Cycle:
Two Case Studies

CASE I: OPPORTUNITY HOUSE

Opportunity House is a program that provides community-based treatment for clients with the dual diagnosis of mild or moderate mental retardation and emotional disturbance. Many of the clients have been in trouble with the law and have been adjudicated to the program in lieu of prison or a state institution. Opportunity House serves approximately twenty men at a time. There is currently a wide client age range (14–43), but the focus is on those between the ages of 18 and 25. Clients live in three strictly supervised group homes in a small town approximately twenty miles from downtown Tampa in Florida. During the day they attend a vocational and academic skills center in Tampa.

Opportunity House is structured along behavior modification lines with graded groups, a point system, and a token economy (Creer and Christian 1976: ch. 7; Drash, Stoffel, and Murdock 1983; Schwartz 1973). Clients move up from "Group 1," progressively acquiring more skills, responsibilities, and privileges. Successful clients are placed in an independent apartment program with minimal staff supervision. One innovation of particular interest is the use of peer groups in the behavior modification system. All resident clients have the right to vote on whether another client is ready to "move up." They form also a kind of appeals court if the staff recommends that a client should be "busted" to a lower group for some rule infraction. Peer groups meet regularly both at the group homes and at the skills center, and they have an important part in the process of developing a sense of independence and responsibility among clients.

Opportunity House was the first program in the state to serve this dually diagnosed population. Its success has made it something of a model program. However, a review of the program's history demonstrates that Opportunity House was not an "agent" of state policy, but rather a creative initiator of policy.

Opportunity House began in 1975 under the auspices of the local Association for Retarded Children (ARC). ARCs are advocacy groups, usually composed of parents or guardians of retarded persons and professionals in the field of mental retardation. They have had a significant impact on the development of an enlightened public consciousness about mental retardation (Holland 1980). The ARC serving the Tampa area was particularly vigorous in the 1970s because its chairperson was a state legislator who had staked out the area of health and human services as his particular concern. He saw to it that the local ARC expanded into the field of direct services and that one of the new programs was Opportunity House, designed to serve delinquent retarded teenagers. The initial plan was designed to serve both sexes, but the program has been limited to men because no funds were provided to establish separate domiciliary facilities for women.

The regional recognition of service needs in this case occurred as a result of close working relationships between a citizen advocacy group and an influential legislator. Out of this partnership there arose a new policy direction, a newly defined clientele in need of services, and a newly defined role of service provision for what had hitherto been a strictly advocacy organization.

During its early years, Opportunity House was a classic example of an agency that implemented policy initiatives. It operated under ARC auspices for three years. At that time, three staff members realized that the program was being abandoned by those who had originally inspired it. ARC had never liked the service delivery role and was taking steps to divest itself of all but its advocacy and community education functions. The state government, having endorsed the program, was unwilling to foster it, and seemed to be letting it languish with insufficient funding. The usual staff response to frustration of this kind is "burnout," but these staff members decided to fight for what they believed in and arranged a separation from the ARC. Opportunity House was reborn as an independent, nonprofit organization under separate contract to the state.

The new Opportunity House had two basic tasks. The state had to be convinced that the client population was a significant one and that it would be more cost efficient to train the young men for independent living in the community rather than to keep them in the state's institutional care for the rest of their lives. In addition, the state had to be convinced to provide adequate funding. These tasks were made more difficult by the local representative of the state's Department of

Health and Rehabilitative Services (HRS), who was oriented toward a medical treatment model of health care. He was impatient with the notion of "rehabilitation" and developmental approaches. Despite these problems, the original Opportunity House staffers, for reasons of personality and political ideology, were not inclined to be compliant bureaucrats. They refused to allow their program to die by inches like good "agents" should.

The confrontation between a small program serving a clientele most people would prefer to ignore and the state health department would not usually have captured public attention in such a way as to effect a major change in policy. However, at the same time that the state was pinching pennies with Opportunity House, it was also supporting a program purporting to serve the same clientele at a cheaper rate. This latter program was run by members of a religious sect with authoritarian tendencies; corporal punishment was their preferred means of behavior modification. Unlike Opportunity House, which demanded a considerable budget to support a well-trained staff and extensive programs of vocational and academic training, the second program seemed relatively inexpensive. For this reason, state officials indicated their intention to move the Opportunity House clients to the other program.

With the aid of a sympathetic local reporter, the Opportunity House staff produced evidence of the physical abuse practiced at the other center, as well as bookkeeping irregularities. The story broke in the press that the state was letting a legitimate program die for lack of funds while supporting a group of untrained religious zealots to the tune of $500,000 per year. There was consequent public outrage not only about the abuse of the poor and helpless clients, but also about the administrative failure to monitor services delivered in the name of the state.

Practicing "confrontation politics," the Opportunity House staff took its clients to the state capital where they camped out in the halls of the legislature. This spectacle inspired legislators to direct HRS to sign a contract with Opportunity House at a "reasonable rate." HRS complied, but with notable bad grace. There was a month lapse during which the staff worked voluntarily without pay. (To date, the staff has not been reimbursed for the wages lost during this period.) Over the years, HRS has also withheld clients deliberately from Opportunity House, but the basic relationship has been stabilized.

It is now accepted state practice to monitor all vendors (i.e., private organizations that deliver community-based services to state clients under contract) for compliance with fiscal regulations and for reasonable client outcomes. (The larger issues of quality assurance in a vendor system of community services are treated comparatively in Angrosino 1981.)

DISCUSSION OF CASE I

The brief review presented above illustrates two significant elements in current state policy (specifically for mentally retarded clients, but easily extended to the mental health system as a whole) that have been established, not by the traditional actors (state executive or legislative authorities) but by the agents of policy, working in conjunction with local advocates. These are as follows:

1. *It is both proper and feasible to set up service programs for dually diagnosed clients.* State policy has traditionally relied on a criterion of unitary diagnosis, such that mentally retarded clients with both problems (not to mention other complications, such as physical handicaps, or involvement with the juvenile justice system) have been excluded. The usual response is the designation of a "primary diagnosis," which means that a caseworker arbitrarily decides which problem is of greater importance, so that the client can be served in at least one system.

2. *The state has a moral as well as a political responsibility to the public to assure that programs funded to serve state clients are upholding acceptable standards of fiscal practice and therapeutic regimen.* The agency was able to establish these principles despite the opposition (or, at best, the passive neutrality) of both the legislature and the organized advocacy community for two main reasons. First, the Opportunity House innovations were part of a process in which the agency moved into an unoccupied service niche. No other agency served these clients who had, in fact, been legislated out of existence by the "unitary diagnosis" criterion. The ARC plan to serve "delinquent" retarded teenagers, not necessarily those with the specific problems grouped under the title "emotional disturbance," meant that no entrenched interests were challenged directly. There was certainly the obstacle of tradition expressed by the feeling that because such a population had not been served previously, it could never be

served. But that feeling is quite different from one that might be expressed by an entrenched bureaucracy which felt its own turf to be directly threatened. In effect, Opportunity House proved that it *could* be done, and started people thinking about the economic and social benefits of doing it. "Why didn't anyone think of this before?" became a potent cry that pushed the issue onto the decision makers' agenda. The state responded primarily by allocating funds to serve this population, but HRS first chose to direct these funds to an agency other than the one that had raised the issue. The new service orientation was established as a priority by the power of the state's budget, but Opportunity House was in danger of being cut off because it had dared to step out of its accepted role.

Second, the independence of Opportunity House meant that it was not part of the bureaucratic establishment and had nothing to lose by taking its case to the "streets" rather than "working through channels." Because it had no stake in the structure, Opportunity House could mobilize the press and civil liberties attorneys, and through them the public. The right of the state to allocate funds for a desirable service to any vendor it chose was not the issue. Rather the issue was whether or not, once having allocated monies, the state had an obligation to see that taxpayer dollars were being spent wisely. No one inside the structure could afford to ask this question, for who could tell where the eye of scrutiny would fall next? In the structural sense, Opportunity House had nothing to lose by taking a moral stance. It knew it was delivering good service and was going to go out of business if *no* state accountability system was established. Because of the dramatic confrontation orchestrated by Opportunity House, the state was forced to accept the principles espoused by the agency. By working without pay when necessary, the staff demonstrated publicly the moral superiority of their own principles. The principles upheld by Opportunity House thus became state policy and went through the stages of the policy cycle outlined earlier, but with the crucial difference that the innovations began with the agency set up to implement an older policy in which inconsistencies had been discerned.

An organization can have a creative part in the policy cycle by making those who hold power more aware of feasible responses to unmet needs and by depicting itself as sufficiently outside the system to engage in meaningful critique, but not so far outside that it is just a gadfly. The state was made to understand that it needed Opportunity House, with all its obstreperous antics, more than Opportunity House needed the state, once a demand had been identified for client services that could not be served by another reputable agency. Opportunity House was able to take the higher ground. The staff had no *personal* stake in the outcome of the confrontation. Rather, the welfare of the agency's clients (and, by extension, all the helpless wards of the state) became the public issue.

The question must certainly arise: now that Opportunity House is an established program with an excellent community reputation and reasonably amicable relations with the state, has it been co-opted? Is it too closely identified with a certain client population to engage in further innovation? Is it too much a part of the system ever again to be willing or able to present itself as a model alternative to state policy? As of this writing (1985) it appears that Opportunity House is determined to keep its activist role alive. It has taken two steps in that direction.

During the past year, the staff has voiced a conclusion that was unthinkable a few years ago: not all clients are capable of "graduation." For some, the severity of the behavioral problems makes it unrealistic to expect them to become independent members of the community, although they can still lead productive lives under close supervision. These clients experience the frustration of learning skills but never being able to graduate, and hence the benefits of the program are vitiated. Current policy posits two options: the institution, or independent living in the community. Opportunity House is now in the process of defining a third alternative: the creation of a special group home in the community (i.e., not on the same campus with the basic group homes) with a degree of supervision intermediate between the group homes and the independent apartment program. Students with irremediable behavior problems could "graduate" successfully to this new kind of living setting without the stigma attached to perennial failure to attain independent living status. Hence, staff are on the cutting edge again by defining new service options for their own current clients, and for those referred directly into this new intermediate group home program from other programs around the state. In other words, Malinowski's equation is operative: one solution generates new needs that require new solutions.

Second, the staff has requested and brought into existence a strong, independent Board of Trustees. More than a standard "letterhead"

Board of community worthies, the Opportunity House Board is comprised of people with active interest in the clients and the rehabilitation program. The Board is involved in long-range planning, and has direct oversight in areas of client services, physical plant, financial management, and community awareness (public relations). Because Board members are mostly persons with their own established reputations in the community and not beholden to HRS, the Board has become a force for maintaining the in-the-system-but-not-of-it status of Opportunity House. The particular nature of the Board makes it possible for Opportunity House to maintain its reputation as a critic and rethinker of HRS policy, even while the program itself operates comfortably within the framework of the HRS system. In sum, the agency created the Board to serve its own needs for a moral arbiter. After establishing a working partnership with HRS, the staff could no longer comfortably perform this role. Thus, staff mobilized the community to serve this need, rather than waiting for the community to demand that the agency perform in a certain way.

CASE II: CHILD WATCH

Child Watch was a local fact-finding and advocacy project organized in response to President Reagan's 1981 budget reductions. The project was organized by the Children's Defense Fund (CDF), an advocacy and lobbying group based in Washington, D.C. In Tampa the project was composed of a coalition of voluntary public service groups. The task of Child Watch was to trace how the loss of federal monies affected local delivery of social services, particularly in the area of health care delivery to children.

"Since 1980, children have come first in budget sacrifice. They lost one of every ten dollars previously provided them by their national government for critical preventive children's and family support programs." (Children's Defense Fund 1984:15). "Children also have been the first victims of poverty. More than 3.1 million children, 3,000 a day, have fallen into poverty since 1979. Their thirty-one percent poverty increase is the sharpest rise in child poverty since poverty statistics have been collected. Less than one-third of these new poor children will be lifted from poverty by economic recovery alone" (Children's Defense Fund 1984:17). The President proposed eleven billion dollars in cuts in programs crucial to children's well-being in 1982; the following year an additional cut of nine billion dollars was proposed. In FY 1984, the Administration asked that more than 3.5 billion dollars be additionally cut and in FY 1985, an additional three billion dollars in cuts was sought.

The lack of a clearly articulated national child health policy made this fiscal restructuring possible; it also provided the impetus for advocacy and lobbying activities resulting in local and national policy changes. The resultant developments in child health policies were generated from outside the traditional policy creation channels. The Child Watch case study provides an opportunity to trace the development of health policy from its inception as a response to severe fiscal budget reductions, through local advocacy activity and centralized nationwide research, to its contribution to the Children's Survival Bill (H.R. 1603, S. 572) introduced in the U.S. Congress in the spring of 1984. Thus the case study is an example of the policy cycle as a social process.

In order to understand policy development within Child Watch as a social process, it is important to review briefly some of the history and structure of child health care policy in the United States. In 1912, President Theodore Roosevelt created the federal Children's Bureau in an effort to improve health care for mothers and children. In 1921 Congress passed the Sheppard-Towner Maternity Act to promote the "welfare and hygiene of maternity and infancy" (Children's Defense Fund 1984:43) by providing federal funding to help states in that effort. The programs incorporated in the Sheppard-Towner Maternity Act later (1935) became the basis of the Title V Maternal and Child Health Program. In 1935 Congress enacted the Aid to Dependent Children (ADC) program as part of the Social Security Act. This program was designed to provide families in which one parent was dead or missing with financial support to raise the children. The cost of the program was shared between state and federal budgets. In 1950 Congress passed the Social Security Act Amendments which specifically created a medical assistance program providing matching federal funds for health care services purchased for ADC children. In the fifteen years between 1950 and 1965, the federal government strengthened this program of medical assistance, which in 1965 became the Medicaid Program. An important aspect of the historical development of child welfare legislation is that it shows the development and institutionalization of a set of attitudes, values, and goals which have been challenged covertly by the Reagan Administration.

Initially, the urgency to analyze the data generated by Child Watch was very real. Data were needed to document the effect of loss of services and to present arguments against further reductions in federal aid for children's health care costs. Research findings had to be available for analysis and presentation before the next budget was presented to Congress. Once this early type of information was sent to Washington, it became obvious that the data raised questions which required continued research. After two phases of the research were completed, the evaluation and public presentation of that information generated local concern about the consequences of loss of federal monies on the welfare of children in the community. Congruent with the third phase of research, a local public awareness and education campaign was undertaken in conjunction with lobbying efforts on behalf of changes in health care policy. Before we describe the details of the activities that went into this project and their implications for policy making, we will note how these activities exemplify the cyclical process of policy creation.

Policy development, viewed from the processual orientation, incorporates the following elements: the identification and analysis of a problem or a problematic situation; the involvement of a decision maker who recommends policy changes; and the implementation of these policy recommendations. Once recommended changes have occurred, evaluation of them and their consequences are analyzed in light of new problems and policy solutions. This model approximates closely the activities that occurred during the operation of Child Watch.

Child Watch expressed a need to document changes in health status as a response to changes in health policy. Human service professionals and others could both anticipate and imagine the effects of loss of federal revenues on local programs to a disadvantaged and voiceless population. However, imagination alone could not provide the kind of statistical data required to document the effects of these budget cuts on local programs. Impetus from a national organization provided the mechanism by which local groups began to gather data which addressed this question. This mechanism took the form of a standardized series of questions to be asked of specific categories of people in health and human services: 250 interviews were conducted in an eighteen-month period. Four topical areas were identified as programs significant to the welfare of children and simultaneously dependent upon federal support: child health; child welfare; day care; and Aid to Families with Dependent Children. Within each topical area, interviews were conducted with program administrators and policy makers, providers, advocates, and clients of these programs.

Decisions were made at CDF that structured the local project. One of these was that local researchers were to focus on the policy makers, those who carry out the policies, and those whose lives were being affected by the policies. Relationships among federal, state, and local policy makers were an explicit part of the research design. The social process of decision making, implementation, and evaluation was, in part, documented by the project because it measured program and policy changes by interviewing the same people about the same programs at three-month intervals.

Child Watch information was applied to policy decisions in several ways. First, information was sent to Washington, where the CDF staff analyzed it. Information was collected with the knowledge that it would be used both locally and nationally. It was therefore possible to seek information about the history of services, changes in programs over the last several years, and other data that would provide a context for understanding the potential, as well as the real, impact of the changes taking place. Knowledge of the intended use of the findings made it possible to collect data that would make the information valuable in policy decisions.

The results of Child Watch were shared with a number of people and organizations. Through CDF, the information was delivered as testimony at the United States Senate Hearings of the Subcommittee on Nutrition of the Committee on Agriculture, Nutrition, and Forestry. State and federal legislators were informed of the project's findings. Television, radio, and newspaper interviews were given; brief summaries were supplied to local newspapers and neighborhood newsletters. During the project, a grassroots coalition of groups was created. Each group received updates of the findings as the research progressed and an analysis of the final conclusions of the research project. CDF also mailed a nationwide newsletter focusing on Child Watch results. This newsletter was sent to each project approximately every three months and reported findings of importance selected from all the Child Watch projects around the nation, thereby providing access to comparative data.

On the basis of the information produced, the Child Watch coalition chose to take an active role in the development of health care policy for children of the poor. This decision was facilitated, in part, by providing documentation of need, and structured, programmatic recommendations to policy makers. Channeling Child Watch information to policy makers occurred in two ways: vertically from the local project to CDF in Washington, and from them to members of Congress. Information also moved horizontally among various projects through the CDF newsletter. It went from the local project to state and local legislators, to the supporting organizations, and to the local public.

Many recommendations made by Child Watch addressed the issue of child health care and the lack of access to care for children of the indigent. As a direct result of this project in Tampa, two pediatricians and several nurses have established free clinics three times a year to treat children of migrant farm workers who otherwise would lack medical care. At the time of the initial research, no local private practice pediatrician would see a Medicaid child in his or her office. Child Watch provided documentation of the inadequacy of child health policy at a time when there was a local initiative to create both a children's hospital and a free-standing children's clinic designed especially to care for poor children. Health care policy that focused explicitly on the provision of health care to children of the poor was an integral part of the founding philosophy for these new institutions. The children's hospital and the clinic are planned for the near future. By focusing attention on a particular problem and documenting the legitimacy of that problem, Child Watch moved actively into the policy process.

DISCUSSION OF CASE II

Policy implications of this research can be examined at several different levels. First is a redefinition of a particular population. Children of the poor, and, more recently, the newly enlarged category of children of the working poor, were reconceptualized as a category of people at risk. In the past, they were ignored easily because they had little power within the political system. Federal programs designed to care for children have been perceived recently as causing deficits in the budget; in truth, these programs are deficit containers if they protect and prepare children for self-sufficiency. Child Watch, by focusing attention on this population, its unmet needs, and the potential social and economic costs associated with lack of preventive health care, highlighted the need for specific policy development on their behalf.

This particular population is a category caught between publicly expressed beliefs in the welfare of all children and the private support of a fiscally conservative government. As local agencies responded to the Child Watch research, an advocacy coalition was created to recognize this category of children. In a sense, the budget cuts provided the opportunity for legitimization of this at-risk population. While the plight of poor children, especially in the area of health care, was acute before the budget cuts, the reductions exacerbated an already intolerable situation so as almost to "force" policy to be written and legislation to be created to protect these children.

The second way in which health policy was influenced, and has the potential for continued influence, is through the coalition of agencies and individuals drawn together in this effort. Child Watch served as a central research and advocacy body which contacted, and was contacted by, individuals concerned about the health of children. Originally, people were contacted to work on the project or to provide information and expertise in the development of a data base. Many of them became sponsors of Child Watch. Sponsors were people with whom we shared our findings, and they supported and gave credibility to our public statements. They formed a loose network, tied by their interest and commitment to the topic. Others joined the coalition because of their professional involvement in child health. Administrators, state and regional elected representatives, and others who were interviewed repeatedly in the process of the research, joined the network and took their professional involvement beyond vocation to advocacy. In this way, Child Watch provided a mechanism to draw people together without binding them in a structural way. The policy implications of this coalition were powerful and immediate. Because of the reasons that people were drawn together, the lack of structural constraints, and their own personal and professional power in the community, changes became possible that otherwise would not have occurred.

Child Watch is but one example of how policy can develop outside traditional channels: it demonstrates how a group structured as a research-based coalition can become an advocate group which helps to redefine the perceptions about a category of people and provides a mechanism to aid adaptation of the community. Because of its structure, Child Watch was able to respond to national political issues as they were translated into health care systems on the local level. Its local application, particularly in the area of health policy, reflected the concern, commitment, and action of individuals and, as such, the social process of policy development and implementation. The next phase of Child Watch incorporates monitoring and evaluation of new services and the consequences of present policy decisions. The analysis of new services and policy solutions will likely engender indentification of new problems, thus continuing the cyclical process of policy development.

Conclusions

The two case studies presented here demonstrate clearly how service and advocacy agencies can function as creative initiators of policy. Each case describes the development of policy as a social process. It is important to note the similarities shared by Opportunity House and Child Watch, both in their structure and in the type of client they serve. In each case, the client population is dually disadvantaged. In the case of Opportunity House the clients were mentally retarded and emotionally disturbed. In the case of Child Watch, the clients were poor and children. Both populations have characteristics that traditionally deny them access to power, and both groups of clients were, until recently, unrecognized or denied recognition as legitimately "needy" populations. The client populations were community based, as opposed to institutionally housed. The survival needs of both groups exceeded their parents/guardians' abilities to provide for them. It is this discrepancy between needs and abilities that makes clients of them. Their inability to speak as their own advocates places them in a position of dependence on others who can present their case in public.

The greatest structural similarity between Opportunity House and Child Watch is that they are external to extant bureaucracies, and yet have credibility in the eyes of those very bureaucracies. In both cases, the agencies provided a mechanism by which people could openly criticize the bureaucratic structure without jeopardizing their jobs or creating internecine antagonism. The two case studies demonstrate how policy can be influenced from the middle level and from the outside: they also show that outside organizations of this type fill voids left by institutional superstructures.

The process described in this essay is not restricted to these two case studies. The two cases themselves encompass many variations. One organization existed for a number of years, while the other was only recently established. One has a paid staff, and the other is strictly volunteer. One began from a grassroots initiative, while the other developed in response to a need perceived in Washington. Yet, between them they exemplify both the social process of policy development and the role an anthropologist can play in it.

Anthropologists working in service agencies are particularly well suited to have an impact on policy decisions because of their methodological and conceptual skills. In the two cases presented here anthropologists responded to local needs by gathering data and conceptualizing problems reflective of issues that were the focus of state and national concern. The result was a legitimization of particular populations as needed and deserving of attention. The process entailed using the anthropologist as a credible outsider to distill basic data from the political and social "noise" and to formulate programmatic policy recommendations based on that information. In the instance of Child Watch, once the population was recognized as a legitimate one with valid problems, local groups served as advocates for better health care. On the national level, a congressional bill was introduced to protect the rights of children. Locally, pediatricians and others were made aware of and developed a concern for the lack of medical care; they began to design both a free-standing outpatient clinic (at no cost to the indigent) and a children's hospital in which some beds are to be reserved for the needy. In the case of Opportunity House, initial identification of a dually diagnosed, legitimate service population was followed by identification of new services that could best serve the needs of that population. These service innovations were underscored by the agency's ability to persuade the state to recognize and systematize a process for monitoring community-based services delivered in its name.

In sum, the model suggested here sees policy as part of a complex feedback process, with solutions to one problem raising new issues to be solved by new solutions which may be developed by players in the policy cycle other than those posited in the classic policy analysis literature. In the cases presented here, the creative change agents were located in programs established to implement older policies. Perceiving new needs and in a position to act on their own initiatives, these agents stimulated important policy shifts. Given current federal orientation toward local initiatives, the fact that both of these programs effectuated change in policy without first seeking the approval of the relevant central authority is an object lesson to applied social scientists. One can have an impact on policy development at the sometimes more accessible middle level of service provision and advocacy without having to be an advisor to the "king."

Applied social scientists can clarify the policy process for agency staff so that they become more aware of their potentially creative roles. They can conduct research that results in a reconceptualization of a given service population so as to legitimize change in the service delivery system. By working with an agency newly armed with a positive identity resulting from its active role in policy development, applied social scientists can work within the new realities of the political system and become effective players in the policy cycle, combining in the process the roles of researcher and advocate.

22

TOWARD A FRAMEWORK
FOR POLICY RESEARCH
IN ANTHROPOLOGY

Pertti J. Pelto
and Jean J. Schensul

T he focus on public policy as a social process is
continued in this essay by Pertti Pelto and Jean
Schensul. Here, however, the emphasis is on the policy research roles
played by practicing anthropologists amidst the variety of settings and
levels where policy is made and implemented. Pelto and Schensul define
the practitioner who attempts to influence policy as a researcher who
takes action in decision-making arenas that are derived from research.
It is the view of these authors that policy advocacy is founded upon

Pertti J. Pelto (Ph.D., University of California, Berkeley) is professor of anthropology
and community medicine at the University of Connecticut. He is a medical anthropologist who has done fieldwork in Finland, Mexico, and in rural and urban settings in the
United States. In Finland, he examined the effects of technological modernization among
Lapland reindeer herders and dietary modernization in urban families. In Mexico, he
and his wife, Gretel, are currently engaged in research on food patterns, malnutrition,
and modernization in rural communities. He is director of the program in medical anthropology at the University of Connecticut, where he and his coworkers have carried
out several applied projects among minority populations, with particular attention to
health care and education.

Jean J. Schensul (Ph.D., Minnesota) is director of research at the Hispanic Health
Council in Hartford Connecticut and associate professor of anthropology at the University of Connecticut. Her fieldwork has been done in Mexico, Peru, and in the United
States. She has done many years of applied work among Puerto Ricans and other
minority groups in Connecticut. Her special interests are in urban applied anthropology
and policy issue in the fields of education and health care. She is a past president of
the Council on Anthropology and Education.

We want to express our appreciation to Elizabeth Eddy for the many thoughtful sug-
gestions which have improved this essay immeasurably. We are indebted also to Maria
Borrero, Executive Director of the Hispanic Health Council, for her consultation on the
Hartford case study.

research as the recommendations and actions that flow from research become operational in the creation or modification of public policy.

Pelto and Schensul summarize two cases in which policy-oriented anthropological research was conducted, recommendations were formulated, and action was taken to assert and defend the recommendations. In the first instance, practicing anthropologists provided research findings about the placement of school children in special education classes to a national agency with a mandate for policies in the area of education for the handicapped. Their recommendations influenced later legislation in this field. In the second instance, practicing anthropologists undertook action-research at the local level in Hartford, Connecticut. In this setting, research findings and recommendations about the policies governing health services for Blacks and Hispanics were taken up directly with health-related organizations in the community.

These cases lead to several conclusions about the roles of practicing anthropologists in the field of public policy and the steps that anthropologists can take to become more effective participants in this important field.

DURING RECENT YEARS anthropologists have engaged in considerable debate about the nature of policy research, whether or not anthropologists have been or should be involved in policy research, and the extent to which they have been influential in the creation or modification of public policy (see essays 17 and 20 in this volume; Stull and Moos 1981). Although there is general agreement among anthropologists that policy relates to decision making and social change, most writing on the subject assumes that the reader knows what policy is. This failure to define "policy" creates confusion. It permits any anthropologist who undertakes research related to contemporary problems to define his or her research as "policy related."

The general rubric of policy research in anthropology now includes a wide diversity of activities, including the Cornell Vicos Project in Peru (see essay 19), social impact assessments (Jorgensen 1981), research on the effects of government projects on local populations (Bee 1982; Gruenbaum 1981), and ethnographic descriptions of communities, schools, and other social settings within which contemporary issues are debated, implemented, or assessed (Burns 1975; Everhart 1975). In addition, there are innumerable examples of anthropological studies in which the final chapter of a book or concluding section of an article presents the implications of the study for policies of one kind or another. Any one or all of these types of research may, in fact, influence policy, but they do not necessarily represent policy research as we use the term here.

Weaver has noted that "many of anthropology's past contributions could be classified as policy-related if one defines policy science as helping decision makers set guidelines for action" (Weaver 1985). We agree that policies are sets of ideas or guidelines for action to be followed by governmental institutions, private organizations, or other public bodies and the individuals within them. They express values or philosophical assumptions about broad social and cultural conditions and are intended to suggest solutions to social problems (see essay 20). For example, federal policies about cultural pluralism in education embody values concerning democracy and suggest particular actions to be taken by school districts and individuals within school systems.

We deliberately use the word *policies* in the plural because in most settings there are multiple, often conflicting policies that may or may not be well articulated and that offer differing implications for action. Indeed, one of the most important contributions that anthropologists can make to the policy field is to articulate existing as well as potential policy alternatives in relation to particular issues.

The sets of ideas or guidelines that comprise policy include rationales or "theories of action." These theories of action contain implicit or explicit causal relationships such as: "if opportunities for getting jobs are equalized, the employment situation of minority groups will be improved." Usually, policy rationales and theoretical frameworks are not articulated as clearly by policy formulators as they would be by social scientists. Nevertheless, they are highly important theories concerning social actions and their consequences (cf. essay 6). Moreover, they are often derived from contemporary social science theory. In some cases, social scientists are invited officially to participate in the rationalization of a policy position. It is not uncommon for social scientists, like physicians and other expert witnesses, to testify on opposing sides in policy disputes although such social science confrontations are usually not documented (see essay 16).

Theories of action embedded in policy formulations are frequently analogous to medical folk beliefs. They may not reflect the best available knowledge, yet they have sufficient credibility to affect political action. The theoretical assumptions underlying policies are important but their lack of clear articulation allows them to become confused with the personal values and ideologies of the policy makers.

In public decision making arenas—in education, health, law enforcement, etc.—there are generally conflicting sets of policies. A change of administration or even lesser changes of personnel are likely to bring about new debates, negotiations, and discussions. Policy negotiations may occur within single settings—for example, within a single administrative unit such as a school or health care facility—or between several such settings. Policy negotiation often involves an entire network of local organizations or institutions and it may also involve discussions between local groups and federal offices. From this perspective, policies are not unchanging "constants." Rather, they are continually changing in relation to particular events, actors, and settings (Patton 1979).

The results of policy formulation at high administrative levels provide guidelines which must be given concrete interpretation at lower levels. The various agencies, organizations, and individuals in local arenas thus become vehicles for action with respect to policy implementation, modification, or even rejection. At the local level, where policy implementation is concretely manifested, the outcomes of policy are generally a blending of the original policy, the personalities of the actors, plus the economic considerations and the effects of specialized interest groups.

Outcomes of policy negotiations are strongly affected by the patterns of power distribution within specific settings and policy-making events. An understanding of power relationships and politics is crucial for an understanding of how policies are formulated and the ways in which compromises are reached between opposing interest groups. Although we are accustomed to thinking of the distribution of power in terms of "two sides" to a particular issue, this is a very unusual situation likely to be found only in highly polarized communities, or perhaps in legislatures at the moment of voting on a particular enactment. Much more usual is the pattern of multiple power sectors and points of view. For example, in urban health care systems, there is a variety of different patient categories, "third party payers," and different providers, each with its own constituencies and interests. Federal agencies also wield power in local settings through funding, monitoring, and indirect influence.

In summary, policy may be conceptualized as a process which may be found, observed, and influenced within a wide range of settings. At one extreme are the meetings and sessions of legislatures and other formal policy-making bodies that usually have no direct hand in implementation. As policy enactments from legislative or other deliberative bodies move closer to the local settings in which implementation takes place, policy-making continues, as each acting organization interprets, refines (or sometimes ignores) the laws, regulations, guidelines, and other expressions of formal policy. As such, policy formulation is neither scientific nor unscientific, although at various levels, the findings and writings of scientists may or may not be utilized. We turn now to the ways in which research enters into arenas of policy formulation and implementation.

Research and Public Policy

Research and public policy may be linked in several ways. First, each party in policy negotiations typically seeks to convince and impress others by presenting facts which support the point of view being advocated, meanwhile questioning facts presented by opponents. Nowadays, it is common for the main protagonists in policy formation to present large masses of statistics and other information to make their case. Often a governmental agency commissions a study to address the implications of a particular piece of legislation, or to define potential policy directions. Alternatively, professional researchers—anthropologists, economists, political scientists, and others—may see their research as having direct policy implications. This may take the form of modifying the underlying theory or theories in a political debate. For example, a major intent of earlier anthropologists attempting to influence policy conerning the "treatment" of racial differences was to change fundamental theoretical assumptions from biological determinism to cultural and environmental relativism (Boas 1948). On the other hand, social science researchers have often sought to affect policy by presenting descriptive information concerning locations of aboriginal hunting grounds, economic activities, sacred places, kinship patterns, or other cultural information (Paredes 1985; Pelto 1980).

Professional anthropologists and other social scientists sometimes seek to affect policy by developing programs or other activities designed to test theory or to establish environments within which new policies can be formulated. For example, in Hartford during the late 1970s medical anthropologists worked with community organizations to establish a health clinic in an underserved neighborhood. The main purpose was to establish a setting which permitted community residents to become involved in local and statewide policies affecting neighborhood health care and other services. Using this approach, some anthropologists have taken a more direct role in affecting the policy formulation process (cf. Borrero, Schensul, and Garcia 1982; Kimball essay 17; Peterson 1974b; Schensul and Schensul 1978). Most anthropologists, however, have not been inclined to take direct action with regard to policy making. The more usual mode has been to publish theoretical materials based on research, hoping that the results will be convincing enough to influence policy makers. There is still considerable debate about the efficacy of "influencing action through thought." Although it appears that anthropological research in the areas of race, culture, ethnicity, and other social issues have played a role in shaping contemporary public opinion and policy, this approach alone has been of limited effectiveness (Stull and Moos 1981; Eddy and Partridge 1978; Hicks and Handler essay 18; Harding and Livesay 1984). As several writers have noted, the form and content of our published work has not interested most primary actors in the policy formulation process.

An alternative strategy is to utilize as the primary point of intervention those arenas of power and decision making where policy issues are debated, generated, and carried out. Most of the literature on knowledge utilization points to this direction as particularly promising. Our contention is that anthropologists as policy researchers can make significant contributions in these settings if the theoretical and ideological frameworks underlying their positions are clarified, and the assumptions of other actors are made explicit. To be effective, these processes must take place in the settings where policies are made and implemented. We are in essential agreement with Kimball (essay 17), who notes that "there is need to make blade edge sharp the distinction between advocacy and data based policy." Anthropologists are not likely to be effective as mere advocates for desired social policies. Rather, we must use our research skills and theoretical perspectives effectively. The communication of our policy-oriented materials must be at the scene of policy making rather than in the groves of academe.

The perspective outlined above enables us to differentiate clearly between research about policy formulation and policy research. The former attempts to analyze the domains of policy as process; the latter involves the researcher as actor in the policy arena. The pages to follow present two case studies which examine these different aspects of the interplay between researchers and the policy arena. The first case describes ethnographic research commissioned by the Federal Bureau of Education for Handicapped (BEH) to examine the implications of special education legislation. The second case illustrates how a combination of research and theory testing influenced material and child health policy in the mid-New England city of Hartford, Connecticut.

Case I: Special Education and the Medical Model

During the period from 1977 to 1979, new federal and state laws were enacted concerning the placement and programming of special education students. This legislation (PL 94–142) was a consequence of strong lobbying by three primary sectors: parents concerned with the availability and appropriateness of special education programs; teachers faced with problems in the teaching of children with special needs; and physicians, psychologists, and other clinicians who viewed the problems of special education from a medical, particularly a psychiatric, perspective.

The legislation reflected three major sets of policies current in the 1970s. First, there was the emphasis given to involving parents in educational decisions affecting their children. In the legislative language, parents were to give "informed consent" before decisions could be made to change the placement of children in any special program. However the legislation did not clearly define "informed consent."

A second set of policies stressed the education of the "whole child." The law required that the child be placed in the "least restrictive environment." This policy, the legal language, and associated federal funding programs enabled the creation of numerous in-school and district programs, regional and local centers, and other alternative programs to meet the needs of individual children or groups of children with special learning problems. The law also created opportunities for teachers to send students off to special programs if they felt unable to offer special instruction to children with learning difficulties.

A third set of policies defined students' learning problems as medically related and therefore treatable with medically based or derived approaches. Thus, the new laws embodied the growing tendency in our society to "medicalize" individual disabilities. This trend is well illustrated by a collection of papers from the proceedings of the Association for Children with Learning Disabilities (Kirk and McCarthy 1975) which includes a section on "medical practices," and a statement by one author that "there is now unequivocal evidence that the appropriate use of stimulants or tranquilizing drugs is an important facet of the management of certain types of children with learning disabilities" (Masland 1975:195).

Direct use of standard medical treatment in the area of learning disabilities and related aspects of special education undoubtedly occurs in only a small minority of cases. Our concern is not with this issue. Rather, we examine a broader policy question based on our finding that the tendencies toward medicalization in special education may undermine the intentions of policies directed toward enhancing parental informed consent.

We became involved in this policy research because in 1977 the federal Bureau of Education for the Handicapped (BEH) funded ethnographic research intended to identify "facilitators and barriers" to parental involvement in special education decision making. The Bureau wanted results which would help to shape further regulations and funding strategies. State officials supported the study because of their interest in understanding and monitoring the already existing state education policies. Our research analyzed the ways in which already formulated federal and state policies were implemented at the local operational level. Before turning to this question, we first present a brief description of the research site, and summarize the highlights of our findings and their implications for special education.

THE RESEARCH SITE AND RESEARCH METHODS

The Breckenridge Elementary School is located in a suburban township in a northeastern state. It serves pupils in kindergarten through fourth grade. The school was chosen by the Bureau for the study because the state had initiated an earlier version of the special education legislation there. Special education programs were already well developed and the school received considerable financial support from the local school district and the state. Moreover, the informed consent of parents and their active involvement in placement decisions concerning their children was established policy, and had been so for some time.

The special education services included a number of different programs for children with learning disabilities, the educably mentally retarded (EMR), and children requiring speech and language therapy. Other remedial programs (Title 1) were also available. Several additional features of the special education program added to its complexity, including an active resource center especially designed for special education students.

Research followed this normal course for school-based ethnography. Relationships were established with administrators, teachers, and other special education support personnel at the district level and in Breckenridge School. This group was interviewed a series of times about the organization and day-to-day activities in special education programming. The special education placement process was observed, using standard ethnographic methods, including interviews, participant observation at meetings, and review of written materials. Following a six-month period of data collection on the special education system, including case monitoring, the research team carried out structured interviews with a random sample of thirty parents of children in the special education program, and thirty households in the regular education program. These interviews obtained demographic data, as well as information concerning parents' knowledge of and experience with special education program placement.

The parents whose children attended Breckenridge represented a predominantly suburban population. They were nearly evenly divided between white collar and blue collar workers in nearby urban workplaces. Less than ten percent of parents in the school were unemployed, and only a handful were minority group members. Black, Hispanic and Oriental families comprised less than five percent of the 600 households in the school's feeder area. In general, these parents viewed the special services program quite favorably. Many parents had collaborated with the school in the past, in seeking more services for children with learning difficulties.

The Breckenridge School had an enrollment of nearly 700 pupils and was larger than most elementary schools in the state. Twelve percent of the children were assigned to special education programs. They were distributed among the several components of the program as follows:

Pupils in learning disabilities resource rooms	49
Educably mentally retarded students	9
Speech, hearing, and language program	69
Intensive learning disabilities program	11
Intensive language program	13
Total	151

The high interest of the school staff in special education was indicated by their active engagement in specialized courses and projects intended to improve the special education program. They were very cooperative with our research.

THE PROCESSING AND PLACEMENT
OF SPECIAL EDUCATION PUPILS

The special education program was administered by a Child Study Team acting under the direction of the school principal. Based on observations of the work of the Child Study Team, and interviews with team members and parents, we discovered several central characteristics of the special education review and placement system. Childrens' learning problems were first observed by the regular classroom teachers who discussed them with members of the Child Study Team. Parents were brought into discussions of a particular child early in the process, because parental permission was required for any testing to be carried out. Following testing, cases were discussed at length in Child Study Team meetings, but parents were rarely invited to participate at this key point in the decision process.

The Child Study Team preferred to keep children in their regular classrooms. Hence programs were scheduled to minimize the number of hours spent in special education programs during the day, as well as the length of the overall placement outside the regular classroom. In addition, the Child Study Team occasionally juggled existing programs to meet the special needs of a child who might require immediate attention but for whom the designated program was not available until later. For example, a student might be placed temporarily in a Title I program until an opening was available in the right special education program. Programming and scheduling depended on available program slots. These continually changed as students were shifted from program to mainstream or to other special education programs. In the Child Study Team meetings, complex issues about alternative placement possibilities were negotiated.

Final decisions about placement were made at the district level meetings of the Pupil Placement Team (PPT). Parents were invited to these meetings and usually attended them. They were carefully prepared for the meeting by the Breckenridge guidance counselor who expected parents to support her at the PPT meeting and to advocate the recommended placement for the child.

Our interviews with a sample of parents indicated that the majority of parents were satisfied with the special education placement process. Most parents played a rather passive role; some of them noting that they left the special education decision-making to the "experts" at the school. Statistically, there was a significant relationship between higher socioeconomic status and level of parental involvement in the PPT meetings and between lower socioeconomic status and placement of students in special education programs. The lower the socioeconomic level of the student in this relatively wealthy community, the more likely the student was to be placed in a special education program, and the less likely the parents were to be actively involved in the placement process. These relationships were not perceived by the staff of the school, who saw themselves as well-trained child advocates in the area of special education.

THE MEDICAL MODEL IN SPECIAL EDUCATION

Only a small minority of cases entailed direct contact with medical doctors or prescribed medication. Nevertheless, certain aspects of the special education process strongly reflected the use of a medical model in professional-client relations. The Child Study Team meetings were reminiscent of medical or psychiatric case conferences. Pupils were referred to as "cases" whose problems were "diagnosed." Programmatic recommendations for individual children were called "prescriptions" or "treatments." Similar to practices in hospitals and other medical settings, additional "tests" were called for in cases in which the diagnosis was unclear.

Our observations of the special education program over a two-year period led us to identify the following key aspects of medical model dynamics in the special education program of Breckenridge:

1. *Complexity and expertise.* The special education system, like the medical system, is a domain of complex and highly specialized information, controlled by experts who require special training and experience in order to utilize this information. Nonexperts can play only marginal, if any, roles in the system.
2. *Clients are defined as individuals with malfunctions.* The treatment focuses on the individual and his or her problems. Aspects of the institutional setting are not called into question.
3. *The experts define their efforts as humanitarian.* They believe that they are helping individuals to improve themselves, to "get well." They often view those who criticize them as misguided due to ignorance, or as ungrateful for the services they have received.
4. *Diagnostic testing is essential for the identification of problems and the prescription of appropriate treatment.* The testing has become increasingly more specialized, technical, and costly. Because they are based on norms and "averages," tests may obscure individual differences.
5. *Relationships between expert personnel and clients is expected to be based on trust and submission to authority.* When patients question or contradict medical authorities, they are

often viewed as a threat or an interference with the proper functioning of "the medical system."

6. *Medical practice is based on scientific knowledge.* The uncertainties of scientific knowledge and disagreement among the experts about the proper diagnosis and treatment of patients are usually hidden from the public.

7. *The expert's first responsibility is to the patient.* Members of the patient's family are not usually involved in the treatment process. Family members are sometimes viewed as causes of the problem, and treatment may be seen as an antidote to their deleterious influence. This may result in feelings of guilt among family members.

Our provisional medical model can be rephrased in terms of *power* in the special education negotiation process. The shift toward medicalization and expertise tends to confer power to those with special knowledge and skills. To the extent that relatively high costs are involved, power also tends to shift toward those who allocate the financial resources. One can hypothesize that families whose children appeared to need special help may feel some sense of shame or inferiority, hence a diminution of social power. At the same time, the persons in schools who are active in special education will tend to discourage the participation of parents, seeing them as lacking the special knowledge needed to understand the problem.

Our research suggested that the policies supporting medicalization of the special education process complemented the search for the "least restrictive environment," but contradicted directly the intent of the legislation regarding informed consent. The medical analogy brings into bold relief some of the social forces that operate against strong parental (or other lay) participation in the special education process. Based on this formulation we predict that any steps toward well-informed parental participation in the special education process, however well conceived, will encounter serious difficulties. We discussed these contradictions with school personnel at the local and district levels in order to increase their awareness of the problem.

IMPLICATIONS FOR POLICY INTERVENTION

Our discussions with school personnel addressed the factors which created an imbalance of power and information flow affecting the decision-making ability of parents in the special education process. For us, the main issue was to find ways to restore some balance of information flow between school personnel and parents (Yoshida et al. 1978). A more equitable balance, we felt, would enable them to play an active role in the special education placement and policy process. This would require the presence of an active, independent organization that could study the special education process in the school and at the district level, and assist parents to raise questions about placement, selection, and monitoring of appropriate alternatives. Such organizations exist among parent groups in many cities, particularly to deal with issues in bilingual/multicultural education, special education, and other school issues (Moore 1977). There were no organizations of this type in the research community when we completed our study.

The vehicles for action in this case were not to be found at the local or state levels; there was little support for change among school officials and parents. However, the Bureau of Education for the Handicapped was interested in the results of our study for the designing of new research and intervention programs. We suggested that they provide funding for the development of parent advocacy groups in the Black and Hispanic communities.

The strength of commissioned research on aspects of proposed new legislation lies in the degree to which the funding agency is committed to developing new policy and is willing to use research results in pushing for policy changes. In some instances, an influential agency may have wide-ranging effects on the educational system (for example, in the case of school desegregation). However, research of this nature often lacks a *local* base for influencing policy implementation. Our second case study describes how a national demonstration project with a local community base influenced local policy in maternal and child health.

Case II: Maternal and Child Health in the Puerto Rican Community

This second case example illustrates policy research in which anthropologists have had direct effects on policy *implementation* at the local level, through research that is coupled with development of new institutional procedures in health care.

The 1970s saw growing awareness that poor women and children, especially among ethnic minorities, experienced poorer health status and poorer health outcomes than middle-class white populations. Research showed that poor Black and Hispanic women had less access to reproductive health care and that infant mortality, low birth weight, infant impairments, and morbidity in the first year of life were significantly more common among these populations (Minority Health Care 1979).

Over the past two decades, a series of national policies have been formulated primarily by physicians and administrators in the health care system. These policies assume that maternal and child health outcomes can be changed simply through increases in the availability and use of health care services. As a result, funding became available for "improved pregnancy outcome" (IPO) programs, which included health education and other outreach to high-risk women. These programs emphasize first-trimester entry to prenatal care, involvement in public nutrition programs, compliance with medical interventions, health education, and postnatal and pediatric check-ups.

This medical intervention model continues to dominate maternal and child health policy and implementation at all levels. Nevertheless, recent statistics show that Blacks and Hispanics continue to lag behind Whites on all maternal and child health indicators. National and state policy makers have continued to support funding for prenatal health services for low income women, but they have been puzzled that the medically sponsored IPO programs have been unable to make a significant difference in maternal and child health outcomes in certain high risk groups. Therefore, they have promoted both research and innovative intervention and prevention programs to determine what factors might improve health service use and outcomes among low-income minority populations.

Social science research has identified several factors that reduce the effectiveness of maternal and child health programs. One set of factors has to do with the organization of public health care. Clinics and hospital emergency rooms are overcrowded and do not offer continuity of care. Service providers are often hurried, and have limited time for education of patients. Many programs lack sufficient bilingual/bicultural staff. Other research points to the importance of social support (relatives, neighbors, and others) for ensuring entry into appropriate health care services and improved health outcomes (Dressler and Bernal 1981; Gottlieb 1982; Schensul and Schensul 1982). Households without effective social support have less access to quality health care.

THE MATERNAL AND CHILD HEALTH/PREVENTION
NETWORK: THE COMADRONA PROGRAM

In 1982 the Hispanic Health Council, a community-based research organization in Hartford's Puerto Rican community, received a Title V national demonstration grant to improve health behaviors and health outcomes among high-risk Puerto Rican women.[1] Although the outcome measures were medical, the program's methodology combined the notions of cultural brokerage (Weidman 1982) and social support networks (Schensul and Schensul 1982; Guarnaccia 1984) as key elements in achieving positive medical outcomes. The project, referred to as the Comadrona Program after the concept of the traditional birth attendant in Puerto Rico, included the following important features: (1) emphasis on ethnic identity and pride through the "Comadrona" staff and culturally appropriate training materials; (2) Puerto Rican staffing and administration; (3) the use of "cultural brokerage" in the form of health education and advocacy on behalf of Puerto Rican women clients who were interacting with health care providers; (4) the development of community, school-based, and volunteer groups and support networks through which women could be identified, supported, and enrolled in health care at an early stage of pregnancy; (5) the development of a data base on pregnancy and prenatal care among Puerto Rican women.

The program staff built an extensive city-wide network of support for the program through their participation in many health-related committees. These included the School Health Task Force, an Infant Mortality/Teen Pregnancy Committee, and a Child Advocacy committee. Program methods and results were shared with members of these committees.

By the end of its second year, the Comadrona program was

1. The program was developed in collaboration with the State Health Department, Division of Maternal and Child Health, under the direction of Estelle Seiker, M.D., and federal funds flowed through the State to the Hispanic Health Council.

showing improvements in first trimester entry to health care, continuity of care, compliance with medication, a decrease in the number of babies with low birth weight, increased rates of breastfeeding, and improvements in familiarity with and use of family planning methods.

Before the success of the program was widely known, the local Health Systems Agency issued a report stating that the city had the fourth highest infant mortality rate among the nation's cities. The report indicated also that Puerto Ricans showed a high incidence of low birth weight babies and teenage pregnancies. These data attracted the attention of the committees mentioned above. The city health department argued that infant mortality could be addressed best through improved prenatal care and general health education. Health care providers on the committees, including school health providers, used the information to campaign for increased funding for medical care and family life education. The medically oriented direction of these committees was supported by the City Health Department, the State Health Department, and local community health clinics. Committee members representing community organizations did not have sufficient power to obtain funding for themselves, nor the philosophical or theoretical framework to promote alternative policies centering on the expansion of social support networks and appeal to ethnic identity as a means of enhancing awareness of health care services and their utilization.

In the meantime, private donor organizations (corporate givers) were seeking a clearly focused program in which to place their health funds. They commissioned two consultants to carry out a needs assessment in the city in the area of maternal and child health. The consultants identified the pressing need for maternal and child health services and health education. A complicated set of negotiations about funding developed among the newly created advisory committees, the city health department, and a consortium of neighborhood clinics. Eventually, a city-wide plan for maternal and infant health care was developed. However, the original consultants retained control of policy making in this city-wide network.

The action plan called for public and private sector monies to be amalgamated in a service and outreach program for high-risk Black and Hispanic women. To appease those concerned with community involvement in maternal and child health care, the program was, to some extent, modeled after the Hispanic Health Council's maternal and child health program insofar as it entailed home visits and health education. It did not, however, include central aspects of the program such as the creation of social support networks and the development of volunteer groups of health promotors and ethnically specific health education materials.

The action plan called also for centralization of all maternal and child health monies, private and public, through a central committee. This left control of maternal and child health policy and funds in the hands of the consultants who continued to act as "brokers" between the private sector donors and the city's neighborhoods. Because the consultants worked closely with the physicians in the city health department, and the program monies were to be spent to support city health department activities, the city health department was closely involved in policy and funding decisions.

The above arrangement was opposed by the independent Black and Hispanic organizations. They argued that the arenas of power and policy making were not easily identifiable and that access to policy making was limited to an "inside group" which failed to include community organization representatives. Secondly, the plan called for consolidation of funds and funding priorities in the area of maternal and child health. Those excluded from the central decision making group were neither able to participate in setting priorities nor to obtain independent funding from local sources. Finally, the models promoted by the action plan did not acknowledge the significance of cultural factors and social networks in the management of pregnancy and postnatal care.

Program staff utilized ethnographic data and case materials from the program to demonstrate the ability of an ethnic organization to promote better health outcomes. These data showed that social support networks, including community and neighborhood groups, plus volunteers could improve early entry into and continuous involvement in prenatal health care. Moreover, health outcomes for mothers and infants with the social and educational supports offered by the Comadrona program were significantly better than outcomes citywide.

Program staff, members of the Hispanic Health Council Board, and volunteers confronted members of the Maternal Services Committee with these program results and requested that participation in the plan be broadened to include community groups. They then mobilized support from organizations and individuals in maternal and child health who had worked with the Hispanic Health Council and the Comadrona program. Data from the Hispanic Health Council program and the theoretical framework of the program were presented to this group. The network then began to seek independent support for community programs that used the concepts of community support networks and ethnicity in staffing and program content.

The debate continues. However, several local foundations have indicated that they will fund individual requests for program support and that they will favor program designs oriented toward community based social support. The leaders of the city action plan have hired senior personnel who favor the development of community networks in the identification of high-risk pregnancy clients. The Hispanic Health Council program model is becoming the basis of training materials which will be disseminated within the city and throughout the state with the support of the State Health Department. Program staff are now participants in the state maternal and child health committee that sets priorities for statewide maternal and child health funding.

THEORETICAL PRINCIPLES AND POLICY ADVOCACY

This case illustrates the ways in which diverse interest groups converged to develop policies concerning maternal and child health. These different interest groups were strongly influenced by a series of research and evaluation results. Clearly, however, research data from the health planning agency and the Hispanic Health Council's maternal and child program would have been less successful except for the several competing local groups whose interests and positions required documentation. In this case, a social science oriented program with ethnographic data was central in providing an alternative for those community organizations interested in combining sociocultural and biomedical strategies in the improvement of pregnancy and infant health outcomes. However, without *prior involvement of program staff in a number of other health policy issues in the city,* the research results stemming from the maternal and child health program would probably have had considerably less influence.

Several theoretical principles arise from the experience of testing and expanding this project:

1. Social support in the form of individual cultural brokerage can improve continuity of prenatal care, raise birth weights, and improve breast feeding rates among high-risk ethnic minority women.
2. The development of community-wide maternal and child health networks can increase overall community access to prenatal care.
3. Health programs directed to particular urban ethnic minorities are unlikely to achieve success unless the programs include considerable investment in research on specific conditions and features in local communities. The significance of the research is enhanced by participation of community residents in the research process.
4. Health programs directed to particular ethnic minorities are unlikely to achieve long-term success unless members of the ethnic minorities are included in policy-making bodies such as health committees, city health departments, and legislative task forces.
5. The effectiveness of ethnic minorities in such local policy-making settings can be enhanced by the carefully thought out presentation of research results.

In contrast to the research on special education at Breckenridge School, the maternal infant health project has been directed to the local community level of policy making. Presentation of the data, and participation in policy discussions, has been primarily within the health-related organizations and facilities in the city. Nevertheless, it is our expectation that the main theoretical principles arising from this research will be widely applicable to health care programs in other ethnic groups and in other regions of the country.

Anthropologists and Policy Research

The results of the two projects described above suggest several key issues for anthropologists interested in policy research in education, health, and other areas. Policy researchers must become quite familiar with the local political settings, or policy arenas, in which policies are modified and implemented. It is necessary to identify the various foci of power, recognizing that political "clout" is likely to be dispersed in different patterns for different policy questions. Thus, the arenas of policy making are likely to be distributed differently in education than in health care, even though some of the actors in the drama may be the same.

Anthropologists should work hard to identify "sympathetic sectors" and constituencies in relation to particular policy issues. These sympathetic sectors may be community groups, "progressive" doctors and health administrators, school-based groups, religious groups, and occasionally legislators. In educational policy making there may be effective constituencies among parent groups, unions, ethnic organizations, or other community organizations.

Our two examples demonstrate the contrast between two policy research strategies: in the Breckenridge school example, we maintained a neutral stance in the research setting in order to maximize the flow of information among different groups and individuals. In the maternal/infant health project, we have been consistently allied with one group—the Puerto Rican community as represented by the Hispanic Health Council. The close working relationships between the research program and the Puerto Rican community have enabled us to translate research results directly into concrete policy suggestions in a population that needs better health care. No matter which of the two strategies they adopt, researchers should know that their most effective weapons in the policy making arena are methodologically sound quantitative and qualitative data.

In both research examples it was possible to identify the most important potential users of research results; at the same time, we kept in mind that all policy-oriented research will encounter opposing forces. The opposing forces may be groups competing for the same scarce resources, individuals and groups fearing loss of prestige and "turf," or perhaps individuals with markedly different philosophies and "theories of action." Some, but not all, of the opposing forces are likely to be influenced by new research data if the materials are presented effectively. In the maternal/infant health project most of our presentations of relevant data have been in oral discussions during committee meetings and other negotiation sessions. The special education data, on the other hand, were transmitted mainly in written form, although we also made oral presentations to teachers and administrators at the school.

Policy research, as noted earlier, is generally composed of *both* descriptive information and theoretical propositions. This type of research gives rise to new theoretical frameworks offering testable options that may be generalized to other issues and locations. For example, our analysis of the medical model in relation to special education suggests a series of hypotheses for testing other arenas. This "middle range theory" is likely to be significant for policy *wherever special education programs are elaborated.* In addition, the basic elements of the medical model suggest parallels in sectors other than special education.

The theoretical foundations of the maternal/infant health program are anchored in social network theory, interrelated with hypotheses about ethnicity as a major social factor. The empirical data on the importance of social support networks in the Puerto Rican population do not, of course, demonstrate that the same programmatic guidelines will be effective in all ethnic populations. Nor have we specified all the contextual conditions affecting program outcomes. However, the theoretical propositions arising from our research point to social support networks as a major program alternative that should not be ignored in health programs.

At certain points in our research, the presentation of "mere" descriptive materials played an important role. At the Breckenridge school, our ethnographic descriptions of the Child Study Team, and the style of decision making concerning "trouble cases," were more important and convincing than the statistical data. In committee meetings and other policy arenas in Hartford, we have been called on often to present information concerning health care seeking, patterns of household structure, and other descriptive data.

Paredes has recently described participation on an advisory council connected with the Gulf of Mexico Fishery Management Council, noting that "most of my comments focused on the need for additional data and for refinements in the presentation of data" (Paredes 1985:177). On the other hand, Paredes and other applied anthropologists working with governmental advisory committees have pushed frequently for recognition of a generalized sociocultural theory which recognizes that all governmental policies have social and cultural effects, and that these effects are often very different for poorer in contrast to wealthier sectors of the population. Thus the modest suggestion by Paredes that fishing regulations be posted in both Spanish and English (in coastal Florida) embodies a complex implicit theoretical model concerning bilingual/bicultural societies. Ethnic group differences and socioeconomic inequalities are not always central elements in policy making, but it appears that a large share of anthropological interest focuses on policy impacts for low-income, socially marginal groups. This includes, of course, the considerable research interest in policy effects on women and women's roles in health, education, agriculture, and other sectors of socioeconomic change.

Ethnographic policy research and policy-implementing action programs are essentially microlevel, practically by definition. However, our case examples are intended to illustrate the strategic importance of research about the *linkages* with macrolevel—state and national level—policy processes. Part of the essential policy research in a given local arena is the analysis of how macrolevel policies and processes impinge on local action settings. In contemporary educational and health care settings, the federal government is *always* an interested party almost always providing at least part of the financial resources for local programs. At the same time, macrolevel economic processes, the flow of cultural influences, mass media effects, and many other phenomena from the wider society all have their manifestations in the local scenes within which specific programs are implemented. A number of anthropologists have commented on the need for more research on the macrosystems which shape the general political/economic environments within which local policy implementation takes place (Chambers 1985; Foster 1969). Analysis of microlevel-macrolevel linkages presents a major challenge for policy-related anthropology of the 1980s.

BIBLIOGRAPHY OF WORKS CITED

Abegglen, James. 1958. "The Japanese Factory System." Glencoe, Ill.: Free Press.

Abt, Clark C. 1979. "Government Constraints on Evaluation Quality." In L. E. Datta and R. Perloff, eds., *Improving Education,* pp. 43–52. Beverly Hills, Calif.: Sage.

Aceves, Joseph B., and H. Gill King. 1978. *Cultural Anthropology.* New York: General Learning Press.

Acland, H. 1979. "Are Randomized Experiments the Cadillacs of Design?" *Policy Analysis* 5:223–241.

Adams, Richard Newbold. 1967. *The Second Sowing.* San Francisco, Calif.: Chandler.

—— 1981. "Ethical Principles in Anthropological Research: One or Many." *Human Organization* 40:155–160.

Adams, Richard N., and Charles C. Cumberland. 1960. *United States University Cooperation in Latin America.* Institute of Research on Overseas Programs. East Lansing, Mich.: Michigan State University Press.

Alers, J. Oscar. 1971. "Well-Being." In Henry Dobyns, Paul Doughty, and Harold Lasswell, eds., *Peasants, Power, and Applied Social Change: Vicos as a Model,* pp. 115–136. Beverly Hills, Calif.: Sage.

Alexander, Linda. 1977. "The Double-Bind: Theory and Hemodialysis." *Archives of General Psychiatry.* 33:1353–1356.

Alland, Alexander. 1981. *To Be Human: An Introduction to Cultural Anthropology.* New York: John Wiley and Sons.

American Anthropological Association. 1980. "Profile of an Anthropologist—Institute for Development Anthropology: Social Equity Must Be Part of Development." *Anthropology Newsletter.* 21(9):4–5.

—— 1976. *Guide to Departments of Anthropology 1976–77.* Washington, D.C.: American Anthropological Association.

—— 1981. *Directory of Practicing Anthropologists.* Washington, D.C.: American Anthropological Association.

Amin, Samir. 1973. *Neo-Colonialism in West Africa.* Harmondsworth, New York: Penguin.

Angrosino, Michael V. 1981. *Quality Assurance for Community Care of Retarded Adults in Tennessee.* Nashville, Tenn.: Center for the Study of Families and Children, Vanderbilt Institute for Public Policy Studies. Mental Health Monograph, Series #11.

Anthropology and the American Indian. 1973. San Francisco, Calif.: Indian Historian Press.

Arensberg, Conrad M. 1941. "Toward a 'Control' System for Industrial Relations: A Review of Management and the Worker." *Applied Anthropology.* 1:54–57.

—— 1942. "Report on a Developing Community, Poston, Arizona." *Applied Anthropology.* 2:2–21.

—— 1947. "Prospect and Retrospect." *Applied Anthropology* 6:1–7.

—— 1951. "Behavior and Organization: Industrial Studies." In John Rohrer and Muzafer Sherif, eds., *Social Psychology at the Crossroads,* pp. 324–352. New York: Harper and Row.

—— 1955. "American Communities." *American Anthropologist* 57:1143–60.

—— 1967. "Upgrading Peasant Agriculture: Is Tradition the Snag?" *Columbia Journal of World Business* 2(1):68–71.

—— 1972. "Culture as Behavior: Structure and Emergence." In Bernard J. Siegal, ed., *Annual Review of Anthropology* 1:1–26. Palo Alto, Calif.: Annual Reviews.

—— 1975. "Discussion of C. Steward Sheppard, The Role of Anthropology in Business Administration." In Bela C. Maday, ed., *Anthropology and Society.* pp. 71–75. Washington, D.C.: Anthropological Society of Washington.

—— 1981. "Cultural Holism Through Interactional Systems." *American Anthropologist* 83:562–581.

—— 1982. "Generalizing Anthropology: The Recovery of Holism." In E. Adamson Hoebel, Richard Currier, and Susan Kaiser, eds., *Crisis in Anthropology: View from Spring Hill,* pp. 109–131. New York: Garland Publishing House.

Arensberg, Conrad M., and Solon T. Kimball. 1938. *Family and Community in Ireland.* Cambridge: Harvard University Press.

—— 1965. *Culture and Community.* New York: Harcourt Brace and World.

Arensberg, Conrad M., and Arthur H. Niehoff. 1964. *Introducing Social Change: A Manual for Americans Overseas.* Chicago: Aldine.

Armstrong, A. J. 1882–85. "Crow Agency Report." Washington, D.C.: U.S. Department of Interior Annual Report, 4 vols.

Artola del Poza, Armando. 1952. "Discurso del Sr. Ministro de Trabajo y Asuntos Indigenas, General de Brigada Don Armando del Poza." *Peru Indigena* 2(5–6):246–248.

Ashby, Sir Eric. 1959. *Technology and the Academics.* London: MacMillan.

Babb, Florence E. 1985. "Women and Men in Vicos, Peru: A Case of Unequal Development." In W. W. Stein, ed., *Peruvian Contexts of Change,* pp. 163–210. New Brunswick, N.J.: Transaction Books.

Bailey, Frederick G. 1960. *Tribe, Caste and Nation.* Manchester, England: Manchester University Press.

—— 1969. *Strategems and Spoils.* Oxford: Blackwell.

Baker, Keith. 1975. "A New Grantsmanship." *American Sociologist* 10:206–219.

Ball, Richard A. 1971. "The Southern Appalachian Folk Subculture as a Tension-Reducing Way of Life." In John D. Photiadis and Harry K. Schwarzweller, eds., *Change in Rural Appalachia: Implications for Action Programs,* pp. 69–79. Philadelphia: University of Pennsylvania Press.

Baltzell, E. Digby. 1964. *The Protestant Establishment: Aristocracy and Caste in America*. New York: Vintage Books.

Barker, Roger B. 1963. *The Stream of Behavior*. New York: Meredith.

Barnard, Chester I. 1938. *The Functions of the Executive*. Cambridge: Harvard University Press.

Barnes, J. A. 1980. *Who Should Know What? Social Science, Privacy and Ethics*. New York: Cambridge University Press.

Barnett, Clifford. 1980. "Commentary on Open Forum: Clinical Anthropology." *Medical Anthropology Newsletter* 12(1):23–25.

—— 1985. "Anthropological Research in Clinical Settings: Role Requirements and Adaptations." In Symposium: Anthropologists in Clinical Settings—A Matter of Style, pp. 56–61. *Medical Anthropology Quarterly* 16(3):59–73.

Barnett, Homer G. 1953. *Innovation, The Basis of Cultural Change*. New York: McGraw-Hill.

—— 1956. *Anthropology in Administration*. Evanston, Ill.: Row, Peterson.

Barnett, Tony. 1981. "Evaluating the Gezira Scheme: Black Box or Pandora's Box." In J. Heyer et al., eds., *Rural Development in Tropical Africa*, pp. 306–324. New York: Saint Martin's.

Barr, Donald A. 1972. "The Professional Urban Planner." *Journal of the American Institute of Planners* 38:155–159.

Barth, Frederick. 1963. *The Role of the Entrepreneur in Social Change*. Northern Norway, Bergen: Scandinavian University Books.

—— 1966. *Models of Social Organization*. London: Royal Anthropological Institute of Great Britain and Ireland. Occasional Paper no. 23.

—— 1967. "On the Study of Social Change." *American Anthropologist* 69:661–669.

Bartoleme, Miquel A., and Alicia M. Barabas. 1984. "Apostles of Ethnocide: Reply to Partridge and Brown." *Culture and Agriculture* 24:5–9.

Bastide, Roger. 1973. *Applied Anthropology*. Alice L. Morton, trans. New York: Harper and Row.

Bateson, Gregory. 1935a. *Naven*. Stanford, Calif.: Stanford University Press (orig. pub. 1936).

—— 1935b. "Culture Contact and Schismogenesis." *Man* 35:178–183.

—— 1972. "Towards a Theory of Schizophrenia." In Gregory Bateson, ed., *Steps to an Ecology of Mind*. Los Angeles: Chandler Publishing Company.

Bateson, Mary Catherine. 1980. "Continuties in Insight and Innovation: Toward a Biography of Margaret Mead." *American Anthropologist* 82:270–277.

Bauer, R., and K. Gergen. 1968. *The Study of Policy Formation*. New York: Free Press.

Beals, Ralph L. 1945. *Cheran: A Sierra Tarascan Village*. Washington, D.C.: Smithsonian Institution, Institute of Social Anthropology, Publication 2.

—— 1969. *Politics of Social Research: An Inquiry into the Ethics and Responsibilities of Social Scientists*. Chicago: Aldine.

Beals, Ralph L., and Harry Hoijer. 1971. *An Introduction to Anthropology*. New York: MacMillan.

Bee, Robert L. 1974. *Patterns and Processes: An Introduction to Anthropological*

Strategies for the Study of Sociocultural Change. New York: Free Press.
—— 1982. *The Politics of American Indian Policy.* Cambridge, Mass.: Schenkman.
Bell, Daniel. 1976. *The Cultural Contradictions of Capitalism.* New York: Basic Books.
Belshaw, Cyril. 1966. "Project Evaluation." *International Development Review* 8(2): 2–6.
—— 1972. "Anthropology." *International Social Science Journal* 24:80–94.
—— 1976. *The Sorcerer's Apprentice: An Anthropology of Public Policy.* New York: Pergamon.
Benedict, Ruth. 1935. *Zuni Mythology.* 2 vols. Columbia University Contributions to Anthropology, 21. New York: Columbia University Press.
—— 1947. *Race: Science and Politics.* New York: Viking.
Benthall, Jonathan. 1985. "The Utility of Anthropology." *Anthropolgoy Today* 1(2):18–20.
Benthall, Jonathan, and Gustaaf Houtman. 1985. "RAIN Attains Majority." *Anthropology Today* 1:1–2.
Bernard, H. Russell, and Pertti Pelto. 1972. *Technology and Social Change.* New York: MacMillan.
Bernstein, Richard J. 1971. *Praxis and Action: Contemporary Philosophies of Human Activity.* Philadelphia: University of Pennsylvania Press.
—— 1978. *The Restructuring of Social and Political Theory.* Philadelphia: University of Pennsylvania Press.
Berreman, Gerald D. 1980. "Comment." *America in the 1980's: Issues for Anthropologists.* Boston, Mass.: Anthropology Resource Center Working Paper #2.
Biderman, Albert D., and Lauriston M. Sharp. 1972. *The Competitive Evaluation Research Industry.* Washington, D.C.: Bureau of Social Science Research.
Bieder, Robert E., and Thomas G. Tax. 1976. "From Ethnologists to Anthropologists: A Brief History of the American Ethnological Society." In John V. Murra, ed., *American Anthropology: The Early Years,* pp. 11–22. New York: West.
Black, Alan. 1968. "The Comprehensive Plan." In William I. Goodman and Eric C. Freund, eds., *Principles and Practice of Urban Planning,* pp. 349–378. Washington, D.C.: International City Managers Association.
Blau, Peter M. 1974. "Parameters of Social Structures." *American Sociological Review* 39:615–635.
Boas, Franz. 1898. "Growth of Toronto Children." *Report of the U.S. Commissioner of Education for 1896–1897,* pp. 1541–1599, Washington, D.C.
——1910. "Changes in Bodily Form of Descendants of Immigrants." Partial report on the results of an anthropological investigation for the U.S. Immigration Commission, Washington, D.C.: Government Printing Office. (Senate Document no.208, 61st Cong.,2d Sess.)
——1911. *The Mind of Primitive Man.* Rev. ed. New York: Free Press. (Orig. pub. New York: Macmillan.)
——1928. *Anthropology and Modern Life.* New York: Norton.
——1948. *Race, Language and Culture.* New York: MacMillan.
Boas, Franz, and Ella Deloria. 1941. *Dakota Grammar.* Memoirs of the National

Academy of Sciences, vol.33. Washington, D.C.: U.S. Government Printing Office.

Boissevain, Jeremy, and John C. Mitchell. 1973. *Network Analysis: Studies in Human Interaction.* The Hague: Mouton.

Bonfil Batalla, Giullermo. 1966. "Conservative Thought in Applied Anthropology." *Human Organization* 25:89–92.

Bonilla y Segura, Guillermo. 1945. *A Report on the Cultural Missions of Mexico.* Federal Security Agency, U.S. Office of Education. Bulletin no. 11. Washington, D.C.: U.S. Government Printing Office.

Bordieu, Pierre. 1977. *Outline of a Theory of Practice.* New York: Cambridge University Press. (Trans. R. Nice.)

Borrero, Maria; Jean J. Schensul; and R. Garcia. 1984. "Research, Training and Organizational Change." *Urban Anthropology* 11:129–153.

Bosk, Charles. 1985. "The Fieldworker as Watcher and Witness.." Hastings Center Report, June 1985, pp. 10–14.

Brace, C. Loring, and M.F. Ashley Montagu. 1965. *Man's Evolution: An Introduction to Physical Anthropology.* New York: Macmillan.

Bradford, Leland P.; Jack R. Gibb; and Kenneth D. Benne, eds. 1964. *T-Group Theory and Laboratory Method: Innovation in Reeducation.* New York: Wiley.

Brown, G. Gordon. 1945. "WRA, Gila River Project, Rivers, Arizona: Community Analysis Section—Final Report." *Applied Anthropology* 4:1–49.

Bunzel, Ruth. 1962. "Introduction." In Franz Boas, *Anthropology and Modern Life,* pp. 4–10. New York: Norton. (Orig. pub. 1928.)

Burnett, Jaquetta Hill. 1968. "Anthropological Study of Disability from Educational Problems of Puerto Ricans." Application for Research Grant, DHEW Social and Rehabilitation Service. Urbana, Ill.: Bureau of Educational Research. (Files of the author.)

——1969. "Event Description and Analysis in the Micro-ethnography of Urban Classrooms." Urbana, Ill.: Bureau of Educational Research. (Files of the author.)

——1970. "Culture of the School." *Council on Anthropology and Education Newsletter* 1:4–13.

——1972. "Event Analysis as a Methodology for Urban Analysis." Anthropological Study of Disability from Educational Problems of Puerto Rican Youth. Final Report: DHEW. SRS Grant no. RD 2969 G69, vol. 2, part 2. Urbana, Ill.: Bureau of Educational Research. (Files of the author.)

——1974. "Social Structures, Ideologies, and Culture Codes in Occupational Development of Puerto Rican Youths. Anthropological Study of Disability from Educational Problems of Puerto Rican Youths." Final Report: DHEW, SRS Grant no.2969 G69, vol.1. Urbana, Ill.: Bureau of Educational Research. (Files of the author).

Burns, Allan. 1975. "An Anthropologist at Work: Field Perspectives on Applied Ethnography." *Council on Anthropology and Education Quarterly* 6(4):28–33.

Burns, Tom. 1954. "The Directions of Activity and Communication in a Departmental Executive Group." *Human Relations* 7:73–97.

California. 1976. "California High Court Rules on Davis Minority Program." *Forum*, October 6. Berkeley: University of California School of Law.

Campbell, Donald T. 1979. "Degrees of Freedom and the Case Study." In T.D. Cook and C.S. Reichardt, eds., *Qualitative and Quantitative Methods in Evaluation Research*. Beverly Hills, Calif.: Sage.

Campbell, Donald T., and Julian T. Stanley. 1963. *Experimental and Quasi-Experimental Designs for Research*. Chicago, Ill.: Rand McNally.

Campbell, Joan. 1971. "Agricultural Development in East Africa: A Problem in Cultural Ecology." Ph.D. diss., Columbia University.

Carnegie Commission on Higher Education. 1973. *Priorities for Action: Final Report*. New York: McGraw-Hill.

Carter, William. 1972. "Review." *Human Organization* 31:460–462.

Casagrande, Joseph B. 1959. "Some Observations on the Study of Intermediate Societies." In Verne F. Ray, ed., *Intermediate Societies, Social Mobility, and Communication*, pp. 1–10. Proceedings of the 1959 Meeting of the American Ethnological Society. Seattle: University of Washington Press.

Castillo, Gelia T. 1983. *How Participatory is Participatory Development? A Review of the Philippine Experience*. Manila, Philippines: Institute for Development Studies.

Caudill, William. 1953. "Applied Anthropology in Medicine." In A.L. Kroeber, ed., *Anthropology Today*, pp. 771–806. Chicago: University of Chicago Press.

——1958. *The Psychiatric Hospital as a Small Society*. Cambridge: Harvard University Press.

Cernea, Michael M. 1979. *Measuring Project Impact: Monitoring and Evaluation in the PIDER Rural Development Project—Mexico*. World Bank Staff Working Paper no. 332. Washington, D.C.: World Bank.

——1983. *A Social Methodology for Community Participation in Local Investments: The Experience of Mexico's PIDER Program*. World Bank Staff Working Paper, no. 598. Washington D.C.: World Bank.

——1985. "Sociological Knowledge for Development Projects." In Michael M. Cernea, ed., *Putting People First: Sociological Variables in Rural Development*, pp. 3–21. London: Oxford University Press.

Cernea, Michael M., ed. 1985. *Putting People First: Sociological Variables in Rural Development*. London: Oxford University Press.

Chaiken, Miriam. 1983. "The Social, Economic and Health Consequences of Spontaneous Frontier Settlement in the Philippines." Ph.D. diss., University of California, Santa Barbara.

Chambers, Erve. 1985. *Applied Anthropology: A Practical Guide*. Englewood Cliffs, N.J.: Prentice-Hall.

Chambers, Robert. 1969. *Settlement Schemes in Tropical Africa: A Study of Organizations and Development*. New York: Praeger.

Champagne, Anthony, and Edward J. Harpham, eds. 1984. *The Attack on the Welfare State*. Prospect Heights, Ill.: Waveland Press.

Chapple, Eliot D. 1941. "Organization Problems in Industry." *Applied Anthropology* 1:2–9.

——1942. "The Analysis of Industrial Morale." *Journal of Industrial Hygiene and Toxicology* 24(7):163–172.

——1949. "The Interaction Chronograph: Its Evolution and Present Application." *Personnel* 25(4):295–307.

——1953a. "Applied Anthropology in Industry." In A.L. Kroeber, ed., *Anthropology Today*, pp. 819–831. Chicago: University of Chicago Press.

——1953b. "The Standard Experimental (Stress) Interview as Used in Interaction Chronograph Investigations." *Human Organization* 12:23–32.

——1970. *Culture and Biological Man: Explorations in Behavioral Anthropology.* New York: Holt, Rinehart, and Winston.

Chapple, Eliot D., and Conrad M. Arensberg. 1940. "Measuring Human Relations: An Introduction to the Study of the Interaction of Individuals." *Genetic Psychology Monographs* 22:3–147.

Chapple, Eliot D., and Carleton S. Coon. 1942. *Principles of Anthropology.* New York: Holt.

Chapple, Eliot D., and Gordon Donald. 1946. "A Method for Evaluating Supervisory Personnel." *Harvard Business Review* 24:197–214.

——1947. "An Evaluation of Department Store Salespeople by the Interaction Chronograph." *Journal of Marketing* 12:173–185.

Chapple, Eliot D., and Erich Lindemann. 1941. "Clinical Implications of Measurements of Interaction Rates in Psychiatric Patients." *Applied Anthropology* 1:1–10.

Chapple, Eliot D., and Leonard R. Sayles. 1961. *The Measurement of Management.* New York: Macmillan.

Chesterfield, Roy. 1986. "Qualitative Methodology in the Evaluation of Early Childhood Bilingual Curriculum Models." In D.M. Fetterman and M.A. Pitman, eds., *Ethnographic Evaluation: Theory, Practice and Politics.* Beverly Hills, Calif.: Sage.

Children's Defense Fund. 1984. *A Children's Defense Budget.* 3d ed. Washington, D.C.: Children's Defense Fund.

Chrisman, Noel J., and Thomas W. Maretzki, eds., 1982. *Clinically Applied Anthropology: Anthropologists in Health Science Settings.* Dordrecht, Holland, and Boston, Mass.: D. Reidel.

Cheuca Sotomayor, Carlos. 1962. "Vicos: Comunidad Individualista." *FANAL* 17(64): 2–11.

CIDER (Centro de Investigacion para el Desarollo Rural). 1979. *Notes on the Preparation of the Zacatecas State Rural Development Plan.* (Mimeo.) Mexico, D.F.

Clifton, James A. 1970. *Applied Anthropology: Readings in the Uses of the Science of Man.* Boston, Mass.: Houghton Mifflin.

Clinton, Charles A. 1975. "The Anthropologist as Hired Hand." *Human Organization* 34:197–204.

——1976. "On Bargaining with the Devil: Contract Ethnography and Accountability in Fieldwork." *Anthropology and Education Quarterly* 8:25–29.

Cochrane, Glynn. 1971. *Development Anthropology.* New York: Oxford University Press.

Cohen, Abner. 1969. *Custom and Politics in Urban Africa: A Study of Hausa Migrants in Yoruba Towns.* Berkeley: University of California Press.

——1974. *Two-Dimensional Man: An Essay on the Anthropology of Power and Symbolism in Complex Society.* Berkeley: University of California Press.

Cohen, Ronald. 1981. "Evolutionary Epistemology and Human Values." *Current Anthropology* 22:201–218.

Coke, James G. 1968. "Antecedents of Local Planning." In William I. Goodman and Eric C. Freund, eds., *Principles and Practice of Urban Planning*, pp. 7–28. Washington, D.C.: International City Managers Association.

Collier, John Jr. 1957. "The Tribe that Slept 400 Years." *Pageant* (13 December), 6:40–47.

Collins, Orvis and June Collins. 1973. *Interaction and Social Structure.* The Hague: Mouton.

Colson, Elizabeth. 1971. *The Social Consequences of Resettlement.* Kariba Studies IV. Manchester: Manchester University Press for Institute for African Studies, University of Zambia.

Cook, Thomas, and Charles S. Reichardt, eds. 1979. *Qualitative and Quantitative Methods in Evaluation Research.* Beverly Hills, Calif.: Sage.

"Convenio Celebrado con la Universidad de Cornell de los EE.UU." 1952. *Peru Indigena* 2(4):85–92.

Court, David. 1982. "The Idea of Social Science in East Africa: An Aspect of the Development of Higher Education" In Laurence D. Stifel et al., eds., *Social Science and Public Policy in the Developing World*, pp. 125–165. Lexington, Mass.: Lexington Books (Heath).

Coward, Raymond T. 1976. "The Involvement of Anthropologists in Contract Evaluation: The Federal Perspective." *Anthropology and Education Quarterly* 7:12–16.

Craf, John R. 1958. *Junior Boards of Executives.* New York: Harper.

Creer, Thomas L., and Walter P. Christian. 1976. *Chronically Ill and Handicapped Children, Their Management and Rehabilitation.* Champaign, Ill.: Research Press, Inc.

Cronbach, Lee, et al. 1980a. *Toward Reform of Program Evaluation: Aims, Methods, and Institutional Arrangements.* Pre-published manuscript.

——1980b. *Toward Reform of Program Evaluation: Aims, Methods, and Institutional Arrangements.* San Francisco, Calif.: Jossey-Bass.

Curtis, C. Michael. 1962. "New Day in Peru." *Cornell Alumni News* (May), no. 64:8–12,18.

Davies, Thomas M. 1974. *Indian Integration in Peru: A Half Century of Experience, 1900–1948.* Lincoln, Neb.: University of Nebraska Press.

Davis, Allison W. 1948. "The Measurement of Mental Systems." *Scientific Monthly* 66:301–316.

Davis, Allison W. and John Dollard 1940. *Children of Bondage.* Washington, D.C.: American Council on Education.

Davis, Allison W.; Burleigh B. Gardner; and Mary R. Gardner. 1941. *Deep South: A Social-Anthropological Study of Caste and Class.* Chicago: University of Chicago Press.

Davis, Gloria Jean. 1976. "Pariqi: A Social History of Balinese Movement to Central Sulawesi, 1907–1974." Ph.D. diss., Stanford University.

——1981. "Promoting Increased Food Production in the 1980s." In Proceedings of the Second Annual Agricultural Sector Symposium, January 5–9, p.284. Washington, D.C.: The World Bank.

DeLaguna, Frederica. 1960. "Method and Theory of Ethnology." In F. DeLaguna, ed., *Selected Papers from the American Anthropologist (1888–1920)*, pp. 782–792. Evanston, Ill.: Row, Peterson.

Delgado O., Carlos. 1969. "An Analysis of 'Arribismo' in Peru." *Human Organization* 28:133–139.

Deloria, Ella. 1944. *Speaking of Indians*. New York: Friendship Press.

Deloria, Vine, Jr. 1969. *Custer Died for Your Sins*. New York: Macmillan.

Densmore, Frances. 1929. *Chippewa Customs*. Washington, D.C.: Bureau of American Ethnology, Bulletin 86.

De Vos, George, and Lola Romanucci-Ross, eds. 1975. *Ethnic Identity: Cultural Continuities and Change*. Palo Alto: Mayfield.

Dickson, William J., and F. J. Roethlisberger. 1966. *Counseling in an Organization*. Boston, Mass.: Harvard University, Graduate School of Business Administration.

Dobyns, Henry F. 1971. "On the Economic Anthropology of Postcolonial National Development." *Current Anthropology* 12:393–394.

——1974. *Hualapai Indians, Prehistoric Indian Occupation within the Eastern Area of the Yuman Complex: A Study in Applied Archaeology*. 3 vols. New York: Garland.

Dobyns, Henry F.; Paul L. Doughty; and Harold D. Lasswell. 1971. *Peasants, Power and Applied Social Change: Vicos as a Model*. Beverly Hills, Calif.: Sage.

Dobyns, Henry F., et al. 1966. *Recommendations for Future Research on the Processes of Cultural Change*. Report to the Office of Technical Cooperation and Research, USAID. Cornell University, Department of Anthropology, Comparative Studies of Culture Change, Ithaca, New York.

——1967a. *Strategic Intervention in the Cultural Change Process*. A Report to the Office of Technical Cooperation, USAID. Cornell University, Department of Anthropology, Comparative Studies in Cultural Change, Ithaca, New York.

——1967b. *Some Principles of Cultural Change*. Report to the Office of Technical Cooperation, USAID. Cornell University, Department of Anthropology, Comparative Studies in Cultural Change, Ithaca, New York.

Dobyns, Henry F.; Carlos Monge M.; and Mario C. Vasquez. 1962. "Summary of Technical-Organizational Progress and Reactions to It." *Human Organization* 21:109–115.

Dobyns, Henry F., and Mario C. Vasquez. 1964. "The Cornell-Peru Project: Bibliography and Personnel." Cornell Peru Project Pamphlet 2. Ithaca, New York.

Dollard, John. 1937. *Caste and Class in a Southern Town*. New Haven: Yale University Press.

Donovan, John C. 1967. *The Politics of Poverty*. New York: Pegasus.

Doughty, Paul L. 1971a. "Human Relations: Affection, Rectitude and Respect." In Henry Dobyns, Paul L. Doughty, and Harold Lasswell, eds., *Peasants, Power and Applied Social Change*, pp. 89–114. Beverly Hills, Calif.: Sage.

——1971b. "Local and National Power Structure in Relation to Vicos, 1951–1966:

An Explanatory Note.'' In Henry Dobyns, Paul L. Doughty, and Harold Lasswell, eds., *Peasants, Power and Applied Social Change*, pp.209–213. Beverly Hills, Calif.: Sage.

——1977. ''Review of Directed Social Change in Peru: A Guide to the Vicos Collection.'' *American Anthropologist* 79:144–146.

——1985. ''Directed Culture Change and the Hope for Peace.'' In M.C. Foster and R.A. Rubenstein, eds., *Peace and War: Cross-Cultural Perspectives*. New Brunswick, N.J.: Transaction Books.

Drake, St. Clair, and Horace R. Cayton. 1945. *Black Metropolis*. New York: Harcourt, Brace.

Drash, Philip W., Cynthia L. Stoffel, and Kevin Murdock. 1983. *A Primer of Behavior Modification for the Human Services*. Tampa, Fl.: Hillsborough Alternative Residential Program and Florida Mental Health Institute.

Dressler, W.W. 1982. *Hypertension and Culture Change: Acculturation and Disease in the West Indies*. Salem, N.Y.: Redgrave.

D'Souza, Frances. 1985. ''Anthropology and Disasters: A Roundup After Six Years.'' *Anthropology Today* 1(1):18–19.

Dye, Thomas R. 1972. *Understanding Public Policy*. Englewood Cliffs: Prentice-Hall.

Eades, J.S. 1981. ''Society for Applied Anthropology, 41st Annual Meeting, 'Rethinking Applied Anthropology.' '' *RAIN* (June), no.44:10–11.

Eaton, G. Gray. 1976. ''The Social Order of Japanese Macaques.'' *Scientific American* 235:96–106.

Ebihara, May. 1985. ''American Ethnology in the 1930s: Contexts and Currents.'' In June Helm, ed., *Social Contexts in American Ethnology*, pp. 101–121. 1984 Proceedings of the American Ethnological Society, Washington, D.C.: American Anthropological Association.

Eddy, Elizabeth, and William Partridge, eds. 1978. *Applied Anthropology in America*. New York: Columbia University Press.

Eder, James F. 1982. *Who Shall Succeed? Agricultural Development and Social Inequity on a Philippine Frontier*. Cambridge: Cambridge University Press.

Eggan, Fred. 1963. ''The Graduate Program.'' In David G. Mandelbaum, Gabriel W. Lasker, and Ethel M. Albert, eds., *The Teaching of Anthropology*, pp.409–419. Washington, D.C.: American Anthropological Association.

Elden, Max. 1979. ''Three Generations of Work-democracy Research in Norway: Beyond Classical Socio-technical Systems Analysis.'' In C.L. Cooper and E. Mumford, eds., *The Quality of Working Life in Europe*, pp. 226–257. London: Associated Business Press.

Ellison, Ralph. 1966. ''An American Dilemma: A Review.'' In *Shadow and Act*, pp.290–302. New York: Signet Books.

Elisberg, D.A. 1977. ''Congressional View of Program Evaluation.'' In E. Chelimsky, ed., *A Symposium on the Use of Evaluation by Federal Agencies*, pp. 67–70. McLean, Va.: Mitre Corporation.

Embree, John. 1943. ''Dealing with Japanese.'' *Applied Anthropology* 2:37–41.

Emener, William G. 1979. ''Professional Burnout.'' *Journal of Rehabilitation* 45:55–58.

Enchenique, Jorge. 1979. "Notes on Peasant Participation in Rural Development Planning." Paper prepared for the Sociological Workshop on Participation, August (mimeo). Washington, D.C.: The World Bank.

Erasmus, Charles J. 1961. *Man Takes Control: Cultural Development and American Aid*. Minneapolis: University of Minnesota Press.

——1985. *In Search of the Common Good: Utopian Experiments Past and Future*. New York: Free Press.

Etzioni, Amitai. 1969. *Latin America: Underdevelopment or Revolution*. New York: Monthly Review Press.

——1971. "Policy Research." *American Sociologist* 6(4):8–12.

——1972. "The Search for Political Meaning." *The Center Magazine* 5(2):2–11.

Evans-Pritchard, E.E. 1940. *The Nuer*. Oxford: Clarendon Press.

——1946. "Applied Anthropology." *Africa* 16:92–98.

Everhart, Robert L. 1975. "Problems of Doing Fieldwork in Ethnographic Evaluation." *Human Organization* 34:205–215.

Fallers, Leonard A. 1974. *The Social Anthropology of the Nation-State*. Chicago: Aldine.

Farvar, M.T., and J.P. Milton. 1972. *The Careless Technology:Ecology and International Development*. New York: Natural History Press.

Ferrell, B.G., and D.W. Compton. 1986. "Use of Ethnographic Techniques for Evaluation in a Large School District: The Vanguard Case." In D.M. Fetterman and M.A. Pitman, eds., *Ethnographic Evaluation: Theory, Practice and Politics*. Beverly Hills, Calif.: Sage.

Fetterman, David M. 1981a. "New Perils for the Contract Ethnographer." *Anthropology and Education Quarterly* 12:71–80.

——1981b. *Study of the Career Intern Program. Final Report—Task C: Program Dynamics: Structure, Function and Interrelationships*. Mountain View, Calif.: RMC Research Corporation.

——1982. "Ibsen's Baths: Reactivity and Insensitivity (A Misapplication of the Treatment-control Design in National Evaluation)." *Educational Evaluation and Policy Analysis* 4:261–269.

——1984a. *Ethnography in Educational Evaluation*. Beverly Hills, Calif.: Sage.

——1984b. "Ethnography in Education Research: The Dynamics of Diffusion." In D.M.Fetterman, ed., *Ethnography and Educational Evaluation*, pp. 21–35. Beverly Hills, Calif.: Sage.

——1984c. "Guilty Knowledge, Dirty Hands and Other Ethical Dilemmas: The Hazards of Contract Research." In David M.Fetterman, ed., *Ethnography in Educational Evaluation*, pp. 211–236. Beverly Hills, Calif.: Sage.

——1985a. "Focusing on a Cross-Cultural Lens in Evaluation." *Evaluation Research Society Newsletter* 9(2):1–5.

——1985b. "The CAE Network." *Anthropology Newsletter* 26(1):8.

——in press a. "Conceptual Crossroads: Methods and Ethics in Ethnographic Evaluation." In D.D.Williams, ed., *Conflicts and Possible Solutions in the Practice of Naturalistic Evaluation*. San Francisco, Calif.: Jossey-Bass, Inc.

——in press b. "Ethnographic Educational Evaluation." In George Spindler, ed., *Educational Anthropology Now*. New York: Academic Press.

——in press c. *Re-evaluating Gifted Education.* Beverly Hills, Calif.: Hoover Press and Sage.

Fetterman, David M. and M.A. Pitman. 1986. *Ethnographic Evaluation: Theory, Practice and Politics.* Beverly Hills, Calif.: Sage.

Finsterbusch, Kurt, and Annabelle Bender Motz. 1980. *Social Research for Policy Decisions.* Belmont,Calif.: Wadsworth.

Firestone, William A., and Robert E. Herriott. 1984. "Multi-site Qualitative Policy Research: Some Design and Implementation Issues." In D.M. Fetterman, ed., *Ethnography in Educational Evaluation,* pp. 63–88. Beverly Hills, Calif.: Sage.

Firth, Raymond. 1951. *Elements of Social Organization.* London: Watts and Company.

——1981. "Engagement and Detachment: Reflections on Applying Social Anthropology to Social Affairs." *Human Organization* 40(3):193–201.

Firth, Raymond ed. 1957. *Man and Culture: An Evaluation of the Work of Bronislaw Malinowski.* London: Routledge and Kegan Paul.

Fischer, John L. 1979. "Government Anthropologists in the Trust Territory of Micronesia." In Walter Goldschmidt, ed., *The Uses of Anthropology,* pp. 238–252. Washington, D.C.: American Anthropological Association.

Fisher, Donald. 1977. "The Impact of American Foundations on the Development of British University Education, 1900–1939." Ph.D. diss., University of California, Berkeley.

Fisher, Joseph. 1969. "Regional Planning: Determining the Public Interest." In Maynard M. Hufschmidt, ed., *Regional Planning: Challenge and Prospects,* pp.3–27. New York: Praeger.

Forde, Daryll. 1953. "Applied Anthropology in Government: British Africa." In A.L. Kroeber, ed., *Anthropology Today,* pp.841–865. Chicago: University of Chicago Press.

Fosdick, Raymond B. 1952. *The Story of the Rockefeller Foundation.* New York: Harper and Brothers.

Foster, George M. 1948. *Empire's Children: The People of Tzintzuntzan.* Washington,D.C., Smithsonian Institution, Institute of Social Anthropology Publication No.6.

——1952. "Relationships Between Theoretical and Applied Anthropology: A Public Health Program Analysis." *Human Organization* 11:5–16.

——1958. *Summary Report.* Wenner Gren-American Anthropological Association Ph.D. Curricula Conference, Washington, D.C., November 23–24 (Mimeographed).

——1962. *Traditional Cultures and The Impact of Technological Change.* New York: Harper and Row.

——1969. *Applied Anthropology.* Boston: Little, Brown.

——1979. "The Institute of Social Anthropology." In Walter Goldschmidt, ed., *The Uses of Anthropology,* pp. 205–216. Washington, D.C.: American Anthropological Association.

Foster, George M., et al. 1979. *Long-Term Field Research in Social Anthropology,* New York: Academic Press.

Frank, Andre Gunder. 1969. *Latin America: Underdevelopment or Revolution.* New York: Monthly Review Press.

Franklin, S.H. 1969. *The European Peasantry: The Final Phase.* London: Methuen.

Frantz, Charles. 1985. "Relevance: American Ethnology and the Wider Society, 1900–1940." In June Helm, ed., *Social Contexts of American Ethnology,* pp. 83–100. 1984 Proceedings of the American Ethnological Society. Washington, D.C.: American Anthropological Association.

Fraser, Thomas M., Jr. 1968. *Culture and Change in India: The Barpali Experiment.* Amherst, Mass.: University of Massachusetts Press.

Frazier, E. Franklin. 1939. *The Negro Family in the United States.* Chicago: University of Chicago Press.

Freeman, Howard E., and Peter H. Rossi. 1984. "Furthering the Applied Side of Sociology." *American Sociological Review* 49:571–580.

Freeman, Howard E., and Clarence C. Sherwood. 1970. *Social Research and Social Policy.* Englewood Cliffs, N.J.:Prentice-Hall.

Fried, Morton H. 1953. *The Fabric of Chinese Society.* New York: Praeger.

Frohock, Fred M. 1979. *Public Policy: Scope and Logic.* Englewood Cliffs: Prentice-Hall.

Fromm, Erich. 1972. "Humanistic Planning." *Journal of the American Institute of Planners* 38:67–71.

Fuchs, Estelle, and Robert J. Havighurst. 1972. *To Live on This Earth: American Indian Education.* Garden City, N.Y.:Doubleday.

Furnivall, John S. 1948. *Colonial Policy and Practice.* Cambridge: Cambridge University Press.

Galloway, George B., and Associates. 1941. *Planning for America.* New York: Holt.

Gans, Herbert J. 1970. "From Urbanism to Policy Planning." *Journal of the American Institute of Planners* 36:223–225.

Gardner, Burleigh B. 1945. *Human Relations in Industry.* Chicago: R.D. Irwin.

——1976. "Doing Business with Management." In Elizabeth M. Eddy and William L. Partridge, eds., *Applied Anthropology in America,* pp. 245–260. New York: Columbia University Press.

Gearing, Fred. 1970. "The Strategy of the Fox Project." In James A. Clifton, ed., *Applied Anthropology,* pp. 113–120. New York: Houghton Mifflin, reprinted from Fred Gearing, R. McC. Netting, and L.R. Peattie, *Documentary History of the Fox Project: 1949–1959,* pp. 294–300. Chicago: University of Chicago, Department of Anthropology.

Geertz, Clifford. 1963a. *Agricultural Involution: The Process of Ecological Change in Indonesia.* Berkeley, Calif.: University of California Press.

——1963b. *Peddlers and Princes: Social Development and Economic Change in Two Indonesian Towns.* Chicago: University of Chicago Press.

——1973. *The Interpretation of Cultures.* New York: Basic Books.

Gillie, F.B. 1967. *Basic Thinking in Regional Planning.* The Hague: Mouton.

Gillin, John. 1947. *Moche: A Peruvian Coastal Community.* Washington, D.C.: Smithsonian Institution, Institute of Social Anthropology Publication No. 3.

Gladwin, Thomas. 1967. *Poverty, U.S.A..* Boston: Little, Brown.

Glaser, Barney G., and Anselm L. Strauss. 1967. *The Discovery of Grounded Theory: Strategies for Qualitative Research.* Chicago: Aldine.

Glazer, Nathan. 1975. *Affirming Discrimination: Ethnic Inequality and Public Policy.* New York: Basic Books.

Glennan, T.K. 1972. "Evaluating Federal Manpower Programs: Notes and Observations." In P.H. Rossi and W. Williams, eds., *Evaluating Social Programs: Theory, Practice and Politics,* pp.187–220. New York: Seminar Press.

Gluckman, Max. 1955. *Custom and Conflict in Africa.* London: Oxford University Press.

Goetz, Judith P., and Margaret D. LeCompte. 1984. *Ethnography and Qualitative Design in Educational Research.* New York: Academic Press.

Goffman, Erving. 1970. *Asylums.* Garden City, New York: Doubleday.

Goldberg, H.E. 1984. "Evaluation, Ethnography, and the Concept of Culture: Disadvantaged Youth in an Israeli Town." In D.M. Fetterman, ed., *Ethnography in Educational Evaluation,* pp.153–173. Beverly Hills, Calif.: Sage.

Goldfrank, Esther. 1943. "Historic Change and Social Character: A Study of the Teton Dakota." *American Anthropologist* 45:67–83.

Goldschmidt, Walter, ed. 1979. *The Uses of Anthropology.* Washington, D.C.: American Anthropological Association.

Gonzalez, Nancie L. 1972. "The Sociology of a Dam." *Human Organization* 31:353–60.

Goodenough, Ward H. 1956. "Componential Analysis and the Study of Meaning." *Language* 32:195–216.

——1963. *Cooperation in Change: An Anthropological Approach to Community Development.* New York: Russell Sage Foundation.

——1969. "Re-thinking Role and Status: Toward a General Model of Relationships." In Stephen A. Tyler, ed., *Cognitive Anthropology,* pp. 311–330. New York: Holt, Rinehart and Winston.

——1971. *Culture, Language and Society.* Reading, Mass.: Addison-Wesley Modular Publications No.7.

Goodland, Robert. 1982. *Tribal Peoples and Economic Development: Human Ecologic Considerations.* Washington, D.C.: World Bank.

Gottlieb, B.H., ed. 1981. *Social Networks and Social Support.* Beverly Hills, Calif.: Sage.

Gottlieb, David. 1974. "Work and Families." *The Journal of Higher Education* 45:535–544.

Gouldner, Alvin W. 1959. "Organizational Analysis." In R.K. Merton, L. Broom, L.S. Cottrell, Jr., eds., *Sociology Today,* pp. 400–428. New York: Basic Books.

Grabow, Stephen, and Alan Heskin. 1973. "Foundations for a Radical Concept of Planning." *Journal of the American Institute of Planners* 39:106–114.

Green, Wayne E. 1975. "Inept Advocates? Lawyers' Competence at Courtroom Work Stirs Growing Debate." *Wall Street Journal* (February 24), 55(92):1,17.

Gruenbaum, Ellen. 1981. "Medical Anthropology, Health Policy and the State: A Case Study of the Sudan." *Policy Studies Review* 1(1):47–65.

Guarnaccia, Peter J. 1984. "Asthma in a Low-Income Community: The Correlates of Illness Severity and Health System Utilization." Ph.D. diss., University of Connecticut.

Guest, Robert A. 1962. *Organizational Change: The Effect of Successful Leadership.* Homewood, Ill.: Irwin and Dorsey Press.

Haas, Theodore H. 1957. "The Legal Aspects of Indian Affairs from 1887–1957." *Annals American Academy of Political and Social Sciences.* 311:12–22.

Habermas, Jurgen. 1971. *Knowledge and Human Interests.* Boston, Mass.: Beacon Press. (Translated by J.J. Shapiro.)

Halbwachs, Maurice. 1930. *Les Causes du Suicide.* Librairie Felix Alcan. (Reprinted New York: Arno Press, 1975.)

Hall, Edward T. 1966. *The Hidden Dimension.* Garden City, N.Y.: Doubleday.

——1976. *Beyond Culture.* Garden City, N.Y.: Doubleday.

Hannerz, Ulf. 1969. *Soulside: Inquiries into Ghetto Culture and Community.* New York: Columbia University Press.

——1974. "Ethnicity and Opportunity in Urban America." In Abner Cohen, ed., *Urban Ethnicity,* pp. 37–76. ASA Monograph 12. London: Tavistock.

Hansen, Art, and Anthony Oliver-Smith, eds. 1982. *Involuntary Migration and Resettlement: The Problems and Responses of Dislocated Peoples.* Boulder: Westview Press.

Hansen Asael T. 1976. "Robert Redfield, The Yucatan Project, and I." In John V. Murra, ed., *American Anthropology: The Early Years,* pp. 167–186. New York: West.

Harbord, J.H. 1960. "The Vicos Experiment: Rehabilitation of the Andean Indian." *Peruvian Times* (August 12) 20(1026):9–11.

Harding, Joseph R., and J. Michael Livesay. 1984. "Anthropology and Public Policy." In George J. McCall and George H. Weber, eds., *Social Science and Public Policy: The Roles of Academic Disciplines in Policy Analysis,* pp. 51–90. Port Washington, New York: Associated Faculty Press.

Hargrove, Erwin C. 1975. *The Missing Link: The Study of the Implementation of Social Policy.* Washington, D.C.: The Urban Institute.

Harris, José. 1977. *William Beveridge: A Biography.* Oxford: Clarendon Press.

Harris, Marvin. 1964. *The Nature of Cultural Things.* New York: Random House.

——1968. *The Rise of Anthropological Theory.* New York: Thomas Y. Crowell.

——1971. *Town and Country in Brazil.* New York: W.W. Norton. (Orig. pub. 1956.)

Haskell, Edward F. 1972. *Full Circle: The Moral Force of Unified Science.* New York: Gordon and Breach.

Hayek, Friedrich A. 1967. "The Intellectuals and Socialism." In Friedrich A. Hayek, ed., *Studies in Philosophy, Politics and Economics,* pp. 178–194. Chicago: University of Chicago Press.

Health Systems Agency North Central Connecticut (HSANC). 1985. "Material Risk Factors." Unpublished document.

Heighton, Robert H., Jr., and Harold L. McPheeters. 1976. *Program Evaluation in the State Mental Health Agency: Activities, Functions and Management Uses.* Washington, D.C.: Department of Health, Education and Welfare. Doc. No. (ADM) 76:310.

Helman, Cecil. 1985. "Anthropology and Clinical Practice." *Anthropology Today* 1(3):7–10.

Hemwall, Martha K. 1984. "Ethnography as Evaluation: Hearing-Impaired Students in the Mainstream." In D.M. Fetterman, ed., *Ethnography in Educational Evaluation*, pp. 133–152. Beverly Hills, Calif.: Sage.

Henry, Jules. 1973. "A Theory for an Anthropological Analysis of American Culture." In Jules Henry, ed., *On Sham, Vulnerability, and Other Forms of Self-Destruction*, pp. 59–81. New York: Random House.

Herskovits, Melville J. 1941. *The Myth of the Negro Past*. New York: Harper.

——1953. *Franz Boas: The Science of Man in the Making*. New York: Scribner's.

Hertzman, Marc, ed. 1984. "Systems Theory and Psychiatry. *Psychiatric Annals* 14 (entire volume).

Hessler, Richard M., and Peter Kong-Ming New. 1972. "Toward a Research Commune?" *Human Organization* 31:449–451.

Heyer, Judith, et al. 1981. *Rural Development in Tropical Africa*. New York: St. Martin's Press.

Hicks, George L., and Phillip E. Leis, eds. 1977. *Ethnic Encounters: Identities and Contexts*. North Scituate, Mass.: Duxbury Press.

Higham, John. 1974. *Strangers in the Land: Patterns of American Nativism 1860–1925*. 2d ed. New York: Atheneum.

Hill, Carol E., ed. 1985. *Training Manual in Medical Anthropology*. Washington, D.C.: American Anthropological Association and Society for Applied Anthropology.

——1986. *Contemporary Health Policy Issues and Alternatives*. Athens: University of Georgia Press.

Hill, Polly. 1985. "The Gullibility of Development Economists." *Anthropology Today* 1(2):10–12.

Hill-Burnett, Jaquetta. 1976. "The Joking Relationship Between Teachers and Puerto Rican Youths in School." Urbana, Ill.: Bureau of Educational Research. (Files of the author.)

Himes, James R. 1972. "The Utilization of Research for Development: Two Case Studies in Rural Modernization and Agriculture in Peru." Ph.D. diss., Princeton University.

——1981. "The Impact in Peru of the Vicos Project." In George M. Dalton, ed., *Research in Economic Anthropology*, pp. 141–209. Greenwich, Conn.: JAI Press, Inc.

Hinsley, Curtis M. 1976. "Amateurs and Professionals in Washington Anthropology, 1879–1903." In John V. Murra, ed., *American Anthropology: The Early Years*, pp. 36–68. New York: West.

——1981. *Savages and Scientists: The Smithsonian Institution and the Development of American Anthropology 1846–1910*. Washington, D.C.: Smithsonian Institution Press.

Hirschman, Albert O. 1981. "The Tolerance of Income Inequality in the Course of Economic Development." In Albert O. Hirschman, ed., *Essays in Trespassing: Economics to Politics and Beyond*. New York: Cambridge University Press.

——1984. *Getting Ahead Collectively: Grassroots Experience in Latin America*. New York: Pergamon Press.

Hobbs, Nicholas. 1979. "Knowledge Transfer and the Policy Process." Manuscript, Vanderbilt Institute for Public Policy Studies.

Hoben, Allan. 1980. "Agricultural Decision-Making in Foreign Assistance: An Anthropological Analysis." In Peggy Bartlett, ed., *Agricultural Decision-Making,* pp.359–375. New York: Academic Press.

——1982. "Anthropologists and Development." In Bernard J. Siegel, ed., *Annual Review of Anthropology* 11:158–166. Palo Alto, Calif.: Annual Reviews, Inc.

Hodgkinson, Harold. 1974. "Adult Development: Implications for Faculty and Administrators." *Educational Record.* 55:263–274.

Holcomb, H. 1974. "Tell Congress Results of Research." *Education Daily* 7(4):313.

Holland, Thomas. 1979. "The Politics of Community Action." In C. Cherington and F. Dybwad, eds., *New Neighbors: The Retarded Citizen in Quest of a Home,* pp.173–184. HHS Publication # (OHOS) 80-21004. Washington, D.C.: U.S. Department of Health and Human Services.

Holmberg, Allan R. 1952a. "Propuesta de la Universidad de Cornell de los EE.UU." *Peru Indigena* 2(4):87–95.

——1952b. "Proyecto Peru-Cornell en las Ciencias Sociales Aplicadas." *Peru Indigena* (5–6):158–166.

——1955. "Participant Intervention in the Field." *Human Organization* 14:23–26.

——1956. "The Vicos Research Proposal." Unpublished manuscript, 51 pages.

——1958. "The Research and Development Approach to the Study of Change." *Human Organization* 17:12–16.

——1960. "Changing Community Attitudes and Values in Peru." In Council on Foreign Relations, *Social Change in Latin America Today,* pp. 63–107. New York: Harper.

——1967. "Algunas Relaciones entre la Privacion Psico-biologica y el Cambio Cultural en los Andes." *American Indigena* 27 (1):3–24.

——1969. "Dynamic Functionalism." In A.A. Rogow, ed., *Politics, Personality and Social Science in the Twentieth Century,* pp. 159–178. Chicago: University of Chicago Press.

——1971. "The Role of Power in Changing Values and Institutions of Vicos." In Henry F. Dobyns, Paul L. Doughty, and Harold Lasswell, eds., *Peasants, Power and Applied Social Change,* pp. 33–64. Beverly Hills, Calif.: Sage.

Holmberg, Allan R., and Henry F. Dobyns. 1969. "The Cornell Program in Vicos, Peru." In Clifford Wharton, ed., *Subsistence Agriculture and Economic Development,* pp. 392–414. Chicago: Aldine.

Holmberg, Allan R., et al. 1962. "Community and Regional Development: The Joint Cornell-Peru Experiment." *Human Organization* 21:107–124.

Homans, George C. 1950. *The Human Group.* New York: Harcourt Brace.

Homans, George C., and David M. Schneider. 1955. *Marriage, Authority and Final Causes: A Study of Unilateral Cross-Cousin Marriage.* New York: Free Press.

Horowitz, Irving L. 1965. "The Life and Death of Project Camelot." *Transaction* 3(1):3–7, 44–47.

——1976. *Ideology and Utopia in the United States, 1956–1976.* London: Oxford University Press.

Horowitz, Irving L., ed. 1974. *The Rise and Fall of Project Camelot.* Rev. ed. Cambridge, Mass.: MIT Press. (Orig. pub. 1967.)

Horsfall, Alexander, and Conrad M. Arensberg. 1949. "Teamwork and Productivity in a Shoe Factory." *Human Organization* 8:13–26.

Howard, Alan. 1970. *Learning To Be Rotuman: Enculturation in the South Pacific.* New York: Teachers College Press.

Howard, Jane. 1984. *Margaret Mead: A Life.* New York: Simon and Schuster.

Huizer, Gerrit. 1969. "Community Development, Land Reform and Political Participation." *American Journal of Economics and Sociology* 28:159–178.

Huse, Edgar. 1975. *Organization Development and Change.* New York: West.

Hyden, Goran. 1980. *Beyond Ujamaa.* Berkeley: University of California Press.

Hymes, Dell, ed. 1964. *Language, Culture and Society.* New York: Harcourt and Brace.

——1969. *Reinventing Anthropology.* New York: Random House.

——1972. "Introduction." In Courtney B. Cadzen, Vera P. John, and Dell Hymes, eds., *Functions of Language in the Classroom,* pp. xi–lvii. New York: Teachers College Press.

Jacobs, Sue-Ellen. 1974. "Action and Advocacy Anthropology." *Human Organization* 33:209–215.

Jacobs, Wilbur R. 1950. *Diplomacy and Indian Gifts: Anglo-French Rivalry Along the Ohio and Northwest Frontiers, 1748–1763.* Stanford, Calif.: Stanford University Press.

——1954. *The Appalachian Frontier: The Edmond Atkin Report and Plan of 1755.* Columbia: University of South Carolina Press.

——1972. *Dispossessing the American Indian.* New York: Scribner's.

——1974. "The Tip of an Iceberg: Pre-Colombian Indian Demography and Some Implications for Revisionism." *William and Mary Quarterly* 31:123–132.

——1975. "Native American History: How It Illuminates our Past." *The American Historical Review* 80(3):593.

James, Bernard J. 1971. "Niche Defense Among Learned Gentlemen: Notes on Organizational Inertia in Universities." *Human Organization* 30:223–228.

Jenkins, W.I. 1978. *Policy Analysis.* New York: St. Martin's Press.

Jenks, Albert E. 1921. "The Relations of Anthropology to Americanization." *Scientific Monthly* 12:240–245.

Johnson, Lyndon B. 1964. Speech at the University of California, Irvine.

Johnson, Thomas M. 1985. "Consultation-Liaison Psychiatry: Medicine as Patient, Marginality as Practice." In Robert A. Hahn and Atwood D. Gaines, eds., *Physicians of Western Medicine: Anthropological Approaches to Theory and Practice,* pp. 269–292. Dordrecht, Holland, and Boston, Mass.: D. Reidel.

Johnson, Thomas M., and Arthur Kleinman. 1984. "Cultural Concerns in Consultation Psychiatry." In Frederick G. Guggenheim and Myron F. Weiner, eds., *Manual of Psychiatric Consultation and Emergency Care,* pp. 275–284. New York: Jason Aronson.

Johnson, Wendell. 1953. "The Fateful Process of Mr. A. Talking to Mr. B." *Harvard Business Review* 31(1):49–56.

Jones, Charles O. 1984. *An Introduction to the Study of Public Policy.* 3d ed. Monterey, Calif.: Brooks/Cole.

Jones, Delmos J. 1970. "Towards a Native Anthropology." *Human Organization* 29:251–259.

——1971. "Social Responsibility and the Belief in Basic Research: An Example from Thailand." *Current Anthropology* 12:347–350.
Jorgenson, Joseph G. 1971. "Indians and the Metropolis." In Jack Waddell and O.M. Watson, eds., *The American Indian in Urban Society*, pp. 66–113. Boston, Mass.: Little, Brown.
——1981. "Social Impact Assessments and Energy Developments." *Policy Studies Review* 1(1):66–86.
Joshi, Vidyut. 1983. *General Report on Studies on Rehabilitation of Submerging Villages*. Surat, Gujarat: Centre for Social Studies.
Kain, John F. 1970. "Rampant Schizophrenia: The Case Study of City and Regional Planning." *Journal of American Institute of Planners* 36:221–223.
Kaplan, David. 1974. "The Anthropology of 'Authenticity': Everyman His Own Anthropologist: An Essay Review." *American Anthropologist* 76:824–839.
Kardiner, Abram, and Edward Preble. 1961. *They Studied Man*. Cleveland, Ohio: World.
Katon, Wayne, and Arthur Kleinman. 1980. "Doctor-Patient Negotiation and Other Social Science Strategies in Patient Care." In Leon Eisenberg and Arthur Kleinman, eds., *The Relevance of Social Science for Medicine*, pp. 253–279. Boston, Mass.: D. Reidel.
Katzman, Martin T. 1977. *Cities and Frontiers in Brazil: Regional Dimensions of Economic Development*. Cambridge: Harvard University Press.
Keesing, Roger M. 1970. "Toward a Model of Role Analysis." In Raoul Naroll and Ronald Cohen, eds., *A Handbook of Method in Cultural Anthropology*, pp. 423–454. Garden City: The Natural History Press.
——1979. *Cultural Anthropology: A Contemporary Perspective*. New York: Holt, Rinehart and Winston.
Keller, A.R. 1881. "Crow Agency Report." Washington, D.C.: Department of the Interior Annual Report.
Kelly, Lawrence C. 1980. "Anthropology and Anthropologists in the Indian New Deal." *Journal of the History of the Behavioral Sciences* 16:6–24.
——1981. "The Society for Applied Anthropology: Its Origins and Early Years." Paper presented at the Society for Applied Anthropology, April 1981, Edinburgh, Scotland. (Files of the author.)
——1985a. "Anthropology in the Soil Conservation Service." *Agricultural History* 59:136–147.
——1985b. "Why Applied Anthropology Developed When It Did: A Commentary on People, Money, and Changing Times, 1930–1945." In June Helm,,ed., *Social Contexts of American Ethnology*, pp.122–138. 1984 Proceedings of the American Ethnological Society. Washington, D.C.: American Anthropological Association.
Kendon, Adam. 1963. "Temporal Aspects of the Social Performance in Two-Person Encounters." Dissertation, Oxford University.
Kennard, Edward A., and Gordon Macgregor. 1953. "Applied Anthropology in Government: United States." In A.L. Kroeber, ed., *Anthropology Today*, pp. 832–840. Chicago: University of Chicago Press.
Kennedy, Timothy. 1984. "Beyond Advocacy: An Animative Approach to Public Participation." Ph.D. diss., Cornell University.

548   Bibliography

Kimball, Solon T. 1946. "The Crisis in Colonial Administration." *Applied Anthropology* 5:8–16.
——1960. "Cultural Influences Shaping the Role of the Child." In *The National Elementary Principal: Those First School Years* 40:8–32.
——1974a. "Comment." *Impact of Science on Society* 24:109–117. Paris: UNESCO.
——1974b. *Culture and the Educative Process.* New York: Teachers College Press.
——1979. "Land Use Management: The Navajo Reservation." In Walter Goldschmidt, ed., *The Uses of Anthropology*, pp.61–78. Washington, D.C.: American Anthropological Association.
Kimball, Solon T., and Marion Pearsall. 1954. *The Talladega Story.* University: University of Alabama Press.
Kimball, Solon T., and John H. Provinse. 1942. "Navajo Social Organization in Land Use Planning." *Applied Anthropology* 1:18–25.
Kirk, S.A., and Jeanne McRae McCarthy, eds. 1975. *Learning Disabilities: Selected ACLD Papers.* Boston, Mass.: Houghton-Mifflin.
Kleinman, Arthur; Leon Eisenberg; and Byron Good. 1978. "Culture, Illness, and Care: Clinical Lessons from Anthropologic and Cross-Cultural Research." *Annals of Internal Medicine* 88:251–258.
Kluckholn, Clyde, and Robert A. Hackenberg. 1954. "Social Science Principles and the Indian Reorganization Act." In William H. Kelly, ed., *Indian Affairs and the Indian Reorganization Act: The Twenty Year Record*, pp. 29–34. Tucson: University of Arizona Press.
Kluckholn, Clyde, and Olaf Prufer. 1959. "Influences During the Formative Years." In Walter Goldschmidt, ed., *The Anthropology of Franz Boas*, pp. 4–28. American Anthropological Association Memoir 89.
Koestler, Arthur. 1967. *The Act of Creation.* New York: Macmillan.
Kohler, Ulrich. 1981. "Integrated Community Development: Vicos in Peru." In George M. Dalton, ed., *Research in Economic Anthropology*, pp. 111–141. Greenwich, Conn.: JAI Press.
Korten David C. 1980. "Community Organization and Rural Development: A Learning Process Approach." In *Public Administration Review* 40:480–511.
Kottak, Conrad P. 1985. "When People Don't Come First: Some Sociological Issues from Completed Projects." In Michael M. Cernea, ed., *Putting People First: Sociological Variables in Rural Development*, pp.325–356. New York: Oxford University Press.
Kroeber, Alfred L. 1959. "Preface." In Walter Goldschmidt, ed., *The Anthropology of Franz Boas*, pp. v–vii. American Anthropological Association Memoir 89.
Kroeber, Theodora. 1970. *Alfred Kroeber: A Personal Configuration.* Berkeley: University of California Press.
Kuhn, Thomas S. 1962. *The Structure of Scientific Revolutions.* Chicago: University of Chicago Press.
Kunkel, J. 1970. *Society and Economic Growth.* New York: Oxford University Press.
Kuznets, Simon. 1980. "The Kuznets Curves." In World Bank, *Poverty and Human Development*, pp. 8–9. New York: Oxford University Press.
Kvaloy, Sigmund. 1984. "Man, Nature and Mechanistic Systems: An Exercise in

Ecophilosophy.'' In Soren Bergstrom, ed., *Economic Growth and the Role of Science*. Eldsbruk: Holms Gards Tryckeri.

Labov, William. 1968. *A Study of the Non-Standard English of Negro and Puerto Rican Speakers in New York City*. Vol. 2: Final Report, Cooperative Research Project No. 3288. Washington, D.C.: Office of Education.

Lako, George Tombe. 1985. ''The Impact of the Jonglei Scheme on the Economy of the Dinka.'' *African Affairs* 84:15–38.

Lantis, Margaret. 1945. ''Applied Anthropology as a Public Service.'' *Applied Anthropology* 4:20–32.

Lasch, Christopher. 1975. ''The Democratization of Culture.'' *Change: The Magazine of Higher Learning* (Summer), 7:14–23.

Lasswell, Harold D. 1968. ''Policy Sciences.'' In *International Encyclopedia of the Social Sciences* 12:181–188. New York: Macmillan.

——1971. ''The Transferability of the Vicos Strategy.'' In Henry Dobyns, Paul L. Doughty, and Harold Lasswell, eds., *Peasants, Power and Applied Social Change*, pp. 167–178. Beverly Hills, Calif.: Sage.

Lauria, Anthony. 1964. ''Respeto, Ralajo, and Interpersonal Relations in Puerto Rico.'' *Anthropological Quarterly* 37:53–67.

Lawler, Edward E. 1973. *Motivation in Organization*. Monterey, Calif.: Brooks-Cole.

Lazes, Peter, and Tony Costanza. 1984. ''Xerox Cuts Costs without Layoffs through Union-Management Collaboration,'' U.S. Department of Labor, Labor-Management Brief (July). (Reprinted from National Productivity Review, Autumn 1983.)

Leacock, Eleanor. 1973. ''The Concept of Culture and Its Significance for School Counselors.'' In F.A. Ianni and E. Storey, eds., *Cultural Relevance and Educational Issues: Readings in Anthropology and Education*, pp. 189–200. Boston, Mass.: Little, Brown.

Leacock, Eleanor, ed. 1971. *The Culture of Poverty: A Critique*. New York: Simon and Schuster.

Leacock, Eleanor; Nancie L. Gonzalez; and Gilbert Kushner, eds. 1974. *Training Programs for New Opportunities in Applied Anthropology*. Washington, D.C.: American Anthropological Association.

Leaf, Murray J. 1979. *Man, Mind, and Science: A History of Anthropology*. New York: Columbia University Press.

LeCompte, Margaret D., and Judith P. Goetz. 1984. ''Ethnographic Data Collection in Evaluation Research.'' In D.M.Fetterman, ed., *Ethnography in Educational Research*, pp.37–59. Beverly Hills, Calif.: Sage.

Leighton, Alexander H. 1945. *The Governing of Men*. Princeton, N.J.: Princeton University Press.

——1959. *My Name Is Legion*. New York: Basic Books.

Lenton, Roberto. 1981. ''A Note on the Relationship Between Action Research and Other Forms of Engineering Research.'' In OJI Agricultural Administration, Network Paper, February 2.

Lesieur, Frederick, ed., 1958. *The Scanlon Plan: A Frontier in Labor-Management Cooperation*. Cambridge, Mass.: Technology Press of MIT.

Lesser, Alexander. 1968. "Franz Boas." *International Encyclopedia of the Social Sciences* 2:99–110. New York: Macmillan.

——1976. "The American Ethnological Society: The Columbia Phase, 1906–1946." In John V. Murra, ed., *American Anthropology: The Early Years*, pp. 126–135. New York: West.

Levin, M., and N. Abend. 1971. *Bureaucrats in Collision: Case Studies in Area Transportation.* Cambridge, Mass.: MIT Press.

Lévi-Strauss, Claude. 1963. *Structural Anthropology.* C. Jacobson and B. Schoepf, trans. New York: Basic Books. (Orig. pub. 1958.)

——1969. *The Elementary Structures of Kinship.* Boston, Mass.: Beacon Press. (Orig. pub. Paris: Presses Universitaires de France, 1949.)

Lewis, Hylan. 1955. *Blackways of Kent.* Chapel Hill: University of North Carolina Press.

Lewis, John P. 1964. *Quiet Crisis in India: Economic Development and American Policy.* Garden City, N.Y.: Doubleday.

Lewis, Oscar. 1951. *Life in a Mexican Village: Tepotzlan Restudied.* Urbana, Ill: University of Illinois Press.

——1966a. *La Vida: A Puerto Rican Family in the Culture of Poverty-San Juan and New York.* New York: Random House.

——1966b. "The Culture of Poverty." *Scientific American* 215:19–25.

Liebow, Eliot. 1967. *Tally's Corner: A Study of Negro Streetcorner Men.* Boston, Mass.: Little, Brown.

Lindblom, C.E., and D.K. Cohen. 1979. *Usable Knowledge.* New Haven, Conn.: Yale University Press.

Linton, Adelin, and Charles Wagley. 1971. *Ralph Linton.* New York: Columbia University Press.

Linton, Ralph. 1936. *The Study of Man.* New York: Appleton.

Linton, Ralph, ed. 1945. *The Science of Man in the World Crisis.* New York: Columbia University Press.

Littlestone, Ralph. 1973. "Planning in Mental Health." In Saul Feldman, ed., *The Administration of Mental Health Services*, pp. 3–28. Springfield, Ill.: Charles C. Thomas.

Livingston, Robert Teviot, and Stanley H. Milberg. 1957. *Human Relations in Industrial Research Management.* New York: Columbia University Press.

Long, Norman, and Bryan Robert, eds. 1978. *Peasant Cooperation and Capitalist Expansion in Central Peru.* Austin, Texas: University of Texas Press.

Lorenz, Konrad. 1966. *On Aggression.* New York: Harcourt Brace and World.

Lowie, Robert H. 1912. "Some Problems in Ethnology of the Crow and Village Indians." *American Anthropologist* 14:60–71.

——1922. "Material Culture of the Crow Indians." *Anthropological Papers of the Museum of Natural History* 225:201–270.

——1935. *The Crow Indians.* New York: Rinehart.

——1937a. "Introduction." In W. Lloyd Warner, ed., *A Black Civilization*, pp. xv–xix. New York: Harper.

——1937b. *The History of Ethnological History.* New York: Farrar and Rinehart.

Loy, Artha Sue. 1974. Appendix B: "Language Study." In J. Hill Burnett, ed.,

Social Structures, Ideologies, and Culture Codes in Occupational Development of Puerto Rican Youth: Anthropological Study of Disability from Educational Problems of Puerto Rican Youths, pp. 315–325. Urbana, Ill.: Bureau of Educational Research. (Files of the author.)

Luomala, Katherine. 1947. "Community Analysis Outside the Centers." Applied Anthropology 6:25–31.

Lurie, Nancy Oestreich. 1955. "Problems, Opportunities, and Recommendations." Ethnohistory 2:357–375.

——1956. "A Reply to 'The Land Claims Cases.' Anthropologists in Conflict." Ethnohistory 3:256–279.

——1957. "The Indian Claims Commission Act." Annals of the American Academy of Political and Social Science 311:56–70.

——1968. "Historical Background." In Stuart Levine and Nancy Lurie, eds., The American Indian Today, pp. 49–81. Deland, Fla.: Everett Edwards.

——1970. "Anthropologists in the U.S. and the Indian Claims Commission." Paper presented at the American Ethnological Society—Northeastern Anthropological Society, Ottawa, May 7–9, 1970.

Luxemburg, Rosa. 1961. The Russian Revolution and Leninism or Marxism. Ann Arbor: Ann Arbor Paperbacks.

Lynch, Barbara D. 1981. The Vicos Experiment: A Study of the Impacts of the Cornell-Peru Project in a Highland Valley. Agency for International Development (LAC/DP), Contract no. LAC-0044-C-00-1023-00. Washington, D.C. Mimeo.

Lynd, Robert S., and Helen M. Lynd. 1929. Middletown: A Study in Contemporary American Culture. New York: Harcourt, Brace.

MacCormick, Carol. 1985. "Anthropology and the Control of Tropical Disease." Anthropology Today 1(3):14–16.

Macgregor, Gordon. 1946. Warriors without Weapons: A Study of the Society and Personality of the Pine Ridge Sioux. Chicago: University of Chicago Press.

Machlup, Fritz. 1976. "Hayek's Contribution to Economics." In Fritz Machlup, ed., Essays on Hayek, pp. 13–59. New York: New York University Press.

MacLean, Paul D. 1968. "Alternative Neural Pathways to Violence." In Larry Ng, ed., Alternatives to Violence, pp. 24–34. New York: Time-Life Books.

Maday, Bela C. 1977. "Anthropologists in the United States Government." Human Organization 36:89–97.

Maday, Bela C., ed. 1975. Anthropology and Society. Washington, D.C.: Washington Anthropological Society.

Madge, Charles. 1968. "Planning, Social: Introduction." In The International Encyclopedia of the Social Sciences 12:125–129. New York: Macmillan.

Mair, Lucy. 1985. "Development Anthropology: Some New Views." Anthropology Today 1(1):19–21.

Makielski, S.R.,Jr. 1973. Beleaguered Minorities: Cultural Politics in America. San Francisco: W.H. Freeman.

Malinowski, Bronislaw. 1922. Argonauts of the Western Pacific. New York: Dutton.

——1929. "Practical Anthropology." Africa 2:23–38.

——1944a. A Scientific Theory of Culture. Chapel Hill: University of North Carolina.

———1944b. *Freedom and Civilization*. New York: Roy Publishers.

———1967. *A Diary in the Strict Sense of the Term*. New York: Harcourt, Brace and World.

Mandelbaum, David G.; Gabriel W. Lasker; and Ethel M. Albert. 1963a. *The Teaching of Anthropology*. Washington, D.C.: American Anthropological Association Memoir 94.

———1963b. *Resources for the Teaching of Anthropology*. Washington, D.C.: American Anthropological Association Memoir 95.

Mangin, William P. 1979. "Thoughts on Twenty-Four Years of Work in Peru: The Vicos Project and Me." In George Foster et al., eds., *Long Term Field Research in Social Anthropology*, pp. 65–84. New York: Academic Press.

Mann, Lawrence. 1972. "Social Science Advances and Planning Applications: 1900–1965." *Journal of the American Institute of Planners* 39:346–358.

Manners, Robert A. 1974. "Introduction to the Ethnohistorical Reports on the Land Claims Cases." In H.F. Dobyns, *Hualapai Indians*, pp. 17–19. New York: Garland.

Maquet, Jacques. 1970. "Objectivity in Anthropology." In James A. Clifton, ed., *Applied Anthropology: Readings in the Uses of the Science of Man*, pp. 254–272. Boston, Mass.: Houghton Mifflin.

March, J.G., and J.P. Olsen. 1976. *Ambiguity and Choice in Organization*. Bergen, Norway: Harald Lyche.

Marcson, Simon. 1960. *The Scientist in American Industry*. New York: Harper and Row.

Margolis, Maxine. 1979. "Green Gold and Ice: The Impact of Frosts on the Coffee Growing Region of Northern Parana, Brazil." In *Mass Emergencies* 4(2):135–144.

Mariategui, Jose Carlos. 1971. *Seven Interpretive Essays on Peruvian Reality*. Austin, Texas: University of Texas Press.

Marotto, R.A. 1986. "Posin' to Be Chosen: An Ethnographic Study of In-school Truancy." In D.M. Fetterman and M.A. Pitman, eds., *Ethnographic Evaluation: Theory, Practice and Politics*. Beverly Hills, Calif.: Sage.

Martin, Phillip; John H. Peterson, Jr.; and Jan P. Peterson. 1975. "Choctaw on-Campus Intensive Education Program at Mississippi State University." *BIA Education Research Bulletin* 3:1–9.

Maruyama, Magorah. 1973. "Human Futuristics and Urban Planning." *Journal of the American Institute of Planners* 39:346–358.

Marx, Karl. 1967. *Capital: A Critique of Political Economy*. vol. 1. Samuel Moore and Edward Aveling, trans. New York: International Publishers. (Orig. pub. 1867.)

Marzal, Manuel M. 1981. *Historia de la Antropologia Indigenista: Mexico y Peru*. Lima: Pontifica Universidad Catolica del Peru, Fondo Editorial.

Masland, Richard L. 1975. "Learning Disabilities: Medical Aspects." In S.A. Kirk and J.M. McCarthy, eds., *Learning Disabilities: Selected ACLD Papers*, pp. 189–198. Boston, Mass.: Houghton-Mifflin.

Mason, Leonard. 1955. "The Characterization of American Culture in Studies of Acculturation." *American Anthropologist* 57:1264–1279.

Maxwell, J.A.; P.G. Bashook; and L.J. Sandlow. 1986. "Combining Ethnographic and Experimental Methods in Educational Research: A Case Study." In D.M.

Fetterman and M.A.Pitman, eds., *Ethnographic Evaluation: Theory, Practice and Politics.* Beverly Hills, Calif.: Sage.

May, Judith V., and Aaron B. Wildavsky, eds. 1978. *The Policy Cycle.* Beverly Hills, Calif.: Sage.

Mayer, Albert, et al. 1958. *Pilot Project India: The Story of Rural Development at Etawah, Uttar Pradesh.* Berkeley, Calif.: University of California Press.

Mayo, Elton. 1940. *The Human Problems of an Industrial Civilization.* New York: Viking (Orig. pub. New York: Macmillan, 1933)

——1945. *The Social Problems of an Industrial Civilization.* Boston, Mass.: Harvard University, Graduate School of Business Administration.

McClelland, David, and D. Winter. 1969. *Motivating Economic Achievement.* New York: The Free Press.

McNickle, D'arcy. 1979. "Anthropology and the Indian Reorganization Act." In Walter Goldschmidt, ed., *The Uses of Anthropology,* pp. 51–60. Washington, D.C.: American Anthropological Association.

Mead, George H. 1934. *Mind, Self and Society.* Chicago: University of Chicago Press.

Mead, Margaret. 1928. *Coming of Age in Samoa.* New York: William Morrow.

——1942. *And Keep Your Powder Dry.* New York: William Morrow.

——1952. "The Training of the Cultural Anthropologist." *American Anthropologist* 54:343–346.

——1953a. "National Character." In A. L. Kroeber, ed., *Anthropology Today,* pp. 642–667. Chicago: University of Chicago Press.

——1953b. *Cultural Patterns and Technical Change.* Paris: UNESCO.

——1955. *Male and Female.* New York: Mentor Books. (Orig. pub. New York: Morrow, 1949.)

——1956. *New Lives for Old: Cultural Transformations—Manus.* New York: New American Library.

——1959. "Apprenticeship Under Boas." In Walter Goldschmidt, ed., *The Anthropology of Franz Boas* pp. 29–45. American Anthropological Association Memoir 89.

——1964a. *Continuities in Cultural Evolution.* New Haven, Conn.: Yale University Press.

——1964b. *Food Habits Research: Problems of the 1960s.* National Academy of Sciences, National Research Council Publication No. 1225.

——1966. *The Changing Culture of an Indian Tribe.* New York: Putnam (Orig. pub. New York: Columbia University Press, 1932.)

——1972. *Blackberry Winter.* New York: Simon and Schuster.

——1973. "Changing Styles of Anthropological Work." In Bernard J. Siegel, ed., *Annual Review of Anthropology* 2:1–26. Palo Alto: Annual Reviews.

——1975. "Discussion." In Bela Maday, ed., *Anthropology and Society,* pp. 13–18. Washington, D.C.: Anthropological Society of Washington.

——1979. "Anthropological Contributions to National Policies During and Immediately After World War II." In Walter Goldschmidt, ed., *The Uses of Anthropology,* pp. 145–157. Washington,D.C.: American Anthropological Association.

Mead, Margaret, and Rhoda Metraux. 1965. "The Anthropology of Human Conflict.'' In Elton B. McNeil, ed., *The Nature of Human Conflict*, pp. 116–138. Englewood Cliffs, N.J.: Prentice-Hall.

Medical Anthropology Newsletter. 1980. "Open Forum: Clinical Anthropology.'' *Medical Anthropology Newsletter* 12(1)):14–25.

Mekeel, Scudder. 1936. *The Economy of a Modern Teton Dakota Community*. New Haven: Yale University Publications in Anthropology, No. 6:1–14.

Mellor, John W. 1962. "The Process of Agricultural Development.'' *Journal of Farm Economics* 44:700–716.

Mendras, Henri. 1970. *The Vanishing Peasant: Innovation and Change in French Agriculture*. Jean Lerner, trans. Cambridge: MIT Press.

Merton, Robert K. 1957. *Social Theory and Social Structure*. Glencoe: Free Press.

Messerschmidt, Donald A. 1984. "Federal Bucks for Local Change: On the Ethnography of Experimental Schools.'' In D.M. Fetterman, ed., *Ethnography in Educational Evaluation*, pp. 89–113. Beverly Hills, Calif.: Sage.

Miller, Paul A. 1973. *The Cooperative Extension Service: Paradoxical Servant. The Rural Precedent in Continuing Education*. A.A. Liveright Memorial Series, Landmarks and New Horizons in Continuing Education 2. Syracuse, N.Y.: Syracuse University.

Miller, Warren. 1973a. "Psychiatric Consultation: Part I. A General Systems Approach.'' *Psychiatry in Medicine* 4:135–145.

——1973b. "Psychiatric Consultation: Part II. Conceptual and Pragmatic Issues of Formulation.'' *Psychiatry in Medicine* 4:251–271.

Mills, C. Wright. 1959. *The Sociological Imagination*. New York: Grove Press.

Mintz, Sidney. 1970. "Foreward.'' In Norman Whitten and John Szwed, eds., *Afro-American Anthropology*, pp. 1–16. New York: Free Press.

Mintzberg, Henry. 1973. *The Nature of Managerial Work*. New York: Harper and Row.

Mirsky, Jeanette. 1937. "The Dakota'' In Margaret Mead, ed., *Cooperation and Competition Among Primitive People*, pp. 382–427. New York: McGraw-Hill. (Reprinted Boston: Beacon Press, 1961.)

Mississippi Band of Choctaw Indians. 1972–73. *Accelerated Progress Through Self-Determination*. 2 vols. Philadelphia, Miss.

Mitchelmore, Peter. 1984. "Uprising in Indian Country: After 150 Years of Poverty and Oppression, The Mississippi Choctaws Have Gone on the Warpath.'' *Reader's Digest* (November), pp.69–76.

Monge Medrano, Carlos. 1952. "Editorial.'' *Peru Indigena* 2(4):3.

Montalvo, Abner. 1967. "Vicos: A Study in Health Culture.'' Ph.D. diss., Cornell University.

Montgomery, Edward, and John W. Bennett. 1979. "Anthropological Studies of Food and Nutrition: The 1940s and the 1970s.'' In Walter Goldschmidt, ed., *The Uses of Anthropology*, pp.217–237. Washington, D.C.: American Anthropological Association.

Moore, Donald, et al. 1977. "Assistance Strategies of Six Groups That Facilitate Educational Change at the School Community Level.'' Manuscript. Chicago: Center for New Schools.

Moore, Sally Falk. 1975. "Epilogue: Uncertainties in Situations, Indeterminates in

Culture." In Sally Falk Moore and Barbara G. Myerhoff, eds., *Symbol and Politics in Communal Ideology*, pp. 210–239. Ithaca, New York: Cornell University Press.

Moran, Emilio F. 1981. *Developing the Amazon*. Bloomington: Indiana University Press.

——1985. *Social Reproduction in Frontier Agroecosystems*. Paper presented at the 1985 Meeting of the Society for Economic Anthropology on Anthropology and the Development Process.

Moravcsik, M.J., and J.M. Ziman. 1975. "Paradisia and Dominatia: Science and the Developing World." *Foreign Affairs* 53:699–724.

Morehouse, T.A. 1969. "The 1962 Highway Act: A Study in Artful Interpretation." *Journal of the American Institute of Planners* 35:160–168.

Morgan, Lewis Henry. 1851. *League of the Ho-de-no-sau-nee, or Iroquois*. Rochester, N.Y.: Sage.

——1871. Systems of Consanguinitity and Affinity of the Human Family. Smithsonian Institution Contributions to Knowledge No. 17, article 2. Washington, D.C.: U.S. Government Printing Office.

——1877. *Ancient Society*. New York: Holt.

Morland, John Kenneth. 1958. *Millways of Kent*. Chapel Hill: University of North Carolina Press.

Morss, Elliot R., et al. 1976. *Strategies for Small Farmer Development*. Boulder, Colo.: Westview Press.

Morss, Elliot R., and Victoria A. Morss. 1982. *U.S. Foreign Aid: An Assessment of New and Traditional Development Strategies*. Westview Replica Edition. Boulder, Colo.: Westview Press.

Moynihan, Daniel P. 1965. *The Negro Family: The Case for National Action*. Washington, D.C.: U.S. Government Printing Office.

Mulhauser, Frederick. 1975. "Ethnography and Policymaking: The Case of Education." *Human Organization* 34:311–314.

Murdock, George P. 1936. *Rank and Potlach among the Haida*. New Haven, Conn.: Yale University Publications in Anthropology No. 13:1–20.

Murphy, Jane, and Alexander Leighton. 1965. *Approaches to Cross-Cultural Psychiatry*. Ithaca, New York: Cornell University Press.

Murray, Albert. 1973. "White Norms, Black Deviation." In J.A. Ladner, ed., *The Death of White Sociology*, pp. 96–113. New York: Random House.

Myerhoff, Barbara G. 1978. *Number Our Days*. New York: Simon and Schuster.

Myrdal, Gunnar. 1944. *An American Dilemma*. 2 vols. New York: Harper.

Nakane, Chie. 1970. *Japanese Society*. Berkeley: University of California Press.

Naroll, Raoul, and R.G. Sipes. 1973. "A Standard Ethnographic Sample: Second Edition." *Current Anthropology* 15:1–2, 111–140.

Nash, Philleo. 1973. "Applied Anthropology and the Concept of Guided Acculturation." In *Anthropology and the American Indian*, pp. 23–31. San Francisco, Calif.: Indian Historian Press.

National Association for the Practice of Anthropology. 1986. Directory of Practicing Anthropologists. Washington, D.C.: American Anthropological Association.

National Planning Board. 1934. *National Planning Board Final Report 1933–1934*. Washington, D.C.: U.S. Government Printing Office.

National Research Council. 1943. Report of the Committee on Food Habits 1941–1943. Bulletin No. 108. Washington, D.C.

——1945. Report of the Committee on Food Habits. *Manual for the Study of Food Habits*. Bulletin No. 111. Washington, D.C.

Naylor, Larry L. 1973. "Applied Anthropology: Approaches to the Using of Anthropology." *Human Organization* 32:363–370.

Nelson, Michael. 1973. *The Development of Tropical Lands: Policy Issues in Latin America*. Baltimore: Johns Hopkins University Press.

Newman, Monroe. 1972. *The Political Economy of Appalachia*. Lexington, Mass.: D.S. Heath.

Niehoff, Arthur H. 1964. "The Primary Variables in Directed Culture Change." Paper presented at the Annual Meeting, American Anthropological Association, Detroit, Mich. Mimeographed. (Files of the author.)

——1966. *A Casebook of Social Change*. Chicago: Aldine.

Norman, J.T. 1954. "Now They Stand Up under Pressure." *Sales Management* 73:36–37ff.

Northrup, F.S.C. 1953. "Cultural Values." In A.L.Kroeber, ed., *Anthropology Today*, pp. 668–681. Chicago: University of Chicago Press.

Nunez del Prado, Oscar (with William F. Whyte). 1973. *Kuyo Chico: Applied Anthropology in an Indian Community*. Chicago: University of Chicago Press.

Oberg, Kalervo. 1956. "Community Center Project at Chonin, Brazil." In Arthur Niehoff, ed., *A Casebook for Social Change*, pp. 78–90. Chicago: Aldine.

Oberg, Kalervo, and Jose Arthur Rios. 1955. "A Community Improvement Project in Brazil." In B. Paul, ed., *Health, Culture and Community*, pp. 349–376. New York: Russell Sage Foundation.

Odum, Howard W. 1964. *Folk, Region, and Society: Selected Papers*. Chapel Hill: University of North Carolina Press.

Officer, James. 1971. "The American Indian and Federal Policy." In Jack Waddell and O. M. Watson, eds., *The American Indian in Urban Society*, pp. 8–65. Boston, Mass.: Little, Brown.

O'Hara, Hazel. 1953. "Science and the Indian." *Natural History* 67(6):268–275,282–283.

Opler, Morris E. 1952. "The Creek 'Town' and the Problem of Creek Indian Political Reorganization." In Edward Spicer, ed., *Human Problems in Technological Change*. pp. 165–180. New York: Russell Sage Foundation.

Ortner, Sherry. 1984. "Theory in Anthropology Since the Sixties." *Comparative Studies in Society and History* 26(1):126–166.

Ozarin, Lucy D. 1982. "Mental Health in Public Health: A Federal Perspective." In M. Wagenfeld, P. Lemkau, and B. Justice, eds., *Public Mental Health*, pp. 30–45. Beverly Hills: Sage.

Paige, Jeffrey M. 1975. *Agrarian Revolution*. New York: The Free Press.

Panday, Triloko Nath. 1972. "Anthropologists at Zuni." *Proceedings of the American Philosophical Society* 116(4):321–336.

Panel on Youth (of the President's Science Advisory Committee). 1974. James Coleman, ed., *Youth: Transition to Adulthood.* Chicago: University of Chicago Press.

Paredes, J. Anthony. 1985. "Any Comments on the Sociology Section, Tony?: Committee Work as Applied Anthropology in Fishery Management." *Human Organization* 44:177–182. (With comments by James M. Acheson, et al.)

Parkin, David J. 1972. *Palms, Wine, and Witnesses.* San Francisco, Calif.: Chandler Publishing.

Partridge, William L., ed. 1984. *Training Manual in Development Anthropology.* Washington, D.C.: American Anthropological Association and Society for Applied Anthropology.

Patton, M.Q. 1979. "Evaluation of Program Implementation." In L. Sechrest, et al., eds., *Evaluation Studies Review Annual*, vol.4. Beverly Hills, Calif.: Sage.

Paul, Benjamin, ed. 1955. *Health, Culture and Community: Case Studies of Public Reactions to Health Programs.* New York: Russell Sage Foundation.

Pearse, Andrew. 1980. *Seeds of Plenty, Seeds of Want: Social and Economic Implications of the Green Revolution.* United Nations Research Institute for Social Development. Oxford: Clarendon Press.

Peattie, Lisa Redfield. 1958. "Interventionism and Applied Science in Anthropology." *Human Organization* 17:4–8.

——1968a. "Reflections on Advocacy Planning." *Journal of the American Institute of Planners* 34:80–88.

——1968b. *The View from the Barrio.* Ann Arbor: University of Michigan Press.

Pelto, Gretl H., and Pertti J. Pelto. 1979. *The Cultural Dimension of the Human Adventure.* New York: MacMillan.

Pelto, Pertti, J. 1980. "Kolttien Porotalouden Vaiheista." *Suomen Antropologi I Finland* 5(1):43–54.

Petersen, William. 1975. "A Demographer's View of Prehistoric Demography." *Current Anthropology* 16:227–245.

Peterson, John H. 1970a. *Socio-Economic Characteristics of the Mississippi Choctaw Indians.* Social Science Research Center Report No. 34. State College: Mississippi State University.

——1970b. "The Mississippi Band of Choctaw Indians: Their Recent History and Current Social Relations." Ph.D. diss., University of Georgia.

——1972. "Assimilation, Separation and Out-Migration in an American Indian Community." *American Anthropologist* 74:1286–1295.

——1973a. "A Very Applied Anthropologist's Report from the Field." Paper presented at the annual meeting of the Southern Anthropological Association. (Files of the author.)

——1973b. "Working for a Tribal Government." Paper presented at the annual meeting of the Central States Anthropological Association. (Files of the author.)

——1974a. "The Operation of a Tribal Planning Center." Paper presented at the annual meeting of the Society for Applied Anthropology. (Files of the author.)

——1974b. "The Anthropologist as Advocate." *Human Organization* 33:311–318.

Peterson, John H., Jr.; Barbara G. Spencer; and Choong S. Kim. 1974. *Choctaw Demographic Survey.* Philadelphia, Miss.: Mississippi Band of Choctaw Indians.

Piddington, Ralph. 1970. "Action Anthropology." In James A. Clifton, ed., *Ap-*

plied Anthropology: Readings in the Uses of the Science of Man, pp. 127–143. Boston, Mass.: Houghton Mifflin.

Piehler, Henry F.; Aaron D. Twerski; A. S. Weinstein; and W.A. Donaher. 1974. "Product Liability and the Technical Expert." *Science* 186:1089–1093.

Pitman, M.A., and M.L. Dolbert. 1986. "The Use of Explicit Anthropological Theory in Educational Evaluation: A Case Study." In D.M. Fetterman and M.A. Pitman, eds., *Ethnographic Evaluation: Theory, Practice and Politics.* Beverly Hills, Calif.: Sage.

Plan Estatal de Desarollo del Estado de Zacatecas (State Development Plan for the the State of Zacatecas). November 1979.

Plog, Fred, and Daniel G. Bates. 1976. *Cultural Anthropology.* New York: Alfred A. Knopf.

Posposil, Leopold. 1963. *The Kapauku Papuans of West New Guinea.* New York: Holt, Rinehart and Winston.

Powdermaker, Hortense. 1939. *After Freedom: A Cultural Study in the Deep South.* New York: Viking.

——1966. *Stranger and Friend: The Way of an Anthropologist.* New York: Norton.

Pressman, Jeffrey, and Aaron Wildavsky. 1973. *Implementation.* Berkeley: University of California Press.

Presthus, Robert. 1974. *Elites in the Policy Process.* London: Cambridge University Press.

Preston, P.W. 1982. *Theories of Development.* London: Routledge and Kegan Paul.

Price, John A. 1985. "The Society of Applied Anthropology in Canada." Unpublished manuscript. (Files of the author.)

Provinse, John H. 1942. "Cultural Factors in Land Use Planning." In Oliver La Farge, ed., *The Changing Indian,* pp. 55–71. Norman: University of Oklahoma Press.

Provinse, John H., and Solon T. Kimball. 1946. "Building New Communities During Wartime." *American Sociological Review* 11:396–410.

Quandt, Sara A., and Cheryl Ritenbaugh. 1986. *Training Manual in Nutritional Anthropology.* Washington, D.C.: American Anthropological Association and Society for Applied Anthropology.

Rachlin, Carol K. 1968. "Tight Shoe Night: Oklahoma Indians Today." In Stuart Levine and Nancy O. Lurie, eds., *The American Indian Today,* pp. 99–114. Deland, Fla.: Everett Edwards Press.

Radcliffe-Brown, A. R. 1922. *The Andaman Islanders.* Cambridge: Cambridge University Press.

——1930 "Applied Anthropology." In *Report of the Twentieth Meeting of the Australian and New Zealand Association for the Advancement of Science,* vol.20:267–280.

Raia, Anthony P. 1974. *Managing by Objectives.* Glenview, Ill.: Scott, Foresman.

RAIN. 1981. "AAG/GAPP." *RAIN* (December),No.47: 13–14.

——1982. "Special Feature on Urban Anthropology." *RAIN* (October), No.52:4–10.

——1984. "Special Section on Social Anthropology and Social and Community Work in the U.K." *RAIN* (August), No.63:2–15.

Rainger, Ronald. 1980. "Philanthropy and Science in the 1830s: The British and Foreign Aborigines' Protection Society." *Man* 15:702–717.

Rappaport, Roy A. 1968. *Pigs for the Ancestors.* New Haven, Conn.: Yale University Press.

——1974. "Obvious Aspects of Ritual." *Cambridge Anthropology* 2(1):1–69.

Read, C. H. 1906. "Anthropology at the Universities." *Man* 38:56–59.

Redfield, Robert. 1930. *Tepotzlan, A Mexican Village: A Study of Folk Life.* Chicago: University of Chicago Press.

——1950. *A Village That Chose Progress: Chan Kom Revisited.* Chicago: University of Chicago Press.

——1955. *The Little Community.* Chicago: University of Chicago Press.

——1956. *Peasant Society and Culture.* Chicago: University of Chicago Press.

Redfield, Robert; Ralph Linton; and Melville Herskovits. 1936. "Memorandum for the Study of Acculturaton." *American Anthropologist* 38:149–152.

Redfield, Robert, and Alfonso Villa Rojas. 1934. *Chan Kom: A Maya Village.* Carnegie Institution of Washington Publication No. 448.

Redfield, Robert, and Milton Singer. 1954. "The Cultural Role of Cities." *Economic Development and Cultural Change* 3:53–73.

Reicken, W.R., et al. 1974. *Social Experimentation: A Method for Planning and Evaluating Social Intervention.* New York: Academic Press.

Rein, Martin. 1971. "Social Policy Analysis as the Interpretation of Beliefs." *Journal of the American Institute of Planners* 37:297–310.

——1979. *Social Science and Public Policy.* New York: Penguin Books.

Reining, Conrad C. 1962. "A Lost Period of Applied Anthropology." *American Anthropologist* 64:593–600.

Richardson, Frederick L. W. 1941. "Community Resettlement in a Depressed Coal Region." *Applied Anthropology* 1:24–53.

——1961. *Talk, Work and Action.* Monograph No. 3. Ithaca, N.Y.: Society for Applied Anthropology.

——1965. "Executive Action—Stimulating Others to Greater Performance." Document 8426, American Documentation Institute, Library of Congress, Washington, D.C.

——1966. "Recollecting vs. 'Live' Recording: Organizational Relationships of a Surgeon." *Human Organization* 25:163–179.

——1975. "Organizational Evolutions from Mating Pairs to Trading Nations." In Steven Polgar, ed., *Population, Ecology, and Social Evolution,* pp. 305–335. The Hague: Mouton.

——1979. "Social Interaction and Industrial Productivity." In Walter Goldschmidt, ed., *The Uses of Anthropology,* pp.79–99. Washington,D.C.: American Anthropological Association.

Richardson, Frederick L.W., and Charles R. Walker. 1948. *Human Relations in an Expanding Company.* New Haven, Conn.: Yale Labor and Management Center.

Richardson, Frederick L. W., and Kenneth White. 1965. "Technical Supplement" to "Executive Action," Document 8425, American Documentation Institute, Library of Congress.

Richardson, F. L. W., et al. 1972. "Committee Meetings—The Non-Rational Process of Conference Discussion." Ms. (Files of the author.)

Roberts, John M. 1951. *Three Navajo Households.* Cambridge, Mass.: Papers of the Peabody Museum of Archaeology and Ethnology, 40(3).

Roberts, Ralph Leon, III. 1975. "Migration and Colonization in Colombian Amazonia: Agrarian Reform or Neo-Latifundismo." Ph.D. diss., University of Syracuse.

Roche, George C. 1976. "The Relevance of F.A. Hayek." In Fritz A. Machlup, ed., *Essays on Hayek*, pp.1–11. New York: New York University Press.

Rodgers, Harrell R., Jr., and Charles S. Bullock, II. 1972. *Law and Social Change: Civil Rights and Their Consequences.* New York: McGraw-Hill.

Rodney, Walter. 1972. *How Europe Underdeveloped Africa.* Dar es Salaam: Tanzania Publishing House.

Roethlisberger, Fritz J., and William J. Dickson. 1939. *Management and the Worker.* Cambridge: Harvard University Press.

Rondinelli, Dennis A. 1969. "Policy Analysis and Planning Administration: Toward Adjunctive Planning for Regional Development." Ph.D. diss., Cornell University.

——1973. "Urban Planning as Policy Analysis: Management of Urban Change." *Journal of the American Institute of Planners* 39:13–22.

Rossi, Peter H., and William F. Whyte. 1964. "The Applied Side of Sociology." In Peter H. Rossi and William F. Whyte, eds., *Applied Sociology.* San Francisco, Calif.:Jossey-Bass.

Rothman, Jack; John L. Erlich; and Joseph G. Teresa. 1976. *Promoting Innovation and Change in Organizations and Communities: A Planning Manual.* New York: Wiley.

Rubin, Irwin M.; Mark S. Plovnick; and Ronald E. Fry. 1975. *Improving the Coordination of Care: A Program for Health Team Development.* Cambridge, Mass.: Ballinger.

Rubin, Morton. 1951. *Plantation County.* Chapel Hill: University of North Carolina Press.

Rubin, Vera. 1961. "The Anthropology of Development." In Bernard J. Siegel, ed., *The Biennial Review of Anthropology*, pp. 120–172. Stanford, Calif.: Stanford University Press.

Ruopp, Phillips. 1953. *Approaches to Community Development.* The Hague: W. Van Hoeve.

Sahlins, Marshall. 1981. *Historical Metaphors and Mythical Realities.* Ann Arbor, Mich.: University of Michigan Press.

Sainsbury, Peter. 1955. *Suicide in London: An Ecological Study.* Maudsley Monographs No. 1. London: Chapman and Hall.

Salisbury, Robert H. 1968. "The Analysis of Public Policy: A Search for Theories and Roles. In A. Ranney, ed., *Political Science and Public Policy.* Chicago: Markham.

Salisbury, Robert H., and John Hienz. 1970. "A Theory of Policy Analysis and Some Preliminary Applications" In I. Sharkansky, ed., *Policy Analysis in Political Science*, pp. 39–60. Chicago: Markham.

Sayles, Leonard. 1964. *Managerial Behavior.* New York: McGraw-Hill.

Schensul, Stephen L. 1974. "Skills Needed in Action Anthropology: Lessons Learned from El Centro de la Causa." *Human Organization* 33:203–209.

——1978. "Advocacy and Applied Anthropology." In George Weber and George McCall, eds., *Social Scientists as Advocates: Views from the Applied Disciplines,* pp. 121–164. Beverly Hills, Calif.: Sage.

——1982. "Helping Resource Use in a Puerto Rican Community." *Urban Anthropology* 11:59–80.

Schoolcraft, Henry R. 1852–57. *Information Respecting the History, Condition, and Prospects of the Indian Tribes of the United States.* 6 vols. Philadelphia, Pa.: Lippincott.

Schwartz, Eugene P., ed. 1973. *Services to the Mentally Retarded Youthful Offender: Manual for Instructors.* St. Louis: University of Missouri—St. Louis Extension Division.

Schwartzman, Helen B., et al. 1984. "Children, Families, and Mental Health Service Organizations: Cultures in Conflict." *Human Organization* 43:297–306.

Scriven, Michael. 1972. "The Methodology of Evaluation." In Carol H. Weiss, ed., *Evaluating Action Programs,* pp. 123–136. Boston, Mass.: Allyn and Bacon.

Scudder, Thayer. 1973. "The Human Ecology of Big Projects: River Basin Development and Resettlement." In B. Siegel, ed., *Annual Review of Anthropology,* pp. 45–55. Palo Alto: Annual Reviews.

——1981. *The Development Potential of New Lands Settlement in the Tropics and Subtropics: A Global State-of-the-Art Evaluation with Specific Emphasis on Policy Implications.* Binghamton, New York: Institute for Development Anthropology.

——1983. "Economic Downturn and Community Unraveling: The Gwembe Tonga Revisited." *Culture and Agriculture* 18:16–19.

——1984a. "Economic Downturn and Community Unraveling, Revisited." *Culture and Agriculture* 23:6–10.

——1984b. *The Development Potential of New Lands Settlement in the Tropics and Subtropics: A Global State-of-the-Art Evaluation with Specific Emphasis on Policy Implications, Executive Summary.* AID Program Evaluation Discussion Paper No. 21. Washington, D.C.: Agency for International Development.

——1985. "A History of Development in the Twentieth Century: The Zambian Portion of the Middle Zambezi Valley." *Cooperative Agreement on Settlements and Resource Systems Analysis.* U.S. Agency for International Development, Clark University and Institute for Development Anthropology. Binghamton, New York: Institute for Development Anthropology.

——1985. "A Sociological Framework for the Analysis of New Lands Settlements." In Michael M. Cernea,ed., *Putting People First: Sociological Variables in Rural Development,* pp.121–153. London: Oxford University Press.

——Forthcoming. "The Institute for Development Anthropology: History and Activities." To be published in the Proceedings of the 1985 Meeting of the Society for Economic Anthropology on Anthropology and the Development Process.

Scudder, Thayer, and Elizabeth Colson. 1982. "From Welfare to Development: A

Conceptual Framework for the Analysis of Dislocated People.'' In Art Hansen and Anthony Oliver-Smith, eds., *Involuntary Migration and Resettlement: The Problems and Responses of Dislocated People*, pp. 267–287. Boulder, Colo.: Westview Press.

Scudder, Thayer, and Kapila P. Wimaladharma. 1985. *The Accelerated Mahaweli Programme (AMP) and Dry Zone Development: Report No. 5.* Cooperative Agreement on Settlements and Resource Systems Analysis. Binghamton, New York: Institute for Development Anthropology.

Shepherd, Ross A. 1981. ''Agrarian Change in Northern Ghana.'' In Judith Heyer et al., eds., *Rural Development in Tropical Africa*, pp.62–88. New York: St. Martin's Press.

Shiloh, Ailon. 1978. ''The Anthropologist as Private Practitioner.'' *American Anthropology* 79:443–445.

——1980. ''Therapeutic Anthropology.'' In *Open Forum: Clinical Anthropology, Medical Anthropology Newsletter* 12(1):14–15.

Shimkin, Demitri, and Peggy Golde. 1983. *Clinical Anthropology: A New Approach to America's Health Problems?* Lanham, Maryland: University Press of America.

Shipeck, Florence C. 1974. ''Anthropologists Shortchanged as Consultants.'' *Newsletter* of the American Anthropological Association 15(8):2.

Simon, E.L. 1986. ''Theory in Educational Evaluation, or What Is Wrong with Generic Brand Anthropology.'' In D.M.Fetterman and M.A. Pitman, eds., *Ethnographic Evaluation: Theory, Practice and Politics*. Beverly Hills, Calif.: Sage.

Simon, Herbert. 1973. ''The Organization of Complex Systems.'' In Howard Pattee, ed., *Hierarchy Theory: The Challenge of Complex Systems*, pp. 3–27, New York: Braziller.

Singer, Milton. 1976. ''Robert Redfield's Development of a Social Anthropology of Civilizations.'' In John V. Murra, ed., *American Anthropology: The Early Years*, pp. 187–260. New York: West.

Sjoberg, Gideon, ed. 1967. *Ethics, Politics, and Social Research.* Cambridge, Mass.: Schenkman.

Sloan, Alfred P., Jr. 1964. *My Years with General Motors.* Garden City, N.Y.: Doubleday.

Smith, A.G., and A.E. Robbins. 1984. ''Multimethod Policy Research: A Case Study of Structure and Flexibility.'' In D.M. Fetterman, ed., *Ethnography in Educational Evaluation*, pp. 115–132. Beverly Hills, Calif.: Sage.

Smith, Allan H., and John L. Fischer. 1970. *Anthropology.* Englewood Cliffs, N.J.: Prentice-Hall.

Smith, Edwin. 1934. ''The Story of the Institute: A Survey of Seven Years.'' *Africa* 7:1–27.

Smith, M. G. 1974. *Corporations and Society.* London: Duckworth and Co.

Smith, Marion. 1959. ''Boas' Natural History Approach to Field Method.'' In Walter Goldschmidt, ed., *The Anthropology of Franz Boas*, pp. 46–60. American Anthropological Association Memoir 89.

South American Handbook. 1961. London: Trade and Travel Publications, Ltd.

Spicer, Edward H. 1940. *Pascua: A Yaqui Village in Arizona.* Chicago: University of Chicago Press.

——1946. "The Uses of Social Scientists by the War Relocation Authority." *Applied Anthropology* 5:16–36.

——1954. *Potam: A Yaqui Village in Sonora.* American Anthropological Association Memoir 77.

——1979. "Anthropologists and the War Relocation Authority." In Walter Goldschmidt, ed., *The Uses of Anthropology,* pp. 217–237. Washington,D.C.: American Anthropological Association.

Spicer, Edward H., ed. 1952. *Human Problems in Technological Change.* New York: Russell Sage Foundation.

Spicer, Edward H., et al. 1969. *Impounded People: Japanese-Americans in Relocation Centers.* Tucson: University of Arizona Press. (Orig. pub. Washington, D.C.: U.S. Government Printing Office, 1946.)

Spindler, George, ed. 1955. *Education and Anthropology.* Stanford, Calif.: Stanford University Press.

——1963. *Education and Culture: Anthropological Approaches.* New York: Holt, Rinehart, and Winston.

Spiro, Melford E. 1955. "The Acculturation of American Ethnic Groups." *American Anthropologist* 57:1240–1252.

Spitz, Rene A. 1945. "Hospitalism: An Inquiry into the Genesis of Psychiatric Conditions in Early Childhood." In *Psychoanalytic Study of the Child* 1:53–74. New York: International Universities Press.

——1946. "Hospitalism: A Followup Report on Investigation Described in Volume I, 1945"; "Anaclitic Depression: An Inquiry into the Genesis of Psychiatric Conditions in Early Childhood II." In *Psychoanalytic Study of the Child,* 2:113–117,312–342. New York: International Universities Press.

SPP (Secretatria de Programacion y Presupuesto). 1980. "Manual de Procedimientos para la Programacion de Inversiones Publicas para el Desarollo Rural" (Manual for the Programming of Public Investments for Rural Development). Mexico, D.F.: SPP, Direccion General de Desarollo Rural Integral, and CIDER.

——1982a. "Manual del Programa de Analisis Socioeconomico de la Comunidad Rural" (Manual for the Program of Socioeconomic Analysis of the Rural Community). Vols. 1 and 2. Mexico, D.F.: SPP, Direccion General de Desarollo Rural Integral, and CIDER.

——1982b. "Manual del Programa de Apoyo a la Formulacion de Proyectos Productivos" (Manual for the Support Program for Formulating Productive Projects). Mexico, D.F.: SPP, Direccion General de Desarollo Rural Integral, and CIDER.

——1982c. "Manual del Programa de Apoyo a la Participacion de la Comunidad Rural" (Manual for the Support Program for Rural Community Development). Mexico, D.F.: SPP, Direccion General de Desarollo Rural Integral.

——1982d. "Manual de Procedimientos para el Control de la Ejecucion" (Manual of Procedures for Monitoring Project Execution). Mexico, D.F.: SPP, Direccion General de Desarollo Rural Integral.

——1982e. "Manual de Procedimientos para el Seguimiento de la Operacion" (Manual of Procedures for Monitoring Project Operations). Mexico, D.F.: SPP, Direccion General de Desarollo Rural Integral.

——1982f. "Lineamientos para la Evaluacion en el PIDER" (Guidelines for PIDER Evaluation). Mexico, D.F.: Direccion General de Desarollo Rural Integral.

Srinivas, M.N. 1968. *Social Change in Modern India*. Berkeley and Los Angeles: University of California Press.

Stack, Carol. 1974. *All Our Kin: Strategies for Survival in the Black Community*. New York: Harper and Row.

Stavenhagen, Rodolfo. 1971. "Decolonizing Applied Social Sciences." *Human Organization* 30:333–357.

Stein, Howard F. 1980. "Medical Anthropology and Western Medicine." *Journal of Psychological Anthropology* 3(2):185–195.

——1985. "Principles of Style: A Medical Anthropologist as Clinical Teacher." *Medical Anthropology Quarterly* 16(3):59–73.

Stein, Leonard. 1967. "The Doctor-Nurse Game." *Archives of General Psychiatry* 16:699–703.

Stein, William W. 1971. "Nuevas Semillas de Papa para Vicos: Cambio Agricola en los Andes." *America Indigena* 31(1):51–83.

——1972a. "Race, Culture and Social Structure in the Peruvian Andes." Summer NDEA Quechua—Aymara Language Institute, University of Pittsburgh (ms. 62 pp.)

——1972b. *Changing Vicos Agriculture*. Special Studies No. 15, Council on International Studies. Buffalo, New York: State University of New York.

Stein, William W.,ed. 1985. *Peruvian Contexts of Change*. New Brunswick, New Jersey: Transaction Books.

Steward, Julian H. 1933. *Ethnography of the Owen's Valley Paiute*. University of California Publications in American Archaeology and Ethnology 33:233–350.

——1938. *Basin-Plateau Aboriginal Socio-Political Groups*. Washington, D.C.: Bureau of American Ethnology Bulletin No. 120.

——1950. *Area Research: Theory and Practice*. Social Science Research Council Bulletin No. 63.

——1955. *Theory of Culture Change: The Methodology of Multilinear Evolution*. Urbana: University of Illinois Press.

——1956. *The People of Puerto Rico*. Urbana: University of Illinois Press.

——1969. "The Limitations of Applied Anthropology: The Case of the Indian New Deal." *Journal of the Steward Society* 1(1):1–17.

Stewart, Elbert W. 1973. *Evolving Life Styles*. San Francisco, Calif.: MacGraw Hill.

Stewart, F. 1975. "A Note on Social Cost-Benefit Analysis and Class Conflict in LDCs." *World Development* 3(1):412–421.

Stewart, Omer C. 1961a. "The Native American Church and the Law with Description of Peyote Religious Services." *Westerners Brand Book*, 17:3–47.

——1961b. "Memorandum of Examples of Dr. Omer C. Stewart Respecting Defendant's Exhibit 113: (1) Non-Southern Paiute References; (2) Titles for Which No Defendant's Exhibit Offered; (3) Secondary Sources by Popular Writer; (4) Scholarly Reports Not Evaluated; and (5) Works Listed in Bibliography Not

Cited in Report." U.S. Indian Claims Commission, Dockets 88 and 130. Typescript.

——1970. "Symposium: Academics, Humanism, and the Ethics of Involvement." Paper presented at the Society for Applied Anthropology, Annual Meeting, Boulder, Colo., April 2, 1970. (Files of the author.)

——1973. "Anthropologists as Expert Witnesses for Indians: Claims and Peyote Cases." In *Anthropology and the American Indian*, pp. 35–42. San Francisco, Calif,: Indian Historian Press.

Stewart, Rosemary. 1967. *Managers and Their Jobs*. New York: Macmillan.

Stirling, Paul. 1982. "Selling Applied Anthropology." *RAIN* (December), No. 53:5–6.

——1983. "Employment in Social Anthropology." *RAIN* (April), No. 55.:8–9.

Stocking, George W., Jr. 1968. *Race, Culture, and Evolution: Essays in the History of Anthropology*. New York: Free Press.

——1974. "The Basic Assumptions of Boasian Anthropology." In George W. Stocking, Jr., ed., *The Shaping of American Anthropology 1883–1911: A Franz Boas Reader*, pp. 1–20. New York: Basic Books.

——1984. "Radcliffe-Brown and British Social Anthropology." In George W. Stocking, Jr., ed., *Functionalism Historicized: Essays on British Social Anthropology*, pp. 131–191. Madison: University of Wisconsin Press.

——1985. "Philanthropoids and Vanishing Cultures: Rockefeller Funding and the End of the Museum Era in Anglo-American Anthropology." In George W. Stocking, Jr., ed., *Objects and Others: Essays on Museums and Material Culture*, pp. 112–145. Madison: University of Wisconsin Press.

Straus, Robert. 1957. "The Nature and Status of Medical Sociology." *American Sociological Review* 22:200–204.

Stubbs, J.M., and C.G.T. Morrison. 1938. *The Western Dinka, Their Land and Their Agriculture*. Khartoum: Sudan Notes and Records.

Studstill, J.D. 1986. "Attrition in Zairian Secondary Schools: Ethnographic Evaluation and Sociocultural Systems." In D.M. Fetterman and M.A. Pitman, eds., *Ethnographic Evaluation: Theory, Practice and Politics*. Beverly Hills, Calif.: Sage.

Stull, Donald D., and Felix Moos. 1981. "A Brief Overview of the Role of Anthropology in Public Policy." *Policy Studies Review* 1:19–27.

Swanton, John R. 1922. *Early History of the Creek Indians and Their Neighbors*. Washington, D.C.: Bureau of American Ethnology Bulletin No.73.

Szwed, John F. 1972. "An American Anthropological Dilemma: The Politics of Afro-American Culture." In Dell Hymes, ed., *Reinventing Anthropology*, pp. 153–181. New York: Vintage.

Talavera T., Luis Guillermo 1961. "Seccion 17: El Problema del Indio. El Experimento de Vicos." *Educacion Civica* (para el Quinto Ano de Secundaria), pp.88–98. Lima: Editorial Leoncio Prado.

Talbert, Carol. 1974. "Experiences at Wounded Knee." *Human Organization* 33:215–217.

Tarnow, Jay D., and Steven E. Gutstein. 1982. "Systematic Consultation in a General Hospital." *International Journal of Psychiatry in Medicine* 12(3):161–185.

Tateishi, John. 1984. *And Justice For All: An Oral History of the Japanese American Detention Camps*. New York: Random House.

Tax, Sol. 1937. "The Social Organization of the Fox Indians." In Fred Eggan, ed., *The Social Anthropology of North American Tribes*, pp. 242–282. Chicago: University of Chicago Press.

——1942. "Ethnic Relations in Guatemala." *America Indigena* 2:43–48.

——1945. "Anthropology and Administration." *America Indigena* 4:21–33.

——1951. *Penny Capitalism: A Guatemalan Indian Economy*. Smithsonian Institution, Institute of Social Anthropology Publication No. 16.

——1958. "The Fox Project." *Human Organization* 17:17–19.

Tax, Sol, ed. 1964. *The Horizons of Anthropology*. Chicago: Aldine.

Taylor, Carol. 1969. *In Horizontal Orbit*. New York: Holt, Rinehart and Winston.

Taylor, Frederick W. 1911. *The Principles of Scientific Management*. New York: Harper and Row.

Tendler, Judith. 1975. *Inside Foreign Aid*. Baltimore: Johns Hopkins University Press.

Thomas, Dorothy S. 1952. *The Salvage*. Berkeley: University of California Press.

Thomas, Dorothy S., and Richard S. Nishimoto. 1946. *The Spoilage*. Berkeley: University of California Press.

Thompson, Bobby, and John H. Peterson, Jr. 1975. "Mississippi Choctaw Identity: Genesis and Change." In John W. Bennett, ed., *The New Ethnicity: Perspectives from Ethnology*, pp. 179–196. 1973 Proceedings of the American Ethnological Society. New York: West.

Thompson, Frank J. 1981. *Health Policy and the Bureaucracy: Politics and Implementation*. Cambridge, M.I.T. Press.

Thompson, Laura. 1951. *Personality and Government: Findings and Recommendations of the Indian Administration Research*. Mexico City: Instituto Indigenista Inter-americano.

——1956. "U.S. Indian Reorganization Viewed as an Experiment in Social Action." In *Estudios Antropologicos publicados en homenaje al doctor Manual Gamio*, pp. 514–522. Mexico City: National Autonomous University of Mexico, Mexican Anthropological Society.

——1970. "Is Applied Anthropology Helping to Develop a Science of Man?" In James A. Clifton, ed., *Applied Anthropology: Readings in the Uses of the Science of Man*, pp. 225–245 Boston, Mass.: Houghton Mifflin.

——1976. "An Appropriate Role for Postcolonial Applied Anthropologists." *Human Organization* 35:1–4.

Thorensen, Timothy H.H. 1975. "Paying the Piper and Calling the Tune: The Beginnings of Academic Anthropology in California." *Journal of Behavioral Sciences* 11(3):257–275.

Tocqueville, Alexis de. 1945. *Democracy in America*. 2 vols. New York: Vintage Books.(Orig. pub. Paris: vol.1, 1834; vol. 2, 1840.)

Trahair, Richard C.S. 1984. *The Humanist Temper: The Life and Work of Elton Mayo*. New Brunswick, N.J.: Transaction Books.

Trow, Martin. 1969. "Elite and Popular Functions in American Higher Education."

In W.R. Niblett, ed., *Higher Education: Demand and Response*, pp. 181–202. London: Tavistock.

———1973. *Problems in the Transition from Elite to Mass Higher Education*. Carnegie Commission on Higher Education. Ann Arbor, Mich.: University Microfilms, reprint.

Turner, Victor. 1957. *Schism and Continuity in an African Society*. Manchester: Manchester University Press.

———1967. *The Forest of Symbols*. Ithaca, N.Y.: Cornell University Press.

———1969. *The Ritual Process: Structure and Anti-Structure*. Chicago: Aldine.

———1974. *Dramas, Fields, and Metaphors: Symbolic Action in Human Societies*. Ithaca, N.Y.: Cornell University Press.

Tyler, Stephen A., ed. 1969. *Cognitive Anthropology*. New York: Holt, Rinehart, and Winston.

Tyler, S. Lyman. 1964. *Indian Affairs: A Study of the Changes in the Policy of the United States Toward Indians*. Provo, Utah: Brigham Young University Press, Institute of American Indian Studies.

UNESCO. 1953. *New Horizons at Tzentzenhuaro: Balance Sheet of a Fundamental Education Centre*. Paris: UNESCO.

U.S. Department of Interior. 1946. *Community Government in War Relocation Centers*. U.S. Department of Interior, War Relocation Authority. Washington, D.C.: U.S. Government Printing Office. (Prepared by Solon T. Kimball.)

U.S. District Court, Northern Mississippi. 1979. Civil Action No. GC-75-147-S.

U.S. Supreme Court. 1978. Cases No. 77-836 and 77-575.

Uphoff, Norman. 1985. "Fitting Projects to People." In Michael Cernea, ed., *Putting People First: Sociological Variables in Rural Development*, pp.359–395. New York: Oxford University Press.

Uphoff, Norman, and Milton Esman. 1974. *Local Organization for Rural Development: Analysis of Asian Experience*. Ithaca, New York: Cornell University Press.

Valentine, Charles A. 1968. *Culture and Poverty: Critique and Counter-Proposals*. Chicago: University of Chicago Press.

———1971. "The 'Culture of Poverty': Its Scientific Significance and Its Implications for Action." In Eleanor Burke Leacock, ed., *The Culture of Poverty: A Critique*, pp. 193–225. New York: Simon and Schuster.

Vance, John T. 1969. "The Congressional Mandate and the Indian Claims Commission." *North Dakota Law Review* 45:325–336.

Van Lawick-Goodall, Jane. 1971. *In the Shadow of Man*. Boston: Houghton Mifflin.

Van Maanen, John. 1973. *The Process of Program Evaluation: A Guide for Managers*. Washington, D.C.: National Training and Development Service Press.

Van Willigen, John. 1980. *Anthropology in Use: A Bibliographic Chronology of the Development of Applied Anthropology*. Pleasantville, N.Y.: Redgrave Publishing Company.

———1986. *Applied Anthropology: An Introduction*. South Hadley, Mass.: Bergin and Garvey.

Van Willigen, John, ed. 1985. "Guide to Training Programs in the Applications of Anthropology." Supplement to *Practicing Anthropology*. Vols. 1 and 2.

Van Willigen, John, and Billie DeWalt. 1985. *Training Manual in Policy Ethnography*. Washington, D.C.: American Anthropological Association and Society for Applied Anthropology.

Vasquez Varela, Mario C. 1952. "La Antropologia Cultural y Nuestro Problema del Indio." *Peru Indigena* 2(5):7–157.

——1961. *Hacienda, Peonaje, y Servidumbre en Los Andes Peruanos*. Lima: Editorial Estudios Andinos.

——1965. *Educacion Rural en el Callejon de Huaylas*. Lima: Editorial Estudios Andinos.

Vayda, Andrew P.,ed. 1969. *Environment and Cultural Behavior: Ecological Studies in Cultural Anthropology*. New York: Natural History Press.

Veblen, Thorstein. 1921. *Engineers and the Price System*. New York: B. W. Huebsch.

Voget, Fred W. 1975. *A History of Ethnology*. New York: Holt, Rinehart and Winston.

Von Neuman, J., and O. Morganstern. 1953. *The Theory of Games and Economic Behavior*. Princeton, N.J.: Princeton University Press.

Wachman, Marvin. 1974. "Needed: An Urban-Grant Approach to Higher Education." *Educational Record* 55(4):242–247.

Wagenfeld, Morton O., and Judith H. Jacobs. 1982. "The Community Mental Health Movement: Its Origins and Growth." In M. Wagenfeld, P. Lemkau, and B. Justice, eds., *Public Mental Health*, pp.46–89. Beverly Hills, Calif.: Sage.

Wagley, Charles. 1941. *The Economics of a Guatemalan Village*. American Anthropological Association Memoir 58.

——1949. *Social and Religious Life of a Guatemalan Community*. American Anthropological Association Memoir 71.

——1953. *Amazon Town: A Study of Man in the Tropics*. New York: Macmillan.

——1972. "Review." *Human Organization* 31:458–459.

Wagley, Charles, and Marvin Harris. 1955. "A Typology of Latin American Subcultures." *American Anthropologist* 57:428–451.

——1958. *Minorities in the New World*. New York: Columbia University Press.

Walker, Charles R. 1962. *Modern Technology and Civilization*. New York: McGraw-Hill.

Walker, Charles R., and Robert A. Guest. 1952. *The Man on the Assembly Line*. Cambridge: Harvard University Press.

Walker, Charles R.; Robert Guest; and Arthur Turner. 1956. *The Foreman on the Assembly Line*. Cambridge: Harvard University Press.

Wallace, Anthony F.C. 1961. *Culture and Personality*. New York: Random House.

——1965. "James Mooney (1861–1921) and the Study of the Ghost-Dance Religion." In James Mooney, ed., *The Ghost-Dance Religion and the Sioux Outbreak of 1890*, pp. v–x. Chicago: University of Chicago Press.

——1967. "Revitalization Movements in Development." In Richard J. Ward, ed., *The Challenge of Development: Theory and Practice*, pp. 448–454. Chicago: Aldine.

——1969. *The Death and Rebirth of the Seneca*. New York: Random House.

——1971. *Administrative Forms of Social Organization*. Reading, Mass.: Addison-Wesley. (McCaleb Module in Anthropology #9.)

Wallace, Tina. 1981. "The Kano River Project." In Judith Heyer et al., eds., *Rural Development in Tropical Africa*, pp. 281–305. New York: St. Martin's Press.

Wallerstein, Immanuel. 1974. *The Modern World System*. New York: Academic Press.

Warner, W. Lloyd. 1941. "Social Anthropology and the Modern Community." *American Journal of Sociology* 46:785–796.

——1962. *The Corporation in the Emergent American Society*. New York: Harper.

Warner, W. Lloyd, and Josiah Low. 1947. *The Social System of the Modern Factory*. New Haven, Conn.: Yale University Press.

Warner, W. Lloyd, and Paul S. Lunt. 1941. *The Social Life of a Modern Community*. New Haven, Conn.: Yale University Press.

Warner, W. Lloyd, and Leo Srole. 1945. *The Social System of American Ethnic Groups*. Yankee City Series, vol. 31. New Haven, Conn.: Yale University Press.

Warner, W. Lloyd, et al. 1964. *Democracy in Jonesville: A Study in Equality and Inequality*. New York: Harper and Row (Harper Torchbooks).

Wax, Murray. 1956. "The Limitations of Boas' Anthropology." *American Anthropologist* 58:46–63.

Wax, Rosalie. 1971. *Doing Fieldwork*. Chicago: University of Chicago Press.

Weaver, Thomas. 1985. "Anthropology as a Policy Science: Part I, A Critique." *Human Organization* 44:97–105.

Weed, Perry L. 1973. *The White Ethnic Movement and Ethnic Politics*. New York: Praeger.

Weidman, Hazel H. 1982. "Research Strategies, Structural Alterations, and Clinically Relevant Anthropology." In Noel J. Chrisman and Thomas W. Maretzki, eds., *Clinically Applied Anthropology*, pp. 201–242. Boston, Mass.: D. Reidel.

Weidman, Hazel H., et al. 1978. "Miami Health Ecology Report." Vol.1. University of Miami Offprint.

Weiss, C.H., ed. 1977. *Using Social Research in Public Policy Making*. Lexington, Mass.: Lexington Books.

Westerman, Floyd. 1969. "Custer Died for Your Sins" (album). New York: Perception Records.

White, Leslie. 1932a. "The Acoma Indians." *Annual Report of the Bureau of American Ethnology* 47:17–192. Washington, D.C.: Bureau of American Ethnology.

——1932b. *The Pueblo of San Felipe*. Memoir no. 38 of the American Anthropological Association. Washington, D.C.: American Anthropological Association.

——1935. *The Pueblo of Santo Domingo, New Mexico*. Memoir no.43 of the American Anthropological Association. Washington, D.C.: American Anthropological Association.

——1942. *The Pueblo of Santa Ana, New Mexico*. Memoir no.60 of the American Anthropological Association. Washington, D.C.: American Anthropological Association.

——1943. "Energy and the Evolution of Culture." *American Anthropologist* 45:335–356.

——1951. "Lewis H. Morgan's Western Field Trips." *American Anthropologist* 53:11–18.

——1959a. "Lewis Henry Morgan: His Life and Researches." In Leslie White, ed., *Lewis Henry Morgan, The Indian Journals, 1859–1862*, pp. 3–12. Ann Arbor: University of Michigan Press.

——1959b. *The Evolution of Culture:The Development of Civilization to the Fall of Rome.* New York: Mcgraw-Hill.

Whitney, Dan. 1985. "Recent Non-Academically Employed Ph.D.s Earn More and Are More Satisfied in Their Work than Academics." *Anthropology Newsletter* 26(4):28,20–23.

Whitten, Norman, and John Szwed. 1970. "Introduction." In Norman Whitten and John Szwed, eds., *Afro-American Anthropology*, pp. 23–60. New York: Free Press.

Whyte, William Foote. 1943. *Street Corner Society.* Chicago: University of Chicago Press.

——1955. *Money and Motivation.* New York: Harper and Row.

——1975. *Organizing for Agricultural Development.* New Brunswick, N.J.: Transaction Books.

——1982. "Social Inventions for Solving Human Problems." *American Sociological Review* 47:1–13.

——1984. *Learning from the Field: A Guide from Experience.* Beverly Hills, Calif.: Sage.

Whyte, William Foote, et al. 1983. *Worker Participation and Ownership: Cooperative Strategies to Strengthen Local Economies.* Ithaca, N.Y.: ILR Press.

Whyte, William Foote, and Damon Boynton, eds. 1983. *Higher Yielding Human Systems for Agriculture.* Ithaca, New York: Cornell University Press.

Wilke, Philip J.; Thomas F. King; and Stephen Hammond. 1975. "Aboriginal Occupation at Tahquitz Canyon: Ethnohistory and Archaeology." In Lowell J. Bean, ed., *The Cahuilla Indians of the Colorado Desert: Ethnohistory and Prehistory.* Ramona: Ballena Press Anthropological Papers No. 3.

Williams, Robin. 1947. *The Reduction of Intergroup Tensions.* New York: Anti-Defamation League.

Willis, William S., Jr. 1970. "Anthropology and Negroes on the Southern Colonial Frontier." In James Curtis and L. Gould, eds., *The Black Experience in America*, pp. 33–50. Austin: University of Texas Press.

——1975. "Franz Boas and the Study of Black Folklore." In John W. Bennett, ed., *The New Ethnicity: Perspectives from Ethnology*, pp. 307–334. 1973 Proceedings of the American Ethnological Society. New York: West.

Wissler, Clark. 1920. "Opportunities for Coordination in Anthropological and Psychological Research." *American Anthropologist* 22:1–12.

Witt, Shirley Hill. 1968. "Nationalistic Trends Among American Indians." In Stuart Levine and Nancy O. Lurie, eds., *The American Indian Today*, pp. 53–75. Deland, Fla.: Everett Edwards Press.

Wolcott, Harry F. 1984. "Ethnographers sans Ethnography: The Evaluation Compromise." In D.M. Fetterman, ed., *Ethnography and Educational Evaluation*, pp. 177–210. Beverly Hills, Calif.: Sage.

Wolf, Eric R. 1955. "Types of Latin American Peasantry: A Preliminary Discussion." *American Anthropologist* 57:452–459.

——1956. "Aspects of Group Relations in a Complex Society: Mexico." *American Anthropologist* 58:1065–1078.

——1969a. "American Anthropologists and American Society." In Southern Anthropological Proceedings no.3, *Concepts and Assumptions in Contemporary Anthropology*, pp. 3–11. Athens, Ga.: University of Georgia Press.

——1969b. *Peasant Wars of the Twentieth Century.* New York: Harper and Row.

——1972. "American Anthropologists and American Society." In Dell Hymes, ed., *Reinventing Anthropology*, pp. 251–263. New York: Vintage.

Wolf, Eric, and Joseph Jorgensen. 1970. "Anthropology on the Warpath in Thailand." *New York Review of Books* (November 19), pp. 26–35.

Wood, Deborah A. 1975. *Directed Cultural Change in Peru: A Guide to the Vicos Collection.* Department of Manuscripts and University Archives. Ithaca, New York: Cornell University Libraries.

Woods, Clyde M. 1975. *Culture Change.* Dubuque, Iowa: William C. Brown Company.

Woodward, C. Vann. 1957. *The Strange Career of Jim Crow.* New York: Oxford University Press.

World Bank. 1981. *Accelerated Development in Sub-Saharan Africa.* Baltimore, Maryland: Johns Hopkins.

Yambert, Karl A. 1980. "Thought and Reality: Dialectics of the Andean Community." In B.S. Orlove and G. Custred, eds., *Land and Power in Latin America*, pp. 55–78. New York: Holmes and Meier.

Yang, Martin C. 1945. *A Chinese Village.* New York: Columbia University Press.

Yankelovich, Daniel. 1974. "Turbulence in the Working World: Angry Workers, Happy Grads." *Psychology Today* 8(7):80–87.

Yoshida, R., et al. 1978. "The Principal and Special Education Placement." *The National Elementary Principal* 56:34–39.

Zborowski, Mark. 1969. *People in Pain.* San Francisco, Calif.: Jossey-Bass.

Zileri Gibson, Enrique. 1961. "A los Comuneros de Vicos, Los Quieren Tracionar." *Caretas* (julio-agosto), 25:16–19.

Zimmerman, William J. 1957. "The Role of the Bureau of Indian Affairs since 1933." *Annals. American Academy of Political and Social Sciences* 311:31–40.

Zola, Irving K. 1966. "Culture and Symptoms: An Analysis of Patients' Presenting Complaints." *American Sociological Review* 31:615–630.

Zorbaugh, Harvey W. 1929. *Gold Coast and Slum: A Sociological Study of Chicago's Near North Side.* Chicago: University of Chicago Press.